...otte of Mecklenburg-Strelitz
1744–1818

...rick of Württemberg
1754–1816

Mary
1776–1857
= Duke of Gloucester
1776–1834

Adolphus,
Duke of Cambridge
1774–1850
= Augusta, Princess
of Hesse
1797–1857

Ernest Augustus,
King of Hanover
1771–1851
= Frederica of Mecklenburg-Strelitz
1778–1841

8
others

George,
Duke of Cambridge
1819–1904

Augusta Caroline
1822–1916
= Frederick William of
Mecklenburg-Strelitz
1819–1904

Mary Adelaide
1833–97
= Francis, Prince of Teck
1st Duke of Teck
1837–1900

Victoria Mary
(Queen Mary)

Adolphus 1st Marquess
of Cambridge
1868–1927

Francis
1870–1910

Alexander,
Earl of Athlone
1874–1957
= Alice, Princess of Albany
1883–1981

Leopold, Duke of
Albany
1853–84
= Helen of
Waldeck-Pyrmont
1861–1922

Beatrice
1857–1944
= Henry of Battenberg
1858–96

Victoria
1840–1901
= Kaiser Frederick III
1831–88

EDWARD VII
1841–1910
= Alexandra of Denmark
1844–1925

= Hon. Sir
A. Ramsay
1881–1972

Charles Edward
Duke of
Saxe-Coburg

Alice
1883–1981
= Alexander,
Earl of Athlone
1874–1957

3s

Victoria Eugenie
(Ena)
1887–1969
= Alfonso XIII
of Spain
1886–1941

3s
4d

Kaiser Wilhelm II
1859–1941

Albert Victor,
Duke of Clarence
1864–92

Alexander
1871

Louise
1867–1931
= Duke of Fife
1849–1912

Victoria
1868–1935

Maud
1869–1935
= Haakon
of Norway
1872–1957

GEORGE V

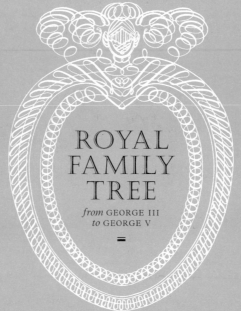

ROYAL
FAMILY
TREE

from GEORGE III
to GEORGE V

=

ROYAL SERVICE

VOLUME II

ROYAL SERVICE

VOLUME II

James Risk

Henry Pownall

David Stanley

John Tamplin

with

Stanley Martin

THIRD MILLENNIUM PUBLISHING
IN ASSOCIATION WITH
VICTORIAN PUBLISHING

Published by Third Millennium Publishing
in association with Victorian Publishing
Copyright © James Risk, Henry Pownall, David Stanley
and John Tamplin 2001

A catalogue record for this book is available
from the British Library

ISBN 1 903942 04 7

Designed and produced by
Pardoe Blacker Limited
a member of the Third Millennium Group
Lingfield · Surrey

Printed in China
by Midas Printing

Contents

Introduction

IN 1996, the centenary year of the institution of the Royal Victorian Order and the Royal Victorian Medal, Volume I of *Royal Service* was published. It recorded the history of the Order, the Medal and the Royal Victorian Chain and all substantive appointments to the Order and substantive awards of the Medal. It also recorded all holders of the Royal Victorian Chain.

This volume completes that history, bringing the appointments and awards up to date and recording all honorary appointments to the Order and all honorary awards of the Medal. It also includes the history of the Royal Family Orders, and an account of various medals and badges of office connected with the Royal Households.

Volume III records the history of the Royal Household Long and Faithful Service Medals, together with a register of all recipients.

In 1951, the Order and Medals Research Society had published with the permission of King George VI, a booklet entitled *The Royal Family Orders, Badges of Office, Royal Household Medals and Souvenirs*. It was compiled by G.P.L. James and was limited to three hundred and fifty copies. It was followed in 1954 by a small supplement edited by R.E. Harbord, with the permission of the Queen. Both publications were the first in their field and have long been out of print.

The authors have thought it right to record their debt to those who first researched this field. It is their work which has led directly to the appearance of these three volumes which cover a wider field and in much greater detail.

London, 2001

Acknowledgements

T HE AUTHORS acknowledge the gracious permission of Her Majesty the Queen in allowing them to compile this record of awards for personal service to the Royal Family and of badges of office; for access to relevant material at Buckingham Palace, the Central Chancery of the Orders of Knighthood at St James's Palace and in the Royal Archives at Windsor Castle; and for the use of photographs in the Royal Photographic Collection.

Many individuals have willingly given their help to the production of this work, and our special thanks go firstly to Her Majesty Queen Elizabeth The Queen Mother, Grand Master of the Royal Victorian Order, for so kindly agreeing to be photographed, and for all the care and trouble that Her Majesty took at the time, the result of which now appears as Plate I in Volume I; secondly, to all the other members of the Royal Family for so readily giving their permission for photographs to be taken of Badges of Office, and to the members of all the various Royal Households, past and present, who gave of their time to ensure that the Badges were made available; thirdly, to the late Earl Mountbatten of Burma, Patron of the Orders and Medals Research Society 1977–9, for his very real interest and practical assistance in the preparation of parts of this book. It is a matter of sadness to us that, because of his tragic death in 1979, he is not able to see the fruits of his help.

Invaluable advice and co-operation has been given by the late Sir Owen Morshead, GCVO, KCB, DSO, MC, Librarian and Assistant Keeper of the Royal Archives 1926–58 and by his successors, the late Sir Robert Mackworth-Young, GCVO 1958–85 and Oliver Everett, Esq., CVO, since 1985. For their interest and encouragement we are very grateful. We are grateful to the Rev. Dr Peter Galloway, OBE for his early contributions to this work.

Special thanks are due to Russell Malloch, Esq. whose original chronological and alphabetical list of substantive appointments to the Royal Victorian Order provided the basis for the Register of the Order, which also appears in Volume I; and to Derek Waters, Esq., CVO for his friendly help over many years. We also wish to record our thanks to the following individuals, without whose help much would have gone unrecorded:

Major Albert Abela, MBE
Jeremy Bagwell Purefoy, Esq., MVO
Lady Balfour
Ronald Barden, Esq.
Lady Anne Bentinck
The late Marcus Bishop, Esq., LVO
The late Marjorie, Countess of Brecknock
Norman Brooks, Esq.
The late Dame Gillian Brown, DCVO, CMG
Harold Brown, Esq., RVM
The Duke of Buccleuch and Queensberry, KT, VRD
Charles Burnett, Esq., Ross Herald
Miss Shirley Bury, Victoria and Albert Museum
His Honour Sir Harold Cassel, Bt. TD, QC
The Trustees of the Chatsworth Settlement, T.S. Wragg and Peter Day, Esqs.

The Honourable Mrs Chaworth-Musters
Hubert Chesshyre, Esq., LVO
Major Sir Peter Clarke, KCVO
Denis Vere Collings, Esq.
Miss Diana Condell, Imperial War Museum
Stephen Connelly, Esq., Spink and Son
The late Group Captain John Constable
The Corporation of Church House
Miss Elizabeth Cuthbert, LVO
Lady de Bellaigue, MVO
Miss Frances Dimond, LVO
Nimrod Dix, Esq.
G.P. Dyer, Esq., Royal Mint
Edward Edwards, Esq.
David Erskine-Hill, Esq.
Dr Margaret Farquhar and Mrs. B.R.L. Graham
Major A.F. Flatow, TD

Mrs Birthe Fraser, Royal Danish Embassy
Mrs Ruth Gardner, LVO, OBE
J.C.G. George, Esq., Kintyre Pursuivant
   of Arms
Robert Golden, Esq.
Ivor Guild Esq., CBE
The late Sir Philip Hay, KCVO and Lady
   Margaret Hay DCVO
John Hayward, Esq.
Air Vice-Marshal Sir Peter Horsley, KCB,
   CBE, MVO, AFC
William Hunt, Esq., TD
Edward Joslin, Esq., LVO
Peter Joslin, Esq.
Michael Kelly, Esq., LVO
Miss Jane Langton, LVO
Hans Levin-Hansen, Esq.
Andrew Litherland, Esq.
J. Little, Esq.
The late Miss Gwynedd Lloyd, CVO
Dr Llewelyn Lloyd, OBE
The Honourable Mrs Lucas
Miss Lorna MacEchern
Richard Magor, Esq.
Philip Mallet, Esq., CMG
The Honourable Mrs P.E. Bromley-Martin
Michael Bromley-Martin, Esq.
Lieut. Colonel Anthony Mather, CVO, OBE
James Methuen-Campbell, Esq.
Michael Naxton, Esq.
The late Lavinia, Duchess of Norfolk,
   LG, CBE
Phillippe O'Shea, Esq., LVO New Zealand
   Herald of Arms Extraordinary
Stephen Patterson, Esq., MVO
Lady Mary Pawle
The late Sir Eric Penn, GCVO, OBE, MC
The late Honourable Mrs Michael Portman

Dr Christopher Rawll
Major-General Sir Desmond Rice,
   KCVO, CBE
Dr D.G.B. Riddick
Harry Robertson, Esq.
Gordon Roberton, Esq., Geoffrey Dodd,
   Esq. and Trevor Chriss, Esq. A.C. Cooper
   Ltd
Miss Charlette Robinson, MVO
Lord Romsey
The Marquess of Salisbury and R.H.
   Harcourt Williams, Esq.
Robert Scarlett, Esq.
Miss Olive Short, CVO
Peter Simkins, Esq., Imperial War Museum
Jonathan Smith, Esq.
Stephen Slater, Esq.
Lars Stevnsborg, Esq.
Mark Stocker, Esq.
Patrick Street, Esq.
W.H. Summers, Esq., LVO formerly the
   Crown Jeweller
HE Dr Konthi Suphamongkhon
The Countess of Sutherland
The Marquess of Tavistock and the Trustees
   of the Bedford Estates
Sir Michael Thomas, Bt.
Sir John Titman, KCVO, DL
Charles Tod, Esq., Wemyss Estates
The late Charles Tozer, Esq.
The Honourable Jane Walsh, MVO
Miss Rachel Wells, LVO
The late Lady Victoria Wemyss, CVO
The late Viola, Duchess of Westminster
Mrs C.C.L. Williams, MBE
John Wilson, Esq.
Thomas Woodcock, Esq., LVO Norroy and
   Ulster King of Arms

The typing of the manuscript was a considerable effort and we owe a great debt of gratitude to Mrs Edward Mountain and Michael Watts, Esq. for undertaking this task in spare moments of their busy lives.

Other contributions are duly recorded in the text. If we have omitted any-one, we apologise unreservedly. It is wholly unintentional.

We are extremely grateful to Elwyn Blacker Esq. and all the staff at Pardoe Blacker, especially Mrs Cindy Edler for their patience, unstinting support and very considerable skills in producing this book.

Photographic credits

Associated Press 101; Authors' Collection 35 (*top*), 47, 56 (*bottom*), 57, 61 (*top right*), 67 (*left*), 68, 69 (*bottom right*), 71, 72, 73 (*top*), 74, 75 (*top left and right*), 76, 78, 79 (*bottom*), 80 (*top*), 81, 82, 83, 84 (*top*), 86 (*bottom left*), 87, 89 (*middle*) 102 (*top*), 122 (*left*); Geoffrey Ballantyne 104; Mr and Mrs Jeremy Bennett 123; Anthony Buckley and Constantine Ltd (*frontispiece*); Camera Press (Snowdon) 31; The Lord Chamberlain's Office 64 (*bottom right*), 89 (*bottom*), 102 (*bottom*), 103 (*right*); College of Arms 90, 91, 92, 93; A.C. Cooper Ltd 68 (*left*), 74, 78, 79 (*bottom*), 80 (*top*), 81, 82, 83, 84 (*top*); Geoffrey Dodd and Trevos Chriss, A.C. Cooper (Colour) Ltd 122 (*left*); A.F. Flatow Collection 26, 58, 126; Duff House Gallery 28; Garrard and Co. Ltd 69 (*top*); J.C.G. George 96, 97; Glendinnings 86 (*top*); Glen Harvey Collection 36; Harvey Photography, Leven 72; Tim Graham Library 63 (*top right*); Hulton Getty Library 63 (*bottom*); Peter Joslin 50 (*top and bottom*), 51, 52; Lord Lichfield 88 (*right*); William Hunt 94; Imperial War Museum 62, 64 (*top*); Peter Lane, Derby 75 (*top left*); The Lord High Almoner 84 (*bottom*); Middlesex County Press 88 (*left*); Hy Money 103 (*left*); Ordenshistorisk Selskab 49, 50 (*middle right*), 125; PA News 64 (*bottom left*), 106; Public Archives Canada 27; Layland Ross, Nottingham 73 (*top*); Royal Collection 15, 16, 17, 21, 23, 25, 29, 30, 32, 33, 34, 35, 67 (*bottom left and right*), 75 (*bottom*), 77, 80 (*bottom*); The Russian Diamond Fund 14; R.J. Scarlett 53, 54, 55, 59, 60, 61 (*left and bottom*); David Sim, Golspie 76; Spink and Son 73 (*bottom*), 86 (*bottom right*), 122 (*right*); Stephen Slater 85; Sotheby 67 (*left top*); Roy Stephens 69 (*bottom left*); Sir Michael Thomas Bt. 56 (*top*); J.M. Thurston 108; The Trustees of the Bedford Estates 66; Philip Way Photography 90, 91, 92; Victoria and Albert Museum Picture Library 13.

CHAPTER ONE

The Royal Family Orders and the Royal Order of Victoria and Albert

═══

WHEN QUEEN ELIZABETH I knighted Sir Francis Drake on the deck of the *Golden Hind* at Deptford in the autumn of 1580 after he returned from his memorable circumnavigation of the globe, she gave him a rich jewel. This device took the form of a lozenge-shaped baroque gold frame of coloured enamels ornamented with diamonds and rubies. One side contained a fine miniature of the Queen by Nicholas Hilliard (1537–1619), who was the first English miniature painter and portrait painter to the Queen, and the other an oval antique onyx cameo. A ring attached to a loop on the upper edge permitted the piece to be suspended by a red and gold cord around the neck.

The Drake jewel was only one of several portrait miniatures of herself that Queen Elizabeth I presented to distinguished men throughout her long reign. They were intended to be used as badges indicating that the wearers enjoyed their Sovereign's personal esteem. In this sense they were the forerunners of today's Royal Family Order, as well as the Royal Victorian Order and the Royal Victorian Chain. The jewelled portrait of the reigning monarch, worn as a form of decoration, eventually emerged in Britain as the private Order still given today by the Queen to ladies of the Royal Family.

THE ARMADA JEWEL which was given by Queen Elizabeth I to Sir Thomas Heneage (? by Nicholas Hilliard, *c.*1588): it is similar to that given to Sir Francis Drake.

At first glance, the connection between the Drake jewel and the Court decoration of today may appear to be somewhat remote. The tradition of wearing the Sovereign's portrait developed strongly in northern Europe during the sixteenth and seventeenth centuries while it tended to lapse in Britain. The Vasa Kings of Sweden rewarded their subjects with oval gold medals, more or less jewelled and enamelled, depending on the rank of the recipients, to be worn from gold chains of varying designs and weights. The practice was also common in Germany and Denmark, and it became the custom to give the royal portrait to ambassadors and other distinguished foreigners. When Elias Ashmole, Windsor Herald, published his monumental work *Institutions and Ceremonies of the Most Noble Order of the Garter* in 1672, he was presented with plain gold medals and chains by the Elector of Brandenburg and the King of Denmark as tokens of their approval of his splendid book.

Like most other traditions, the form and use of the royal portrait changed over the years. During the eighteenth century it was largely replaced by admission to newly established orders of knighthood. When the Kings of France wished to make a private gift they used gold snuff boxes often carrying a finely painted miniature of the donor or his crowned cypher in diamonds. Where France led, other princes and kings, whose titles could not compare in antiquity with those of the House of Capet, soon followed. The use of the portrait presentation snuff box perhaps reached its highest point at the Congress of Vienna in 1814. Naturally enough, the great Duke of Wellington received several fine ones, now on display in the Apsley House Museum in London.

There remained two countries which, then as now, were strongly wedded to peculiarities of their own, however much they may have made use of foreign practices that suited their convenience from time to time. These were Russia and Britain. It is to the former that we can trace the more immediate antecedents of the British Royal Family Orders. When the Tsar and later Emperor, Peter the Great (1672–1725), set about bringing his country into the mainstream of European life, he took advantage of everything he found useful in the West, from British and Dutch shipbuilding to German and Swedish Court etiquette. In the 1690's he adopted the jewelled Imperial portrait as the principal honour that could be awarded within his redesigned Empire. Whilst this was followed by the creation of the Order of Saint Andrew in 1698, it was the jewelled portrait that took precedence.

Although established at a time when its use was fast dying out in other countries, the Imperial miniature remained the greatest honour the Russian Sovereign could confer, right down to the collapse of the monarchy in 1917. This Badge took the form of a small portrait of the reigning monarch framed in diamonds, surmounted by an imperial crown and worn from a bow of blue ribbon on the left breast.★ The Imperial Portrait Order has one characteristic that made it entirely different from other similar institutions found elsewhere. It could be conferred on either men or women. When conferred on men, the Badge was worn senior to the Star of the Order of Saint Andrew. Needless to say, it was an extremely rare distinction.

THE JEWELLED IMPERIAL PORTRAIT ORDER OF TSAR PETER THE GREAT. An early eighteenth-century example from the collection of the Russian Diamond Fund in Moscow.

★ See Y. Dujenko, E. Smirnova (and others), *Treasures of the USSR Diamond Fund.* Moscow, 1967. No pagination or plate numbers. This well illustrated book is the catalogue of an exhibition held that year to commemorate the 50th anniversary of the Revolution. Several pieces of Imperial insignia are shown.

FIELD MARSHAL GEBARDT VON BLÜCHER
(1742–1819) by Sir Thomas Lawrence.Over the ribbon
of the Order of the Black Eagle he wears George IV's
Family Order which the Prince Regent presented to
him on his arrival in London. He also wears the Iron
Cross and the stars of the Orders of Maria Theresa of
Austria and St George of Russia.

MATVEI IVANOVITCH, COUNT PLATOFF (1757–1818),
painted by Lawrence. The Count is in the uniform of
a Cossack General and wears George IV's Family
Order, together with the ribbon and star of the Order
of St Andrew, the badges of the Orders of St Anne
and St George of Russia, the Red Eagle of Prussia and
the Order of St John of Jerusalem.

In 1794, Lord Grenville wrote to King George III suggesting that he confer
'a gold chain, to which the picture of your Majesty set round with diamonds
should be pendant'[1] on a certain General Paoli (1725–1807), a Corsican who
had led the resistance to the French conquest of Corsica in 1768. 'So peculiar
a mark of distinction, only so lately imagined by your Majesty & conferred
only for the most eminent public services, would be the most desirable grati-
fication which he could receive'.[2] The King was happy to oblige. 'I . . . approve
. . . his having a gold chain with my picture set in diamonds for him to wear
on all public occasion. I desire the D. of Portland will order Duval the jeweller to prepare the setting, and that Collins★ may have orders to paint the
picture.'[3] Whether any further pictures were made and awarded is uncertain,
but this honour almost certainly marks the restoration of a custom begun by
Queen Elizabeth I, the extension of the continental practice to the English
Court, and the beginning of the most recent period of personal honours
given by the Sovereign.

★ Richard Collins (1755–1831) miniature painter.

The end of the Napoleonic Wars ushered in a period of economic and social upheaval in Britain. The leaven of change even penetrated the Court circle of the Prince Regent (later King George IV). The honours system itself reflected European influences when the Order of the Bath was divided up into three military classes and one civil class. After assuming the Regency in 1811, George Prince of Wales was at last able to give free rein to some of his natural predilections. He liked making gifts. Many of these were pieces of jewellery for ladies and a variety of badges or medals embodying the insignia of the Prince of Wales for men.

In the spring of 1814 the Regent looked forward to playing host to the Emperor of Russia, the King of Prussia, Prince Metternich representing the Austrian Emperor, and many of the senior military officers who had done so much to bring down Bonaparte's Empire. During this visit he departed from British tradition in the field of honours. The Russian and Prussian sovereigns and their staffs landed at Dover on 6 June 1814. Proceeding to London they were received at Carlton House the next day. The Regent immediately invested the Prussian Field Marshal Prince Blücher with a jewelled miniature to be worn around the neck by a Garter blue ribbon.[4] The miniature was a painted enamel of the Regent surrounded by brilliants of good size and surmounted by a crown in diamonds and enamel. Later he gave a similar Badge to General Count Platoff, hetman (captain) of the Don Cossacks. Both pieces are shown in the Lawrence pictures of Blücher and Platoff in the Waterloo Chamber at Windsor.[5]

There is no documentary evidence that, in presenting these two Badges, the Russian practice was deliberately being imitated. Nevertheless, the Russian example was near at hand. It should not be forgotten that the Emperor Alexander I was the most powerful Sovereign in Europe and thought to be the most dangerous. The employment of his own portrait by the Regent, according to the Russian custom, could be construed as a compliment to his somewhat unpredictable guest. It is significant that Count Platoff wore the Badge attached to a bow of ribbon on his breast in the Russian fashion while Prince Blücher did not.[6]*

British monarchs had long followed the general custom of presenting plain miniatures and snuff boxes as gifts on suitable occasions and were to continue to do so after the Prince Regent's imaginative innovation in 1814. Just where that innovation would lead was soon to be made apparent. The jewelled royal portrait as a decoration for distinguished soldiers was never used again. Instead King George IV somewhat informally established what we have since come to think of as a private Order for ladies of the Royal Family. These included his sisters, and later his two nieces. Exactly how many were

* Count Platoff wears the Regent's portrait attached to a bow of Garter blue ribbon between the Stars of St Andrew and St George.

(above) THE ROYAL FAMILY ORDER OF KING GEORGE IV (1820–30); the reverse showing the King's cypher in small brilliants and rose-cut diamonds.

(right) THE ROYAL FAMILY ORDER OF KING GEORGE IV. The portrait by Bone shows the King wearing the Garter Star and the Golden Fleece; *(top)* the Badge of the Queen of Württemberg; *(bottom left)* a smaller version; *(bottom right)* the Badge of Grand Duchess Augusta of Mecklenburg-Strelitz.

given is not clear. The first to receive it was his eldest sister the Princess Royal, Charlotte Augusta Matilda, Queen of Württemberg.

One of his nieces, Princess Victoria, received hers from 'Uncle King' in August 1826 when she was seven years old and staying with her mother and step-sister Princess Feodore at Cumberland Lodge in Windsor Great Park. Forty-six years later Queen Victoria recorded the event among a few random memories of her childhood:

> 'In the year '26 George IV asked my Mother, my Sister and Me down to Windsor for the first time; he had been on bad terms with my poor Father when he died. We went to Cumberland Lodge, the King living at the Royal Lodge. Aunt Gloucester was there at the time. When we arrived at the Royal Lodge the King took me by the hand, saying 'Give me your little paw'. He was large and gouty, but with a wonderful dignity and charm of manner. He wore the brown wig which was so much worn in those days. Then he said he would give me something for me to wear, and that was his picture set in diamonds, which was worn by the Princesses as an Order to a blue ribbon on the left shoulder. I was very proud of this – and Lady Conyngham pinned it on my shoulder. Her husband was Lord Chamberlain and constantly there, as well as Lord Mt. Charles as Vice-Chamberlain. None of the Royal Family or general visitors lived at Royal Lodge, but only the Conyngham family; all the rest at Cumberland Lodge.'[7]

There were no Statutes written for the new Order, nor did there seem to be any standard pattern for the Badges. The largest and most ornate was the Queen of Württemberg's. The centre was an enamelled portrait of the King in Field Marshal's uniform by Bone, set in an arabesque frame of small diamonds, which in turn was surrounded by a floral wreath executed in brilliants, the whole surmounted by a diamond imperial crown with a red enamel cap. This was suspended from the left shoulder by a bow of light blue watered silk ribbon. While the Bone enamel was virtually the same for all the surviving Badges, the form given to the frames was quite different, although generally similar in style.* That of Augusta, Duchess of Cambridge is smaller and less ornate than the one just described. What appears to have been another very interesting specimen was in the hands of a London jeweller in 1953. The provenance of this latter piece and its present whereabouts are unknown.†

While there do not seem to have been any grades to the Family Order, the Badges the King gave his nieces, Princess Victoria of Kent and Princess Augusta of Cambridge, were much simpler than those presented to his sisters. Although Cecil Woodham-Smith in her biography of Queen Victoria

---

* The Bones were a family of miniaturists whose prominent members, Henry Bone and Henry Pierce Bone, flourished in the years 1755–1855. They specialized in painted enamels and were patronized by all the reigning monarchs from King George III to Queen Victoria.

† The cover of the 6 June 1953 Coronation issue of the *Illustrated London News* reproduces a small colour photograph of the Queen within a diamond frame. The original of the frame was illustrated on page 901 of the magazine, where it was described as a 'diamond pendant containing an enamel miniature of George IV which we reproduce on this page, the design of the frame incorporating a crown and the floral emblems of England, Scotland, and Ireland, and it is possible that it may have been given by George IV to a close personal friend. It recalls the diamond framed portraits known as Royal Family Orders which British Sovereigns give ladies of the Royal Family as personal gifts, of which the portraits of George V and George VI, worn by the Queen and members of the Royal family are examples.' The Badge mentioned here was undoubtedly one of King George IV's, but there is no record of the King having given the Family Order to 'a friend'.

PRINCESS VICTORIA wearing the Royal Family Order of King George IV, c.1826–7. The miniature is attributed to Anthony Stewart (1773–1846) and was the first to be painted of the princess. It is in the Methuen Collection.

described the Badge as being the same as those worn by the King's sisters, the statement is not correct. Nonetheless the Badge was certainly similar to a type used before. Thanks to the accurate brush of Sir Thomas Lawrence (1769–1830), the most successful English portrait painter of his day, we know that it resembled those given to Prince Blücher and Count Platoff in 1814.

King William IV did not continue the tradition of the private Order established by his brother. But Queen Victoria's memory of her thrilling gift from the King on that summer's visit to Royal Lodge was to influence later events.

The Prince Consort's admiration for the Renaissance probably influenced the design of what began in 1856 as the Badge of an unofficial family Order.

Princess Victoria, Princess Royal and later German Empress, the eldest daughter of the Queen and Prince Albert, was confirmed on 20 March 1856. During the nineteenth century confirmation in the Church of England was, after baptism, regarded as the second most important step in a young person's life. The rite was solemnly prepared for, made the occasion of grave celebration within the confines of each family, and accompanied by presents to commemorate the event. Queen Victoria refers in her Journal to some of the Princess's presents,

> 'a diamond necklace and earrings, and a beautiful cameo, of our profiles (taken from the Exhibition Medal in 1851) cut in cornelian, handsomely set round in diamonds, attached to a white moire silk bow, to be worn on the left shoulder.'

The cameo bearing the double portrait of Victoria and Albert was engraved by Tommaso Saulini of Rome from Wyon's obverse of the Great Exhibition medals. The cameo is framed with a border interrupted at intervals by projections, a summary rendering of a Renaissance cartouche.

The Princess wore her badge at her marriage on 25 January 1858, posing with her parents for a daguerrotype before they left Buckingham Palace for the ceremony in the Chapel Royal.

Princess Alice was the next recipient when she was confirmed in her turn on 21 April 1859. To her daughter in Berlin, the Queen wrote, 'She (Princess Alice) will tell you of her presents; such fine ones; from us the Order.–'[8] Mr Fulford says in his footnote that in her diary the Queen added, 'From us the family Order (our cameo with diamonds).' His observation that 'This is probably the earliest example of the gift of the Queen's private family order' was not correct.

Thanks to Winterhalter's portraits of both the Princess Royal and Princess Alice, we know both Badges were of the same design and workmanship. In this they differed from King George IV's which, with the two exceptions of those given to his nieces, were not of the same design. Like the King's, Queen Victoria's Family Order was not provided with Statutes of any kind. In the event, only the two Princesses were ever given the private Order by their parents. Then, on 14 December 1861, the Prince Consort died.

After the Prince's death, the Queen devoted a great deal of time and thought to the question of appropriate memorials. Several of these such as the Albert Hall and the Albert Memorial in London, were to bulk large in the public eye, as they still do. Others were confined to the Royal circle. As early as 28 December 1861 Sir Charles Phipps, Keeper of the Privy Purse, conveyed the Queen's commands to Mr Albert Woods on the subject of the private Order.* After referring to the two appointments hitherto made he wrote,

> 'This Order, being purely a family Order, requires no public recognition or record – but the Queen wishes its establishment with rules for it to be formally and regularly engrossed. All female descendants of Victoria and Albert are to be entitled to receive it after confirmation – son's wives and grandson's wives and exceptionally it may be given to other Queens or Princesses of foreign houses connected by blood or friendship. With the exception of the two original possessors, viz. The Crown Princess of Prussia and the Princess Alice who received the Order from both the Queen and the Prince – the Badge would not be hereditary.... The expenses of this Order to be borne by the Sovereign, or by the Sovereign and Queen Consort as the case may be.'[9]

Sir Charles also informed Woods that the new distinction was to be called 'The Royal Order of Victoria and Albert in commemoration of the happy marriage.' Woods' agile pen quickly produced a set of Rules and Regulations that met Her Majesty's approval. They were promulgated on 10 February 1862, the twenty-second anniversary of the Queen's wedding. The original decoration already given to the two eldest daughters provided the model for the Badge of the new Order, and these ladies were declared members. Their younger sisters were to be eligible 'from, and immediately after, the solemn Rite of Confirmation...

(opposite) THE ROYAL ORDER OF VICTORIA AND ALBERT (1862–1901). *(top)* Worn by Queen Victoria, it is the only cameo to be cut with the head of the Prince Consort in front; *(bottom)* First Class badge worn by Queen Alexandra.

* Albert William Woods, (1816–1904). Lancaster Herald, 1841–70. Appointed Garter 1869. Also an officer of the Orders of the Bath, Star of India, Indian Empire, St Michael and St George, and Victoria and Albert. Knighted 1869. CB 1887, KCMG 1890, KCB 1897, GCVO 1903.

according to the Rites and Ceremonies of the Church of England.' Princess
Alexandra of Denmark was also given it in March 1863 upon her marriage to
the Prince of Wales. But of the members of foreign Houses connected by
blood or friendship, the first to receive it was Augusta, Queen of Prussia and
German Empress, and then not until 8 May 1872.

At the time of its foundation in 1862 there was little to distinguish the
institution from King George IV's Order of some forty years earlier, other
than the 'Rules and Regulations', the most important section of which would
seem to have been a memorial to the late Prince Consort. Although the
Badge followed the pattern already established, there was one significant
exception. Queen Victoria had never worn the private Order as long as it
remained a distinction for Princesses of the Royal House. The establishment
of an order confined within a set of written rules created a somewhat different situation and, as Sovereign, the Queen assumed a Badge that was quite
original. The onyx cameo was cut with the Prince Consort's profile to the
fore rather than taking second place as it did on all the other Badges. This
unique Badge is now in the Royal Collection at Windsor.

The second half of the nineteenth century saw a vast growth of the Empire
accompanied by a necessary increase in the Honours available to the Crown.
Military campaigns generated a series of handsome medals that carried the
message of optimism and expansion to all classes. For the higher ranks in the
military, and increasingly the civil services, during the decade between 1860
and 1870, a new Order, the Order of the Star of India, was created, and the
Order of Saint Michael and Saint George, was freed from its limitation to the
people of Malta and the Ionian Islands and adapted as the Diplomatic and
Colonial Order.

The Queen herself was hardly immune to the yeasty trend of the times.
Only a little over two and a half years after the new Family Order had been
created, Her Majesty decided on 10 October 1864, to add a second class.

It could be conferred upon those 'who now hold, or may hereafter hold the
Offices of Mistress of the Robes, Lady of the Bedchamber, or other Offices in
the Household ... and also upon Ladies not of Royal Rank, nearly connected
with Ourself or Our Family, as We, Our Heirs and Successors, shall from time
to time think fit.'[10] Just a year later on 29 November 1865 a third class was
added for Women of the Bedchamber and any other Ladies of a similar rank.
Thus it was that, in a short space of time, the old concept of a private family
distinction changed. The Royal Order of Victoria and Albert emerged as a
reward that included provision for personal services rendered by those closely
associated with the Sovereign who was, for the time being, a Queen Regnant.

A casual examination of the regulations, however, will disclose certain anom-
alies. One did not proceed up the promotional ladder from being a Woman to
becoming a Lady of the Bedchamber. Both the Household appointments and
appointments to the Order were made in accordance with social rank. There
could be no promotion from the Third to the Second Class. The First Class
was still reserved for Royal persons. The Badges reflected the different posi-
tions of the recipients. That of the Second Class consisted of a shell cameo of
the Queen and the Prince Consort framed with a diamond at the four points
of the compass and pearls in between, the whole surmounted by a jewelled
crown, while the Third Class was a crowned and jewelled cypher VR and A.
All these devices were to be returned by the heirs after the death of the
holder.

(opposite) THE ROYAL
ORDER OF VICTORIA
AND ALBERT.
(top) THIRD CLASS
(1862–80);
(centre) SECOND CLASS
(1880) worn by Princess
Helena Victoria and
(bottom) FOURTH
CLASS (1880–1901).

It was not until about the middle of 1877 that a problem was perceived. What, if any, were to be the post nominal initials assigned to the members of the Royal Order of Victoria and Albert? Heretofore there had been none. But connected with the Queen's assumption of the title of Empress of India, plans were under way for the establishment of two new Orders. These were the Crown of India for wives of Indian Princes and the wives of high ranking British Indian officials, and the Order of the Indian Empire as an honour junior to the Star of India. As usual in matters of this kind, the invaluable Sir Albert Woods was consulted by Sir Henry Ponsonby, the Queen's Private Secretary. On 5 May Sir Albert reduced his puzzled thoughts to paper in his usual elegant hand. He had a fixation about the word 'Member' and could see no way out of including an 'M' for the two Ladies' Orders. The best he could do for the Victoria and Albert Order was to suggest:

M V&A (FC)   or   I (FC) V&A
M V&A (SC)   or   M (SC) V&A
M V&A (TC)   or   M (TC) V&A.

With considerable prescience he noted, 'This would not, I fear, be understood – I see no other way of defining the classes.' For the Crown of India he proposed M.C.I. The other Indian Order presented no problem because there were to be no Members but rather Companions. So, C.I.E. was an obvious choice.[11]

The Private Secretary, a man of elemental common sense, would have nothing to do with 'M'. He briskly reduced the Crown of India to a simple C.I. But his touch with regard to the Victoria and Albert was less sure. He observed, 'Nothing as regards the Victoria and Albert. They may place after their names in the Peerage, "Lady of the Order of Victoria and Albert."' Although Sir Henry generally threaded his way through such mazes with experienced ease, in this instance he slipped up. The Queen in her turn did not agree with him and opted for a sensible 'V. A.' without the other additional letters that so puzzled Garter King of Arms.

As the long reign progressed, Queen Victoria found herself with a number of granddaughters of whom she was very fond. Perusal of the Rules showed that there was no way these young ladies could be given the Order. This, Her Majesty felt, was rather hard and directed that steps be put in motion to expand the Order by another class. Those invaluable servants, Albert Woods and Henry Ponsonby, bent their collective minds to the matter. What ensued was a flurry of correspondence between the two in the course of which exactly what the Queen wanted became less and less clear. Finally, on 20 January 1880, after summarizing the then limitations the Queen minuted rather plaintively to Sir Henry, 'Well, I have felt that it is strange that my own gd. children (not British Psses) & nieces etc. cannot have it – & therefore I wish a smaller form of the 1st large badge to be established for grand children & Relations – not Crowned heads: like the Psses. of Prussia, Hesse & S. Holstein, Pss. Leiningen, the Pss. Hermann Hohenlohe – the Dcss. of Teck & Pss. Augusta of Saxe-Coburg etc.'[12]

With this thorny question settled Sir Albert was able to turn his mind to the details. The new Class was to be inserted after the old First Class and before the Second and Third, thus demoting the latter by one. It was, in brief, to be a lesser version available only for junior members of the Royal Family. Some of the Rules, now obsolete, were changed and confirmation was no longer a requirement for membership. But the question of nomenclature

became complicated. It is not exactly clear from the correspondence who eventually proposed that the Classes should run Royal, First, Second, and Third, but the inference is that Sir Henry was responsible. Fortunately, Woods was always fairly sound on such matters, and on 2 March 1880, he came down strongly for a simple numerical designation from First to Fourth.[13] The Queen was happy to accept the arrangement.

Sir Albert also dealt with the new Badge. In his opinion the piece could be either larger or smaller than the former Second Class. Sir Henry settled the matter. He minuted to the Queen on Woods' letter, 'The size will be smaller but the value greater than the 2nd Class (i.e., the Third as it became).[14] In the end it emerged as a small onyx cameo in a crowned frame of small brilliants. The following schedule of costs supplied by the Privy Purse Office is instructive:

1st Class	Signor Ronca for Cameo on onyx	26.5s
	Messrs. Garrard for mounting it	320.
		£346.5s
2nd Class	Signor Ronca for Cameo on shell	7.7s
	Messrs. Garrard for mounting it	50.
		£57.7s
3rd Class	Messrs. Collingwood for Monogram Badge. each.	£30 -

The Classes listed above were, of course, those used before the addition of the new Second Class. In passing the information on to the Queen, Ponsonby was able to add the cost of the new Badge. Signor Ronca charged £26 for an onyx cameo and the price of the mounting by Garrard came to £55, or a total of £81 for the completed piece.[15] It is easy to see why these devices were to be

(top left) QUEEN ALEXANDRA wearing the Royal Order of Victoria and Albert, the Royal Family Order of King Edward VII and the Royal Family Order of King Christian IX of Denmark. *(bottom left)* QUEEN MARY wearing the Royal Order of Victoria and Albert and the Royal Family Order of Edward VII.
(right) LOUISE MARGARET, DUCHESS OF CONNAUGHT, as Colonel-in-Chief of the 8th Brandenburg Regiment wearing the Order of Louisa (Prussia), the Order of Victoria and Albert (as a medal), the Order of the Crown of India, the Order of St John, a hidden medal and the Queen Victoria Jubilee Medal.

returned to the Queen, for re-issue, by the heirs of the recipients, particularly when one considers the value of money at the time. After 1901, however, King Edward VII and King George V allowed them to be retained in the families of the wearers.

After 1880 there were no further changes in the arrangement of the Order during the rest of the reign. Nevertheless, an interesting idea did come up for discussion. In many foreign ladies' Orders the Badge was worn to a sash for the First Class decoration and suspended to a bow on the left shoulder for the Second Class. Of these the Russian Order of St Catherine was a striking example, and the Portuguese St Isabella another. Both of these distinctions the Queen herself had received almost fifty years before. Now Her Majesty became concerned that the First Class Victoria and Albert worn on the shoulder by the British princesses did not show up very well compared with the striking sashes of the Russian and Portuguese Orders. The idea of using a sash for the Family Order had a certain appeal. At this point the Prince of Wales was asked to look over the Rules and Regulations and give an opinion. On 19 February 1888 Sir Henry reported that the Prince 'didn't much like the idea of a Grand Cordon because the Order of Victoria and Albert as he saw it was unique in being the only (United Kingdom) Order worn on the shoulder.'[16] The Queen was not particularly pleased with this reply and was disposed to argue the point. She had her way, and members of the First Class were allowed to wear the v.a. Badge from a sash two and one quarter inches in width on ceremonial occasions, and from a bow on lesser occasions. HRH the Duchess of Connaught wore her v.a. from a sash at the Coronation of King Edward VII, at the opening of the first Parliament of the Union of South Africa in 1910 and on other occasions in accordance with the Ninth of

THE DUKE AND DUCHESS OF CONNAUGHT at the opening of the first Parliament of the Union of South Africa, 4 November 1910. The Duchess wears the Royal Order of Victoria and Albert suspended from a sash.

THE DUKE AND
DUCHESS OF FIFE,
c.1910. The Princess
Royal is wearing the
Royal Family Order of
Edward VII and Queen
Alexandra's 'Order'.
The Duke wears the
Royal Victorian Chain,
the Stars of the Order of
the Thistle, the Royal
Victorian Order and the
Order of St John with
the Jubilee Medal 1897,
Coronation Medal 1902
(*hidden*), Volunteer
Officers' Decoration and
the Commemorative
Medal of the Golden
Wedding of King
Christian IX and Queen
Louise of Denmark
1892.

the Rules and Regulations of the Order. At the State Opening of Parliament
in the United Kingdom on 14 February 1901, HRH Princess Louise, Duchess
of Argyll, is recorded as wearing the Order from a sash.[17]

A close examination of Queen Victoria's private decoration for ladies raises
an interesting question. Was it an Order at all in the generally accepted sense of
that word? It certainly carried the title, and it was regulated by a formal set of
rules explaining to whom it could be given and describing the devices to be
worn by recipients. Beyond these surface details the institution was endowed
with special characteristics that set it apart from others bearing the title
'Order'. The system of lateral entry with the grade being given based entirely
on social rank froze the members within their respective classes. On only one
occasion did the Queen make a promotion in the Order, that of Augusta, German Empress and Queen of Prussia, wife of her grandson the Emperor
William II. She was given the Second Class on her marriage in 1881 and promoted to the First Class in 1890 after her husband had become Emperor.

Until the last years of her reign, the strict rules regarding admission to the Third Class and Fourth Class were maintained. The Third Class was conferred only on Mistresses of the Robes and Ladies of the Bedchamber from 1864 to 1880. In that year the Queen conferred it on the Duchess of Marlborough 'for special services as wife of the Lord Lieutenant of Ireland'. Between then and the end of her reign the Queen conferred it on three further wives of Lords Lieutenant of Ireland and on three Vicereines of India, generally at the termination of their husbands' terms of office. She also gave the Third Class to the Marchioness of Salisbury in 1893 after the resignation of her husband as Prime Minister. The Fourth Class remained the preserve of Women of the Bedchamber, though towards the end of her reign the Queen began to give it to Extra Women of the Bedchamber as well. There might have been a further broadening out after the Queen's death had the Order been continued.

That the Queen expected her Order to survive her own reign is quite clear. The preamble to the rules stated that it had been founded 'for Us Our Heirs and Successors.'[18] Nevertheless, King Edward VII did not continue the Order. It was not abolished but simply allowed to lapse and it can only be concluded that the King's decision in this matter was correct. The more closely one looks at the Royal Order of Victoria and Albert, the more it can be seen to have two quite separate and unrelated components. The first two

THE ROYAL FAMILY ORDER OF KING EDWARD VII (1901–10). (*left*) the reverse containing the King's cipher; (*below left*) the Order worn by Queen Alexandra, and (*below right*) the Order worn by other recipients.

classes resembled King George IV's Family Order, while the third and fourth classes were little more than two graduated badges of office for ladies-in-waiting. Additionally, he could hardly be expected to have the same interest in the numerous Royal European female relations possessed by his mother. The last surviving member of the Royal Order of Victoria and Albert was HRH Princess Alice, Countess of Athlone who died on 3 January 1981 in her ninety-eighth year. She was, at that time, in the unique position of having two sets of insignia of the Order, being effectively promoted from the Second Class to the First Class long after the Order ceased to be awarded. She received the Second Class from Queen Victoria on 9 April 1898 at the time of her confirmation. On the death of her mother, the Duchess of Albany, in 1922, King George V gave Princess Alice permission to retain and wear the Duchess's insignia of the First Class and she wore it on appropriate occasions until the end of her life. On 31 January 1966, as Chancellor of the University of the West Indies, she laid the foundation stone of the John F. Kennedy College of Arts and Science. Sixty-five years after this long-forgotten Order had ceased to be conferred, and by which time she was the sole surviving recipient, the plaque celebrating the occasion carefully records her as 'HRH Princess Alice, Countess of Athlone, GCVO, GBE, VA.'

The decision not to continue with the Order did not resolve the need for something to replace it. Because of its peculiar dual nature, the Order of Victoria and Albert had served both its purposes and something was needed

THE ROYAL FAMILY ORDER OF GEORGE V worn by Princess Alice, Duchess of Gloucester; (*below*) the reverse of the badge.

PRINCESS ALICE,
COUNTESS OF
ATHLONE, wearing the
Royal Order of Victoria
and Albert and the
Royal Family Orders of
King George V and
Queen Elizabeth II.
Princess Alice also had
the Royal Family Order
of King George VI.

THE ROYAL FAMILY ORDER OF KING GEORGE V was made in four sizes and was suspended from a plain light blue watered ribbon. The largest size was worn by Queen Mary and Queen Alexandra. These photographs, (*opposite and above*) taken by Garrard *c.*1911, prior to bestowal, illustrate the differences in the sizes.

THE ROYAL FAMILY
ORDER OF KING
GEORGE VI worn by
Princess Alice, Duchess
of Gloucester.
(*above*) The reverse of
the badge.

to take its place. The first step was formally to separate the two functions
performed by the Order. The King followed the example of George IV and
established a new Family Order, suspended from a ribbon bow of his racing
colours, for the Queen Consort and British princesses, to replace the First
and Second classes. The Third and Fourth Classes of the Royal Order of
Victoria and Albert had effectively functioned as badges of office for the
Mistress of the Robes, Ladies of the Bedchamber and Women of the
Bedchamber, for whom new badges of office were designed. (These are dealt
with in Chapter V.) The badge of King Edward VII's new Order given to
Queen Alexandra contained his miniature set in a crowned diamond frame
that bore a close resemblance to the device originally given to the Princess
Royal by his great uncle. A similar but smaller badge was given only to his
immediate family and presented to his sisters and sisters-in-law and daughters and daughter-in-law. All were made by Garrard in time for the King's
Coronation, in 1902.

This tradition has been followed in succeeding reigns with the colour of the
ribbon being individual to each monarch.

The Royal Family Order of King George V was suspended from a plain
light blue watered ribbon wider than that worn on his father's badge. The

THE ROYAL FAMILY
ORDER OF QUEEN
ELIZABETH II (*right*)
size one worn by
Princess Margaret;
(*below right*) size two
worn by Princess Alice,
Duchess of Gloucester;
(*below left*) the reverse
of the badge.

THE QUEEN wearing the Royal Family Order of King George V and King George VI, together with the insignia of the Order of the Crown of the Realm (Darjah Utama Seri Mahkota Negara) of Malaysia, during the State Visit to Malaysia in 1989.

order was made in four sizes and more widely distributed than that of the previous reign. The largest size was worn by Queen Mary and Queen Alexandra and the first awards were made in time for the Coronation in 1911.

King George VI's Family Order was suspended from a pink watered ribbon the same width as that of his father but only made in the two sizes. Two large and five smaller badges were supplied by Garrard in May 1937 and the first presentations were made by the King at a family lunch at Buckingham Palace two days before the Coronation.

The Family Order of Queen Elizabeth II is suspended from a yellow silk watered ribbon the same width as on her father's order, and has been made in two sizes. The larger size was given to Queen Mary and Queen Elizabeth The Queen Mother. These and five smaller badges were given at Christmas 1952. It is interesting to note that Queen Mary held the remarkable distinction of being awarded every Royal Family Order from that of Queen Victoria to that of her great-great-granddaughter. In every case, the portrait used has remained the same throughout the reign, taking no account of the advancing age of the monarch.

MEMBERS OF THE ROYAL ORDER
OF VICTORIA AND ALBERT

═══

Instituted 10 February 1862.
Enlarged 10 October 1864, 15 November 1865 and 15 March 1880.
No awards made after 1901.

SOVEREIGN: Her Majesty Queen Victoria

FIRST CLASS

20 March 1856	HIM **Victoria** Adelaide Mary Louisa, German Empress and Queen of Prussia (Princess Royal of Great Britain and Ireland). *Daughter of Queen Victoria, wife of Frederick III of Germany. Born 21 November 1840. Died 5 August 1901.*
21 April 1859	HRH The Princess **Alice** Maud Mary, Grand Duchess of Hesse and by Rhine (Princess Alice of Great Britain and Ireland). *Daughter of Queen Victoria, wife of Louis IV, Grand Duke of Hesse. Born 25 April 1843. Died 14 December 1878.*
17 April 1862	HRH The Princess **Helena** Augusta Victoria, Princess Christian of Schleswig-Holstein (Princess Helena of Great Britain and Ireland). *Daughter of Queen Victoria, wife of Prince Christian of Schleswig-Holstein. Born 25 May 1846. Died 9 June 1923.*
9 March 1863	HM Queen **Alexandra** (formerly HRH The Princess of Wales). *Daughter of King Christian IX of Denmark, wife of Albert Edward, Prince of Wales later King Edward VII. Born 1 December 1844. Died 20 November 1925.*
21 January 1865	HRH The Princess **Louise** Caroline Alberta, Duchess of Argyll. *Daughter of Queen Victoria, wife of John, 9th Duke of Argyll. Born 18 March 1848. Died 3 December 1939.*
8 May 1872	HIM Marie Louise **Augusta** Catherine, German Empress and Queen of Prussia. *Daughter of Charles, Duke of Saxe-Weimar-Eisenach, wife of Emperor William I of Germany. Born 30 September 1811. Died 7 January 1890.*
8 January 1874	HRH The Princess **Beatrice** Mary Victoria Feodore, Princess Henry of Battenberg. *Daughter of Queen Victoria, wife of Prince Henry of Battenberg. Born 14 April 1857. Died 26 October 1944.*
22 January 1874	HR and IH **Marie** Alexandrovna, Reigning Duchess of Saxe-Coburg and Gotha (Duchess of Edinburgh and Grand Duchess of Russia). *Daughter of Emperor Alexander II of Russia, wife of Alfred, Duke of Edinburgh. Born 17 October 1853. Died 25 October 1920.*
25 June 1875	HIM **Maria** Alexandrovna, Empress of Russia. *Daughter of Louis II, Grand Duke of Hesse, wife of Emperor Alexander II of Russia. Born 8 August 1824. Died 9 June 1880.*
30 November 1875	HM Queen **Louise** Wilhelmina Frederica Caroline Augusta Julie, Queen of Denmark. *Daughter of Landgrave William of Hesse-Cassel, wife of King Christian IX of Denmark, (mother of Queen Alexandra). Born 31 October 1851. Died 20 March 1926.*
25 June 1878	HM Queen **Marie** Alexandrina Wilhelmina Catherine Charlotte Theresa Henrietta Louisa Paulina Elizabeth Frederica Georgina, Duchess of Cumberland and Teviotdale and Queen of Hanover. *Daughter of John, Duke of Saxe-Altenburg, wife of George, Duke of Cumberland (King George V of Hanover). Born 14 April 1818. Died 9 January 1907.*
22 August 1878	HM Queen **Marie** Henriette Ann, Queen of the Belgians. *Daughter of Joseph, Archduke of Austria, wife of King Leopold II of the Belgians. Born 23 August 1836. Died 19 September 1902.*
12 March 1879	HRH The Princess **Louise Margaret** Alexandra Victoria Agnes, Duchess of Connaught and Strathearn. *Daughter of Prince Frederick Charles of Prussia, wife of Arthur, Duke of Connaught and Strathearn, son of Queen Victoria. Born 25 June 1860. Died 14 March 1917.*

26 April 1882	HRH The Princess **Helena** Frederica Augusta, Duchess of Albany. *Daughter of George, Prince of Waldeck-Pyrmont, wife of Leopold, Duke of Albany, son of Queen Victoria. Born 17 February 1861. Died 1 September 1922.*
3 March 1885	HRH The Princess **Louise** Victoria Alexandra Dagmar, (Duchess of Fife), Princess Royal. *Daughter of King Edward VII, wife of Alexander Duff, Duke of Fife. Born 20 February 1867. Died 4 January 1931.*
6 August 1886	HRH The Princess **Victoria** Alexandra Olga Mary of Wales. *Daughter of King Edward VII. Born 6 July 1868. Died 3 December 1935.*
10 March 1888	HM Queen **Maud** Charlotte Mary Victoria, Queen of Norway, Princess Maud of Wales. *Daughter of Edward VII, wife of King Haakon VII of Norway. Born 26 November 1869. Died 20 November 1938.*
10 July 1889	HM Queen **Maria Christina**, Queen Regent of Spain. *Daughter of Charles, Archduke of Austria, wife of King Alphonso XII of Spain. Born 21 July 1858. Died 6 February 1929.*
27 February 1890	HRH The Princess **Louise** Marie Elizabeth of Prussia, Grand Duchess of Baden. *Daughter of Emperor William I of Germany, wife of Frederick I, Grand Duke of Baden. Born 3 December 1838. Died 23 April 1923.*
8 August 1890	HIM **Augusta Victoria** Frederica Louise Feodora Jenny, German Empress and Queen of Prussia. *Daughter of Frederick, Duke of Schleswig-Holstein-Sonderburg-Augstenburg, wife of Emperor William II of Germany. Born 22 October 1858. Died 11 April 1921. (promoted from 2nd Class)*
9 December 1890	HM Queen **Elizabeth** of Romania. *Daughter of Hermann, Prince of Wied, wife of King Carol I of Romania. Born 29 December 1843. Died 3 March 1916.*
6 July 1893	HM Queen **Mary**, Duchess of York. *Daughter of Francis, Duke of Teck, wife of King George V. Born 26 May 1867. Died 24 March 1953.*
24 May 1896	HIM **Victoria** Alix Helena Louise Beatrice, Empress of Russia. *Daughter of Louis IV, Grand Duke of Hesse, wife of Emperor Nicholas II of Russia. Born 6 June 1872. Died 16 July 1918.*
25 April 1898	HM Queen **Wilhelmina** Helena Pauline Marie of the Netherlands. *Daughter of King William III of the Netherlands, wife of Henry, Duke of Mecklenburg-Schwerin. Born 31 August 1880. Died 28 November 1962.*

SECOND CLASS

31 March 1880	HIH Princess **Elizabeth** Alexandra Louise Alice, *Daughter of Louis IV, Grand Duke of Hesse, wife of Serge, Grand Duke of Russia. Born 1 November 1864. Died 17/18 July 1918.*
16 August 1880	HRH Princess Victoria Elizabeth Augusta **Charlotte**, Duchess of Saxe-Meiningen. *Daughter of Emperor Frederick III of Germany, wife of Bernard, Duke of Saxe-Meiningen. Born 24 July 1860. Died 1 October 1919.*
27 February 1881	HIM **Augusta Victoria** Frederica Louise Feodora Jenny, German Empress and Queen of Prussia, (from 1888). *Born 22 October 1858. Died 11 April 1921 (promoted to 1st Class 8 August 1890)*
21 March 1883	HRH Princess **Irene** Maria Louisa Anna. *Daughter of Louis IV, Grand Duke of Hesse, wife of Prince Henry of Prussia. Born 11 July 1866. Died 11 November 1953*
12 April 1883	HRH Princess Frederica Wilhelmina Amelia **Victoria**. *Daughter of Emperor Frederick III of Germany, wife of Prince Adolf of Schaumburg-Lippe and subsequently of Mr Alexander Zubkov. Born 12 April 1866. Died 13 November 1929.*
27 June 1884	HGDH Princess **Mary** Amelia of Leiningen. *Daughter of Leopold, Grand Duke of Baden, wife of Ernest, Prince of Leiningen. Born 20 November 1834. Died 21 November 1899.*
21 June 1887	HH Princess **Victoria** Louise Sophie Augusta Amelia **Helena** of Schleswig-Holstein (later known as HH Princess Helena Victoria). *Daughter of Prince Christian of Schleswig-Holstein. Born 3 May 1870. Died 13 March 1948.*
20 August 1887	HM Queen **Sophie** Dorothea Ulrica Alice of Greece. *Daughter of Emperor of Frederick III of Germany, wife of King Constantine I of Greece. Born 14 June 1870. Died 13 January 1932.*

25 April 1888	HRH Princess **Margaret** Beatrice Feodora. *Daughter of Emperor William II of Germany, wife of Frederick, Landgrave of Hesse. Born 22 April 1872. Died 22 January 1954.*
25 May 1890	HH Princess Franziska Josepha **Louise** Augusta **Marie** Christina Helena of Schleswig-Holstein, (later known as HH Princess Marie Louise). *Daughter of Prince Christian of Schleswig-Holstein, wife of Prince Aribert of Anhalt. Born 12 August 1872. Died 8 December 1956.*
15 May 1891	HM Queen **Marie** Alexandra Victoria of Romania. *Daughter of Alfred, Duke of Edinburgh, wife of King Ferdinand I of Romania. Born 29 October 1875. Died 18 July 1938.*
15 May 1891	HIH Princess **Victoria Melita**. *Daughter of Alfred, Duke of Edinburgh, wife of Ernest Louis, Grand Duke of Hesse and later Grand Duke Cyril of Russia . Born 25 November 1876. Died 2 March 1936.*
6 July 1893	HRH Princess **Mary Adelaide** Wilhelmina Elizabeth. *Daughter of Adolphus, Duke of Cambridge, wife of Francis Duke of Teck (mother of Queen Mary). Born 27 November 1833. Died 27 October 1897.*
8 March 1895	HRH Princess **Alexandra** Louise Olga Victoria. *Daughter of Alfred Duke of Edinburgh, wife of Ernest, Prince of Hohenlohe-Langenburg. Born 1 September 1878. Died 16 April 1942.*
5 March 1898	HRH Princess **Margaret** Victoria Augusta Charlotte Norah, Crown Princess of Sweden. *Daughter of Arthur Duke of Connaught, wife of Gustaf Adolf, Crown Prince of Sweden (later King Gustaf V). Born 15 January 1882. Died 1 May 1920.*
9 April 1898	HRH Princess **Alice Mary** Victoria Augusta Pauline. *Daughter of Leopold, Duke of Albany, wife of Alexander Cambridge, 1st Earl of Athlone. Born 25 February 1883. Died 3 January 1981.*
	HRH Princess **Beatrice** Leopoldine Victoria.* *Daughter of Alfred, Duke of Edinburgh (later Duke of Saxe Coburg and Gotha), wife of Alphonso, Infante of Spain, Duke of Galliera. Born 20 April 1884. Died 13 July 1866.*

THIRD CLASS

5 November 1864	Elizabeth, Duchess of Wellington. *Mistress of the Robes 1861–8 and 1874–80 Born 27 September 1820. Died 13 August 1904.*
28 November 1864	Jane Frederica Harriot Mary, Countess of Caledon. *Lady of the Bedchamber 1858–78. Born 17 January 1825. Died 30 March 1888.*
26 January 1865	Jane, Baroness Churchill. *Lady of the Bedchamber 1854–1900 Born 1 June 1826. Died 25 December 1900.*
27 February 1865	Jane, Marchioness of Ely. *Lady of the Bedchamber 1851–89 Born 3 December 1821. Died 11 June 1890.*
13 March 1865	Susanna Stephania, Duchess of Roxburghe. *Lady of the Bedchamber 1865–95. Acting Mistress of the Robes January to July 1886 Born 28 August 1814. Died 7 May 1895.*
20 March 1365	Frances, Countess of Gainsborough. *Lady of the Bedchamber 1837–72 Born 20 November 1814. Died 12 May 1885.*
27 March 1865	Frances Elizabeth, Viscountess Jocelyn. *Lady of the Bedchamber 1841–65 Born 8 February 1820. Died 26 March 1880.*
3 May 1865	Elizabeth Jane, Baroness Waterpark. *Lady of the Bedchamber 1864–90 Born 26 February 1816. Died 15 September 1894.*
19 May 1865	Caroline Augusta, Countess of Mount Edgcumbe. *Lady of the Bedchamber 1840–54 and 1863–65. Born 22 January 1808. Died 2 November 1881.*
24 May 1865	Anne, Duchess of Atholl. *Lady of the Bedchamber 1854–97, Mistress of the Robes 1852–3, Acting Mistress of the Robes January to July 1886 Born 17 June 1814. Died 18 May 1897.*
6 February 1866	Harriet Elizabeth Georgina, Duchess of Sutherland . *Mistress of the Robes 1837–41, 1846–52, 1853–58, 1859–61. Born 21 May 1806. Died 27 October 1868.*
10 February 1868	Eliza Horatia Frederica, Viscountess Clifden. *Lady of the Bedchamber 1867–72 Born 16 July 1833. Died 23 April 1896.*

* There would appear to be no record of the date of the award of the Order to Princess Beatrice of Saxe-Coburg and Gotha as she then was. The strong probability is that she was given it at the time of her Confirmation in July 1899.

16 December 1868	Elizabeth Georgiana, Duchess of Argyll. *Mistress of the Robes 1868–70 Born 30 May 1824. Died 25 May 1878.*
29 January 1870	Anne, Duchess of Sutherland and Countess of Cromartie. *Mistress of the Robes 1870–74. Born 21 April 1829. Died 25 November 1888.*
11 May 1872	Blanche Julia, Countess of Mayo, *Lady of the Bedchamber 1872–74 Born 21 November 1826. Died 31 January 1918.*
8 April 1873	Eliza Amelia, Countess of Erroll. *Lady of the Bedchamber 1873–1901 Born 24 February 1829. Died 11 March 1916.*
8 May 1873	Julia Janet Georgina, Baroness Abercromby. *Lady of the Bedchamber 1874–85 Born 26 January 1840. Died 8 December 1915.*
26 November 1878	Ismania Catherine, Baroness Southampton. *Lady of the Bedchamber 1878–1901 Born . Died 18 August 1918.*
12 August 1879	Charlotte Anne, Duchess of Buccleuch. *Mistress of the Robes 1841–46 Born 10 April 1811. Died 28 March 1895.*
3 May 1880	Frances Anne Emily, Duchess of Marlborough. *Born 15 April 1822. Died 16 April 1899. Conferred for special services as wife of the Lord Lieutenant of Ireland.*
6 May 1880	Elizabeth, Duchess of Bedford. *Mistress of the Robes 1880–83, Acting Mistress of the Robes January to July 1886. Born 23 September 1818. Died 22 April 1897.*
2 July 1881	Louisa Jane, Duchess of Abercorn. *Born 8 July 1812. Died 31 March 1905.*
21 May 1883	Anne Emily, Duchess of Roxburghe. *Mistress of the Robes 1883–85 Born 14 November 1854. Died 20 June 1923.*
28 June 1885	Charlotte Frances Frederica, Countess Spencer. *Born 28 September 1835. Died 31 October 1903. Conferred on the resignation of Earl Spencer as Lord Lieutenant of Ireland.*
4 July 1885	Louisa Jane, Duchess of Buccleuch. *Mistress of the Robes 1885–February 1886, August 1886–92, 1895–1901. Born 16 August 1836. Died 17 March 1912.*
17 April 1886	Emily Theresa, Baroness Ampthill. *Lady of the Bedchamber 1885–1901 Born 9 September 1842. Died 22 February 1907.*
25 January 1889	Harriet Georgina, Marchioness of Dufferin and Ava. *Born 5 February 1843. Died 25 October 1936. Conferred on her return from India at the termination of the Marquess of Dufferin and Ava's Viceroyalty.*
7 July 1889	Cecilia Maria Charlotte, Viscountess Downe. *Lady of the Bedchamber 1889–1901 Born 17 November 1838. Died 26 May 1910.*
10 March 1891	Louisa Jane, Countess of Antrim. *Lady of the Bedchamber 1889–1901 Born 15 February 1855. Died 2 April 1949.*
2 August 1893	Georgina Caroline, Marchioness of Salisbury. *Born . Died 20 November 1899. Conferred on the resignation of the Marquess of Salisbury as Prime Minister.*
11 March 1894	Maud Evelyn, Marchioness of Lansdowne. *Born 17 December 1850. Died 21 October 1932. Conferred on her return from India at the termination of the Marquess of Lansdowne's Viceroyalty.*
3 October 1895	Edith, Countess of Lytton. *Born 15 September 1841. Died 17 September 1936. Conferred on her return from India at the termination of the Earl of Lytton's Viceroyalty.*
19 April 1900	Beatrix Jane, Countess Cadogan. *Born 8 August 1844. Died 9 February 1907. Conferred on the occasion of Queen Victoria's visit to Ireland.*
1901*	Verena Maud, Viscountess Churchill. *Lady of the Bedchamber 1901 Born 6 April 1865. Died 25 December 1938.*

FOURTH CLASS

17 November 1865	Lady Caroline Barrington. *Woman of the Bedchamber 1837–75 Born 30 August 1799. Died 18 April 1875.*
11 March 1866	Catherine Mary, The Honourable Mrs Robert Bruce. *Woman of the Bedchamber 1862–63 and 1866–89. Born 8 October 1824. Died 3 December 1889.*
4 April 1866	Lady Augusta Frederica Elizabeth Stanley. *Woman of the Bedchamber 1861–63 Born 3 April 1822. Died 1 March 1876.*
23 August 1866	The Honourable Mrs George Campbell. *Woman of the Bedchamber 1837–73 Born 30 June 1802. Died 14 October 1873.*

* Exact date of conferment is unknown.

23 August 1866	Caroline Emilia Mary, The Honourable Lady Hamilton-Gordon. *Woman of the Bedchamber 1855–1901. Born 31 March 1830. Died 29 January 1909.*
23 August 1866	Frances, Viscountess Chewton. *Woman of the Bedchamber 1855–1901 Born 29 August 1816. Died 11 April 1902.*
23 August 1866	Lady Sarah Elizabeth Lindsay. *Woman of the Bedchamber 1859–90 Born 23 September 1813. Died 16 December 1890.*
23 August 1866	Mary, Lady Codrington. *Woman of the Bedchamber 1856–85 Born 22 December 1814. Died 28 June 1898.*
12 November 1866	Lady Charlotte Copley. *Woman of the Bedchamber 1837–66 Born 22 October 1810. Died 10 August 1875.*
2 December 1869	Mary Frederica, The Honourable Lady Biddulph. *Honorary Woman of the Bedchamber 1857–75 and Lady in Attendance on Princess Beatrice 1875–96 Born 2 May 1824. Died 23 October 1902.*
8 May 1872	Caroline Eliza, The Honourable Mrs Charles Grey. *Extra Woman of the Bedchamber 1870–90. Born 20 March 1814. Died 4 November 1890.*
20 June 1872	Frances Mary, Viscountess Forbes. *Woman of the Bedchamber 1837–74 Born 21 October 1810. Died 25 December 1877.*
2 January 1874	Lady Elizabeth Philippa Biddulph. *Woman of the Bedchamber 1874–77 Born 15 November 1834. Died 13 January 1916.*
1 January 1875	The Honourable Flora Isabella Clementina Macdonald. *Woman of the Bedchamber 1847–74. Born 1822. Died 21 December 1899.*
15 April 1875	Anne Carmichael, The Honourable Mrs George Hope. *Woman of the Bedchamber 1875–77. Born 27 January 1824. Died 28 May 1877.*
18 July 1877	Nina Maria, The Honourable Mrs George Ferguson of Pitfour. *Woman of the Bedchamber 1877–1901. Born 4 September 1841. Died 5 June 1923.*
2 August 1877	The Honourable Horatia Frances Charlotte Stopford. *Woman of the Bedchamber 1877–1901. Born 25 January 1835. Died 6 February 1920.*
27 January 1880	The Honourable Emily Sarah Cathcart. *Extra Woman of the Bedchamber 1880–91, Woman of the Bedchamber 1891–1901. Born 29 November 1834. Died 16 February 1917.*
26 January 1885	Charlotte Sobieski Isabel, Lady Cust. *Woman of the Bedchamber 1885–99 Born 20 May 1835. Died 13 June 1914.*
14 May 1885	Magdalen, The Honourable Mrs Gerald Wellesley. *Extra Woman of the Bedchamber 1882–1901. Born 30 September 1831. Died 30 September 1919.*
23 July 1885	Mary Elizabeth, The Honourable Lady Ponsonby. *Maid of Honour 1853–61, Extra Woman of the Bedchamber 1895–1901. Born 21 September 1832. Died 16 October 1916.*
30 October 1888	Ina Erskine, Duchess of Argyll. *Extra Woman of the Bedchamber 1888– Born . Died 24 December 1925.*
2 May 1889	Lady Geraldine Harriet Anne Somerset. *Lady in Waiting to HRH The Duchess of Cambridge. Born 19 June 1832. Died 22 January 1915.*
25 May 1889	The Honourable Harriet Lepel Phipps. *Woman of the Bedchamber 1889–1901 Born 22 January 1841. Died 7 March 1922.*
20 August 1890	Georgina, Mrs Townshend Wilson. *Extra Woman of the Bedchamber 1890–1894 Born 3 December 1826. Died 26 December 1894.*
10 December 1891	Frances Jemima, Mrs John Drummond of Megginch. *Extra Woman of the Bedchamber 1891. Born 9 February 1818. Died 22 December 1891.*
21 August 1894	The Honourable Caroline Cavendish. *Extra Woman of the Bedchamber 1894–1901 Born 11 November 1826. Died 25 January 1910.*
15 February 1895	Georgina Elizabeth, Lady Cowell. *Extra Woman of the Bedchamber 1894–1901 Born 5 February 1846. Died 3 November 1927.*
16 October 1895	Marie Constance, The Honourable Lady Mallet. *Extra Woman of the Bedchamber 1895–1901. Born 8 February 1862. Died 5 March 1934.*
12 December 1895	Victoria Matilda Susan, The Honourable Mrs Alaric Grant. *Extra Woman of the Bedchamber 1895–1901. Born 8 November 1857. Died 4 November 1938.*
24 June 1897	Miss Ethel Henrietta Maria Cadogan. *Woman of the Bedchamber 1897–1901 Born 31 December 1853. Died 30 December 1930.*
24 August 1899	Helen, Mrs John Haughton. *Woman of the Bedchamber 1899–1901 Born 1866. Died 10 April 1925.*

RECIPIENTS OF
THE ROYAL FAMILY ORDERS

═══

THE ROYAL FAMILY ORDER OF KING EDWARD VII

SIZE ONE

HM Queen Alexandra

SIZE TWO

HRH The Princess of Wales (later HM Queen Mary)
HRH Princess Louise, Duchess of Fife (later HRH The Princess Royal)
HRH Princess Victoria
HRH Princess Maud of Denmark (later HM Queen Maud of Norway)
HRH Princess Christian of Schleswig-Holstein-Sonderburg Augustenburg
HRH Princess Louise, Duchess of Argyll
HRH Princess Henry of Battenberg
HIH Duchess Marie of Saxe-Coburg and Gotha (Duchess of Edinburgh)
HRH The Duchess of Connaught
HRH The Duchess of Albany

THE ROYAL FAMILY ORDER OF KING GEORGE V

SIZE ONE

HM Queen Mary
HM Queen Alexandra

SIZE TWO

HRH The Duchess of York (later HM Queen Elizabeth the Queen Mother)
HRH The Duchess of Gloucester (Princess Alice, Duchess of Gloucester)
HRH The Duchess of Kent (Princess Marina, Duchess of Kent)
HRH Princess Mary, Countess of Harewood (later HRH The Princess Royal)
HRH Princess Victoria
HRH Princess Louise, Duchess of Fife (HRH The Princess Royal)
HM Queen Maud of Norway
HRH Princess Henry of Battenberg
HRH Princess Louise, Duchess of Argyll
HRH Princess Christian of Schleswig-Holstein
HIH Duchess Marie of Saxe-Coburg and Gotha (Duchess of Edinburgh)
HRH The Duchess of Connaught
HRH The Duchess of Albany

SIZE THREE

HRH Princess Elizabeth of York (later HM Queen Elizabeth II)
HRH Princess Margaret of York (later HRH Princess Margaret, Countess of Snowdon)

SIZE FOUR

HRH Princess Alice, Countess of Athlone
The Marchioness of Cambridge
HRH Princess Arthur of Connaught (Duchess of Fife)
HH Princess Maud of Fife (Countess of Southesk)
HRH Crown Princess Margaret of Sweden
Lady Patricia Ramsay

THE ROYAL FAMILY ORDER OF KING GEORGE VI

SIZE ONE

HM Queen Elizabeth (later HM Queen Elizabeth The Queen Mother)
HM Queen Mary

SIZE TWO

HRH Princess Elizabeth (later HM Queen Elizabeth II)
HRH Princess Margaret (later HRH Princess Margaret, Countess of Snowdon)
HRH The Princess Royal (Princess Mary, Countess of Harewood)
HRH The Duchess of Gloucester (Princess Alice, Duchess of Gloucester)
HRH The Duchess of Kent (Princess Marina, Duchess of Kent)
HRH Princess Alexandra of Kent

THE ROYAL FAMILY ORDER OF QUEEN ELIZABETH II

SIZE ONE

HM Queen Elizabeth The Queen Mother
HM Queen Mary

SIZE TWO

HRH Princess Margaret, Countess of Snowdon
HRH Princess Alice, Duchess of Gloucester
HRH Princess Marina, Duchess of Kent
HRH The Princess Royal (Princess Mary, Countess of Harewood)
HRH Princess Alice, Countess of Athlone
HRH Princess Alexandra, the Honourable Mrs Angus (later the Hon Lady) Ogilvy
HRH The Princess Royal
HRH The Duchess of Kent
HRH The Duchess of Gloucester
HRH The Princess of Wales

THE RULES AND REGULATIONS
OF THE ROYAL ORDER OF
VICTORIA AND ALBERT 1887

====

VICTORIA R.I.

VICTORIA, by the Grace of God, of the United Kingdom of Great Britain and Ireland, Queen, Defender of the Faith, Empress of India, and Sovereign of the Royal Order of Victoria and Albert, To all to whom these Presents shall come, Greeting: WHEREAS We were graciously pleased by Warrant under Our Sign Manual, and countersigned by one of Our Principal Secretaries of State, bearing date the tenth day of February, in the Twenty-fifth year of Our Reign, in consideration of the Happiness We had experienced in Our married state, for a period of more than twenty-one years, and the blessings which it had pleased Almighty God to Bestow upon Us and Our Dearly Beloved and ever to be lamented Husband, His Royal Highness FRANCIS ALBERT AUGUSTUS CHARLES EMANUEL, THE PRINCE CONSORT, Duke of Saxony, Prince of Saxe Coburg Gotha, We resolved to commemorate our happy Marriage by the Institution of a Family Order of Distinction, to be enjoyed by Our Most Dear Children, the Princesses of Our Royal House, and by such other Princesses upon whom We from time to time should confer the same, We did institute, constitute, and create a family Order of Distinction, to be for ever thereafter named, styled, and designated 'THE ROYAL ORDER OF VICTORIA AND ALBERT'.

AND WHEREAS We were further pleased in and by the said Warrant to make rules and ordinances for the government of the same, wherein certain powers were reserved to Us; AND WHEREAS We were pleased by Warrants bearing date respectively the tenth day of October, one thousand eight hundred and sixty-four, the fifteenth day of November, one thousand eight hundred and sixty-five, and the fifteenth day of March, one thousand eight hundred and eighty, to make certain alterations in Our said Order, and to make rules and regulations in that behalf; AND WHEREAS We think fit to make new rules and ordinances for the government of the said Order. Now, We exercising the power vested in Us, do hereby, within certain exceptions hereinafter specified, annul, abrogate, and repeal all and every the said rules and ordinances, with the intention of making, ordaining and establishing the following rules and ordinances, as well as of confirming such portion as may concern the vested rights of any person or persons, and of renewing such other portions thereof as may be specially set forth, or referred to, in the following rules: NOW, KNOW YE, that we have made, ordained and established, and by these Presents under Our Sign Manual, do make, ordain, and establish, the following rules and ordinances, which shall from henceforth be observed and kept within the said Order.

First. – That the Order shall henceforth as heretofore be styled and designated 'The Royal Order of Victoria and Albert,' and that the tenth day of February of every year shall henceforth be taken and deemed to be the Anniversary of the institution of the said Order.

Second. – It is ordained that the said Royal Order shall consist of the Sovereign and of four several Classes, to be styled, respectively, the First Class, the Second Class, the Third Class, and the Fourth Class.

Third. – That we, Our Heirs and Successors, Kings and Queens Regnant of the United Kingdom of Great Britain and Ireland, shall be Sovereigns thereof.

Fourth. – We do declare and ordain that the Daughters, the Wives of the Sons, the Daughters of the Sons, and the Wives of the Sons of the Sons of Us, Our Heirs and

Successors, together with such Queens and Reigning Princesses of Foreign Houses connected by Blood to or in amity with Us, Our Heirs and Successors, shall be eligible to be admitted into the First Class of Our said Order whenever We are graciously pleased to declare the same. And We do hereby declare that the existing Members of the First Class of Our aforesaid Order of Victoria and Albert shall be Members of this Class, and be entitled to continue to wear the Decoration as heretofore and now worn by them.

Fifth. –That from and immediatley after the Solemn rite of Confirmation shall have been received by the Daughters, or by the Daughters of any Son of Us, Our Heirs and Successors, they shall become eligible to be nominated by Us, Our Heirs and Successors, Members of the First Class of the Order.

Sixth. –That it shall be competent for Us, Our Heirs and Successors, to confer the Decoration of the Second Class of the Order upon such of the Female descendants, and upon such of the Wives of the Male descendants of Us and Our said Dearly Beloved Consort; also upon other Female members of Our Royal House, and of Royal or Princely Foreign Families connected by Blood to, or in amity with, Us as We shall think fit.

Seventh. –That it shall be competent for the Sovereign of the Order to confer the Decoration of the Third Class upon such of the Ladies as have held, now hold, or may hereafter, hold the Office of Mistress of the Robes, Lady of the Bed-chamber, or other Office in the Household of the Queen Regnant, or Queen Consort of these Realms, and also upon Ladies not of Royal rank, nearly connected with Ourself or Our Royal Family, as We, Our Heirs and Successors, shall from time to time appoint. And it is Our Will and Pleasure that the several Ladies heretofore appointed by Us to the then Second Class of the Order shall be, and We do hereby declare them to be, Members of the Third Class of Our said Royal Order of Victoria and Albert, with all the rights and privileges to that Class belonging, in as full and ample a manner as if they had been so named and appointed by Us.

Eighth. – That it shall be competent for the Sovereign of the Order to confer the Decoration of the Fourth Class upon such Ladies as have held, now hold, or may hereafter hold the Office of Bed-chamber Women, or other Office in the Household of the Queen Regnant, or Queen Consort of these Realms, as also upon any other Ladies of a similar rank, as We our Heirs and Successors, shall from time to time think fit. And it is Our Will and Pleasure that the several Ladies heretofore appinted by Us to the then Third Class of the Order shall be, and We do hereby declare them to be, Members of the Fourth Class of Our said Royal Order of Victoria and Albert, with all the rights and privileges to that class belonging, in as full and ample a manner as if they had been so named and appointed by Us.

Ninth. – That the Decoration of the First Clas of the Order shall consist of an Onyx Cameo having Our Royal Effigy, and also that of Our Dearly Beloved Consort, conjointly thereon in an ornamental Oval set with Diamonds, surmounted by an Imperial Crown in precious stones; that the said Badge should be worn on all occasions of State or high Ceremony by the Members of this Class of the Order, suspended to a white moire Riband of two inches and a quarter in width passing from the right shoulder obliquely to the left side; or, on ordinary occasions, attached to a like Riband of an inch and a half in width, tied in a bow, on the left shoulder, as heretofore authorised and sanctioned.

Tenth. – That the Decoration of the Second Class of the Order shall consist of a like Cameo to the First Class, but of smaller size, encircled with Diamonds, and the Imperial Crown enamelled in proper colours attached to a white moire Riband of an inch in width, tied in a bow, and shall be worn on the left shoulder.

Eleventh. – That the Decoration of the Third Class of the Order shall be similar to that of the First Class, except that it shall be smaller, ornamented with Pearls and Diamonds, and the Imperial Crown enamelled in proper colours attached to a white moire Riband, and shall be worn in the same manner as those appertaining to the Second Class of Our said Order.

Twelfth. – That the Decoration of the Fourth Class of the Order shall consist of an oval-shaped Monogram, composed of the letters V.R. and A. (being Our Royal Cypher and the initial of Our Dearly Beloved Consort) in Gold, pierced and ornamented with Pearls and Diamonds, suspended from an Imperial Crown enamelled in proper colours, and ornamented with Diamonds, attached to a white moire Riband, and shall be worn in the same manner as those appertaining to the Third Class of Our said Order.

Thirteenth. – That no mistake may arise with respect to the said Decorations, We have directed that representations thereof shall be emblazoned and hereunto annexed.

Fourteenth. – That the said Order shall be conferred by personal investiture with the Insignia upon such Queens and Princesses as We, Our Heirs and Successors, may be pleased to nominate and appoint thereto, but in the absence from England of any Illustrious Personage so nominated and appointed, it shall be competent for Us, Our Heirs and Successors, to transmit the Decoration of the Order with an Autograph Letter.

Fifteenth. – We are pleased to declare that the expense attending the Order shall be borne by the Sovereign, or by The Sovereign and Queen Consort conjointly for the time being, and We do hereby further declare that the Decoration conferred upon any of the Princesses of Our Royal House (save and except Our most dear Daughter, Her Imperial Highness the Crown Princess of Germany and Prussia, who had, prior to the establishment of the original regulations for the government of the Order received the Decoration from Us), or of any Foreign House, or any other Lady admitted into either of the Classes of Our said Order, shall, in the event of Her or Their decease, be returned to Us, Our Heirs and Successors.

Sixteenth. – That a Register shall be kept in which the names of the Royal and Illustrious Princesses and others who may be admitted into this Order shall be enrolled, with the date of their respective admissions, and that a Registrar may be appointed by Us for the fulfilment of this duty.

Given at our Court at Osborne, under Our Sign Manual, this thirty-first day of December, in the Fifty-first year of Our Reign, and in the year of Our Lord One thousand eight hundred and eighty-seven.

By Her Majesty's Command,

HENRY MATTHEWS.

CHAPTER TWO

The King Edward VII's Medal for Science, Art and Music

KING EDWARD VII'S
MEDAL FOR SCIENCE,
ART AND MUSIC;
obverse and reverse
(enlarged).

THIS MEDAL had a short life of about four years; it was instituted in 1902 and no awards were apparently made after 1906, although there is a record of a further award in Denmark in 1910.

It has not been possible to establish the reason for its institution, but by the wording in the exergue ('For Science Art & Music') and by examination of a roll of the recipients, it was clearly intended to be bestowed on a class of person that hitherto had not been recognized to any wide degree by the Sovereign with an honour. The only surviving documentary references to the medal are four letters between the Honourable Sidney Greville* and Arthur Davidson†, all dated January 1903. These state that 'there is to be a new medal for "Science & Art" given both by the King and Queen, and both have agreed not to give it without the consent of the other'; there is then some discussion on the shades of the red and blue in the ribbon which continued throughout the four letters. In the event a ribbon of scarlet moire was decided upon with a central stripe of dark blue, three-eighths of an inch wide, with white stripes, one-eighth of an inch wide set in one-eighth of an inch from each border.

The medal itself, suspended from the ribbon by a ring, bears the conjoint heads of King Edward VII and Queen Alexandra on the obverse and a group of symbolic figures on the reverse. The circumference of the medal is formed of sprays of laurel.

There was also mention as to whether 'there should be anything on the velvet case such as a crown – or the two monograms of King and Queen side by side stamped in gold. Fraser says people so appreciate (?) something on the case.' In practice a blue velvet box was used on which was stamped a gold crown.

The Royal Archives contains a list of recipients, bound in a foolscap blue leather volume. This records the names of eleven individuals who received the medal. However a further, unrecorded, award to Sir James Gildea is known; there may well have been other recipients whose names are not on record. All the recipients received their medals in the years 1903 to 1906, but for some reason the medal then ceased to be awarded. This is rather sad as in its short life the medal, given to certain persons, distinguished in their own fields of

---

* The Honourable (Sir) Sydney Robert Greville, (KCVO), CVO, (1866–1927), Private Secretary to Queen Alexandra.

† Colonel (Sir) Arthur Davidson, (GCVO, KCB), CB, CVO, (1856–1922) Assistant Private Secretary to King Edward VII. The correspondence between Greville and Davidson is in the Royal Archives at Windsor Castle (RA PP Ed. VII 16428/1–4).

art and music, served a good purpose. The reasons for the institution and the demise of the medal are now a matter of speculation. There is the possibility that it was intended to be a junior Order of Merit which had been instituted in 1902. That Order was for arts, science and literature, and the medal for science, art and music. The overlap is plain to see. In the event, the majority of the twelve known recipients of the medal were musicians; none was an artist, and most were overseas nationals. Given the existence of the Order of Merit, it is not easy to know who the recipients of the medal might have been. Apart from three awards by Queen Alexandra when on a private visit to Copenhagen in April 1903, and the award to Sir James Gildea at an unknown date, all the other recipients were musicians who generally received the medal after performing before the King and Queen at private concerts. It was given as a private award by the King and Queen with little ceremony (but was noted in the Court Circular in some cases). Gildea's entry in *Who was Who* confirms the personal aspect by describing it as 'the King Edward and Queen Alexandra Personal Gold Medal'. As he was neither an artist, musician nor a scientist, but a militia officer and fund raiser – the founder of S.S.A.F.A. – his personal friendship with Queen Alexandra is possibly his reason for being awarded the medal.

As far as is known, no further medals were awarded after 1906. The final note on the medal is a comment in the Register that six ladies' and eighteen men's medals were sent to the Royal Mint on 8 February 1911 to be melted down.

RECIPIENTS OF
KING EDWARD VII'S MEDAL FOR
SCIENCE, ART AND MUSIC

NIELS FINSEN
(1860–1904).

FERDINAND MELDAHL
(1827–1908).

The first three awards of the medal, as listed in the Register, were made to Danes in 1903 when Queen Alexandra was on a private visit to Denmark to visit her father, King Christian IX, on his 85th birthday.

(1) PROFESSOR NIELS RYBERG FINSEN, *c.*April 1903. Born 15 December 1860 in Torshavn, Faroe Islands; died 24 September 1904 in Copenhagen, where buried. Son of Hannes Christian Steingrim Finsen (1828–1892), Lord-Lieutenant of the Faroe Islands, and Johanne Sophie Caroline Christine Formann (1833–1864). Married on 29 December 1892 to Ingeborg Dorothea Balslev (1868–1963). A distinguished physician, he received his M.D. from the University of Copenhagen in 1890. He then began his research on the effect of light, sunlight and artificial ultraviolet light on living organisms. In 1895–1896 he demonstrated the virtual cure of skin tuberculosis, *lupus vulgaris*. In 1890 he began the radiation treatment of cancer, and in the same year he established his own Institute and Hospital in Copenhagen which still exists as part of the Rigshospitalet (University Hospital of Copenhagen). Finsen became a professor in 1898, and was awarded the Nobel Prize for Medicine in 1903, donating a large part of the prize money to his Institute. He was appointed a Knight of the Dannebrog in 1899, receiving the Silver Badge of the same Order in 1904, and the Medal of Merit in Gold in 1903. Finsen also received honours from Russia, Prussia, Venezuela and France.

(2) FERDINAND MELDAHL, *c.* April 1903. Born 16 March 1827 at Frederiksberg; died 3 February 1908 in Copenhagen, buried in Lyngby. Son of Heinrich Joachim Meldahl (1776–1840), an iron founder, and Benedicte Louise Hansen (1796–1845). Married on 9 June 1860 to Caroline Amalie Raeder (1838–1906). He was the foremost Danish architect of his day. He began work as a moulder in his father's iron foundry, but in 1842 he became apprenticed to a bricklayer. In 1844 he began to study architecture at the Royal Academy of Arts in Copenhagen. He won the Academy's silver medals: in 1851 its small medal and in 1853 the great gold medal. In 1858 he became a Fellow of the Academy and from 1864–1905 he was Professor of Architecture; he was President and Director of the Academy 1873–1890 and 1899–1902. He was Royal Inspector of Buildings 1865–1902, and became a Councillor of State in 1867. In 1892 he received the title of Kammerherre (Chamberlain) to the King. Appointed a Knight of the Dannebrog in 1861, he was promoted Commander in 1874 and Grand Cross in 1904. He was honoured by Russia, Sweden, Siam, Norway, Prussia, Austria, Portugal, Italy, Mecklenburg, Greece and Hesse.

Meldahl's knowledge and interests were wide-ranging, covering every aspect of architecture. He was a leading member of the Copenhagen Building Association and exercised great influence over planning in the city; he had a particular interest in public and private buildings with social connotations and designed the Institute for the Blind. His work in designing or restoring buildings included manor houses, castles, churches, schools, hospitals and guild-

(*left*) DAME HELEN
MELBA (1861–1931).
(*right*) DAME MARIE
ALBANI (1847–1930).

halls. He supervised the restoration of Frederiksborg Castle after a fire in the years 1860–1875, Rosenborg Castle 1866–1890, and Christiansborg Castle after the fire of 1884.

(3) HENRI CARL AUGUST GLAESEL, 22 April 1903. Born 19 March 1853; died 1921. Son of Julius Glaesel (1813–1874), secretary of the railways in Jutland, and Henriette Danchell (1831–1916). He was married on 15 May 1888 to Ingeborg Fritsche. Glaesel was Inspector and Secretary for the State Furniture Commission which looks after the state furniture in the Royal castles and palaces. Appointed a Knight of the Dannebrog in 1898, he later received the Silver Badge of the Order. He was also decorated by Russia,

HENRI CARL AUGUST
GLAESEL (1853–1921).

(*left*) EDOUARD DE
RESKE (1853–1917).
(*right*) JEAN DE RESKE
(1850–1925).

(left) MARIE CECILIA JANOTHA (1856–1932), who is wearing her medal.
(right) CHARLES CAMILLE SAINT-SAENS (1835–1921).

Italy, Mecklenburg, France, Greece, Prussia and Siam. He was a councillor of the Borough of Frederiksborg 1901–1904, and President of the Federation of Danish Architects.

(4) DAME HELEN MELBA (Mrs Charles Nesbitt Frederick Armstrong), GBE 9 June 1904. Born 1861, died 1931. DBE 1918, promoted GBE 1927. Known as Dame Nellie Melba; née Mitchell. Australian soprano. She received the Medal at Buckingham Palace after performing at a state concert in honour of the Archduke Frederick Ferdinand of Austria. She had trained under Madame Marchesi and performed with both Jean de Reske and Edouard de Reske, three other recipients of the Medal. Her award is noted in *D.N.B.*, *Grove's Dictionary of Music and Musicians* and *The Times* 10 June 1904.

(5) JEAN DE RESKE. 6 July 1904. Born 1850, died 1925. Polish tenor. Honorary MVO, 4th Class, *London Gazette*, 2 June 1899. Together with his brother Edouard was received by the King and Queen at Buckingham Palace on 6 July 1904 and presented with the Medal. Refs.: *The Times* 7 July 1904; *Who was Who*; *Grove*.

(6) EDOUARD DE RESKE. 6 July 1904. Born 1853, died 1917. Polish bass. Honorary M.V.O., 4th Class, *London Gazette*, 20 July 1900. Received his Medal with his elder brother, q.v. Refs.: *Who was Who*.

(7) DAME MARIE LOUISE CECILE EMMA ALBANI (Mrs Ernest Gye), DBE 13 July 1904. Born 1847, died 1930. Known as Madame Albani; née Lajeunesse. Canadian soprano. DBE 1925. The bestowal of her Medal is noted in *The Times* of 9 July 1904: 'His Majesty the King has been graciously pleased to confer upon Mme Albani the Order of Merit for Art, Science and Music'.

(8) MARIE CECILIA NATALIA JANOTHA. 13 July 1904. Born 1856, died 1932. Known as Madamoiselle Janotha. Polish pianist and composer. She 'had the honour of playing upon the Pianoforte before the Queen this afternoon' and was presented with the Medal on that occasion. (*The Times*, 14 July 1904)

(left) JOSEPH HOLLMAN (1852–1927). *(right)* MATHILDE MARCHESI DE CASTRONE (1821–1913).

(9) CHARLES CAMILLE SAINT-SAENS. 14 July 1906. Born 1835, died 1921. French composer, organist and pianist. His Medal was presented at Buckingham Palace on 14 July 1906 after he performed before the Queen with Joseph Hollman 'and received from Their Majesties the Medal for Music, Art and Science' (*sic*) (*The Times*, 16 July 1906).

(10) JOSEPH HOLLMAN. 14 July 1906. Born 1852, died 1927. Dutch cellist. Received his Medal with Mons. Saint-Saens as noted. (See *Black and White* of 21 July 1906 for illustration.)

(11) MATHILDE MARCHESI DE CASTRONE. 15 July 1906. Born 1821, died 1913. Née Graumann. Known as Madame Marchesi. German mezzo-soprano and teacher. 'Madame Marchesi had the honour of being received by the Queen and presented by Their Majesties with the Medal for Music, Art and Science.' (*The Times*, 16 July 1906)

(12) LIEUT.-COLONEL AND HONORARY COLONEL SIR JAMES GILDEA, Kt., GBE, KCVO, CB, KSTJ. Born 1838, died 1920. Founded in 1885 what is now S.S.A.F.A. In his entry in *Who was Who* he recorded that he had 'the King Edward and Queen Alexandra Personal Gold Medal'. Among his existing awards is the King Edward VII Medal for Science, Art and Music, and presumably he was referring to this when he speaks of the 'Personal Gold Medal'. The Medal is in fact silver-gilt. The date of the award to Gildea is unknown. According to the Court Circular in *The Times* he was received in audience by Queen Alexandra on two occasions during the period of bestowal (1903–1910), on 1 April 1906 and on 13 April 1909. It is possible he may have received the Medal on either occasion.

COLONEL SIR JAMES GILDEA CVO CB (1838–1920).

There is a further name given in Danish records – but *not* in the Register in the Royal Archives. This is NIELSINE CAROLINE PETERSEN, 15 July 1910. Born 10 July 1853; died 26 November 1916. Sculptor. Permission to wear the Medal granted on 15 July 1910 (*State Gazette* of 27 July 1910); it is also recorded in the *State Calendar* (1916). Received a Danish Gold Medal for Art, the French Palmes d'Academiques, and the Russian Medal of Merit in Gold.

CHAPTER THREE

Commemorative Medals and Royal Souvenirs

—

NATICAL
THANKSGIVING, 1872,
obverse and reverse.

F OR MORE THAN A HUNDRED YEARS it has been customary for members of the Royal Family to give presents on their tours abroad and on other special occasions. Over the years a remarkable variety of gifts, including badges or medals, has been presented as tokens of remembrance or souvenirs. It is with the medals and badges that this chapter is concerned.[1]

In December 1871, Albert Edward, Prince of Wales, then aged 30, became gravely ill with typhoid fever and for some weeks lay close to death at Sandringham. Eventually, however, he recovered and a Service of National Thanksgiving for that recovery was held on 27 February 1872. A badge commemorating the event was distributed and is illustrated here.

In October 1875 the Prince of Wales travelled to Brindisi from where his party set sail for India in HMS *Serapis* accompanied by the Royal Yacht. The tour covered much of the Indian sub-continent and also Ceylon.[2]

The badge presented on this occasion is oval. The obverse bears the portrait of the Prince of Wales surrounded by a laurel wreath and the reverse shows the Prince of Wales's plume encircled by the Garter and the collar of the Order of the Star of India. The whole is surrounded by the words: HRH ALBERT EDWARD PRINCE OF WALES 1875–6 and surmounted by a crown. It

ALBERT EDWARD,
PRINCE OF WALES'S
TOUR OF INDIA,
1875–76, obverse and
reverse of the large medal.

was made by Phillips Bros. of Cockspur Street and was struck in two sizes: 48 in the larger size, in gold , and 165 in silver; an unknown quantity were also struck in white metal. The obverse of the smaller medal bears the insignia on the larger medal in miniature with the letters 'A' to the left and 'E' to the right.

ALBERT EDWARD, PRINCE OF WALES'S TOUR OF INDIA, 1875–76, obverse and reverse of the small medal.

On 16 March 1901 the Duke and Duchess of York, set sail in the P. and O. liner *Ophir*, temporarily commissioned in the Royal Navy, to visit Australia and New Zealand, a visit to which Queen Victoria had given her consent before her death. They sailed via Gibraltar, Malta, Port Said, Colombo and Singapore and visited Melbourne, Brisbane and Sidney before New Zealand and Mauritius. They returned home by South Africa and Canada, docking at Portsmouth on 1 November 1901. Eight days later the Duke was made Prince of Wales. A small medal was presented during this long and successful tour.

On 19 October 1905 the Prince and Princess of Wales, set sail for India on board the battleship HMS *Renown*. They sailed through the Mediterranean and the Suez Canal and on to Bombay, touring much of the sub-continent as well as Burma.

COLONIAL TOUR BY THE DUKE AND DUCHESS OF CORNWALL AND YORK IN HMS OPHIR, 1901, obverse and reverse.

On this occasion, too, medals in two sizes were presented. The obverse of the large medal bears the conjoined effigies of the Prince and Princess and the reverse shows the Prince's plume surrounded by the Garter and the collar of the Order of the Star of India, surmounted by a crown and surrounded by the words: 'HRH THE PRINCE AND PRINCESS OF WALES VISIT TO INDIA 1905-6'. Sixty-nine medals struck by Elkington & Co in silver were presented. The smaller medals were struck in gold and silver. The obverse is of a similar design to that presented by the King when he was Prince of Wales in 1875, with the appropriate initials; the reverse bears the inscription shown.

INDIAN TOUR BY THE PRINCE AND PRINCESS OF WALES, 1905–06. *(above)* The small medal, obverse and reverse. *(left)* The large medal, obverse and reverse.

INDIAN TOUR BY KING
GEORGE V AND QUEEN
MARY, 1911-12, obverse
and reverse.

In 1910 King George V suggested that he should hold his Coronation Durbar in Delhi in person. On 11 November 1911, the King and Queen boarded the new P. and O. liner *Medina*, which had been temporarily commissioned in the Royal Navy. On arrival at Bombay the King-Emperor became the first English monarch to visit the East since Richard Coeur de Lion and the only King-Emperor to visit India. On 12 December 1911, the King-Emperor and the Queen-Empress held the most splendid of the three Imperial Durbars. It was also the last. They returned to Portsmouth on 5 February 1912. The small medal presented on this occasion is illustrated.

In 1921 Edward, Prince of Wales, accompanied by his suite which included Lieutenant the Lord Louis Mountbatten, set sail in the battle cruiser HMS *Renown* for India via Aden. The tour covered more of the sub-continent than did earlier tours and again included Burma. On this occasion 84 medals, struck in silver by Elkington & Co. were presented.

VISIT TO NEW ZEALAND BY THE PRINCE OF WALES, 1920, obverse and reverse.

INDIAN TOUR BY THE PRINCE OF WALES, 1921–2, obverse and reverse.

(left) VISIT TO BOMBAY BY THE PRINCE OF WALES, 1921, obverse and reverse.

THE PRINCE OF WALES' TOUR TO INDIA: DELHI, 1921. *(seated left to right)* Lieut. Col. C.O. Harvey, CVO, CBE, MC., Central India House; Sir Godfrey Thomas Bt, CVO; Sir Geoffrey de Montmorency, KCVO, CIE, CBE, Indian Civil Service; The Earl of Cromer, KCIE, CVE; HRH The Prince of Wales; Vice-Admiral Sir Lionel Halsey, GCVO, KCMG, CB; Colonel R.B. Wolgan CSI, CVO, DSO; Captain Dudley North, CMG, CVO, RN; Lieut. Col. Frederick O'Kinealy, CIE, CVO, Indian Medical Service. *(back row left to right)* D. Petrie Esq, CIE, CVO, CBE, Indian Police; Surgeon Cdr. A.C.W. Newport, MVO, RN; H.A.F. Metcalfe Esq, MVO, Indian Civil Service; Lieut. The Hon. Bruce A.A. Ogilvy, MC, Life Guards; Captain The Hon. Piers Legh, MVO, OBE, Grenadier Guards; Lieut. The Lord Louis Mountbatten, MVO, RN; Captain F.S. Poynden, MVO, OBE, MC, 9th Gurkha Rifles; Captain E.D. Metcalfe, MC; 3rd Skinners House.

On the day after war was declared, 4 September 1939, with many misgivings and little enthusiasm Queen Mary and her staff set off from Sandringham for Badminton House, the Gloucestershire home of her niece and her husband, the Duke and Duchess of Beaufort. There she spent the next five years, returning to London in 1945.

Never since her marriage had Queen Mary had so much freedom, taking every opportunity of meeting and talking with ordinary people in more relaxed circumstances than protocol would normally allow. Throughout this period, Queen Mary distributed the enamelled souvenir to

QUEEN MARY'S SOUVENIR, (1940–45).

those who had performed some service and to those whom she met, for example Servicemen and others engaged on war-work to whom she had given a lift in her car.

On 1 February 1947, King George VI and Queen Elizabeth, accompanied by Princess Elizabeth and Princess Margaret set sail in the new battleship HMS *Vanguard* for Cape Town, in the Union of South Africa, the youngest of the Dominions. The ten-week tour covered thousands of miles of the Union and included a visit to the Rhodesias where the King performed the State Opening of Parliament in Salisbury, Southern Rhodesia.

SOUTH AFRICAN TOUR BY
KING GEORGE VI AND
QUEEN ELIZABETH, 1947,
obverse and reverse.

On 21 April, three days before the end of the tour, Princess Elizabeth came of age and broadcast to the British Commonwealth and Empire, dedicating her life to the service of the Imperial Commonwealth and all its peoples. The Royal Family returned to Britain in *Vanguard* at the beginning of May. The medal presented during this tour is illustrated.

COMMONWEALTH TOUR BY
QUEEN ELIZABETH II AND
THE DUKE OF EDINBURGH,
1953–54, obverse and reverse.

Coronation and Jubilee Medals

==

ALTHOUGH MEDALS to commemorate Coronations have been struck since 1547, it was not until Queen Victoria's Jubilee in 1887 that medals were struck to be suspended from a ribbon and worn with other decorations and medals. Today, they are worn in chronological order and take precedence after war medals and before those for long service.

This chapter deals only with the medals more generally awarded and not with those awarded, for example, to mayors and police officers.[1] The figures given for the numbers struck are the initial figures, and are approximate, since they do not include the small numbers struck subsequently.

THE MAHARAJAH OF NABHA, wearing *(on the right)* the Stars of the Order of the Star of India *(above)* and of the Order of the Indian Empire (GCSI and GCIE); *(on the left)* The Prince of Wales's Tour of India Medal 1875–76, Empress of India Medal 1877 and *(below)* Delhi Durbar Medal 1903.

The Delhi Imperial Assemblage Commemorative Medal (more commonly called The Empress of India Medal 1877) was struck to commemorate Queen Victoria's assumption of the title Empress of India on 1 January 1877. It was the first such medal intended to be worn by some. It is 2.3in. in diameter, the obverse bearing the bust of Queen Victoria wearing the Star of the Order of the Star of India. The legend EMPRESS OF INDIA on the reverse is in Persian, English and Nagri. It was struck in gold and silver, for wearing (though not officially by serving British Servicemen) and in copper unmounted. It was designed and engraved by George Gammon Adams who had been articled to William Wyon. It is not known for certain where the medals were struck or in what numbers.

EMPRESS OF INDIA MEDAL, 1877, obverse and reverse.

Queen Victoria's Jubilee Medal 1887. The medal was designed by Sir Joseph Edgar Boehm and Clemens Emptmeyer[2] and about 1,745 were struck in, it is believed, Vienna. It was awarded in gold (133) to members of the Royal Family and certain foreign guests, in silver (1,012) to the Royal Household, other distinguished guests, serving officers and officials and in bronze (600)[3] to certain men in the Royal Navy and the Army. When worn by ladies, the medal is attached to a bow of the same ribbon.

Queen Victoria's Diamond Jubilee Medal 1897 is the same as that for 1887 except that, on the reverse, the inscription reads: IN COMMEMORATION OF THE 60TH YEAR OF THE REIGN OF QUEEN VICTORIA 20 JUNE 1897. The ribbon too is identical. Seventy-three gold medals, 3,040 silver and 1,890 bronze were awarded in a similar way to those in 1887. To those

(right) QUEEN VICTORIA'S JUBILEE MEDAL, 1887, obverse and reverse.
(far right) QUEEN VICTORIA'S DIAMOND JUBILEE MEDAL, reverse, and the bars worn with the medal – top, ladies; bottom, gentlemen.

who had already received the 1887 medal, a bar, bearing the date 1897, of gold, silver or bronze, was awarded and worn on the 1887 medal. When worn by ladies, the medal is attached in the same way as before to a bow of the same ribbon.

King Edward VII's Coronation Medal 1902 was struck to commemorate the Coronation on 26 June 1902. On the 15 June, however, the King was taken ill and the ceremony postponed to 9 August. The medal which is ovoid 1.325in by 1.225in, was awarded in a similar way to those of the previous reign. It was designed by E. Fuchs and 9,547 were struck, 3,493 in silver and 6,054 in bronze by Elkington & Co. The reverse bears the original date: 26 June 1902. When worn by ladies, the medal is attached to a bow of the same ribbon.

King George V's Coronation Medal 1911 was designed by Sir Bertram Mackennel and was struck, in silver only, at the Royal Mint. It was more widely distributed than those of previous reigns, a total of 15,901 having been struck. When worn by ladies, the medal is attached to a bow of the same ribbon.

King George V's Silver Jubilee Medal 1935 was designed by Sir William Goscombe John, RA, and was struck, in silver only, at the Royal Mint. It was widely distributed throughout the British Empire, a total of 85,234 having been struck. When worn by ladies, the medal is attached to a bow of the same ribbon, whose white stripe signifies silver.

King George VI's Coronation Medal 1937. On 11 December 1936, King Edward VIII abdicated before his Coronation and was succeeded by his brother, the Duke of York, whose Coronation took place on 12 May 1937. The medal was designed by Mr Percy Metcalfe and was struck in silver at the Royal Mint, 90,279 being distributed throughout the British Empire. When worn by ladies, the medal is attached to a bow of the same ribbon.

Queen Elizabeth II's Coronation Medal 1953 was designed by Sir Cecil Thomas and was struck, in silver, at the Royal Mint. It was distributed throughout the British Commonwealth, a total of 129,051 having been struck.

On Coronation Day, Mount Everest was climbed for the first time and to commemorate the occasion, Her Majesty The Queen presented to the fourteen members of the Expedition the Coronation Medal with the words: MOUNT EVEREST EXPEDITION engraved on the rim.

When worn by ladies, the ordinary medal is attached to a bow of the same ribbon.

Queen Elizabeth II's Silver Jubilee Medal 1977 was designed by Mr David Wynne and was struck in silver at the Royal Mint. It was awarded throughout the British Commonwealth, a total of 47,158 having been struck. The Canadian version was struck at the Royal Canadian Mint. Its reverse

THE CORONATION MEDAL, 1902, obverse and reverse.

THE CORONATION MEDAL, 1911, obverse and reverse.

THE SILVER JUBILEE MEDAL, 1935, obverse and reverse.

THE CORONATION MEDAL, 1937, obverse and reverse.

THE CORONATION
MEDAL, 1953, obverse
and reverse.

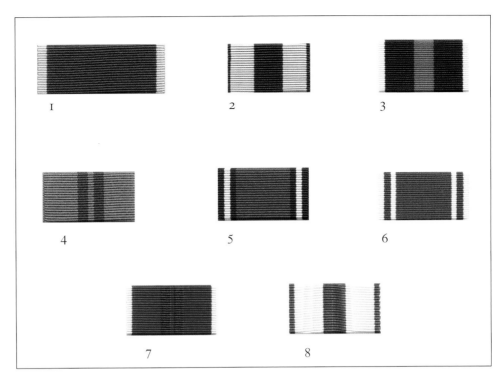

CORONATION AND JUBILEE MEDAL RIBBONS:

1. Empress of India Medal, 1877
2. Queen Victoria's Jubilee Medals, 1887 and 1897
3. King Edward VII's Coronation Medal, 1902
4. King George V's Coronation Medal, 1911
5. King George V's Silver Jubilee Medal, 1935
6. King George VI's Coronation Medal, 1937
7. Queen Elizabeth II's Coronation Medal, 1953
8. Queen Elizabeth II's Silver Jubilee Medal, 1977

was designed by Mrs Dora de Pédery Hunt and bears a representation of a maple leaf with, above it, the word: CANADA and, below it, the Royal cypher surmounted by a crown with, to the left of it, 1952 and to the right 1977. When worn by ladies, the medal is attached to a bow of the same ribbon. The medals were forwarded with a certificate.

THE SILVER JUBILEE MEDAL, 1977, obverse and reverse; *(right)* Canadian reverse.

CHAPTER FIVE

Badges of Office

T HIS CHAPTER deals with the principal badges of office worn, rather than carried, by the office-holders in the Royal Household, from the reign of Queen Victoria to the present day.

They include the badges of office of Personal Aides-de-Camp to the Sovereign, the Lord Chamberlain, the Lord Great Chamberlain, the Ladies in attendance, the Equerries, the Ecclesiastical Household, the honorary Physicians to the Sovereign, Lord Lieutenants, the Captain of The Honourable Corps of Gentlemen at Arms, the College of Arms, the Marshal of the Diplomatic Corps, Diplomatic Officers, The Abbey Court and High Constables and Guard of Honour of Holyrood House and the Harpist to the Prince of Wales.

AIDES-DE-CAMP TO THE SOVEREIGN

Aides-de-camp (ADC) derives from the French for camp or field assistants. Today in the armed services they are of comparatively junior rank and assist those of more senior rank.

The office of aide-de-camp to the Sovereign is given to certain members of the Royal Family as a reward or an honorary distinction. Among the present holders are the Prince of Wales, Captain Mark Phillips and the Duke of York. The Sovereign also appoints senior members of each of the armed services as ADCs for a period, and those appointed form part of the Queen's Household. At present they are the First and Principal Naval Aide-de-Camp and the Flag Aide-de-Camp, four Aides-de-Camp General and two Air

(left) EPAULETTTE worn by Prince Louis of Battenberg, 1st Marquess of Milford Haven (1854–1921). *(right)* EPAULETTTE worn by Lord Louis Mountbatten, later Earl Mountbatten of Burma (1900–79).

(above left) EARL MOUNTBATTEN OF BURMA; the cyphers can be seen on the right shoulder. *(right)* THE PRINCESS ROYAL, Colonel of the Blues and Royals and Gold Stick, at the ceremony of Trooping the Colour in 1999. The cypher as a Personal ADC can be seen on the left shoulder.
(left) THE PRINCE OF WALES as Colonel of the Welsh Guards at the Ceremony of Trooping the Colour. On the right epaulette is the Sovereign's cypher worn as a Personal ADC to the Queen.

Aides-de-Camp. All wear the Sovereign's cypher on each shoulder, in a gold or silver coloured metal depending on the type of uniform being worn.

The cyphers of previous reigns may be worn during the current reign and, in such cases, those on the right shoulder are worn in the formation shown, whilst those on the left shoulder have the VR and ER cyphers in reverse order. The late Prince Henry, Duke of Gloucester, wore the cyphers of four Sovereigns: GR, EVIIIR, GVIR and EIIR. In certain uniforms there was insufficient room to wear them other than in a square formation as follows:

GR EVIIIR

GVIR EIIR

It is particularly interesting to note that the late Earl Mountbatten of Burma (1900–79) and his father, between them, served as Personal ADC; to the Sovereign in each reign from Queen Victoria's to the present. The cyphers are also attached to the aiguillette tags.

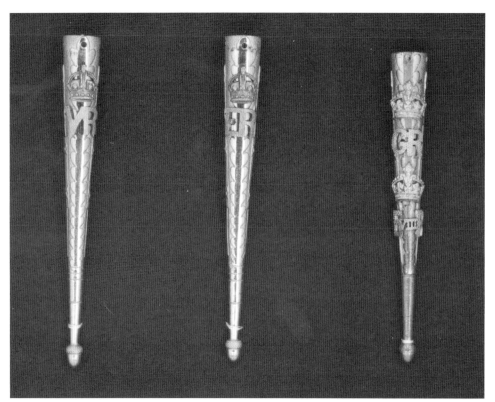

AIGUILETTE TAGS, bearing the Sovereign's cyphers: (*left to right*) Queen Victoria, Edward VII, George V and Edward VIII.

THE QUEEN AND PRINCE PHILIP, arriving at Westminster Hall on 5 May 1995, the 50th anniversary of the end of the Second World War. The Lord Great Chamberlain, the Marquess of Cholmondeley is wearing his badge of office.

THE KEY, on a blue ribbon, which is worn by the Lord Great Chamberlain on his right hip.

THE LORD GREAT CHAMBERLAIN AND
THE LORD CHAMBERLAIN

The Lord Chamberlain, is head of the Queen's working household, and the Lord Great Chamberlain who is responsible for royal affairs in the Palace of Westminster. The Lord Chamberlain is also Chancellor of the Royal Victorian Order.

On ceremonial occasions both carry a white staff and wear a key on a blue ribbon on the right hip pocket as does the Lord Chamberlain to Queen Elizabeth. The origin of the key is uncertain but is reputed to be the key to the chest containing the Sovereign's money and other valuables which, in the twelfth and thirteenth centuries, was the responsibility of the King's Chamberlain as he was then called.

The present Lord Chamberlain, Lord Luce, was appointed in 2000.

The Lord Great Chamberlain is an hereditary office. In 1902 the House of Lords held that the office was jointly vested in the families of the Marquess of Cholmondeley, the Marquess of Lincolnshire and the Earl of Ancaster. King Edward VII agreed that the position should be held for the duration of a reign, the first having a two-part right and the second and third a single part each. Thus, the Marquess of Cholmondeley holds office in every other reign and the Earl of Ancaster and the Marquess of Lincolnshire (Carringtons) sharing every other reign. The current holder is the Marquess of Cholmondeley.

THE LADIES IN ATTENDANCE

'Those who have the privilege of being appointed Lady in Waiting serve Her Majesty out of love and loyalty. The badge of office, which is chosen individually by each successive Queen, is its own reward.'[1]

From Norman times, Queens, both regnant and consort, and female members of the Royal Family, have been attended by Ladies in Waiting. Over the centuries the role of Ladies in Waiting has changed beyond all recognition as have their titles. Four of the less quaint titles, however, remain to this day: the Mistress of the Robes, the Ladies of the Bedchamber and the Women of the Bedchamber.

Before the reign of Henry VIII, there were Great Ladies, Ladies of the Privy Chamber and of the Presence, Maids of Honour (who chaperoned the unmarried girls in royal service) and Chamberers. Also attending the Queen were Ladies with delightful titles and unusual responsibilities: the Mistress of the Sweet Coffers, for example, was responsible for the sweet herbs kept amongst the Queen's linen; and the Laundress of the Body saw to the cleanliness of the Queen's underclothes. Legend has grown around some Queens and their Ladies in Waiting. For instance it is said that when Mary, Queen of Scots, caught a fever, her Ladies made her a mixture of oranges saying *Marie est malade*. Thus was marmalade born!

In the reign of Queen Elizabeth I the senior lady was styled the First Lady of the Bedchamber, a title later changed to Mistress of the Robes and, as such, she was in charge of the Queen's wardrobe. The position of Mistress of the Robes was often combined with that of Groom of the Stole, originally Groom of the Stool namely, the close stool for even the divine right of Kings could not free the Stuarts from the necessity of performing the most human functions and as such someone had to be responsible for the provision of chamber pots and the disposal of their contents.'[2]

Until the late nineteenth century, there was often a political element in the appointments to the Queen's Household. Some, like Sarah, Duchess of Marlborough, wielded great influence over the Queen. Having been Maid of Honour to Mary of Modena, second wife of King James II, she became Lady in Waiting to Princess Anne, after whose accession to the throne in 1702, she was appointed Mistress of the Robes, Groom of the Stole and Keeper of the Privy Purse. 'There never was a more absolute favourite in a Court,' wrote Gilbert Burnet, Bishop of Salisbury.

The influence of the Duchess over the Queen seems to have gone to her head and the relationship between the two women ended unhappily. After a particularly unpleasant row, the Duke persuaded his wife to write an apology to the Queen. Nonethe-less the Queen demanded the return of the gold key of the Bedchamber which was then the badge of office of the Mistress of the Robes. When the Duke relayed this message to the Duchess, she threw it on the floor, insisting that he should return it himself at once. Thus ended a long friendship.

(left) SARAH, DUCHESS OF MARLBOROUGH, wearing her badge of office as Mistress of the Robes to Queen Anne – by Sir Godfrey Kneller.

It is uncertain when the gold key ceased to be the badge of office of the Mistress of the Robes, but it was still in use by the Duchess of St Albans, Mistress of the Robes and Groom of the Stole to Queen Caroline, consort of King George II.

Some Ladies in Waiting held their posts in name only. Perhaps the best example was Nell Gwynn, mistress of King Charles II, and nominally Lady of the Bedchamber to his wife, Queen Catherine. A number of Ladies in Waiting married their Sovereign. Elizabeth Woodville married King Edward IV, and Anne Boleyn, Jane Seymour and Catherine Howard married King Henry VIII.

During the reign of King George III (1760–1820), the duties of the Ladies in Waiting became less humble and they were on duty for shorter periods. During Queen Victoria's reign (1837–1901) a new respectability showed itself at Court, but there was still a political element in the appointments to the Queen's Household. This caused a minor political incident in 1839 when the young Queen refused to follow tradition and replace the Ladies of the Household with those sympathetic to the politics of the incoming Tory Prime Minister, Sir Robert Peel. Without a change of Ladies, Sir Robert refused to take office, the Queen kept her Ladies, and the minority Whig Government of Lord Melbourne remained in power even though it had lost the confidence of Parliament. The incident, known thereafter as the Bed-chamber Crisis, effectively began the process of diminishing political influence on the appointments in the Household, though the Prime Minister continued to nominate ladies for the office of Mistress of the Robes.

MRS BERNARD MALLET (Marie Mallet), Maid of Honour to Queen Victoria 1887–91, Woman of the Bedchamber.

Queen Victoria was very particular as to whom she had in her Household, so much so that in 1886 and 1892 the office of Mistress of the Robes remained vacant for a time because the Prime Minister of the day, William Gladstone, was unable to find any lady who was willing to take on the job and of whom the Queen approved. A sort of political element appeared again at the end of Queen Victoria's reign when Marie Mallet, one of her Ladies in Waiting, found that she was having to read State papers to the Queen, whose eyesight was beginning to fail.

Since the turn of the century, the political element has totally disappeared and the role of the Lady in Waiting has entirely changed. Over the years the number of Maids of Honour has declined until the present day when they are only appointed for special occasions. The last to fill the position on a long term basis was the Honourable Jean Bruce. She was promoted to Woman of the Bedchamber in 1935 and her former position was not thereafter filled.

At least one Lady in Waiting founded dynasties which achieved fame in later generations. Countess Julie von Hauke was Lady in Waiting to the Tsarina of Russia when she married the Tsarina's brother, Prince Alexander of Hesse. She was given the title Princess of Battenberg, a town near Wiesbaden in Germany. Their eldest son, Prince Louis, married Queen Victoria's granddaughter, Princess Victoria. They were the parents of Earl Mountbatten of Burma, and the grandparents of the Duke of Edinburgh. Their third son, Prince Henry, married Queen Victoria's daughter, Princess Beatrice, and had three sons and a daughter, Victoria Eugenie (Ena), who married King Alfonso XIII of Spain, and was grandmother to King Juan Carlos I.

Danger has befallen Ladies in Waiting. In 1900, Miss Charlotte Knollys, a Woman of the Bedchamber to Queen Alexandra, and the Queen's favourite Lady in Waiting, was in attendance on the Princess of Wales, as she then was,

THE BADGE of a Maid of Honour to Queen Victoria; (*above*) the two types of reverse; the second type post-1877, when Queen Victoria assumed the title of Empress of India.

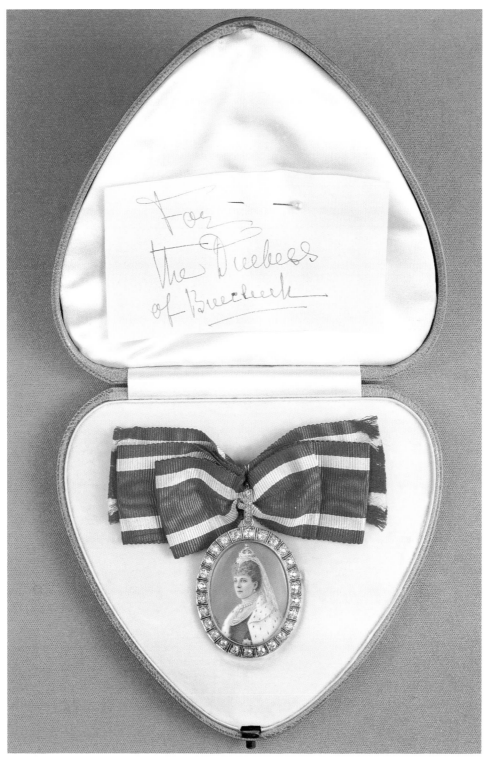

BADGE of the Mistress of the Robes to Queen Alexandra. Worn by Louise, Duchess of Buccleuch, 1902–12, with card from the Queen.

(*above*) BADGE of a Lady in Waiting to Princess Helena, Princess Christian of Schleswig Holstein. This badge was later used for a Lady in Waiting to Princess Helena Victoria.
(*below*) BADGE of a Lady in Waiting to Princess Marie Louise. Both badges were worn by Mrs Phyllis Murray, MVO, who was Lady in Waiting to both Princess Helena's daughters in succession, 1947–48 and 1948–56.

during the visit by the Prince and Princess to Brussels. While they waited in the train, an anarchist fired twice at the Prince. As Miss Knollys wrote to Queen Victoria, one bullet missed, passing between the Prince and the Princess and ending between herself and Sir Sydney Clarke. In 1901 Miss Knollys was raised to the rank of a Baron's daughter by Royal Warrant. In December 1903, the Honourable Charlotte Knollys saved Queen Alexandra from a fire at Sandringham. The Grand Duchess Augusta of Mecklenberg-Strelitz asked 'What Order will the King decorate Charlotte with to reward such readiness of thought and action?'

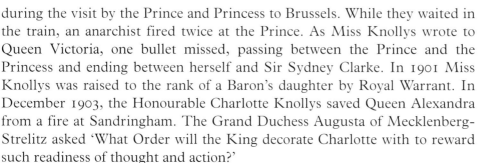

BADGE of the Mistress
of the Robes to Queen
Alexandra. Garrard's
photograph in the year
of manufacture (1914).

(left) THE MARQUESS
AND MARCHIONESS OF
SALISBURY in 1937.
Lady Salisbury was a
Lady of the Bedchamber
to Queen Alexandra
1907–10. Lord Salisbury
was ADC to King
Edward VII 1903-10,
King George V 1910–29,
and was High Steward
at the Coronation of
George VI in 1937.
(right) EDITH,
COUNTESS OF LYTTON.
Lady of the Bedchamber
to Queen Victoria and
Queen Alexandra.

In March 1974 the Princess Royal and Captain Mark Phillips, attended by a Lady in Waiting, Miss Rowena Brassey, and a police officer, Inspector James Beaton, were returning to Buckingham Palace in a car driven by Mr Alexander Callender. In The Mall a young man made an attempt to kidnap the Princess. He fired a revolver at the Inspector, wounding him in the shoulder. The Princess and Captain Phillips managed to hold their door closed whilst the Inspector entered their car on the other side and shielded the Princess with his body. When the gunman was about to fire into the car, the Inspector raised his hand directly into the line of fire. The gunman fired, wounding him in the hand, and then fired again, wounding him in the stomach. He fell unconscious out of the car. With the arrival on the scene of several other policemen, the gunman was brought down with a rugger tackle and arrested. In July awards for bravery were announced (*London Gazette*, 5 July 1974). These included the George Cross to Inspector Beaton and the Queen's Gallantry Medal to Mr Callender. On 15 August, the Princess's birthday, the Queen announced the appointment of the Princess as a Dame Grand Cross of the Royal Victorian Order, Captain Phillips as a Commander, and Miss Brassey as a Member of the 4th Class (now Lieutenant). All three received their insignia from the Queen on 14 October. The bravery awards were presented on 26 November 1974.

Today the Ladies of the Household are the Mistress of the Robes, the Ladies of the Bedchamber and the Women of the Bedchamber, with such Extra Ladies and Extra Women as may from time to time be required. The Mistress of the Robes remains the senior Lady and the office is usually held by a Duchess. Her duties are principally ceremonial, although she arranges the duties of the other Ladies. The Ladies of the Bedchamber accompany the Queen on important occasions and on overseas visits. They do not attend her on a day-to-day basis. This is the task of the Women of the Bedchamber who are on duty for two weeks at a time. Their duties are varied, accompanying the Queen on less important occasions, making telephone calls for her, and answering letters.

None of the Ladies in Waiting receives a salary, counting their appointment an honour. All the ladies have badges of office which are worn on the more important occasions. The Ladies in Waiting to most of the other Ladies of the Royal Family have similar badges, though more modest in design. They are all illustrated in this chapter.

The current position of today's Ladies in Waiting has been described by Anne Somerset in words that can hardly be improved upon: 'Royal Service is a profession with a long and distinguished pedigree, even though it is true that in the past some ladies combined a career at Court with pursuit of the oldest profession of all. On the whole, however, these were the exceptions, and it would be unjust to overlook those generations of Ladies in Waiting who for centuries oiled the wheels of monarchy by rendering ungrudging service to the Crown. It is their mantle which has fallen on the Ladies in Waiting of the present Queen, who follow in the very best traditions of royal servants over the ages. . . . (and) since the Queen's accession her Ladies in Waiting have ensured that, far from having to discharge her responsibilities in solitary splendour, she can always rely on the support of a group of utterly dependable women, whose loyalty is beyond question, and who have dedicated their lives to her service.'[3]

LIST OF LADIES IN WAITING

The following list includes only some of the Ladies in Waiting who would have worn the badges described in the text. *Queen Victoria's Maids of Honour have been grouped to show the order of succession.*

HM QUEEN VICTORIA

MISS ALINE MAJENDIE, Maid of Honour to Queen Victoria.

THE HONOURABLE LUCIA WHITE (later Viscountess Galway), Maid of Honour to Queen Alexandra.

MAIDS OF HONOUR

Miss Matilda Paget 1837
The Honourable H.E. Pitt 1837
Miss E. Stanley 1841
Miss H.L. Phipps 1862
Miss A. Loftus 1889
Miss M. Hardinge 1892
The Honourable J. Harbord 1894

Miss C.M. (later Lady Caroline) Somers-Cocks 1837
Miss E.F. Lennox 1849
Miss M. Seymour 1850
Miss L.F. Gordon 1856
Miss H.C. Stopford 1857
Miss A.G. Lambart 1877
Miss M. Okeover 1884
The Honourable L. Brownlow 1887
Miss M. Adeane 1887
Miss M. Hughes 1891

The Honourable M. Dillon 1837
Miss H.J. Anson 1838
The Honourable G. Liddell 1841
The Honourable A. Napier 1845
The Honourable Flora Macdonald 1847
Miss E.C. Paget 1874
Miss A. Majendie 1894

Miss S. M. Cavendish 1837
Miss C. Hamilton 1842
Miss C. M. Dawson 1845
Miss B. Byng 1851
The Honourable L.C. Lyttleton 1863
Miss F. (later Lady Florence) Seymour 1864
The Honourable M.E. Pitt 1870
The Honourable F.L. Fitzroy 1883
Miss B. Lambart 1890

Miss M. Paget 1837
Miss E. Cathcart 1855
Miss E. H. Cadogan 1880
Miss S. Edwardes 1897

Miss A.M. Murray 1837
Miss M. Bulteel 1853
Miss V. Stuart-Wortley 1861
The Honourable A. Cavendish 1863
Miss E. Lascelles 1863
Miss M.L. Lascelles 1865
Miss E. Moore 1881

Miss H Lister 1837
Miss L.M. Kerr 1844
The Honourable F.M. Drummond 1872

BADGE of the Mistress of the Robes to Queen Alexandra. Worn by Winifred Anna, Duchess of Portland, 1913–25: *(left)* the obverse and *(right)* the reverse. The brooch of crossed and reversed 'A's was not part of the original badge.

MAIDS OF HONOUR *(continued)*

    The Honourable M.A. Spring-Rice 1837
    The Honourable Frances Devereux 1841
    Miss C.F. Cavendish 1847
    Miss V.M.S. Baillie 1881
    Miss C.H. Kerr 1884
    The Honourable R.P. Hood 1886
    Miss M.E.A. Byng 1894

HM QUEEN ALEXANDRA

MISTRESSES OF THE ROBES

    The Duchess of Buccleuch 1901–16
    The Duchess of Portland 1916–25

LADIES OF THE BEDCHAMBER

    The Countess of Antrim 1901–25
    The Countess of Lytton 1901–07
    The Countess of Gosford 1901–25
    The Lady Suffield 1901–13
    The Marchioness of Lansdowne 1907–13 *(Extra* 1913–25)
    The Marchioness of Salisbury 1908–13 *(Extra* 1913–25)
    The Countess of Derby 1910–13 *(Extra* 1913–25)
    The Marchioness of Lincolnshire 1913–25

EXTRA LADIES OF THE BEDCHAMBER

    The Countess of Macclesfield 1901–25
    The Dowager Countess of Morton 1901–08
    The Lady Hardinge of Penshurst 1913–15

BADGE of a Lady of the Bedchamber to Queen Alexandra. Worn by Ivy, Duchess of Portland. The badge of the Dannebrog is in white enamel with red enamel border and on each arm the reversed cypher 'A' surmounted by a crown in gold. Superimposed across the centre of the cross is the letter 'A' crossed and reversed and set with diamonds. The Cross is surmounted by a crown in gold and set with diamonds in the arches and fleur-de-lis and cross-patee. The base of the crown is set with emeralds, rubies, diamonds and a sapphire. The badge was made by Rowland and Fraser of Regent Street.

REVERSE OF A BADGE of a Lady of the Bedchamber to Queen Alexandra. Worn by The Honourable Charlotte Knollys.

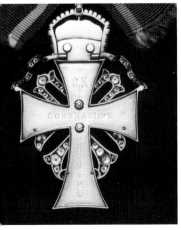

WOMEN OF THE BEDCHAMBER

The Honourable Mrs Charles Hardinge 1901–10
Lady Emily Kingscote 1901–07
The Honourable Charlotte Knollys 1901–25
Lady Alice Stanley 1901–10

MAIDS OF HONOUR

The Honourable Mary Dyke 1901–06
The Honourable Sylvia Edwardes 1901–10
The Honourable Dorothy Vivian 1901–05
The Honourable Violet Vivian 1901–25
The Honourable Margaret Dawnay 1907–10
The Honourable Blanche Lascelles 1907–13
The Honourable Ivy Gordon-Lennox 1913
The Honourable Lucia White 1920–26

HM QUEEN MARY

MISTRESSES OF THE ROBES

> The Duchess of Devonshire 1910–17 *and* 1921–53
> The Duchess of Sutherland 1917–21

LADIES OF THE BEDCHAMBER

> The Countess of Shaftesbury 1910–12 (*Extra* 1912–53)
> The Countess of Minto 1912–36 (*Extra* 1936–39)
> The Lady Ampthill 1912–53
> The Lady Desborough 1912–17 *and* 1926–36 (*Extra* 1917–26 *and* 1936–53)
> The Countess Fortescue 1915–26 (*Extra* 1926–29)
> The Countess of Airlie 1917–53 (*Extra* 1910–17)

EXTRA LADIES OF THE BEDCHAMBER

> The Countess of Bradford 1910–36
> The Lady Lamington 1910–45

WOMEN OF THE BEDCHAMBER

> Lady Eva Dugdale 1910–36 (*Extra* 1936–)
> Lady Mary Forbes-Trefusis 1910–27
> Lady Katherine Coke 1910–21
> Lady Bertha Dawkins 1910–45
> Lady Isobel Gathorne-Hardy 1915–21
> Lady Joan Verney 1921–36 (*Extra* 1936–)
> Lady Elizabeth Dawson 1921–
> Lady Cynthia Colville 1924–53
> Lady Elizabeth Hesketh-Prichard 1926–
> Lady Elizabeth Motion 1927–37 (*Extra* 1937–53)
> Lady Katherine Hamilton 1927–30 (*Extra* 1930–53)
>   (Lady Katherine Seymour from 1930)
> Lady Victoria Weld-Forester 1930– (*Extra* –1953)
> Lady Constance Milnes-Gaskell 1937–53
> The Honourable Margaret Wyndham 1939– (*Extra* –1953)
> Lady Cecily Vesey 1951–53

EXTRA WOMAN OF THE BEDCHAMBER

> Lady Jean Bruce 1935–39

MAIDS OF HONOUR

> The Honourable Sybil Brodrick 1911–32
> The Honourable Venetia Baring 1911–19
> The Honourable Katherine Villiers 1911–19

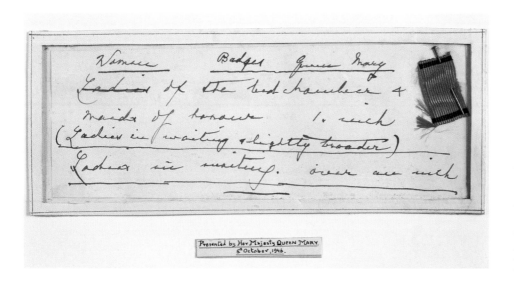

QUEEN MARY'S NOTE on the ribbon of the badge of Her Majesty's Women of the Bedchamber and Maids of Honour. Written during the 1939–45 war to G.P.L. James. Now in the collection of Henry Pownall.

BADGE of the Mistress of the Robes to Queen Mary.
Worn by Evelyn, Duchess of Devonshire, 1910–53.
(right) Evelyn, Duchess of Devonshire.

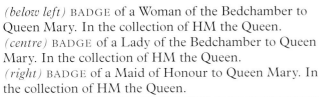

(below left) BADGE of a Woman of the Bedchamber to
Queen Mary. In the collection of HM the Queen.
(centre) BADGE of a Lady of the Bedchamber to Queen
Mary. In the collection of HM the Queen.
(right) BADGE of a Maid of Honour to Queen Mary. In
the collection of HM the Queen.

BADGE worn by Eileen, Duchess of Sutherland, Mistress of the Robes to Queen Mary 1917–21.

MAIDS OF HONOUR *(continued)*
> The Honourable Mabel Gye 1911–21
> The Honourable Ursula Lawley 1913–32
> The Honourable Jean Bruce 1927–35

EXTRA MAID OF HONOUR
> The Honourable Elizabeth Cadogan 1915–32

HM QUEEN ELIZABETH THE QUEEN MOTHER

MISTRESSES OF THE ROBES
> The Duchess of Northumberland 1937–64
> The Duchess of Abercorn 1964–90

LADIES OF THE BEDCHAMBER
> The Countess Spencer 1937–72
> The Countess of Halifax 1937–44 (*Extra* 1944–76)
> The Viscountess Hambleden 1937– 1994
> The Lady Nunburnholme 1937–53
> The Dowager Lady Harlech 1945–53 (*Extra* 1953–84)
> The Countess of Scarbrough 1949–53 (*Extra* 1953–79)
> The Lady Grimthorpe 1973–

WOMEN OF THE BEDCHAMBER
> Lady Helen Graham 1937–39 (*Extra* 1939–53)
> Lady Katherine Seymour 1937–60
> The Lady Hyde 1937–61 (*Extra* 1961–71)

BADGE of the Mistress of the Robes to Queen Elizabeth The Queen Mother. An identical badge was worn during the reign of King George VI.

(below left) BADGE of a Lady of the Bedchamber to Queen Elizabeth the Queen Mother.
(below right) BADGE of a Woman of the Bedchamber. Identical badges were worn during the reign of King George VI.

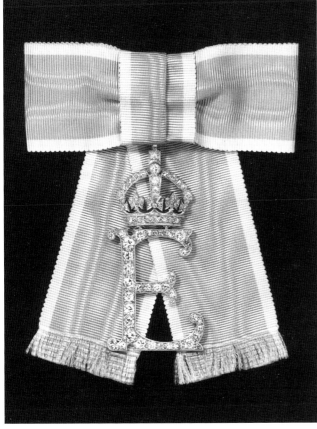

WOMEN OF THE BEDCHAMBER *(continued)*
> The Honourable Mrs Geoffrey Bowlby 1937–44
>   (*Extra* 1952–88)
> Lady Delia Peel 1939–49 (*Extra* 1949–77)
> Lady Jean Rankin 1947–82 (*Extra* 1982–)
> The Honourable Mrs John Mulholland 1950–84
>   (*Extra* 1984–85)
> Lady Mary Harvey 1961–63
> Lady Caroline Douglas-Home 1963–64
> Ruth, Lady Fermoy 1960–93 (*Extra* 1956–60)
> Mrs Patrick (later Dame Frances) Campbell-Preston 1968–
> Lady Angela Oswald 1983– (*Extra* 1981–83)
> Lady Elizabeth Basset 1982– 1993 (*Extra* 1959–82)
> The Honourable Mrs Rhodes 1993–
> Mrs Michael Gordon-Lennox 1993–

EXTRA WOMEN OF THE BEDCHAMBER
> Lady Victoria Weymss 1937–94
> Miss Jane Walker-Okeover 1985–
> Lady Penn
> Lady Margaret Colville 1949–
> Mrs Martin Leslie

HRH THE PRINCESS MARY, THE PRINCESS ROYAL

LADIES IN WAITING
> Miss Dorothy Yorke 1937–39 (*Extra* 1939–53)
> Miss Sybil Kenyon-Slaney 1937–48 (*Extra* 1948–62)
> The Lady Carrington 1939–40 (*Extra* 1940–48)
> The Lady Lloyd 1942–48 (*Extra* 1948–62)
> Miss Gwynedd Lloyd 1948–65
> The Honourable Mrs Francis Balfour 1948–65
> The Honourable Mary Lampson 1948–52
> The Lady Paynter 1952–62 (*Extra* 1962–65)
> Mrs Cuthbert 1954–63
> Dame Mary Colvin 1962–65
> The Honourable Mrs John Thorold 1963–65

EXTRA LADY IN WAITING
> The Countess of Cavan 1943–65

HRH PRINCESS ALICE, DUCHESS OF GLOUCESTER

LADIES IN WAITING
> Lady Winnifred Cecil 1937–40
> Miss Eva Sandford 1937–48
> The Honourable Gwendolen Meysey-Thompson 1940–48
> Miss Dorothy Meynell 1947–59 (*Extra* 1959–92)
> Mrs Cedric Holland 1951–69 (*Extra* 1969–88)
> Dame Jean Maxwell-Scott 1959–
> Miss Jane Egerton–Warburton 1975–84 (*Extra* 1984–)
> Mrs Michael Harvey 1984–

EXTRA LADY IN WAITING
> Lady Cecily Vesey 1947–51
> The Honourable Jane Walsh 1969–96
> Miss Diana Harrison 1974–

BADGE of a Lady in Waiting to Princess Mary, the Princess Royal, Countess of Harewood (1897–1965). Worn by Miss Gwynedd Lloyd and made by Plante of Bury Street.

BADGE of a Lady in Waiting to Princess Alice, Duchess of Gloucester (1901–). Made by Garrard.

THE COUNTESS OF BRECKNOCK wearing her badge as Lady in Waiting to Princess Marina, Duchess of Kent, May 1937.

HRH PRINCESS MARINA, DUCHESS OF KENT

LADIES IN WAITING

The Lady Herbert 1937–49 (*Extra* 1949–60)
The Countess of Brecknock 1937–39
The Lady Rachel Davidson 1943–65
The Countess of Birkenhead 1949
Lady Constance Milnes-Gaskell 1954–61 (*Extra* 1961–64)
The Lady Balfour 1961–68
Lady Rachel Pepys 1962–68

EXTRA LADY IN WAITING

The Countess of Pembroke and Montgomery 1960–68

HRH THE PRINCESS ELIZABETH, DUCHESS OF EDINBURGH

LADIES IN WAITING

Lady Margaret Colville 1946–49
Lady Margaret Hay 1948–53
The Honourable Mrs Andrew Elphinstone 1949–53
Lady Alice Egerton 1949–53
Lady Palmer 1949–53
Lady Abel-Smith 1949–53

EXTRA LADY IN WAITING

Lady Maria Strachey 1948–53

HRH THE PRINCESS MARGARET, COUNTESS OF SNOWDON

LADIES IN WAITING

Miss Jennifer Bevan (Mrs John Lowther) 1948–52
    (*Extra* 1952–70)
Honourable Iris Peake (Hon. Mrs Dawnay) 1952–62
    (*Extra* 1962–64)
Miss Fiona Middleton (Lady Aird) 1960–63 (*Extra* 1963–)
Miss Jane Allday 1963–64
Mrs Robin Benson 1964–65 (*Extra* 1965–)
Lady Juliet Smith (Townsend) 1965–71 (*Extra* 1971–)
The Honourable Annabel Hoyer Millar 1971–74
The Honourable Mrs Whitehead 1971–75 and 1993–
    (*Extra* 1975–93)

(left) BADGE of a Lady in Waiting to Princess Marina, Duchess of Kent. Worn by Lady Balfour. The badge is believed to have been designed by the Duchess's husband.
(right) BADGE of a Lady in Waiting to Princess Elizabeth. Worn before HRH's accession to the throne in 1952.

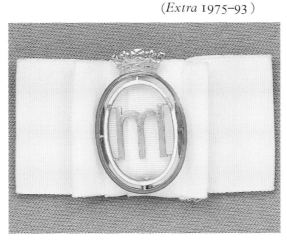

LADIES IN WAITING *(continued)*
>The Honourable Davina Woodhouse 1975–80 (*Extra* 1980–88)
>Miss Elizabeth Paget 1979–82

EXTRA LADIES IN WAITING
>Lady Elizabeth Cavendish 1954–
>The Honourable Mrs Wills 1970–
>Mrs Jane Stevens 1970–79 *and* 1983–
>Lady Juliet Townsend 1971–
>The Lady Glenconner 1971–
>The Countess Alexander of Tunis 1979–
>Mrs Charles Vyvyan 1981–

BADGE of a Lady in Waiting to Princess Margaret, Countess of Snowdon.

HM QUEEN ELIZABETH II

MISTRESSES OF THE ROBES
>The Duchess of Devonshire 1953–66
>The Duchess of Grafton 1967–

LADIES OF THE BEDCHAMBER
>Lady Palmer
>The Countess of Leicester 1953–71 (*Extra* 1971–72)
>The Countess of Euston (later Duchess of Grafton) 1953–67
>Patricia Marchioness of Abergavenny 1966–87
>   (*Extra* 1960–66 *and* 1987–)
>The Countess of Cromer 1967–72 (*Extra* 1974–93)
>The Lady Fairfax of Cameron 1967–69
>The Countess of Airlie 1973–
>The Lady Farnham 1987–

WOMEN OF THE BEDCHAMBER
>Lady Margaret Hay 1953–75
>Lady Alice Egerton 1953–59
>Lady Rose Baring 1953–72 (*Extra* 1973–93)
>Mrs John (later Lady) Dugdale 1973–
>The Honourable Mary Morrison 1960–

(left) BADGE of the Mistress of the Robes to Queen Elizabeth II.
(right) BADGE worn by Ladies of the Bedchamber and Women of the Bedchamber to Queen Elizabeth II.

WOMEN OF THE BEDCHAMBER *(continued)*
>Lady Susan Hussey 1960–
>Lady Abel Smith 1974–87 (*Extra* 1987–)
>The Lady Elton 1987–
>Mrs Christian Adams 1997–

EXTRA WOMEN OF THE BEDCHAMBER
>The Honourable Mrs Andrew Elphinstone 1953–
>>(later Mrs John Woodroffe from 1980)
>Mrs Michael Wall 1981–
>Mrs Robert de Pass 1987–

(left) BADGE of a Lady in Waiting to the Princess of Wales. Made by Collingwood *(right)* BADGE of a Lady in Waiting to the Duchess of York. Made by Garrard, the badge is formed by an enamelled white rose of York. It was designed by the Duke of York.

HRH THE PRINCESS OF WALES

LADIES IN WAITING
>Miss Anne Beckwith-Smith 1981–90

EXTRA LADIES IN WAITING
>The Honourable Mrs Vivian Baring 1981–93
>Mrs George West 1982–97
>The Viscountess Campden 1991– 1997 (*Extra* 1985–91)
>Mrs Max Pike 1991–97 (*Extra* 1986–91)
>Mrs Duncan Byatt 1991–97 (*Extra* 1986–91)

HRH THE DUCHESS OF YORK

LADIES IN WAITING
>Mrs John Spooner 1986–96
>Mrs John Floyd 1986–96

HRH THE PRINCESS ANNE, THE PRINCESS ROYAL

BADGE OF A LADY IN WAITING TO THE PRINCESS ROYAL Made by Garrard, the badge is of diamonds on an off-white ribbon.

LADIES IN WAITING
>Lady Carew-Pole 1970–74 *and* 1986– (*Extra* 1974–86)
>Miss Rowena Brassey 1970–77
>Mrs Andrew Feilden 1970–86 and 1990– (*Extra* 1986–90)
>Miss Victoria Legge-Bourke 1974–86 (*Extra* 1986–)
>Mrs Malcolm Innes 1977–86 (*Extra* 1986–)
>The Honourable Mrs Legge-Bourke 1978– 98 (*Extra* 1998–)
>Mrs Malcolm Wallace 1986–
>Mrs Timothy Holdernesse-Roddam 1986–
>The Countess of Lichfield 1986–88 (*Extra* 1979–86 *and* 1988–)
>Mrs Charles Ritchie 1986–
>Mrs David Bowes-Lyon 1991–
>Mrs William Nunneley
>The Honourable Mrs Louloudis 1997–

(left) BADGE of a Lady in Waiting to the Duchess of Gloucester, designed by the Duke of Gloucester.
(right) THE GOLD AND SILVER EMBROIDERED BADGE of a lady in waiting to the Duchess of Gloucester presented by the Royal School of Needlework in 1985 to Her Royal Highness, Patron of the School.

HRH THE DUCHESS OF GLOUCESTER

LADIES IN WAITING

Mrs Michael Wigley 1973–
Miss Jennifer Thomson 1974–77 (*Extra* 1977–)
Miss Susanna Cryer 1978–79 (*Extra* 1979–80)
The Honourable Mrs Munro 1980–88
Mrs Euan McCorquodale 1980–
Mrs Howard Page 1984–
The Lady Camoys 1988–94 (*Extra* 1994–)

HRH PRINCESS ALEXANDRA, THE HONOURABLE LADY OGILVY

LADIES IN WAITING

Lady Moyra Campbell 1954–66 (*Extra* 1966–69)
Lady Mary Mumford 1964–

EXTRA LADIES IN WAITING

Dame Mona Mitchell 1969–
The Honourable Lady Rowley 1970– 1997
Lady Mary Colman 1970–
Lady Caroline Waterhouse 1970–79
Mrs Peter Afia 1987–
Lady Nicholas Gordon Lennox (1981–84 and 1990–

HRH THE DUCHESS OF KENT

LADIES IN WAITING

Miss Fiona Pilkington 1968–69
Mrs Alan Henderson 1967–79 *and* 1992–94 (*Extra* 1979–92 and 1994–)
Miss Carola Goodman-Irvine (later Mrs Law) 1979–81
Mrs David Napier (née Jane Pugh) 1970–79 (*Extra* 1979–82)
Mrs Colin Marsh (née Sarah Partridge) 1983–
Mrs Peter Wilmot-Sitwell 1993–94 (*Extra* 1974– 93)
Mrs Peter Troughton 1991–
Mrs Julian Tomkins 1994–
Mrs Richard Beckett 1994–

(above) BADGE of a Lady in Waiting to Princess Alexandra, the Honourable Lady Ogilvy. The brooch which forms this badge originally belonged to Queen Alexandra.
(below) BADGE of a Lady in Waiting to the Duchess of Kent. Made by Spink and Son in 1971.

EQUERRIES

An equerry was originally a 'Gentleman of the egnerory', an officer in charge of the stables of the Royal Household. Today they are the gentlemen and ladies in attendance on members of the Royal Family.

In the same way as the Ladies in attendance wear a badge of office on appropriate occasions so the Gentlemen, when in uniform, wear the cypher of the particular member of the Royal Family. Like the Sovereign's cypher they are in a gold or silver coloured metal, depending on the type of uniform being worn. They are worn below the wearer's badges of rank, if any, on each shoulder.

Equerries in attendance on the late Princess Royal (Princess Mary, Countess of Harewood), on the late Prince George, Duke of Kent, and on the late Prince Henry, Duke of Gloucester, wore no cypher, nor do those in attendance on the present Duke of Gloucester and Duke of Kent.

CYPHERS of members of the Royal Family:
 1. King George V
 2. Queen Mary
 3. Edward, Prince of Wales
 4. King Edward VII
 5. King George VI
 6. Queen Elizabeth
 7. Princess Elizabeth, Duchess of Edinburgh and the Duke of Edinburgh
 8. Princess Margaret
 9. Queen Elizabeth II
10. Prince Philip, Duke of Edinburgh
11. Charles, Prince of Wales
12. Prince Andrew, Duke of York

CYPHERS of members of the Royal Family:
1. Prince Edward
2. Cypher of the Princess Royal
3 Princess Alexandra, the Honourable Lady Ogilvy
4. Princess Marina, Duchess of Kent.
The badge at 5 was originally designed for equerries to the late Duke of Kent when Governor-General designate of Australia at the outbreak of war in 1939. Shortly after war was declared, the Duke began active service with the RAF. After his death in 1942, the badge was adapted and altered as illustrated, the words being removed from the Garter. Thereafter it was used as a cap badge for Princess Marina's chauffeur.

THE LORD HIGH ALMONER

All Royal charities were originally controlled by the King's Almoner to whom money was assigned from the sale of the goods of felons and from deodands (something forfeited to the Crown as having caused the death of a human being).

Though the office is likely to have existed at an earlier time, the first recorded appointment of Almoner is found in 1103. By the middle of the fifteenth century the title became that of Great Almoner and shortly afterwards that of High Almoner; officially it remains so to this day. The holder has, however, long since been referred to as the Lord High Almoner and since the sixteenth century the office has usually been held by a diocesan bishop. The duties of the Lord High Almoner are now restricted to assisting the Sovereign in the distribution of Maundy money on Maundy Thursday (the Thursday before Easter Sunday) each year.

This ceremony originally consisted of the washing of the feet of twelve or more poor men to commemorate the washing of the twelve disciples' feet at the last supper, when Jesus rose 'from supper and laid aside his garments and took a towel and girded himself and began to wash the disciples' feet and to wipe them with the towel wherewith he was girded' (John 13 v. 4–5). The ceremony had been performed from very early times. In England, the King used to wash the feet of as many poor men as he was years old and then distributed money, food and clothing to them. However the Lord High Almoner, Sub-Almoner,[3] Secretary and Assistant Secretary still wear during the service linen towels over their right shoulders and tied round the waist.

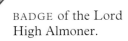

BADGE of the Lord High Almoner.

Thereafter the Sovereign used to delegate the washing to the Almoner. During the reign of Charles II, the washing and distribution of food and clothing was discontinued and was replaced by the distribution of money. Today the specially minted Maundy money is distributed in soft leather purses (the red containing money replacing the clothing of earlier times, the white containing the sets of silver Maundy coins), to as many men and women as the Sovereign is years old. Originally the service was held in the Chapel Royal at Whitehall and later in Westminster Abbey. Today the Service is held annually at a different cathedral church, but still bears a resemblance to the services held in the reign of Elizabeth I.

The present seal of the Royal Almonry depicts a three-masted ship in full sail at sea. It is of uncertain date but is thought to derive from the seal of Stephen Payne who was Dean of Exeter (1415–1419) and Almoner to Henry V (1414–1419). Payne's seal depicts the Almoner under a canopy, holding in his arms a ship on wheels. An alms box, in the form of a silver ship on wheels which could be passed down a long table, was often used in the fifteenth and sixteenth centuries.

The Lord High Almoner possessed no badge of office until 1976 when the present badge was made by Spink and Son of London for the Right Reverend David Say, Bishop of Rochester (1961–1988) and Lord High Almoner (1970–1988). It is made of 9-carat gold and red enamel and is worn at the neck suspended from a burgundy coloured ribbon. It is circular and the obverse shows the traditional three-masted ship in full sail at sea surrounded by the words 'SIGILL: ELEEMOSYN (Seal of the Almonry): ELIZABETHAE: II: D: G: BRITT: OMNIUM REGINA: F: D: . The outer rim bears the words: LORD HIGH ALMONER. The reverse is plain except for the London hallmark for 1976. A similar embroidered badge is worn by the Secretary and Assistant Secretary on the left upper arm of their gowns.

LORD HIGH ALMONERS (From the accession of Queen Victoria)
The Honourable Edward Harcourt 1808–1847 (Archbishop of York 1807–1847)
Samuel Wilberforce 1847–1869 (Bishop of Oxford 1846–1869 and Bishop of Winchester 1869–1873)
The Honourable Gerald Wellesley 1870–1882 (Dean of Windsor 1854–1882)
Lord Alwyne Compton 1882–1906 (Dean of Worcester 1879–1886 and Bishop of Ely 1886–1905)
Joseph Armitage Robinson 1906–1933 (Dean of Westminster 1902–1911 and Dean of Wells 1911–1933)
Cosmo Gordon Lang 1933–1945 (Archbishop of Canterbury 1928–1942)
Edward Sydney Woods 1946–1953 (Bishop of Lichfield 1937–1953)
Edward Michael Gresford Jones 1953–1970 (Bishop of St Albans 1950–1969)
Richard David Say 1970–1988 (Bishop of Rochester 1961–1988)
John Bernard Taylor 1988–1997 (Bishop of St Albans 1980–1995)
Nigel Simeon McCulloch 1995– (Bishop of Wakefield 1992–)

THE COLLEGE OF CHAPLAINS

The Clerk of the Closet is head of the College and advises the Sovereign on the appointment of Royal Chaplains. The office is an ancient one: the Closet was the private apartment of the Sovereign and the Clerk, 'usually a Reverend, Sober and Learned Divine'[4] was probably the private confessor of

BADGE of the Clerk of the Closet.

BADGES of Chaplains to King Edward VII, Queen Alexandra and King George V.

the Sovereign with access to the private apartment. He was involved with the spiritual life of the Sovereign,' his influence varying with the religious climate of the period. Many have exercised important influence at the heart of the Royal Household in a post obscure to many, unknown to most and, until now, something of a mystery even to those familiar with the Clerk and his duties in the late twentieth century'[5].

The first known Clerk was Edward Atherton in 1437. The present Clerk, the Right Reverend Johnathan Bailey, Bishop of Derby, is the 56th holder of the office.

Until 1986, the Clerk wore a Chaplain's badge, which replaced an earlier embroidered scarf in 1906. The badge worn by the Clerk after 1906 was

(*below left*) BADGE of a Chaplain to the Queen and badge of a Priest-in-Ordinary to the Queen. (*below right*) THE REVD ARTHUR FULLER, CVO 1942 (MVO 1935) Chaplain to the Forces and later Domestic Chaplain to George V, Edward VIII and George VI, wearing the badge.

BADGES of Civil Honorary Physicians. These badges were approved by King George VI in 1938. They are of silver gilt, bearing the Royal cypher and Crown within a wreath of laurel and oak leaves, at the base of which is a representation of the serpents of Asclepius, the Greek god of medicine and son of Apollo. They were made by Elkington & Co Ltd but, since 1987 have been made by Toye, Kenning & Spencer Ltd. Honorary Physicians and Surgeons in the Services wear aiguilettes bearing the Sovereign's cypher which is also on the shoulder straps in uniform.

pinned to the left side of his black scarf. Since a Bishop was seldom in convocation robes wearing a scarf, Bishop Bickersteth wore his, with the Queen's permission, on his cassock below the collar.

On 21 April 1986, The Queen's sixtieth birthday, the first Clerk's badge was presented by the Lord Chamberlain, in the Vestry of St George's Chapel, Windsor, to the Right Reverend John Bickersteth, the first Bishop of Bath and Wells to hold the office. The badge is the same as the Chaplain's badge with the addition of the words: CLERK OF THE CLOSET inscribed on a scroll beneath the Royal cypher. It is suspended from a scarlet ribbon so that the badge hangs just below the collar. The badge was referred to for the first time in the Court Circular when it was recorded that on 25 October 1989 the Bishop of Chelmsford 'had the honour of being received by Her Majesty upon his appointment as Clerk of the Closet to the Queen and received his badge of office'.

The College, founded in Edward VII's reign, consists of thirty-six serving clergy (or chaplains) of the Church of England with a meritorious record who have been recommended by the Clerk of the Closet to serve the Sovereign and the Household. They receive no stipend but a fee on the occasions when they are summoned to preach at one of the Royal Chapels or at Windsor.

Extra Chaplains are those who have attained the retiring age of 70 and have been so appointed in recognition of particularly long and distinguished service.

Priests-in-Ordinary are not members of the College of Chaplains but of the Staff of Her Majesty's Chapels Royal. There are three and each is appointed on the recommendation of the Dean of the Chapels Royal. They attend by monthly rota at the statutory services held in the Chapels Royal or on such other occasions as are commanded by the Sovereign. They share with the Sub-Dean (who is also Domestic Chaplain at Buckingham Palace) the responsibility for maintaining these services and for the pastoral care of Her Majesty's Household and staff. Each of them holds a position in the Church or in academic life, for example, as a diocesan official or a school chaplain. The Deputy Clerk of the Closet, an office in existence by the middle of the seventeenth century, the Chaplains to the Queen, the extra Chaplains, the Dean and the Sub-Dean of the Chapels Royal and the Domestic Chaplains wear a badge of silver gilt and enamel consisting of the Royal cypher set within an oval frame of laurel and oakleaves. The Priests-in-Ordinary wear an identical badge except that it is made of silver.

The badge is worn on the left side of the scarf when the Chaplain is officiating at divine service and may also be worn below any decorations on appropriate occasions. They are given to the recipient who may retain them on retirement. Should the Chaplain or Priest be appointed a Dean or a Bishop, he may continue to wear the badge if he wishes to do so.

CLERKS OF THE CLOSET (during the period covered by this book)

1827	Robert James Carr, Bishop of Chichester and of Worcester
1837	Edward Stanley, Bishop of Norwich.
1849	John Graham, Bishop of Chester.
1865	Henry Philpott, Bishop of Worcester.
1891	Randall Thomas Davidson, Bishop of Rochester and of Winchester. (later Archbishop of Canterbury).
1903	William Boyd Carpenter, Bishop of Ripon.
1918	Hubert Murray Burge, Bishop of Oxford.
1925	Thomas Banks Strong, Bishop of Oxford.

1937   Cyril Forster Garbett, Bishop of Winchester.
            (later Archbishop of York).
1942   Percy Mark Herbert, Bishop of Norwich.
1963   Roger Plumpton Wilson, Bishop of Chichester.
1975   William Gordon Fallows, Bishop of Sheffield.
1979   John Monier Bickersteth, Bishop of Bath and Wells.
1989   John Waine, Bishop of Chelmsford.
1996   Jonathan Sansbury Bailey, Bishop of Derby

LORD LIEUTENANTS

In each of the counties of England, Wales, Scotland and Northern Ireland, the Queen is represented by a Lord Lieutenant, who is appointed by the Sovereign by patent under the Great Seal as the permanent local representative of the Crown. As such Lord Lieutenants take precedence over all others in the county or district during their term of office.

The office was first created in the reign of King Henry VIII and originally the holder was the military representative of the Sovereign and head of the local militia. Today the Lord Lieutenant remains the county representative of the Sovereign. The duties of the office include recommendations for honours and for the appointment of magistrates, and the appointment of Deputy Lieutenants. The Lord Lieutenant is the head of the Commission for the Peace for the County and was often the Custos Rotulorum appointed by the Crown to keep the records of the County Sessions.

The ceremonial dress of a Lord Lieutenant consists of a dark blue jacket with scarlet gorget and patches, a crimson and silver sash, dark blue trousers with scarlet stripes, and a dark blue cap with two rows of silver oakleaf embroidery on the peak. The badges of rank and buttons bear the crown above

LORD LIEUTENANTS' BADGES: English type. Worn by Lavinia, Duchess of Norfolk, Lord Lieutenant of West Sussex 1975–90 *(left)*. Irish type. Worn by Viola, Duchess of Westminster, Lord Lieutenant of County Fermanagh 1979–86 *(right)*.

LORD LIEUTENANTS'
BADGES: Scottish type.
Worn by Councillor Dr
Margaret Farquhar CBE
JP Lord Lieutenant of
the City of Aberdeen,
the Lord Provost
(above). Welsh type.
Worn by Wing-
Commander Mrs
C.C.L. Williams, Lord
Lieutenant of South
Glamorgan *(below)*.

BADGE OF OFFICE (for
a lady) of the Captain of
Her Majesty's Body-
guard of the Honourable
Corps of Gentlemen at
Arms. Worn by
Baroness Llewelyn –
Davies of Hastoe

the Rose, Prince of Wales's Plume of three feathers, Thistle or Shamrock, according to country.

This uniform was inappropriate in 1975 for the first lady to be appointed. Lavinia, Duchess of Norfolk (who became the first non-Royal Lady of the Garter in June 1990) succeeded her late husband as Lord Lieutenant of West Sussex. She was followed in 1978 by Baroness Phillips as Lord Lieutenant of Greater London, in 1979 by Viola, Duchess of Westminster of County Fermanagh in Northern Ireland, in 1985 by Mrs Williams of South Glamorgan, in 1994 by Mrs Mary Fagan of Hampshire and Lady Mary Holborow of Cornwall, in 1995 by Mrs Robin Cracroft-Eley of Lincolnshire and in 1997 by Mrs Sarah Goad of Surrey. Latterly the following appointments have been made: 1998 Lady Juliet Townsend, LVO (Northamptonshire), The Honourable Mrs Legge-Bourke, LVO (Powys), Dr June Paterson-Brown (Roxburgh, Ettrick and Lauderdale) and Lady Gass (Somerset). 1999 Mrs Margaret Dean (Fife) and 2000 Mrs Andrew Stewart-Roberts (East Sussex) and Lady Carswell (County Borough of Belfast).

As a result of the 1975 appointment, a badge of office was devised to replace the uniform worn by men. For English counties, the badge consists of a Tudor rose enamelled in red and white with an 18 carat gold centre and gold tracery round the petals, the whole surmounted by a crown set with pearls, emeralds, sapphires and a ruby. For the counties of Northern Ireland the rose is replaced by a green enamelled sprig of shamrock on a white enamelled background with gold tracery. For Welsh counties, the rose is replaced by the Prince of Wales's plume in white enamel with the motto in gold lettering on a blue enamelled scroll on a red enamelled background. For the counties and certain cities of Scotland the thistle replaces the rose, shamrock or Prince of Wales's plume.

All the badges were made by Spink & Son and are worn from a ribbon bow of white with a maroon stripe towards each edge, the colours being the same as those of the men's sash.

THE HONOURABLE CORPS OF GENTLEMEN AT ARMS

In 1485, King Henry VII formed the Valecti Gardi (Corporis) Domini Regis, The King's Body Guard of the Yeoman of the Guard. In 1509 his son and successor, Henry VIII, raised its strength and instituted another bodyguard of nobles and gentry, the Gentlemen Spears who, in 1539, were renamed Gentlemen Pensioners. Both guards shared the duty of being 'continuously near His Majesty's person'.

King William IV (1830–1837) restored the military character of the Pensioners and renamed them The Honourable Corps of the Gentlemen at Arms. It has remained so to this day, though now the duties of guarding the Sovereign are purely ceremonial.

The uniform consists of scarlet coat, blue trousers and gilt metal helmet crowned by white swans' feathers. The Corps consists of the

Captain, Lieutenant, Standard Bearer, Clerk of the Cheque and Adjutant, Harbinger and twenty-six Gentlemen of the Corps.

The appointment of the Captain is a political one, and held by the Government Chief Whip in the House of Lords. In the Labour Government of 1974–1979, the appointment was held for the first time by a lady, Baroness Llewelyn-Davies of Hastoe. To replace the traditional uniform, a badge was devised for a lady Captain. It consists of the badge of the Corps in white and yellow gold and enamel, the crown and portcullis set with brilliant cut diamonds, all mounted on a ribbon bow of red and blue, the colours of the Corps.

THE OFFICERS OF ARMS

The Corporation of the Kings, Heralds and Pursuivants, more commonly known as the College of Arms, forms part of the Royal Household. It consists of three Kings of Arms, six Heralds and four Pursuivants, each of whom is appointed by letters patent on the nomination of the Earl Marshal.

The Officers of Arms-in-Ordinary are:

GARTER'S JEWEL. The obverse and the reverse are the same.

> Kings of Arms: Garter, Clarenceux and Norroy and Ulster.
> Heralds: Chester, Lancaster, Richmond, Somerset, Windsor and York.
> Pursuivants: Bluemantle, Portcullis, Rouge Croix and Rouge Dragon.

The Corporation dates from 1484 with their functions governed by a later charter granted by Queen Mary in 1555. They grant arms on behalf of the Sovereign and keep the official register of arms and genealogies.

Each Officer is also empowered to conduct his own private practice in relation to heraldic and genealogical research.

They are most frequently seen by the public at ceremonies such as the Garter Service at Windsor and the State Opening of Parliament at Westminster. In Scotland, the Officers of Arms-in-Ordinary are officers of the Court of the Lord Lyon King of Arms in Edinburgh. Under Lord Lyon there are at present three Heralds and two Pursuivants:

> Heralds: Albany, Rothesay and Ross.
> Pursuivants: Kintyre and Unicorn.

ENGLISH HERALDS' AND PURSUIVANTS' JEWEL.

There are other titles which are in use from time to time: Marchmont, Islay and Snowdoun Herald and Dingwall, Carrick, Bute and Ormonde Pursuivant. The two Extraordinary titles are Falkland and Linlithgow Pursuivant.

The duties of the Scottish Officers of Arms are similar to their English counterparts though, unlike the latter, Lord Lyon has a judicial function determining claims to armorial bearings.

There are a number of Officers of Arms Extraordinary, in England and in New Zealand. Canada has three Heralds-in-Ordinary as part of an heraldic executive established under the authority of the Queen of Canada.

The Irish Officers of Arms, Dublin Herald, Cork Herald and Athlone Pursuivant were Officers of Arms of the Order of St Patrick, their offices having been founded in 1783 by letters patent under the Great Seal of Ireland. They were part of the Vice-regal Household.

On the deaths of the then incumbents the offices were allowed to lapse (Dublin Herald in 1890 and Cork Herald in 1880). With the revision of the Statutes of the Order in 1905, the offices were re-established. The fifth and last Dublin was Major Guillamore O'Grady who was appointed in 1908. He was the last Irish Herald to take part at a Coronation, that of King George VI in 1937. He died in 1952. The sixth and last Cork, Richard Keith, was appointed in 1911. In July 1952, with commendable tact and sensitivity, he resigned before the impending Coronation. The eleventh and last Athlone, George Burtchaell was appointed in 1908 and died in office in 1921.

The jewel for the officers was not provided for in the Statutes and Ordinances until the Statutes of 1905. It shows the Cross of St Patrick gules, on a field argent encircled with the motto of the Order, the whole enamelled in their proper colours. It was worn round the neck from a sky blue ribbon. The badge illustrated is that worn by Major O'Grady.

KINGS, HERALDS AND PURSUIVANTS OF ARMS
(from 1837)

ENGLAND AND WALES

GARTER KING OF ARMS
Sir Ralph Bigland 1831–38
Sir William Woods 1838–42
Sir Charles George Young 1842–69
Sir Albert William Woods 1869–1904
Sir Alfred Scott-Gatty 1904–18
Sir Henry Farnham Burke 1919–30
Sir Gerald Woods Wollaston 1930–44
Sir Algar Henry Stafford Howard 1944–50
The Hon. Sir George Rothe Bellew 1950–61
Sir Anthony Richard Wagner 1961–78
Sir Alexander Colin Cole 1978–92
Sir Conrad Marshall Fisher Swan 1992–95
Peter Llewellyn Gwynn-Jones 1995–

THE JEWELS of Norroy King of Arms (left) and Ulster King of Arms (right), obverses and reverses.

CLARENCEUX KING OF ARMS

William Woods 1831–38
Edmund Lodge 1838–39
Joseph Hawker 1839–46
Francis Martin 1846–48
James Pulman 1848–59
Robert Laurie 1859–82
Walter Aston Blount 1882–94
George Edward Cokayne 1894–1911
Sir William Henry Weldon 1911–19
Charles Harold Athill 1919–22
William Alexander Lindsay 1922–26
Gordon Ambrose de Lisle Lee 1926–27
Sir Arthur William Steuart Cochrane 1928–54
Archibald George Blomefield Russell 1954–55
Sir John Dunamace Heaton-Armstrong 1956–67
John Riddell Bromhead Walker 1968–78
Sir Anthony Richard Wagner 1978–95
John Philip Brooke-Little 1995–97
David Hubert Boothby Chesshyre 1997–

NORROY KING OF ARMS (NORROY AND ULSTER KING OF ARMS FROM 1943)

Edmund Lodge 1822–38
Joseph Hawker 1838–39
Francis Martin 1839–46
James Pulman 1846–48
Edward Howard Gibbon 1848–49
Robert Laurie 1849–59
Walter Aston Blount 1859–82
George Edward Cokayne 1882–94
William Henry Weldon 1894–1911
Henry Farnham Burke 1911–19
Charles Harold Athill 1919
William Alexander Lindsay 1919–22
Gordon Ambrose de Lisle Lee 1922–26
Arthur William Steuart Cochrane 1926–28
Gerald Woods Wollaston 1928–30
Algar Henry Stafford Howard 1930–44
Sir Gerald Woods Wollaston 1944–57

THE JEWEL of
Clarenceux King of
Arms. Obverse *(left)*
and reverse *(right)*.

Aubrey John Toppin 1957–66
Richard Preston Graham-Vivian 1966–71
Walter John George Verco 1971–80
John Philip Brooke Brooke-Little 1980–95
David Hubert Boothby Chesshyre 1995–97
Thomas Woodcock 1997–

CHESTER HERALD

Walter Aston Blount 1834–59
Edward Stephen Dendy 1859–64
Henry Murray Lane 1864–1913
Thomas Morgan Joseph-Watkin 1913–15
Arthur William Steuart Cochrane 1915–26
John Dunamace Heaton-Armstrong 1926–55
James Amold Frere 1956–60
Walter John George Verco 1960–71
David Hubert Boothby Chesshyre 1978–95
Timothy Hugh Stewart Duke 1995–

LANCASTER HERALD

George Frederick Beltz 1822–41
Albert William Woods 1841–69
George Edward Cokayne (formerly Adams) 1869–82
Edward Bellasis 1882–1922
Archibald George Blomefield Russell 1922–54
John Riddell Bromhead Walker 1954–68
Francis Sedley Andrus 1972–82
Peter Llewellyn Gwynn-Jones 1982–95
Robert John Baptist Noel 1999–

RICHMOND HERALD

Joseph Hawker 1803–38
James Pulman 1838–46
Matthew Charles Howard Gibbon 1846–73
Henry Harrington Molyneux-Seel 1873–82
Arthur Staunton Larken 1882–89
Charles Harold Athill 1889–1919
Gerald Woods Wollaston 1919–28
Henry Robert Charles Martin 1928–42
Anthony Richard Wagner 1943–61
Robin Ian Evelyn Milne Stuart de la Lanne-Mirrlees 1962–67
John Philip Brooke Brooke-Little 1967–80
Michael Maclagan 1980–89
Patric Laurence Dickinson 1989–

SOMERSET HERALD

James Cathrow-Disney 1813–54
William Courthope 1854–66
James Robinson Planché 1866–80
Stephen Isaacson Tucker 1880–87
Henry Farnham Burke 1887–1911
Everard Green 1911–26
George Rothe Bellew 1926–50
Michael Roger Trappes-Lomax 1951–67
Rodney Onslow Dennys 1967–82
Thomas Woodcock 1982–97

WINDSOR HERALD

Francis Martin 1819–39
Robert Laurie 1839–49
George Harrison Rogers-Harrison 1849–80
William Henry Weldon 1880–94
William Alexander Lindsay 1894–1919
Algar Henry Stafford Howard 1919–31
Alfred Trego Butler 1931–46
Richard Preston Graham-Vivian 1947–66
Alexander Colin Cole 1966–70
Theobald David Mathew 1978–97
William George Hunt 1999–

YORK HERALD

Charles George Young 1820–42
Edward Howard Gibbon 1842–48
Thomas William King 1848–72
John von Sonnentag de Havilland 1872–86
Alfred Scott-Gatty 1886–1904
George William Marshall 1904–05
Gordon Ambrose de Lisle Lee 1905–22
The Hon. Philip Plantagenet Cary 1922–32
Aubrey John Toppin 1932–57
Charles Murray Kennedy St Clair, Lord Sinclair 1957–68
Conrad Marshall John Fisher Swan 1968–92
Peter Brotherton Spurrier 1992–93
Henry Edgar Paston-Bedingfeld 1993–

WILLIAM HUNT,
Portcullis Pursuivant
(later Windsor Herald)
wearing the jewel.

BLUEMANTLE PURSUIVANT

George Harrison Rogers-Harrison 1831–49
Henry Murray Lane 1849–64
Henry Harrington Molyneux-Seel 1864–73
Edward Bellasis 1873–82
Charles Harold Athill 1882–89
Gordon Ambrose de Lisle Lee 1889–1905
Gerald Woods Wollaston 1906–19
The Hon. Philip Plantagenet Cary 1919–22
Edmund Richard Clarence Armstrong 1923
Aubrey John Toppin 1923–32
Richard Preston Graham-Vivian 1932–47
James Arnold Frere 1948–56
John Philip Brooke Brooke-Little 1956–70
Francis Sedley Andrus 1970–73
Peter Llewellyn Gwynn-Jones 1973–82
Terence David McCarthy 1983–91
Robert John Baptist Noel 1992–99

PORTCULLIS PURSUIVANT

James Pulman 1822–38
Albert William Woods 1838–41
George William Collen 1841–78
Arthur Staunton Larken 1878–82
William Alexander Lindsay 1882–94
Thomas Morgan Joseph-Watkin 1894–1913
Keith William Murray 1913–22
George Rothe Bellew 1922–26
Alfred Trego Butler 1926–31

Anthony Richard Wagner 1931–43
Charles Murray Kennedy St Clair 1949–57
Alexander Colin Cole 1957–66
Michael Maclagan 1970–80
Peter Brotherton Spurrier 1981–92
William George Hunt 1992–99

ROUGE CROIX PURSUIVANT

Robert Laurie 1823–39
William Courthope 1839–54
James Robinson Planché 1854–66
John von Sonnentag de Havilland 1866–72
Stephen Isaacson Tucker 1872–80
Henry Farnham Burke 1880–87
George William Marshall 1887–1904
Arthur William Steuart Cochrane 1904–15
Archibald George Blomefield Russell 1915–22
Henry Robert Charles Martin 1922–28
Philip Walter Kerr 1928–47
John Riddell Bromhead Walker 1947–54
Walter John George Verco 1954–60
Rodney Onslow Dennys 1961–67
David Hubert Boothby Chesshyre 1970–78
Thomas Woodcock 1978–82
Henry Edgar Paston-Bedingfeld 1983–93
David Vines White 1995–

ROUGE DRAGON PURSUIVANT

Thomas William King 1833–48
Edward Stephen Dendy 1848–59
George Edward Adams (later Cokayne) 1859–70
William Henry Weldon 1870–80
Alfred Scott Gatty 1880–86
Albert William Woods 1886–93
Everard Green 1893–1911
Algar Henry Stafford Howard 1911–19
Alexander Warren Dury Mitton 1919–22
John Dunamace Heaton-Armstrong 1922–26
Eric Neville Geijer 1926–41
Michael Roger Trappes-Lomax 1946–51
Robin Ian Evelyn Milne Stuart de la Lanne-Mirrlees
    1952–62
Conrad Marshall John Fisher Swan 1962–70
Theobald David Mathew 1970–78
Patric Laurence Dickinson 1978–89
Timothy Hugh Stewart Duke 1989–1995
Clive Edwin Alexander Cheesman 1998–

ARUNDEL HERALD EXTRAORDINARY

Dermot Michael Macgregor Morrah 1953–74
Rodney Onslow Dennys 1982–93
Alan Roger Dickins 1998–

BEAUMONT HERALD EXTRAORDINARY

Francis Sedley Andrus 1982–

BLANC COURSIER HERALD EXTRAORDINARY

Walter Aston Blount 1831–57

BRUNSWICK HERALD EXTRAORDINARY
Albert William Woods 1841–57

FALCON HERALD EXTRAORDINARY
Henry Frederick Stephenson 1813–58

MALTRAVERS HERALD EXTRAORDINARY
Joseph Jackson Howard 1887–1902
The Rt Hon Sir William Bull Bt 1922–31
Arthur Oswald Barron 1937–39
Aubrey John Toppin 1966–69
Francis John Steer 1972–78
John Martin Robinson 1989–

MOWBRAY HERALD EXTRAORDINARY
Edward Howard Gibbon 1842

NEW ZEALAND HERALD EXTRAORDINARY
Phillippe Patrick O'Shea 1978–

NORFOLK HERALD EXTRAORDINARY
Albert William Woods 1841
Hugh Stanford London 1953–59
George Drewry Squibb 1959–94
David Rankin-Hunt 1994–

SURREY HERALD EXTRAORDINARY
Edward Stephen Dendy 1856–59
Charles Alban Buckler 1880–1905
Sir Walter John George Verco 1980–

WALES HERALD EXTRAORDINARY
Francis Jones 1963–93
Michael Powell Siddons 1994–

CARNARVON PURSUIVANT EXTRAORDINARY
Keith William Murray 1911–13

FITZALAN PURSUIVANT EXTRAORDINARY
Albert William Woods 1837–38
Gerald Woods Wollaston 1902–06
Algar Henry Stafford Howard 1911
Alexander Colin Cole 1953–57
Charles Wilfred Scott-Giles 1957–82
John Martin Robinson 1982–89
Alastair Andrew Bernard Reibey Bruce of Crionaich 1998–

HOWARD PURSUIVANT EXTRAORDINARY
John Henry Bruce Bedells 1992–98

SCOTLAND

LORD LYON KING OF ARMS
The 10th Earl of Kinnoull 1804–66
George Burnett 1866–90
Sir James Balfour Paul 1890–1927
George Sitwell Campbell Swinton 1927–29
Sir Francis James Grant 1929–45

THE BADGE of Lord Lyon King of Arms. On ceremonial duties, Lord Lyon wears the badge with the obverse (*above*) showing. When acting as King of Arms of the Order of the Thistle, it is worn with the reverse (*below*) showing.

BADGE worn by the
Heralds and Pursuivants
of Scotland: the obverse
and (*bottom*) the reverse.

Sir Thomas Innes of Learney 1945–69
Sir James Monteith Grant 1969– 1981
Sir Malcolm Innes of Edingight 1981–2001
Robin Orr Blair 2001–

ALBANY HERALD

David Littlejohn 1837–59
James Sinclair 1859–78
(vacant 1878–83)
John Spence 1883–85
Robert Spence 1885–1909
William Rae Macdonald 1909–23
George Sitwell Campbell Swinton 1923–27
Sir Thomas Wolseley Haig 1927–35
Thomas Innes of Learney 1935–45
Sir Francis James Grant 1945–53
Charles Ian Fraser of Reilig 1953–61
Sir Rupert Iain Moncrieffe of that Ilk 1961–85
John Alexander Spens 1985–

ISLAY HERALD

John Cook 1811–51
Henry Wilson 1851–84
(vacant 1884–1981)
John Inglis Drever Pottinger 1981
(vacant)

MARCHMONT HERALD

William Anderson 1836–74
(vacant 1874–84)
John Grant 1884–85
Andrew Ross 1885–1901
(vacant 1901–25)
John Home Stevenson 1925–39
John William Balfour Paul of Cakemuir 1939–57
James Montieth Grant 1957–69
Sir Thomas Innes of Learney 1969–71
Malcolm Rognvald Innes of Edingight 1971–81
Sir James Monteith Grant 1981–82
David Maitland Maitland-Titterton 1982–89

ROSS HERALD

David Taylor 1825–39
George Goldie 1839–60
Andrew Gilman 1860–79
(vacant 1879–1901)
Andrew Ross 1901–25
(vacant 1925–88)
Charles John Burnett 1988–

ROTHESAY HERALD

James Lorimer of Kellyfield 1822–68
(vacant 1868–79)
James William Mitchell 1879–98
Francis James Grant 1898–1929
Sir John Mackintosh Norman Macleod 1929–39
Harold Andrew Balvaird Lawson 1939–81
Sir Crispin Hamlyn Agnew of Lochnaw 1986–

SNOWDOUN HERALD
> David Alexander 1828–45
> James Cook 1845–60
> William Robert Montignani 1860–83
> (vacant since 1883)

ROTHESAY HERALD EXTRAORDINARY
> Harold Andrew Balvaird Lawson 1981–85

BUTE PURSUIVANT
> David Littlejohn 1833–38
> William Goodall Bayley 1838–51
> Walter Ferguson 1851–84
> Robert Spence Livingstone 1884–85
> Andrew Ross 1885–88
> John Thomas Loth 1888–99
> James Keir Lamont 1899–1901
> (vacant since 1901)

CARRICK PURSUIVANT
> William Dunnett 1836–55
> Henry Wilson 1855–64
> Archibald Thorburn 1864–72
> (vacant 1872–79)
> John Spence 1879–83
> John Grant 1883–84
> William Macfarlane Wylie 1884–86
> Francis James Grant 1886–98
> William Rae Macdonald 1898–1907
> Sir Duncan Alexander Dundas Campbell 1907–26
> Thomas Innes of Learney 1926–35
> Sir Alexander Hay Seton 1935–39
> Alexander James Stevenson 1939–46
> James Monteith Grant 1946–57
> Malcolm Rognvald Innes of Edingight 1957–72
> David John Wilson Reid of Robertland 1972–73
> (vacant until 1992)
> Mrs Elizabeth Ann Roads 1992–

DINGWALL PURSUIVANT
> John Neill 1830–64
> Samuel Bough 1864–78
> (vacant 1878–1939)
> Charles Ian Fraser of Reilig 1939–53
> (vacant 1953–83)
> Charles John Burnett 1983–88

KINTYRE PURSUIVANT
> Robert Hamilton 1821–59
> William Robert Montignani 1859–60
> John Jeffers Wilson 1860–66
> Hugh Gray Tibbetts 1866–69
> (vacant 1869–1953)
> Sir Rupert Iain Moncrieffe of that Ilk 1953–55
> Charles Eliot Jauncey of Tullichettle 1957–73
> (vacant 1973–86)
> John Charles Grossmith George 1986–

ORMONDE PURSUIVANT

> George Goldie 1835–40
> Andrew Paterson 1840–55
> John Brown 1855–79
> (vacant 1879–1971)
> David Maitland Maitland-Titterton 1971–82

UNICORN PURSUIVANT

> James Cook 1825–45
> James Sinclair 1845–59
> Andrew Gillman 1859–60
> Stuart Moodie Livingstone 1860–1902
> John Home Stevenson 1902–25
> Sir John Macintosh Norman Macleod 1925–29
> Harold Andrew Balvaird Lawson 1929–39
> Gordon Dalyell 1939–55
> Sir Rupert Iain Moncrieffe of that Ilk 1955–61
> John Inglis Drever Pottinger 1961–81
> Sir Crispin Hamlyn Agnew of Lochnaw 1981–86
> Alistair Lorne Campbell of Airds 1987–

FALKLAND PURSUIVANT

> John William Balfour Paul of Cakemuir 1927–39
> (vacant since 1939)

FALKLAND PURSUIVANT EXTRAORDINARY

> David Hugh Montgomerie Boyle 15–29 October 1962,
>   28 June – 11 July 1963
> Charles John Shaw of Tordarroch 10 June – 31 August 1966
> David Maitland Maitland-Titterton 1969–71
> Lord James Douglas-Hamilton 7–14 July 1973
> Peter de Vere Beauclerk Dewar 2–10 July 1975
> Francis Henderson Coutts 20–27 May 1977,
>   30 June– 7 July 1979
> Peter de Vere Beauclerk Dewar 1–10 July 1982,
>   1–10 July 1984,
>   28 June–8 July 1987
> William Edward Peter Louis Drummond-Murray of
>   Mastrick June–July 1990
> Reginald John Maiden July 1994

LINLITHGOW PURSUIVANT EXTRAORDINARY

> John Inglis Drever Pottinger 1953
> Elizabeth Ann Roads 24–31 March 1987

IRELAND

ULSTER KING OF ARMS

> Sir William Betham 1820–53
> Sir Bernard Burke 1853–92
> Sir Arthur Vicars 1893–1908
> Sir Nevile Wilkinson 1908–40
> Thomas Ulick Sadleir (acting) 1940–43

NORROY AND ULSTER KING OF ARMS

> (See under England and Wales)

DEPUTY ULSTER KING OF ARMS

Molyneaux Cecil John Betham 1839–80
Sir Henry Farnham Burke 1889–93
George Dames Burtchaell 1910–11 and 1915–21
Thomas Ulick Sadleir 1921–43

HERALDS AND PURSUIVANTS

CORK HERALD

Molyneaux Cecil John Betham 1829–80
(The office of Cork Herald was abolished in 1880 and was
    revived in 1905)
Peirce Gun Mahony 1905–10
Captain Richard Alexander Lyonal Keith 1910–52
(vacant since 1952)

DUBLIN HERALD

Captain Sheffield Philip Fiennes Betham 1834–90
(The office of Dublin Herald was abolished in 1890 and was
    revived in 1905)
Francis Richard Shackleton 1905–07
Major Guillamore O'Grady 1908–52
(vacant since 1952)

ATHLONE PUSUIVANT

William Crawford 1829–65
Captain Robert Smith 1865–82
Bernard Louis Burke 1883–92
John Edward Burke 1892–99
Henry Claude Blake 1899–1907
Francis Bennett-Goldney 1907
George Dames Burtchaell 1908–21
(vacant since 1921)

JUNIOR PURSUIVANT

Alfred Betham 1825–41
William Heron 1829–after 1837
Joseph Cotton Walker 1830–
Joseph Baker in 1837
William Skeys
    (afterwards Skey) 1839–48
Robert Smith 1840–65
Francis Betham 1841–
Charles Patrick MacDonnell 1850–70
Columbus Patrick Drake 1854–89
George Frith Barry 1865–91

CORK PURSUIVANT

Major Gerald Achilles Burgoyne 1924–36

DEPUTY ATHLONE PURSUIVANT

Joseph Nugent Lentaigne 1874–82
Bernard Louis Burke 1882–83

THE JEWEL worn by Irish Heralds in their capacity as Heralds of the Order of Saint Patrick. This particular jewel was made for Dublin Herald and was probably made in 1905 when the office was revived under the revised Statutes of the Order.

MASTER OF THE CEREMONIES AND MARSHAL OF THE DIPLOMATIC CORPS

The office of Master of the Ceremonies was created by James I, its special functions being to enforce the observance of the etiquette of the Court, to arrange the reception of foreign potentates and ambassadors and to assist the Lord Chamberlain in the ordering of all entertainments at the Palace. Any connection between the Sovereign and an Ambassador would be arranged through the Master of Ceremonies. All applications for presentations and attendances at Courts and Levées by members of the Corps were made by the accredited envoy through the same official who would submit the list to the Lord Chamberlain. The Master of the Ceremonies also had duties at the time of Coronations, Jubilees and other State Occasions and was sometimes taken in personal attendance on the Sovereign. In 1920 it was felt that the title was something of a misnomer and it was changed in that year to Marshal of the Diplomatic Corps. It remains so to this day.

In peacetime, the badge is worn with the side showing the emblem of peace to the front; in time of war, the badge is worn the other way round.

MASTERS OF THE CEREMONIES SINCE 1820

1818–46	Sir Robert Chester, Kt.
1847–76	Colonel the Honourable Sir Edward Cust, KCH
1876–90	General Sir Francis Seymour, Bt. KCB
1890–93	Major General Sir C. C. Teesdale, VC, KCMG
1893–1903	Colonel the Honourable Sir William Colville, KCVO, CB
1904–07	Colonel Sir Douglas Dawson, KCVO, CMG
1907–20	The Honourable Sir Arthur Walsh (later Lord Ormathwaite), KCVO

MARSHALS OF THE DIPLOMATIC CORPS

1920–34	Major General Sir John Hanbury-Williams, GCVO, KCB, CMG
1934–45	Lieutenant General Sir Sidney Clive, GCVO, KCB, CMG, DSO
1946–50	Sir John Berkeley Monck, GCVO, CMG

THE MARSHAL OF THE DIPLOMATIC CORPS, Lieut. Gen. Sir John Richards KCB KCVO, wearing his badge. Accompanying him is the High Commissioner for India on presentation of his credentials, March 1990.

1951–61	Major General Sir Guy Salisbury-Jones, GCVO, CMG, CBE, MC
1962–71	Rear Admiral the Earl Cairns, KCVO, CB
1972–81	Major General Lord Michael Fitzalan-Howard, GCVO, CB, CBE, MC
1982–92	Lieutenant General Sir John Richards, KCB, KCVO
1993–2001	Vice Admiral Sir James Weatherall, KCVO, KBE
2001–	Sir Anthony Figgis, KCVO, CMG

ASSISTANT MASTERS OF THE CEREMONIES SINCE 1820

1820–21	Sir Robert Chester
1822–23	William John Crossbe Esq
1824–26	Henry Mash Esq
1826–45	Thomas S. Hyde Esq
1845–47	Colonel Sir Edward Cust
1847–55	Major General William Cornwall
1855–80	Colonel Charles Bagot
1881–87	Augustus Lumley-Savile Esq
1887–1900	Lieutenant Colonel William Chaine
1901–19	Sir Robert Synge, KCMG, MVO

VICE MARSHALS OF THE DIPLOMATIC CORPS

1921–34	Sir Hubert Montgomery, KCMG, CB, CVO
1934–45	Sir John Berkeley Monck, KCVO, CMG
1947–57	Sir Marcus Cheke, KCVO, CMG
1958–66	Dugald Malcolm Esq, CVO, TD
1965–73	A.L. Mayall Esq, CMG, CVO
1974–76	John Curle Esq, CMG, CVO
1977–82	Roger du Boulay Esq, CMG, CVO
1983–86	The Honourable Eustace Gibbs, CMG
1987–92	Roger Hervey Esq, CMG
1993–97	Anthony Figgis Esq, CMG
1997–99	Philip Astley Esq, LVO
1999–	Mrs Kathryn Frances Colvin

ARTHUR HENRY JOHN WALSH, later Baron Ormathwaite, GCVO, Master of the Ceremonies to King Edward VII and King George V, 1907–20, wearing the badge.

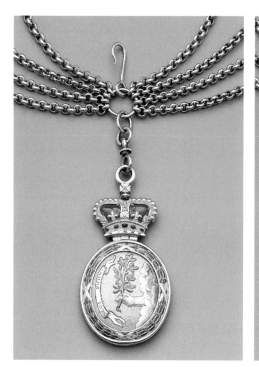

BADGE of the Marshal of the Diplomatic Corps: peacetime, obverse (*left*); wartime, reverse (*right*).

HER MAJESTY'S AMBASSADORS AND DIPLOMATIC SERVICE OFFICERS

The full dress uniform worn by the Officers of the British Diplomatic Service has been well known for many decades: the dark blue coatee with embroidery of oakleaf and acorn design on the collar and cuffs, dark blue trousers with gold oakleaf lace on the seams, and a black beavercocked hat with black silk cockade and white ostrich feathers.

This uniform was inappropriate when ladies were appointed to posts in the Diplomatic Service in which uniform would normally be worn. In 1976 the first lady, Miss Anne Warburton, CVO (later Dame Anne Warburton, DCVO, CMG) was so appointed as Ambassador to Denmark, and a badge of office was devised to replace the traditional uniform worn by men. The badge is of gilt, one and three-eighths inches wide, and is worn from a ribbon bow of Garter blue.

DAME GILLIAN BROWN DCVO, CMG, HM's Ambassador to Norway, 1981–3, wearing the diplomatic badge. (*right*) A BADGE worn by Lady Diplomatic Officers.

THE ABBEY COURT AND THE HIGH CONSTABLES AND GUARD OF HONOUR OF HOLYROOD HOUSE

In the sixteenth century, James IV built for himself and his Queen, Margaret Tudor, the Palace of Holyroodhouse, close to the earlier Abbey of Holy Rood.

The Coronation of Charles I as King of Scotland took place at Holyrood in 1633, after which much rebuilding was put in hand and it became the official royal residence in Scotland.

In 1646, the King appointed the Duke of Hamilton and his successors as Hereditary Keepers of the Palace. After the Act of Union of 1707, there being no royal residents, it was occupied by the Hereditary Keepers and a number of noblemen. Like the owners of other large estates in Scotland, the Dukes of Hamilton were entitled to maintain a baronial court. Most courts did not survive the 1745 Rising but the Abbey Court did and the Hereditary Keeper kept his right to hold regular court sittings and to appoint a Bailie as judge in the Abbey Court. The position remains so to this day.

The Bailie, still appointed by the Duke of Hamilton, appoints not only the Moderator of the High Constables, whose duties were to keep order within the Palace precincts, but also the Guard of Honour whose duty was to keep order during the election of the representative Scottish peers to the House of Lords. Today the High Constables and the Guard of Honour are one body, and their duties are largely ceremonial.

The obverse of the badge of office of the Bailie, made in 1954 by Hamilton & Inches of Edinburgh, consists of a silver oval medallion with, in the centre, the badge of Holyrood, a stag's head beneath a Latin cross. The stag is set with a ruby eye on a blue enamelled plaque surrounded by a wreath of thistles, the whole surmounted by an Imperial Crown in gold with a red enamelled Cap of Maintenance with a border collet set with two sapphires, two diamonds and a ruby.

The reverse bears the cypher TMM, surrounded by the inscription: 'INSIGNIA BALLIRI DE HOLYROOD UNACUM PALATII DE HOLYROODHOUSE' 'Thomas Menzies McNeil'. It is worn round the neck from a blue

THE BADGE of the Moderator of the High Constables of Holyrood House.

ribbon and is contained in a fitted case of old Cadzow oak traditionally planted by King David I in about 1140.

The obverse of the badge of the Moderator of the Holyrood High Constables, made in Edinburgh in 1877, consists of a silver gilt curved lozenge-shaped medallion, bearing the coat of arms of Scotland surrounded by borders of twisted rope and of trefoil and bead decorations.

The reverse bears the coat-of-arms of the Hereditary Keeper, the Duke of Hamilton and Brandon above the inscription: 'Presented to the High Constables and Guard of Honour of Holyrood House by William Ford, Esquire of Ferneyside. Moderator 1875–1878 to be worn by his successors in office as their insignia. 30th November, 1877'.

It is worn suspended from a silver gilt chain set centrally in which is a George III gold guinea of 1790 and, three links above it, to right and left are two George III half-guineas (on right 1777 and on the left 1801), each coin being set in a silver gilt collet and joined together by two silver gilt chain festoons.

THE BADGE of the High Constables of Holyrood House.

In 1822, George IV visited the Palace and it became again a royal residence. He also decreed that the Lord High Commissioner to the Church of Scotland might have the use of it for the duration of the annual General Assembly.

It was Queen Victoria who began the custom, which has been continued by all subsequent sovereigns, of staying at the Palace for a period during the summer. King George V and Queen Mary initiated the annual garden parties held at the Palace.

The administration of the Palace is in the control of the Superintendent under the Master of the Household.

THE BADGE of the Bailie of the Abbey Court and Palace of Holyrood House.

MISS CATRIN FINCH
wearing the brooch.

HARPIST TO THE PRINCE OF WALES

In order to give support and recognition to a young harpist and to encourage appreciation of the harp and the harpist, the Prince of Wales has recreated the tradition of harpists being appointed to the Royal Court by appointing a 'Harpist to the Prince of Wales'. The earliest recorded Royal Harpist was one in the 15th century; in 1788, Edward Jones was appointed Harpist to the Prince of Wales and the last Royal Harpist was John Thomas appointed by Queen Victoria in 1871.

In May 2000 Miss Catrin Finch was the first in the welcome new tradition to be appointed, for a period of two years, and made her debut performance on 11 May at a private dinner given by the Prince of Wales in Port Talbot. For the period of the appointment the harpist will be given a neck decoration or brooch, to the design of which the Prince of Wales made a significant contribution.

THE BROOCH of the
Harpist to the Prince
of Wales.

THE EQUERRY'S SWORD
is used to open the
telegram from the Queen
on 4 August 2000.
left to right, the postman,
Mr Anthony Nicholls,
Captain William de
Rouet, MVO, Captain
Sir Alastair Aird, GCVO,
Mr William Tallon, RVM
and bar, with Queen
Elizabeth The Queen
Mother, Grand Master
of the Royal Victorian
Order. The promotions
and appointments to the
Order to celebrate the
occasion are listed on
page 121.

CHAPTER SIX

The Royal Victorian Order
and The Royal Victorian Medal

THE FIRST PART of this chapter covers the appointments and awards made since those on the occasion of the Queen's Official Birthday in 1996, which are recorded in *Royal Service,* Volume I, and up to and including the One Hundredth Birthday of Queen Elizabeth The Queen Mother. Also in this part are recorded those errors and omissions in Volume I, of which the authors have been made aware.

The second part of the chapter covers the honorary appointments to the Order and honorary awards of the Medal since 1896 up to, and including, 13 March 2000 (Commonwealth Day) when the retiring Secretary General of the Commonwealth was appointed GCVO.

PART I

Since the publication in 1996 of Volume I the authors have been made aware of and wish to record the following corrections and additions:

page 157   1 January 1973, James Starritt, delete all after semi-colon

202   11 June 1998, for John George Fennell read John Cregg Fennell

228   Button W.D., for Miss read Mrs

241   at 8.1902 add PUSEY, George Henry, *Boy Signalman* RN; *for gallantry in trying to save the life of a shipmate on HMS* Victory

276   9 May 1942, for Coates Mission read Coats Mission

281 and 359   at 1.1.1951 for SEARLES read SEARIES

313   16 June 1989, for C.J. Airey read C.J. Airy

319   Cunningham, J.H.D., for 26.7.34 read 26.7.24

322   Fennell, for J.G. read J.C.

323   Gordon-Lennox, for H.C. read C.H.

334   O'Shea, P.P., for 7.11.95 read 1.11.95

242 and 356   at 20.9.1904 add NOWELL, Frederick, *House Steward to the Marchioness of Dufferin and Ava: HM's visit to Clandeboye in 1903*

304 and 352   HOATH, Miss Peggy Gladys, for 31.12.84 read 31.12.94

34 and 35 the following further information on the Coats Mission and the Morris Detachment has been obtained:

The Coats Mission and the Morris Detachment
In 1940, after Dunkirk, a detachment of one officer and nine other ranks from the XII Royal Lancers was hurriedly assembled as a mobile armed guard for the protection of the Royal Family.

The original members included Lieutenant W.A. Morris, Sergeant J. Thurston and Trooper J.H. Rosling who were later joined by Lieutenant M. Humble-Crofts of the Northamptonshire Yeomanry. They became known as the Morris Detachment, which itself formed part of the Coats Mission. This was comprised of a company from the Coldstream Guards and detachments from the Royal Signals, the Royal Military Police, the Royal Army Medical Corps and the Royal Army Service Corps, under the command of Lieutenant Colonel J.S. Coats.

For the next two years the Morris Detachment was in close, almost daily, contact with the Royal Family, protecting them wherever they went – in London, at Windsor, Sandringham, Glamis and Balmoral. In 1942, the Household Cavalry was able to take over their duties. On 10 May 1942, the King and Queen with Princess Elizabeth and Princess Margaret inspected the Morris Detachment, after which Major Morris and Lieutenant Humble-Crofts were appointed Members of the Royal Victorian Order and Staff Sergeant Major Thurston, Lance Corporal Rosling and Trooper Porter were awarded the Royal Victorian Medal. At the same time Staff Sergeant Major Thurston was decorated with the Military Medal which he had earned in France in 1940.

As Major Morris wrote in the Regimental Journal in 1946, each 'was proud of the honour to have served the Royal Family so closely, to have got to know them and to realise and appreciate the tremendous task and work that they were doing. . . .'

THE MORRIS DETACHMENT, a photograph taken shortly before the handover to the Household Cavalry in 1942. Major Morris is seated in the centre with Lieutenant Humble-Crofts on his right and Staff Sergeant Thurston on his left. Trooper Porter is standing at far left in the third row and Trooper Rosling is in the back row, sixth from the left.

APPOINTMENTS AND AWARDS
TO THE ROYAL VICTORIAN ORDER
since 1966

═══

GCVO

1997

1 January   AIRD, Captain Sir Alastair Sturgis, KCVO, *Private Secretary and Comptroller to Queen Elizabeth The Queen Mother*

FITZPATRICK, General Sir (Geoffrey Richard) Desmond, GCB, DSO, MBE, MC, *Gold Stick*

1998

12 February   CAMOYS, Ralph Thomas Campion George Sherman Stonor, Lord, *on appointment as Lord Chamberlain and Chancellor of the Order*

13 June   FORD, Sir Edward William Spencer, KCB, KCVO, ERD, *Secretary and Registrar of the Order of Merit*

31 December   SOMERLEYTON, Savile William Francis Crossley, Lord, KCVO, *lately Master of the Horse*

1999

2000

3 August   COOPER, Major General Sir Simon Christie, KCVO, *on relinquishing appointment as Master of the Household*

DCVO

1998

31 December   DEVONSHIRE, Deborah Vivien, Duchess of, *Trustee, Royal Collection Trust*

1999

9 November   **State Visit to Africa of the Queen and the Duke of Edinburgh**
FORT, Dame Maeve Geraldine DCMG, *British High Commisioner, Pretoria*

KCVO

1996

25 October   BUXTON, Aubrey Leyland Oakes, Baron, of Alsa, MC

30 October   **State Visit to Thailand of the Queen and the Duke of Edinburgh**
HODGE, James William, CMG, *HM Ambassador to Thailand*

7 November   WAINE, The Rt. Revd. John, *on retirement as Clerk of the Closet*

4 December   MAYNE, The Very Revd. Michael (Clement Otway), *Dean of Westminster and of the Order of the Bath, on retirement*

1997

1 January   LOWTHER, John Luke, CBE, *Lord Lieutenant of Northamptonshire*

27 March   TAYLOR, The Rt. Revd. John Bernard, *lately Bishop of St Albans, Lord High Almoner*

14 June   JAMES, John Nigel Courtenay, CBE, *Secretary and Keeper of the Records, Duchy of Cornwall*
THORNTON, Richard Eustace, OBE, *Lord Lieutenant of Surrey*

15 July	MACKAY-DICK, Major General Ian Charles, MBE, *General Officer Commanding London District*
6 October	GIBBS, Lieut. Col. Peter Evan Wyldbore, CVO, *on retirement as Private Secretary to the Princess Royal*
7 October	**State Visit to Pakistan of the Queen and the Duke of Edinburgh** DAIN, David John Michael, CMG, *British High Commissioner to Pakistan*
13 October	**State Visit to India of the Queen and the Duke of Edinburgh** GORE-BOOTH, The Hon. Sir David Alwyn, KCMG, *British High Commissioner to India*
31 December	JANVRIN, Robin Berry, CB, CVO, *Deputy Private Secretary to the Queen* MORLEY, Lieutenant Colonel John St Aubyn Parker, Earl of, *Lord Lieutenant of Devon* PEAT, Michael Charles Gerrard, CVO, *Keeper of the Privy Purse and Treasurer to the Queen* SHEPPARD, Allen John George, Lord, of Didgmere, *lately Chairman of Business in the Community* WILLS, Colonel Sir John Vernon, Bt., TD, *Lord Lieutenant of Somerset and former Lord Lieutenant of Avon*

1998

13 June	HOBBS, Major General Michael Frederick, CBE, *lately Director, Duke of Edinburgh's Award* OSWALD, William Richard Michael, CVO, *Director, Royal Studs*
24 July	MITCHELL, The Very Revd. Patrick Reynolds, *on retirement as Dean of Windsor*
4 August	BLANCH, Malcolm, CVO, *on retirement as Clerk Comptroller to Queen Elizabeth The Queen Mother*
17 September	**State Visit to Brunei Darussalam of the Queen and the Duke of Edinburgh** CALLAN, Ivan Roy, CMG, *High Commissioner in Brunei*
20 September	**State Visit to Malaysia of the Queen and the Duke of Edinburgh** MOSS, David Joseph, CMG, *High Commissioner in Kuala Lumpur*
13 October	VICKERS, Lieutenant General Sir Richard Maurice Hilton, KCB, LVO, OBE, *on retirement as Gentleman Usher to HM*
21 October	NICHOLLS, Nigel Hamilton, CBE, *on retirement as Clerk of the Privy Council*
31 December	DIGBY, Edward Henry Kenelm, Lord, *Lord Lieutenant of Dorset* CARR-ELLISON, Colonel Sir Ralph Harry, TD, *Lord Lieutenant of Tyne and Wear* SELLORS, Patrick John Holmes, LVO, *Surgeon-Dentist to the Queen*

1999

19 April	**State visit to Korea of the Queen and the Duke of Edinburgh** BROWN, Stephen David Reid, *HM Ambassador to the Republic of Korea*
12 June	DOWNWARD, Major General Peter Aldcroft, CB, DSO, DFC, *Governor of the Military Knights of Windsor* HOWES, Christopher Kingston, CB, CVO, *Second Commissioner and Chief Executive, Crown Estate* ROSS, Lieutenant Colonel Walter Hugh Malcolm, CVO, OBE, *Comptroller, Lord Chamberlain's Office*
11 July	PALMER, General Sir Charles Patrick Ralph, KBE, *Constable and Governor of Windsor Castle*
31 December	MERIFIELD, Anthony James, CB, *Ceremonial Officer, Cabinet Office*

2000

17 June	RIDLEY, Michael Kershaw, CVO, *Clerk of the Council, Duchy of Lancaster*

but see also page 121

CVO

1996

23 July	HORNE, Christopher Malcolm, *for personal services, Coutts & Co.*
30 October	**State Visit to Thailand of the Queen and the Duke of Edinburgh** FELL, Richard Taylor, *Counsellor, British Embassy, Bangkok*

1997

1 January	CAWS, Richard Byron, CBE, *lately Crown Estate Commissioner* GILBERT, Philip Stephen, OBE, *Broadcaster* HOLDSWORTH, Sir George Trevor, *Trustee, Duke of Edinburgh's Award Scheme*
19 February	MARSH, Commander Robert, QPM, *Commander, Royalty and Diplomatic Protection Group, Metropolitan Police, on retirement*

14 June	COX, Stephen James, *Director General, Commonwealth Institute* HOME, The Earl of, CBE, *for personal services* HOWES, Christopher Kingston, CB, *Second Commissioner and Chief Executive, Crown Estates* CHAMBERLAYNE-MACDONALD, Major Nigel Donald Peter, LVO, OBE, *lately Gentleman Usher to HM*
23 June	**HM's Visit to Canada** CARLE, Jean, *Operations Co-ordinator, Prime Minister's Office*
7 October	**State Visit to Pakistan of the Queen and the Duke of Edinburgh** DOREY, Gregory John, *Counsellor (Economic), British High Commission in Pakistan* WATT, James Wilfrid, *Deputy British High Commissioner in Pakistan*
13 October	**State Visit to India of the Queen and the Duke of Edinburgh** DRAPER, Brigadier Robin Anthony, OBE, *Defence Adviser, British High Commission, New Delhi* PERCHARD, Colin William, OBE, *Minister (Cultural Affairs), British High Commission, New Delhi*
11 December	MORROW, Commodore Anthony John Clare, RN, *at decommissioning of HMY Britannia*
31 December	CURWEN, Charles Roderick, LVO, OBE, *Official Secretary, Office of Governor General of Victoria, Australia* HUNT-DAVIS, Brigadier Miles Garth, CBE, *Private Secretary to the Duke of Edinburgh* DOWNES, Giles Patrick Stretton, *Partner, Sidell Gibson Partnership, for services in connection with restoration of fire damage at Windsor Castle* HALL, Colonel Thomas Armitage, OBE, *Lieutenant, Body Guard of the Honourable Corps of Gentlemen at Arms* MATHER, Lieutenant Colonel Anthony Charles McClure, OBE, *Secretary, Central Chancery of Orders of Knighthood and Assistant Comptroller, Lord Chamberlain's Office* MAXWELL, Robert James, CBE, *lately Secretary and Chief Executive of The King's Fund* PINCHIN, Malcolm Cyril, *lately Trustee, Duke of Edinburgh's Award* ROBERTS, Hugh Ashley, LVO, *Director of Royal Collection and Surveyor of the Queen's Works of Art*

1998

4 March	HARDING, Air Vice-Marshal Peter, CB, CBE, AFC, *on relinquishing appointment as Defence Services Secretary*
13 June	FLEMING, Thomas Kelman, OBE, *Broadcaster* GEORGE, Sir Richard William, *Vice-Chairman, The Prince's Trust* GWYNN-JONES, Peter Llewellyn, LVO, *Garter Principal King of Arms* PARSONS, John Christopher, LVO, *Deputy Keeper of the Privy Purse and Deputy Treasurer to HM* WIGHTMAN, John Watt, CBE, RD *and Bar*, WS, *Solicitor to HM in Scotland* WOODHOUSE, Charles Frederick, *Solicitor to the Duke of Edinburgh* WORRALL, Eric Arthur, *lately Deputy Director, Duke of Edinburgh's Award Scheme*
20 September	**State Visit to Malaysia of the Queen and the Duke of Edinburgh** PARKINSON, Howard, *Counsellor (Commercial), British High Commission, Kuala Lumpur*
13 October	VICKERS, Lieutenant General Sir Richard Maurice Hilton, KCB, LVO, OBE, *on retirement as a Gentleman Usher to HM*
15 December	HOLMES, John Eaton, CMG, *lately Principal Private Secretary to the Prime Minister*
31 December	HIGHAM, Commander Michael Bernard Shepley, RN, *lately Grand Secretary, United Grand Lodge of England* JENNINGS, Peter Nevile Wake, *Serjeant at Arms, House of Commons* SCLATER, John Richard, *Member of the Council, Duchy of Lancaster*

1999

19 April	**State Visit to Korea of the Queen and the Duke of Edinburgh** MARSH, Derek Richard, *Counsellor and Deputy Head of Mission*
12 June	HOLROYD, John Hepworth, CB, *Secretary for Appointments to the Prime Minister* LAMPORT, Stephen Mark Jeffrey, *Private Secretary and Treasurer to the Prince of Wales* MACMILLAN, The Very Revd. Gilleasbuig, *Chaplain to the Queen in Scotland and Dean of the Order of the Thistle*
14 July	FULFORD-DOBSON, Captain Michael, RN, *Gentleman Usher to the Queen*
29 July	ASTLEY, Philip Sinton, LVO, *on relinquishing post of Vice Marshal of the Diplomatic Corps*
8 November	**Visit to Africa of the Queen and the Duke of Edinburgh** MACKLEY, Ian Warren, CMG, *British High Commioner, Accra*
9 November	GASS, Simon Lawrence, CMG, *British Deputy High Commioner, Pretoria*
15 November	EVERETT, Bernard Jonathan, *British High Commioner, Maputo*
31 December	JENKINS, Surgeon Rear Admiral Ian Lawrence, *Overseas Tour Doctor to the Prince of Wales* MACLEAN, The Honourable Sir Lachlan Hector Charles Bt, *lately Adjutant, Royal Company of Archers* WOODHOUSE, Ronald Michael, *Trustee, The Prince's Trust*

2000

21 March	**Visit to Australia of the Queen and the Duke of Edinburgh** SAMUELS, HE the Honourable Gordon Jacob, AC, *Governor of New South Wales*
24 March	GOBBO, HE the Honourable Sir James Augustine, AC, *Governor of Victoria*
30 March	GREEN, HE Sir Guy Stephen Montague, KBE AC, *Governor of Tasmania*
1 April	BAGLEY, Roger Thomas, LVO, *Commonwealth Visit Director* JEFFERY, Major General Philip Michael, AC MC, *Governor of Western Australia*
17 June	CAIRNS, Simon Dallas Cairns, Earl, CBE, *Receiver General of the Duchy of Cornwall* KNOTT, Kevin John Selwyn, LVO, *Deputy Secretary, Duchy of Cornwall and Deputy Treasurer to the Prince of Wales* PUGSLEY, John Edward, *Member of the Prince's Council* REYNOLDS, Graham, *for services to the Royal Collection* WALKER, Richard John Boileau, *for services to the Royal Collection* WIGHT, Robin, *Chairman, Duke of Edinburgh's Award, Charter for Business*

but see also page 121

CVO (Ladies)

1997

1 January	CAVENDISH, The Lady Elizabeth Georgina Alice, LVO, *Extra Lady in Waiting to Princess Margaret, Countess of Snowdon*
31 December	ELTON, Lady (Susan Richenda), *Lady in Waiting to the Queen* FARNHAM, Lady (Diana Marion), *Lady in Waiting to the Queen*

1998

12 June	MURPHY, Mrs Lucy Annora, LVO, *Information Officer, Household of Queen Elizabeth The Queen Mother* MURDO-SMITH, Mrs Felicity Margaret Salisbury, LVO, *Information Officer, Press Office, Buckingham Palace*
31 December	MITCHELL, The Honourable Dame Roma Flinders, DBE, AC, *lately Governor of South Australia*

1999

2000

but see also page 121

LVO

1996

24 July	MCGURK, James, MVO, *Insignia Clerk, Central Chancery of the Orders of Knighthood*
1 August	NOBLE, Charles Patrick Neville, MVO, *Assistant to the Surveyor of the Queen's Pictures*
30 October	**State Visit to Thailand of the Queen and the Duke of Edinburgh** FIELDEN, Colonel James Drew, MBE, *Defence Attaché, British Embassy, Bangkok* RYDER, Martin Frederick John, *First Secretary (Management), British Embassy, Bangkok* STOKES, Dr Nigel Antony David, *First Secretary (Political), British Embassy, Bangkok*

1997

1 January	BLAIR, Hamish, *Senior Executive Officer, Scottish Office* BLAIR, Captain Robert Neil, RN, *Private Secretary to the Duke of York and to Princess Alexandra, the Hon. Lady Ogilvy* BROWN, Laurence Albert, *for services to the Royal Collection* BUTTRESS, Donald Reeve, *Surveyor of the Fabric, Westminster Abbey* FRAHM, Bernard Joseph, MVO, *for services to the Crown on Royal Visits to New Zealand* LAIDLAW, Commander Thomas Dixon, QPM, *Metropolitan Police* PERCIVAL, Allan Arthur, *lately Press Secretary to the Prince of Wales* SUTHERLAND, Alexander Hay, *Chief Publicity Officer, Scottish Office*

14 June	AZIZ, Khalid, *lately Chairman, Prince's Trust (Hampshire) and The Prince's Youth Business Trust (Southern Counties)* BOND, John David, MVO, *lately Keeper of the Savill and Valley Gardens, Windsor* BRISCOE, Dr John Hubert Daly, *Apothecary to Royal Household, Windsor* CHAMBERLAYNE, Michael Thomas, *for personal services* FFYTCHE, Timothy John, *Surgeon-Occulist to Royal Household* TILTMAN, John Hessel, *Director of Property Services, Royal Household* JEPHSON, Michael Charles William Norreys, MVO, *Chief Clerk, Master of the Household's Department*
23 June	**HM's Visit to Canada** CLEVELAND, Assistant Commissioner David Grant, RCMP, *Canadian Police Officer to the Queen* FEU, Ernesto, *Ontario Visit Co-ordinator* JENKINS, Robert John, *Newfoundland and Labrador Visit Co-ordinator* KNAPP, David George, *Broadcasting Co-ordinator, CBC*
7 October	**State Visit to Thailand of the Queen and the Duke of Edinburgh** HITCHENS, Timothy Mark, *First Secretary (Political), British Embassy, Bangkok*
13 October	**State Visit to India of the Queen and the Duke of Edinburgh** PALMER, Sidney Hodgson, *Deputy British High Commissioner, Madras* WILDASH, Richard James, *First Secretary (Chancery), British High Commission, New Delhi*
30 October	GIMSON, Simon John Timothy, *on relinquishing appointment as Special Assistant to the Private Secretary*
5 November	KOOPS, Eric Jan Leendert, *Chairman, World Fellowship of the Duke of Edinburgh's Award Scheme and Trustee of the International Award*
31 December	BLUNDEN, Commander Jeremy Jonathan Frank, RN, *HMY* Britannia DICKER, Ivor John, *Solicitor to the Duchy of Lancaster* FROST, Alan John, *Director, Donald Insall Associates, for services in connection with restoration of fire damage at Windsor Castle* GIBBINS, Michael Edward Stanley, *Controller to the late Diana, Princess of Wales* JONES, Simon Alan, *Managing Director, Gardiner & Theobald Management Services, for services in connection with restoration of fire damage at Windsor Castle* MARTIN, Commander Simon Charles, RN, *HMY* Britannia MONEY, Brian Walter, *lately Head of Royal Matters Unit, FCO* NEARY, Martin Gerard James, *Organist and Master of Choristers, Westminster Abbey: for services in connection with the funeral of the late Diana, Princess of Wales*

1998

22 March	MOXON, The Revd. Canon Michael Anthony, *Chaplain, Royal Chapel, Windsor Great Park*
26 April	MAJOR, John, *Land Agent, Sandringham Estate, on relinquishing appointment* COWELL, Joseph, MVO *Superintendent, Royal Collection, Hampton Court Palace*
13 June	HOWELL, Brian Neale, *Forestry Consultant to Sandringham Estate* HYND, Neil Robertson, *Regional Director, Properties in Care, Historic Scotland* RICKETTS, Sidney William, *Senior Veterinary Consultant to the Royal Studs* TWINING, Samuel Humfrey Gaskell, OBE, *lately Honorary Treasurer, Royal Warrant Holders Association*
20 September	BRIDGES, Stephen John, *First Secretary, British High Commission, Kuala Lumpur*
31 December	ABLITT, John Leveson-Gower, *Member of The Prince's Trust.* BLAIR, Robin Orr, *Purse Bearer to the Lord High Commissioner* FANCOURT, Edward George, MVO, RVM, *lately Senior Conservator, Royal Collection* HALL, The Revd. Canon George Rumney, *Domestic Chaplain to the Queen at Sandringham* HANSFORD, Neil Martin, *Treasury Accountant, HM Treasury* HODGETTS, Captain David Percy Langley, *lately Secretary to Lieutenant Governor of Guernsey* MOORE, The Revd. Canon Michael Mervlyn Hamond, *Chaplain, Chapel Royal, Hampton Court Palace* STEWART, John Barry Bingham, OBE, *High Constable of Holyroodhouse*

1999

19 April	**State Visit to Korea of the Queen and the Duke of Edinburgh** CROOKS, Colin James, *Second Secretary, British Embassy, Seoul*
12 June	BOOTH, The Revd. William, *Sub-Dean of HM Chapels Royal and Domestic Chaplain* BUNBURY, Dr Michael Charles de St Pierre, *Medical Practitioner* BURGESS, Chief Inspector Stephen Orme, MVO, *Royalty Protection Department, Metropolitan Police* COOK, Robert, MVO, *lately Inventory Clerk, Windsor Castle* FOX, Frederick Donald, *Milliner* HUNTINGDON, William Edward Robin Hastings Bass, Earl of, *Racehorse Trainer* METCALFE, Malcolm, *Member, Canadian Steering Committee, Duke of Edinburgh's Commonwealth Study Conference* ROBSON, The Revd. John Phillips, *Chaplain of the Queen's Chapel of the Savoy and Chaplain of the Royal Victorian Order* TAYLOR, Robert Forbes, *Trustee, UK Fund of Duke of Edinburgh's Commonwealth Study Conference*

29 July	ACLAND, Lieutenant Colonel Sir Christopher Guy Dyke, Bt., MVO, *on retirement as Deputy Master of the Household*
15 November	LIVESEY, Geoffrey Colin, OBE, *Deputy Head of Mission, Maputo*
31 December	CORBETT, Simon Mark, *lately HSBC Investment Management* FERGUSON, Colonel Iain Alexander, OBE, *lately Vice Chairman and Director, Royal Tournament* GRAPES, David Alan, *Farm Consultant to Sandringham Estate and Royal Farms, Windsor* HAYWOOD-TRIMMING, Superintendent Colin Leslie, MVO, *lately Royalty Protection Dept., Metropolitan Police* WALKER, Graham Arthur James, *lately Treasurer, Royal Jubilee Trusts and The Prince's Trust*

2000

21 March	LONSDALE, Clifford Donald, OAM, *New South Wales Director of Protocol*
28 March	BONSEY, Martin Charles Brian, *Official Secretary, Government House, Canberra*
1 April	SKIPWORTH, Kevin Leslie, *Official Secretary, Government House, Perth*
17 June	BARBER, Gerald William Priestman, *Joint Headmaster, Ludgrove School* ENGLAND, Barrie, *former Deputy Head, Protocol Division, Foreign and Commonwealth Office* GRIFFITHS, George Albert, MVO, *Fire, Health and Safety Manager, Royal Household* MARSTON, Charles Nicholas John, *Joint Headmaster, Ludgrove School* MAYFIELD, Lieutenant Colonel Richard, DSO, *Queen's Body Guard of the Yeomen of the Guard* NEWELL, Robert Fraser, *Director, Royal Overseas League* PARKER, Michael Trevor, MVO, *Assistant to Master of the Household* POPPLEWELL, Richard John, MVO, *Organist, Choirmaster and Composer, HM Chapels Royal* RISING, Major Robert Philip, RM, *Secretary, Royal Yacht Squadron* SANDS, Richard Martin, *former Honours Secretary, Foreign and Commonwealth Office*
28 June	ROBINSON, Superintendent David John, MVO, *on retirement as the Queen's Police Officer*

but see also page 121

LVO (Ladies)

1997

1 January	LICHFIELD, Leonora Mary, the Countess of, *Extra Lady in Waiting to the Princess Royal*
14 June	LOULOUDIS, The Hon. Mrs Madeleine, *Assistant Private Secretary to the Princess Royal*
7 October	**State Visit to Pakistan of the Queen and the Duke of Edinburgh** GIBSON, Miss May Fyfe, *First Secretary, British High Commission Office, Karachi*
31 December	NUNNELEY, Mrs Caroline Anne, *Lady in Waiting to the Princess Royal* PAYNE, Miss Claudia Ann Wyndham, MVO, *lately Secretary to Secretary and Keeper of the Records of Duchy of Lancaster*

1998

13 June	VYVYAN, Mrs Elizabeth Frances, *Lady in Waiting to Princess Margaret, Countess of Snowdon*
9 November	GOLDTHORPE, Mrs Debra Kay, *HM Consul, Durban*
31 December	AUTON, Mrs Cherril Diana, *Sales Ledger Administrator, Royal Household* BULL, Miss Deborah Jean, *Secretary to the UK Trustees, Duke of Edinburgh's Commonwealth Study Conferences* BELLAIGUE, Sheila Loraine, Lady de, MVO, *Registrar, Royal Archives, Windsor Castle* FERGUS, Miss Sheena Mary, MVO, *Secretary to the Master of the Household* HOLDERNESS-RODDAM, Mrs Jane Mary Elizabeth, *Lady in Waiting to the Princess Royal* KITCHENER-FELLOWES, Mrs Emma Joy, *Lady in Waiting to Princess Michael of Kent*

1999

28 April	FRANCIS, Mrs Mary Elizabeth, *lately Deputy Private Secretary to the Queen*
12 June	RITCHIE, Mrs Araminta Mary, *Lady in Waiting to the Princess Royal*

2000

1 April	LOGAN, Miss Patricia Jane, MVO, *Executive Officer, Commonwealth Visits*

17 June   RHODES, The Honourable Mrs Margaret, *Lady in Waiting to Queen Elizabeth The Queen Mother*
RUSSELL-SMITH, Miss Penelope, *Deputy Press Secretary to the Queen*

MVO

1996

30 October   **State Visit to Thailand of the Queen and the Duke of Edinburgh**
GARRETT, Martin, *Second Secretary, British Embassy, Bangkok*

1997

1 January   BOOTH, Frederick, *Chief Heraldic Painter, College of Arms*
BUTLER, Matthew Nicholas, *lately Assistant Private Secretary to the Prince of Wales*
ELLIOTT, Reginald, *Higher Executive Officer, Crown Estate, Windsor*
JACKSON, Norman William, *Chief Yeoman Warder, HM Tower of London*
MASSON, Alexander, *Head Gamekeeper, Balmoral Estate*
PEPPER, John Ronald, *lately of Collingwood & Co Ltd*
ROBINSON, Inspector Stephen Lionel, *Royalty and Diplomatic Protection Department, Metropolitan Police*
STEWART, William Albert, *Head Warden, Palace of Holyroodhouse*
TABOR, Lieutenant Colonel Patrick John, *lately Equerry to the Prince of Wales*

14 June   BAXTER, James Duncan, *lately Chairman, The Prince's Youth Business Trust (Cheshire) – deceased, to be dated 22 May 1997*
BROCK, Peter Leonard, *Headmaster, Royal School, Windsor Great Park*
CRAKER, Sergeant Graham Leonard, *Royalty and Diplomatic Protection Department*
EDWARDS, Richard Julian Ashton, *Gentleman of the Chapel Royal, St James's Palace*
MESTON, William Anderson, *Secretary, Braemar Royal Highland Society*
SAMPLER, Sidney John, *Secretary, Royal Travel Office*
SHARP, Sergeant. David John, *Royalty Protection Department, Metropolitan Police*

23 June   **HM's Visit to Canada**
BASTIEN, Lieutenant Commander Jean Yves, CD, *Canadian Equerry to the Queen*
MUNNOCH, Scott Norman, *Operations Consultant, Ontario*
THIVIERGE, André, *Media Co-ordinator*

23 July   GURUNG, Captain Govinde, *Queen's Gurkha Signals: Queen's Gurkha Officer*
GURUNG, Captain Narbahadur, BEM, *The Royal Gurkha Rifles: Queen's Gurkha Officer*
RICHARDS, Lieutenant Colonel Anthony Charles, *on relinquishing appointment as Equerry to the Duke of Edinburgh*

13 October   **State Visit to India of the Queen and the Duke of Edinburgh**
HICKSON, Philip John, *Third Secretary (Chancery), British High Commission, New Delhi*

31 December   COLE, Captain David Charles, RN, *HMY Britannia*
EVANS, Robert Eric, QPM, *lately Chairman, North Wales Committee of The Prince's Trust*
NEAL, Brian, *Gentleman of the Chapel Royal Choir, Windsor Great Park*
PATTERSON, Stephen James, *Computer Systems Manager, Royal Collection*
ROWLEY, Philip, *Site Manager, Higgs and Hill Special Contracts: for services in connection with restoration of fire damage at Windsor Castle*
GORDON-SMITH, George Edmund, *Clerk to Lieutenancy of Greater London*
SMITH, Richard William Lowestoft, *lately Honorary Treasurer, Chapel Royal, St James's Palace*
WATSON, Christopher Michael, *Project Manager, Gardiner & Theobald Management Services in connection with restoration of fire damage at Windsor Castle*
WHARFE, Inspector Kenneth Anstey, *Royalty Protection Department, Metropolitan Police (formerly with the late Diana, Princess of Wales)*
WHITE, Warrant Officer Robert Ernest, *HMY Britannia*

1998

13 June   BEST, Sergeant Roger Edward, *Royalty Protection Department, Metropolitan Police*
CAESAR, Gerald Arthur, JP, *lately Chairman, The Prince's Youth Business Trust, Lancashire*
HARDY, Ian, *Information Systems Manager, Royal Household*
HARRIS, Inspector William Maurice, *Royalty Protection Department, Metropolitan Police*
HUNT, Kevan, *lately Chairman, The Prince's Youth Business Trust, Nottinghamshire*
MACRAE, Inspector Iain, *Royalty Protection Department, Metropolitan Police*
MANN, Lionel Thomas, RVM, *Royal Chef*
MARSHALL, Allen James, *Superintendent's Assistant, Royal Mews, Buckingham Palace*
MCCARTNEY, Martin Francis, *Operations Director, Town and County Catering*
PINDRED, George Chesterton, *lately Regional Director, The Prince's Youth Business Trust, Yorkshire and Humberside*

22 July	LIMBU, Captain Khemkumar, *The Royal Gurkha Rifles: Queen's Gurkha Officer* GURUNG, Captain Narainbahadur, *The Royal Gurkha Rifles: Queen's Gurkha Officer*
10 August	WILLIAMSON, Lieutenant Commander Toby, RN, *on retirement as Equerry to the Queen*
17 October	**State Visit to Brunei Darussalam of the Queen and the Duke of Edinburgh** MALONE, Philip, *Third Secretary, British High Commission*
20 September	**State Visit to Malaysia of the Queen and the Duke of Edinburgh** ORD-SMITH, Robin Jeremy, *Second Secretary, British High Commission, Kuala Lumpur*
31 December	AMADI, Emmanuel Oribi, *lately Director of Fund-raising, The Prince's Trust* HASSALL, George, *Business Liaison Director, Rover Group Limited* LARNDER, Sergeant Christopher John, *Royalty Protection Department, Metropolitan Police* MACEWAN, Major Andrew Charles Burrell, *lately Temporary Equerry to Queen Elizabeth The Queen Mother* MCGIVERN, John Simon, *Managing Director, Unitech Complete Computing* SKAN, Jonathan Anthony, *lately Assistant Private Secretary to the Prince of Wales* SPENS, John Alexander, RD, *Albany Herald of Arms*

1999

12 June	BROWN, Roy, *Maintenance Manager, Buckingham Palace and Royal Mews* COOPER, Norman Robert, *Gentleman of the Chapel Royal, St James's Palace* MARSHALL, Squadron Leader Jeremy David, *lately Pilot, 32 (The Royal) Squadron, RAF* REEVE, Chief Superintendent David Stanley, *Norfolk Constabulary*
20 July	GURUNG, Captain Dharambahadur, *The Royal Gurkha Rifles: Queen's Gurkha Officer* LIMBU, Captain Chitraj, *The Queen's Own Gurkha Transport Regiment: Queen's Gurkha Officer*
29 July	TARRAN, Lieutenant Commander Martin Richard Mitchell, RN, *on completion of service as Equerry to the Duke of Edinburgh*
8 November	**Visit to Africa of the Queen and the Duke of Edinburgh** COPE, Brian Roger, *Second Secretary (Management), British High Commission, Accra* NITHAVRIANAKIS, Michael Stephen, *Second Secretary (Chancery), British High Commission, Accra*
9 November	OAKLEY, Matthew Edward, *Third Secretary (Political), British High Commission, Cape Town*
31 December	BETTLES, Inspector Trevor Christopher Raymond, *Royalty Protection Department, Metropolitan Police* DUGGAN, Terence Edwin, *Pilot, The Queen's Helicopter Flight* HAMILTON, Robert Gray, RVM, *Yeoman of the Royal Pantries, Royal Household* LANE, Mark James, *Head Gardener, Buckingham Palace* LAVERY, Commander John Patrick, RN, *lately Equerry to the Prince of Wales* BAGWELL PUREFOY, Jeremy Patrick, *Insignia Clerk, Central Chancery of the Orders of Knighthood* SMITH, Alan John, *lately of The Prince's Trust* THOMLINSON, Inspector Andrew Wallace, *Royalty Protection Department, Metropolitan Police* WALFORD, Peter Ludlow, *lately Royal Household Liaison Officer, Rover cars*

2000

24 March	**Visit to Australia of the Queen and the Duke of Edinburgh** MORRISON, Paul Francis, *Senior Protocol Officer, Department of the Premier and Cabinet*
28 March	DAVIDSON, Lieutenant Commander Kevin James, *Senior Adviser to the Governor General*
1 April	BURR, Lieutenant Colonel Richard Maxwell, *Australian Equerry to the Queen*
17 June	COLLINS, Robert Bruce, *Deputy Clerk of the Lieutenancy, Leicestershire* HALL, Inspector David Stephen, *Royalty Protection Department, Metropolitan Police* KINGSMILL, Superintendent Roger Derek, *Royalty Protection Department, Metropolitan Police* MANNING, Major Ian Gordon, *former Honorary Secretary, Grand Military Race Committee* SMITH, Roy Alan, *Deputy Keeper of the Records, Duchy of Lancaster* THAIN, Norman, *Clerk of Works, Balmoral Estate* WHEELDON, Gerard Anthony, *Royal Estates Branch, Department for Culture, Media and Sport* WILSON, Wing Commander James Edward Sissmore, *former Accountant to Princess Margaret, Countess of Snowdon*
19 July	GURUNG, Captain Bhimbahadur, *The Royal Gurkha Rifles, Queen's Gurkha Officer*

but see also page 121

MVO (Ladies)

1996

25 October
GIACOMETTI, Mrs Angela Thirze Margaret, *for personal services to the Duke of Edinburgh's World Wide Fund for Nature*

30 October
State Visit to Thailand of the Queen and the Duke of Edinburgh
PURDY, Miss Samantha Louise, *Second Secretary (Political), British Embassy, Bangkok*

1997

1 January
BAILEY, Miss Christian Mary, *Curator to the Prince of Wales*
BROWN, Miss Ann Teresa, MBE, *lately of British Overseas Trade Board*
CLARK, Miss Pamela Margaret, *Deputy Registrar, Royal Archives, Windsor*
HAMPTON, Mrs Valerie Winifred, *Personal Secretary to Princess Alexandra, the Hon. Lady Ogilvy*
HUNTER-CRAIG, Miss Claire Elizabeth, *Secretary, Household of the Duke of Edinburgh*
SLY, Miss Eileen Margaret, *lately of the Westminster Abbey Trust*
SUTCLIFFE, Mrs Prudence Sarah, *Assistant Curator, Print Room, Windsor Castle*

14 June
GRAYSON, Mrs Carole, *Secretary, Yorkshire Survey, Duchy of Lancaster*
GREEN, Miss Margaret Elizabeth, *Administrator, Property Services, Royal Household*
TINEY, Miss Rosemary Jetta, *Manager, operational scheduling (long haul), British Airways*
WYCHERLEY, Miss Ann, *Assistant Secretary, Royal Warrant Holders' Association*

23 June
BASTRASH, Mrs Danielle, *Logistics Officer, HM's Visit to Canada*

7 October
State Visit to Pakistan of the Queen and the Duke of Edinburgh
BANKS, Mrs Jacinta Mary Catharine, *British High Commission, Islamabad*
FOWLER, Miss Joanna, *British High Commission, Islamabad*

13 October
State Visit to India of the Queen and the Duke of Edinburgh
WILDASH, Mrs Elizabeth Jane, *First Secretary (Political), British High Commission, New Delhi*

31 December
BISHOP, Mrs Pamela Alice, *Personnel Director and Administrator, Government House, Canberra*
BURFIELD, Miss Lilian Joyce Amelia, *Couture Fitter, Hardie Amies Ltd*
DUNLOP, Mrs Hazel Margaret, *Assistant Property Administrator, Royal Household*
GOODALL, Miss Sarah Lucy Georgina, *Secretary to the Prince of Wales's Household*
JOHNSON, Mrs Gail Elizabeth, *Financial Controller, Royal Collection*
JONES, Mrs Lettice, *Secretary to Chapter Clerk, College of St George, Windsor*
MCCREERY, Mrs Alexandra Gray, *Secretary to Private Secretary to the Duke of Edinburgh*
MIDDLEBURGH, Mrs Gillian Lesley, *Chief Clerk, Private Secretary's Office*
MOORE, Mrs Jeanie Elizabeth, *lately Vice Chairman, Devonshire Committee of The Prince's Trust*
MOORE, Mrs Margaret Audrey, *Secretary to the Lord Chamerlain*
WILSON, Mrs Beverley Ann, *Clerk of the Lieutenantcy, City of Edinburgh*

1998

13 June
DOVE, Miss Lucy Mary, *Secretary to Comptroller, Lord Chamberlain's Office*
LAING, Mrs Audrey Margaret, *Deputy Visitor Manager, Windsor Castle*
NORRAD, Mrs Corinne Albert, *Principal Secretary to Lieutenant Governor of New Brunswick*
SHARMA, Mrs Chander Kanta, *Invoice Clerk, Property Services, Royal Household*
WILLIAMS, Mrs Manon Bonner, *Assistant Private Secretary to the Prince of Wales*

1999

19 April
State Visit to Korea of the Queen and the Duke of Edinburgh
SPARROW, Mrs Rosalyn Louise, *First Secretary, British Embassy, Seoul*

12 June
ASPREY, Miss Helen Elizabeth, *Secretary to the Equerry to the Duke of Edinburgh*
CLARK, Mrs Jean Young, *Secretary to the Crown Equerry*
GORDON, Mrs Anne Rae, *Secretary to the Lord Lieutenant of Tyne and Wear*
HOLLAND, Mrs Maureen Patricia, *Secretary, Household of Princess Margaret, Countess of Snowdon*
MCNEILE, Miss Fiona Frances, *Secretary, Royal Farms, Windsor*
SHARP, Mrs Lisa Penelope, *Secretary, Household of Prince Edward*
YAXLEY, Mrs Amanda Charlotte, *lately Personnel and Administration Manager, Household of the Prince of Wales*

31 December
COPEMAN, Mrs Patricia Anne, *Bookshop Manager, St George's Chapel, Windsor Castle*
PORTER, Mrs Marilyn Jean, *Assistant Clerk to the Lieutenancy, Dorset*
ROBINSON, Miss Charlette Helen, *Administrator, Privy Purse Office*
SILLARS, Miss Clare Margaret, *Information Officer, Press Office, Buckingham Palace*
STEVENS, Mrs Jacqueline Mary, *Secretary to the Comptroller to Queen Elizabeth The Queen Mother*
WARD, Miss Rosemary, *Senior Assistant Chief Accountant, Royal Household*

2000

28 March	KELLY, Mrs Malveen Eileen, *Receptionist and Anniversaries Officer, Government House, Canberra*
30 March	BIRKETT, Ms Fiona Mary, *Deputy Visit Director, Tasmania*
	ROBERTSON, Mrs Kaye Elizabeth, *Invitations Secretary, Government House, Hobart*
1 April	KEADY, Ms Dale, *Deputy Chief of Protocol, Perth*
17 June	GRANT, Miss Sybil Alexandra, BEM, *Personal Secretary to GOC London District and the Household Division*
	LLOYD, Miss Patricia Ann, *Personnel Officer, Royal Household*

RVM (Gold)

1997

| 31 December | WEBSTER, Alexander, RVM, *Head Gardener, Castle of Mey* |

1998

| 31 December | BRIDGES, Raymond Frederick, RVM, *lately Motor Mechanic, Sandringham Estate* |

2000

| 28 March | **Visit to Australia of the Queen and the Duke of Edinburgh** |
| | HEENAN, James Joseph, RVM, *Butler, Government House, Canberra* |

BAR TO RVM (Silver)

1997

14 June	WILCOCK, Reginald, RVM, *Deputy Steward and Page of the Presence to Queen Elizabeth The Queen Mother*
19 December	DORAN, Miss Mary, RVM, *Housemaid to Queen Elizabeth The Queen Mother*
	GROVES, David Malcolm, RVM, *lately Manager of Reprographic Unit*
	PERRY, Michael, RVM, *Valet to the Duke of York*

1998

| 13 June | WILLIAMS, Eric, RVM, *Manager, Reprographic Unit* |
| 19 December | HARROD, Graham John, RVM, *lately Painter, Sandringham Estate* |

1999

| 3 December | OATES, Alfred Francis, RVM, *Coachman, Royal Mews, Buckingham Palace* |
| 31 December | LEWIS, Ronald John, RVM, *Travelling Yeoman, Household of the Prince of Wales* |

RVM (Silver)

1996

| 30 October | WILLIAMS, Miss Prue Miriam, *Personal Assistant to Second Secretary, British Embassy, Thailand: State Visit of the Queen and the Duke of Edinburgh* |
| 27 November | GIBBS, Mrs Rena, *Telephonist, Royal Household* |

1997

1 January	HART, John Nelson, *Gamekeeper, Sandringham Estate*
	HODSON, Keith, *Stud Hand, Royal Studs*
	JAMES, PC Anthony Claud, *Royalty and Diplomatic Protection Group, Metropolitan Police*
	KERR, John Trodden, *Leading Palace Attendant, Windsor Castle*

KING, Leading Marine Engineer Mechanic (Mech.) Andrew Kevin, *HMY* Britannia
LINES, Richard Clive, *Painter, Sandringham Estate*
MORRIS, Musician William Huw, *HMY* Britannia
MURRELL, Sergeant Paul Andrew George, *Norfolk Constabulary*
RICHES, Peter Leonard, *Foreman Gardener, Crown Estate, Windsor*
SHRUBB, PC Mervyn John, *Royalty and Diplomatic Protection Group, Metropolitan Police*
WETHERILL, David, *Sacristan, St George's Chapel, Windsor*
WILLISON, John Herbert, *formerly of Truefitt and Hill*
WINSTONE, A/PO Marine Engineer Mechanic (Electrical) Barry John, *HMY* Britannia

14 June
BATTERBEE, Malcolm Douglas, *Carpenter, Sandringham Estate*
BROOKS, PC Robert, *Royalty and Diplomatic Protection Group, Metropolitan Police*
BURRELL, Paul, *Butler to Diana, Princess of Wales*
CHONG, Peter, *Chief Gilder, Master of the Household's Department*
CRITCHLOW, Leonard, *Assistant Keeper, Valley Gardens, Crown Estate, Windsor*
DODGE, Miss Pauline Marie, *Senior Telephone Operator, Royal Household*
GARRAWAY, Peter Christopher Noel, *lately Assistant Bailiff, Ascot Racecourse*
HISLOP, AB (Missile) Stephen Ernest, *HMY* Britannia
HOWARTH, Divisional Sergeant Major Harold Sheldon, *Queen's Bodyguard of the Yeomen of the Guard*
KEIR, Allan, *Senior Gardener, Palace of Holyroodhouse*
KLUTH, John Frederick George, *Furniture Manager, Town and Country Caterers*
LOVELL, Barrie Thomas, *Valet to the Duke of Edinburgh*
RAYNER, PO Marine Engineering Mechanic (Mech) David Tony, *HMY* Britannia
STONE, David Eric, *for services to the Royal Household*
STUTTARD, PC Graham Kenneth, *Royalty and Diplomatic Protection Group, Metropolitan Police*
SULLIVAN, Terence Peter, *Fitter, Crown Estate, Windsor*
WHARRAM, A/Leading Seaman (Missile) David John, *HMY* Britannia

23 June
BOISVERT, Master Warrant Officer Jean, *Transportation Officer, HM's visit to Canada*
HUMES, Sergeant Robert Ronald, RCMP, *File Co-rdinator, Newfoundland, HM's visit to Canada*
LEGRAND, Richard, *Maître d'Hotel, Rideau Hall, HM's visit to Canada*

24 July
OATES, Lawrence Edward George, *Royal Mews, Buckingham Palace*

31 December
BENNETT, PO Michael John, *HMY* Britannia
BONICI, Tonino, *Palace Foreman, Buckingham Palace (later gazetted as Honorary; see also p.312 post)*
CAWS, Leading Seaman Patrick Bryan, *HMY* Britannia
CHARMAN, PO Gary Edward, *HMY* Britannia
CLARKE, Sidney Charles *Chauffeur, Leverton & Sons, for services in connection with the funeral of Diana, Princess of Wales*
CLOUGH, George Bernard, *Decorator, Hare & Humphreys, for services in connection with restoration of fire damage at Windsor Castle*
ELLIOTT, Philip Roland, *Foreman, Fencing and Engineering Department, Crown Estate, Windsor*
GRIFFIN, David Martin, *Chauffeur to Princess Margaret, Countess of Snowdon*
HOPE, CPO Steven John, *HMY* Britannia
INGRAM, PO Anthony, *HMY* Britannia
JOY, Jonathan Warner, *Plasterer, A.G. Joy & Son, for services in connection with restoration of fire damage at Windsor Castle*
MCGEE, James, *Head Storekeeper, Crown Estate, Windsor*
PLAYFORD, Rodney Robin, *lately Farrier to Royal Studs, Sandringham*
ROSSITER, Divisional Sergeant Major Lionel George, MBE, *2nd Division, Queen's Body Guard of the Yeomen of the Guard*
ROWE, PO David Christopher, *HMY* Britannia
SLADE, PC Michael Edwin, *Royalty Protection Department, Metropolitan Police*
SMITH, Marshall, *lately Senior Fire Prevention Officer, Windsor Castle*
SPRUCE, Norman James, *lately Gardener, Sandringham Estate*
VENABLES, Miss Clare, *Plasterer, St Blaise, for services in connection with restoration of fire damage at Windsor Castle*
WRIGHT, Musician John Zopara Leo, *HMY* Britannia
WRIGHT, Jonathan Wilfred, *Project Supervisor, Taylor Made Joinery (Bildeston) Ltd, for services in connection with restoration of fire damage at Windsor Castle*

1998

7 May
MURPHY, Hugh Joseph Anthony, *Harness Cleaner, Royal Mews, Buckingham Palace*

13 June
ASHWORTH, Robert Peter, *lately Senior Horological Conservator, Windsor Castle*
BUNN, Robin Victor, *Royalty Protection Department, Metropolitan Police*
CATTLE, David Charles, *Assistant Superintendent of Parks, Home Park, Windsor*
CHAMBERS, Robert John Rogerson, *Horse-box Driver, Royal Mews, Buckingham Palace*
CHRISTIAN, Alan, *Reprographic Operator, Royal Household*
COOK, Phillip Raymond, *Senior Dining Room Assistant, Royal Household*
DIXON, John Alfred, *Verger, Royal Chapel, Windsor Great Park*
GUILEMETTE, Marcel, *Maître d'Hotel and Administrative Assistant to Lieutenant Governor of Quebec*

NORTHBROOK-HINE, Miss Susan Bridgett, *Dining Room Assistant, Royal Household*
POOLE, Derek George, *Messenger, Buckingham Palace*
POWER, Gerard, *Gilder, Buckingham Palace*
STANDEN, Roger Edward, *Foreman Basement Cleaner, Buckingham Palace*
STEVENS, Brian William, *lately Joiner, Royal Household*
STUTTARD, PC James Clifford, *Royalty Protection Department, Metropolitan Police*
WILLIAMS, Alan Edward, *lately Divisional Sergeant Major, 2nd Division, Queen's Bodyguard of the Yeomen of the Guard*

20 September HEALY, Warrant Officer Class 2 Martin Vincent, *Adjutant General's Corps (SPS), State Visit to Malaysia*

31 December AMBROSE, Barry Russell, *Tractor Driver, Crown Estate, Windsor*
BIGSBY, Robert Paul, *Deputy Chief Steward, Royal Train*
BINT, Divisional Sergeant Major Walter Harry, *Queen's Bodyguard of the Yeomen of the Guard*
BRYANT, PC Stephen Charles, *Royalty Protection Department, Metropolitan Police*
CARLIN, PC Joseph Kevin, *Royalty Protection Department, Metropolitan Police*
COTTRELL, Richard George, *Driver, Gardens Department, Crown Estate, Windsor*
DAY, Joseph Walter Frank, *lately Royal Mews, Buckingham Palace*
GILLENDER, PC Paul George, *Royalty Protection Department, Metropolitan Police*
HAZELL, Divisional Sergeant Major Charles Thomas Hugh BEM, *Queen's Bodyguard of the Yeomen of the Guard*
HOLLIS, Miss Margaret Elsie, *Housemaid, Government House, Adelaide*
MOOTOO, Raymond Claud Cyril, *Electrician, Buckingham Palace*
SOULARD, Stephen Michael, *Senior Gardener, Kensington Palace*
STEWART, Mrs Agnes Annie Watt, *Lady's Maid, Household of the Lord High Commissioner*
WALKERDINE, Divisional Sergeant Major Ronald David, *lately Queen's Bodyguard of the Yeomen of the Guard*

1999

12 April BENEFER, David James, *Glasshouse Manager, Sandringham Estate*
BIRCH, Yeoman Warder Peter, *Chapel Clerk, Chapel Royal, HM Tower of London*
BLOMFIELD, Gerald, *Hairdresser*
COX, James Albert, *Maintenance Officer, Windsor Castle*
MARSHALL, Stephen Henry Ronald, *Assistant Yeoman of the Royal Pantries*
MCDONALD, James Alexander, *Painter, Balmoral Estate*
PITHERS, David Arthur, *Woodman, Crown Estate, Windsor*
ROWLANDS, Robert, *Stud Groom, Royal Studs*
SEYMOUR, Colin John, *Painter, Crown Estate, Windsor*
THOMAS, John, *Estate Maintenance, Yorkshire Survey, Duchy of Lancaster*

31 December BULL, Malcolm Joseph, *Craftsman Fitter, Crown Estate, Windsor*
D'ARCY, Brian James, *Chief Exhibitor, Jewel House, HM Tower of London*
ELDRIDGE, Leonard Byron, *Building Supervisor, Property Section, Buckingham Palace*
GOLDSMITH, Nigel George, *Deputy Assistant to the Master of the Household 'C' Branch*
HAMILTON, Mrs Doris Gay, *Housekeeper, Frogmore House, Windsor*
HOLT, Mrs Dora Ann, *Daily Lady, Windsor Castle*
KEY, David Edward, *Chauffeur to the Duke of Edinburgh*
MOYSES, Miss Hilary Sybil, *lately Senior Housemaid, Windsor Castle*
STANLEY, Brian Alan Ernest, *Stud Groom, Royal Paddocks, Hampton Court*

2000

1 April NEWLAND, Andrew John

17 June BOGGIS, Ivan Richard, *Tractor Driver, Sandringham Estate*
BRENT, Anthony Gerald, *Storekeeper and Messenger, Windsor Castle*
CHAMPION, Leslie, *former Fire Surveillance Officer, Buckingham Palace*
CLIFFORD, Terence, *former Senior Fire Precautions Officer, Buckingham Palace*
D'ARCY, Police Constable Desmond Joseph, *Royalty Protection Department, Metropolitan Police*
EMERY, John Gilbert, *Livery Porter, Windsor Castle*
ESSON, Mrs Hazel Ann, *Head Housemaid, Balmoral Castle*
FICE, Leighton Daniel, *Divisional Sergeant Major, Queen's Body Guard of the Yeomen of the Guard*
FROMONT, Mark, *Sous chef, Royal Household*
HENDERSON, Mrs Sheila, *former Senior Sales Assistant, Palace of Holyroodhouse*
IVES, David Allen, *Woodman, Crown Estate, Windsor*
JACKSON, William Verron, *former Groundsman, Ascot Racecourse*
LISTER, Barrie, *former Assistant Manager, Royal Studs*
JACKSON, William Verron, *former Groundsman, Ascot Racecourse*
LISTER, Barrie, *Former Assistant Manager, Royal Studs*
MILLS, Edward Peter, *Leading Polisher, Royal Household*
PHILLIPS, Henry Thomas, *Assistant to the Crown Jeweller*
POWELL, Mrs Olga Joyce, *for services to the Prince of Wales*
YOUNG, Frederick Alan, *Craftsman Welder, Crown Estate, Windsor*

but see also page 121

ROYAL VICTORIAN CHAIN

1997

17 December   AIRLIE, David George Coke Patrick Ogilvy, *Earl of*, KT, GCVO, *on retirement as Lord Chamberlain*

ROYAL VICTORIAN ORDER

On the occasion of the Celebration of Her Majesty The Queen Mother's One Hundredth Birthday, the Queen was graciously pleased to make the following promotions in, and apppointments to, the Order and to award the following Medal:

KCVO

2000

4 August   PARKER, Major Michael John, CVO, CBE, *Producer of the Queen Elizabeth The Queen Mother Centenary Tribute*
WEBB-CARTER, Major General Evelyn John, OBE, *Chairman of the Queen Elizabeth The Queen Mother Centenary Tribute Committee*

CVO

2000

4 August   FLETCHER, Miss Fiona Margaret, LVO, *Secretary to the Ladies in Waiting to Queen Elizabeth The Queen Mother*
GILL, Ian George, LVO, *Registrar and Seneschal of the Cinque Ports*
WINDHAM, Captain Ashe George Russell, LVO, *Chairman of the Castle of Mey Trust*

LVO

2000

4 August   BROWNE, Colonel William Toby, *Organiser of the Queen Elizabeth The Queen Mother Tribute and Parade Commander*

MVO

2000

4 August   ROUET, Captain William Jonathan de, *Irish Guards; Equerry to Queen Elizabeth The Queen Mother*
MASON, Warrant Officer Class 1 (Garrison Sergeant Major) Alan George, MBE, *Parade Sergeant Major, Queen Elizabeth The Queen Mother Centenary Tribute*

RVM (Silver)

2000

4 August   BAGWELL PUREFOY, Mrs Emma Mary, *Assistant to the Producer of the Queen Elizabeth The Queen Mother Centenary Tribute*

PART II

Towards the end of her reign, Queen Victoria considered the possibility of instituting a personal Order. She had made a number of visits abroad during which she had come into contact with many foreign nationals of many different stations in life, who had rendered service of one sort or another to her and she had been in the habit of rewarding such service with gifts, both large and small.

However, there was no Order which she could appropriately give as foreign sovereigns did. Eventually, on 24 April 1896, the *London Gazette* announced the institution of the Royal Victorian Order and later in the same year, the Royal Victorian Medal. The history of both is recorded in *Royal Service, Volume 1*.

The Statutes provided for honorary appointments and awards and the first such appointments to the Order were made on 8 May 1896 and the first awards of the Medal on 30 June 1896. The insignia for honorary members and recipients is identical to those for substantive ones. The makers of the insignia of the Order are Collingwood & Co. Ltd., now of New Bond Street. The medals are struck by the Royal Mint. In 1951, King George VI decided to distinguish honorary awards of the Medal by the addition of a central white stripe in the ribbon. Sir Robert Knox obtained four samples of variations on the existing ribbon from Dalton, Barton & Co.Ltd of Coventry, two with a red stripe in the centre and two with a white one. The King chose the one with the broader white stripe *(below)*.[1] The additional Statute incorporating the description of the new ribbon was dated 15 October. Ribbons for honorary recipients were provided with the Continental form of rosettes and bows *(below left)*, together with the regular ribbons in the boxes of issue

CONTINENTAL STYLE of rosettes and bows for MVO 4th and 5th classes *(below)*.

THE ROYAL VICTORIAN MEDAL with the ribbon for honorary medalists.

which were stamped HON. The supplying of rosettes and bows and the stamping of the boxes ceased on 2 December 1955.

All appointments were inserted in the *London Gazette* until 1 July 1911 when King George V decided that honorary appointments should no longer be gazetted. Thereafter they were included in the printed Registers up to and including 1913, after which they were recorded in separate red volumes in 1930, 1935, 1940, 1952, 1958 and 1960.

Throughout their existence both the Order and the Medal have commemorated service rendered during events great and small, sometimes in circumstances which were unusual and sometimes when the Sovereign wished to reward service which, for one reason or another, was not being recognised by other awards.

There is a startling change in the distribution of honorary awards over the years. In the reign of King Edward VII, the Order was distributed more widely and more freely. With the advent of the Order of the British Empire in 1971 and the simultaneous broadening of the use of the Order of St Michael and St George, the distribution of the Royal Victorian Order became more limited, both in numbers and scope.

The first unusual award was made in the year of the Order's institution. On 16 June 1896 one of the best known maritime disasters of its time occurred; in poor visibility the SS *Drummond Castle*, on her way to England from Cape Town with a crew of 102 and 247 passengers, struck rocks off the island of Molène, off the Brittany coast and foundered within minutes. Only one passenger and two crew members were saved many hours later, the passenger by the crew of a small French fishing boat and the crew by another ship from Molène. During the next few days bodies were washed ashore and funerals held. The local population performed wonders, recovering and caring for bodies, administering the last rites and, when possible, making coffins.[2] On 20 June the French Ambassador sent his country's condolences to the Queen at Balmoral, to which Her Majesty replied, expressing her deep gratitude for the 'touching manner in which all possible respect and attention had been shown by the people of Brittany to the remains of those who were lost...'

So serious was the disaster that an Inquiry was held at the Guildhall in Westminster (now Middlesex Crown Court). A relief fund was opened and rewards were given to the local population. The Queen had been deeply moved by the disaster and quickly approved the institution of a medal as a token of her gratitude and that of the nation. Sea Gallantry Medals and Lloyd's Bronze Medals were also awarded. At the end of April 1897, at the spot where the *Drummond Castle* went down, there were moving ceremonies on board ship at which the Queen was represented by the First Secretary at the British Embassy. Between 26 and 29 April a number of other ceremonies took place where the commemorative medals were presented. At the last two ceremonies the British Ambassador himself presented the medals, having been prevented from doing so on the earlier occasions as he was in attendance on the Queen. In a speech he announced that he had specific instructions from the Queen to convey to the Breton people the grateful thanks which she and the British people felt and her wish that the medals would be a constant reminder to the recipients of Her Majesty's sentiments. Those sentiments had already been exemplified during the previous month by the appointment as Hon KCVO of Vice-Admiral Barrera, the Maritime Prefect of Brest.

In December 1901, John Philip Sousa, the American composer and bandmaster was awarded the Royal Victorian Medal when he and his band visited Britain during their European tour. He composed, *inter alia*, over one hundred marches.

In 1911 the Delhi Durbar ceremony took place on 12 December. On the following day King George V and Queen Mary heard of the wreck off the Moroccan coast of the P&O liner *Delhi*. On board were the Princess Royal (Princess Louise, the King's eldest sister), her husband the Duke of Fife and their two daughters Princess Alix and Princess Maud en route to Egypt and the Sudan. *Delhi* had gone aground in heavy seas and distress signals had been sent out. First to arrive was the French cruiser *Friant*, followed by HMS *Edinburgh*, under the command of Rear-Admiral Sir Christopher

Lieutenant Hans Peter Langkilde, 5 Regiment Danish Army and his wife. He was appointed MVO on 22 July 1907 when attached to HQ Gymnastic Staff at Aldershot. He was born in 1879, retired as a Lieutenant Colonel and died in 1948

Cradock, and the battleship HMS *London*. The Fifes refused to leave the ship before other passengers and were finally rescued having jumped into a boat sent out by *Edinburgh*. Several passengers and crew were lost. Sadly the Duke of Fife died six weeks later from pleurisy in Egypt. These events were also recognised by the award of gallantry medals, including again the Sea Gallantry Medal, and by appointments to the Order on 23 January 1912 of Rear-Admiral Lequerre (Hon CVO) and Rear-Admiral Drujon (Hon MVO IV). British appointments are to be found recorded in Volume 1 and dated 28 February, 5 March and 13 March 1912.

Marconi (Il Marchese Guglielmo Marconi), the inventor of a practical method of communicating intelligence without the use of connecting wires between the sending and receiving points, was appointed Hon GCVO. Despite the curvature of the earth he had succeeded in 1901 in receiving, in Newfoundland, signals sent from Cornwall. Thereafter he had patented the magnetic detector and the horizontal directional aerial. His pioneering work was responsible for much of what today we take for granted. His appointment as a GCVO was on 24 July 1914, King George V having found time to make the appointment during the dreadful days of suspense between the murder in Sarajevo by a Serbian of Archduke Francis Ferdinand and his wife, the Duchess of Hohenberg, and the outbreak of the Great War in August. As can be seen in the register in this volume the murdered couple had visited the King and Queen at Windsor, only eight months previously.

On 27 February 1929 appointments as Hon MVO IV and V were made to officials of the Italian and French State Railways in connection with the Prince of Wales's journey of nearly seven thousand miles in nine days, which was, in those days, a remarkable feat accomplished with the considerable help of the railways. In November 1928, King George V had become dangerously ill with an acute form of septicaemia, the source being an abscess on the lung. At the time, the Prince was undertaking a tour of Africa. Hence the hurriedly arranged emergency journey. The King recovered but had to have a prolonged convalescence which included, famously, a stay at Bognor. After a relapse, the King again recovered during 1930 but his health was never again robust.

Political changes preceding the outbreak of the Second World War caused an unusual conferment of the accolade. On 17 December 1937, Baron Georg Franckenstein, the Austrian Minister in London since 1920, was received in private audience by King George VI and given the insignia of a GCVO. After the German absorption of Austria in March 1938, the anglophile Franckenstein sought permission to remain in Britain and was duly naturalised. In July 1938, he was again received in private audience and received the accolade, becoming Sir George Franckenstein as a substantive rather than an honorary member of the Order. He was killed in an air crash in 1953.

In time of war consideration is always given to the forfeiture of British honours held by citizens of enemy countries. This was done in 1917, shortly after the outbreak of war in 1914, and again on 23 August 1940 the *London Gazette* recorded the King's command to remove from the list of honorary members of the Orders of Chivalry ... 'of all persons therein who are of German or Italian nationality'. A similar notice in the *London Gazette* in February 1942 cancelled awards to citizens of Bulgaria, Finland, Hungary, Japan, Romania and Siam. Under this heading came, for example, King

ROBERT RECKDORF'S MEDALS (*left to right*) King Frederick IX's Medal of Recompense (1961), King Gustav VI Adolf's Medal of Recompense (Sweden, 1952), King Haaken VII's Commemorative Medal (Norway, 1950), Royal Victorian Medal, silver (Great Britain, 1957) – see page 294 –, Medal of Honour in silver of the House Order of Orange (Netherlands, 1953), Medal of Honour of Foreign Affairs in silver (France, 1955), and Emperor Haile Selassie I's Commemorative Medal in silver (Ethiopia, 1954).

ROBERT RECKDORF, (1907–82), Footman to Queen Alexandrine of Denmark until 1952 and thereafter in the service of Prince Knud.

Carol II of Romania appointed a GCVO on 28 November 1925 when attending the funeral of Queen Alexandra, and his son Crown Prince Michael, appointed a GCVO on 15 November 1938 when on a visit to Britain. King Michael's later heroic role in dismissing his pro-Nazi prime minister Marshal Antonescu in 1944 and transferring his country to the Allies' side, did the King much credit, a factor which was ignored by the post-war Communist government who ill-used the King. After the war, King Carol asked if he could wear his insignia as a Knight of the Garter and as a GCVO and was given permission. On 10 July 1947 King George VI and Queen Elizabeth announced the betrothal of Princess Elizabeth to Lieutenant Philip Mountbatten, RN, son of the late Prince Andrew of Greece and of Princess Andrew (Princess Alice of Battenberg). Amongst those invited to attend the wedding of the Princess and Lieutenant the Duke of Edinburgh, KG RN was King Michael of Romania. He was similarly given permission to wear his GCVO insignia.

During the present reign the majority of honorary appointments to the Order and honorary awards of the Medal have been made on the occasion of State Visits although, as can be seen from the Registers, there have been a number of exceptions, particularly in the case of retiring doyens of the Diplomatic Corps.

HONORARY MEMBERS OF
THE ROYAL VICTORIAN ORDER

═══

GCVO

1896

8 May	**Queen Victoria's visit to Cimiez** HENRY, Monsieur Arsène, *Prefect of the Alpes Maritimes*
30 June	**Coronation of Emperor Nicholas II of Russia** DASHKOV, Count Hilarion Vorontsov, *Minister of the Imperial Russian Court* DE RICHTER, General Otto, *Commandant of the Imperial Russian Headquarters* PAHLEN, Count Constantine, *Arch Grand Marshal of Russia.* DOLGOROVKY, Prince Alexis, *Grand Master of the Ceremonies* GALITZIN, Major-General Prince Dimitri, *Staff of the Emperor of Russia*
21 July	**Wedding of Prince Charles of Denmark to Princess Maud of Wales** MOLTKE, Count Joachim, *Comptroller and Treasurer to the Crown Prince and Crown Princess of Denmark*
5 August	**Emperor Kuang-Hsü of China's Mission** CHANG, HE Li Hung, *Special Envoy from China*
31 October	**Emperor Nicholas II of Russia's visit to Queen Victoria at Balmoral** BENCKENDORF, Major-General Count Paul, *Master of the Household to the Emperor*

1897

6 March	SECKENDORFF, HE Count Götz Burkhard, *Comptroller of the Household to the German Empress Frederick*
26 March	MONTENEGRO, HH Prince Nicholas I, Hospodar of
28 March	**The Duke of Connaught's visit to Berlin** VON MÜLLER, Lieutenant-General Edward, *Inspector General of Rifles, Berlin, in attendance on HRH*
26 April	BATTENBERG, HSH Prince Francis Joseph of
30 June	MENSDORFF-POUILLY, Count Arthur August von
28 July	SPAIN, HM King Alfonso XIII of (aged 11)
26 August	**The Attendance of the Duke of Connaught at the French Manoeuvres** DE NEGRIER, General François, *Member of the Supreme War Council*

1898

1899

29 September	PRUSSIA, HRH Prince Frederick Leopold of
21 November	GERMANY, HIM Wilhelm II, German Emperor and King of Prussia
23 November	**Visit to Britain of the German Emperor** BÜLOW, Count Bernard von, *Foreign Secretary, in attendance on the German Emperor* EULENBERG, Count August zu, *Grand Marshal of the Court, in attendance on HIM* PLESSEN, General Hans von, *ADC General in attendance on HIM* SENDEN-BIBRAN, Admiral Baron Gustav von, *Admiral à la Suite in attendance on HIM*

1900

31 March	ERBACH-SCHÖNBERG, Colonel Gustavus Ernst, Count of, *Colonel à la Suite of the Grand Ducal Hessian Army* WOELLWARTH-LAUTERBURG, Freiherr August von, *Chamberlain and Grand Marshal of the Court of the King of Württemberg*
28 June	**The Khedive's visit to Queen Victoria at Windsor** EGYPT, HH Prince Abbas Pacha, Khedive of
16 July	REUSS, HSH Prince Henry XXX of, *Infantry Regiment von Wittich No 83*
20 December	ARNIM, General Gustav Carl Heinrich Ferdinand Emil von, *à la Suite of the Garde-Jäger Battalion*

1901

18 January	**The Duke of Connaught's visit to Berlin for the Bicentenary of the Foundation of the Kingdom of Prussia** KESSEL, HE Lieutenant-General Gustav von, *ADC General to German Emperor*
27 January	SAXE-COBURG AND GOTHA, HRH The Duke of (Duke of Albany) *(reinstated 14 January 1933)*
1 February	METTERNICH, HE Count Paul Wolff, *German Ambassador in London*
2 February	DENMARK, HRH Prince Charles (Christian Frederik Charles George Waldemar Axel) of, (later King Haakon VII of Norway)
8 March	HELLENES, HM King George I of the DENMARK, HRH Frederik (Christian Frederik William Charles) Crown Prince of (later King Frederik VIII)
	King Edward VII's visit to Cronberg REISCHACH, HE Baron Hugo von, *Marshal of the Court of the German Empress Frederick*
	King of Portugal attending the Funeral of Queen Victoria FICALHO, HE the Count of, *in attendance on King Carlos of Portugal*
	The Grand Duke's visit to Britain RUSSIA, HIH Grand Duke Michael Michaelovitch of
16 August	**HRH's visit to Britain** GREECE, HRH Prince Nicholas of
11 October	**King Edward VII's visit to Denmark** DENMARK, HRH Prince Christian (Christian Charles Frederick Albert Alexander William) of DENMARK, HRH Prince Harald Christian Frederick of SCHLESWIG-HOLSTEIN-SONDERBURG-GLÜCKSBURG, HH Prince John of
	King Edward VII's visit to Cronberg MENSDORFF-POUILLY-DIETRICHSTEIN, Count Albert Victor Julius Joseph Michael von, *First Secretary, Austro-Hungarian Embassy in London (reinstated 15 Sept 1927)* LINDEQUIST, General von, *Commanding XVIII Army Corps, Germany* WEDEL, Ernst Count von, *Master of the Horse to The German Emperor*
	King Edward VII's visit to Copenhagen OXHOLM, HE Monsieur Oscar Siegfrid Christian O'Neill, *Marshal of the Court to King Christian IX of Denmark* CASTENSKJOLD, Monsieur Ludwig, *Chamberlain and Geheim-Konferenzraad to King Christian IX of Denmark*

1902

2 May	SIAM, HRH Maha Vajirarudh, Crown Prince of
6 June	ESTERHAZY, Lieutenant-General HSH Prince Louis, *Captain of the Hungarian Bodyguard Vienna, Military Attaché to Austro-Hungarian Embassy in London*
	The Duke of Connaught's visit to Madrid to attend the Enthronement of King Alfonso XIII ALBA DE TORMES, Duke of, *Lord of the Bedchamber and a Grandee of Spain* SOTOMAYER, Duke of, *Great Chamberlain to the King of Spain*
22 August	**Coronation of King Edward VII** GREECE, HRH Prince Andrew of
	Coronation of King Edward VII and on Retirement STAAL, HE Baron Georges de, *Russian Ambassador in London*
19 November	**Visit of King Carlos of Portugal to Windsor** SOVERAL, HE The Marquis de, *Portuguese Minister in London*

1903

7 April	**King Edward VII's visit to Portugal** OPORTO, HRH The Infante Alphonso, Duke of LIMA, Senhor Wencelau de, *Minister for Foreign Affairs* TAROUCA, Lieutenant-Colonel Count, *Chamberlain attached to King Edward VII* ARNOSO, Count d', *Private Secretary to King Carlos*
27 April	**King Edward VII's visit to Italy** ABRUZZI, HRH Prince Luigi Amedeo of Savoy, Duke d' FRIGERIO, Vice-Admiral Giovanni Galeazzo, *Commander-in-Chief, Mediterranean Squadron, Naples*
30 April	TURIN, HRH Vittorio Emanuele of Savoy, Count of GENOA, HRH Prince Tomasso of Savoy, Duke of ZANARDELLI, HE Signor Giuseppe, *President of the Council, Italy*

MORIN, Vice-Admiral Enrico Constantino, *Minister for Foreign Affairs, Italy*
VAGLIA, HE General Emilio Ponzio, *Lord Steward to King Vittorio Emanuele III*
GIANOTTI, HE Count Cesare, *Master of the Household*
BRUSATI, HE General Ugo, *First ADC to the King*
PEDOTTI, HE General Ettore, *Commanding 10th Army Corps, attached to King Edward VII*
PANSA, HE Signor Alberto, *Italian Ambassador in London*
SONNINO, Don Prospero Colonna, Prince of, *Syndic of Rome*

4 May	**King Edward VII's visit to France**

COMBES, HE Monsieur Emile, *President of the Council*
DELCASSE, HE Monsieur Theophile, *Minister of Foreign Affairs*
CAMBON, HE Monsieur Paul, *French Ambassador in London*
DEVILLE, Monsieur Alphonse, *President of the Municipal Council of Paris*
SELVES, Monsieur Justin de, *Prefect of the Seine*
LÉPINE, Monsieur Louis, *Prefect of Police*
FOURNIER, Admiral François Ernest, *attached to King Edward VII*
CROIX, General Henri de la, *attached to King Edward VII*

10 July	**Visit to Britain of President Loubet of the French Republic**

COMBARIEU, Monsieur Abel, *Secretary General and Chief of the Household*
DUBOIS, General Emile, *Chief of the Military Household*

9 October	**King Edward VII's visit to Vienna**

AUSTRIA-HUNGARY, HI and RH The Archduke Ludwig Victor of
AUSTRIA-HUNGARY, HI and RH The Archduke Leopold Salvator of
AUSTRIA-HUNGARY, HI and RH The Archduke Franz Salvator of
AUSTRIA-HUNGARY, HI and RH The Archduke Rainer of
GOLUCHOWSKI VON GOLUCHOWO, HE Agenor Maria Adam, Count, *Minister of the Imperial and Royal House and Minister for Foreign Affairs*
LIECHTENSTEIN, HSH Field Marshal Rudolf, Prince von und zu, *First Lord Steward and Acting Master of the Horse to the Emperor of Austria, King of Hungary*
MONTENUOVO, Alfred Adam Wilhelm Johann Maria, Prince von, *Second Lord Steward to HIM*
PAAR, HE Eduard Maria Nikolaus, Count, *General of Cavalry, Senior ADC to HIM*
BECHTOLSHEIM, HE Anton, Baron von, *General of Cavalry, attached to King Edward VII*

21 November	**Visit of King Vittorio Emanuele III and Queen Elena of Italy to Windsor**

TITTONI, HE Tomasso, *Italian Secretary of State for Foreign Affairs*

29 December	**HIH's visit to Windsor**

RUSSIA, HIH Grand Duke Wladimir Alexandrovitch of, *Chief of the Military Household of the Emperor of Russia*

1904

10 February	**Marriage of Princess Alice of Albany with Prince Alexander of Teck**

BENTHEIM UND STEINFURT, HSH Alexis Charles Ernest Louis Ferdinand Eugene Bernard, Prince
WIED, HSH William Frederick Hermann Othon Charles, Hereditary Prince of
BILFINGER, General HE Herman Baron von, *General ADC to the King of Württemberg*
REISCHACH, Major-General HE Eck Baron von, *Lord Chamberlain to the Queen of Württemberg*

23 March	**Funeral of the Duke of Cambridge**

MONTECUCCOLI, Vice-Admiral Rudolf, Count, *Representing the Emperor of Austria, King of Hungary*

18 April	**King Edward VII's visit to Denmark**

SWEDEN AND NORWAY, HRH Oscar Charles William, Duke of West Gotland and Prince of
SCHLESWIG-HOLSTEIN-SONDERBURG-GLÜCKSBURG, HH Prince Albert Christian Adolphus Charles Eugene of
DEUNTZER, Johan Henrik, *President of the Council and Minister of Foreign Affairs*
DANNESKJOLD-SAMSÖE, HE Christian Frederick, Count
BILLE, HE Monsieur Frants Ernst de, *Danish Minister in London*
MELDAHL, Ferdinand, *Chamberlain to the King of Denmark*
ARENDRUP, Major-General Christian Henrik, *attached to King Edward VII*

21 April	**The Prince of Wales's visit to Austria**

AUERSPERG, Prince Franz Joseph von, *Chamberlain to the Emperor of Austria, King of Hungary*
DOBRZ, Lieutenant-General Wenzel Freiherr Kotz von, *Chamberlain to the Emperor of Austria, King of Hungary*

28 April	**The Prince of Wales's visit to Württemberg to confer the Order of the Garter on the King**

NEURATH, Constantin Freiherr von, *Lord Chamberlain to the King*

13 May	**HE's visit to Britain on a Special Mission from the King of Württemberg**

VARNBÜLER VON UND ZU HEMMINGEN, HE Baron Dr Justizrath Axel, *Counsellor of State and Chamberlain to the King*

11 June	**Archduke Frederick's visit to Britain**

BIGOT DE SAINT-QUENTIN, Major-General Anatol, Count, *Comptroller to Archduke Frederick of Austria*

1 July	**King Edward VII's visit to Kiel**
	PRUSSIA, HRH Prince William Eitel Frederick Christian Charles of
	PRUSSIA, HRH Prince Augustus William Henry Günther Victor of
	PRUSSIA, HRH Prince Oscar Charles Gustavus Adolphus of
	PRUSSIA, HRH Prince Joachim Francis Humbert of
	KOESTER, Admiral Hans Louis Raymond von, *Commander-in-Chief and Inspector General of the Imperial German Navy*
	TIRPITZ, Admiral Alfred von, *Minister of Marine*
	BOCK UND POLACH, Lieutenant-General Frederick William Charles von, *Commanding 9th Army Corps*
	EISENDECHER, Vice-Admiral Charles John George von, *Imperial German Navy*
	SECKENDORFF, Vice-Admiral Baron Albert von, *Master of the Household to Prince Henry of Prussia*
	RICHTHOFEN, Baron Oswald Samuel Constantine von, *Minister of Foreign Affairs in Germany*
	BÜCHSEL, Vice-Admiral William Gottlieb Charles, *Chief of Staff, Imperial German Navy*
6 September	**King Edward VII's visit to Marienbad**
	BULGARIA, HRH Ferdinand Maximilien Charles Leopold Marie, Prince of Saxe-Coburg and Gotha, Reigning Prince of
	TRAUTMANSDORFF-WEINSBERG, HSH Charles John Népomucène Ferdinand, Prince
	TOLNA, HE Tassilo, Count Festétics de
	COUDENHOVE, HE Charles, Count, *Governor of Bohemia*
	KIELMANSEGG, HE Eric Louis Frederick Christian, Count, *Governor of Lower Austria; Chamberlain to the Emperor of Austria, King of Hungary*
21 November	**Visit to Britain of King Carlos and Queen Amélie of Portugal**
	PORTUGAL, HRH Manuel Marie Philippe Charles Amelio Louis Michel Raphael Gabriel Gonzaque Xavier Francois d'Assise Eugène, Duc de Beja,
	VILLAÇA, Antonio Eduardo, *Minister for Foreign Affairs*
	RIBEIRA GRANDE DA CAMARA, Don José Maria Goncalves Zarco, Comte da, *Lord Chamberlain to Queen Amélie*
	CAPELLO, Rear-Admiral Hermengildo de Brito, *Aide-de-Camp to King Carlos*
4 December	**Visit to Rome of Prince Arthur of Connaught to represent HM at the Christening of the Prince of Piedmont**
	QUINTO, Lieutenant-General Felice Avogrado dei Conti di
30 December	**The General's visit to Britain on a Special Mission from the King of Saxony**
	BROIZEM, General Hermann von

1905

8 March	**Visit to Britain of the Prince of Bulgaria**
	BOURBOULON, Robert Alphonse André, Count de, *Lord Chamberlain to HRH*
23 March	**The Duke of Connaught's visit to Portugal**
	FIGUEIRÒ, Count Antoine, *Chamberlain to Queen Amélie*
24 March	MONTELLANO, Don Felipe Falcó y Osorio, Duke of, *Chamberlain to King Carlos*
17 April	**King Edward VII's cruise in the Mediterranean**
	JONNART, HE Charles, *Governor General of Algeria*
19 April	SERVIÈRE, General Armand Théodore, *Commanding 19th Army Corps*
	PERCIN, Rear-Admiral Jean Joseph Gaston Chevalier de, *Naval Commander-in-Chief, Algiers*
12 May	SWEDEN AND NORWAY, HRH Oscar Frederick William Olaf Gustavus, Duke of Scania and Prince of
6 June	**Visit to Britain of King Alfonso XIII of Spain**
	VILLA-URRUTIA, HE Wenceslao Ramirez de, *Minister for Foreign Affairs*
	BERNABÉ, HE Don Luis Polo de, *Spanish Ambassador in London*
	SANTO MAURO, HE Mariano de Henestrosa y Mioño, Duke of, *Lord in Waiting*
	BASCARAN Y FEDERICO, HE General José de, *Chief of the Military Household*
6 June	**Visit to Berlin of Prince Arthur of Connaught to represent HM at the Marriage of the Crown Prince of Prussia and the Duchess Cecilie of Mecklenburg-Schwerin**
	LOEWENFELD, Lieutenant-General HE Alfred von, KCVO, *Aide-de-Camp to Wilhelm II, German Emperor and King of Prussia*
15 June	**Marriage of Princess Margaret of Connaught and Prince Gustav Adolph of Sweden and Norway**
	BADEN, HRH Prince Frederick William Louis, Hereditary Grand Duke of
	SWEDEN, HRH Charles William Louis, Duke of Sudermania & Prince of
	SWEDEN, HRH Eugene Napoleon Nicolas, Duke of Nericia, Prince of
	BILDT, HE Charles Nicolas Daniel, Baron de, *Swedish Minister in London*
	GYLDENSTOLPE, Major-General Count August Gustav Fersen, *Master of the Horse to King Oscar II of Sweden*
	FREYSTADT, HE Baron Leopold von, *Lord Chamberlain to the Grand Duke of Baden*
	PRINTZKÖLD, Otto Hack Roland de, *Lord Chamberlain to King Oscar*
	BOUTROS GHALI PACHA, *Egyptian Minister for Foreign Affairs*

4 July	Visit to Britain of Prince and Princess Arisugawa of Japan HAYASHI, HE Viscount Tadasu, *Japanese Minister in London* SAITOW, Momotaro, *Treasurer of the Household of Emperor Mutsuhito of Japan*
11 October	Visit to Glücksburg of Prince Arthur of Connaught to represent HM at the Marriage of the Duke of Saxe-Coburg and Gotha, Duke of Albany and Princess Victoria Adelaide of Schleswig-Holstein-Sonderburg-Glücksburg SCHLESWIG-HOLSTEIN-SONDERBURG-GLÜCKSBURG, HH Prince Frederick Ferdinand George Christian Charles William, Duke of,
9 November	WEHYNITZ UND TETTAU, HSH Charles Rudolph Ferdinand André, Prince Kinsky von
27 November	Visit to Britain of King George I of the Hellenes MÉTAXAS, HE Monsieur Dimitry George, *Greek Minister in London* THON, Nicholas, KCVO, *Keeper of the Privy Purse to King George I*

1906

18 February	Visit to Denmark of the Lord Chamberlain to represent HM at the Funeral of King Christian IX RABEN-LEVETZAU, HE Frederick Christopher Otto, Count, *Chamberlain to the late King Christian IX of Denmark*
20 February	Special Mission of Prince Arthur of Connaught to Japan to invest the Emperor with the Order of the Garter SANENORI, The Marquis Tokudaiji, *Grand Chamberlain and Lord Keeper of the Privy Seal to Emperor Mutsuhito of Japan* MITSUAKI, Viscount Tanaka, *Minister of the Household* SEI, General Baron Okazawa, *Chief Aide-de-Camp* UJITOMO, Count Toda, *Grand Master of Ceremonies*
24 April	King Edward VII's visit to Greece THEOTOKY, George, *President of the Council and Prime Minister of Greece* SKOUSÈS, Alexander, *Minister of Foreign Affairs* PAPPARIGOPOULO, Michael, *Master of the Household* PAPPADIAMANTOPOULOS, Major-General Jean, *Aide-de-Camp to King George I of the Hellenes* ZOTOS, Rear-Admiral Cosmas, *attached to King Edward VII*
6 June	Visit of the Prince of Wales to Madrid to represent HM at the Marriage of the King of Spain and Princess Victoria Eugenie of Battenberg HIJAR, HE Alfonso de Silva y Campbell, Duc de, *attached to the Prince of Wales* LÉCERA, HE Jaime de Silva y Campbell, Duc de, *Chamberlain to King Alfonso XIII of Spain, attached to Princess Henry of Battenberg (Princess Beatrice)* MINA, HE Manuel Falcó Osorio d'Adda y Gutierrez de los Rios, Marquis de la, *Master of the Horse* PACHECO, HE Lieutenant-General Juan Pacheco y Rodrigo, Marquis de, *Commandant General of the Alabarderos* MORET Y PRENDERGAST, HE Segismundo, *President of the Council of Ministers* CASTRO, HE Juan Manuel Sáuchez y Gutierrez, Duc d'Almadovar del Rio de, *Minister of Foreign Affairs*
14 August	SAAVEDRA Y SALAMANCA, Jose, Marquis of Viana, Count of Urbasa and Marquis del Valle de la Paloma, *Master of the Horse*
29 August	Visit of Prince Christian of Schleswig-Holstein to Germany to represent HM at the Christening of the Son of the Crown Prince of Prussia SCHOLL, HE General Frederick von, KCVO, *ADC General to Wilhelm II, German Emperor and King of Prussia*
8 September	SCHWARTZKOPPEN, Lieutenant-General Maximilian von, *attached to the Duke of Connaught at German manoeuvres*
20 September	Visit of the Duke of Connaught to Karlsruhe to invest the Grand Duke with the Order of the Garter and to represent HM at the Celebration of the Golden Wedding of the Grand Duke and Grand Duchess BRAUER, HE Arthur von, *Lord Chamberlain to the Grand Duke of Baden* ANDLAW, Camill, Count von, *Master of the Household* BIEBERSTEIN, Adolf, Baron Marschall von, *President of the Ministry of the Grand Ducal House* BOECKLIN VON BOECKLINSAN, HE Lieutenant-General Adolf, Baron, *attached to the Duke of Connaught*
9 November	SAXE-COBURG AND GOTHA, HRH Prince Philip of
13 November	Visit to Windsor of King Haakon VII and Queen Maud of Norway NANSEN, HE Doctor Fridtjof, *Norwegian Minister in London* RUSTAD, Frederick Frantz Michael Wilhelm, *Master of the Household to King Haakon*

1907

28 January	HOHENZOLLERN, HSH Prince Charles Arthur Antony Frederic William Louis of, *Commanding 1st Regiment of Prussian Dragoon Guards*
9 April	King Edward VII's visit to Spain SPAIN, HRH Prince Don Fernando Maria de Baviera, Infante of

YBARRONDO, HE Don Ventura Garcia Sancho é, Marquis de Aguilar de Campoó, *Lord Chamberlain to Queen Christina of Spain*
MAURA, HE Don Antonio, *Prime Minister*
ALLENDESALAZAR, HE Don Manuel, *Minister of Foreign Affairs*
FERRANDIZ, HE Don Joseph, *Minister of Marine*
PILARES, Rear-Admiral Don Ramon Auñon y Villalon, Marquis de, *Governor of Cartagena*

7 May	**Visit to Britain of General Prince Sadanaru Fushimi representing Emperor Mutsuhito of Japan** KOMURA, HE Baron Jutaro, *Japanese Ambassador in London* NAGASAKI, Michinori Seigo, *Councillor of the Court of Emperor Mutsuhito of Japan* NISHI, HE General Baron Kwanjiro, *Inspector General of Military Education*
18 May	**Visit to Madrid of Prince Arthur of Connaught to represent HM at the Christening of the Prince of Asturias** ARION, HE Don Joaquin Fernandez de Cordova y Osma, Duke of, *Lord of the Bedchamber to King Alfonso XIII of Spain*
10 June	OLDENBURG, HRH Friedrich August, Grand Duke of HESSE, HRH Alexander Friedrich, Landgrave of
13 June	**Visit to Britain of King Frederik VIII and Queen Louise of Denmark** BROCKENHUUS SHACK, Frands Axel Vilhelm, Comte de, *Master of the Household to King Frederik* BARDENFLETH, Rear-Admiral Frederik Carl Christian, *Chamberlain to Queen Louise*
15 June	**Representing the German Emperor at the Unveiling in London of the Statue of the late FM the Duke of Cambridge** HAHNKE, HE Field Marshal Wilhelm von, *Governor of Berlin*
27 June	MICHEL, General Victor Constant, *Commanding 2nd Army Corps, French Army*
3 August	**Visit of the Norwegian Coast Squadron to Cowes** OLSEN, Rear-Admiral Carl Otto, *Commander-in-Chief, Coast Squadron*
14 August	**King Edward VII's visit to Wilhelmshöhe** WÜRTTEMBERG, General HRH Duke Albert of, *Commanding XIth Army Corps* HOHENLOHE-LANGENBURG, General HSH Hermann Ernest Francis Bernhard, Prince of
15 August	**King Edward VII's visit to Ischl** BAVARIA, HRH Prince Leopold of AEHRENTAHL, HE Baron Alois Lexa von, *Minister for Foreign Affairs of Austria-Hungary*
6 September	**King Edward VII's visit to Marienbad** ISVOLSKY, HE Alexander, *Minister for Foreign Affairs of Russia*
28 September	**Visit of the Duke of Connaught to Vienna** BRUDERMANN, General of Cavalry Ritter Rudolf, *attached to HRH*
9 November	TORRECILLA, The Marquis de la, *Lord Chamberlain to King Alfonso XIII of Spain*
12 November	**Visit to Windsor of German Emperor Wilhelm II and German Empress Augusta Victoria** EINEM, HE General Charles von, *Minister for War* SCHOEN, HE William Edward von, *Secretary of State for Foreign Affairs* HÜLSEN-HAESELER, HE General Dietrich, Count von, *Chief of HIM's Military Cabinet* MÜLLER, HE Vice-Admiral George Alexander von, CVO, *Chief of HIM's Naval Cabinet* KNESEBECK, HE Bodo Hugo Bernhard Paridam von dem, KCVO, *Chamberlain and Deputy Grand Master of Ceremonies to HIM*
18 November	BENCKENDORFF, HE Alexander Philip Constantine Louis, Count de, *Russian Ambassador in London*
19 December	**Visit of Prince Arthur of Connaught to Stockholm to represent HM at the Funeral of King Oscar II of Sweden** LENNMAN, Rear-Admiral Frederick William

1908

30 January	**Visit of Prince Arthur of Connaught to Stockholm to represent HM at the Funeral of King Oscar II of Sweden** PALANDER OF VEGA, HE Vice-Admiral Adolf Arnold Louis, *ADC to the late King Oscar*
6 February	SAN PEDRO, Benalua y de las Villas, Duke of, *Chamberlain to King Alfonso XIII of Spain*
4 March	CHERVACHIDZE, HE George, Prince, *Comptroller of the Household of the Empress Marie Feodorovna of Russia*
25 April	**King Edward VII's visit to Denmark** DENMARK, HRH Prince Christian Frederik William Valdemar Gustavus of FRIJS, Mogens Christian, Count Krag Juel Vind-, KCVO, *Chamberlain to King Frederik VIII of Denmark, attached to King Edward VII* KÜHNEL, Lieutenant-General Arnold August Blichert, *Commanding 1st District*
27 April	**King Edward VII's visit to Sweden** LINDMAN, HE Arvid, *Prime Minister*

TROLLE, HE Eric de, *Minister for Foreign Affairs*
WRANGEL, HE Herman, Count, *Swedish Minister in London*
ESSEN, HE Frederick, Baron von, *Marshal of the Realm to King Gustav V of Sweden*
LILLIEHÖÖK, Charles Malcolm, *Master of the Household*
STENBOCK, Albert Magnus Otto, Count, *Lord of the Bedchamber attached to King Edward VII*

2 May	**King Edward VII's visit to Christiania** CHRISTOPHERSEN, HE William Christopher, *Minister for Foreign Affairs* HANSEN, Lieutenant-General Ole, *Commander-in-Chief, Norwegian Army, attached to King Edward VII*
29 May	**Visit to London of President Fallières of the French Republic** PICHON, Stephen, *Minister for Foreign Affairs* LANES, Jean, *Secretary General to the President* MOLLARD, Armand, KCVO, *Minister Plenipotentiary and Director of Protocol* JAURÉGUIBERRY, Vice-Admiral Horace Anne Alfred, *Commander-in-Chief of French Northern Squadron*
10 June	**King Edward VII's visit to Russia** OLDENBURG, HH Prince Peter Alexandrovitch of STOLYPINE, HE Peter, *President of the Council of Ministers* FRÉEDÉRICKSZ, HE General Baron Wladimir, KCVO, *Minister of the Imperial Court* DIKOFF, HE Admiral Jean, *Minister of Marine* ZAKAMELSKY, HE General Baron Alexander Meller, *Governor General of the Baltic Provinces*
27 July	GEOFFRAY, Léon Marcel Isidore, *on retirement as Minister Plenipotentiary, French Embassy in London*
18 August	**King Edward VII's visit to Cronberg** JENISCH, HE Martin Johan, Baron von, *Minister in attendance on Wilhelm II, German Emperor and King of Prussia*
21 August	**King Edward VII's visit to Ischl** AUSTRIA-HUNGARY, General HI and RH the Archduke Eugene of AUSTRIA-HUNGARY, HI and RH the Archduke Joseph Augustus of BAVARIA, Captain HRH Prince George of BAVARIA, Lieutenant HRH Prince Conrad of HANDEL, HE Erasmus, Baron von, *Governor of Upper Austria* PERSTORFF, HE Francis von Schiessl, *Chief of the Imperial Cabinet of Franz Josef, Emperor of Austria and King of Hungary*
17 November	**Visit to Windsor of King Gustav V and Queen Victoria of Sweden** THOTT, Count Tage Alexis Otto, *Master of the Court Hunt* DYRSSEN, Rear-Admiral William, *Inspector of the Fleet*

1909

12 February	**King Edward VII's visit to Berlin** PRUSSIA, HRH Prince Adalbert Ferdinand Berengar Victor of BÜLOW, General Charles William Paul von, *Commanding the 3rd Army Corps* BELOW, Lieutenant-General von, *Commanding the 1st Division of Guards* SCHENCK, Lieutenant-General Dedo Charles Henry von, *Commanding the 2nd Division of Guards* USEDOM, Vice-Admiral Guido von, KCMG, *attached to King Edward VII*
26 April	**King Edward VII's visit to Catania** SAN GIULIANO, HE Antonio, Marquis di, *Italian Ambassador in London*
7 June	**Visit to Britain of HIH** JAPAN, Field Marshal HIH Prince Morimasa Nashimoto of
22 June	**Special Mission to announce to the King the Sultan's Accession to the Throne** LOUFTI BEY, HE Ismail, *First Chamberlain to Sultan Mehmed V of Turkey*
13 July	GREECE, HRH Prince Christopher of
20 July	**The Anniversary of HRH's Birthday** GREECE, HRH Prince George of
21 July	JAPAN, HIH Prince Kuni of
5 August	**Visit of Emperor Nicholas II and Empress Alexandra Feodorovna of Russia** BÉLOZERSKY, Lieutenant-General Constantin, Prince Bélosselsky, *General ADC to HIM* HENDRIKOFF, HE Basile, Count, *Grand Master of the Ceremonies in attendance on Her Imperial Majesty*
16 November	**Visit to Windsor of King Manoel II of Portugal** BOCAGE, HE Carlos Roma du, *Minister for Foreign Affairs* SABUGOSA, Antonio Vasco de Mello Silva Cezar a Menezes, Count de, *Lord Steward to King Manoel* FAYAL, Luiz Coutinho Borges de Medeiros, Marquis de, *Lord-in-Waiting* LAVRADIO, José d'Almeida Corrèa de Sá, Marquis de, *Private Secretary*
20 November	FONG, HE Lord Li Ching, KCVO, *Chinese Minister in London*

1910

25 January	**Visit of HIH to Windsor** JAPAN, Admiral of the Fleet HIH Prince Hiroyasu Fushimi of, *Chief of the Naval General Staff*
	LIGNE, HE Louis Eugène, Prince de, *Special Ambassador from King Albert of the Belgians*
25 February	IRGENS, HE Monsieur Johannes, CVO, *on relinquishing appointment as Norwegian Minister in London*
8 June	CUMBERLAND, HRH Prince George William Christian Albert Edward Alexander Frederick Waldemar Ernest Adolphus of

1911

22 April	**Visit of Prince Arthur of Connaught to represent HM at the Jubilee Celebration of Italian Unity** GIROLA, Lieutenant-General Arnoldo, *Commanding 3rd Italian Corps*
22 June	**King George V's Coronation** BADEN, HGDH Prince Maximilian of BAVARIA, HRH Prince Rupert of BRUNSWICK-LÜNEBURG, HRH Duke Ernest Augustus of BULGARIA, HRH Prince Boris, Prince of Tirnovo and Crown Prince of, *(re-instated 15 September 1927)* CHINA, HIH Prince Tsai Chen of JAPAN, HIH Prince Yorihito of JONQUIÈRES, Vice-Admiral Eugène de Fauque de, *Representative of French Republic* MECKLENBURG-STRELITZ, HRH The Hereditary Grand Duke of MECKLENBURG-SCHWERIN, HRH The Grand Duke of MONACO, HSH The Hereditary Prince of MONTENEGRO, HRH The Crown Prince of RAS KASSA, HH, *Representing Emperor Menelik II of Ethiopia* RUSSIA, HIH The Grand Duke Boris Vladimirovitch of SAXE-COBURG AND GOTHA, HH Prince Leopold of SAXONY, HRH Prince John George of SCHLESWIG-HOLSTEIN, HH Duke Ernst Günther of SERVIA, HRH The Hereditary Prince Alexander of (later King Alexander I of Yugoslavia) SIAM, HRH The Prince Chakrabongse of
8 August	**On relinquishing appointment of Military Attaché to Austro-Hungarian Embassy** LIECHTENSTEIN, Major HSH Prince Frederick von und zu
7 September	ETHIOPIA, HRH Lij Yasu of (later Emperor)
22 November	**Visit to Egypt of King George V and Queen Mary en route to India** TURKEY, HIH Prince Ziaeddin Effendi of

1912

24 January	**Visit to Malta of King George V and Queen Mary** BOUÉ DE LAPEYRÈRE, Vice-Admiral Gaston, *Commanding French Squadron at Malta*
31 January	**Visit to Gibraltar of King George V and Queen Mary** SPAIN, General HRH Don Carlos de Bourbon, Infante of, GCB
21 March	**Special Mission to HM from Sultan Mehmed V of Turkey** TEWFIK PASHA, HH, *Turkish Ambassador in London*
22 July	**HIH's visit to London** RUSSIA, HIH The Grand Duke George Michaelovitch of
12 September	**Visit of Prince Arthur of Connaught to Japan to represent HM at the Funeral of Emperor Mutsuhito** SAKAMOTO, Vice-Admiral (Retired) Baron Toshiatsu, *Chief of Naval Education* TOGO, Admiral, Count (later Marquis) Heihachiro, OM, *Former Chief of Naval Staff*
21 September	SLATIN PASHA, Lieutenant-General Rudolph Charles Baron von, KCMG, CB, *on his visit to Balmoral (re-appointed 1928)*
23 September	SAZONOW, HE Serge, *Russian Minister for Foreign Affairs*
20 November	BRETEUIL, Marquis de, *on his visit to Windsor Castle*

1913

24 May	**Visit of King George and Queen Mary to Berlin to attend the Marriage of the Duke of Brunswick and Lüneburg and Princess Viktoria Luise of Prussia** BETHMANN-HOLLWEG, HE Theobald Theodor Frederick Alfred von, *Imperial Chancellor* FÜRSTENBERG, HSH Max Egon, Prince zu, *Lord Great Chamberlain to Wilhelm II, German Emperor and King of Prussia*

HUTIER, HE Lieutenant-General Oscar Ernest von, *Commanding 1st Division of Prussian Guards*
JAGOW, HE Hangott von, *Chief of Police, Berlin*
JAGOW, HE Gottlieb von, *Imperial Secretary of State for Foreign Affairs*
KROSIGK, HE Vice-Admiral Günther von, *attached to the King*
LICHNOWSKY, HSH Prince Charles Max, *German Ambassador in London*
LYNCKER, HE Lieutenant-General Maximilian, Baron von, *Master of the Household*
PLETTENBERG, HE General Charles, Baron von, *General Officer Commanding Regiments of the Guard*
ROEDER, HE Baron Eugene Alexander Henry von, *Vice-Grand Master of Ceremonies*
WERMUTH, HE Adolphus Louis, *Chief Burgomaster, Berlin*

26 May   **Visit of King George and Queen Mary to Neu-Strelitz**
BODDIEN, HE Captain William von, *Master of the Horse to the Grand Duke of Mecklenberg-Strelitz*
MALTZAN, HE Lieutenant-General Adolphus Frederick Joseph Otto (Baron zu Wartenberg und Genzlin),
    Lord Chamberlain to the Grand Duke of Mecklenberg-Strelitz

11 June   **Special Mission from Argentine Republic**
SALAS, HE Dr Don Carlos, *Special Ambassador*

24 June   **Visit to Britain of President Poincaré of the French Republic**
FAVEREAU, Vice-Admiral Charles Eugène
BEAUDEMOULIN, General Antoine, *attached to President Poincaré of the French Republic*

    HRH's visit to Britain
HOHENZOLLERN, HRH William Augustus Charles Peter Ferdinand Benedictus, Prince of

21 July   **Mission to HM to Announce the Accession of King Constantine I of the Hellenes**
PALLIS, General Agamemnon, *Chief of Military Household*
ZAIMIS, HE Alexander, *President of the Council of Ministers*

26 September   CURIÈRES DE CASTELNAU, General Edward de, *Chief of the French Deputation at the Army Exercise at Althorp*

17 November   **Visit to Windsor of the Archduke Francis Ferdinand of Austria-Hungary**
RUMERKIRSCH, HE Charles, Baron, *Master of the Household to HI and RH*

1914

24 April   **King George V's visit to France**
DELANNEY, Marcel François, *Prefect of the Seine*
DOUMERGUE, Gaston, *President of the Council*
ESPÉREY, Marshal Louis Felix Marie François Franchet d', *Commanded 1st Army Corps*
GOYON, Paul Auguste Pierre Chassaigne, *President, Municipal Council of Paris*
JOFFRE, Marshal Joseph Jacques Cesaire, *Chief of General Staff (later Generalissimo)*
LE BRIS, Vice-Admiral Pierre Ange Marie

9 May   **Visit to Britain of King Christian X of Denmark**
ROSENBORG, HH Prince Aage, Count of
SCAVENIUS, Erik Julius Christian, *Danish Minister of Foreign Affairs*

24 July   MARCONI, Guglielmo, *Senator of Italy and Inventor*

1915

12 February   YOUSSOUPOFF, HE Felix, Prince (Count Soumarakoff-Elston), *Chief of Mission to HM from Emperor Nicholas*
    II of Russia

11 November   IMPERIALI, HE Marquis Guglielmo, *Italian Ambassador in London*

1916

1 April   **Visit to London of the Crown Prince Regent of Serbia**
BOSHKOVITCH, HE Monsieur Mathias, *Serbian Minister in London*
JANKOVITCH, HE Dragomir, *Chief of Civil Cabinet*
YOVANOVITCH, Yovan, *Deputy Minister of Foreign Affairs*

3 November   **The Installation of HRH as Crown Prince of Japan**
JAPAN, HRH The Crown Prince of (later Emperor Hirohito; reinstated 7 May 1975 during the State Visit to
    Japan)

1917

1918

28 October   **Visit to London of Admiral Prince Yorihito of Higashi Fushimi**
SHIBA, General Goro, KCVO, CB, *Commander of the Tokyo Garrison*

30 November	**King George V's State Visit to France** AUTRAND, Auguste Alexandre Guillaume, *Prefect of the Seine* DUPARGE, General Paul Louis, GCMG, *Military Secretary and Chief of Military Household of the French President* MARTIN, Richard William, KBE, CMG, *Chief of Protocol* RAUX, Fernand Jérôme Urbain, *Prefect of Police, Paris*

1919

18 February	**On relinquishing Appointment of Greek Minister in London** GENNADIUS, HE Monsieur Johannes
4 November	**Visit to London of Shah Ahmed Mirza of Persia** ALA-ES-SALTANEH, HH Prince Mirza Mehdi Khan, *Persian Minister in London* NOSRAT-ES-SALTANEH, HIH Prince
12 November	**Visit to London of President Poincaré of the French Republic** PÉNELON, General Marie Jean-Baptiste, *Secretary General of the Presidency*
25 November	**Reception by HM of a Uruguayan Mission** BUERO, Dr Juan Antonio, *Uruguayan Minister for Foreign Affairs*

1920

1921

9 February	**On Retirement as Minister Plenipotentiary and Counsellor of French Embassy in London** FLEURIAU, Aimé Joseph de
19 March	MURAT, HH Joachim Napoleon, Prince
9 May	**Visit to Britain of The Crown Prince of Japan** HAYASHI, HE Baron Gonsuke, *Japanese Ambassador in London* IRYIE, Viscount Tamemori, *Chief Equerry to HIH* MIURA, Dr Kinnosuke, *Physician to the Japanese Court* NARA, General Takeji, Baron, *Chief ADC to the Emperor* OGURI, Admiral Kozaburo, GCMG, *Commanded Japanese Third Fleet* TAKESHITA, Admiral Isamu, KCB
20 June	**Visit to Britain of King Alfonso XIII of Spain** MERRY DEL VAL, Marquess (HE. Don Alfonso Merry del Val y Zulueta), *Spanish Ambassador in London* SOMERUELOS, Major The Marquess de, (Don Pedro Diez de Rivera y Figueroa), *in attendance on HM*
4 July	**Visit to Britain of King Albert I and Queen Elisabeth of the Belgians** LANNOY, Comte de, *Grand Marshal of the Court* MERODE, Comte Jean de, *Grand Marshal of the Court* MONCHEUR, HE Baron, *Belgian Ambassador in London*

1922

22 April	**Visit by the Prince of Wales to Japan** MAKINO, Count Nobuaki, *Minister of Imperial Household* TAKAHASHI, Korekiyo, *Prime Minister* UCHIDA, Count Yasuya, *Minister of Foreign Affairs*
13 May	**King George V's visit to Belgium** ARSCHOT SCHOONHOVEN, Count d', *Chef du Cabinet of King Albert I of the Belgians* BIEBUYCK, Lieutenant-General Aloise, GCMG, *ADC to King Albert I of the Belgians* BRABANT, HRH Prince Leopold, Duke of, (later King Leopold III) FRANCK, Louis, *Minister of the Colonies* JONGHE, Lieutenant-General Count d'Ardoye, KCB, KCMG LIPPENS, Maurice Auguste Eugène Charles Marie Ghislain, *Governor General of the Congo* MAX, Adolphe Eugène Henri Jean, GBE, *Minister of State and Burgomaster of Brussels*
9 June	**The Duke of York's visit to Belgrade for the Marriage of Alexander I, King of the Serbs, Croats and Slovenes to Princess Marie of Roumania** SERBIA, HH Prince Paul of, (later Prince Regent)

1923

14 May	**King George V's visit to Italy** DEBONO, HE General Emilio, *Director General, Italian Police* BOREA D'OLMO, HE Giovanni Battista, Duke of, *Prefect of the Palace, Rome*

CONTARINI, HE Senator Salvatore, *Secretary General, Ministry of Foreign Affairs*
GIORGIO, General HE Antonio di, KCMG
MATTIOLI PASQUALINI, HE Count Alessandro, *Minister of the Italian Court*
MOLA, Vice-Admiral Vittorio, KCMG, CB, *ADC General to King Vittorio Emmanuele III of Italy*
PIEDMONT, HRH Umberto of Savoy, Prince of (later King Umberto II)

4 November   **Visit to Britain of King Gustav V of Sweden for the Wedding of the Crown Prince of Sweden and Lady Louise Mountbatten**
LEWENHAUPT, Count Claes Axel August
PALMSTIERNA, HE Baron Erik, *Swedish Minister in London*
RALAMB, Baron Claes Erik

24 December   NORWAY, HRH the Crown Prince of (later King Olav V)

1924

13 May   **King George V's visit to Belgium**
DE CEUNINCK, Lieutenant-General Armand Leopold Théodore, KCB, KCMG

15 May   **Visit to Britain of King Ferdinand I of Roumania and Queen Marie**
ANGELESCU, General Paul, CB, *Chief of Military Household of King Ferdinand and Marshal of the Court*
TITILESCU, HE Monsieur Nicolas, *Romanian Minister in London*

29 May   **Visit to Britain of King Vittorio Emanuelle III of Italy**
MONACO, Admiral Roberto, Duke of Longano, DSO, *ADC to King of Italy*
TOMASI DELLA TORRETTA, HE Pietro, Il Marchese (Dei Principi di Lampedusa), *Italian Ambassador*

1925

24 April   **King George V's visit to France**
PAINLEVÉ, Paul, *President of the Council of Ministers*

11 November   **Visit to Britain of King Alfonso XIII of Spain**
BENDAÑA, HE Don Lorenzo Pineyro Fernandez, Marquis of Villavicencio, *Lord Steward and Chamberlain to Queen Victoria Eugenie of Spain*

28 November   **The Funeral of Queen Alexandra**
BELGIUM, HRH Prince Charles of
DENMARK, HRH Prince Axel of
EVERS, HE Vice-Admiral Anton Ferdinand Mazanti, GBE
GREECE, HRH Prince George of
ROUMANIA, HRH Crown Prince Carol of, (later King Carol II)

1926

8 June   **HRH's visit to Britain**
SWEDEN, HRH Prince Gustavus Adolphus of

1927

19 May   **Visit to Britain of President Doumergue of the French Republic**
FOUQUIÈRES, Pierre Becq de, KCVO, *Introducteur des Ambassadeurs*
MICHEL, Jules, *Secretary General of the French Presidency*

6 July   **Visit to Britain of King Fuad I of Egypt**
IZZET PASHA, General HE, Aziz, *Egyptian Minister in London*
ZOULFIKAR PASHA, HE Said, *Grand Chamberlain to HM*

14 December   **HRH's visit to London**
DENMARK, HRH Crown Prince Frederik of, (later King Frederik IX)

1928

15 March   **Visit to Britain of King Amanullah of Afghanistan**
ALI AHMED KHAN, HE, *Governor of Kabul*
ALI MUHAMMAD KHAN, HE, *Afghan Minister in Rome*
GHULAM SADIQ KHAN, HE, *Acting Afghan Foreign Minister*
MUHAMMAD HASSAN KHAN, *Chamberlain to King Amanullah*
MUHAMMAD YAKUB KHAN, HE, *Minister of the Afghan Court*
SHER AHMED KHAN, HE, *President of the Council of State*
SHUJA-ED-DOWLEH, HE, *Afghan Minister in London*

1929

25 April	**For services to the late Empress Marie Feodorovna of Russia** AMDRUP, HE Vice-Admiral Georg Carl, *Royal Danish Navy*
10 May	**The Duke of Gloucester's Garter Mission to Japan** IKKI, Baron Kitokuro, *President of the Privy Council* OKADA, Admiral Keisuke, *Minister of Marine* SHIRAKAWA, General Yoshinori, *Minister of War* SUZUKI, Admiral Kantaro, *Grand Chamberlain to Emperor Hirohito*
15 June	**In recognition of services to the Russian Imperial Family** BARK, Pierre, (later Sir Peter Bark, Kt, 1935), *former Russian Minister of Finance*
21 December	**Visit to Britain of King Christian X of Denmark** AHLEFELDT-LAURVIG, HE Count Preben Ferdinand, *Danish Minister in London*

1930

28 June	**Visit of HIH to Britain** JAPAN, Lieutenant HIH Prince Nobuhito Takamatsu of ABO, Admiral Baron Kiyokazu, KCMG, CVO MATSUDAIRA, HE Tsuneo, *Japanese Ambassador in London*
29 October	**For services to Queen Maud of Norway** VOGT, HE Monsieur Paul Benjamin, *Norwegian Minister in London*
30 October	**Visit of the Duke of Gloucester to Ethiopia to represent HM at the Coronation of Emperor Haile Selassie I of Ethiopia** ETHIOPIA, HIH Maridazmach Asfa Wossen, GBE, Crown Prince of

1931

17 May	**Visit of the Duke and Duchess of York to the French Colonial Exhibition, Paris** REYNAUD, Paul, *Minister for the Colonies*
3 June	SWINDEREN, HE Jonkheer Rencke de Marees van, *Netherlands Minister in London*

1932

1933

20 June	**Visit to Britain of King Feisal I of Iraq** NURI PASHA AL SAID, *Minister for Foreign Affairs* JA'FAR PASHA EL ASKERI, HE, CMG, DSO, *Iraqi Minister in London*

1934

13 June	**Visit of the Special Mission to announce the Accession of King Leopold III of the Belgians** DE CARTIER DE MARCHIENNE, HE Baron, *Belgian Ambassador in London* D'URSEL, Duc, *Head of Special Mission*
26 July	**On retirement from post of Polish Ambassador in London** SKIRMUNT, HE Monsieur Constantin

1935–1936

1937

11 May	**Visit of HRH to London for Coronation of King George VI** GREECE, HRH Paul, Crown Prince of, (later King Paul I)
22 July	REGIS DE OLIVEIRA, HE Senhor Raul, GBE, *Brazilian Ambassador in London*
16 November	**Visit to Britain of King Leopold III of the Belgians** CORNET DE WAYS-RUART, Comte Louis Benoit Marie Ghislain TILKENS, Lieutenant-General August Constant, CMG, CVO
17 December	FRANCKENSTEIN, HE Baron George, *Austrian Minister in London, (Substantive GCVO on 23 July 1938 on acquiring British nationality)*

1938

2 February   THAILAND, HRH Prince Chula Chakrabongse of, *Hon ADC to King Ananda Mahidol of Thailand*

19 July   **Visit of King George VI and Queen Elizabeth to France**
CHAUTEMPS, Camille, *Vice-President, Council of Ministers*
CORBIN, HE Monsieur Charles, GBE, *French Ambassador in London*
DARLAN, Vice-Admiral Jean Louis Xavier François, *Vice-President, Marine Council*
GAMELIN, Général Maurice Gustave, CMG, *Vice-President, War Council*
SARRAUT, Albert, *Minister for the Interior*
VUILLEMIN, Général de Division Joseph, DSO, *Vice-President, Air Council*

26 October   THAILAND, HRH Prince Aditya Dibhabha of, *President of the Council of Thailand*

15 November   **Visit to Britain of King Carol II of Roumania**
ROUMANIA, HRH Michael, Crown Prince of, (later King Michael I), *(Reinstated 20 November 1947)*
GRIGORCEA, HE Basile, *Romanian Minister in London*
STIRCEA, HE Baron Jean, *Grand Master of Ceremonies*
UDARIANU, HE Ernest, *Grand Chamberlain to King Carol (Reinstated 11 September 1950)*

1939

1940

1 June   **800th Anniversary of Portuguese Independence**
MONTEIRO, HE Senhor Armindo Rodrigues de Sttau, *Portuguese Ambassador in London*

1941–1942

1943

10 November   **Visit of HRH to Britain**
IRAQ, HRH Abdul Ilah, Regent of, GCMG

1944–1945

1946

24 September   **Visit of a Special Mission from Nepal**
RANA, HE General Shamsher Jang Bahadur, GBE, KCSI, KCIE, *Minister and Commander-in-Chief of Nepal*

10 December   LUXEMBOURG, HRH Charlotte, Grand Duchess of, *on returning to Luxembourg after wartime exile in Britain*

COLBAN, HE Monsieur Erik, *on retirement from post of Norwegian Ambassador in London*

1947–1949

1950

7 March   **Visit to Britain of President Auriol of the French Republic**
MASSIGLI, René Lucien Daniel KBE, *French Ambassador in London*

21 November   **Visit to Britain of Queen Juliana of the Netherlands**
NETHERLANDS, HRH Bernhard, The Prince of the, GBE
BAUD, Jean Chrétien, Baron, CVO, *Grand Officer on special service to Queen Juliana*
VAN TUYLL VAN SEROOSKERKEN, Baroness Cornelie Marie, *Grand Mistress to Queen Juliana*
ROST VAN TONNINGEN, Vice-Admiral Nicolaas Albertus, CBE, *Master of the Military Household*
MICHIELS VAN VERDUYNEN, HE Jonkheer Edgar Frederik Marie Justin, *Netherlands Ambassador in London*
VAN TUYLL VAN SEROOSKERKEN VAN ZUYLEN, Baron Frederik Christiaan Constanijn, *Lord Chamberlain*

1951

8 May   **Visit to Britain of King Frederik IX and Queen Ingrid of Denmark**
REVENTLOW, HE Eduard Vilhelm Sophus Christian, Count, *Danish Ambassador in London*
DANNESKIOLD-SAMSØE, Dowager Countess Fanny, *Grand Mistress to Queen Ingrid*
VEST, Commodore Johan Vilhelm Filip, KCVO, *Marshal of the Court*

5 June	**Visit to Britain of King Haakon VII of Norway**
	PREBENSEN, HE Monsieur Per Preben, CBE, *Norwegian Ambassador*

1952

6 May	MONIZ DE ARAGAO, HE Senhor José Joaquim de, CBE, *Brazilian Ambassador in London and Doyen of the Diplomatic Corps*
24 September	IRAQ, HM King Feisal II of, on his visit to Balmoral

1953

2 April	**On conclusion of King Hussein's stay in Britain**
	JORDAN, HM King Hussein I of
19 December	**Visit of the Queen and the Duke of Edinburgh to Tonga**
	TONGA, HM Queen Salote Tupou, GBE, of

1954

28 June	**State Visit to Britain of King Gustav VI Adolf and Queen Louise of Sweden**
	CEDERSCHIÖLD, Lieutenant-General Hugo Montgomery, KBE, MVO
	HÄGGLÖF, HE Mr Bo Gunnar Richardson, *Swedish Ambassador in London*
	RALAMB, Baroness Louise Elizabeth Charlotta, *Mistress of the Robes*
	WETTER, Rear-Admiral Sten Erik Pison, Royal Swedish Navy, *First Marshal of the Court*
14 October	**State Visit to Britain of Emperor Haile Selassie I**
	HARAR, HIH Prince Makonnen, Duke of
	RETTA, HE Ato Abbebe, *Ethiopian Ambassador in London*
	HABTE-WOLD, HE Ato Aklilou, *Foreign Minister*
	WOLDE-YOHANNES, HE Wolde Guiorguis, *Minister of Justice*

1955

24 June	**State Visit of the Queen and the Duke of Edinburgh to Norway**
	NORWAY, HRH Harald, Prince of, (later King Harald V)
	BOMMEN, Arne Vincent, KCVO, *Private Secretary to King Haakon VII of Norway*
	JACOBSEN, Vice-Admiral Johannes Espeland, OBE, *Commander-in-Chief, Royal Norwegian Navy*
	SMITH-KIELLAND, Lieutenant-Colonel Ingvald Marillus Emil, KCVO, *Lord Chamberlain*
	MOTZFELDT, Major-General Birger Frederik, CVO, OBE, *Air Commander, Norway*
25 October	**State Visit to Britain of President Craveiro Lopes of the Republic of Portugal**
	DE BRION, Rear-Admiral Nuno Frederico, CVO, OBE, *Commander-in-Chief, Naval Home Forces*
	THEOTONIO PEREIRA, HE Senhor Pedro, *Portuguese Ambassador in London*
	FARRAJOTA ROCHETA, HE Manuel, *Director General, Political Affairs, Foreign Ministry*

1956

8 June	**State Visit of the Queen and the Duke of Edinburgh to Sweden**
	EKEBERG, HE Lars Birger, *Marshal of the Realm*
	HESON ERICSON, Vice-Admiral Stig, *Commander-in-Chief, Royal Swedish Navy*
	FRIIS, Lieutenant-General Torsten, *Governor of Royal Palaces*
	VON HEIDENSTAM, Rolf Magnus, KCVO, *Lord in Waiting*
	RUDEBECK, Mme. Carin Helen Astrid, *Mistress of the Robes*
	RUDEBECK, Nils Fredrik Louis, KCVO, KBE, *Grand Chamberlain*
16 July	**State Visit to Britain of King Feisal II of Iraq**
	BAKIR, HE Abdullah, *Chief of the Royal Diwan*
	KADRY, HE Tahsin, KCVO, OBE, *Chief Master of Ceremonies*
	ZEID, HRH Al-Amir Ibn Al-Hussein, GBE, *Iraqi Ambassador in London*

1957

18 February	**State Visit of the Queen and the Duke of Edinburgh to Portugal**
	BOTELHO, General Afonso Talaia Lapa de Sousa, *Commanding National Republic Guard*
	BRAZÃO, Eduardo, KCVO, *Director National Secretariat of Information*
	REBELO VALENTE DE CARVALHO, General José Maria, MC, *Military Governor of Lisbon*
	PEREIRA DA CUNHA, Vasco, *Secretary General, Ministry of Foreign Affairs*
	PALMELLA, HE Domingos de Souza e Holstein Beck, Duke of, *Former Ambassador in London*
	PALMELLA, Maria do Carmo Pinheiro de Souza e Holstein Beck, Duchess of
	PINA, General Luiz Maria da Camara, OBE, *Former Chief of Army Staff*

8 April	**State Visit of the Queen and the Duke of Edinburgh to France** BILLÈRES, René, *Minister of Education* CHAUVEL, HE Monsieur Jean-Michel, GCMG, *French Ambassador in London* GILBERT, Jules, *Minister of the Interior* BOURGÈS-MAUNOURY, Maurice Jean Marie, DSO, *Minister of National Defence*
21 May	**State Visit of the Queen and the Duke of Edinburgh to Denmark** ANDERSEN, Lieutenant-General Tage, *Commander-in-Chief, Royal Danish Air Force* BARDENFLETH, Gunnar, *Private Secretary to King Frederik IX of Denmark* STEENSEN-LETH, HE Mr Vincens, *Danish Ambassador in London*

1958

25 March	**State Visit of the Queen and the Duke of Edinburgh to the Netherlands** NETHERLANDS, HRH Beatrix Wilhelmina Armgard, Crown Princess of the, (later Queen Beatrix) VAN WICKEVOORT CROMMELIN, Mme. Marie-Louise Johanna Daisy, *Mistress of the Robes* VAN HARDENBROEK, Gijsbert Carel Duco, Baron, *Grand Master of the Household* PAHUD DE MORTANGES, Lieutenant-General Charles Ferdinand, *Master of the Military Household* DE SMETH VAN PALLANDT, Baroness Louise Adolphine Jacqueline, *Lady of the Bedchamber* STIKKER, HE Mr Dirk Uipko, GBE, *Netherlands Ambassador in London* REPELAER VAN DRIEL VAN DER WILLIGEN, Mme. Wilhelmina Adolphine, *Lady in Waiting*
13 May	**State Visit to Britain of President Gronchi of Italy** MOCCIA, HE Oscar, *Secretary General of the Italian Presidency* ZOPPI, HE Conte Vittorio, *Italian Ambassador in London*
20 October	**State Visit to Britain of President Heuss of the Federal Republic of Germany** HERWATH VON BITTENFELD, HE Herr Hans-Heinrich, *German Ambassador in London* BLEEK, Karl Theodor, *State Secretary to the Presidency*

1959

5 May	**State Visit to Britain of Mohammad Reza Shah Pahlavi, Shahanshah of Iran** GHARAGOZLOU, HE Mohsen, *Director General of Court Protocol* GHODS-NAKHAI, HE Mr Hossein, *Iranian Ambassador in London*

1960

5 April	**State Visit to Britain of the President of the French Republic and Madame de Gaulle** DE COURCEL, Louis Geoffroy, Baron, MC, *Secretary General of the Presidency*
16 July	**State Visit to Britain of King Bhumibol Adulyade and Queen Sirikit of Thailand** MALAKUL, HE Mom Luang Peekdhip, *Thai Ambassador in London*
19 July	NARONG, General Luang Sura, *Chief ADC General* SRIVISAR, HE Phya, *Privy Counsellor*
17 October	**State Visit to Britain of King Mahendra and Queen Ratna of Nepal** MALLA, Major-General Sher Bahadur, *Principal Military Secretary* MANANDHAR, HE Rama Prasad, CBE, *Nepalese Ambassador in London* RAJBHANDARY, Kaji Pushpa Raj, *Principal Personal Secretary*

1961

26 February	**State Visit of the Queen and the Duke of Edinburgh to Nepal** RANA, Shamsher Jang Bahadur, General Nir, KBE, *Commander-in-Chief, Royal Nepal Army* SINGH, Sarda Hangsa Man, *Principal secretary*
2 March	**State Visit of the Queen and the Duke of Edinburgh to Iran** ALAVI MUQADDAM, HE Lieutenant-General Mehdi Coli, *Minister of the Interior* ALA, Hussain, CMG, *Minister of the Court*
29 April	**State Visit of the Queen and the Duke of Edinburgh to Italy** ANDREOTTI, Dr Giulio, *Minister of Defence* FOLCHI, Professor Alberto Enrico, *Minister of Tourism* SCELBA, Mario, *Minister of the Interior*

1962

10 July	**State Visit to Britain of President Tubman of Liberia and Mrs Tubman** ANDERSON, Senator James Ande Norman, *President of Liberian Senate* BREWER, HE Mr George Tilmon, *Liberian Ambassador in London*

16 October   **State Visit to Edinburgh of King Olav V of Norway**
SKAUG, HE Mr Arne, *Norwegian Ambassador in London*

1963

14 May   **State Visit to Britain of King Baudouin I and Queen Fabiola of the Belgians**
DE LIGNE, HH Princess Philippine Marie Cecile Doulce, OBE, *Lady in Waiting to Queen Fabiola*
DU PARC LOCMARIA, Gatien Gabriel Jean Marie, Comte, CVO, *Master of Court Ceremonies*
SCHÖLLER, André Marie Louis, *Grand Marshal of the Court*
DE THIER, HE Monsieur Jacques, *Belgian Ambassador in London*

9 July   **State Visit to Britain of King Paul I and Queen Frederika of the Hellenes**
CAROLOU, Madame Mary C., *Grand Mistress to Queen Frederika*
MELAS, HE Mr Michael, *Greek Ambassador in London*

1964

26 May   **State Visit to Britain of President Abboud of the Republic of the Sudan**
HUSSEIN, HE Amin Ahmed, *Sudanese Ambassador in London*

1965

1 February   **State Visit to Ethiopia of the Queen and the Duke of Edinburgh**
ALEMAYEHOU, HE Haddis, *Ethiopian Ambassador in London*
KASSA, HH Dejazmach Asseratte Medhin, *Governor General of Eritrea*
MENGESHA, Lieutenant-General Merid, *Of the Suite attached*
SEYOUM, Dejazmach Mengesha, *Governor General of Tigre*
SILESHI, HE Ras Mesfin, *Deputy Governor General of Shoa Province*
WOLD, HE Taffara Worq Kidane, *Minister of the Imperial Court*

18 May   **State Visit to Germany of the Queen and the Duke of Edinburgh**
BLANKENHORN, HE Herr Herbert Adolf Heinrich, *German Ambassador in London*
ETZDORF, Hasso von, *Ambassador attached to The Queen's suite*

13 July   **State Visit to Britain of the President of Chile and Señora de Frei**
SANTA CRUZ, HE Señor Don Victor Ralph Andrew, *Chilean Ambassador in London*

1966

9 May   **State Visit to Belgium of the Queen and the Duke of Edinburgh**
LIÈGE, HRH Prince Albert of, (later King Albert II)
VAN DEN BOSCH, HE Jean Baptiste Emanuel Remie Marie, Baron, *Belgian Ambassador in London*
BOUSSEMAERE, Lieutenant-General Paul Marcel Charles, *Military Chief of the Household*
MOLITOR, André Philippe Jules, *Private Secretary*
LIMBURG-STIRUM, Charles Gaetan, Count de, *Master of the Household*

17 May   **State Visit to Britain of the President of the Federal Republic of Austria and Frau Jonas**
SCHÖNER, HE Dr Josef Andreas, *Austrian Ambassador in London*
TRESCHER, Dr Karl, *Chief of Cabinet of the President*

20 May   SCHWARZENBERG, Dr Johannes Erkinger, *Formerly Austrian Ambassador in London*

19 July   **State Visit to Britain of King Hussein I of Jordan and Princess Muna Al Hussein**
NASSER, HH The Sharif Hussein bin, *Chief of Royal Hashemite Cabinet*
AL-SATI, HE Dr Shawkat, *Private Physician*
NUSEIBEH, HE Mr Anwar, *Jordanian Ambassador in London*

1967

9 May   **State Visit to Britain of King Faisal of Saudi Arabia**
AL-HELAISSI, HE Sheikh Abdulrahman, *Saudi Arabian Ambassador in London*
PHARAON, HE Dr Rashad, *Counsellor to King Faisal*

1 November   **State Visit to Britain of the President of Turkey and Madame Sunay**
BAYÜLKEN, HE Mr Umit Halük, *Turkish Ambassador in London*

1968

1 November   **State Visit to Brazil of the Queen and the Duke of Edinburgh**
ABREU-SODRÉ, Roberto, *Governor of São Paulo*
CORREA AFFONSO DA COSTA, HE Senhor Sergio, *Brazilian Ambassador in London*
NEGRÃO DE LIMA, Dr Francesco, *Governor of State of Guanabara*

PACHECO, Deputy Rondon, *Head of President's Civil Household*
PORTELLA DE MELLO, Brigadier-General Jayme, *Head of President's Military Household*

11 November **State Visit to Chile of the Queen and the Duke of Edinburgh**
PEREZ-ZUJOVIC, Edmundo, *Minister of the Interior*

22 November CLASEN, HE Monsieur André, *Luxembourg Ambassador in London, as Doyen of the Diplomatic Corps*

1969

22 April **State Visit to Britain of President Saragat of Italy**
ORLANDI-CONTUCCI, Corrado, *Head of Protocol*
MANZINI, HE Signor Raimondo, *Italian Ambassador in London*

5 May **State Visit to Austria of the Queen, the Duke of Edinburgh and Princess Anne**
JIRESCH, Dr Roland, *Head of Department, Chancellor's Office*
PLATZER, Dr Wilfried, *Permanent Under Secretary, Ministry of Foreign Affairs*

15 July **State Visit to Britain of President Kekkonen of Finland and Madame Kekkonen**
HANNIKAINEN, Heikki Juhani, *Chief of Protocol*
WARTIOVAARA, HE Mr Otso Uclevi, *Finnish Ambassador in London*

1970

9 March **The Queen's Visit to Tonga**
TONGA, HM King Taufa'ahau Tupou IV of, KCMG, KBE

1971

5 October **State Visit to Britain of Emperor Hirohito and Empress Nagako of Japan**
IRIE, HE Sukemasa, *Grand Chamberlain*
SHIMA, HE Shigenobu, *Grand Master of Ceremonies*
USAMI, HE Takeshi, *Grand Steward of the Imperial Household*
YUKAWA, HE Mr Morio, *Japanese Ambassador in London*

18 October **State Visit to Turkey of the Queen, the Duke of Edinburgh and Princess Anne**
KUNERALP, HE Mr Zeki, *Turkish Ambassador in London*
TAGMAÇ, General Memduh, *Chief of the General Staff*

7 December **State Visit to Britain of King Zahir of Afghanistan**
MAHMUD-GHAZI, HRH Sardar Zalmay, *Afghan Ambassador in London*
WALI, HRH General Sardar Abdul, *Commander, Central Forces*

1972

10 February **State Visit to Thailand of the Queen and the Duke of Edinburgh**
CHARUSATHIAN, General Prapass, *Deputy Chairman National Executive Council and Chairman Reception Committee*
DISKUL, Admiral Prince Galwarnadis, *ADC General*
ISRASENA NA AYUDHA, Kalya, *Lord Chamberlain*
SUPHAMONGKHON, Dr Konthi, *Thai Ambassador in London*
YUGALA, HRH Prince Phanubhandhu, *Senior Prince of the Chakri Dynasty*

22 February **State Visit to Malaysia of the Queen, the Duke of Edinburgh and Princess Anne**
HAMZAH BIN HAJI ABU SAMAH, Dato HJ, *Minister in Attendance*
AZIZ BIN YEOP, HE Tan Sri Abdul, *Malaysian High Commissioner in London*

29 February **State Visit to Brunei of the Queen, the Duke of Edinburgh and Princess Anne**
OMAR ALI SAIFUDDIN, Duli Yang Teremat Mulia Paduka Seri Bejawan Sultan Sir Muda, KCMG, *Father of the Sultan*

11 April **State Visit to Britain of Queen Juliana and Prince Bernhard of the Netherlands**
GEVERS, HE Baron Willem Johan Gysbert, *Netherlands Ambassador in London*
LYNDEN, HE Baron Jacob Jan Lodewyk van, *Grand Master of the Household*
SCHAPER, HE Lieutenant-General Heye, DFC, *Adjutant-General and Chief of the Military Household*
SWEERTS DE LANDAS WYBORGH, HE Baroness Elisabeth Lucie, *Mistress of the Robes*

15 May **State Visit to France of the Queen and the Duke of Edinburgh**
FREY, M. Roger, *Minister of Regional Development*
JOBERT, M. Michel, *Secretary General of the Presidency*
JUILLET, M. Pierre Armand, *Chargé de Mission of the Presidency*

13 June **State Visit to Britain of Grand Duke Jean and Grand Duchess Charlotte of Luxembourg**
MUYSER, M. Guy de, *Marshal of the Court*
PHILIPPE, HE Monsieur André, *Luxembourg Ambassador in London*

17 October	**State Visit to Yugoslavia of the Queen and the Duke of Edinburgh** KOMAR, Dr Slavko, *Minister in Attendance* VIDIC, HE Mr Dobrivoje, *Yugoslav Ambassador in London*
24 October	**State Visit to Britain of President Heinemann of the Federal Republic of Germany and Frau Heinemann** SPANGENBERG, Herr Dietrich Georg Otto Gerhard, CBE, *Head of Federal Presidency* HASE, HE Herr Karl Günther von, KCMG, *German Ambassador in London*

1973

3 April	**State Visit to Britain of President Echeverria of Mexico and Señora de Echeverria** GAVITO, HE Señor Vicente Sanchez, *Mexican Ambassador in London*
5 June	**Visit to Portugal by the Duke of Edinburgh for 600th Anniversary of the Anglo-Portuguese Alliance** DE FARIA, HE Senhor Antonio Leite, *Portuguese Ambassador in London*
11 December	**State Visit to Britain of President Mobuto of Zaïre** KANINDA, HE Monsieur Mpumbua Tshingomba, *Zaïrean Ambassador in London*

1974

30 April	**State Visit to Britain of Queen Margrethe II of Denmark and Prince Henrik** DENMARK, HRH Henrik, The Prince of KRISTIANSEN, HE Erling Engelbrecht, *Danish Ambassador in London* KNUTH-WINTERFELDT, Count Kield, *Lord Chamberlain*
9 July	**State Visit to Britain of the Yang DiPertuan Agong and the Raja Permaisuri Agong of Malaysia** ZAHIRUDDIN BIN SYED HASSAN, HE Tan Sri Syed, *Malaysian High Commissioner in London*

1975

24 February	**State Visit to Mexico of the Queen and the Duke of Edinburgh** MARGÁIN, HE Senhor Lic Hugo Benigno, *Mexican Ambassador in London* PALENCIA, Señor Lic Mario Moya, *Minister of the Interior* CERVANTES DEL RIO, Señor Lic Hugo, *Minister of the Presidency*
7 May	**State Visit to Japan of the Queen and the Duke of Edinburgh** JAPAN, HRH Crown Prince Akihito of, (later Emperor Akihito) MORI, HE Mr Haruki, *Japanese Ambassador in London* NAKAGAWA, Toru, *Head of Suite of Honour*
8 July	**State Visit to Britain of King Carl XVI Gustaf of Sweden** MURRAY, Lieutenant-General Charles Gustaf Uno Malcolm, *Head of the King's Staff* VON DER ESCH, Carl Gosta Bjorn Joachim, *Lord Chamberlain* WACHTMEISTER, Count Thomas, *Retiring Lord Chamberlain* JÖDAHL, HE Mr Ole, *Swedish Ambassador in London*

1976

4 May	**State Visit to Britain of President Geisel of Brazil and Senhora Geisel** CAMPOS, HE Senhor Roberto de Oliveira, *Brazilian Ambassador in London*
24 May	**State Visit to Finland of the Queen and the Duke of Edinburgh** WRIGHT, Professor Georg Henrik von, *Head of Suite* TÖTTERMAN, HE Dr Richard, *Finnish Ambassador in London*
22 June	**State Visit to Britain of President Giscard d'Estang of the French Republic and Madame Giscard d'Estang** PIERRE-BROSSOLETTE, M. Claude Jean François, *Secretary General of the Presidency* BEAUMARCHAIS, HE M. Jacques, *French Ambassador in London*
8 November	**State Visit to Luxembourg of the Queen and the Duke of Edinburgh** LUXEMBOURG, HRH Prince Henri of, (later Grand Duke Henri) THORN, M. Gaston Egmont Jean, GCMG, *Prime Minister and Minister for Foreign Affairs*

1977

1978

22 May	**State Visit to Germany of the Queen and the Duke of Edinburgh** FRANK, Dr Paul, *State Secretary* RUETE, HE Herr Hans Hellmuth, *German Ambassador in London*

24 October	**On relinquishing position of Doyen of the Diplomatic Corps** DIMECHKIÉ, HE Monsieur Nadim, *Lebanese Ambassador in London*
14 November	**State Visit to Britain of President Eanes of Portugal** GRANADEIRO, Senhor Henrique, *Head of the President's Household* MARTINS, HE Senhor Armando, *Portuguese Ambassador in London*

1979

28 February	**Visit of the Queen to Eastern Arabia** OMAN, HM Sultan Qaboos bin Said, GCMG, Sultan of
16 May	**State Visit to Denmark of the Queen and the Duke of Edinburgh** SØLVHØJ, Hans Juul, *Lord Chamberlain* WAHL, Mogens Erik, *Chamberlain and Private Secretary* CHRISTIANSEN, HE Mr Jens, *Danish Ambassador in London*

1980

14 October	**State Visit to Italy of the Queen and the Duke of Edinburgh** MACCANICO, Dott.Antonio, *Secretary General of the Presidency* CAGIATI, HE Signor Andrea, *Italian Ambassador in London*
21 October	**State Visit to Tunisia of the Queen and the Duke of Edinburgh** FAROUK, HE Madame Fäika, *Tunisian Ambassador in London*
27 October	**State Visit to Morocco of the Queen and the Duke of Edinburgh** MOROCCO, HRH Crown Prince Sidi Mohammed of, (later King Mohammed VI) MOROCCO, HRH Princess Lalla Meriem of, *King's eldest daughter* EL ALAOUI, General Moulay Hafid, *Minister of the Court* FILALI, HE M. Abdellatif, *Moroccan Ambassador in London*
18 November	**State Visit to Britain of King Birendra and Queen Aishwarya of Nepal** SINGHA, HE Mr Jharendra Narayan, CVO, *Nepalese Ambassador in London*

1981

5 May	**State Visit to Norway of the Queen and the Duke of Edinburgh** WERRING, Mrs Else, *Mistress of the Robes* GRØNVOLD, Mr Odd, *Lord Chamberlain* JACOBSEN, HE Mr F.H., *Norwegian Ambassador in London* HAMRE, General Sverre, *Chief of Defence Staff*
9 June	**State Visit to Britain of King Khaled of Saudi Arabia** AL-NOWAISER, HE Sheikh Mohammed Abdullah, *Chief of the Royal Court* ALMANQOUR, HE Sheikh Nasser Hamad, *Saudi Arabian Ambassador in London* ABDUL WAHAB, HE Sayyid Ahmed, *Chief of Royal Protocol*

1982

16 March	**State Visit to Britain of Qaboos bin Al Said, Sultan of Oman** HABIB, HE Malallah Ali, *Ambassador of Oman in London*
16 November	**State Visit to Britain of Queen Beatrix and Prince Claus of the Netherlands** NETHERLANDS, HRH Prince Claus of the HEEMSKERCK, HE Madame C. Bischoff van, *Mistress of the Robes* JONKMAN, HE Mons. P.J.H., *Master of the Household* HUYDECOPER, HE Jonkheer Jan Louis Reinier, KCVO, *Netherlands Ambassador in London*

1983

25 May	**State Visit to Sweden of the Queen and the Duke of Edinburgh** RUDHOLM, Riksmarskalken Herr Sten, *Marshal of the Realm* SYNNERGREN, Stabsschefen General Stig, *Principal ADC* WACHTMEISTER, Statsfrun Grevinnan Alice Trolle–, *Mistress of The Robes* LEIFLAND, HE Mr Leif, *Swedish Ambassador in London*

1984

26 March	**State Visit to Jordan of the Queen and the Duke of Edinburgh** RAAD bin Zeid El-Hussein, HRH Prince, *Lord Chamberlain* HIKMAT, HE Yanal Omar, *Chief of Royal Protocol*

KASIM, HE Marwan S., *Chief of Royal Hashemite Court*
ABU ODEH, HE Adnan Sa'id, *Minister, Royal Hashemite Court*
TABBARAH, HE Hani Bahjat, *Jordanian Ambassador in London*
JORDAN, HRH Crown Prince Hassan bin Talal of
JORDAN, General HRH Prince Mohammad bin Talal of

10 April **State Visit to Britain of Shaikh Isa bin Sulman Al-Khalifa, Amir of Bahrain**
AL-KHALIFA, HE Mr Abdul Rahman bin Faris, *Ambassador of Bahrain in London*
AL-DOSARI, Mr Yousif Rahma, *Head of the Amiri Court*

23 October **State Visit to Britain of the President of the French Republic and Madame Mitterand**
ATTALI, M. Jacques, *Special Adviser to the President*
MARGERIE, HE M. Emmanuel de, *French Ambassador in London*

1985

22 February **On relinquishing position of Doyen of the Diplomatic Corps**
RICART, HE Señor Alfredo, *Dominican Ambassador in London*

26 March **State Visit to Portugal of the Queen and the Duke of Edinburgh**
HALL-THEMIDO, HE Dr Joao, *Portuguese Ambassador in London*

16 April **State Visit to Britain of Life President Dr Banda of Malawi**
KADZAMIRA, Miss Cecilia Tamanda Eve, *Official Hostess*
MKONA, HE Mr Callisto Matekenya, *Malawi High Commissioner in London*

11 June **State Visit to Britain of President de la Madrid of Mexico and Señora de la Madrid**
CUEVAS CANCINO, HE Señor Francisco, *Mexican Ambassador in London*

12 November **State Visit to Britain of Shaikh Khalifa bin Hamad Al-Thani, Amir of Qatar**
AL KAWARI, HE Issa Ghanim, *Minister of Information and Director of the Amir's Office*
AL-KA'ABI, HE Sherida Sa'ad Jubran, *Qatar Ambassador in London*

1986

17 February **State Visit to Nepal of the Queen and the Duke of Edinburgh**
NEPAL, HRH Princess Prekshya Rajya Laxmi Devi Shah of
PANDEY, HE Mr Ishwar Raj, *Nepalese Ambassador in London*

22 April **State Visit to Britain of King Juan Carlos I and Queen Sofia of Spain**
FERNANDEZ CAMPO, Señor Sabino, *Secretary General of HM's Household*
COTONER Y COTONER, Marques de Mondejar Nicolas, *Head of HM's Household*
PUIGCERVA ROMA, Tte. General Gonzalo, *Head of HM's Military Office*
PUIG DE LA BELLACASA, HE Señor Jose Joaquin, *Spanish Ambassador in London*

1 July **State Visit to Britain of President von Weizsäcker of the Federal Republic of Germany and Freifrau von Weizsäcker**
BLECH, Herr Dr Klaus Wolfgang Gunther, KCMG, *State Secretary, Head of Federal Presidency*
WECHMAR, HE Freiherr Rüdiger von, CBE, *German Ambassador in London*

1987

24 March **State Visit to Britain of King Fahd of Saudi Arabia**
SAUDI ARABIA, HRH Prince Saud Al-Faisal bin Abdulaziz of, GCMG

11 June **On relinquishing position of Doyen of the Diplomatic Corps**
MAMBA, HE Senator the Hon. George Mbikwakhe, *High Commissioner for Swaziland in London, as Doyen of the Diplomatic Corps*

14 July **State Visit to Britain of King Hassan II of Morocco**
MOROCCO, HRH Princess Lalla Asmaa of
GUEDIRA, M. Ahmed-Reda, KBE, *Counsellor to HM*
MOROCCO, HRH Prince Moulay Rachid of
ZENINED, HE M. Abdesselam, *Moroccan Ambassador in London*

1988

12 April **State Visit to Britain of King Olav V of Norway**
BUSCH, HE Mr Rolf Trygave, *Norwegian Ambassador in London*
HAGEN, Knut Magne, GCMG, *Private Secretary*

12 July **State Visit to Britain of President Evren of Turkey**
GÜMRÜKÇÜOGLU, HE Mr Rahmi Kamil, *Turkish Ambassador in London*

17 October **State Visit to Spain of the Queen and the Duke of Edinburgh**
SPAIN, HRH Felipe, Prince of Asturias and Infante of
BARRA, Lieutenant-General Jaime, *Head of Military Household*

8 November	**State Visit to Britain of President Abdou Diouf of Senegal and Madame Abdou Diouf** KA, HE Mr Djibo, *Minister of Planning and Co-operation* FALL, HE General Idrissa, MBE, *Senegalese Ambassador in London*

1989

9 May	**State Visit to Britain of President Babangida of Nigeria and Mrs Babangida** DOVE-EDWIN, HE Mr George, *Nigerian High Commissioner in London*
18 July	**State Visit to Britain of Shaikh Zayed bin Sultan Al-Nahyan, President of United Arab Emirates** SULTAN, bin Zayed Al-Nahyan, HH Shaikh, *Chairman Abu Dhabi Public Works Department* SULAIMAN, HE Dr Khalifa M., *Ambassador of the United Arab Emirates in London*

1990

28 February	PANAYIDES, HE Mr Tasos, *High Commissioner for Cyprus, as Doyen of the Diplomatic Corps*
25 June	**State Visit to Iceland of the Queen and the Duke of Edinburgh** AGUSTSSON, HE Mr Helgi, *Icelandic Ambassador in London* SIGMUNDSSON, Mr Kornelius, *Private Secretary to the President*
23 October	**State Visit to Britain of President Cossiga of Italy and Signora Cossiga** BERLINGUER, Ambassador Sergio, CBE, LVO, *Secretary General of the Presidency* BIANCHERI, HE Signor Boris, *Italian Ambassador in London* FERRETTI, Ambassador Franco, *Head of Protocol*

1991

1992

9 June	**State Visit to France of the Queen and the Duke of Edinburgh** DORIN, HE M. Bernard Jean Robert, *French Ambassador in London* LANG, M. Jack Mathieu Emile, *Mayor of Blois*
19 October	**State Visit to Germany of the Queen and the Duke of Edinburgh** MEYER-LANDRUT, HE Dr Andreas Bruno, *State Secretary* RICHTHOFEN, HE Hermann Manfred Georg, Freiherr von, *German Ambassador in London*
3 November	**State Visit to Britain of the Sultan of Brunei Darussalam and the Raja Isteri** BRUNEI-DARUSSALAM, HRH Prince Jefri Bolkiah of, *Minister of Finance* MUSTAPHA, HE Pengiran Dato Haji, *High Commissioner in London*

1993

23 March	**On relinquishing position of Doyen of the Diplomatic Corps** AL-RAYES, HE Mr Ghazi, *Ambassador of Kuwait in London*
27 April	**State Visit to Britain of President Soares of Portugal and Senhora Soares** NUNES BARATA, Ambassador Joao Diogo Correia Saraiva, CBE, *Chief of the Cabinet* MOREIRA, Professor Adriano Jose Alves, *Vice-President of the Parliament* VAZ PEREIRA, HE Senhor Antonio Augusto, Marques da Costa, *Portuguese Ambassador in London* SAMPAIO, Jorge Fernando Branco, *Mayor of Lisbon* SYDER SANTIAGO, Ambassador Antonio Manuel, *Chief of Protocol* DURAO BARROSO, HE Senhor Jose Manuel, *Minister of Foreign Affairs*

1994

18 March	**On relinquishing position of Doyen of the Diplomatic Corps** ROSALES-RIVERA, HE Dr Mauricio, *Ambassador of El Salvador in London*
5 July	**State Visit to Britain of King Harald V and Queen Sonja of Norway** FORBERG, Mr Lars Petter, *Marshal of the Court* VRAALSEN, HE Mr Tom, *Norwegian Ambassador in London*

1995

23 May	**State Visit to Britain of Sheikh Jabir al-Ahmed al Jabir Al-Sabah, Amir of Kuwait** AL-ATIQI, Mr Abdulrahman, *Counsellor in the Office of the Amir* AL-RIFAE, Mr Mohammed, *Counsellor in the Office of the Amir* AL-DUWAISAN, HE Mr Khaled, *Ambassador of Kuwait in London*

17 October	State Visit to Britain of the President of the Republic of Finland and Mrs Ahtisaari
	BLOMQVIST, HE Mr Leif, *Finnish Ambassador in London*
	KALELA, Mr Jaako, *Secretary General to President*

1996

13 March	BARBARITO, HE Archbishop Luigi, *Apostolic Nuncio, as Doyen of the Diplomatic Corps*
17 May	State Visit to Britain of the President of the French Republic and Madame Chirac
	GUEGUINOU, HE Monsieur Jean, *French Ambassador in London*
28 October	State Visit to Thailand of the Queen and the Duke of Edinburgh
	THAILAND, HRH Crown Prince Maha Vajiralongkorn of
	THAILAND, HRH Princess Maha Chakri Sirindhorn of
	THAILAND, HRH Princess Chulabhorn of

1997

| December | State Visit to Britain of the President of the Federative Republic of Brazil and Senhora Cardoso |
| | BARBOSA, HE Senhor Rubens Antônio, *Brazilian Ambassador in London* |

1998

26 May	State Visit to Britain of Emperor Akihito and Empresss Michiko of Japan
	HAYASHI, HE Mr Sadayuki, *Japanese Ambassador in London*
	KAMAKURA, HE Sadame, *Grand Steward of the Imperial Household*
	WATANABE, HE Makoto, *Grand Chamberlain to the Emperor*
	KARITA, HE Yoshio, *Grand Master of the Ceremonies*
1 December	State Visit to Britain of the President of the Federal Republic of Germany and Frau Herzog
	STAUDACHER, Wilhelm, *State Secretary, Head of the Office of the President*
	VERHEUGEN, Günter, *Minister of State*
	MOLTKE, HE Herr Gerbhardt von, *German Ambassador in London*

1999

19 May	HAMMOUD, HE Monsieur Mahmoud, *Ambassador of Lebanon, as Doyen of the Diplomatic Corps*
22 June	State Visit to Britain of the President of the Republic of Hungary and Madame Arpad Göncz
	STUMPF, Istvan, *Minister in the Prime Minister's Office*
	SZENTIVÁNYI, HE Gabor, *Hungarian Ambassador in London*

2000

16 February	State Visit to Britain of Queen Margrethe II of Denmark and Prince Henrik
	POULSEN, HE Mr Ole Lønsmann, *Danish Ambassador in London*
	HASLUND-CHRISTENSEN, H.E. Major-General Søren, *Lord Chamberlain*
13 March	ANYAOKU, H.E. Chief Eleazar Chukwuemeka, *on retirement as Secretary-General of the Commonwealth*

DCVO & KCVO

1896

8 May	The Queen's visit to Cimiez
	MALAUSSENA, M. le Comte Alziary de, *Mayor of Nice*
30 June	Coronation of Emperor Nicholas II of Russia
	FREDERICKS, Baron Vladimir, *Equerry to the Imperial Russian Court*
	BENCKENDORF, Major-General Count Paul, *Acting Master of the Household*
5 August	Emperor Kuang-Hsü of China's Special Mission
	FONG LI CHING, *in attendance on Li Hung Chang, Special Ambassador to England*
27 August	LUH LOH FUNG, *First Secretary of Li Hung Chang's special mission*

1897

| 26 March | For services on the Occasion of the disaster to the *Drummond Castle* |
| | BARRERA, Vice-Admiral Edouard Pierre Antoine, *Commander-in-Chief and Maritime Prefect of Brest* |

| 28 March | REISCHACH, Hugo, Freiherr von, *Master of the Household to the German Empress Frederick* |

28 March   REISCHACH, Hugo, Freiherr von, *Master of the Household to the German Empress Frederick*

30 June   MENSDORFF-POUILLY-DIECHTRICHSTEIN, Count Albert Victor Julius Joseph Michael von, *Austro-Hungarian Ambassador in London*

12 September   SECKENDORFF, Admiral Baron Albert, *Master of the Household to Prince Henry of Prussia*

1898

5 May   MONTENEGRO, HRH Crown Prince Danilo Alexander of
LEININGEN, HSH Prince Edward Frederick Maximilian John of
ERBACH-SCHOENBERG, Count Gustavus Ernest, Count of

Queen Victoria's visit to Cimiez
GEBHART, General Paul, *Governor of Nice*
LE ROUX, Mons. Gabriel, *Prefect of the Maritime Alps*

26 August   **The Duke of Connaught's attendance at French Military Manoeuvres**
HAGRON, General Alexis Auguste Raphael
CROZIER, Mons. Philippe Marius, *Chief of Protocol*

1899

9 May   **Queen Victoria's visit to Cimiez**
MAIGRET, Vice-Admiral le Comte de, *Maritime Prefect, Cherbourg*

24 June   STRENGE, HE Carl Friedrich von, *Minister of State of the Duchies of Saxe-Coburg and Gotha*

23 November   **HIM's visit to Queen Victoria**
SCHOLL, Major-General Friedrich von, *Aide-de-Camp to the German Emperor*
KNESEBECK, Baron Bodo von dem, *Deputy Master of the Ceremonies*

1900

7 May   **Visit of the Duke of York to Berlin**
ARNIM, Major-General Ferdinand Gustav Hans von, *of 4th Regiment of Prussian Foot Guards*

20 December   HÄNEL, Dr Friedrich Albert, *Geheimer Justizrath, Professor at the University of Kiel*

1901

2 February   **Funeral of Queen Victoria**
LEUTHOLD, HE Professor von, *Surgeon General, Guard Corps and Physician in attendance on the German Emperor*
WEDEL, Count von, *Master of the Horse to the German Emperor*

8 March   PINHA, Vice-Admiral, *in attendance on King Carlos of Portugal*
D'ARNOSO, Count, *Private Secretary to King Carlos*
REINECK, General, *in attendance on King George I of the Hellenes*
DASCHKOFF, Colonel Dimitri, *in attendance on the Hereditary Grand Duke Michael Alexandrovitch of Russia*
THON, Intendant General, *in attendance on King George I of the Hellenes*

King Edward VII's visit to Cronberg
RENVERS, Dr Professor, *Consulting Physician to the Empress Frederick of Prussia*

28 May   **The sending of a deputation from the Emperor to King Edward VII with Colonial equipment for HM's inspection**
MOLTKE, General Count von, *in attendance on the German Emperor*

11 October   **King Edward VII's visit to Denmark**
ZACHARIAE, Rear-Admiral George Hugh Robert
ROSENSTAND, Mons. Frants Wilhelm Ferdinand, *Chamberlain to King Christian IX of Denmark*

1902

14 March   **Visit of the Prince of Wales to Berlin**
LOEWENFELD, Major-General Alfred von, *ADC to the German Emperor*
ROEDER, Eugen von, *Master of the Ceremonies and Chamberlain to the German Emperor*

9 November   ECKHARDSTEIN, Baron Hermann von, *Counsellor and First Secretary of the German Embassy, (created CVO on 28 May 1901 but wrongly gazetted as KCVO, an error which was not corrected.)*

20 December   **Visit of King Carlos to Windsor Castle**
CAPELLO, Rear-Admiral Guilherme Augusto de Brito, *ADC to the King of Portugal*

1903

7 April **King Edward VII's visit to Portugal**
CAPELLO, Rear-Admiral Hermengilde de Brito, *ADC to the King of Portugal*
FERREIRA DO AMARAL, Rear-Admiral Francisco Joaquim, *President of the Royal Geographical Society, Lisbon*
PEREIRA DA CUNHA, Dr Manuel Augusto, *Civil Governor of Lisbon*
DUARTE E SILVA, Colonel Antonio, *Commanding Portuguese Cavalry Regiment No 3*
VEIGA, Señor Francisco Maria da, *Police Magistrate in charge of Police attached to King Edward*
PIMENTEL, Señor Fernando Eduardo de Serpa, *Master of the Household to King Carlos*
D'AVILA, Antonio Jose, Count d'Avila e Bolama, *Lord Mayor of Lisbon*
ALMEIDA, Señor Antonio Joaquim Simoes de, *President, Commercial Association of Lisbon*

13 April **King Edward VII's visit to Gibraltar**
ABDELSADOK, Cid Abderrahman Ben, *Governor of Fez; Special envoy from the Sultan of Morocco*

30 April **King Edward VII's visit to Italy**
CORSINI, Pier Francesco (Dei Principi), Marchese di Lajatico, *Crown Equerry to King Vittorio Emanuele III of Italy*
MAJO, Major-General Pio Carlo di, *Aide-de-Camp*

4 May **King Edward VII's visit to France**
MOLLARD, Mons. Armand, *Director of Protocol, France*

9 October **King Edward VII's visit to Vienna and Marienbad**
CHOLONIEWSKI-MYSZKA, HE Edouard, Count, *Master of Ceremonies to the Emperor of Austria*
KIELMANSEGG, HE Erich Ludwig Friedrich Christian, Count, *Governor of Lower Austria*
LÜTZOW UND SEEDORF, HE Heinrich Joseph Rudolf Gottfried, Count Lützow zu Drey, *Under-Secretary of State for Foreign Affairs*
KAPOS-MÈRE, Kajetan Mérey von, *Under-Secretary of State for Foreign Affairs*
BELLEGARDE, Colonel HE August Maria Rudolf Emanuel Franz, Count, *Master of the Household*
GUDENUS, HE Leopold, Baron von, *Oberjägermeister*
JEDINA, Rear-Admiral Leopold, Ritter von, *attached to King Edward*

1904

10 February **The Marriage of Princess Alice of Albany with Prince Alexander of Teck**
DE WEEDE, Jonkheer Rudolf Everard Willem, *Lord Chamberlain to the Queen Mother of the Netherlands*

18 April **King Edward VII's visit to Denmark**
FRIJS, Julius Benedictus, Count Krag Juel Vind-, *Acting Master of the Horse to King Christian IX*
OLDENBURG, Waldemar, *Over Präsident of Copenhagen*
DANNESKJOLD-SAMSÖE, Christian Conrad Sophus, Count, *Director of the Royal Theatre*
LEMVIGH, Colonel Waldemar Edward, *Commanding Danish Life Guards*
FRIJS, Mogens Christian, Count Krag Juel Vind-
PETERSEN, Eugen, *Chief Commissioner of Police*

28 April **The Prince of Wales's visit to Württemberg**
RÖDER, Major-General Hermann Reinhard, Freiherr von, *Commanding 27th Cavalry Brigade*

1 July **King Edward VII's visit to Kiel**
FISCHEL, Rear-Admiral Max, *Admiral Superintendent of Dockyard, Kiel*
BAUDISSIN, Rear-Admiral Frederick,Count von, *ADC to the German Emperor attached to King Edward VII*
ENGELBRECHTEN, Colonel Maximilian George Frederick Charles von, *Commanding 36th Infantry Brigade*

6 September MENSDORFF-POUILLY, HSH Hugo Alphonse Eduard Emanuel Joseph John Vanceslas, Prince von Dietrichstein zu Nickolsburg, *ADC to Emperor Franz-Joseph of Austria*

King Edward VII's visit to Marienbad
HABRDA, John, Baron von, *Chief Commissioner of Police, Vienna*

9 November BRETEUIL, Henry Charles Joseph, Marquis de
LAU D'ALLEMAND, Alfred Thérèse Armand, Marquis du

21 November **Visit to Britain of King Carlos and Queen Amélie of Portugal**
LANCASTRE, Don Antonio Maria de, *Physician to Their Majesties*

1905

8 March TZOKOW, Dimitry, *Diplomatic Agent of The Prince of Bulgaria*

24 March **The King of Spain's visit to Britain**
BOADO Y MONTES, Commodore Don Leopoldo, *ADC to King Alfonso XIII of Spain*

19 April **HM's Cruise in the Mediterranean**
BAILLOUD, General Maurice Camille, *Commanding the Division at Algiers*

23 April TORCY, General Louis Joseph Gües de, *Commanding the Division at Constantine*

19 May	On relinquishing appointment of Military Attaché to the Imperial Russian Embassy YERMOLOFF, Major-General Nicolas
9 June	The King of Spain's visit to Britain LEON, Colonel Milans del Bosch y Carrio Joaquin Mario, *ADC to King Alfonso XIII*
4 July	Visit of Prince and Princess Arisugawa of Japan ITO YUKICHI, *Master of the Household of Prince Arisugawa of Japan*
19 July	Visit of the Duke of Connaught to Coburg and Gotha to represent HM at the Coming of Age of the Duke of Saxe-Coburg and Gotha RUEXLEBEN, HE Frederick von, *Grand Marshal of the Court of the Duke of Saxe-Coburg and Gotha*
11 October	Visit of Prince Arthur of Connaught to Glücksburg to represent HM at the Marriage of the Duke of Saxe-Coburg and Gotha, Duke of Albany and Princess Victoria Adelaide of Schleswig-Holstein-Sonderburg-Glücksburg RECKE, Carl, Baron von der, *Controller to the Duke of Schleswig-Holstein-Sonderburg-Glücksburg*

1906

18 February	Visit of Lord Chamberlain to Denmark to represent HM at the Funeral of King Christian IX ROTHE, Charles Adolph, *Chamberlain to King Christian IX of Denmark* VEDEL, Axel, *Chamberlain to King Christian IX of Denmark*
20 February	Special Mission of Prince Arthur of Connaught to Japan to invest the Emperor of Japan with the Order of the Garter TAKAMASA, The Marquis Kido, *Grand Chamberlain to the Crown Prince of Japan and Master of Ceremonies*
15 March	KATAOKA, Vice-Admiral Shichiro, *Commander-in-Chief, First Squadron, Imperial Japanese Navy*
16 April	HM's visit to Corfu METAXAS, André, *Prefect of Corfu*
24 April	HM's visit to Greece DIMOPOULO, Major-General Jean, *Commanding the troops at Athens* CONDOURIOTIS, Captain George, Royal Hellenic Navy, *ADC to King George of the Hellenes, attached to the Prince of Wales*
22 May	VILLALOBAR, M.I. Don Rodrigo de Saavedra y Vinent Cueto y O'Neill, Marquis de, CVO, *Counsellor of the Spanish Embassy*
6 June	Visit of the Prince of Wales to Madrid to represent HM at the Marriage of King Alfonso XIII of Spain and Princess Victoria Eugenie of Battenberg PERPIÑAN, HE Emilio de Ojeda y, *Under Secretary of State for Foreign Affairs*
18 June	Visit of the Duke of Connaught to Sweden VIRGIN, Major-General Otto William, *attached to HRH*
22 June	Visit of the Prince of Wales to Trondhjem to represent HM at the Coronation of the King of Norway BORRESEN, Rear-Admiral Urban Jacob Rasmus, *Chief of the Royal Norwegian Naval Staff, attached to HRH*
15 August	HM's visit to Kronberg FLOTOW, Theodor, Baron von, *Comptroller to Prince Frederick Charles of Hesse*
20 September	Visit of the Duke of Connaught to Karlsruhe to invest HRH with the Order of the Garter and to represent HM at the Golden Wedding of the Grand Duke and Duchess of Baden SPONECK, Major-General Count von, *Master of the Horse to the Grand Duke of Baden* BECKHOLTZ, HE William Offensandt von, *Constable of the Palace*

1907

9 February	DETAILLE, Edouard, *Member of the Institute of France*
23 February	On relinquishing appointment of Naval Attaché at German Embassy COERPER, Rear-Admiral Charles William Henry, CVO
9 April	HM's visit to Spain MORGADO, Captain Don José, Royal Spanish Navy, *Commandant General of the 2nd Division* MONTANEZ, Captain Don Emilio Fiol y, Royal Spanish Navy, *Commandant General of the Arsenal, Cartagena* ROBLEDO, Señor Don Manuel Ledesma y, *Physician to King Alfonso XIII of Spain*
7 May	Visit to England of General Prince Sadanaru Fushimi representing Emperor Mutsuhito of Japan BABA, Saburo, *Grand Master of the Household*
13 June	Visit to London of King Frederik VIII and Queen Louise of Denmark HOVGAARD, Captain Andreas Peter, *Naval ADC to the King of Denmark*
27 June	MARION, General Charles Louis Raoul, *Commanding 3rd Cavalry Division, French Army*
3 August	Visit of the Coast Squadron of the Royal Swedish Navy to Cowes EHRENSVÄRD, Commodore Count Carl August

14 August	**HM's visit to Wilhelmshöhe** BITTER, Colonel Max von, MVO, *attached to King Edward VII*
7 October	**Visit of the Duke of Connaught to Karlsruhe to represent HM at the Funeral of the Grand Duke of Baden** SCHICKFUS, Lieutenant-General HE Emil von, *Commanding 29th Division, German Army*
12 November	**Visit to Windsor of the German Emperor and Empress, King and Queen of Prussia** INGENOHL, Rear-Admiral Ernest Henry Frederick, *Commanding HIM's Yacht Hohenzollern*

1908

30 January	WACHTMEISTER, Count Carl Axel Baltzar, *Equerry to the late King Oscar II of Sweden*
25 April	**HM's visit to Denmark** WARMING, John Eugene Bulow, *Chancellor of Copenhagen University* OXHOLM, Charles Arthur George O'Neill, *Chamberlain to King Frederik VIII of Denmark, attached to King Edward*
27 April	**HM's visit to Sweden** PEGELOW, Frederick William Henrik, *Director General of Swedish State Railways* HINTZE, Theodore, *Chief Commissioner of Police* ROSENBLAD, Colonel Charles, Baron, *Commanding Swedish Dragoons of the Guard, attached to King Edward* PEYRON, Captain Frederick Maurice de, CVO, Royal Swedish Navy, *Chamberlain to the Queen of Sweden, attached to Queen Alexandra*
2 May	**HM's visit to Norway** GRÖNVOLD, Hans Aimar Mow, *Private Secretary to King Haakon VII of Norway* MELLBYE, John Egeberg, *attached to King Edward VII*
10 June	**HM's visit to Russia** NILOFF, HE Vice-Admiral Constantine, *Chief of the Naval Staff to the Emperor of Russia* GORTCHACOW, HSH Prince Constantine, *attached to Queen Alexandra* DEDULINE, Major-General Wladimir, *Governor of the Palace* MOSSOLOFF, Major-General Alexander, *Chief of the Chancery of the Ministry of the Court* ESSEN, Rear-Admiral Nicholas, *Commanding Naval Flotilla at Reval* HEIDEN, Rear-Admiral Alexander, Count, *attached to King Edward VII* SAVINSKY, Alexander, *Master of the Ceremonies* ORLOFF, Prince Wladimir, CVO, *ADC and Chief of the Military Cabinet of HIM* KOROSTOWETZ, Colonel Ismael de, *Governor of Estonia*
21 August	**HM's visit to Ischl** GLÜCKMANN, HE Lieutenant-General Charles, *Commanding 3rd Division, Austro-Hungarian Army* COLARD, Major-General Hermann von, *Commanding 6th Infantry Brigade, Austro-Hungarian Army*
23 September	**On relinquishing appointment of Military Attaché at Japanese Embassy** SHIBA, Major-General Goro, CVO
26 September	KOZIELL, Stanislas Poklewski, CVO, *Counsellor to the Imperial Russian Embassy*
17 November	**Visit to Windsor of King Gustav V and Queen Victoria of Sweden** THOTT, Baron Otto Gustave Erik, CVO, *Chamberlain to King Gustav V* ROSENBLAD, Eberhard, *Equerry of the Court*

1909

12 February	**HM's visit to Berlin** DOHNA, Major-General Alphons, Count zu, *Commanding the Cavalry Division of Guards* MARSCHALL, Major-General Wolf, Baron, CVO, *attached to King Edward VII* ESEBECK, Walter Asmus Charles Frederick Eberhard, Baron von, *Deputy Master of the Horse to the German Emperor, King of Prussia* KIRSCHNER, Martin Charles Augustus, *Chief Burgomaster of Berlin*
29 April	**HM's visit to King Vittorio Emanuele III of Italy at Baia** GARELLI, Rear-Admiral Aristide, CVO, *ADC General to the King of Italy*
5 August	**Visit of Emperor Nicholas II of Russia** CHAGHIN, Rear-Admiral John, CVO, *Commanding Imperial Yacht Standart* **HM's visit to Marienbad** LIECHTENSTEIN, HSH Prince Edouard Victor von und zu, *Prefect of Marienbad* BRONN, Lieutenant-Colonel Charles George, Baron von, CVO, *Equerry to The Emperor of Austria, King of Hungary* SLATIN PASHA, Lieutenant-General Baron Sir Rudolf Charles, KCMG, CVO, CB, *of the Egyptian Army: Inspector General of Anglo-Egyptian Sudan* HELMER, Gilbert John, CVO, *Abbot of Tepl (Did not receive the honour of Knighthood)*

16 November	Visit to Windsor of King Manoel II of Portugal PIMENTEL, Captain D. Fernando de Serpa, CVO, *ADC to King Manoel II*
20 November	LIANG-CHANG, HE Sir Chentung, KCMG, *Member of the Privy Council of China and of the Imperial Naval Commission*

1910

1911

6 April	Garter Mission of Prince Arthur of Connaught to the Prince Regent of Bavaria WURTZBURG, Colonel HE Louis Charles Veit, Baron von, *Chamberlain to King of Bavaria*
22 April	Visit of Prince Arthur of Connaught to Rome to represent HM at the Jubilee Celebration of Italian Unity TROMBI, Lieutenant-General HE Count Vittorio, *Honorary ADC to the King of Italy*
15 May	Visit to England of the German Emperor, King of Prussia for the Unveiling of the Queen Victoria Memorial ILBERG, Dr Friedrich Wilhelm Carl von, *Physician to HIM*
7 September	FITAURARI, HE Hapta Giorgis, *Minister for War, Abyssinia*
23 November	King George V and Queen Mary's visit to Egypt en route to India ISMAIL DJENAY BEY, *Master of Ceremonies to Sultan of Turkey*
2 December	Mission of Prince Alexander of Teck to Bangkok to represent HM at the Coronation of the King of Siam SRIVARAWONGS, Phya, *Assistant Private Secretary to the King of Siam* VIJITVONGS VUDDHIKRAI PHYA, Lieutenant-General Phya, *ADC to the King of Siam* BHIJAI SONGKRAM, Major-General Phya, *ADC to the King of Siam*

1912

24 January	TM's visit to Malta MOREAU, Rear-Admiral Paul, *commanded 2nd Division of 2nd Squadron, French Fleet*
30 January	TM's visit to Gibraltar MEHEMMED, ben Mohammad el Guebbas Cid, *of the Mission from the Sultan of Morocco*
31 January	MUNOZ COBO SERRANO, HE Lieutenant-General Don Diego, *Governor of Algeciras* SANTALO Y SAENZ DE TEFADA, Vice-Admiral Don Enrique, *commanded Spanish Squadron*
23 May	Visit of Prince Arthur of Connaught to Copenhagen to represent HM at the Funeral of King Frederik VIII of Denmark ARENDRUP, Major-General Albert, *Chamberlain to the King of Denmark*
12 September	Visit of Prince Arthur of Connaught to Japan to represent HM at the Funeral of Emperor Mutsuhito INABA, Viscount Masanao, *Master of Ceremonies to The Emperor*

1913

24 May	TM's visit to Berlin to attend the Marriage of the Duke of Brunswick and Luneburg and Princess Viktoria Luise of Prussia BAERECKE, Dr Herman, *Commissioner of Police, Berlin* CHELIUS, Major-General Oscar von, *General ADC to the German Emperor, King of Prussia* GONTARD, Major-General Hans Albert Henry Frederick Augustus von, *General ADC to the German Emperor, King of Prussia* WANGENHEIM, HE Ernest Maximilian Leon, Baron von, *Chamberlain to HIM*
26 May	TM's visit to Neu-Strelitz YORRY, Captain George von, *Chamberlain to the Grand Duke of Mecklenberg-Strelitz*

1914

24 April	HM's visit to France PICHON, Adolphe, *Secretary General in the Household of the President of the French Republic* ROUYER, Vice-Admiral Albert, *Commanded French Naval Escort*

1915

15 February	On leaving the Russian Embassy in London to take up the appointment of Russian Minister in Persia ETTER, Nicholas de

1916

26 May   **Visit of the Prince of Wales to the Italian Front**
BITETTO, Vice-Admiral Luigi Cito Filomarino, Principe di, *ADC General*

1917

5 July   **Visit of the Duke of Connaught to Italy**
MERLI MIGLIETTI, Lieutenant-General Count Giulio, *ADC*

1918

21 September   **On relinquishing appointment as Naval Attaché, French Embassy, London**
LOSTENDE, Rear-Admiral Mercier de

28 October   **Visit to London of Prince Yorihito of Higashi Fushimi**
HONDA, Kumataro, *Counsellor of Japanese Embassy in London*
IIDA, Vice-Admiral Hisatsune, *Naval Attaché, Japanese Embassy in London*
TANAKA, General Kunishige, CB, *Military Attaché, Japanese Embassy in London*

30 November   **HM's visit to France**
LABUSSIERE, André Michel
RENAULT, Lieutenant-Colonel Conrad Edmond
RIEUX, Colonel Ernest Marie de, *ADC to President*
VERDINI, Colonel Alexandre Louis Sauveur, *Military Commandant of the Elysée*

1919

28 July   **Reception by HM of a Sudanese Mission**
ALI EL MIRGHANI, El Sayed, KCMG

4 November   **The Shah of Persia's visit to Britain**
ASSADOLLAH MIRZA CHOHAB-ED-DOWLEH, HH Prince, *Master of Ceremonies to HIM*
MOFAKHAMED DOWLEH, HE, *Persian Minister in Italy*
MOHAMMED HUSSEIN MIRZA, General HH Prince, *ADC*

5 November   **Reception by HM of a Chilean Mission**
IÑIGUEZ, Don Pedro Felipe

1920

5 July   **For services rendered to the late Crown Princess of Sweden**
RUDEBECK, Captain Nils Frederik Louis de

7 December   **Visit to Britain of King Christian X of Denmark**
GJERNALS, Colonel Christian Frederik, *Chief of the Military Household to HM*

1921

9 May   **Visit to London of the Crown Prince of Japan**
ITAMY, Lieutenant-General Matsuo, *Military Attaché, Japanese Embassy*
TAGUCHI, Rear-Admiral Hisamori, *of Japanese Third Fleet*

4 July   **Visit to London of King Albert I and Queen Elizabeth of the Belgians**
DE RIDDER, Alfred

1922

22 April   **Prince of Wales's visit to Japan**
YOSHIDA, Lieutenant-General Toyohiko, CB, CMG, *attached to Prince of Wales's Suite*
HYAKUTAKE, Admiral Saburo, KCMG, *Commanded Japanese Third Squadron*

13 May   **HM's visit to Belgium**
COSTERMANS, Henri Jules Charles Adolphe
GONNE, Louis Charles Jérôme, *Director General, Ministry of Justice*
INGENBLEEK, Jules
RAMAIX, Gaston Marie Joseph Athanase Ghislain de

9 June   **The Duke of York's visit to Belgrade for the Marriage of King Alexander I of the Serbs, Croats and Slovenes and Princess Marie of Roumania**
DAMIANOVITCH, General Yevrem Y., *ADC to the King*

18 October	The Duke of York's visit to Bucharest to represent HM at the Coronation of King Ferdinand I of Roumania
	MIRCESCU, General Ludovic, CMG, *attached to HRH*

1923

14 May	HM's visit to Italy

ACERBO, HE Giacomo, *Under Secretary of State of the President of the Council*
CITO DI TORRECUSO, Colonel Duke Ferdinand, CMG, *Chamberlain to the Queen of Italy*
COSTA DI TRINITA, Count Paolo, *Chamberlain to the Queen of Italy*
CREMONESI, Filippo, *Royal Commissioner for the City of Rome*
GUERRIERI, Count Edgardo, *Master of the Hunt to King Vittorio Emanuele III*
JORI, General Ilio, CB, *ADC General*
MACCHI DI CELLERE, Count Carlo, *Master of Ceremonies*
MONTALTO, Don Massimo, Duke of Fragnito, *Master of Ceremonies*
MONTASINI, Brigadier-General Emilio, *Senior ADC to the Duke of Aosta*
PANTANO, Edoardo, *President of the International Institute of Agriculture*
PUGLIESE, Lieutenant-General Emanuele, CB, DSO, *Commanding Military Division, Verona*
RICCI, Corrado, *President of the Royal Institute of Archaelogy, Rome*
SANCTIS, Vittorio Emmanuele de, *Secretary General to the Minister of the Italian Court*
SOLARO DEL BORGO, Nobile Alberto (Dei Marchesi di Borgo San Dalmazzo), *Master of the Horse*
ZOCCOLETTI, Doctor Riccardo, *Prefect of Rome*

4 November	The Wedding of the Crown Prince of Sweden and Lady Louise Mountbatten

OTRANTE, Charles Louis Fouché, Duke d', *Equerry to King Gustav V of Sweden*
POSSE, Colonel Count Göran Edvard Henning, *Chief of Military Staff of the Crown Prince*
SANDGREN, Carl Johan, *Private Secretary to King Gustav V*

1924

15 May	Visit to Britain of King Ferdinand I and Queen Marie of Roumania
	RADESCU, General Nicolas, CMG, *ADC to King Ferdinand*
25 June	Visit to Britain of the Sultan of Perak
	PERAK, HH Paduka Sri Sultan Iskandar Shah, Sultan of, KCMG
28 June	Visit to Britain of King Christian X of Denmark
	COLD, Rear-Admiral Frederik, *Chief of Naval Staff to King Christian X of Denmark*

1925

10 July	Visit to Britain of the Besar of Negri Sembilan
	NEGRI SEMBILAN, HH Yang-di-Pertuan, Besar of, KCMG
22 July	On relinquishing appointment of French Military Attaché
	PANOUSE, Brigadier-General Artus Henri Louis, Vicomte de la, KCMG, CB
18 August	The Prince of Wales's visit to Uruguay
	BUIST, Brigadier-General William Camilo
14 September	The Prince of Wales's visit to Chile
	SEARLE, Rear-Admiral Alfredo Ricardo
	CHARPIN, General Pedro
23 September	The Prince of Wales's visit to Argentina
	DAIREAUX, Rear-Admiral Don Carlos
	VACAREZZA, Brigadier-General Don Juan Esteban
28 November	Funeral of Queen Alexandra
	CONDIESCO, General Nicolas, DSO, *ADC to the Crown Prince of Roumania*
	GRUT, Major-General Torben, *Chief of Military Staff of King Christian X of Denmark*

1926

1927

19 May	Visit to Britain of President Doumergue of the French Republic
	DESPRÈS, Brigadier-General Ambroise Marie Félix Maurice
	PEYCELON, Gilbert
	VEDEL, Rear-Admiral Marie Joseph Fernand Adolphe
6 July	Visit to Britain of King Fuad I of Egypt
	ANIS PASHA, HE Amin, *Deputy Chief of Royal Cabinet*

HASSANEIN BEY, HE Ahmed Mohamed, MBE, *First Chamberlain to the King*
SHAHIN PASHA, HE Dr Mohamed, *Physician to the King*

1928

15 March — **Visit to Britain of King Amanullah of Afghanistan**
GHULAM DASTAGIR KHAN, Brigadier-General, *General Officer in charge of Afghan Palaces*
HABIBULLA KHAN, Lieutenant-General, *Assistant Afghan Minister for War*

1929

10 May — **The Duke of Gloucester's Garter Mission to Japan**
MATSUDAIRA, Viscount Keimin, CBE, *Secretary to Imperial Cabinet*
NINOMIYA, Major-General Harushige, DSO, *Director of Intelligence, Japanese Army*
OHMINATO, Vice-Admiral Naotaro, CMG, *Japanese Navy Department*
SAIONJI, Hachiro, *Imperial Mews Department*
SEKIYA, Teizaburo, *Imperial Japanese Household*
TOKUGAWA, Iyemasa, OBE, *Imperial Japanese Diplomatic Service*
YOSHIDA, Shigeru, *Under Secretary of State, Foreign Affairs*

11 June — **For Services in connection with the Prince of Wales's Journey from Africa to England (Dec 1928)**
DESPRET, Maurice Jules Antoine

7 December — **Visit to Britain of King Christian X of Denmark**
DALBERG, Colonel Olüf, *Military Household of the King of Denmark*

1930

28 June — **Visit to London of Prince Takamatsu of Japan**
HORI, Yoshiatsu
ISHIKAWA, Iwakichi, *Comptroller of the Household*
YAMAGATA, Commander Takeo, *Master of Ceremonies*

30 October — MULUGETA, Ras, CBE (HE Dejazmach Kassa)

1931

11 February — **Visit of the Prince of Wales to Peru**
MONTAGNE, Colonel Ernesto, *Minister of Foreign Affairs*

22 February — **Visit of the Prince of Wales to Chile**
SCHROEDERS, Rear-Admiral Edgardo von, *Minister of Marine*

8 March — **Visit of the Prince of Wales to Brazil**
FRAGOSO, General Augusto Tarso, *Chief of Staff, Brazilian Army*

13 March — **Visit of the Prince of Wales to Argentina**
FLIESS, Vice-Admiral Don Enrique
SARTORI, General of Division Don Emilio

1932

28 August — **Visit to Balmoral of the King of the Hellenes**
LEVIDIS, Major Dimitri, *Private Secretary*

5 October — HEIDENSTAM, Captain Rolf von

26 October — **Visit of the Prince of Wales to Denmark**
GYLDENKRONE, Commodore Baron Einar Marius, CVO, *Chamberlain to King Christian X of Denmark*

13 December — **Visit of King Christian X of Denmark to Britain**
TRAMPE, Captain Count Christopher, *Master of Ceremonies*

1933

20 June — **Visit of King Feisal I of Iraq to Britain**
TASHIN BEG QADRI, *Chief Master of Ceremonies to King of Iraq*

1934

13 June — **Member of Special Mission to announce the Accession of King Leopold III of the Belgians**
VAN STRYDONCK, Lieutenant-General Victor Jean Clement

15 September	**Visit to Britain of Queen Marie of Roumania** ZWIEDINEK, Colonel Eugène, *Master of the Court*
27 November	**For his services to the Grand Duchess Xenia Alexandrovna of Russia in the Settlement of the Halila Property** RYTI, Risto
28 November	**The Marriage of The Duke and Duchess of Kent** STRENOPOULOS, Germanos Pandeli, *Metropolitan of Thyateira and Exarch of West and Northern Europe*

1935–1936

1937

16 November	**Visit of King Leopold III of the Belgians to Britain** CAPELLE, Baron Robert PAPEIANS DE MORCHOVEN, Charles

1938

9 January	**The Marriage of the Crown Prince Paul of Greece and Princess Friederike of Hanover** PAPPARIGOPOULO, Vice-Admiral Etienne, *attached to the Duke of Kent*
19 July	**TM's visit to France** BILLOTTE, General Gaston Henri Gustave, CB, *Military Governor of Paris* BOURRET, General Victor, *Commander Paris Military Region* BOUSCAT, General (Air) Rene, *Chief of Air Ministry* BRACONNIER, General Joseph Eugène Charles, *Military Secretary General of the Presidency* VILLEY-DESMESERETS, Lieutenant Achille Joseph Henri, *Prefect of the Seine* DEVIN, Vice-Admiral Léon Henri, *Commander-in-Chief, Prefect Maritime* FAILLIOT, René Georges Henri, *Former President of the Municipal Council, Paris* LANGERON, Roger, *Prefect of Police, Paris* LAUNAY, Gordon Henri Adolphe de, *President, Municipal Council, Paris* LOZE, Maurice Henry, *Chief of Protocol* MAGRE, André, *General Secretary of the Presidency* RIVET, Vice-Admiral Léon, *Prefect Maritime, Cherbourg*
15 November	**Visit to Britain of King Carol II of Roumania** CHEVALIER DE FLONDOR, Constantin, *Marshal of the Roumanian Court* GHYKA, Matila, MC, *Minister, Roumanian Legation* MIHAIL, General de Brigade Gheorghe, *Premier ADC*

1939

21 March	**Visit to Britain of President Lebrun of the French Republic** CAMBON, Roger Paul Jules, *Counsellor, French Embassy* BRESSY, Pierre Gaston Prosper, *Minister Plenipotentiary*
18 July	ANTITCH, Milan, *Minister of the Royal Court of Yugoslavia*

1940

1 June	**800th Anniversary of Portuguese Independence** MOTTA, General Amilcar de Castro Abreu, *Head of Military Household of the President*

1941–1945

1946

10 May	WAHBA, Sheikh Hafiz, *Ambassador of Saudi Arabia*

1947

1948

11 October	**Visit of Princess Margaret to the Netherlands to represent HM at the Inauguration of Princess Juliana as Queen** VAN HOLTHE, Admiral Jonkheer Edzard Jacob, CBE

1949

1950

7 March   **Visit to Britain of President Auriol of the French Republic**
BAUDET, Philippe, *Minister, French Embassy, London*
DUMAINE, Jacques, CVO, *Minister*
FORGEOT, Jean, *Secretary General to the President*
GROSSIN, General Paul Joseph Roger, *Military Secretary General to the Presidency*
KOSCZUISKO-MORIZET, Jacques, *Director of the Cabinet of the President*
VERBRUGGE VAN'S GRAVENDEEL, Madame Louise Odilie, *Lady in Waiting to the Queen*

1951

8 May   **Visit to Britain of King Frederik IX and Queen Ingrid of Denmark**
SCHACK, Countess Karin Brigitte Ulrica Henny Ellen, *Lady in Waiting*
ANDRESON, Commodore Helge Christian Marius, *ADC*
VESTBIRK, Jens Anthon, *Consul-General for Denmark*

5 June   **Visit to Britain of King Haakon VII of Norway**
BOMMEN, Arne Vincent, *Private Secretary*
SMITH-KIELLAND, Lieutenant-Colonel Ingnald Marillus Emil, *Marshal of the Court*

1952–1953

1954

28 June   **State Visit to Britain of King Gustav VI Adolf and Queen Louise of Sweden**
STEUCH, Mlle Brita Charlotte Louise Wilhelmina, *Lady in Waiting to Queen Louise*
HALLENBORG, Carl Albert Magnus, *Consul-General for Sweden, London*

14 October   **State Visit to Britain of Emperor Haile Selassie I of Ethiopia**
SILASHI, HE General Dedjazmach Masfin
TAFARA-WORQ, HE Ato Kidane Wold, MVO, *Private Secretary*

1955

24 June   **State Visit to Norway of Queen Elizabeth II and the Duke of Edinburgh**
ANDVORD, Captain Richard, Norwegian Army, *Chamberlain and Equerry*
ØSTGAARD, Colonel Nikolai Ramm, Norwegian Army, *Chief Military Household to Crown Prince*

25 October   **State Visit to Britain of President Craveiro Lopez of Portugal**
FRANCA, Colonel Bento da, *Head of President's Military Establishment*
SARMENTO RODRIGUES, Captain Manoel Maria, OBE, *commanded the 'Bartolomeu Dias'*

1956

8 June   **State Visit to Sweden of the Queen and the Duke of Edinburgh**
REUTERSWÄRD, Mlle Carolina Elisabeth Christina, *Lady in Waiting*
WETTER, Mme Maja
ANDERBERG, Rear-Admiral Erik Magnus, *Commanding Officer, East Coast Naval District*
DYRSSEN, Major-General Gustaf Peder Wilhelm, *Military Governor of Stockholm*
ESSEN, Baron Fritz Wilhelm von, *Master of the Horse*
LAGERBERG, Joen, *Chief Master of Ceremonies*
LEWENHAUPT, Count Carl Gustaf Sixtenson, *Lord in Waiting*
LJUNGDAHL, Lieutenant-General Axel Georg, CBE, *Commander-in-Chief, Royal Swedish Air Force*

16 July   **State Visit of King Feisal II of Iraq to Britain**
AL-ASKARI, Tarik, *Iraqi Minister at Court of St James's*

1957

18 February   **State Visit of the Queen and the Duke of Edinburgh to Portugal**
BARRETO, Lieutenant-Colonel Alvaro de Salvaçao, OBE, *Lord Mayor of Lisbon*
OREY PEREIRA COUTINHO, Luis Maria José d', *Private Secretary to the President*
CUNHA, Colonel Mario Raphael, *Commandant General, Public Security Police*
CARREIRO DE FREITAS, Anthero, *Chief of Protocol*
PINTO DE LEMOS, Abilio, *Assistant Political Director General*
GUSMÃO MADEIRA, Mário, *Civil Governor of Lisbon*
SÁ NOGUEIRA, Commander Salvador de, OBE, *Military and Air Attaché*

8 April	State Visit of the Queen and the Duke of Edinburgh to France

BENEDETTI, Jean-Baptiste, *Chief of Police (North)*
BORDENEUVE, Jacques, *Secretary, Ministry of Foreign Affairs*
DUFRESNE DE LA CHAUVINIÈRE, Emile Edouard, *Chief of Protocol*
GANEVAL, Général de Corps d'Armée Jean Joseph Xavier Emile, MC, *Secretary General (Military) to the President*
GENEBRIER, Roger Pierre, MVO, *Chief of Police*
MORLIÈRE, Général de Corps d'Armée Louis Constant, *Commander 1st (Paris) Region*
PELLETIER, Emile Amedée, OBE, *Chief of Police (Seine)*
RUAIS, Pierre Adolphe Emile, *President, Municipal Council, Paris*
THOMAS, Eugène, *Secretary of State for the PTT*
MERVEILLEUX DU VIGNAUX, Charles Henri, *Secretary General (Civil) to the President*

21 May	State Visit of the Queen and the Duke of Edinburgh to Denmark

AHLEFELDT-LAURVIG, Countess Thea Ottilia
BOAS, Vilhelm, *Permanent Under Secretary of State, Ministry of Justice*
CHRISTENSEN, Sigurd, *Under Secretary of State, Ministry of Foreign Affairs*
GREVE, Commodore Svend Bernhard Vilhelm Johannes, *Principal Naval ADC*
GYTH, Colonel Volmer Leopold Undset, OBE, *Principal ADC*
HVALKOF, Major-General Frode Lund, *Commander-in-Chief, Copenhagen*
NEHENDAM, Dean Michael Nicolaj, *Clerk of the Closet*
PONTOPPIDAN, Rear-Admiral Svend Erik, OBE, *Flag Officer, Coastal Defences*
SCHAUMBURG, Major Ernst Maria Eegholm, *Master of the Horse*
WEIKOP, Ove Vilhelm, *Mayor of Copenhagen*
WERN, Captain Holger Eigil, MVO, *Royal Danish Navy, Master of Ceremonies*

1958

25 March	State Visit of the Queen and the Duke of Edinburgh to the Netherlands

ROELL, Jonkvrouwe Catharina Elisabeth Boudewina, *Private Secretary*
VAN ZINNICQ BERGMANN, Lieutenant-Colonel Robert Jacques Emile Marie, CVO, DFC, *ADC and Master of the Household*
FORTUYN, Rear-Admiral Gerrit Bernard, *Commander-in-Chief, Netherlands Home Station*
GRAAFF, Frans Adriaan de, *Private Secretary to Prince Bernhard*
HALL, Gijsbert van, *Burgomaster of Amsterdam*
BISCHOFF VAN HEEMSKERCK, Major Willem Frederick Karel, *Crown Equerry and ADC*
VAN DER HOEVEN, Jan, *Private Secretary*
KLAASESZ, Jan, *Queen's Commissioner, South Holland*
KOLFSCHOTEN, Henri Anthony Melchior Tieleman, *Burgomaster of The Hague*
PANHUYS, Jonkheer Willem Ernest van, *Head of Foreign Minister's Cabinet*
PRINSEN, Marinus Jacobus, *Queen's Commissioner, North Holland*
LYNDEN VAN SANDENBURG, Count Constant Theodore Emmo van, *Queen's Commissioner for Utrecht*
SICKINGHE, Jonkheer Pieter Feyo Onno Rembt., *Superintendent Amsterdam and Hague Royal Palaces and Director of Royal Archives*
VAN WALSUM, Gerard Ewout, *Burgomaster of Rotterdam*

13 May	State Visit to Britain of President Gronchi of Italy

BIGI, HE Admiral Luciano, *Military Counsellor*
CIPPICO, HE Tristram Alvise, *Diplomatic Counsellor*
PRUNAS, Don Pasquale, *Minister-Counsellor, Italian Embassy*

20 October	State Visit to Britain of President Heuss of the Federal Republic of Germany

BOTT, Hans, *Deputy Under-Secretary of State to Presidency*
BRAUN, Baron Sigismund Maximilian Wernher Gustav Magnus, Freiherr von, *Chief of Protocol Department*
RITTER, Joachim-Friedrich, *Minister at German Embassy*

1959

5 May	State Visit to Britain of the Shahanshah of Iran

AFKHAMI, Admiral Houshang, *ADC*
ATABAI, Abolfath, *Master of the Hunt*
AYADI, Major-General Doctor Abdolkarim, *Special Physician*
ESHTODAKH, Major-General Issa, *ADC*
GHAVAM, Mohamed, *Iranian Minister, London*
NASSIRI, Major-General Nemat, *ADC*
SADRI, Doctor Mohsen, *ADC*

1960

5 April	State Visit to Britain of President de Gaulle of the French Republic and Madame de Gaulle

GROUT DE BEAUFORT, Général de Corps d'Armée Guy, *Chief Staff Officer*
BROUILLET, René Alexis, *Director of the Secretariat of the President*

CHANCEL, Ludovic Charles, *Chief of Protocol*
MARCHAL, Contre-Amiral Victor Bernard, *Naval Attaché*
WAPLER, Arnauld, *Minister, French Embassy*

19 July	**State Visit to Britain of King Bhumibol Adulyade and Queen Sirikit of Thailand** ISARASENA, Kalya, *Grand Chamberlain*
17 October	**State Visit to Britain of King Mahendra and Queen Ratna of Nepal** RAJBHANDARY, Meersubba Madhusudan, *Private Secretary*

1961

26 February	**State Visit of the Queen and the Duke of Edinburgh to Nepal** KHANAL, Professor Yadu Nath, *Secretary of Ministry of Foreign Affairs* KHATRI, Major-General Padam Bahadur, *Secretary of Ministry of Defence* PANT, Doctor Yadav Prasad, *Secretary of Ministry of Finance* RANA, General Arjun Shamsher Jang Bahadur, *ADC General* RANA, General Arun Shamsher Jang Bahadur, *ADC General* RANA, General Kiran Shamsher Jang Bahadur, KBE, *ADC General* RANA, Major-General Kshetra Bikram, CIE, *Secretary of the Home Ministry* RANA, General Nara Shamsher Jang Bahadur, *ADC General* RANA, General Samrajya Shamsher Jang Bahadur, *ADC General* SHAH, Lieutenant-General Surendra Bahadur, *Chief of Staff of the Army* SHRESTHA, Mir Subba Ishwari Man, *Secretary to the King* MAN SINGH, Sardar Prakat, OBE, *Chief of Protocol*
2 March	**State Visit of the Queen and the Duke of Edinburgh to Iran** AKBAR, HE Muhammad, *Master of Ceremonies at the Imperial Court of Iran* FOROUD, HE Sayyed Fathollah, *Mayor of Tehran* HIRAD, HE Rahim, *Head of Imperial Private Secretariat* KIA, Lieutenant-General Ali NABIL, HE Fazlullah, *Master of the Court of the Empress* QARAGUZLU, Hussein Ali, *Civil Aide* ADL TABATABAI, HE Murteza, *Chief of Protocol*
29 April	**State Visit of the Queen and the Duke of Edinburgh to Italy** MOCCIA, Madame Alfina, *in charge of domestic arrangements at Palace of Quirinale* FRACASSI DI TORRE ROSSANO, Marchesa Maria CATENACCI, Corrado Francesco Eduardo, *Counsellor of State* CHECCHIA, General Alfonso, *Commander Central Military Region* CIOCCETTI, Doctor Urbano, *Mayor of Rome* FERRI, General Guido, *President, Italian Red Cross* PECORI GIRALDI, Admiral Conte Corso, *Chief of Naval Staff* GUALANO, General Antonio, *Chief of Army Staff* NAPOLI, General Silvio, *Chief of Air Staff* REMONDINO, General Aldo, *Military Counsellor to President of the Council* ROBERTI, Conte Guerino, *Minister Plenipotentiary* ROSSI, General Aldo, *Chief of Staff* VICARI, Angelo, *Chief of Police*

1962

10 July	**State Visit to Britain of the President of the Republic of Liberia and Mrs Tubman** DUKULY, The Hon. Momolu, *Adviser on International Affairs* MORGAN, The Hon. James Edwin, CVO, *Chief of Protocol*
16 October	**State Visit to Edinburgh of King Olav V of Norway** GRØNVOLD, Odd, MVO, *Marshal of the Court* PETTERSEN, Commodore Thorleif, MBE, *Principal ADC to the King* THORESEN, Captain Wilhelm Oscar, OBE, *Commanding HM Yacht* Norge

1963

14 May	**State Visit to Britain of King Baudouin I and Queen Fabiola of the Belgians** GRAAFFE, Jacques, *Minister Counsellor* HENRY, Major-General Albert Victor Ghislain, *Chief of Air Staff and ADC* KERREMANS, Charles Amand Oscar, *Minister attached to Grand Marshal*
9 July	**State Visit to Britain of King Paul I and Queen Frederika of the Hellenes** DOXIADIS, Thomas, *Physician* PAPANICOLAOU, Sophocles, *Comptroller of Civil List*

1964

26 May **State Visit to Britain of President Abboud of the Republic of the Sudan**
EL DAW, Sayed Ahmed Hassan, *Lord Chamberlain*

1965

1 February **State Visit to Ethiopia of the Queen and the Duke of Edinburgh**
DESTA, Princess Sebla-Wengel, *Of the Suite attached*
ABAI, Fitaurari Haregot, *Lord Mayor of Asmara*
ABEBE, Ato Mesfin, *Assistant Minister, in charge of Protocol*
AMANUEL, HE Fitaurari Worqneh Walde, *Vice-Minister, Imperial Court*
BERHE, Fitaurari Tesfai Yohannes, *Deputy Governor General of Eritrea*
DEMISSE, Brigadier-General Assefa, *Principal ADC*
DOUBBALA, Major-General Diresie, *Commissioner of Police, Addis Ababa*
HEYWOT, Ato Zande Gabre, *Lord Mayor of Addis Ababa*
MARIAM, Major-General Debebe Haile, *Commanding Officer, Imperial Bodyguard*
SELASSIE, Lieutenant-General Nega Haile, *Governor General of Begemdir and Simien*
SELASSIE, Dejazmach Tschai Ingus, *Governor General of Gojjam*

12 February **State Visit to the Republic of Sudan of the Queen and the Duke of Edinburgh**
BAGHIR, Sayed Baghir el Sayed Mohammed, *Under Secretary, Ministry of Foreign Affairs*
EL KHAWAD, Major-General Mohammed Ahmed, *Commander-in-Chief*

18 May **State Visit to Germany of the Queen and the Duke of Edinburgh**
BOEHM, Brigadier-General Karl Eberhard, *Military Member of German Suite specially attached*
EINSIEDLER, Albert, *Deputy Head, Office of the Federal President*
HOLLEBEN, Ehrenfried von, *Chief of Protocol Department*
HÖLZL, Professor Dr Josef, *State Secretary, Ministry of the Interior*
OEFTERING, Professor Dr Heinz Maria, *First President, Federal German Railroad*
TRETTNER, General Heinrich, *Inspector General of the Bundeswehr*

13 July **State Visit to Britain of the President of Chile and Señora de Frei**
CISTERNAS, General Pedro, *Chief of General Staff, Chilean Army*

1966

9 May **State Visit to Belgium of the Queen and the Duke of Edinburgh**
DE LIGNE, HRH Princess Leontine, *Lady in Waiting*
CLERDENT, Pierre Charles Jean Joseph OBE, *Governor of Province of Liège*
DANLOY, Major-General Georges Marie Gérard Urbain Joseph, MBE, *ADC*
DECLERCK, Richard August Frans, *Governor of the Province of Antwerp*
DESSART, Lieutenant-General Ulisse Maximilien Joseph, *Chief of Staff, Armed Forces*
ENGELEN, Lieutenant-General Ernest Victor Louis Eugène, *ADC*
PARC LOCMARIA, Antoine Guillaume F.M.G., Comte du, *Master of the Household*
DE MERODE, HRH Prince Werner Paul Marie Ghislain, *Minister Plenipotentiary*
NAZE, Fernand Marcel, *Keeper of the Privy Purse*
NÉEFF, Jean Fernand Marie Joseph Eugène Benoit Ghislain de, *Governor of the Province of Brabant*
ROMAN, Colonel Pierre Victor Edouard, MC, *ADC to the King of the Belgians*
OUTRYVE D'YDEWALLE, Pierre Joseph Marie Ghislain van, *Governor of Province of West Flanders*

17 May **State Visit to Britain of the President of the Federal Republic of Austria and Frau Jonas**
ENDER, Dr Rudolf, *Chief of Protocol*

19 July **State Visit to Britain of King Hussein I of Jordan and Princess Muna Al Hussein**
EL-HUSSEIN, HRH Prince Ra'ad Zeid, *Principal Secretary*
AL-SATI, HE Iklil, *Grand Master of Ceremonies*

1967

9 May **State Visit to Britain of King Faisal of Saudi Arabia**
ALSAYED ALY, HE Dr Rifat, *Personal Physician*
NOWAISER, HE Sheikh Mohamed, *Head of the Private Secretariat*
ABDUL WAHAB, HE Ahmed, *Chamberlain and Chief of Protocol*

1 November **State Visit to Britain of the President of Turkey and Madame Sunay**
ALPAN, HE M. Cihad, *Secretary General, Presidential Office*

1968

1 November **State Visit to Brazil of the Queen and the Duke of Edinburgh to Brazil**
AMARAC MURTINHO, Wladimir do, *Chief Ministry Official, Brazilia*

BARROS, Carlos Jacyntho, *Chief of Ceremonial*
CHERMONT, Jayme Sloan, *Gentleman attached to the Queen*
DA COSTA GOMIDE, Wadjô, *Mayor of Brazilia*
MAGALHÃES FIGUEIREDO, Rear-Admiral Sylvio de, *Gentleman attached to the Duke of Edinburgh*
VIANNA MOOG, Brigadier-General Olavo, *Gentleman attached to the Queen*

11 November　**State Visit to Chile of the Queen and the Duke of Edinburgh**
BARROS GONZÁLEZ, Admiral Ramón, *Commander-in-Chief of the Navy*
CASTILLO, General Sergio, *Commander-in-Chief of the Army*
ERRÁZURIZ WARD, General Maximo, *Commander-in-Chief of the Air Force*
FERNANDEZ DIAS, Manuel, *Lord Mayor of Santiago*
FONTECILLA CONCHA, Mariano, *Director of Protocol*
HUERTA CELIS, General Vicente, *Director General of Caribineros*
JORQUERA GOYCOLEA, Rear-Admiral Pedro, *Chief of Defence Staff*
LARRAIN GARCIA-MORENO, Sergio, *President, Chilean-British Institute*
OELCKERS-HOLLSTEIN, Colonel Emilio, *Director General, Security Services*
RIVERA-MANNHEIM, Rear-Admiral Quintilio, *Naval ADC to the Queen*
VICENTE VICENTE, Enrique, *Prefect of Valparaiso*

1969

22 April　**State Visit to Britain of President Saragat of Italy**
RICCIULLI, Pasquale, CMG, *Minister at Italian Embassy*
STADERINI, Ettore, *Diplomatic Adviser*

5 May　**State Vvisit to Austria of the Queen, the Duke of Edinburgh and Princess Anne**
BACH, General Albert Friedrich, *In attendance on the Queen*
BEROLDINGEN, Dr Lukas, *Head of Protocol, Chancellor's Office*
CALICE, Dr Heinrich Franz Rudolf, *Gentleman-in-Attendance on the Queen*
HOLAUBEK, Josef, *Police President of Vienna*
KORAB, Dr Wilhelm, *Deputy Director, President's Private Office*
MEZNIK, Dr Friedrich, *Head of Information, Chancellor's Office*
PETERLUNGER, Dr Oswald, *Head of Security*
WINTERSTEIN, Dr Claus, *Head of Protocol*

15 July　**State Visit to Britain of the President of Finland and Madame Kekkonen**
EHRNROOTH, Mrs Louise, *Lady-in-Waiting to Mme Kekkonen*
LEVO, Colonel Urpo Jurva, CBE, *ADC*
TÖTTERMAN, Dr Richard Evert Björnson, OBE, *Secretary General to the President*

1970

1971

5 October　**State Visit to Britain of Emperor Hirohito and Empress Nagako of Japan**
KITASHIRAKAWA, Madame Sachiko, *Chief Lady in Waiting*
NAKASHIMA, Nobuyuki, *Minister Plenipotentiary, Japanese Embassy*
NISHINO, Dr Shigetaka, *Chief Physician*
TOKUGAWA, Yoshihiro, *Vice Grand Chamberlain*

18 October　**State Visit to Turkey of the Queen, the Duke of Edinburgh and Princess Anne**
BARLAS, HE Ekrem, *Mayor of Province of Ankara*
BATUR, General Muhsin, *Commander of Air Force*
EKEN, General Kemalettin, *Commander of Gendarmerie*
EYICEOGLU, Admiral Celal, *Commander of Naval Forces*
GURLER, General Faruk, *Commander of Land Forces*
HALEFOGLU, Vahit, *attached to the Queen*
KIRTETEPE, Sedat, *Director General of Security*
TUMER, Vice-Admiral Nejat, *attached to the Duke of Edinburgh*
VERSAN, HE Veysel, *First Deputy Secretary General of Protocol*

7 December　**State Visit to Britain of King Zahir of Afghanistan**
GHAUSSY, HE Dr Saadollah, *Chef de Protocol*
WAZIR, Lieutenant-General Mirza-Khan, *First ADC*

1972

10 February　**State Visit to Thailand of the Queen and the Duke of Edinburgh**
RANGSIT, HSH Princess Vibhavadi, *Member of the Thai Suite*
BHAKDI, Luang Dithakar, *Member of the Thai Suite*
CHARUSATHIARA, Lieutenant-General Champen, *Deputy ADC General*

KRARIKSH, Poonperm, *Master of the Household*
LADAWAN, Mom Luang Thawisan, *Principal Private Secretary*
SUWANRATH, Puang, *Under Secretary of State for the Interior*
SITAKALIN, Vice-Admiral Abhai

22 February **State Visit to Malaysia of the Queen, the Duke of Edinburgh and Princess Anne**
SHARIFF BIN HAJI IBRAHIM, Datuk Haji Mohamed, *Comptroller of the Royal Household and Private Secretary*
SALLEH BIN ISMAEL, Tan Sri Dato Mohamed, *Inspector General of Police*
MUSTAPHA BIN TUNKU BESAR BURHANUDDIN, Tunku, *Grand Chamberlain*

11 April **State Visit to Britain of Queen Juliana and Prince Bernhard of the Netherlands**
HUYDECOPER, Jonkheer Jan Louis Reinier, *Minister at Netherlands Embassy*

15 May **State Visit to France of the Queen and the Duke of Edinburgh**
BALLADUR, Edouard, *Assistant Secretary General of the Presidency*
CHERIOUX, Jean Georges Adolphe Emile, *President, Council of Paris*
COINTAT, Michel, *Minister of Agriculture*
DOUBLET, Maurice Charles H., *Prefect, Paris Region*
LENOIR, Jacques, *Chief of Police*
MARCELLIN, Raymond, *Minister of the Interior*
PONS, Bernard Claude, *Minister of State for Agriculture*
SENARD, Jacques, *Chief of Protocol, Quai d'Orsay*
THENOZ, General Michel, *Chief of Staff of the Presidency*
VERDIER, Jean, *Prefect of Paris*

13 June **State Visit to Britain of the Grand Duke Jean and Grand Duchess Charlotte of Luxembourg**
MEYERS, Mme Félix, *Lady in Waiting*
KONSBRUCK, M. Guillaume, *Chamberlain*

17 October **State Visit to Yugoslavia of the Queen and the Duke of Edinburgh**
KOSTIC, Dr Dejan, *Chief of Protocol*
MELOVSKI, Milos, *Adviser to President on Foreign Affairs*
SMODLAKA, Dr Sloven, *Acting Chief of Protocol*
VOJINOVIC, Lieutenant-Colonel General Aleksander, *attached to the Queen*
VRHUNEC, Marko, *Chief of President's Cabinet*

24 October **State Visit to Britain of President Heinemann of the Federal Republic of Germany**
CASPARI, Herr Professor Doktor Fritz Eduard, *Deputy Head, Federal Presidency*
SCHMIDT-PAULI, Herr Doktor (Kurt) Edgar Richard Paul von, *Minister Plenipotentiary*
PODEWILS, Count Max, *Chief of Protocol*

1973

3 April **State Visit to Britain of President Echeverria of Mexico**
BERNAL, Ambassador Joaquin, OBE, *Director General of Protocol*
CASTENADA GUTIERREZ, General Jesus, *Chief of Presidential Staff*

11 December **State Visit to Britain of President Mobutu of Zaïre**
RWEMA, Citoyen Bisengimana, *Director of Presidential Office*

1974

30 April **State Visit to Britain of Queen Margrethe II of Denmark and Prince Henrik**
JORGENSEN, Lieutenant-Colonel Ulf Gabel, *Master of Ceremonies to Queen of Denmark*
SCHULZE, Captain Aage Oscar, *First Principal Naval ADC*
GRÜNER, Colonel Christian Gustav Ulrik, *Chamberlain and Principal Staff Officer*
WILLUMSEN, Kjeld, *Minister Plenipotentiary*
DENMARK, HRH Prince Georg of, *Defence Attaché, Royal Danish Embassy*

9 July **State Visit to Britain of the Yang DiPertuan Agung and the Raja Permaisuri Agung of Malaysia**
ISMAIL BIN MOHAMMED, Encik, *Deputy High Commissioner*
MALEK, Datuk Abdul, *Chief of Protocol*
PILLAY, Datuk Dr Raghava Paremeswaran, *Royal Physician*

1975

24 February **State Visit to Mexico of the Queen and the Duke of Edinburgh**
GUTIÉRREZ BARRIOS, Señor Fernando, *Deputy Minister of the Interior*
OVALLE FERNÁNDEZ, Señor Lic Ignacio, *Deputy Minister of the Presidency*
FUENTE RODRIGUEZ, General de Brigade DEM Juan Antonio de la, *Equerry attached to the Queen*
GONZALEZ SOSA, Señor Licenciado Ruben, *Deputy Minister of Foreign Affairs*
ZAPATA LOREDO, Señor Licenciado Fausto, *Deputy Minister of the Presidency*

7 May **State Visit to Japan of the Queen and the Duke of Edinburgh**
MASAKI, Hideki, *Interpreter to the Emperor*

SHIMADZU, Hisanaga, *Superintendent Akasaka Palace*
TOMITA, Tomohiko, *Vice-Grand Steward, Imperial Household*
UCHIDA, Hiroshi, *Chief of Protocol*

8 July **State Visit to Britain of King Carl XVI Gustaf of Sweden**
ÅKERREN, Bengt Olof, *Minister Plenipotentiary*
COLLIANDER, Colonel Bengt Peter Erland, *Marshal of the Court*

1976

4 May **State Visit to Britain of President Geisel of Brazil and Senhora Geisel**
RIBEIRO, Jorge Carlos, *Head of Protocol*

24 May **State Visit to Finland of the Queen and the Duke of Edinburgh**
VALTANEN, Major-General Jaakko, *Adjutant General, Finnish Defence Forces*
KLENBERG, *First ADC*
SIIPONEN, Professor Kauko, *Secretary General to the President*
SUNELL, Ambassador Ossi, *Head of Protocol*

22 June **State Visit to Britain of President Giscard d'Estaing of France and Mme Giscard d'Estaing**
BOUCHARD, M. Jean-Max Pierre Paul, *Minister-Counsellor*

8 November **State Visit to Luxembourg of the Queen and the Duke of Edinburgh**
FRANTZ, Lieutenant-Colonel Germain, *Chamberlain to the Grand Duke*
GREDT, M. Réné, *President, Grand Duke's Estates Administration*
NEUMAN-SIMONS, Madame Andrée, *Lady in Waiting*

1977

1978

22 May **State Visit to Germany of the Queen and the Duke of Edinburgh**
DÖRING, Herr Paul, *Head of Division, President's Office*
DIEDRICH, Herr Willi Edmund, *Chief of Protocol*
EICKHOFF, Dr Ekkehard, *Head of Division, President's Office*
FRANZKE, Dr Peter, *Head of the President's Private Office*
HOLZHEIMER, Herr Franz Hermann Joseph, *Deputy Chief of Protocol*
FREVERT-NIEDERMEIN, General Major Alexander Heinrich, *Honorary Escort*
SCHOELLER, Herr Franz Joachim, *Head of Protocol*

1979

16 May **State Visit to Denmark of the Queen and the Duke of Edinburgh**
ANDERSEN, Rear-Admiral Fritz Carl Heisterberg, *Flag Officer attached to Duke of Edinburgh*
IVERSEN, Colonel Sven-Aage, *First and Principal Naval ADC*
KØNIGSFELDT, Albert Wulff, *Chief of Protocol*
SANDER-LARSEN, Captain Jirgen Vilhelm, *First and Principal Naval ADC*

1980

14 October **State Visit to Italy of the Queen and the Duke of Edinburgh**
CALENDA, Ambassador Carlo, *Diplomatic Counsellor to President*
GUAZZARONI, Ambassador Cesidio, *Counsellor for EC Affairs to President*
MARALDI, Ministro Guglielmo Guerrini, *Deputy Chief of Protocol*
GUIDI, Ministro Marcello, *Chief of Protocol*
BERNARDINI, General Umberto, *President's Military Adviser*

State Visit to Tunisia of the Queen and the Duke of Edinburgh
BOURGUIBA, M. Habib, Junior, *Special Adviser to President*
LAOUITI, M. Allala, *Head of President's Private Office*
KAROUI, M. Abdelmajid, *Director of Presidential Protocol*

State Visit to Morocco of the Queen and the Duke of Edinburgh
MOROCCO, HRH Prince Moulay Abdullah of, *King's brother*
MOROCCO, HRH Princess Lalla Aicha of, *King's sister and ex-Ambassador in London*

18 November **State Visit to Britain of King Birendra and Queen Aishwarya of Nepal**
SINGH, Raja Kumar Deepak Jung Bahadur, *King's brother-in-law*
RAYAMAJHI, Lieutenant-General Dana Gambhir Singh, *Military Secretary*
THAPA, Chiran Shumsher, *Press Secretary*
SINGH, Gehendra Man, *Personal Secretary*
SHRESTHA, Neer Subba Narayan Prasad, *Private Secretary*

1981

5 May   **State Visit to Norway of the Queen and the Duke of Edinburgh**
SMITH-KIELLAND, Mr Ingvald Mareno, *Master of the Household*
HAGEN, Mr Magne, *Deputy Private Secretary*
RØKKE, Colonel Gunnbjørn, *Chief, King's Military Staff*
LIED, Mr Finn, *Chairman, Statoil*
HELSETH, Vice-Admiral R., *Commander South Norway*

1982

16 March   **State Visit to Britain of Qaboos bin Al Said, Sultan of Oman**
AL-MA'AMARI, Brigadier Ali Majid, *First ADC and President of Palace Office*
LANDON, Brigadier James Timothy Whittington, *Counsellor, Omani Embassy, Special Adviser to the Sultan*

16 November   **State Visit to Britain of Queen Beatrix of the Netherlands and Prince Claus**
GRAAFF, Mlle. F.M.de, DBE, *Director of the Queen's Cabinet*
OSIECK, Captain P.W., Royal Netherlands Navy (Retired), *Master of Ceremonies*
TIELEMAN, Mr A.F., *Minister, Netherlands Embassy*

1983

25 May   **State Visit to Sweden of the Queen and the Duke of Edinburgh**
TALLROTH, Tore, *Grand Master of Ceremonies*
AHREN, Lennart, *Marshal of the Court*
LOWENHIELM, Major-General Frederik, *Master of Ceremonies*
BIORCK, Professor Gunnar, *Senior Physician to Royal Household*
FOGELMARCK, Dr Stig, *Keeper of the Royal Collections*
SKIOLDEBRAND, Hans, *Crown Equerry and Master of the Horse*
LEWENHAUPT, Gosta, Count, *Lord in Waiting*
ALGERNON, Rear-Admiral Carl, *Principal ADC*
SILLEN, Ambassador Jan Af, *Chief of Protocol*

1984

26 March   **State Visit to Jordan of the Queen and the Duke of Edinburgh**
DAJANI, HE Major-General Rajai Kamel Wafa, *Secretary General, Royal Hashemite Court*
FARRAJ, Major-General Dr Samir Elias, *King Hussein's Physician*
JORDAN, HRH Prince Abdullah bin Al Hussein of

23 October   **State Visit to Britain of the President of the French Republic and Madame Mitterand**
VAUZELLE, M. Michel, *Spokesman for President*
FERRIERE, M. Jacques Gaultier de la, *Chief of Protocol*
VEDRINE, M. Hubert, *Diplomatic Adviser*
GRENIER, M. Alain, *Minister, French Embassy*

1985

25 March   **State Visit to Portugal of the Queen and the Duke of Edinburgh**
GUIMARAES, Dr Jose Maria Caldeira de Sousa, *Head of President's Civil Household*
HORTA, Vice-Admiral Henrique Silva, *Head, President's Military Household*
SOARES, Ambassador Joaquim Renato Correa Pinto, *Chief of Protocol*
PINTO, General Antonio Avelino Pereira, *Military Escort*

16 April   **State Visit to Britain of Life President Dr Banda of Malawi**
KADZAMIRA, Miss Mary Lilian Chimwemwe
NGWIRI, John R., *Secretary to President and Cabinet*

11 June   **State Visit to Britain of President de la Madrid of Mexico and Señora de la Madrid**
ALONSO, Señor Manuel, *Press Secretary*
BERMADEZ DAVILA, General de Brigade DEM Carlos Humberto, *Chief of Presidential Staff*
GAMBOA PATRON, Señor Emilio, *Private Secretary*

12 November   **State Visit to Britain of Shaikh Khalifa bin Hamad Al-Thani, Amir of Qatar**
AL NOAIMI, Mr Yousef Issa, *Director, Amiri Protocol Department*
AL-WOHAIBI, Mr Abdulrahman A, *Minister Plenipotentiary*

1986

17 February   **State Visit to Nepal of the Queen and the Duke of Edinburgh**
KHANAL, Mr Ranjan Raj, *Principal Secretary*
PANDEY, Lieutenant-General Rishi Kumar, *Military Secretary, Royal Palace*
BANDEL, Mr Lain Singh, *Chancellor, Royal Nepal Academy*

22 April	**State Visit to Britain of King Juan Carlos I and Queen Sophia of Spain**
	BENAUIDES, Señor Jose Ignacio, *Minister Counsellor, Spanish Embassy*
	BLANCO, Señor Manuel, *Head of Security, HM's Household*
	ESCUDERO, Señor Alberto, *Head of Protocol, HM's Household*

1 July	**State Visit to Britain of President von Weizsäcker of the Federal Republic of Germany and Freifrau von Weizsäcker**
	SCHONFELD, Herr Peter Hans Klaus, CMG, *Principal Private Secretary*
	SCHENK, Herr Dr Reinhold, CMG, *Head of Department, Federal Presidency*
	SCHULENBURG, Graf Werner Ludwig Botho Hubertus von der, *Chief of Protocol*
	STEIN, Freiherr Hans H.B.F.W. von, *Minister, Federal German Embassy*

1987

14 July	**State Visit to Britain of King Hassan II of Morocco**
	MOROCCO, HRH Prince Moulay Hassan ben Driss of, KBE
	FREJ, M. Abdelfattah, KBE, *Private Secretary*
	SMILI, M. Bensalem, *Minister of Fisheries*

1988

12 April	**State Visit to Britain of King Olav V of Norway**
	ENGLUND, Brigadier Ole Christian, *Senior Principal Equerry*
	FLAKSTAD, Gunerius, *Marshal of the Court*

17 October	**State Visit to Spain of the Queen and the Duke of Edinburgh**
	FERREIRO, Lieutenant-Colonel José Luis, CVO, *Head of Security*
	GUARDIA, Don Julio de la, *Director, Royal Palaces*
	CHAVARRI, Don Tomas, *Head of State Protocol*
	FRESNO, Don Nicolas Martinez, *Head of Protocol of Presidency*
	URBINA, Don José Antonio de, *Head of Protocol, Ministry of Foreign Affairs*
	POOLE PEREZ-PARDO, Vice-Admiral Fernando, *Senior Military Officer in attendance*

8 November	**State Visit to Britain of President Abdou Diouf of Senegal and Madame Abdou Diouf**
	SAGNA, HE Mr Famara Ibrahima, *Minister of Industrial Development*
	KA, Madame Fatoumata, *Vice-President, National Assembly*

1989

| 18 July | **State Visit to Britain of Shaikh Zayed bin Sultan Al-Nahyan, President of the United Arab Emirates** |
| | AL-RUMAITHY, HE Khamis Butti, *Director of President's Office* |

1990

23 October	**State Visit to Britain of President Cossiga of Italy and Signora Cossiga**
	DOMINEDO, Ambassador Giovanni, *Diplomatic Adviser*
	VACIAGO, Signor Alessandro, *Cultural Adviser*
	MOSINO, Signor Enzo, *Internal Affairs Adviser*
	MASALA, Signor Alfredo, *Chef du Cabinet*
	FALCONI, Signor Livio Muzi, *Minister, Italian Embassy*

1991

1992

9 June	**State Visit to France of the Queen and the Duke of Edinburgh**
	FORRAY, Le Général d'Armée Gilbert
	GADAUD, M. André, *Chief of Protocol*
	MANAGE, M. Gilles Marie Marcel
	QUESNOT, Général de Division Christian
	SAUTTER, M. Christian
	TIBERI, M. Jean

19 October	**State Visit to Germany of the Queen and the Duke of Edinburgh**
	ADE, Dr Karl Meinhard, *Deputy State Secretary*
	BUCHRUCKER, Herr Hasso, *Under Secretary, President's Office*
	DELLMANN, Dr Hansjorg, *Head, President's Private Office*
	METZGER, Herr Ernst Peter, *Deputy Chief of Protocol*
	SEEMANN, Dr Heinrich, *Chief of Protocol*

3 November **State Visit to Britain of the Sultan of Brunei Darussalam and the Raja Isteri**
ANAK HAJI IDRIS, PISD Pengiran, *The Sultan's brother-in-law*
MOHAMMED NAWAWI, Pehin Dato Haji, *Private Secretary*

1993

1994

5 July **State Visit to Edinburgh of King Harald V and Queen Sonja of Norway**
HARLEM, Mrs Lise, *Master of the Household*

1995

23 May **State Visit to Britain of Sheikh Jabir al-Ahmad al Jabir Al-Sabah, Amir of Kuwait**
AL-SHATTI, Ibrahim, *Director of Office of Amir*

17 October **State Visit to Britain of the President of Finland and Mrs Ahtisaari**
KASURINEN, Lieutenant-Colonel Kari, *First ADC*

1996

14 May **State Visit to Britain of the President of the French Republic and Madame Chirac**
COLONNA, Madame Catherine, *President's Spokesman*
JOUANNEAU, Monsieur Daniel, *Chief of Protocol*
TAIX, Monsieur Jean-Paul, *Minister Counsellor, French Embassy*

28 October **State Visit to Thailand of the Queen and the Duke of Edinburgh**
VAJARODAYA, Mr Keokhwan, *Lord Chamberlain*
AYUTHYA, Mr Chirayu Israngkun Na, *Grand Chamberlain*
SIKKAIMONTON, General Dumrong, *Chief ADC General*
KASEMSRI, ML Birabhongse, *Principal Private Secretary*
KASEMSANT, Thanpuying Suprapada, *Principal Private Secretary*
TONGYAI, Mom Rajawongse Tongnoi, *Deputy Principal Private Secretary*
RAYANANONDA, HE Mr Vidhya, *Thai Ambassador in London*

1997

December **State Visit to Britain of the President of the Federative Republic of Brazil and Senhora Cardoso**
MOREIRA, Minister Valter Pecly, *Head of Protocol of the Presidency*

1998

26 May **State Visit to Britain of Emperor Akihito and Empress Michiko of Japan**
ABE, Mrs Yasuko, *Acting Chief Lady in Waiting to the Empress*

1 December **State Visit to Britain of the President of the Federal Republic of Germany and Frau Herzog**
PLANITZ, Bernhard Edler von der, *Chief of Protocol*

1999

22 June **State Visit to Britain of the President of the Republic of Hungary and Madame Arpad Göncz**
SZUNYOGH, Károly, *State Secretary, Office of the President*

2000

16 February **State Visit to Britain of Queen Margrethe II of Denmark and Prince Henrik**
EUGEN-OLSEN, Lieutenant Colonel Christian, *Master of Ceremonies and Chamberlain*
KJELDSEN, Berno, Minister, *Royal Danish Embassy*

CVO

1896

30 June **Coronation of Emperor Nicholas II of Russia**
KOTSCHOUBEY, Captain Prince Victor, *ADC to HIM*
RIBEAUPIERRE, Count Georges de, *Equerry to the Imperial Court*
BOBRINSKY, Count Georges, *Captain of Cavalry Guard, ADC to Minister of War*

21 July **The Marriage of Princess Maud of Wales to Prince Charles of Denmark**
BULL, Captain Otto, *First ADC to the Crwon Prince of Denmark, Chamberlain to the King of Denmark*

31 October ECHAPPARRE, Nicolas Dubreuil, *Secretary, Chancery of the Russian Imperial Court*

1897

28 March **The Duke of Connaught's visit to Berlin**
BÖCKELBURG, Colonel von Vollard, *Colonel of the Ziethen Hussars (Brandenburg), No.3.*

30 June SECKENDORFF, Admiral Baron Albert, *Master of the Household to Prince Henry of Prussia*
ANGELI, Herr von, *Portrait Painter*

2 July FALKENHAYN, Lieutenant-Colonel von, *HM's Prussian Regiment of Dragoons of the Guard*

28 November **The Duke of York's visit to Coburg**
SAFFT, Major Victor von, *Commanding Coburg Battalion of the 6th Thüringen Infantry Regt. No. 95*

1898

5 May **The Queen's visit to Cimiez**
SAUVAN, Monsieur Honoré, *Mayor of Nice*
PAOLI, Monsieur Xavier, MVO, *Special Commissary, French Ministry of the Interieur*

26 August **Attendance of the Duke of Connaught at French Military Manoeuvres**
HEUSSEY, Lieutenant-Colonel Comte Jules Charles du Pontavice de, *Military Attaché in London*

1899

23 November RAUCH, Lieutenant-Colonel Fritz von

The Emperor's visit to Britain
PRITZELWITZ, Lieutenant-Colonel Kurt von, *ADC to the Emperor of Germany, King of Prussia*
HALLERMUND, Captain Count Oskar von Platen zu, *ADC to the Emperor of Germany, King of Prussia*

26 December KLEHMET, Herr Reinhold, MVO, *German Representative on the Greek Debt at Athens*

1900

9 August SERRA, Captain Luigi, Italian Navy, *ADC to the King of Italy*

1901

18 January **The Duke of Connaught's visit to Berlin**
TROTHA, Major Dietrich von
SCHWERIN, Herr Hofrath Gustav

2 February **The Emperor's visit to Britain**
GRÜMME, Captain von, *Naval ADC to the German Emperor, King of Prussia*

8 March **Funeral of Queen Victoria**
BASTO, Commander Pinto, *In attendance on King Carlos of Spain*

King Edward's VII's visit to Cronberg
HEYSE, John, Geheimer Hofrath, *Secretary to the Privy Purse of the late Empress Frederick*
SPIELHAGEN, Frederick, Leibarzt, *Physician to the late Empress Frederick*
LAUÉ, *District Railway Inspector*

28 May RAUCH, Lieutenant-Colonel Nicolaus von, *Commanding 5th (Prince Blücher of Wahlstatt) Hussar Regiment*

23 July **Visit to Britain of Grand Duke Michael Michaelowitch of Russia**
STOECKL, Baron Alexandre de, *In attendance on HIH*

| 11 October | JACOBI, Colonel von, *Commanding Von Gerstorff Regiment No. 80 at Wiesbaden* |
| | SCHULENBURG, Colonel von der, *Commanding 2nd Hussar Regiment (Queen Victoria of Prussia) at Posen* |

King Edward VII's visit to Cronberg
WEDEL, Captain Edgard von, *Chamberlain to the late Empress Frederick*

King Edward VII's visit to Hamburg
MEISTER, Herr von, *Landrath of the Obertaunus District*
HOEBER, Geheim Rath, *Doctor of Medicine*

King Edward VII's visit to Denmark
VIND-FRIJS, Count Julius Krag Juel, *Master of the Horse to King Christian of Denmark*
RÖRDAM, Lieutenant-Colonel Christian Holger, *Intendant of the Civil List*
WEDELLSBORG, Baron A. Wedell, *Lieutenant-Colonel Commanding Danish Hussars of the Guard*

1902

14 March	**The Prince of Wales's visit to Berlin**
	PLUESKOW, Lieutenant-Colonel Carl von, *Commanding 8th (Prussian) Cuirassiers*
2 May	VAMBERY, Professor Arminius
6 June	**The Duke of Connaught's visit to Madrid**
	SILVELA, Commandant Manuel, *Chamberlain to King Alfonso XIII of Spain*
22 August	**The King's Coronation**

BELNAY, Colonel Commandant Johann von, *Austro-Hungarian Imperial and Royal Hussar Regiment, No.12 Edward VII*
EROPKIN, Colonel Ippolit Aleksievitch, *27th (Kieff) King Edward VII Russian Dragoon Regiment*
DUART E SILVA, Colonel Antonio, *Portuguese Cavalry Regiment, No.3 of King Edward VII*
LOEBENSTEIN, Major Commandant Guido Robert von, *1st Regiment of Dragoons of the Guard, (Queen Victoria of Great Britain and Ireland)*

For Services in connection with the erection of the Monument and Hospital in memory of the late Empress Frederick
KANNENGIESSER, Carl, *Commercial Attaché, Wiesbaden*

| 14 October | ROEDERN, Major Count Bolko, *Prussian Cuirassier Regiment of the Guard* |
| | SALMUTH, Major Freiherr Hans von, *2nd Prussian Regiment Field Artillery of the Guard* |

The King's Coronation
SAINT-SAENS, Monsieur Camille, *Composer of the Coronation March*

9 November	MARTINO, Chevalier Eduardo de, MVO, *Marine Painter*
30 December	**Visit to Britain of the German Emperor**
	ILBERG, Dr Friedrich, MVO, *Physician to HIM*

1903

| 7 April | **King Edward VII's visit to Portugal** |

ALBUQUERQUÉ, Lieutenant-Colonel Alfredo Augusto José de, MVO, *Assistant Master of the Horse to King Carlos of Portugal*
SARMENTO, Colonel Jose Antonio de Moraes, *Commissioner of Police, Lisbon*
PINTO, Señor Arthur da Costa, *Mayor of Cascais*
PORTO, Colonel Antonio de Vasconcellos, *ADC to King Carlos of Portugal, Engineer-in-Chief, Portuguese Railways*

30 April	**King Edward VII's visit to Italy**
	GARELLI, Captain Aristide, *Royal Italian Navy, attached to King Edward VII*
4 May	**King Edward VII's visit to France**

CHABAUD, Commandant Victor Luois Eugène, *ADC to the President of the French Republic*
ROUJOUX, Baron de, *Assistant Director of Protocol*
DERVILLÉ, Monsieur Stéphane Dervillé, *Chairman of the Paris, Lyon and Mediterranean Railway*
GAY, Monsieur Joseph, *Chairman of Western Railway of France*

| 10 July | **Visit to Britain of President Loubet of the French Republic** |

BOEHME, Post Captain Jean, *Commanding French Cruiser Guichen*
HUGUET, Commander Albert, *Naval ADC to the President*
POULET, Mons Henri, *Chief of the Judicial Department of the Presidency*

| 21 July | **On retirement from the post of Naval Attaché at the German Embassy** |
| | COERPER, Captain Carl Wilhelm Heinrich |

King Edward VII's visit to Portugal
CHAPUY, Monsieur Paul Ernest Victor, *Director-General, Royal Company of Portuguese Railways*

| 9 October | **King Edward VII's visit to Austria** |
| | LOEBENSTEIN VON AIGENHORST, Heinrich Ritter, *Director of the Ceremonies to the Emperor of Austria, King of Hungary* |

HABRDA, Johann Ritter von, *Commissioner of Police, Vienna*
KINSKY VON WCHINITZ UND TETTAU, Captain Ferdinand Vincenz Rudolf, Count, *Crown Equerry and Chamberlain*
LUEGER, Dr Carl, *Burgomaster of Vienna*
DIETRICHSTEIN ZU NIKOLSBURG, (Count Mensdorff-Pouilly), Colonel HSH Hugo Alfons Eduard Emanuel Joseph Johann Wenzeslaus, Prince von, *ADC to HIM and attached to King Edward VII*

King Edward VII's visit to Marienbad
OTT, Dr Ernst Karl Eduard Hans, *For Medical Services to King Edward VII*

21 November **Visit of King Vittorio Emanuele III and Queen Elena of Italy to Windsor**
PALIERI, Lieutenant-Colonel Gonsalvo, *ADC*
TODINI, Major Dominique, MVO, *ADC*
TOZZONI, Count Francois Joseph, *Master of Ceremonies*
QUIRICO, Dr Jean, *Physician*
CALABRINI, Marquis Carlo, *Chamberlain to the Queen*
COSTA CARRUDI TRINITA, Count Paul, *Chamberlain to the Queen*

29 December **Visit to Windsor of the Grand Duke Wladimir of Russia**
BELOZERSKY, Prince Serge, *ADC to HIH*
ETTER, Alexandre de, *attached to the Suite of the Grand Duchess, Chamberlain to the Emperor of Russia*
ROHDENDORFF, Lieutenant-Colonel Louis, *attached to the Grand Duke Wladimir Alexandrowich*

1904

10 February **The Marriage of Princess Alice of Albany to Prince Alexander of Teck**
PAUW, Ridder Maarten Iman (Heer van Wieldrecht en Darthuyzen), *Chamberlain to the Queen Mother of the Netherlands*
APELL, Colonel Friedrich Wilhem von, *ADC to the Reigning Prince of Waldeck Pyrmont*
HADELN, Baron Heinrich von, *Private Secretary to the Reigning Prince*

23 March **The Funeral of the Duke of Cambridge**
OSTEN, Kurt Max von der, *Master of the Household of the Prince Albrecht of Prussia*
GROTE, Gernand Alexander Albrecht Otto, Count, *Master of the Household to the Duke of Cumberland*
TILLY, Colonel Arthur von, *Commanding the Infantry Regiment von Goeben (2 Rhineland) No.28*

18 April **King Edward VII's visit to Denmark**
PAULLI, Rev. Jacob Peter Mynster, *Domestic Chaplain to the King of Denmark*
SVENDSEN, Christen, *Postmaster General of Denmark*
KIAER, Colonel Hans Frederik August, *Commanding the Danish Hussars of the Guard*
BLIXEN-FINECKE, Captain Wilhelm Carl Anna Otto Gunnar Axel, Baron, *Danish Life Guards*
PETERSEN, Professor Thorvald Saxo Viggo, *Physician*
SCHOU, Professor Jens, *Surgeon*
KONOW, Commander Henri, *attached to King Edward VII*
NIESSEN, Charles Anton, *British Consul at Cologne*
BRUYNE, Pieter Louis de, MVO, *British Vice-Consul, Flushing*

21 April **The Prince of Wales's visit to Vienna**
NEUMANN, Colonel Franz, *Commanding Austro-Hungarian Artillery Regiment, 'George Prince of Wales' No. 12*
HÜBER, Captain Maurice, Austro-Hungarian Imperial Navy, *Military Household of the Emperor of Austria, King of Hungary*

28 April **The Prince of Wales's visit to Stuttgart**
SODEN, Colonel Franz, Baron von, *Commanding Infantry Regiment, 'Kaiser Friedrich' (7th Württemberg) No.125*
VISCHER-IHINGEN, Lieutenant Richard Gustav Adolf von, *Chamberlain to the King of Württemberg*

11 June **Visit to London of the Archduke Frederic of Austria**
PRÓNAY VON TÓTH-PRONA UND BLATNICZA, Captain Gyùla, *Chamberlain to the Emperor of Austria, King of Hungary, ADC to the Archduke*

1 July **The King's visit to Kiel**
MOLTKE, Captain Henry Charles Leonard, Count von, Imperial German Navy, *Chief of Staff to Prince Henry of Prussia*
MÜLLER, Captain George Alexander von, *Naval ADC to the German Emperor, attached to King Edward VII*
POSCHMAN, Captain Adolph, *Chief of Staff to Admiral von Koester*
KONOPACKI, Colonel John Hermann, *Commanding 85th Regiment of Infantry*
ZEDLITZ-TRÜTZSCHLER, Robert, Count, *Chamberlain to the German Emperor, King of Prussia*
SYDOW, Lieutenant-Colonel Otto John Henry von, *Surgeon*
ZITZEWITZ, Lieutenant-Colonel Wedig Otto Rudolph von, *Commanding the 15th Regiment of Hussars*
BODDIEN, Lieutenant-Colonel Harry Ernest Leopold, *Commanding the 16th Regiment of Hussars*
BITTER, Lieutenant-Colonel Max von, *Commanding the 5th Regiment of Hussars*
TRÄGER, Major Alfred Louis Conrad, *Commanding the 9th Train Battalion (Schleswig-Holstein)*
HOEPPNER, Major Ernest William Arnold, *Staff Officer, 9th Army Corps*
KLEYENSTÜBER, Major Paul Robert, *Commanding the 1st Division of the 45th Artillery Regiment*
FUSS, Tobias August Paul, *Chief Burgomaster, Kiel*
SCHROETER, Henry Charles Sigismund von, *Chief of Police, Kiel*

LAUENSTEIN, George Charles Frederick Gustav, *Postmaster, Kiel*
GALSTER, Max Charles Frederick Gustav, *Harbour Master, Kiel*
BALCK, Major William, MVO, *Commanding Infantry Regiment von Courbière (2nd Posenches)*
LOEWE, Charles, *President of the Imperial Canal Office, Kiel*
PIRALY, Frederick Charles August Maximilian, *Traffic Director, Imperial Canal Office, Kiel*

12 August	ROSCHER, Captain Henry Gustav Theodor, *Director of Hamburg Police*
6 September	**Christening of the Cesarewitch**

SLATIN, Major-General Rudolph Charles Ritter von, KCMG, CB, MVO Egyptian Army, *Inspector of the Anglo-Egyptian Sudan*
ORLOFF, Colonel Wladimir, Prince, *ADC to Emperor Nicholas II of Russia, attached to Prince Louis of Battenberg*

The King's visit to Marienbad
KERZL, Dr Joseph, *Physician to the Emperor of Austria, King of Hungary*

9 November	**Visit to Britain of Prince George of Greece**

LEMBESSIS, Captain Kimon Jean, *ADC to HRH*

21 November	**Visit to Britain of King Carlos of Portugal**

CAMARA MANOEL, Jeronymo Pinheiro de Almeida da, *Counsellor, Portuguese Legation in London*
CABRAL, Antonio da Costa, *First Secretary, Portuguese Legation in London*

4 December	**Visit of Prince Arthur of Connaught to Rome representing HM at the Christening of the Prince of Piedmont**

SAINT PIERRE, Commander Eugenio, Baron di

1905

10 January	SERPA-PIMENTEL, Captain D. Fernando de
27 February	**Prince Arthur of Connaught's visit to Berlin representing the King at the Berlin Protestant Cathedral**

KESZYCKI, Lieutenant-Colonel Heinrik von, *Commanding Hussar Regiment von Zieten (Brandenburg) No.3*
SCHMETTOW, Major Eberhard, Count von, *ADC to the German Emperor, King of Prussia*

17 March	GARCIA, Manuel, *Prefect at Algiers*
19 April	**The King's visit to Algeria**

ROSTAING, Joseph Arthur, *Prefect at Algiers*
PLANTIE, Eugène Jean, *Prefect at Constantine*

The King's Return from the Mediterranean
SARTIAUX, Albert, *Director of North of France Railway*

6 June	**Visit to Britain of King Alfonso of Spain**

VILLALOBAR, M.I. Don Rodrigo de Saavedra y Vinent Cueto y O'Neill, Marquis of, *Chamberlain*
GROVE, Don Juan Loriga y Herrera-Dávilla, Count del, *ADC*
ELORRIAGA-TEJADA, Lieutenant-Colonel Don Mauricio, *Orderly Officer*
AYBAR, Lieutenant-Colonel Don Miguel de Castejou y Elio, Count of, *ADC*
DIAZ DE IGLESIAS, Captain Don Manuel, *Naval Attaché, Spanish Embassy in London*
MANZANOS, Lieutenant-Colonel Don Francis Xavier de, *Military Attaché, Spanish Embassy in London*

6 June	**Visit of Prince Arthur of Connaught to Berlin representing the King at the Marriage of the Crown Prince of Prussia and the Duchess Cecilie of Mecklenburg-Schwerin**

LÜTTWITZ, Major Arthur, Baron, *Commanding No.76 Infantry Regiment, Hamburg (2 Hanseatic)*

15 June	**Marriage of Princess Margaret of Connaught and Prince Gustav Adolph of Sweden and Norway**

THOTT, Otto Gustaf Erik, Baron, *Chamberlain to the Crown Prince*
PEYRON, Captain Frederick Maurice de, *Chamberlain to the Crown Princess*
CEDERSTRÖM, Rolf Sixten Christer Thuve, *Chamberlain and Comptroller to Prince Eugene of Sweden*
RALAMB, Klas Erik, Baron, *Chamberlain and Comptroller to Prince Gustav Adolph*
MUNTHE, Dr Axel, *Physician to the Crown Princess of Sweden and Norway*

4 July	**Visit to Britain of Prince and Princess Arisugawa of Japan**

MARUO, Kinsaku, *Chamberlain to the Crown Prince of Japan, Guardian of the Japanese Princes, Member of the Private Council of the Imperial Household*
OSAWA, Captain Kishichiro, *ADC to the Prince*

19 July	**Visit of the Duke of Connaught to Coburg and Gotha to represent the King at the Celebration of the Coming of Age of the Duke of Saxe-Coburg and Gotha**

EBART, Paul von, *Chamberlain to the Duke of Saxe-Coburg and Gotha*
BISMARCK, Lieutenant-Colonel Claus von, *6th Thüringian Infantry Regiment No.95*

8 September	**The King's visit to Marienbad**

PEZELLEN, Carl, MVO, *Prefect of Marienbad*
HELMER, Gilbert John, *Abbot of Tepl*
BREITENBACH, Paul Justin von, *President of the Royal Railway Board of Direction, Cologne*
FRANKL, Commander Paul Edler von Seeborn, *Commandant of the Military Kurhaus*

26 September	UTSUNOMIYA, Colonel Taro, *Military Attaché, Japanese Embassy, London*
23 November	BELLAN, Leopold Désiré, *President of Paris Municipal Council*
27 November	**Visit to Britain of the King of the Hellenes** MILLIOTTI-COMNÈNE, Major Constantine, MVO, *ADC to King George I of the Hellenes* CERNOWITZ, Leo Kumo Mac Mahon, Count de, *Equerry*
23 December	AMADE, Albert Gérade Léo D', *Military Attaché, French Embassy in London*
	On relinquishing appointment of Naval Attaché, Japanese Embassy in London KABURAKI, Captain Makoto
30 December	**The Duke of Connaught's visit to Stockholm** PLATEN, Colonel Philip Christopher von, *Commanding The Crown Prince of Sweden's Regiment of Hussars. In attendance on the Duke of Connaught*

1906

18 February	**Visit of the Lord Chamberlain to Denmark to represent HM at the Funeral of King Christian IX of Denmark** CARSTENSEN, Commander Carl William Edward, Royal Danish Navy
20 February	**Garter Mission of Prince Arthur of Connaught to the Emperor of Japan** TAKARABE, Captain Takeshi, Imperial Japanese Navy, *Assistant Minister of Marine* INABA, Viscount Nagayuki, *Master of Ceremonies*
15 March	SENGE, Baron Takatomi, *Governor of Tokyo* OMORI, Shoichi, *Governor of Kioto* CHIKAMI, Kiyoomi, *Governor of Kagoshima*
16 April	**The King's visit to Corfu** COLLAS, Démetrius, *Mayor of Corfu*
24 April	**The King's visit to Greece** SOUTZO, Lieutenant-Colonel Alexander, *Commander of the Cavalry School, Athens, attached to King Edward VII* THÉOCHARIS, Captain Théocharis, *Commanding the Royal Yacht* Amphitrite MERCOURIS, Spiros, *Mayor of Athens* DAMALA, Paul Ambrose, *Mayor of Piraeus* BOULTZOS, Lieutenant-Colonel Constantine, *Commissioner of Police, Athens* SOTIRIADES, George, *Treasurer of the Household*
31 May	**The Mission to King Edward VII to announce the Accession of King Frederik VIII of Denmark** ROSENKRANTZ, Hans Carl Oluf, Baron, *Master of the Hounds*
6 June	**The Prince of Wales's visit to Madrid representing HM at the Marriage of the King of Spain** RIVERO GONZALEZ O'NEALE SOTO, Don Joaquin Maria, *Chamberlain to the King*
9 August	**On relinquishing the post of German Military Attaché in London** SCHULENBERG, Captain Count Frederick von der
	Visit to Britain of King Alfonso of Spain BARRIERE Y PEREZ, Captain Joaquin, *ADC and Commanding the Royal Yacht* Giralda
15 August	**The King's visit to Cronberg** MARX, Henry Augustus Ernest von, *Landrat at Hamburg*
	Prince Christian of Schleswig Holstein's visit to Germany to represent the King at the Christening of the Son of HI and RH MELLENTHIN, Lieutenant-Colonel Frederick Charles Ernest von, *Commanding the Prussian Guard Uhlan Regiment No.3*
20 September	**Visit of the Duke of Connaught to Karlsruhe to invest the Grand Duke of Baden with the Order of the Garter on behalf of the King and representing HM at the Celebration of the Golden Wedding of the Grand Duke and Duchess of Baden** DÜRR, Colonel Karl, *Personal ADC to the Grand Duke of Baden, attached to the Duke of Connaught* BOHLEN UND HALBACH, Gustav von, *Chamberlain to the Grand Duke, attached to the Duke of Connaught*
27 September	**For Services rendered to British Military Attachés during the Russo-Japanese War** SATO, Colonel Tadayoshi WATANABE, Colonel Kazuo
13 November	IRGENS, Johannes Herr, *Secretary, Norwegian Legation in London*
30 November	TOSTI, Francesco Paolo, MVO

1907

4 January	SCHWARZ, Captain Joseph, Ritter von, *Lately Austro-Hungarian Naval Attaché in London*

9 April	**King Edward VII's visit to Spain**
	SUANCES Y CALVO, Captain Don Angel, *Royal Spanish Navy, ADC to King Alfonso of Spain*
	ZARCO, Don Ramon Fernandez de Cordova, Marquis, *ADC to the Infante of Spain*
	MATZ, Captain Don Rudolph, *Royal Spanish Navy, Chief of Staff, Cartagena*
	HACÁR Y MENDIVIL, Captain Don Leopoldo, *Royal Spanish Navy*
	SANCHEZ Y LOBATON, Captain Don Adriano, *Royal Spanish Navy*
	LE SENNE, Captain Don Gabriel, *Royal Spanish Navy*
	MIRANDA Y CORDONIE, Captain Don Angel, *Royal Spanish Navy*
	AGUIRRE Y CORVETTO, Captain Don Miguel, *Royal Spanish Navy*
26 April	SALINAS, Professor Antonio, *Director, National Museum, Palermo*
29 April	BALLANTI, Cesare, *Chief of Police, Naples*
7 May	**Visit to Britain of General Prince Sadanaru Fushimi representing the Emperor of Japan**
	SHIBA, Colonel Goro, *Military Attaché, Japanese Embassy in London*
	MATSUISHI, Colonel Yasuji, *Director of 2nd Department, General Satff*
	TOCHINAI, Captain Sojiro, *Naval Attaché, Japanese Embassy*
	MUTSU, Count Hirokichi, *First Secretary, Japanese Embassy*
18 May	**Visit of Prince Arthur of Connaught to Madrid to represent HM at the Christening of the Prince of Asturias**
	AGULLA Y RAMOS, Lieutenant-Colonel Joaquin, *ADC to King Alfonso of Spain*
	JAQUOTOT Y GARCIA, Colonel Don Francisco Maria Joaquin
	FUENTE Y CASTRILLO, Colonel Don Antonio Maria de la
	MORAGAS Y TEGERA, Colonel Don José Maria Ricardo Luis
	BLANCO, Colonel Don Enrique Alfredo Fernández
13 June	**Visit to Britain of King Frederik VIII and Queen Louise of Denmark**
	GOTSCHALK, Commander Frederik Ludwig Franz, *ADC*
	CASTONIER, Captain Edgar Oscar Nonus de, *ADC*
14 June	RICHTER, Hans, MVO, *Doctor of Music*
15 June	**Unveiling of Statue of the late Field Marshal the Duke of Cambridge**
	LOEBEN, Colonel Richard von, *Commanding German Infantry Regiment von Goeben, No.23*
27 June	MASSENBACH, Captain Fabian, Baron von, *ADC to the Grand Duke of Hesse*
30 July	HUGO, Lieutenant-Colonel George Emil Constantine Charles von, *Commanding 8th (Count Gessler) Cuirassiers, German Army*
3 August	**Visit of the Coast Squadron of the Royal Swedish Navy to Cowes**
	EKSTRÖM, Captain Arthur, *ADC to King Oscar of Sweden*
	LIDBECK, Commander Gustaf Henrik
14 August	**HM's visit to Wilhelmshohe**
	RIBBECK, Major Hans George von, *1st Regiment of Dragoon Guards (Queen Victoria of Great Britain and Ireland) attached to King Edward VII*
	DALWIGH ZU LICHTENFELS, Baron Alexander von, *Commissioner of Police, Cassel*
	HM's visit to Ischl
	BRONN, Major Charles George, Baron von, *ADC to the Emperor of Austria, King of Hungary*
	MARGUTTI, Major Albert Alexander, MVO, *Orderly Officer to the Principal ADC*
	PRILESZ, Carl Prileszky von, *Comptroller of the Household of the Emperor*
	MESSERKLINGER, Johann, *Director of the Austrian Railways*
14 August	SENDEN, Major Carl Otto, Baron von, *ADC to the German Emperor, King of Prussia*
	Visit to Vienna of the Duke of Connaught
	SZONTAGH, Colonel Arthur, *Commanding Austrian Hussar Regiment No.4*
6 September	**HM's visit to Marienbad**
	LIECHTENSTEIN, HSH Prince Edward Victor von und zu, *Prefect of Marienbad*
	PAHLEN, Count Peter, *Chamberlain to Emperor Nicholas II of Russia, attached to the Russian Minister for Foreign Affairs*
12 November	**Visit to Windsor of the Emperor and Empress of Germany, King and Queen of Prussia**
	MARSCHALL, Colonel Wolf, Baron, *ADC*
	REBEUR-PASCHWITZ, Captain Hubert von, *Naval ADC*
	EISENHART-ROTHE, John von, *Deputy Chief of HIM's Civil Cabinet*
	HATZFELDT-WILDENBURG, Count Paul Hermann Karl Hubert von, *Acting Private Secretary to the Secretary of State for Foreign Affairs*
	WINTERFELD, Hans Charles von, *Chamberlain to Her Imperial Majesty*
	STUMM, William August von, *Counsellor, German Embassy in London*
	TRUMMLER, Captain George, *Commanding HIM's Ship* Scharnhorst
	PHILIPP, Commander Otto Charles Anton, *Commanding HIM's Ship* Könningsberg
18 November	POKLEWSKI-KOZIELL, Stanislas, *Counsellor, Russian Embassy in London*

1908

30 January	**To announce the Accession of King Gustav V of Sweden** THURDIN, Commander Richard August, *attached to Special Envoy to King Edward VII*
19 March	CEBOLLINO, Colonel José Ruiz, *Commanding (Spanish) Zamora Regiment No.8*
26 March	**Visit of the Prince of Wales to Cologne to inspect the Regiment, of which HRH is Colonel-in-Chief** KEUDELL, Major Rudolf Hermann Friedrich Georg von, *Kürassier Regiment Graf Gessler (Rheinisches) No.8*
14 April	**HM's visit to Biarritz** HENNION, Cebstin, MVO, *Principal Commissioner, Paris* **HM's visit to Denmark** ENGELBRECHT, Lieutenant-Colonel Frederick Charles John, MVO, *Commanding Danish Hussars of the Guard, attached to King Edward VII*
2 May	**HM's visit to Norway** KNAGENHJELM, Jacob Roll, *Deputy Master of the Household to King Haakon VII of Norway* EGEBERG, Doctor Theodore Christian, *Physician to King Haakon* STEFFENS, Colonel Nicolai Jacob, *Chief ADC to King Haakon* KNOFF, Colonel Thomas Hans, *Director of the Norwegian Geographical Insititute, attached to King Edward VII* BEICHMANN, Fridtjov Bernt, *Chief Commisioner of Police, Christiania* BERGLAND, Captain Alfred, *ADC to King Haakon*
29 May	**Visit to Britain of President Fallières of the French Republic** KERAUDREN, Captain Jules Jean Marie, *Naval ADC to the President* LASSON, Lieutenant-Colonel Henri Alfred, *ADC to the President* VARENNE, Louis Paul Marc, *Chief Private Secretary* DUTASTA, Paul Eugène, *1st Secretary, Diplomatic Service and Private Secretary to the Minister for Foreign Affairs*
10 June	**HM's visit to Russia** WIASEMSKY, Prince Nicolas, *Commanding the Imperial Yacht* Polar Star BEHR, Captain Felix, *Russian Naval Attaché in London* CHAGIN, Captain Jean, *ADC to the Emperor, Commanding the Imperial Yacht* Standart DRENTELN, Captain Alexander, *ADC to the Emperor* BOTKINE, Dr Eugène, *Physician to the Emperor* SPIRIDOVITCH, Colonel Alexander, *Chief of Police, attached to the Imperial Court* GERASIMOFF, General Alexandre ROUSSINE, Captain Alexander Ivanovitch, *Assistant Chief of Naval Staff* KAUTZ, Dr Georg, *President of the 'Kaiser Wilhelm Canal'*
26 June	**HM's Birthday** FLAMENG, François, *Member of the Institute of France*
18 August	**HM's visit to Cronberg** MALTZAHN, Axel Albrecht, Baron von, MVO, *Spa Director, Homburg* JACOBI, Professor Louis, *Director of the Saalburg Museum*
21 August	**HM's visit to Ischl** SALBURG, Count Julius, *Prefect of Gmunden* HOYOS, Henry, Count, *Chamberlain and ADC to the Emperor of Austria, King of Hungary* KOHOUT, Colonel Charles, *Commanding 59th Infantry Regiment (Archduke Rainer)* NEPALLECK, William, MVO, *Director of Court Ceremonies to the Emperor* UMLAUFT, Anton, *Inspector of the Imperial Gardens*
4 September	**HM's visit to Marienbad** HAUCK, Adalbert, MVO, *Chairman, Bavarian State Railways* TONDELIER, Charles François Victor, *Chairman, Belgian State Railways* SCHMIDT, Rudolf, *President of Board of Directors, Prussian State Railway*
17 November	**Visit to Windsor of King Gustav V and Queen Victoria of Sweden** RUDBECK, Baron Reinhold Hugo Joseph, *Chamberlain to Queen Victoria* BECK-FRIIS, Baron Carl Augustin, *Counsellor, Swedish Legation in London*
11 December	**Visit to Britain of the Grand Duke Michael Alexandrovitch of Russia** MORDVINOFF, Lieutenant-Colonel Anatole de, *ADC to HIH*

1909

12 February	**HM's visit to Berlin** GELLHORN, Colonel Charles von Wrochem, *Commanding Zieten Hussar Regiment* BÄRENSPRUNG, Major Felix von, *Commanding 1st Regiment of Dragoons of the Guard 'Queen Victoria of Great Britain and Ireland' attached to King Edward VII* ZEDLITZ UND LEIPE, Major Frederick, Baron von, *1st Regiment of Dragoons of the Guard 'Queen Victoria of Great Britain and Ireland'* WIDENMANN, Commander Charles William, MVO, *Naval Attaché, German Embassy in London* OSTERTAG, Major Roland Frederick William, MVO, *Military Attaché, German Embassy in London*

REICKE, George Gotthilf Paul, *Burgomaster of Berlin*
MICHELET, Edward Henry Paul, *Chairman, Municipal Council, Berlin*
FRIEDHEIM, Otto Charles Anton, *Commissioner of Police*
BAERECKE, Hermann, *Commissioner of Police*

15 April	**HM's visit to Biarritz**
	FORSANS, Pierre, MVO, *Mayor of Biarritz*
	MOFFRE, Francis Marie Monique Henry, *Director of the Midi Railway*
29 April	**HM's visit to King Vittorio Emanuele and Queen Elena of Italy at Baia**
	GUICIADINI, Count Ludovico, *Chamberlain to the Queen of Italy*
	CAETANI, Livio, *Counsellor of Legation*
	AGLIÉ, Colonel Count Oberto San Martino d', *Principal ADC to the Duke of Aosta*
	TRIFARI, Count Eugenio, *Royal Italian Navy*
	SELBY, Major Gualtiero, *ADC to the King of Italy*
	TORRECUSO, Duke Ferdinand Cito di, *Master of Ceremonies*
25 June	**HM's Birthday**
	TUXEN, Professor Laurits Regner, *Painter*
5 August	**Visit of Emperor Nicholas II and Empress Alexandra Feodorovna of Russia**
	ETTER, Nicholas de, *Counsellor, Imperial Russian Embassy*
	KOERBER, Captain Louis, *Naval Attaché, Imperial Russian Embassy*
	DÉMIDOFF, Elim, *attached to the Russian Minister for Foreign Affairs*
	PONOMAREFF, Captain Vladimir, *Imperial Russian Navy*
	OUGRUMOW, Captain Alexis, *Imperial Russian Navy*
16 November	**Visit to Windsor of King Manoel II of Portugal**
	ASSECA, Captain Salvador Correa de Sá, Viscount d', MVO, *Officier d'Ordonnance to HM*
	BREYNER, Dr Thomas de Mello, *Physician to HM*
	BANDEIRA, Antonio Carlos dos Santos, *Secretary to the Portuguese Minister of Foreign Affairs*
10 December	**On relinquishing the Post of Naval Attaché, Austro-Hungarian Embassy**
	WAWEL, Captain Napoleon Louis Edler von

1910

25 January	**Visit of Field Marshal Viscount Kitchener to Japan**
	ASANO, Nagayuki, MVO, *Master of Ceremonies to the Emperor, attached to Viscount Kitchener*
	KIYOKAWA, Commander Junichi, *Equerry in Waiting to Prince Hiroyasu Fushimi of Japan*
	To announce the Accession of King Albert I of the Belgians
	LANTSHEERE, Lieutenant-Colonel Auguste Marie Joseph Maurice de, *attached to the Special Envoy to King Edward VII*
21 February	**Visit to Britain of Prince Henry of Prussia**
	USEDOM, Lieutenant Ernest Richard Detlef von, Imperial German Navy, *Equerry to HRH*
7 March	KUTNER, Professor Robert, *Director of the Empress Frederick's Institute for Medical Education, Berlin*
21 May	**Funeral of King Edward VII**
	WORAFKA, Colonel Theodor, Ritter von, *Commanding 1st Cavalry Brigade of which HM was Colonel-in-Chief*
	UCKERMANN, Lieutenant-Colonel Franz Gustav Conrad von, *5th German Hussar Regiment (Prince Blucher von Wahlstatt) of which HM was Colonel-in-Chief*
	HEIDBORN, Colonel Hermann, *Curassier Regiment, Graf Gessler (Rhienschen) No.8 of which HM was Colonel-in-Chief*
	RIBEIRO, Colonel Joaquim Jose, Junior, *Portuguese Cavalry Regiment No.3 King Edward VII of which HM was Honorary Colonel*
	DRAGOMIROFF, Colonel Abraham, *Russian Hussar Regiment 9th (Kieff) King Edward VII of which HM was Honorary Colonel*
	FAURA Y GAVIOT, Colonel Don Enrique, *Spanish Zamora Regiment No.8 King Edward VII, of which HM was Honorary Colonel*

1911

23 January	**On relinquishing the appointment of Naval Attaché, French Embassy**
	LOSTENDE, Captain Henry Maurice, Baron Mercier de
21 February	**On relinquishing the appointment of Military Attaché, Japanese Embassy**
	HIGASHI, Lieutenant-General Otohiko
	On relinquishing the appointment of Naval Attaché, Italian Embassy
	RESIO, Captain Arturo
15 May	**Unveiling of the Queen Victoria Memorial**
	KÜHLMANN, Richard von, *Counsellor, German Embassy*
	HOLZING-BERSTETT, Major Max Reinhard Albert, Freiherr von, *ADC to German Emperor*

| 9 June | On relinquishing the appointment of Naval Attaché, Japanese Embassy |
| | KATO, Admiral Hiroharu, KCMG, |

| 12 June | HM's Coronation |
| | VIGNAU, Emanuel Wilhelm Eduard Hans von, *Chamberlain to the Dowager Duchess of Saxe-Coburg and Gotha* |

| 2 December | Mission of Prince Alexander of Teck to Bangkok to represent HM at the Coronation of the King of Siam |
| | SCHÖNING, Captain Knud, Royal Siamese Navy, *Commander, Royal Siamese Yacht* |

1912

| 23 January | For assistance in rescue work on the occasion of the wreck of the SS *Delhi* on 13 December 1911 |
| | LEQUERRÉ, Rear-Admiral André Paul Marie |

24 January	TM's visit to Malta
	HABERT, Rear-Admiral Jules Armedée Augustin Marie, *Commander of the French Battleship* Danton
	LEJAY, Rear-Admiral Gustave, *Commander French Battleship* Justice
	PIGEON DE SAINT PAIR, Rear-Admiral Frederick George, *Commander French Battleship* Verité

| 30 January | TM's visit to Gibraltar |
| | MOKRI, Cid el Hadj Mokhtar, *Of the Mission from the Sultan of Morocco* |

31 January	DE LA MESA DE ASTA, Señor Don Lorenzo Pineiro Fernandez de Sillancencio, Marquis, *ADC to Don Carlos de Bourbon, Infante of Spain*
	HOYOS, HE Lieutenant-Colonel Don José De Hoyos y Vinent, Marquis de (Viscount de Manzanera), *ADC to Don Carlos de Bourbon, Infante of Spain*
	ANTON É IBOLÉON, Captain Don Gabriel, *Commander Spanish Cruiser* Carlos V
	MARQUEZ DE PRADO, HE Vice-Admiral Don Miguel, *Commander Spanish Cruiser* Cataluña
	MARTINEZ ANIDO, HE Lieutenant-General Don Severano, *In attendance on Don Carlos de Bourbon, Infante of Spain*
	MORENO Y ELIZA, Captain Don Salvador, *Commander Spanish Cruiser* Pelayo

| 16 February | On reliquishing appointment of Military Attaché to the French Embassy |
| | HUGUET, Colonel Victor Jacques Marie |

| 29 June | Special Mission to HM to announce the Accession of King Christian X of Denmark |
| | VIND, Ove Holger Christian, *Member of the Mission* |

12 September	Visit of Prince Arthur of Connaught to Japan to represent HM at the Funeral of Emperor Mutsuhito
	YOSHIZAWA, Kenkichi
	YOSHIDA, Lieutenant-Colonel Toyohiko, CB, *Ordnance Committee*

| 23 September | Mission of Prince Alexander of Teck to Bangkok to represent HM at the Coronation of King Vajiravudh of Siam |
| | SCHILLING, Maurice, Baron, Royal Siamese Navy, *Commander Royal Siamese Yacht* |

1913

| 2 April | Visit of Prince Alexander of Teck to Athens to represent HM at the Funeral of King George of the Hellenes |
| | CHARALAMBIS, Lieutenant-Colonel Anastase |

| 12 April | On relinquishing appointment of Naval Attaché, Italian Embassy |
| | LOVATELLI, Captain Max |

24 May	TM's visit to Berlin to attend the Wedding of the Duke of Brunswick and Lüneberg and Princess Viktoria Luise of Prussia
	BEISSEL VON GYMNICH, Lieutenant-Colonel Richard, Count
	BAUMBACH, Lieutenant-Colonel Ewald von
	CARNAP, Moritz August Gustav von, *Deputy Master of Ceremonies to the German Emperor, King of Prussia*
	ESTORFF, Lieutenant-Colonel Charles Otto von, *Equerry to HIM*
	EVERTS, Allard Gerrit Antony, *Traffic Manager, Netherlands Railways*
	GEYER, Albert Hermann, *Inspector of Royal Buildings*
	HENNINGER, Dr Eugene Charles Frederick Ferdinand, *Chief of Special Police attached to the King*
	MUTIUS, Lieutenant-Colonel Maximilian von, *Equerry to HIM*
	PALESKE, Captain Clemens Adalbert William Bernhard, Baron von, *Equerry to HIM*
	SPEE, Lieutenant-Colonel Heribert Octavian Joseph Antonio Francis Xavier Hubert Maria, Count von, *Commanding Prussian Cuirassier Regiment*
	VOORHOEVE, John Marinus, *Chairman, Board of North Brabant and German Railway Company*

26 May	TM's visit to Neu-Strelitz
	BLÜCHER, Ernest von, *Chamberlain to the Grand Duke of Mecklenberg-Strelitz*
	KRELL, Major Conrad von, *Equerry to the Grand Duke*
	WUSSOW, Colonel Max Robert Otto von, *Chief of Military Department of the Grand Duke*

| 30 May | On relinquishing the appointment as Naval Attaché, Japanese Embassy in London |
| | IDE, Captain Kenji |

3 June	**Visit to London of the Empress Marie Feodorovna of Russia** DOLGOROUKY, Colonel Prince Serge, *ADC to Emperor Nicholas II of Russia*
11 June	**Special Mission to HM from the Argentine Republic** SALAS Y ORONO, Don Gabino, *First Secretary to Mission* URIBURU, Colonel José, *Military Attaché to Mission*
24 June	**Visit to Britain of President Poincaré of the French Republic** ALDEBERT, Colonel Francis Ernest, *attached to President Poincaré of the French Republic* PANOUSE, Lieutenant-Colonel Artus Henri Louis, Vicomte de la, *Military Attaché, French Embassy* FLEURIAU, Aimé Joseph de, *Counsellor*
4 July	SAINT-SEINE, Commander Jean Charles Just Bénigne, Comte de, *Naval Attaché, French Embassy*
21 July	**On relinquishing appointment of Military Attaché to French Embassy** BAGNANI, Lieutenant-Colonel Ugo
	Mission to Announce the Accession of King Constantine I of the Hellenes PALI, Alexis, *Hellenic Foreign Office*
30 July	**On relinquishing appointment of Naval Attaché at the Russian Embassy** REIN, Captain Nicolas de

1914

18 March	**Visit to Copenhagen of the Prince of Wales** ANDERSEN, Commodore Edward Emil
24 April	**HM's visit to France** AUBERT, Général de Division Charles, *Military Staff of the President* CHANOT, Pierre Adolphe Francis, *Chief of the Municipal Police, Paris* EXELMANS, Vice-Admiral Louis Remy Antoine, *Commander French Cruiser* Marseillaise GRANDCLÉMENT, Rear-Admiral Gaston Marie Raoul, *Naval Staff of the President* JOUFFROY, Général de Division Louis Pierre Marie, *Military Staff of the President* LAURENT, Emile Marie, *Secretary General to the Prefecture of Police, Paris* PAQUETTE, Général de Division Gabriel Alexandre, *Military Staff of the President* ROTHSCHILD, Baron Edouard de, *Chairman North of France Railways* VIARD, Captain Lucien Armand, *Commander of the French Cruiser* Amiral Aube
9 May	**Visit to Britain of King Christian X of Denmark** GROVE, Commodore Peter Albert, *Commander Danish Royal Yacht* Dannebrog KAUFFMANN, Colonel Axel Otto Tage Niels Basse, *Chamberlain to the King of Denmark*
15 June	**On relinquishing command of the Spanish Zamora Regiment** LANZA-ITURRIAGA, General of Division Guiltermo

1915

12 February	**The Mission to HM from Emperor Nicholas II of Russia** KOUTOUSOF, Serge, Comte Golenistchef, *Member of the Mission*
15 May	**On relinquishing appointment of Naval Attaché to Japanese Embassy** ABO, Admiral Baron Kiyokazu, KCMG
7 June	KEDROFF, Captain Michel, Imperial Russian Navy, *attached to the British Grand Fleet during the War*

1916

1 April	**Visit to London of the Crown Prince of Serbia** MICHAÏLOVITCH, Colonel Tchedomir, *Physician to HRH*

1917

28 June	**On relinquishing appointment of Military Attaché to the Italian Embassy** GREPPI, Colonel Edoardo, CB
14 July	**HM's visit to His Army in the Field** WATIGNY, Ernest Henri Desiré, *French Technical Adviser*
18 December	**On retirement from Command of the Spanish Zamora Regiment** SOSA ARBELO, Brigadier-General Don Alfredo

1918

2 April	**Visit of the Duke of Connaught to Athens to invest King Alexander I of the Hellenes with the Order of the Bath** MÉLAS, George, *Chef du Cabinet, Ministry of Foreign Affairs* NEGROPONTE, Lieutenant-General James, *Commander XIII Division Greek Army*

29 June	**Prince Arthur of Connaught's Mission to Japan** FURUYA, Shigetsuna, *Japanese Consul-General at Ottawa* IMAMURA, Rear-Admiral Nobujiro, CMG, *Staff Commander, Japanese Naval General Staff* MIMURA, Rear-Admiral Kinzaburo, *Imperial Japanese Navy*
6 July	**Visit to Britain of King Albert I of the Belgians** TILKENS, Lieutenant-General Auguste Constant, CMG
28 October	**Visit to Britain of Admiral Prince Yorihito** AMENOOMIYA, Surgeon Vice-Admiral Ryoshichiro, *attached to General Staff* MAYEDA, Colonel Marquis Toshinari, MC NANGO, Rear-Admiral Jiro, *ADC to Prince Yorihito* YOSHIDA, Isaburo, CB, *First Secretary, Japanese Embassy in London*
30 November	**HM's State visit to Paris** CARRÉ, Ferdinand Maurice, *Sous chef du protocole* CROISET, Lieutenant-Colonel Antoine Charles Paul, *20th Battalion of Chasseurs* LE MARCHAND, Georges Hubert, Secretary, Municipal Council of Paris POINTEL, Georges Joseph Marie, Member of Municipal Council of Paris PORTIER, Commander Paul Maurice René, *Officier d'Ordonnance*

1919

28 July	**Reception by HM of a Sudanese Mission** ABD EL RAHMAN MOHAMMED AHMED EL MAHDI, El Sayed, KBE YUSEF EL HINDI, El Sherif, MBE
4 November	**Visit to Britain of the Shah of Persia** LOKMAN-ED-DOWLEH, Docteur, *Chief Physician to HIM* MOIN-OL-MOLK, *Private Secretary to HIM*
12 November	**Visit to Britain of President Poincaré of the French Republic** BLAVIER, Brigadier-General Ernest Henri Jules, *attached to the President* NODET, Brigadier-General Henri, *Officier d'Ordonnance*
25 November	**Reception by HM of a Uruguayan Mission** NOGUEIRA, Julian, *attached to the League of Nations* CAMPOS, Colonel Alfredo R.
1 December	**Visit of the Prince of Wales to the United States of America** BIDDLE, Brigadier-General John, KCB O'RYAN, Major-General John Francis, KCMG, *Commander New York Division, US Army*

1920

1921

9 May	**Visit to Britain of the Crown Prince of Japan** HATTORI, Paymaster Rear-Admiral Kunimitsu, *Of Japanese Third Fleet* KAMEI, Count Koretsune, *Chamberlain to Crown Prince* KANNA, Rear-Admiral Norikazu, CBE, *Captain of HIJMS Katori* KOBAYASHI, Vice-Admiral Seizo, CB, *Naval Attaché, London* NAGAI, Matsuzo, CBE, *Counsellor at Embassy, London* OYAMA, Rear-Admiral Takeshi, *Captain of HIJMS Kashima* SAWADA, Setsuzo, *Secretary to Foreign Office, Tokyo* SEKI, Rear-Admiral Shigemitsu, *Chief Engineer, Third Fleet* TATENO, Surgeon Rear-Admiral Itaru TSUCHIYA, Viscount Masanao, *Chamberlain to HIH* YAMAMOTO, Rear-Admiral Shinjiro, *Of the Household*
4 July	**Visit to Britain of King Albert and Queen Elizabeth of the Belgians** GÉRARD, Max Leo MASKENS, Charles Louis Leon, *Counsellor, Belgian Embassy* MATON, Major-General Rodolphe Jean Alfred, CB, *Military Attaché* OVERSTRAETEN, Lieutenant-Colonel Raoul François Casimir van TRAUX DE WARDIN, Baron de, *Secretary to the Queen*

1922

22 April	**The Prince of Wales's visit to Japan** HYAKUTAKE, Admiral Saburo, KCMG, *Commander Japanese 3rd Squadron* MARUO, Captain Takeshi, *Commander HIJMS Ohi* MIGITA, Rear-Admiral Kumagoro, *Commander HIJMS Kuma*

NAKANOMIKADO, Marquis Tsuneyasu, *attached to HRH's Suite*
TACHINO, Vice-Admiral Tokujiro, *Commander HIJMS* Kiso
TSUNADO, Major-General Masanosuke, CIE, DSO, *attached to HRH's Suite*

13 May	**HM's visit to Belgium**

BINJÉ, Colonel Marcel Henri Florent, *Commander 1st Regiment of Grenadiers*
DAVIGNON, Viscount Henri, *Honorary Secretary, Anglo-Belgian Union*
DAVIGNON, Viscount Jacques, *Chef du Cabinet, Ministry of Foreign Affairs*
HENNIN DE BOUSSU-WALCOURT, Lieutenant-Colonel Raoul Léon Camille Joseph de, *Ordinance Officer*
JOLLY, Lieutenant-General Viscount Hubert Théodore Marie Joseph Ghislain, *Commander 1st Regiment of Guides*
MEEÙS, Major Count André François Marie Eugène de, *Ordinance Officer*

HM's visit to War Cemeteries
OUDRY, Brigadier-General Léopold Charles Anne, CB, *Commanding 8th Regiment of Infantry*

TM's visit to Brussels
PARC, Viscount Gustave du, *attached to the Queen*

HM's visit to Brussels
PATOUL, Chevalier Maurice de, *Marshal of the Court*
SWAGERS, Major-General François, DSO, *of the 6th Division, ADC to King of the Belgians*

9 June	**The Duke of York's visit to Belgrade for the Marriage of King Alexander I of the Serbs, Croats and Slovenes**

YOVITCHITCH, Lieutenant-Colonel Milan Alexander, MC, *Equerry and Assistant Marshal of the Court*

28 July	**On retirement from Command of the Spanish Zamora Regiment**

GOMEZ, Colonel José

18 October	**Visit to Bucharest of the Duke of York to represent HM at the Coronation of King Ferdinand I of Roumania**

DRAGALINA, Commander Virgil Alexandru, *attached to HRH*

1923

28 April	**The Prince of Wales's visit to Belgium**

VINÇOTTE, Colonel Jules Henri, Baron, DSO, *attached to HRH*

14 May	**HM's visit to Italy**

BERTINI, Cesare, *Chief of the Police Force, Rome*
BESI, Doctor Luigi, *ADC General's Office, Rome*
BIANCHIERI, Edmond, *Director of the Royal Secretariat*
CAVRIANI, Marquis Giuseppe, *Chief of Ceremonial Department*
FILANGIERI, (Di Candida Gonzaga) Count Diego, *Chamberlain to the Duchess d'Aosta*
FUROLO, Gicacchino, CBE, *Inspector General of Police*
GIANNINI, Amedeo, *Head of Press Bureau, Ministry for Foreign Affairs*
MESSE, Lieutenant-Colonel Giovanni, *ADC to King Vittorio Emanuele III of Italy*
NOVARI, Brigadier-General Luigi, *Commander Royal Carabinieri*
PAULUCCI, Di Calboli Barone, Marchese Giacomo, *Chief of Cabinet, Ministry for Foreign Affairs*
PIGNOCCO, Luigi, *Of the Ministry of the Italian Court*
SANT' ELIA, Lieutenant-Colonel Count Luigi di, *Master of Ceremonies*

23 October	**Visit of the Duke of York to Belgrade for the Christening of the Heir Apparent of the King of the Serbs, Croats and Slovenes and for the Wedding of Prince Paul**

CHRISTITCH, Brigadier-General Nicola, MC, *attached to HRH*

4 November	**Visit to Britain of the King of Sweden for the Wedding of the Crown Prince of Sweden and Lady Louise Mountbatten**

AKERBLOM, Commander Nils Louis, *ADC to the King of Sweden*
EKLUND, Commodore John Axel Fredrik, *Royal Swedish Navy*
REUTERSWÄRD, Patrik Carl Rheinhold de, *Counsellor, Swedish Embassy*
SALANDER, Lieutenant-Colonel Gunnar Ludvig Malkolm, *ADC to King of Sweden*

1924

15 May	**Visit to Britain of King Ferdinand I of Roumania**

ANTONESCU, Colonel Jon, CMG, *Chief of the Military Household*
CONSTANTINESCU, Constantin, *Private Secretary to Minister of Foreign Affairs*
DJUVARA, Radu T., *Counsellor, Roumanian Legation*
KOSLINSKI, Captain Georges, *ADC to King Ferdinand*
SKELETTI, Lieutenant-Colonel Emil, *ADC to King Ferdinand*

29 May	**Visit to Britain of King Vittorio Emanuele III of Italy**

BISCIA, Captain Count Giuseppe Antonio Raineri, *Naval Attaché, Italian Embassy*
COCCO, Sennen, *Italian Public Security Office*

MARZANO, Lieutenant-Colonel Carlo, *ADC to HM*
MOLOSSI, Umberto, *Inspector General of Italian Police*
PREZIOSI, Gabriele, *First Counsellor, Italian Embassy*
RIGGI, Major-General Virginio Luigi, CMG, *Military Attaché, Italian Embassy*
RUSPOLI, Don Eugenio (dei Principi), MC, *Master of Ceremonies*
SCARONI, Major Silvio, DFC, *Air Attaché, Italian Embassy*
TALIANI, Francesco, CBE, *Second Counsellor, Italian Embassy*

25 June   **Visit to Britain of the Regent of Kedah**
              KEDAH, HH Tunku Ibrahim, Regent of, CMG

1925

18 August   **The Prince of Wales's visit to Uruguay**
              CARBAJAL, Commander Carlos

23 September **The Prince of Wales's visit to Argentina**
              GUERRICO, Don Ezequiel Fernandez, *Secretary to President*

1926

27 March   **Funeral of the Queen Mother of Denmark**
              ROTHE, Colonel Vilhelm, *attached to Prince Arthur of Connaught representing HM*

9 October   **On relinquishing appointment of Spanish Military Attaché**
              RICH FONT, Brigadier-General Don Fernando de

1927

19 May   **Visit to Britain of President Doumergue of the French Republic**
              BARBIER, Ernest, *Administrateur de l'Agence Havas*
              BOYVE, Lieutenant-Colonel Robert de, 6th Spahis, *attached to the President*
              CAMBON, Roger Paul Jules, *Counsellor, French Embassy*
              PHILIPPE, Lieutenant-Colonel Louis Auguste Julien, *attached to the President*
              THIERRY, Adrien Joseph, *Counsellor, French Embassy*
              THOUROUDE, Captain Fernand Emile, DSC, *Naval Attaché, French Embassy*

6 July   **Visit to Britain of King Fuad I of Egypt**
              KHAIRY BEY, Colonel Ibrahim, *ADC to King of Egypt*
              SEKALY BEY, Achille, *Director of European Service, Council of Ministers*
              SIDAROUSS BEY, Sesostris George, *Counsellor, Egyptian Legation*

15 September **Visit of the King of Bulgaria to Balmoral**
              DRAGONOFF, Lieutenant-Colonel Parvan, *ADC to the King*
              HANDJIEFF, Georges, *Private Secretary to the King*

1928

15 March   **Visit to Britain of King Amanullah of Afghanistan**
              ABDUL TAWAB KHAN TARZI, Colonel, *Brother of Queen Souriya of Afghanistan*
              ABDUL WAHAB TARZI, *Brother of Queen Souriya of Afghanistan*
              GHULAM YAHYA KHAN, *Assistant Secretary, Afghan Foreign Office*
              MUHAMMAD AMIN KHAN, *Assistant Secretary, Afghan Foreign Office*
              RUFQI BEY, Dr, *Turkish Physician to the King*

30 October   **Visit of the Duke of York to Copenhagen to represent HM at the Funeral of the Empress Marie**
              GYLDENKRONE, Captain Baron Einar Marius, Royal Danish Navy, *attached to HRH*

1929

22 March   **Visit of the Duke and Duchess of York to Oslo to represent HM at the Wedding of Crown Prince Olav**
              HANSEN, Captain Sigurd Scott, Royal Norwegian Navy, *attached to the Duke of York*

10 May   **The Duke of Gloucester's Garter Mission to Japan**
              OKABE, Viscount Nagakabe, OBE, *Vice Grand Master of Ceremonies*
              YAMAGATA, Commander Takeo, *Master of Ceremonies*

1930

8 January   **The Duke of York's visit to Rome for the Wedding of the Crown Prince of Italy**
              GRAZIANI, Colonel Carlo, MC, Italian Air Force, *attached to HRH*

30 October   **Visit of the Duke of Gloucester to Addis Ababa to represent HM at the Coronation of Emperor Haile Selassie I of Ethiopia**
              GABRE, Mariam Dejazmach

NASIBU, Dejazmach
WOLDE, Tsadik Bitiradad

1931

22 February   **Visit of the Prince of Wales to Chile**
MERINO, Captain Don Julio, *Chilean Navy*
GARFIAS, Colonel Carlos

9 March   **Visit of the Prince of Wales to Portugal**
CARVALHAES, Lieutenant-Colonel Augusto de Azvedo e Lemos Esmeraldo de, *Chief of Staff, Ministry of War*
LOURENCO, Captain Agostinho da C. Pereira, *Director of Police*

13 March   **Visit of the Prince of Wales to Argentina**
STEWART, Captain Don Francisco

1932

5 October   **Visit of the Prince of Wales and Prince George to Sweden**
HAMILTON, Lieutenant-Colonel Count Carl Gustav

1933

20 June   **Visit of King Feisal of Iraq to Britain**
MOHAMMAD, Ata Amin, *of Iraq Legation, London*

1934

13 June   **Special Mission to announce the Accession of King Leopold III of the Belgians**
DU PARC, Viscount Alain Maurice, *Member of Mission*

18 June   **Visit of Princess Juliana of the Netherlands to Windsor Castle**
BAUD, Baron Jean Chrétian

21 November   **Visit of the Duke of Kent to Belgrade to attend the Funeral of the late King Alexander of Yugoslavia**
STOYANOVITCH, Colonel Douchan, *attached to HRH*

1935

22 May   **Visit to Stockholm of Prince Arthur of Connaught to represent HM at the Wedding of the Crown Prince of Denmark and Princess Ingrid of Sweden**
ECKEROTH, Colonel Gunnar

1936

1937

16 November   **Visit to Britain of King Leopold III of the Belgians**
LE GHAIT, Edouard Raymond Charles Alfred
DU PARC, Vicomte Gatien Gabriel Jean Marie
VAN DEN HEUVEL, Major Fernand Joseph Marie
LANTSHEERE, Vicomte Theophile Pierre de

1938

19 July   **State Visit to France of King George VI and Queen Elizabeth**
BERTHOIN, Capitaine Yves Jean Marie Pierre, *Secretary General, Ministry of the Interior*
BROHAN, Rear-Admiral Gabriel, *Commander of Second Flotilla*
FERRY, Marie Alfred René, *Director of the Cabinet*
FOURNIER, Lieutenant-Colonel Pierre Theodore Jules, *Air Attaché, French Embassy, London*
GAMBIER, Général de Brigade Paul, *Commandant, First Air Division*
HUISMAN, Capitaine Aviateur Georges, *Director General des Beaux Arts*
KRANZ, Capitaine de Vaisseau Gabriel Léon Marie Joseph Firmin, *of the Staff of the President of the Republic*
LELONG, Général de Brigade Albert, *Military Attaché, French Embassy, London*
JACQUIN DE MARGERIE, Roland, *First Secretary, French Embassy, London*
MOITESSIER, Pierre Jean Joseph, *Director General of the Surété Nationale*
PENNES, Général de Division Roger Jean Eugène, *Commander First Aviation Corps*
ROBIEN, Louis Marie Anne Joseph de, *Director of Personnel, Ministry for Foreign Affairs*
ROCHARD, Gabriel Auguste Léon, CBE, *Prefect, Pas de Calais*

TAVERA, Rear-Admiral Charles, *Director, Ministry of Marine*
DU TOUR, Capitaine de Vaisseau Edouard Marc Antoine, *Naval Attaché, French Embassy, London*

15 November **Visit to Britain of King Carol II of Roumania**
DEM DIMANCESCO, Captain Dimit, MC, *Counsellor, Roumanian Legation, London*
DUMITRESCU, Capitaine de Vaisseau George St, *Military Attaché, Roumanian Legation, London*
FILITTI, Lieutenant-Colonel Constantin, *ADC to King Carol II*
MILHAILESCU, Lieutenant-Colonel Michel, *ADC to King Carol II*
NICOLAU, Lieutenant-Colonel Constantin, *Air Attaché, Roumanian Legation*

1939

21 March **Visit to Britain of President Lebrun of the French Republic**
DENIS DE RIVOYRE, Contre-Amiral Camille Louis Marie Claude, *Naval Attaché, French Embassy*
TASSIN, Général Charles, MVO, *attached to Suite of the President*

1940

1 June **The Duke of Kent's visit to Lisbon for the 800th Anniversary of Portuguese Independence**
BRION, Captain Nuno Frederico de, OBE, *Commanding Submarine Flotilla*
VIANNA, Henrique da Guerra Quaresma, CBE, *Chief of Protocol*

1941–1947

1948

11 October **Visit of the Princess Margaret to the Netherlands to represent HM at the Inauguration of Princess Juliana as Queen**
LYNDEN, Major Jacob Jan Lodewyk, Baron van
TETS, Jonkvrouwe Digna Hendrika van

1949

1950

7 March **Visit to Britain of President Auriol of the French Republic**
ADAM, Contre-Amiral Marcel Jules, CBE, *Naval Attaché, French Embassy*
ANDRÉ, Gérard, *First Secretary, French Embassy*
BLOUET, Capitaine de Vaisseau Jacques, *ADC*
DE BOURBON-BUSSET, Jacques Louis Robert Marie, Comte, *Director of the Cabinet, Ministry of Foreign Affairs*
DUROSOY, Général de Brigade Maurice Armand, *Military Attaché, French Embassy*
POUYADE, Colonel Aviateur Pierre, *Air Attaché at the Presidency*
LE ROY, Jean Edouard, *Counsellor, French Embassy*
STEHLIN, Général de Brigade Aérienne Paul, *Air Attaché, French Embassy*

21 November **Visit to Britain of Queen Juliana of the Netherlands**
ROO VAN ALDERWERELT, Colonel Joan Karel Hendrik de, *Military Attaché, Royal Netherlands Embassy*
ZINNICQ BERGMANN, Captain Robert Jacques Emile Marie van, DFC, *Master of the Household*
MULOCK VAN DER VLIES BIK,Commander Pieter Andrea, *Naval Attaché, Royal Netherlands Embassy*
GEVERS, Baron Willem Johan Gijsbert, *Counsellor, Royal Netherlands Embassy*
HOLTZ, Colonel Herman Frederick Carel, *Military Air Attaché, Royal Netherlands Embassy*
KARNEBEEK, Jonkheer Abraham Pieter Cornelis van, *Counsellor, Royal Netherlands Embassy*
HEECKEREN VAN MOLECATEN, Baron Walraven Jacob van, *Private Secretary, Royal Netherlands Embassy*
SCHOCH, Dr Herman Constantyn, *First Secretary, Netherlands Embassy*

1951

8 May **Visit to Britain of King Frederik IX and Queen Ingrid of Denmark**
DENMARK, HH Captain Prince Georg Valdemar Carl Axel of, *Acting Military Attaché, Danish Embassy*
JEGSTRUP, Commodore Johannes Harald Jensen, *Naval Attaché, Danish Embassy*
KNUTH, Count Eggert Adam, *Counsellor, Danish Embassy*
BUSCK-NIELSEN, Torben, *Secretary, Danish Embassy*
ORUM, Colonel Torben Ploug Aagesen, *Air Attaché, Danish Embassy*

5 June **Visit to Britain of King Haakon of Norway**
ERIKSEN, Captain Hans Thorleif, *Commanding Officer, Royal Yacht* Norge
MOTZFELDT, Colonel Birger Fredrik, OBE, *Air Attaché, Norwegian Embassy*
MUNTHE, Colonel Adolph Fredrik, *Military Attaché, Norwegian Embassy*
VOGT, Svend Borchmann Hersleb, *Counsellor, Norwegian Embassy*

1952

1953

2 May **Visit of the Duke of Gloucester to Baghdad to attend the Accession Ceremony of King Feisal II of Iraq**
GHAZI MOHAMMAD DAGHISTANI, Brigadier, *Military Attaché, Iraqi Embassy*

1954

28 June **State Visit to Britain of King Gustav VI Adolph and Queen Louise of Sweden**
ASTRÖM, Carl Sverker, *Counsellor, Swedish Embassy*
FALK, Colonel Arthur Valdemar, Royal Swedish Air Force, *Air Attaché, Swedish Embassy*
HAMMARLING, Karl Vilgot Valentin, *Counsellor, Swedish Embassy*
HEDQVIST, Brigadier Tor, *Military Attaché, Swedish Embassy*
KLEEN, Eric Wilhelm Erland, *Counsellor, Swedish Embassy*
STARCK, Captain Magnus Oscar, Royal Swedish Navy, *ADC*
THAM, Commodore Gustaf Sebastian, *Naval Attaché, Swedish Embassy*

14 October **State Visit to Britain of Emperor Haile Selassie I of Ethiopia**
DENEKE, Colonel Makonnen, *Aide-de-Camp*
MAKONNEN, L Indalkachaw, *Press Secretary*
SAHLOU, Ato Petros Mikael, *Counsellor, Ethiopian Embassy*

1955

24 June **State Visit to Norway of the Queen and the Duke of Edinburgh**
BRAADLAND, Commodore Magne, Royal Norwegian Navy, *Principal ADC (Navy)*
BRUN, Colonel Johannes Schwartz, *Chief ADC*
ENGVIK, Colonel Ottar Birting, OBE, Royal Norwegian Air Force, *ADC*
PETERSSON, Lieutenant-Colonel Axel Jacob Thaulow, *Commanding Officer, The King's Guard*
SKALMERUD, Sigurd Svein, *Chief Commissioner of Police, Oslo*
SUNDE, Colonel Leif, *Commandant, Fortress of Akershus*

25 October **State Visit to Britain of President Craveira Lopes of the Republic of Portugal**
HORTA, Doctor Ricardo, *President's Personal Physician*
LUCENA, João de, *Counsellor, Portuguese Embassy*
MIMOSO, Rui Braz, *Of the Ministry of Foreign Affairs*
SA NOGUEIRA, Colonel João Carlos, *Military and Air Attaché*
RAMALHO ROSA, Commander João, *Naval Air Attaché*

1956

8 June **State Visit to Sweden of the Queen and the Duke of Edinburgh**
ADLERCREUTZ, Per Thomas Fredrik, *Chamberlain to the King*
BEXELIUS, Anton Herbert, *First Keeper of the Privy Purse*
BORLIND, Captain Ove Hugo Kristian, *Marshal of the Court*
CERVELL, Colonel Frank-Rutger, Royal Swedish Air Force, *Commander, Fighter Section*
FORSSELIUS, Erik Johan Emil, *General Police Superintendent*
DE GEER, Baron Gustaf Gerard, *Master of Ceremonies*
HORN, Lieutenant-Colonel Jan Carlsson von, *ADC to the King*
MARTENS, Captain Gustaf Harald Märten, *President, City Board of Administration, Stockholm*
NORINDER, Captain Tryggve Lennart, Royal Swedish Navy, *Escort Commander*
PALMSTIERNA, Baron Doctor Bo Carl-Fredrik Kule, PH D., *Private Secretary to the King*
PLATEN, Baron Carl Eric von, *Assistant Master of the Horse*
HÄRD AF SEGERSTAD, Lieutenant-Colonel Fredrik Adolf Bertil
SETTERWALL, Doctor Ake Carl Erik, PH D., *Keeper of the Royal Collection*
STACKELBERG, Count Fritz Carl Louis, *Head of Protocol, Ministry of Foreign Affairs*
STEDINGK, Colonel Gustaf Magnus, Baron von, *Military District Commander, Stockholm*
THAM, Carl Wilhelm Sebastian, *Chamberlain to the Queen*
WACHTMEISTER, Count Nils, *Assistant Master of the Horse*

16 July **State Visit to Britain of King Feisal II of Iraq**
ALI, Colonel Sadiq Haj, *Senior Military Attaché*
JAMIL, Brigadier Nuri, *Chief ADC to HM*

1957

18 February **State Visit to Portugal of the Queen and the Duke of Edinburgh to Portugal**
TAVARES DE ALMEIDA, Albino, OBE, *Head of Press Section*

ESTEVES BEJA, Lieutenant-Colonel Carlos, *Director, Lisbon Airport*
NEWTON DA FONSECA, Captain Ruy, OBE, *Port Captain and Pilot, Lisbon*
PASTOR DE MACEDO, Luiz, *Deputy Lord Mayor, Lisbon*
SILVEIRA MACHADO, Colonel José Frederico, *Commanding Anti-Aircraft Regiment, Queluz*
MENDONÇA, João Pinto de, *Ajuda Palace Staff*
DIAS PIRES MONTEIRO, Lieutenant-Colonel Fernando, *National Republican Guard*
CHARTERS LOPES VIEIRA DA CAMARA OLIVEIRA, Filipe, *of the President's Secretariat*
RATO, Captain João Moreira, *Escort Commander*
CONCEIÇÃO DA ROCHA, Captain José, OBE, *Naval Liaison Officer, Royal Yachts*
CORREA DA SILVA, Joaquim, *Head of Press Service*
SERRA DOS SANTOS-TENREIRO, Commander Henrique Ernesto, *Organiser of Activities on the Tagus and at Nazare*

8 April | **State Visit to France of the Queen and the Duke of Edinburgh**
ALBAYEZ, Georges, OBE MVO, *Director of Travel Services, Ministry of the Interior*
BAECQUE, Francis Georges Henri de, *Director and General Secretary (Civil) of the Presidency*
BÉGARD, Maurice Emile, MVO, *Director of Security*
BOULEY, Général de Division, Jean Claude Louis Victor, DSO, *Commanding 2nd (Lille) Division*
BOUVET, Général de Brigade Georges Regis, *Commander, Paris Area*
CHANEL, Mme Jacqueline Jeanne Marie de Crouy
COCHIN, Denys François, *of the Municipal Council, Paris*
CRESSATY, Général, *ADC to the President*
DOR, Colonel, *ADC to the President*
DUPONT, Capitaine de Vaisseau Jean Leon Albert, *Naval Commandant, Paris*
FRIOL, Henri, *Director of the Cabinet*
JAUJARD, Jacques, KBE, *Director General of Arts*
LAURENT, Augustin, *Mayor of Lille*
LAUZIN, Général de Division (Aérienne) Henri Emanuel Charles, *Commander, Paris Air Region*
LETERRIER, Colonel Auguste Gabriel Alphonse, *Lille Area Commander*
MAIREY, Jean Marie Albert, *Director General, National Security*
MASSON, Colonel Henry Charles Paul, *Versailles Area Commander*
PELABON, Colonel André, *Officer Commanding Garde Republicaine*
PROVO, Victor Emery Georges, *Mayor of Roubaix*
REYNAL, Georges Jean Charles, *Chief of Information Service (Civil)*
CHAMPETIE DE RIBES, Edmond Marie Pierre, *Syndic, Municipal Council, Paris*
ROUMAGNAC, Charles Yrieix René, *Treasurer and Paymaster General*
SALLES, Georges Adolphe, KBE, *Director of French Museums*
SÉRIGNAN, Général de Brigade Pierre Charles, *Commandant of Police, 1st Region*
TETREL, Capitaine de Vaisseau Henry, *ADC to the President*
TRIPARD, Colonel Jacques Louis Charles, *Chief of Office of Military Governor of Paris*

21 May | **State Visit to Denmark of the Queen and the Duke of Edinburgh to Denmark**
AUGSBURG, Lieutenant-Colonel Ejner Hugo, *Gentleman of the Bedchamber*
BRØNDSTED, Henning Andreas, *General Administrator, Royal Theatre, Copenhagen*
CLEMMESEN, Alfred Johan Carl Christian, *Vice-Chairman, City Council, Copenhagen*
HENDRUP, Aage Wilhelm Munch, *General Manager, Port of Copenhagen*
MOLTKE-HUITFELDT, Count Adam Nicolas, *Head of Protocol Department*
HEIDE-JØRGENSEN, Svend Erling, *Commissioner of State Police*
HYE-KNUDSEN, Johan August, *Conductor Royal Theatre, Copenhagen*
KRISTENSEN, Sigvald, *Head of Press Section*
LARSEN, Eivind Frederick Hans, *Commissioner of Police, Copenhagen*
LAUESEN, George Schiønmann, *Comptroller, Lord Chamberlain's Office*
PREIL, Ernst Helmuth, *Comptroller of the Civil List*
WESCHE, Captain Hans-Henrik Oskar, *Commanding, 1st Frigate Squadron*

1958

25 March | **State Visit to the Netherlands of the Queen and the Duke of Edinburgh**
TAETS VAN AMERONGEN, Colonel Jan Joost Carel, Baron, *Commander, Amsterdam Garrison*
VAN BEINUM, Eduard Alexander, *Conductor, Amsterdam Concertgebouw Orchestra*
BEYER, Captain Bernard Arent Wessel, *Pilotage Commissioner, Rotterdam District*
DIJKSTRA, Brigadier Gerrit, *Military Governor of the Capital*
DE GRAEFF, Jonkheer Dirk Georg, *Chamberlain and Master of Ceremonies*
HARDENBERG, Herman Frederick Christiaan, *Under Secretary of State, Foreign Minister and Protocol Department*
KARNEBEEK, Commodore Armand van, *Commander, Netherlands Training Squadron*
LENNEP, Jonkheer Frans Johan Eliza van, *Chamberlain to the Queen*
MANDELE, Karel Paul van der, *Chamberlain to the Queen*
MOLEN, Hindrik Jans van der, *Chief Commissioner, Amsterdam Police*
RANITZ, Jonkheer Constant Johan Adriaan de, *Burgomaster of Utrecht*
ROELL, Jonkheer Eric Willem, *Chamberlain to the Queen*
SESINK, Catharinus, MVO, *Chief Commissioner, Security Service, Royal Household*
STAAL, Henri Marie Conrad Antoine, *Chief Commissioner, Rotterdam Municipal Police*

STEENSMA, Captain Jan Julius, *Pilotage Commissioner, Amsterdam District*
THIJSSE, Johannes Theodor, *Director, Hydraulics Laboratory, Delft*
GUALTHÉRIE VAN WEEZEL, Lieutenant-Colonel Johan Hendrik Albert Karel, *Chief Constable, Municipal Police, The Hague*

13 May **State Visit to Britain of President Gronchi of Italy**
BORROMEO, Conte Giovanni Ludovico, *Counsellor, Italian Embassy*
BRENGOLA, Rear-Admiral Silvano, *Naval Attaché, Italian Embassy*
COLESANTI, Doctor Mario, *Physician to the President*
GEMME, Colonel Giovanni, *Military Attaché, Italian Embassy*
PELOSI, Colonel Giuseppe, *Air Attaché, Italian Embassy*
DE STEFANO, Vincenzo, *Head, Control Department of the Presidency*

20 October **State Visit to Britain of President Heuss of the Federal Republic of Germany**
CASPARI, Fritz, *Counsellor, German Embassy*
HEPP, Brigadier-General Leo, *Military Counsellor to the Presidency*
PLOETZ, Colonel Hans Georg Werner von, *Air Attaché, German Embassy*
RÖHRIG, Georg, *Counsellor at the Presidency*
TSCHIRSCHKY, Fritz-Gunther von, *Counsellor, German Embassy*

1959

5 May **State Visit to Britain of the Shahanshah of Iran**
ESFANDIARI, Colonel Mohammad Hady, *Military Air and Naval Attaché*

1960

5 April **State Visit to Britain of the President of the French Republic and Madame de Gaulle**
BONNEVAL, Colonel Gaston Armand, Comte de, *ADC to the President*
DAILLE, Capitaine de Vaisseau Gerard Roger Eugène Ambroise, DSC, *Staff Officer to the President*
HURÉ, Francis, *Second Counsellor, French Embassy*
LEFRANC, Pierre Abel, *Specially attached to Secretariat of the President*
MAILLARD, Pierre Albert Jean, *Technical Counsellor to the Presidency*
BAUGNIES DE SAINT-MARCEAUX, Colonel Frederic Jacques Jean Gaston, *Air Attaché, French Embassy*
SIMON, Colonel Jean, DSO, MC, *Military Attaché*
TINÉ, Jacques Wilfrid Jean Francis, *First Counsellor*

19 July **State Visit to Britain of King Bhumibol Adulyade and Queen Sirikit of Thailand**
CHARYAVIBHAJ, Luang Pramodya, *Counsellor, Royal Thai Embassy*
DAVIVONGS, Captain Mom Rajawongs Bhandhum, Royal Thai Navy, *ADC to the King*
KANTARAT, Group Captain Panieng, *Air Attaché, Royal Thai Embassy*
KITIYAKARA, Mom Rajawongs Kittinadda, *Private Secretary to the King*
KRAIRIKSH, Poonperm, *Private Secretary to the Queen*
LABANUKROM, Suchin, *Counsellor, Royal Thai Embassy*
RANGSIT, HSH Princess Vibhavadi, *Lady in Waiting*
SANITWONGSE, Colonel Mom Luang Chinda, *Physician*
SONSOMSOOK, Colonel Vijit, *Military Attaché, Royal Thai Embassy*
THAVARADHARA, Group Captain Kaivul, *ADC to the King*

17 October **State Visit to Britain of King Mahendra and Queen Ratna of Nepal**
RANA, Colonel Rabi Shamsher Jang Bahadur, *Military Attaché, Royal Nepalese Embassy*
RANA, Mrs Rani Swetaprava, *Lady in Waiting*
SINGH, Renu Lal, *Press Secretary*
SINGHA, Jharendra Narayan, *First Secretary, Royal Nepalese Embassy*

1961

26 February **State Visit to Nepal of the Queen and the Duke of Edinburgh**
BASNYAT, Brigadier-General Singha Bahadur, *Director of Military Operations*
JOSHI, Sardar Ratna Bahadur, *Secretary to the King*
JOSHI, Sardar Surya Man, *Personal Secretary to the King*
KARKI, Colonel Nar Bahadur, *Chief Engineer*
KUNWAR, Colonel Samar Raj, *Assistant Military Secretary*
PRADHAN, Jyan Bahadur, *Director of Nepalese Aviation*
PRASAI, Tej Bahadur
RANA, Brigadier-General Bhakta Narsingh, *Brigade Commander*
RANA, Major-General Dazzle Jang, *Adjutant General*
RANA, Brigadier-General Maheshwar Shamsher
RANA, Colonel Min Shamsher Jang Bahadur
SHAH, Brigadier-General Mohan Bikram, *Military Secretary to the King*
SHAH, Brigadier-General Punya Ratna
SHAH, Major-General Ranga Bikram, *Commander of the Royal Guard*

SHARMA, Dhundi Raj, *Inspector General of Police*
SHARMA, Surendra Raj, *Director of Publicity of the Government*
SHRESTHA, Dwarika Das
SHRESTHA, Colonel Janak Raj
THAPA, Colonel Chutra Bahadur, *Assistant Military Secretary*

2 March   **State Visit to Iran of the Queen and the Duke of Edinburgh**
ARBABI, HE Hushang, *Under Secretary and Director General of Civil Aviation*
ARDALAN, HE Rear-Admiral Mohammad, *Commander-in-Chief, Southern Naval Forces*
DAVALLU, Hasan, *Of the Tehran Municipality*
NOURY ESFANDIARY, Ali, *Head of Translation Department, Ministry of Foreign Affairs*
FORUGHI, Mohsen, *Dean, Fine Arts Faculty*
GITY, Khalil, *Civil Aide*
JAM, HE Brigadier-General Feridun, *Commandant, Military Academy*
KHADEMI, Brigadier-General Ali Mohammad, *Chief of Staff, Imperial Air Force*
KHALATBARI, HE Brigadier-General Ziaeddin, *Deputy Chief of Police, Tehran*
ALAVI-KIA, HE Brigadier-General Hassan, *Deputy Chief of Security and Special Adjutant*
MUBASSER, HE Brigadier-General Muhsen, *Chief of Tehran Police*
NASERI,Ghulam Ali Saif, *Civil Adjutant*
HASHEMI-NEJAD, Colonel Mohsen, *Chief of Staff, Imperial Guard*
OVEISSI, HE Brigadier-General Gholam-Ali, *Commander of Imperial Guard*
SABETI, Doctor Hasan, *Deputy Chief of Protocol*
SHAFA, Shoja-ed-Din, *Cultural Counsellor, Imperial Court*

29 April   **State Visit to Italy of the Queen and the Duke of Edinburgh**
AMATUCCI, Aster, *Security Officer*
LEQUIO DI ASSABA, General Tomasso, *President, Federation of Equestrian Sports*
BORROMEO, Contessa Egidia
CESCHI, Professor Carlo, *Cultural Affairs Department*
DE FERRARI, Marchese Gio Paolo, *Assistant Chief of Protocol*
FIRMI, Doctor Vincenzo, *Director of Education*
WINSPEARE GUICCIARDI, Vittorio, *Head, Co-ordination Branch, Foreign Office*
LATINI, Carlo, *Superintendent, Rome Opera House*
MARESCA, Adolfo, *Protocol Department*
MENADA, Sister Paola, *National Inspector of Red Cross*
PERUCCA ORFEI, Rear-Admiral Emanuele Filiberto
PERRETTI, Doctor Mario, *President, Society of Racecourse, Capanelle*
SALARIS, General Renato, *Commandant, Fiumicino Airport*
MARIENI SAREDO, Alessandro, *Head of Press Office, Ministry of Foreign Affairs*
SPERANZA, Vincenzo, *Head of Protocol*
STEFANO, Doctor Salvatore di, *Chief of Police*
STAFANO, Vincenzo di, *Head, Control Department of the Presidency*
UNGARO, General Bruno, Italian Air Force, *Assistant Military Adviser*
VITO, Italo de, *Head, General Affairs Branch of the Presidency*

1962

10 July   **State Visit to Britain of the President of the Republic of Liberia and Mrs Tubman**
BAKER, Colonel Nathaniel HS, *Chief Executive, Action Bureau*
DENNIS, Francis Alfonso, *Counsellor, Liberian Legation*

16 October   **State Visit to Edinburgh of King Olav of Norway**
HAUGLAND, Arne, *Counsellor, Norwegian Embassy*
KOREN, Finn Synnøvson, *Norwegian Consul in Glasgow*
ULSTEIN, Egil, DFC, *Counsellor, Norwegian Embassy*
WARLOE, Captain Christian, *Commander, HNMS* Bergen

1963

14 May   **State Visit to Britain of King Baudouin I and Queen Fabiola of the Belgians**
STRYDONCK DE BURKEL, Colonel Yves Auguste Marie Ghislain van, *Military, Naval and Air Attaché*
DEBÊCHE, Colonel Albert Denis, Belgian Air Force, *Equerry to Queen Fabiola*
VALKENEER, Claude Alexandre Alberic de, *Press Officer*

9 July   **State Visit to Britain of King Paul and Queen Frederika of the Hellenes**
ARGENTI, Doctor Philip Pandely, *Cultural and Educational Counsellor*
CHOIDAS, Constantine Stilpon, *Head of Greek Cabinet*
PHOCAS-COSMETATOS, Marino, *Minister, Greek Embassy*
DRACOULIS, Jason, *Counsellor, Greek Embassy*
FRAGISKOS, Group Captain Marios Jhon, *Master of the Royal Household*
KAPSAMBELIS, George Peter, *Counsellor, Greek Embassy*
KARYDIS, Group Captain Evangelos, *Air Attaché, Greek Embassy*
MORALIS, Captain George, Royal Hellenic Navy, *ADC to the King*
STAVRIDIS, Captain Marios, Royal Hellenic Navy, *Naval Attaché, Greek Embassy*

1964

26 May   **State Visit to Britain of President Abboud of the Republic of the Sudan**
EL BAKRI, Sayed Mohamed Kamal, *Counsellor, Sudanese Embassy*
GHANDOUR, Colonel Muzzamil Salman, *Military, Naval and Air Attaché*
EL KAMALI, Brigadier Mustafa Ahmed, *ADC*
MAHMOUD, Brigadier Doctor Mahmoud Hussein, *Medical Officer*
SOGHAYER, Sayed Bushra Abdel Rahman, *Cultural Attaché*

1965

1 February   **State Visit to Ethiopia of the Queen and the Duke of Edinburgh**
ABIYAHOY, Nebureid Makuria, *Governor, Axum Area*
ASFAW, Woizero Terework, *Of the Suite attached*
AZIZI, Brigadier-General Zeremariam, *Commissioner of Police, Eritrea*
HAILE, Doctor Minasse, *Chief of Political Department in Cabinet of Emperor*
KIDANE, Ato Habte Mariam Gebre, *Governor of Bahr Dar*
LEMMA, HE Ato Menasse, *Chief of Economic Affairs in Cabinet of Emperor*
LEMMA, Colonel Tafesse, *Second ADC to Emperor*
MAKONNEN, Dejazmach Adena, *Governor of Woggera District*
MELKE, Colonel Tadesse, *of the Suite attached*
MESHESHA, Dejazmach Kassa, *Governor, Gondar Area*
MERID, Colonel, *Administrator, Jubilee Palace*
ADMASSOU RETTA, Blatta Tekleselassie, *Privy Purse*
TESSEMA, Brigadier Shiffera, *Divisional Commander, Eritrea*
WASSIE, Dejazmach Raya

12 February   **State Visit to the Sudan of the Queen and the Duke of Edinburgh**
SAID, Sayed Abdul Rahim, *Commissioner, Blue Nile Province*
SIDRA, Sayed Lewis, *Commissioner of Police*
EL TAHIR, Sayed Ibrahim, *Commissioner, Khartoum Province*
WAGIEALLAH, Sayed Suleiman, *Commissioner, Kordofan Province*

18 May   **State Visit to Germany of the Queen and the Duke of Edinburgh**
ARENS, Bernward Christian Anton, *Of the Federal Post Office*
DANIELS, Wilhelm, *Mayor of Bonn*
DEHNERT, Captain Hans, *Commanding, German Naval Escort*
DIERKSMEIER, Theodor, *Chief Architect, Federal Railways*
ETZDORF, Frau Katharina von, *of the Suite specially attached*
HUBER, Otto, *In charge of Telephone arrangements*
KNICKENBERG, Rudolf, *Head of Section, Protocol Department*
KÖBLE, Fritz, *Officer for Orders, Federal President's Office*
MÜLLER, Helmut Paul Ernst, *Protocol Officer, President's Office*
MUFF, Eberhard Karl Ludwig, *Protocol Officer, Baden-Württemberg*
NEIDSTEIN, Freiherr Philipp von Brand zu, *Protocol Officer, Bavaria*
NOEBEL, Hans-Heinrich, *Head of Section for State visits*
OESTERHELT, Gerhard, *Head of Federal Security Police*
PLEHWE, Friedrich Carl von, *Head of UK Section, Federal Foreign Ministry and specially attached*
RAEDERSCHEIDT, Erich, *Press Officer to the President*
REUTER, Karl, *Head of Security Section, Ministry of Interior*
SCHAUER, Hans, *Private Secretary to Head of President's Office*
SEHRBROCK, Hermann, *Private Secretary to the Federal President*
HIRSCHFELD-SKIDMORE, James Carl Theodor, *Head of Protocol, Ministry of Defence*
TEETZEN, Willy, *Secretary, Board of Federal Railways*
WEBER, Heinz, *Interpreter*
WELCZECK, Graf Johannes, *Deputy Chief of Protocol*
WITTICH, Wilhelm Karl, *Protocol Officer, Niedersachsen*

13 July   **State Visit to Britain of the President of Chile and Señora de Frei**
CARVAJAL, Captain Patricio, Chilean Navy
GUERRERO SALCEDO, Colonel Felix Edouardo

1966

9 May   **State Visit to Belgium of the Queen and the Duke of Edinburgh**
MONCEAU DE BERGENDAL, Major-General (Air) Ivan Georges Arsène Felicieu du, DFC AND BAR, *Commander, Tactical Air Force*
VAN DAMME, Pierre Marie Joseph Gustave Antoine, *Burgomaster of Bruges*
DELWAIDE, Leonard Herman Joseph, *Deputy Alderman of Antwerp*
DETIEGE, Andreas Frans Theodor, *Deputy Alderman of Antwerp*
DONNET, Major-General (Air) Michael Gabriel Libert Marie, Baron, DFC, *Deputy Chief of Staff*
GITS, Josse Adolphe Philogone Joseph, MBE, *Assistant Protocol Department*

GRAAS, Colonel André François Léopold, *Commander, Special Gendarmerie of the Palaces*
GRYSE, André Aimé Gaston de, *Chief Commissioner of Police, Brussels*
SAINT-HUBERT, Lieutenant-Colonel Edouard Léon Mathilde Joseph Marie Ghislain de, *ADC*
LALOUX, Rene Adolphe Marie Charles, *Managing Director, Fabrique Internationale at Herstal*
PAELINCK, Paul Marie Henri, *Secretary to the Queen of the Belgians*
PEEMANS, Jacques A.M., *Assistant Private Secretary*
POSCH, Major Christian Louis Ernest Marie Ghislain, Baron de, *Commander of the Royal Palaces*
PUTMAN, Lucas Emiel Pauwel Rachel Maria, *Assistant in Grand Marshal's Department*
SEYNAVE, Maurice Eugène Marie Joseph, *Deputy Head of Protocol Department*
THIBAUT DE MASIÈRE, Colonel Gilbert A.M.P., *ADC to the Prince of Liège*
VANDERBORGHT, Emile, *Assistant Private Secretary*

17 May **State Visit to Britain of the President of the Federal Republic of Austria and Frau Jonas**
BUTLER-ELBERBERG, Lieutenant-Colonel Hans Egon Franz, *Defence Attaché, Austrian Embassy*
FISCHER, Doctor Franz, *Head, Press Department of the Presidential Cabinet*
MAYER, Professor Frau Auguste, *Lady in Waiting to Frau Margaretha Jonas*
ALEXANDER, Doctor Karl Otto, *Counsellor, Austrian Embassy*
TRUXA, Lieutenant-Colonel Doctor Raimond, *ADC to the Federal President*

19 July **State Visit to Britain of King Hussein I of Jordan and Princess Muna Al Hussein**
HIKMAT, Faridon Omar, *Counsellor, Jordanian Embassy*
KURDI, Colonel Mahmoud, *Military, Naval and Air Attaché*
NASSER, HH The Sharifa Huzeima, *Lady in Waiting to Princess Muna*
SHAKER, HH The Sharif Zeid bin, *ADC to the King*

1967

9 May **State Visit to Britain of King Faisal of Saudi-Arabia**
AZZAM, Salem, *Counsellor at the Royal Saudi Embassy*
AL BAIZ, Abdul Rahman, *Counsellor at the Royal Saudi Embassy*
AL HARITHY, Major-General Mashour, *Defence Attaché*
IBRAHIM, Mohamed Nouri, *Counsellor at the Royal Saudi Embassy*
KHOUJA, Colonel Akram
MALAIKA, Ibrahim

1 November **State Visit to Britain of the President of Turkey and Madame Sunay**
ENGIN, Brigadier-General Recai, *Senior Service Attaché*
GÜNEN, Zeki, *Counsellor at Embassy*
OZBAHADIR, Colonel Turgut, *First ADC to the President*
SÜNMEZ, Nejat Mesih, *Press Counsellor at Embassy*

1968

1 November **State Visit to Brazil of the Queen and the Duke of Edinburgh**
ASSIS DE ARAGÃO, Professor José, *Deputy Chief of President's Household (Civil)*
BARBOSA SOARES, Lael Simoes, *Chief of Ceremonial to Governor of Guanabara*
BARREIROS, Jose, *attached to Protocol Department*
CAMARA MODG, Senhora Maria de Lourdes da, *Lady attached to the Queen*
COVAS PEREIRA, Colonel José Maria, *Security Officer*
MASSA DA COSTA, Colonel Lourival, *Deputy Chief of the Military Household*
NASCIMENTO E SILVA, Senhora Maria Hortencia, *Lady attached to the Queen*
OLIVEIRA LACERDA, Luiz Horácio, *Chief of Ceremonial Department*
PESSOA FRAGOSO, João Carlos, *Of the Ceremonial Department*
BRAGA TEISERA, Colonel Silton, *Head of Security Police, Brasilia*
TABAJARA DE OLIVEIRA, João, *Chief of Ceremonial to Governor of São Paulo*
FLORES NETTO, Francisco Thompson, *Of the Ceremonial Department*
WEINSCHENCK, Guilherme, *Deputy Chief of Ceremonial*

11 November **State Visit to Chile of the Queen and the Duke of Edinburgh**
BRAUN PAGE, Victor, *President, Anglo-Chilean Society*
BUZETA MUÑOZ, Captain Oscar, *Director of Naval School*
GUIMPERT GARCIA, Captain Daniel, *Chilean Navy, Liaison Officer*
LAGARINI FREIRE, Julio, *Assistant Director of Protocol*
LIRA GOMEZ, Ricardo, *Assistant Director of Protocol*
MAHN, Brigadier-General Alfredo, *Commander of Garrison, Santiago*
SEPULVEDA GALINDO, General José, *Chief of Carabineros*
VALDES PHILLIPS, Pablo, *Civil ADC to the Queen*
WOOLVETT, Colonel Eric, *Military ADC to the Queen*

1969

22 April **State Visit to Britain of President Saragat of Italy**
GIUNCHIS, Professor Giuseppe, *Physician to the President*

MALGERI, Enzo, *Minister (Commercial) at Embassy*
SARAGAT, Giovanni Giuseppe Eugenio, *attached to Diplomatic Counsellor*

5 May   **State Visit to Austria of the Queen and the Duke of Edinburgh**
BANDION, Doctor Josef, *Senior Official, President's Private Office*
BUCHSBAUM, Doctor Herbert, *Official (Antique Furniture), Ministry of Building and Technology*
CHRISTELBAUER, Rudolf, *Senior Official, President's Private Office*
HANDLER, Colonel Johann, *Director, Spanish Riding School*
LEHRNER, Doctor Heinrich Josef Cornel, *Master of Provincial Stables*
NIGISCH, Hans, *Head of Section, Chancellor's Office*
RAINER, Brigadier Doctor Bruno, *Officer in Attendance on the Duke of Edinburgh*
RUDOFSKY, Doctor Hans Georg, *Of the Protocol Department*
SCHLUMBERGER, Frau Marie Helene, *Lady in Waiting to the Queen*
SKALNIK, Doctor Kurt, *Senior Oficial, President's Private Office*
STERNBERG, Doctor Otto, *Press Office, Chancellor's Office*
TRUXA, Lieutenant-Colonel Doctor Raimund, *ADC to the President*

15 July   **State Visit to Britain of the President of Finland and Madame Kekkonen**
SLOTTE, Ulf-Erik Alexander, *Counsellor, Finnish Embassy*
STENIUS, Göran Erik, *Counsellor, Finnish Embassy*
TUOMINEN, Lieutenant-Colonel Keijo Kalervo, *Second ADC to the President*
VITIKKA, Captain Olavi Israel, Finnish Navy, *Military, Naval and Air Attaché*

1970

1971

5 October   **State Visit to Britain of Emperor Hirohito and Empress Nagako of Japan**
HARA, Hidezo, *Counsellor, Japanese Embassy*
ICHIMURA, Madame Kikue, *Lady in Waiting*
KURODA, Minoru, *Master of Ceremonies*
MATSUDAIRA, Kiyoshi, *Chamberlain*
MUSHAKOJI, Madame Fujiko, *Lady in Waiting*
NAKAMURA, Seiichi, *Master of Ceremonies*
NISHIWAKI, Toshihiko, *Counsellor, Japanese Embassy*
TAKAHASHI, Shotaro, *Minister, Japanese Embassy*
TAKEDA, Yasuo, *Chief of General Affairs, Imperial Household*

18 October   **State Visit to Turkey of the Queen, the Duke of Edinburgh and Princess Anne**
ATABEK, Gürbüz, *Director of Security, Province of Izmir*
DEMIREL, Ismail Hakki, *Director of Security, Province of Ankara*
DISLIOGLU, Sulhi, *Chef du Cabinet, President's Office*
EGELI, Colonel Ramiz, *Commandant, Cavalry School, Istanbul*
ERDEM, Orhan, *Director of Security, Province of Istanbul*
HALEFOGLU, Mrs Fatma Zehra, *attached to the Queen*
KILIÇ, Altemur, *Director General (Information), Prime Minister's Office*
KURTBAY, Yalçin, *Director General, Protocol*
TOPA, Colonel Hüseyin, *1st ADC to the President*
URGA, Doctor Rifki Kamil

7 December   **State Visit to Britain of King Zahir of Afghanistan**
HOMSYUN, Doctor Mohammed, *Physician to the King*
SHAH WALI, Lieutenant-Colonel, *2nd ADC to the King*
SULAIMAN, Abdul Ali, *First Secretary, Afghan Embassy*

1972

10 February   **State Visit to Thailand of the Queen and the Duke of Edinburgh**
BEKANAN, Police Lieutenant-General Pote, *Assistant Director General, Police Department*
CHIRAROCHANA, Major-General Sitthi, *Special Security Officer*
DHANABHUMI, Major-General Porn, *Member of the Thai Suite*
DIVAVEJA, Air Vice-Marshal Chalerm, *Member of the Thai Suite*
LOACHALA, Police Lieutenant-General Chumpol, *Commissioner, Central Investigation Bureau*
MAHONONDA, Police Major-General Narong, *Member of the Thai Suite*
MANGKLARATANA, Police Lieutenant-General Chamras, *Commissioner, of Provincial Police*
PANKONGCHUEN, Police Lieutenant-General Monchai, *Commissioner, Metropolitan Police*
PANYARACHUN, Police Major-General Surajit, *Member of the Thai Suite*
PRAVITRA, Police Major-General Chetchandra, *Member of the Thai Suite*

22 February   **State Visit to Malaysia of the Queen, the Duke of Edinburgh and Princess Anne**
ASIAH binte Tengku Muda Chik, *Lady in Waiting to Raja Pirmaisuvi Agong*
SALEHA binte Ahmad, Che, *Malaysian Lady in Waiting to the Queen*
MERICAN bin Sutan, Dato, *Deputy Commissioner of Police*

MOHAMED ZAID bin Mohamed Salleh, Captain Malaysian Navy, *Malaysian ADC to the Queen*
SHAHUDDIN MOHAMED TAIB, Inche, *Chief of Protocol*

29 February   **State Visit to Brunei of the Queen, the Duke of Edinburgh and Princess Anne**
MOHAMMED, Prince, *Brother of the Sultan*
ISA bin Ibrahim, OBE, *Sultan's General Adviser*
ABDUL MOMIN bin Pengiran Othman, Yang Amat Mulia Pengiran Setia Jaya Pengiran Haji, *Sultan's Private Secretary*

13 March   **State Visit to the Maldives of the Queen and the Duke of Edinburgh**
HILMY DIDI, Ahmed, *Minister of Fisheries*
SHIHAB, Ibrahim, *Attorney General*

11 April   **State Visit to Britain of Queen Juliana and Prince Bernhard of the Netherlands**
DE BEAUFORT, Jonkheer Romain, *First Secretary, Netherlands Embassy*
LINDEN, Colonel Jean Eugéne Etoy van der, *Miltary Attaché*
WIJNEN, Dirk Jan van, *Counsellor at the Embassy*

15 May   **State Visit to France of the Queen and the Duke of Edinburgh**
BAUDOUIN, Denis Gustave Charles, *Technical Adviser at Presidency*
REGNAULD DE BELLESCIZE, Capitaine de Fregate Etienne Marie Jean de, *attached to the Duke of Edinburgh*
BERNARD, Jean-René, *Technical Adviser at Presidency*
CHAUBARD, Pierre, *Prefect of Yvelines*
DOMERG, Henri, *Technical Adviser at the Presidency*
DUPUY, Madame Anne-Marie, *Head of Cabinet at Presidency*
ERIAU, Jean-Gabriel, *Prefect of Rouen*
ERIGNAC, René Jean Louis, *Prefect of Vaucluse*
JUILLET, Madame Annick, *attached to the Queen*
KEMP, Gérald Sylvère van der, *Head Curator at Versailles*
LAPORTE, Jean George Marcel, *Prefect of Bouches du Rhône*
LARCHÉ, Jean Marie André, *Protocol Department*
LENCQUESAING, Colonel Hervé Jacques Albéric de, *attached to the Queen*
MONTARRAS, Alain Lucien, *Head of Department for State visits*
PRUVOST, Gérard Jean, *Protocol Department*
RAIMOND, Jean-Bernard, *Technical Adviser*
SALTET, Marc Louis Lionel, *Architect in Chief, Versailles*
LA TOUR DU PIN CHAMBLY DE LA CHARGE, Jean Marie Louis, Comte de, *Protocol Department*
ZIEGLER, Henri Alexandre Léonard, CBE, *S.N.I.A.S.*

June   **State Visit to Britain of Grand Duke Jean and Grand Duchess Charlotte of Luxembourg**
HALL, M. François, *ADC to Grand Duke*

17 October   **State Visit to Yugoslavia of the Queen, the Duke of Edinburgh and Princess Anne**
KVEDER, Mrs Kordija, *attached to Princess Anne*
LUKIC, Rade, *Assistant Chief of Protocol*
MIHAJLOVIC, Captain Ljubisa, *attached to the Duke of Edinburgh*
PAPOVIC, Dragan, *Director of Security Department*
RAKOCI, Stjepan, *Chief of Section, Organisation of visit*
STIPIC, Luka, *Director, Centre for Selection of Horses, Djakovo, Croatia*
VELASEVIC, Veljko, *Chief of Protocol, President's Office*

24 October   **State Visit to Britain of President Heinemann of the Federal Republic of Germany**
BLAU, Herr Doktor Hagen, *Counsellor, German Embassy*
SCHMIDT-DORNEDDEN, Herr Horst, *Ministry Counsellor for Foreign Affairs*
MULLER-GERBES, Herr (Heinz) Geert, *Head of Press Department of Presidency*
GIESDER, Herr Doktor Manfred Joachim Anton, *Counsellor, German Embassy*
GRUNER, Herr Werner Wolfgang, *Liaison Officer to President*
GABLENTZ, Herr Otto Martin von der, *Counsellor, German Embassy*
LOHMEYER, Frau Doktor Brigitte, *Cultural Attaché, German Embassy*

20 December   UTTER, John, *Comptroller to the Duke of Windsor 1959–72*

1973

3 April   **State Visit to Britain of President Echeverria of Mexico**
CANTÚ, Señor Armando, *Minister Counsellor*
AROAZ, Señor Manuel de, *Counsellor*
PEYREFITTE, Rear-Admiral José Blanco, *Naval Attaché*
DESVIGNES, Señor Alain Charles, *Counsellor*
DESVIGNES, Señora Maria Esther Echeverria de, *Interpreter*
AZUARA SALAS, Doctor Tomas Ismael, *Personal Physician*

11 December   **State Visit to Britain of President Mobuto of Zaïre**
MITIMA KANENO, Citoyen Murairi
LEMA, Citoyen Mena, *Conseilleur Juridique*
MOKOLO WA MPOBMO, Citoyen, *Chef du Protocol*

MUDIAYI, Citoyen Lieutenant-Colonel Mwanba Djobo, *Conseilleur Principal*
TUKUZU, Citoyen Colonel Gusu-Wo Angbaduruka
VITA, Citoyen Mpembele Zi
DJEMBA YUMBULA, Citoyen Albert, *Conseilleur Economique*

1974

15 February   **Visit to New Hebrides of the Queen and the Duke of Edinburgh**
LANGLOIS, Robert Jules Amedee

30 April   **State Visit to Britain of Queen Margrethe II of Denmark and Prince Henrik**
ARMFELT, Countess Wava Kitty, *Lady in Waiting to Queen of Denmark*
JESSEN, Captain Niels Finn Zoffmann, *Commanding HMY* Dannebrog
AGERBAK, Harry, *Minister Plenipotentiary*
SONDERGAARD, Bent, *Minister-Counsellor (Economic)*

9 July   **State Visit to Britain of the Yang diPertuan Agung of Malaysia and the Raja Permaisuri Agung**
CHENG, Hor Soon, Encik, *Information Attaché*
ZAWAWI bin Haji Mohamed, Encik Abdullah, *Counsellor and Head of Chancery*
WAN ISMAIL BIN MOHAMED Salleh, Brigadier-General, *General ADC*

1975

24 February   **State Visit to Mexico of the Queen and the Duke of Edinburgh**
BREMER MARTINO, Señor Licenciado Juan Jose, *Private Secretary*
CARRILLO OLEA, Ten. Coronel de Infanteria DEM Jorge, *of the Presidential General Staff*
PELLICER LOPEZ, Señor Juan, *Chief of Protocol*
SANCHEZ, General de Brigada DEM Ramon Mota, *Commander, Presidential Guard*
GUTIERREZ SANTOS, General de Brigada DEM Daniel, *Director General of Police, Mexico City*
BERNAL, Doctor Ignacio, *Director of National Museum of Anthropology*

7 May   **State Visit to Japan of the Queen and the Duke of Edinburgh**
FUKADA, Hiromu, *Interpreter to Emperor*
KODAMA, Masato, *Deputy Superintendent, Akasaka Palace*
KOSAKA, Takashi, *Director of General Affairs Division, Imperial Household*
NAKAGAWA, Mrs Sachiko, *Member of Suite of Honour*
NOMURA, Chusaku, *Deputy Chief of Protocol*
OHNO, Mrs Misako, *Interpreter to Empress*
TANIGUCHI, Sadakazu, *Director of Western European Division, Ministry of Foreign Affairs*
UCHIDA, Mrs Emiko, *Member of Suite of Honour*
UEDA, Koichi, *Master of Ceremonies*
YAMAGUCHI, Takaji, *Master of Ceremonies*
YAMAMOTO, Iwao, *Of the Board of Chamberlains*
YASUI, Yoshiro, *Vice-Grand Master of Ceremonies*
YAMANOUCHI, Kazuhiko

8 July   **State Visit to Edinburgh of King Carl XVI Gustaf of Sweden**
ARNÖ, Lars Gunnar, *Counsellor, Swedish Embassy*
PLATEN, Baron Carl Gustaf Johan Axel von, *Counsellor, Swedish Embassy*

1976

4 May   **State Visit to Britain of President Geisel of Brazil and Senhora Geisel**
BARRETO, Sr. Humberto Esmeraldo, *Head Press Adviser*
COSTA, Sr. Ronaldo, *Minister-Counsellor, Brazilian Embassy*
CALMAN DE SÁ, Sr. Angelo, *Chairman, Bank of Brazil*
FERREIRA, Sr. Heitor Aquino, *Private Secretary*
LIMA, Colonel Wilberto Luiz, *Special Adviser*
PEREIRA-LIRA, Sr. Paulo Hortenzio, *Chairman, Central Bank of Brazil*
MOURAO, Colonel Americo Soverchi, *Head, Medical Service of the Presidency*
NEIVA, Lieutenant-Colonel Antonio Fernandes, *Head, Communications Service*
RAFFAELI, Sr. Marcello, *Minister-Counsellor, Brazilian Embassy*
REIFSCHNEIDER, Rear-Admiral Telmo Becker, *Naval Adviser, Brazilian Embassy*
RODRIGUES, Captain Edouardo de Oliveira, *Naval ADC*
VIANNA, Sr. Marcos Pereira, *Chairman, National Bank for Economic Development*

24 May   **State Visit to Finland of the Queen and the Duke of Edinburgh**
WRIGHT, Mrs Elizabeth von, *of the President's Suite*
TIKKA, Commander Juha, *Chief of Naval Operations*
KALELA, Mr Jaakko, *Special Foreign Affairs Adviser*
SIHVO, Lieutenant-Colonel Sami, *Second ADC*
WÄCHTER, Major Lasse, *Third ADC*
AUERO, Mr Olli, *Protocol Department*
MÄKELÄINEN, Miss Eva-Christina, *Deputy Head of Protocol*

22 June	**State Visit to Britain of President Giscard d'Estaing of France and Madame Giscard d'Estaing** BEAUCHAMPS, M. Xavier Réné Antoine Goyou, *Technical Counsellor* FLOHIC, Contre-Amiral François Leon, *Armed Forces Attaché, French Embassy* FREYCHE, M. Michel Gabriel, *Financial Counsellor, French Embassy* ROBIN, M. Gabriel, *Technical Counsellor* SAUZAY, M. Philippe Pierre WAHL, M. Jean Henri, *Commercial Counsellor, French Embassy*
8 November	**State Visit to Luxembourg of the Queen and the Duke of Edinburgh** CLAUDE, M. André, CBE, *Chief of Information* GUTENKAUF, Dr Jean, *Doctor in attendance* MEUNIER, Major Eugene, *ADC to the Grand Duke* WAGNER, Lieutenant-Colonel Jean-Pierre, *Assistant Commander of Gendarmerie*

1977

23 November	**For Services to the Study of British Orders, Decorations and Medals (particularly those in the Royal Collection)** RISK, James Charles

1978

22 May	**State Visit to Germany of the Queen and the Duke of Edinburgh** FUCHS, Captain Hans-Henning, *Chief of Protocol, Ministry of Defence* HARTMANN, Dr Jurgen Otto, *Chief of Protocol, Rheinland-Pfalz* MAURER, Kapitan zur See Horst-Dieter, *Liaison Officer, President's Office* TER-NEDDEN, Dr Jurg, *Head of Section, President's Office* OTTINGER, Dr Johannes, *Head of Group, President's Office* PATZOLD, Herr Ernst-Günter, *Of Press and Information Office* SCHMIDT, Herr Egon, *Head of Section, President's Office* SPATH, Dr Franz Josef Liborius, *Head of Section, President's Office* PUTTKAMER, Herr Eberhard von, *Deputy Head of Section, Protocol* SCHACKY, Freiherr Erwin von, *Head of Section, Protocol* SELCHOW, Herr Wolfgang Hans-Rudiger von, *Deputy Chief of Protocol, Berlin* SEEMANN, Dr Heinrich, *Head of Section, President's Office*
14 November	**State Visit to Britain of President Eanes of Portugal** BARROCO, Lieutenant-Colonel Jose Manuel Vaz, *Head, President's Office* VIEGAS GONCALVES CORREIA, Coronel-Medico Jose Manuel Nobre, CBE, *President's Doctor* SILVA COSTA, Senhor Manuel Maria da, *Counsellor* ESTEVENS, Tte Coronel (Aerea) Geraldo Jose, *Counsellor* CALDAS FARIA, Senhor Manuel, *Consul-General* MAIA GONCALVES, Coronel Manuel Joaquim Alvaro, *Military and Air Attaché* SERPA GOUVEIA, Captain Ildeberto Manuel, *Naval Attaché* ALVES MACHADO, Senhor Pedro, *Minister-Counsellor*

1979

16 May	**State Visit to Denmark of the Queen and the Duke of Edinburgh** BARDENFLETH, Mrs Alette Ingeborg Henriette, *Lady in Waiting* BERNSTORFF-GYLDENSTEEN, Countess Bente, *Lady in Waiting* NIELSEN, Ingo Emil, *Treasurer to the Queen* PORSDAL, Jirgen Helge, *Comptroller, Lord Chamberlain's Office* THOMSEN, Kaj Straarup, *Assistant Private Secretary* FOGH-ANDERSEN, Major Henrik, *Chamberlain*

1980

14 October	**State Visit to Italy of the Queen and the Duke of Edinburgh** PISCITELLO, Dott. Sergio, *Chief of Protocol* JACOBUCCI, Ministro Michele, *Chief of Press Office* ANTONELLI, Dott. Armando, *Deputy Administration Secretary General of the Presidency* CARBONI, Dott. Giuseppe, *Of the Presidency* JORIO, Amm. Carlo, *Deputy Military Adviser* MALLARDO, Prefetto Vincenzo, *Deputy Chief of Protocol, Council of Ministers* FERRARA, General Arnaldo, *Security Counsellor to President* EPIFANIO, Dott. Giovanni, *Director General of Inspectorate of Public Security* MURGO, Ministro Emanuele Scammacca del, *Deputy Chief of Diplomatic Protocol* ZUCCONI, Ministro Gaetano, *President's Assistant Diplomatic Counsellor* **State Visit to Tunisia of the Queen and the Duke of Edinburgh** ANNABI, M. Hédi, *Head of Tunisian Press Agency*

AMMAR, Madame Sayda ben, *Lady in Waiting*
OUESLATI, Colonel Abdellaziz, *Aide-de-Camp*

18 November   **State Visit to Britain of King Birendra and Queen Aishwarya of Nepal**
SHRESTHA, Lieutenant-Colonel Dr Khagendra Bahadur, *Physician*
MALLA, Lieutenant-Colonel Shanta Kumar, *ADC*
RANA, Prabal Shumsher Jungbahadur, *Deputy Chief of Protocol*
SHAH, Mrs Krishna, *Lady in Waiting*
PANDAY, Mr Mohan Bahadur, *First Secretary and Head of Chancery, Nepalese Embassy*
SHAH, Lieutenant-Colonel Shankar Bikram, *Military Attaché*

1981

5 May   **State Visit to Norway of the Queen and the Duke of Edinburgh**
GRØNVOLD, Mrs Ellinor, *Lady in Waiting*
SEIP, Mrs Gøran, *Lady in Waiting*
SIMONSEN, Colonel Sverre I, *Principal ADC*
HATLEM, Commodore Ole B., *Principal ADC*
BARR, Colonel Terje, *Principal ADC*
KAVLI, Dr T. Guthorm, *Director, Royal Palace Administration*
EVJU, Mrs Marie, *Lady in Waiting, attached to HM*
LANGLETE, Lieutenant-Colonel Kare, *Commanding Queen's Guard*

9 June   **State Visit to Britain of King Khalid of Saudi Arabia**
AL-KHOWAITER, Dr Hamad, *of HM's Secretariat*
AL-NOWAISER, HE Abdulrahman, *of HM's Secretariat*
AL-SHAWWAF, HE Hassan, *of HM's Secretariat*
AL-TURKI, Abdulaziz Mansour, *Cultural Attaché*
AL-UMARI, HE Abdul Aziz, *of HM's Secretariat*
ABDULKARIM, HE Abdullah bin, *Interpreter*
ISMAEL, Brigadier-General Abdullah, *Defence Attaché*

1982

16 March   **State Visit to Britain of Qaboos bin Al Said, Sultan of Oman**
AL HOSNI, HE Sheikh Ahmed Sultan, *Deputy President in Diwan of Protocol*
AL KALBANI, Lieutenant-Colonel Ibrahim Sulayum, *Royal Guard Brigade*

16 November   **State Visit to Britain of Queen Beatrix of the Netherlands and Prince Claus**
ALBLAS, Lieutenant-Colonel P.A. Blusse van Oud, *Master of the Household*
GOUDSWAARD, Madame H.G., *Lady in Waiting*
SPIERENBURG, Colonel E., *Chief of Security of Royal House*
BEUSEKOM, Captain G. van, RNLN, *Defence Attaché*
HEESTERMANS, Colonel M.F.E., *Military Attaché*
ZWAAN, Mr J.P. Kleiweg de, *Counsellor*

1983

25 May   **State Visit to Sweden of the Queen and the Duke of Edinburgh**
PALMSTIERNA, Friherrinnan Elisabeth, Baroness, *Comptroller of Duke of Halland's Household*
OLSSON, Fru Elisabeth, *Lady in Waiting*
LILLIECREUTZ, Brigadier Friherre Frederik, Baron, *ADC to Duke of Edinburgh*
BAUSCH, Mr Christian, *Deputy Chief of Protocol*

1984

26 March   **State Visit to Jordan of the Queen and the Duke of Edinburgh**
AL-FAIZ, Colonel Hamidi, *Commander Royal Bodyguard Battalion*
SALMAN, Brigadier Theeb Sulieman, *Commander Hussein Bin Ali Brigade*
TALHOUNI, Adnan Bahjat, *Assistant Chief of Protocol*
ABU TAYEH, Fawaz Mohammad Audeh, *Assistant Chief of Protocol; Technical Adviser*

23 October   **State Visit to Britain of President Mitterand of the French Republic and Madame Mitterand**
GUIGOU, Mme Elisabeth
COTTIN, Mme Christine, *Head, President's Press Office*
BOURGOIN, Captain, French Navy, *ADC*
VEYRAC, Contre Amiral Olivier de, *Defence Attaché*
SCHNEITER, M. Bertrand, *Financial Minister*
CARRIERE, M. Guy Carron de la, *Commercial Minister*
ROUX, M. Jean-François, *Consul General*

1985

25 March **State Visit to Portugal of the Queen and the Duke of Edinburgh**
PIMENTEL, Lieutenant-Colonel Jose Manuel Tavares, *Head of President's Cabinet*
LETRIA, Dr Joaquim, *President's Spokesman*
MENDES, Dr Luis Filipe de Castro, *Adviser on Foreign Affairs*
SARMENTO, Commandante Arthur Junqueiro, *Military Adviser*
CORREIA, Dr Jose Viegas, *President's Doctor*
FERREIRA, Lieutenant-Colonel Rogerio Coutinho, *Security Adviser*

16 April **State Visit to Britain of Life President Dr Banda of Malawi**
MKWAMBA, Tennyson Jack Kasoka, *Counsellor, Malawi High Commission*

11 June **State Visit to Britain of President de la Madrid of Mexico and Señora de la Madrid**
BERLANGA, Señor Andres Massieu, *Deputy Private Secretary*
STEGER CATANO, Señor Raphael, *Minister, Mexican Embassy*
LOPEZ ORTEGA DE DREIER, Señora Maria de los Angeles, *Minister, Mexican Embassy*
CARDONA MARINO, General de Brigada Arturo, *Deputy Chief, Presidential Staff*
COMPEAN PALACIOS, Señor Manuel, *Director, Foreign Press Relations*
RUIZ, General de Brigada Leobardo, *Personal Doctor*

12 November **State Visit to Britain of Shaikh Khalifa bin Hamad Al-Thani, Amir of Qatar**
AL-SAIRAFI, Dr Shawki, *Private Doctor*
AL-JAIDHA, Mr Mohamed Yousef, *Counsellor*
AL-MALKI, Mr Ibrahim Mohamed, *Assistant Director, Amiri Protocol*

1986

17 February **State Visit to Nepal of the Queen and the Duke of Edinburgh**
PANDEY, Mr Narendra Raj, *Private Secretary, Royal Palace*
SHAH, Mrs. Bhinda Swari, MVO, *Secretary, Ministry of Foreign Affairs*
SINGH, Mr Arjun Bahadur, *Chief of Protocol*
PANDEY, Dr Mrigendra Raj, *Physician*
JOSHI, Mr Hira Bahadur, *Joint Secretary*
THAPA, Colonel Tara Bahadur, *ADC*
SHAH, Lieutenant-Colonel Vivek Kumar, LVO, *ADC*

22 April **State Visit to Britain of King Juan Carlos and Queen Sofia of Spain**
SALGADO ALBA, Señor Alberto, *Physician*
CARBAJAL, Señor Jose Ignacio, *Minister, Spanish Embassy*
ARANDA CARRANZA, Señor Eduardo, *Minister (Consular) Spanish Embassy*
CARVERA, Colonel Jose Antonio, *ADC*
CARRANZA, Captain Jose Luis de, *Defence and Naval Attaché; Spanish Embassy*
LAIGLESIA DEL ROSAL, Señor Eduardo de, *Counsellor; Spanish Embassy*
LOPEZ DE LETONA, Señor Jose Antonio, *Counsellor (Press); Spanish Embassy*
VERANO FABADO, Colonel Pedro, *Assistant Defence (Air) Attaché, Spanish Embassy*
MARTI-FLUXA, Señor Ricardo, *Counsellor; Spanish Embassy*
GARCIA, Señor Ignacio, *Counsellor, Spanish Embassy*
GARRIGUES, Señor Eduardo, *Counsellor (Cultural); Spanish Embassy*
GUTIERREZ, Señor Fernando, *Head, President's Press Office*
SOUSA AMELL, Señor Julio, *Minister (Cultural); Spanish Embassy*
MONTOJO GONZALEZ-TREVILLA, Colonel Jose Maria, *ADC*
VILLEGAS, Señor Jose, *Treasurer*
CORTES, Señor Ricardo, *Minister, (Economic), Spanish Embassy*

1 July **State Visit to Britain of President von Weizsäcker of the Federal Republic of Germany and Freifrau von Weizsäcker**
BRACKLO, Herr Dr Eike Edzard, *Minister-Counsellor*
ECKERT, Herr Heinrich, *Counsellor*
ENGELHARD, Herr Michael Rudolf, *First Counsellor, Federal Presidency*
HAAS, Herr Dr Gottfried, *Counsellor*
KONIG, Herr Gunther Julius Rudolf Kurt, *Counsellor*
PFLUGER, Herr Dr Friedbert, *Head of Press Office, Federal Presidency*
SAND, Oberst Wolfgang, *Liaison Officer, Federal Presidency*
SCHUBACH, Herr Jorg, CBE, *Head of Security Police*
NEUBRONNER, Herr Georg-Heinrich von, *Counsellor*
WALDOW, Herr Dr Adolf Friedrich Bernd von, *Counsellor*

1987

14 July **State Visit to Britain of King Hassan II of Morocco**
ALAOUI, Moulay Youssef
BENMANSOUR, M. Abdelwahhab, *Moroccan Royal Cabinet*

BENNANI, M. Abdelkrim, *Office of Private Secretary*
BERBICH, Professor Abdellatif, CBE, *Moroccan Royal Cabinet*
BOUCHENTOUF, M. Khalid, *Husband of Princess Lalla*
EL M'RINI, M. Abdelhak, CBE, *Moroccan Royal Cabinet*
EL MEDIOURI, M. Mohamed, CBE, *Of Security*
JAIDI, M. Abdeslam, *Moroccan Royal Cabinet*
LAGHZAOUI, Mme Aicha, *Of the non-official suite*
MANSOURI, M. Ben Ali, *Of the non-official suite*
METQAL, Colonel Abdelghani, *Moroccan Royal Cabinet*
ZEMMOURI-ROCHDI, Colonel Ahmed, CBE, *Moroccan Royal Cabinet*
SINACEUR, Colonel Mohammed Abdeslam, CBE, *Moroccan Royal Cabinet*
SKIREDJ, Colonel-Major Boubker, CBE, *ADC*

1988

12 April

State Visit to Britain of King Olav of Norway
GRAM, Major Thomas Andreas, *Equerry*

17 October

State Visit to Spain of the Queen and the Duke of Edinburgh
SANTOS GONZALEZ, Colonel José, *Head of Royal Guard*
CALVA, Lieutenant-Colonel Felicia, *ADC to the King*
BENITO GONZALEZ, Lieutenant-Colonel José, *in command of Motorcades*
LOS ARCOS GALBETE, Don José Luis, *Deputy Head, State Protocol*
LACLAUSTRA, Don Arturo, *Deputy Head, Presidency Protocol*
LEAL CASTILLO, Lieutenant-Colonel José Antonio, *ADC to the King*
BARRIOS, Donna Cristina, *Deputy Chief of Protocol*

8 November

State Visit to Britain of President Abdou Diouf of Senegal and Madame Abdou Diouf
DIATTA, HE Mr Bruno, *Head of Protocol of the President*
MBAYE, Mr Babacar, *Diplomatic Counsellor*
FAYE, Monsieur Amadou, *First Counsellor*
SOURANG, Monsieur Abdou, *First Counsellor*
MENDY, Monsieur Henri, *First Counsellor*

1989

18 July

State Visit to Britain of Sheikh Zayed bin Sultan Al-Nahyan, President of the United Arab Emirates
NUSSEIBEH, HE Zaki Anwar Zaki, *Adviser to President*
HINDI, HE Mohamed bin, *Assistant Under Secretary for Protocol*
AL-KHUMEIRI, HE Mattar Khamis, *Assistant Under Secretary, Private Department*
MOUSA AL HASHIMI, HE Abdulla Al Sayed Mohammed

1990

23 October

State Visit to Britain of President Cossiga of Italy and Signora Cossiga
ORTONA, Signor Ludvico, *Press Adviser*
GROLLA, Dr Cesaro, *Physician*
GORI, Signor Sandro, LVO, *Head of Protocol*
BRUNO, Signor Alberto, MVO, *of the Presidency*

1991

1992

9 June

State Visit to France of the Queen and the Duke of Edinburgh
ANDRIEU, M. Jacques
CHASSIGNEUX, M. Pierre Claude Georges, *Prefect of Bordeaux*
DEMATTEIS, M. Raymond, *Chief of Security*
GOISBAULT, M. Hugues Claude, *Assistant to Chief of Protocol*
LAUVERGEON, Madame Anne
LEBLOND, M. François Jean Louis
MUSITELLI, M. Jean
SEILLER, M. Jean François, *Prefect of Blois*
VIOT, Ambassadeur Jacques Edmond

19 October

State Visit to Germany of the Queen and the Duke of Edinburgh
BRUNNER, Herr Hans Joerg, *Visit Co-ordinator*
KELLEIN, Brigadegeneral Dieter Hans, *Honorary Escort*

3 November

State Visit to Britain of the Sultan of Brunei Darussalam and the Raja Isteri
SUHAIMI, Pengiran Haji, *Private Secretary to Prince Jefri*

JAEFAR, Pengiran Anak Haji, *The Sultan's Brother-in-Law*
YAHYA, Haji, *of Private Secretary's Office*
PUTEH

1993

27 April   **State Visit to Britain of President Soares of Portugal and Senhora Soares**
SERRANO CALEIRO, Mrs. Maria Estrela, *Press Adviser*
VENTURA MARTINS, Carlos Manuel, *Press Adviser*

1994

5 July   **State Visit to Britain of King Harald and Queen Sonja of Norway**
BECH, Jon, *Minister, Norwegian Embassy*
BRAATHEN, Øystein, *Minister Counsellor, Norwegian Embassy*
BRAKSTAD, Knut, *Personal Secretary*
GULLAKSEN, Mrs Nina Houge, *Lady in Waiting to the Queen*
SKEIE, Nikolai, *Consul-General in Edinburgh*

1995

23 May   **State Visit to Britain of Sheikh Jabir al-Ahmad al Jabir Al-Sabah, Amir of Kuwait**
AL-MISHARI, Abdulrazzak, *Deputy Director of Office of the Amir*

17 October   **State Visit to Britain of the President of Finland and Mrs Ahtisaari**
JALKANEN, Mr Timo, *Chief of Protocol*
RUSI, Mr Alpo, *Adviser to the President*
KARUMAA, Commander Antero, *Senior ADC*

1996

14 May   **State Visit to Britain of the President of the French Republic and Madame Chirac**
MENAT, Monsieur Pierre, *Technical Adviser*
JONG, Colonel de, *ADC*
THIERY, Monsieur Christopher, LVO, *Interpreter*
KERSAUSON, Rear-Admiral de, *Defence Attaché, French Embassy*
LOUIS, Monsieur Oliver, *Minister Counsellor, French Embassy*
BOUFFANDEAU, Monsieur Jean-François, *Consul-General*
RICHARD, Madame Evelyne, LVO, *President's Press Office*

28 October   **State Visit to Thailand of the Queen and the Duke of Edinburgh**
HEMATHAT, Mr Pratuang, *Director, Royal Chamberlain's Division*
KAMPEEPAN, General Sayan, *Assistant Chief, ADC General*
KRAIRIKSH, Mr Chittrapat, *Deputy Principal Private Secretary*
CHATRAPONG, Kunying Rattanaporn, *Assistant Principal Private Secretary*
KRAIRIKSHA, Khunying Busaya, *Lady in Waiting*

1997

December   **State Visit to Britain of the President of the Federative Republic of Brazil and Senhora Cardoso**
LIMA, Sérgio Eduardo Moreira, *Minister-Counsellor, Brazilian Embassy in London*
SANTOS, Eduardo dos, *Minister-Counsellor, Brazilian Embassy in London*
CAMPOS, Paulo César de Oliveira, *Deputy Head of Protocol*

1998

26 May   **State Visit to Britain of Emperor Akihito and Empress Michiko of Japan**
MURAKAMI, Tokumitsu, *Director-General of General Affairs Division, Imperial Household*
CHIZAWA, Haruhiko, *Chamberlain to the Emperor*
SATO, Masahiro, *Chamberlain to the Emperor*
KIMURA, Masahiro, *Master of the Ceremonies, Imperial Household*
HAMAMOTO, Mrs Matsuko, *Lady in Waiting to the Empress*

1 December   **State Visit to Britain of the President of the Federal Republic of Germany and Frau Herzog**
MOHN, Frau Liz, *of Bertelsmann AG*
MALTZAHN, Baron Paul von, *Minister-Counsellor, German Embassy in London*

1999

22 June	State Visit to Britain of the President of the Republic of Hungary and Madame Arpad Goncz
	ILLICH, Lajos, *Chief of Protocol, Ministry of Foreign Affairs*
	JUHÁSZ, Sándor, *Minister Plenipotentiary, Hungarian Embassy*

2000

16 February	State Visit to Britain of Queen Margrethe II of Denmark and Prince Henrik
	HAUEN, Mrs Anita van, *Lady in Waiting to the Queen of Denmark*
	NIELSEN, Knud, *Counsellor (Press and Cultural Affairs), Danish Embassy*
17 June	FITZGIBBONS, Harold Edward (Harry), *Chairman of the Trustees, The Prince of Wales's Innovation Trust*

MVO IV & LVO

1896

8 May	Queen Victoria's visit to Cimiez
	ESCOURROU, Mons. Albert, *attached to Minister of the Interior*
	PAOLI, Mons. Xavier, *attached to Minister of the Interior*
	CHARDON, Mons. Louis Arsène Paul, *Chef de l' Exploitation de Chemins de fer de l'ouest*
	LAMOLÈRE, Mons. Ludovic de, *Inspector General of Railway Movements, Paris to Lyon and the Mediterranean*
30 June	Coronation of Emperor Nicholas II of Russia
	ORLOFF, Lieutenant Jean, *Cossacks of the Guard of the Emperor*
	BRINKEN, Captain Baron Leopold von den, *Guard Grenadier Regiment*
	LUNDH, Lieutenant-Colonel Robert, *Superintendent, Imperial Stables, Moscow*
	DOUBRAVINE, Captain Alexander, *Finnish Regiment of the Guard*
31 October	Emperor Nicholas II's visit to Balmoral
	DIETZE, Mons. Emile Gilbert, *Special Commissary of French Railway Police*
	RATCHKOVSKY, Mons. Pierre de, *Officer for special missions at the Russian State Police Department*
	RODENDORF, Captain Louis, *Russian Feldjäger's Corps*
23 November	SLATIN PASHA, Colonel, *of the Egyptian Army*
28 November	WERTHERN, Captain Baron Wolf von, *Chamberlain to the Duke of Saxe-Coburg and Gotha*

1897

5 January	GABLENZ, Heinrich, Freiherr von, *Captain of the 11th Austrian Hussar Regt. (Prince Windisch-Graetz), in attendance on Prince Philip of Coburg*
	BRUYNE, Mons. Pieter L., de
30 June	TOSTI, Signor Paolo
2 July	ARNIM, Major von

1898

5 May	GAMBART, Monsieur Ernest
11 June	MARTINO, Chevalier Eduardo de, *Marine Painter to Queen Victoria*
26 August	The Duke of Connaught's visit to France to attend Military Manoeuvres
	CHODRON de COURCEL, Lieutenant Louis Alphonse, *9th Dragoons Regiment*

1899

25 May	RESZKE, Mons. Jean de
23 November	Visit to Britain of Wilhelm II, the German Emperor, King of Prussia
	KLEHMET, Herr Reinhold
	ILBERG, Doctor Friederich

1900

28 June — **Visit to Windsor of Prince Abbas Pasha, Khedive of Egypt**
CHEFIK BEY, Ahmed, *Private Secretary to the Khedive.*
BEY IZZET, Aziz, *ADC to the Khedive*
KAUTSKI BEY, Doctor, *Physician to the Khedive*
YAWER BEY, *Staff Officer to the Khedive*

16 July — RESZKE, Mons. Edouard de

1901

25 February — PFYFFER-HEYDEGG, Herr Georg von, *German Secretary to Queen Victoria*

18 March — **Funeral of Queen Victoria**
CHÉRÉMÉTEFF, Captain Count Dmitri, *in attendance on the Grand Duke Michael Alexandrovitch of Russia*
BOECK, Captain Ernst, *ADC to King Christian IX of Denmark*
FUCHS, Herr Emil, *Sculptor and painter*

28 May — RENTZELL, Captain Richard von, *1st Regiment. (Queen Victoria's) of Dragoons of the Guard*
COURTH, Captain Carl, *5th (Prince Blücher of Wahlstatt) Hussar Regiment.*
USEDOM, Lieutenant Eggert von

11 October — YORRY, Lieutenant von, *1st Garde Dragoner Regiment (Queen Victoria)*
MALTZAHN, Baron von, *Kur Direktor of Homburg*
LUDWIG, Herr Felix, *Director of Postal Dept. Homburg*

King Edward VII's visit to Denmark
BENZON, Captain Christian, *Danish Hussars of the Guard*
CASTERSKIOLD, Captain Anton, *Danish Hussars of the Guard*
ENGELBRECHT, Captain Frederick C.J., *Danish Hussars of the Guard*
HOLM, Justisrand Waldmar, *Secretary to Hof Marshal Oxholm*

24 December — LEINHAAS, Captain Gustav, *of the Royal Landwehr Cavalry*

1902

14 March — RAMPOLD, Commander Paul, *of the Imperial German Admiralty*

6 June — LAVIÑA, Señor D. Frederica, *Director of Posts, Spain*

22 August — **King Edward's VII's Coronation**
ALBUQUERQUE, Lieutenant-Colonel Alfredo Augusto José de, *Portuguese Cavalry Regt. No 3 of King Edward VII*
KOCH, Lieutenant-Colonel Ludwig, *Austro-Hungarian Imperial and Royal Regiment No 12 Edward VII*
LYNAR, Captain Friedrich Rochus, Count zu, *1st Regt. of Dragoons of the Guard 'Queen Victoria of Great Britain and Ireland'*
RATHENOW, Captain Karl Wilhelm Nicolaus von, *5th Regt. of Hussars 'Prince Blücher von Wahlstatt'*
DRENIAKIN, Captain Nikolai Nikolaievitch, *27th (Kieff) King Edward VII Russian Dragoon Regiment*
LARCHER, Captain Fernando, *Portuguese Cavalry Regt. No.3 of King Edward VII*
GUILLEAUME, Captain Adalbert, *Austro-Hungarian Imperial and Royal Hussar Regt. No.12 Edward VII*

30 December — **Visit to Britain of Wilhelm II German Emperor, King of Prussia**
TAEGEN, Geheimer Hofrathein Julius, *of the German Imperial Foreign Office*

1903

7 April — **King Edward VII's visit to Portugal**
GUERREIRO, Major Jose Garcia, *ADC to King Carlos of Portugal*
SEABRA de LACERDA, Major Antonio Vaz Correia, *Ordinance Officer to King Carlos*
DA SILVA, Major Joao Diaz, *Assistant Commissioner of Police, Lisbon*
RAMOS, Captain Jocio Luiz, *Cavalry Régiment. No.3 of King Edward VII*
SALEMA, Lieutenant Victorino Augusto da Silva, *Cavalry Regiment. No.3 of King Edward VII*
VALLE, Lieutenant Augusto, *Royal Portuguese Navy*

27 April — **King Edward VII's visit to Naples**
SERRANO, Lieutenant the Marquis Roberto Lubelli di, *ADC to the Duke d'Abruzzi*

30 April — **King Edward VII's visit to Rome**
TODINI, Major Domenico, *ADC to King of Italy, attached to King Edward VII*
PREMOLI, Conte Luigi, *Master of the Ceremonies to the King of Italy*
ALESSANDRO, Captain Ulderico d', *Commanding Royal Body Guard, Rome*
SESSI, Cavalier Uff. Avv. Paolo, *Inspector-General of Police, Rome*

4 May — **King Edward VII's visit to France**
LOCQUET, Mons. Henri, *of the Office of Works, Paris*

30 June	BALCK, Major William, *of the Prussian Great General Staff*

10 July **Visit to Britain of President Loubet of the French Republic**
LOUBET, Mons. Paul, *Secretary to the President of France*

9 October **King Edward VII's visit to Austria**
COMNÈNE, Captain Milliotti, *ADC to King George I of the Hellenes*
GOREYR VON BESANETZ, Ferdinand, Baron, *Assistant Commissioner of Police, Vienna*
POLT, Carl, *Head of Detective Corps, Vienna*
NEPALLECK, Herr Wilhelm Friedrich, *Secretary. to Master of Ceremonies to Franz Joseph, Emperor of Austria, King of Hungary*
MARGUTTI, Albert Alexander, *Orderly Officer to the Senior ADC to the Emperor*
SEIPT, Herr Leopold, *Jagdverwalter to the Emperor*
WORLITZKY, Herr Franz Edler von, *Clerk Comptroller at the Hofburg*
NICKLAS, Herr Anton, *Inspector of the Police, Vienna*
TUCEK, Herr Hofrath Jaromir, *Director of the Austrian Imperial Railway*
KHITTEL, Herr Hofrath Jaroslav, *Director of the Austrian Imperial Railway*
MADER, Herr Eduard, *of the Paymaster's Department. at the Hofburg*
GEBHARDT, Herr Theodor, *of the Paymaster's Department at the Hofburg*
FORSTNER, Captain Ernst, *No.8 Austrian Infantry Regiment, Commanding Guard of Honour, Vienna*
STRAUSS, Herr Johann, *Conductor of the Imperial Band, Vienna*
ZYARSKY VON KOTWIEZ, Major Alexander, *of the Hungarian Life Guards*
PEZELLEN, Herr Carl, *Prefect of Marienbad*

9 November BENIGNI, Corvetten Capitan Rudolph, Ritter von, *attached to Lord Methuen's special mission to Vienna.*

21 November **Visit of King Vitorio Emanuele III of Italy to Windsor**
COMOTTO, Signor Ferdinando, *Chief of Secretariat of HM*
BOSISIO, Signor Jean, *Chief of the Private Service of HM*
ALBERTI, Count Degli, *Attaché to the Italian Secretary of State for Foreign Affairs*

1904

10 February **Marriage of Princess Alice of Albany with Prince Alexander of Teck**
MOHN, Major Alfred, *ADC to the King of Württemberg*
GILLHAUSEN, Captain Curt von, MVO, *Equerry to the Duke of Saxe-Coburg-Gotha*

23 March **Funeral of the Duke of Cambridge**
SCHULENBURG, Major Count Anton von der, *ADC to Prince Albrecht of Prussia (Regent of Brunswick)*
BERGE UND HERRENDORFF, Captain Joachim von, *ADC to Prince Albrecht of Prussia (Regent of Brunswick)*
LIVONIUS, Major Louis von, *Chamberlain to the Hereditary Grand Duke of Mecklenburg-Strelitz*
NEUHAUSS, Major Carl, *28th Regiment of Prussian Infantry of which His late Royal Highness was Colonel*
WINIKER, Captain Oskar, *28th Regiment of Prussian Infantry of which His late Royal Highness was Colonel*

18 April **King Edward VII's visit to Denmark**
DAHLERUP, Captain Joachim Wilhelm Bang, *Danish Life Guards*
ESMANN, Captain Sigvord Theobald Thorvald, *Danish Hussars of the Guard*
LE MAIRE, Professor Doctor Christen Martin Wittüsen, *Resident Surgeon to King Christian IX of Denmark*
HAARLOEV, Thorwald Jorgen Henrik, *Traffic Superintendent, Copenhagen*
KRAG, Carl Mauritz Gotthold Rosenberg, *Controller to the Crown Prince and Secretary to Prince Charles of Denmark*
PETERS, Carl Ferdinand Valentin, *Traffic Superintendent, Altona*
GERVIN, Adrianus Marius, *Traffic Superintendent, Flushing*

21 April **Visit of the Prince of Wales to Austria**
OTTENFELD, Captain Joseph Ritter Otto von, *Artillery Regiment 'George, Prince of Wales' No.12*

14 June **Visit to Britain of Prince John of Glücksburg**
KRIEGER, Captain Waldemar, *Chamberlain to King Christian IX of Denmark, in attendance on HH*

1 July **King Edward VII's visit to Kiel**
VIGNAU, Hans Eduard Wilhelm Emanuel von, *Chamberlain to the Duchess of Saxe-Coburg and Gotha*
FUCHS, Emil, *Harbourmaster, Holtenau*
GILBERT, Frederick, *Acting Harbourmaster, Brunsbüttelkoog*

5 July RICHTER, Doctor Hans, *Musical Director, Covent Garden Opera*

5 July **King Edward VII's visit to Kiel**
SCHWIND, Commander Herwath Schmidt von, *Naval ADC to Prince Henry of Prussia*
LEVETZOW, Commander Kurt Christian Hugo Ferdinand William von, *Imperial German Navy*
JASPER, Commander John Peter Gilbert, *Imperial German Navy*
BLUNCK, Christian, *Councillor to the Prussian Railway Administration at Altona*
EULENBURG, Count Victor zu, *Third Secretary, German Embassy*
BUBENDEY, John Frederick, *Director of Harbour Works, Kiel*
UTHEMANN, Lieutenant-Captain Alfred Edward David John, *Imperial German Navy*
SCHOLLMEYER, Captain George Richard, *75th Regiment of Infantry*
SCHLEMMER, Lieutenant-Captain Ferdinand, *Imperial German Navy*

ZOLLIKOFER-ALTENKLINGEN, Captain Frederick William Julius Deodat von, *76th Regiment of Infantry*
MICHELSEN, Lieutenant-Captain Andrew Henry, *Imperial German Navy*
BISMARCK-BOHLEN, Captain Hans, Count von, *1st Prussian Regiment of Foot Guards*
DELUPIS, Captain Carl Ritter Dojmi Di, *15th Regiment of Hussars*
ZGLINITZKI, Captain Paul Theodore Francis Charles von, *31st Regiment of Infantry*
BULOW, Lieutenant-Captain Frederick von, *Naval ADC to Prince Henry of Prussia*
SCHLICHTING, Captain Hans Bernhard von, *1st Train Battalion*
SCHEEFER, Max, *Secretary to the Imperial German Chancellor*
SARTORI, August Louis Andrew, *British Vice-Consul at Kiel*
WALDMANN, Hofrath Adolf, *Secretary to Lord Steward's Department*

12 August   ORPHANIDIS, Captain Panajiotis, *attached to the Crown Prince of Greece, Duke of Sparta*

6 September   BESOLD, Doctor Gustav Henry Anton, *Director of the Falkenstein Sanitorium*

19 October   **Visit of Prince Christian of Schleswig-Holstein to Saxony to represent HM at the Funeral of the King of Saxony**
WENSE, Captain Otto Charles Louis Bodo Tage von der, *Brigade Major, 23rd Saxon Cavalry Brigade*

21 November   **Visit to Britain of King Carlos and Queen Amélie of Portugal**
FARIA, Carlos de Castro, *Second Secretary, Portuguese Legation*
NASCIMENTO, Mario do, *Attaché, Portuguese Legation*
REIS, Jayme Batalha, *Commercial Attaché, Portuguese Legation*
ASSECA, Lieutenant Salvador Correa de Sá, Viscount, *Private Secretary to Minister for Foreign Affairs, Portugal*

4 December   **Visit of Prince Arthur of Connaught to represent HM at the Christening of the Prince of Piedmont**
BIANO, Captain Francesco Pescara, *47th Regt. of Italian Infantry*

Special Mission from The King of Saxony
OMPTEDA, Major Otto, Baron von, *ADC to General von Broizem*

27 December   **Visit of Prince Arthur of Connaught to Coburg to represent HM at the Funeral of the Duchess Alexandrine of Saxe-Coburg and Gotha.**
KANTER, Captain Bruno Georg Felix, *6th Thuringian Infantry Regt. No.95*

1905

10 January   **Visit of the Duke of Connaught to Lisbon**
CAMARA, Lieutenant Francisco de Paula Maria Anna do Loretto Figueira Freire da, *Portuguese Cavalry Regt. No.1 (King Victor Emmanuel's Lancers)*

27 February   **Visit of Prince Arthur of Connaught to Berlin to represent HM at Opening of the Protestant Cathedral**
BRUNING, Lieutenant Rüdiger von, *Adjutant, Hussar Regt. von Zeiten (Brandenburg) No.3*
LUCKEN, Lieutenant Theodor von, *Adjutant, Hussar Regt. von Zeiten (Brandenburg) No.3*
ARNIM, Captain Oscar von, *Commanding Guard of Honour*

8 March   **Visit to Britain of the Prince of Bulgaria**
DRANDAR, Wladimir, *Private Secretary to HRH*
CHÈVREMONT, Paul Emile Alexandre Marie de, *Asstistant Private Secretary to HRH*
NIKYPHOROFF, Stephan, *1st Secretary Bulgarian Diplomatic Agency in London*

17 April   **King Edward VII's Cruise in the Mediterranean**
BOISSIÈRE, Lieutenant Jacques, *ADC to Governor-General of Algeria*

19 April   ALTAIRAC, Frederic Jacques, *Mayor of Algiers*

21 April   CHOISNET, Eugène Etienne Henry, *Assistant Prefect at Bougie*

23 April   POILLEUX, Jules, *Director of the Algerian Railways*

4 May   BERQUET, Laurent Ennemond, *General Manager, Paris, Lyon and Mediterranean Railway*
BOUVERAT, Louis, *Traffic Manager, North of France Railway*
DALTROFF, Gustave, *Assistant Commissioner of Police, Paris*
FINIDORI, Jean Baptist, *Assistant Commissioner of Police, Paris*
MURAT, Jean Achille, *Police Superintendent, Paris*

6 June   **Visit to Britain of King Alfonso XIII of Spain**
SPOTTORNO, Señor Don Ricardo, *Third Secretary, Spanish Embassy, London*
ALABERN Y RASPALL, Doctor José, *Physician to the King of Spain*

Visit of Prince Arthur of Connaught to Berlin to represent HM at the Marriage of the Crown Prince of Prussia and the Duchess Cecilie of Mecklenburg-Schwerin
GROTE, Captain Karl, Baron, *Queen Elizabeth's Grenadier Guard Regiment, No.3*
HARLEM, Captain Fritz von, *Superintendent of the Imperial Stables, Berlin*

15 June   **Marriage of Princess Margaret of Connaught and Prince Gustavus Adolphus of Sweden and Norway**
CHAMPS, Commander Charles Léon de, *ADC to Prince William of Sweden and Norway*
SILFVERSWÄRD, Captain Ernest Lars Isaac de, *ADC to the Crown Prince of Sweden and Norway*
POSSE, Captain Göran Edward Henning, Count, *ADC to Prince Gustavus Adolphus of Sweden and Norway*

4 July	**Visit to England of Prince and Princess Arisugawa of Japan** HISHIDA, Major Kikujiro, *ADC to Prince Arisugawa*
19 July	**Visit of the Duke of Connaught to Coburg and Gotha to represent HM at the Celebration of the Coming of Age of the Duke of Saxe-Coburg and Gotha** KOENIG, Captain Godefroi von, *6th Thüringer Infantry Regt. No.95*
11 August	**Visit of the French Fleet** MERCIER DE LOSTENDE, Captain Henri Maurice, Baron
8 September	**King Edward VII's visit to Marienbad** DIETL, Doctor Wenzel, *Burgomaster of Marienbad* DORNER, Johann Hermann Franz, *Member of the Royal Railway Board of Direction, Cologne* ENGERINGH, Maurice, *General Manager, Netherlands State Railway* EVERTS, Allard Gerrit Anton, *Inspector of the Netherlands State Railway* OPEL, Richard, *Member of the Board of Direction, Bavarian State Railway* SCHOBER, Hans, MVO, *Assistant Commissioner, Austrian Police*
11 October	**Visit of Prince Arthur of Connaught to Glücksburg to represent HM at the Marriage of the Duke of Saxe-Coburg and Gotha, Duke of Albany, and Princess Victoria Adelaide of Schleswig-Holstein-Sonderburg-Glücksburg** SCHACK, Lieutenant Marcel von, *Gardes du Corps, in attendance on the Duke of Saxe-Coburg and Gotha*
27 November	**Visit of King George I of the Hellenes to Britain** PALI, Captain Antoine Constantin, *ADC to Prince Nicholas of Greece*

1906

18 February	**Visit of the Lord Chamberlain to Denmark to represent HM at the Funeral of King Christian IX** HOLTEN-NIELSEN, Captain Einar, *21st Danish Infantry Regiment*
20 February	**Special Mission of Prince Arthur of Connaught to Japan to invest the Emperor with the Order of the Garter** NAGAYUKI, Asano, *Master of Ceremonies to the Emperor of Japan* NAOMICHI, Watanabe, *Master of Ceremonies to the Emperor of Japan* SEIICHIRO, Count Terashima, *Private Secretary to the Minister for Foreign Affairs* SUZUKI, Captain Gizo, *1st Infantry Regiment, Imperial Guard*
15 March	OZAKI, Yukio, *Mayor of Tokyo* SAIGO, Kikujiro, *Mayor of Kioto* AOYAMA, Ro, *Mayor of Nagoya* KAMIMURA, Keikichi, *Mayor of Kagoshima*
2 April	**King Edward VII's visit to Paris and Biarritz** HENNION, Cebstin, *Principal Commissioner of Police, Paris* FORSANS, Pierre, *Mayor of Biarritz*
16 April	**King Edward VII's visit to Corfu** PAPHALIAS, Major Démétrius, *Prefect of Police, Corfu*
24 April	**King Edward VII's visit to Greece** VOURNASOS, Christos, *President, Municipal Council, Athens* ZOCHIOS, Lieutenant Gérassimos, *Royal Hellenic Navy, attached to King Edward VII* PAPPARIGOPOULOS, Lieutenant Etienne, *Royal Hellenic Navy, attached to the Prince of Wales* TROUPAKIS, Captain Nicolas, *Hellenic Gendarmerie* BAKAS, Captain Théodore, *Hellenic Gendarmerie* BERATES, Lieutenant Demetrios, *Harbour Master of the Piraeus*
7 May	**King Edward VII's visit to Paris** PIÉRON, Louis Alphonse Eugène, *Chief Engineer, North of France Railway*
30 May	**Mission to HM to announce the Accession of King Frederik VIII of Denmark** MOLTKE, Count Eiler Frederick Ernest, *Lieutenant Royal Danish Life Guards*
6 June	**Visit of the Prince of Wales to Madrid to represent HM at the Marriage of the King of Spain and Princess Victoria Eugenie of Battenberg** PORTILLO, Major Don Eduardo Vico y, *Commanding Royal Escort* TOGORES, Major Juan Perez Seoane y Roca de, *ADC to the King of Spain* MARTORELL, Captain Pedro Alvarez de Toledo, Marquis of, *attached to Prince Alexander of Battenberg*
22 June	**Visit of the Prince of Wales to Trondhjem to represent HM at the Coronation of King Haakon VII of Norway** LORENTZEN, Captain Lorenz Martin, *Royal Norwegian Navy, attached to the Prince of Wales*
7 September	**King Edward VII's visit to Marienbad** KOEHLER, Anselm, *Prior of Tepl* BLÜTHGEN, Arthur, *General Manager, Austrian Railway at Eiger*
8 September	**The German Manoeuvres** SCHLIEFFEN, Captain Hermann, Count von, *attached to the Duke of Connaught* WENTZKY UND PETERSHEYDE, Lieutenant Arthur Frederick von, *attached to the Duke of Connaught*

20 September	Visit of the Duke of Connaught to Karlsruhe to invest the Grand Duke of Baden with the Order of the Garter and to represent HM at the Celebration of the Golden Wedding of the Grand Duke and Duchess of Baden SKOPNIK, Major Julius Carl Ferdinand von, *attached to HRH*
27 September	For Services to English Military Attachés during the Russo-Japanese War SHIMAUCHI, Captain Kunhiko, *Imperial Japanese Army* TANAKA, Captain Shojiro, *Imperial Japanese Army*
13 November	Visit to Britain of King Haakon VII of Norway KRAG, Captain Hjalmar, *ADC to HM*

1907

28 January	OSTERTAG, Captain Roland Frederic William, *Military Attaché, German Embassy*
5 March	Mission of Prince Alexander of Teck to The Hague to invest the Prince of the Netherlands with the Order of the Bath MUHLEN, Lieutenant Jonkheer Johan Carl Ferdinand von, *Naval ADC to the Queen of the Netherlands*
9 April	King Edward VII's visit to Spain BARREDA, Commander Don Joaquin Gomez de, *Royal Spanish Navy* SOLANA, Lieutenant Don Manuel Andujar, *Royal Spanish Navy* ESPINOSA Y LEON, Lieutenant Don Antonio, *Royal Spanish Navy* HARTLEY, Lieutenant Don Manuel Somoza, *Royal Spanish Navy* LIZANA, Lieutenant Don Serapio Ros, *Royal Spanish Navy* HONTORIA, Manuel Gonzalez, *of the Spanish Foreign Office* GUZMAN Y FERNANDEZ, Lieutenant Don Enrique, *Royal Spanish Navy* MIRANDO Y QUARTIN, Pedro de, *of the Spanish Foreign Office*
7 May	Visit to Britain of Prince Sadanaru Fushimi of Japan representing the Emperor KATO, Commander Hiroharou, *ADC to the Minister of the Imperial Navy* HIGASHI, Major Otohiko, *ADC to the Minister of the Imperial Navy* UDAKA, Captain Tadataka, *Adjutant, War Office, Japan* IWAI, Dr Teizo, *Physician*
10 May	King Edward VII's visit to Biarritz MANGE, Alfred, *Traffic Manager, Chemin de fer d'Orleans*
18 May	Visit of Prince Arthur of Connaught to Madrid to represent HM at the Christening of the Prince of Asturias ENRIQUEZ, Captain Adolfo Diaz RODRIGUEZ, Lieutenant-Colonel Don Tomás Luis Palacio PAEZ-JARAMILLO Y ALVAREZ, Lieutenant-Colonel Don Frederico Julián Mauricio SERRANO Y UZQUETA, Lieutenant-Colonel Don Arturo ARACIL, Captain Don Emilio Cesareo Roque Hernandez HIDALGO Y ANTÚNEZ, Captain Don Manuel MONTERO Y PEREZ, Captain Don Valerio Miquel AROCA, Captain Miquel Mariano Gonzalez ALONSO Y CASTRO, Captain Don Carlos Mariano PINEDA Y MONSERRAT, Don Luis de, *Equerry to the King of Spain*
10 June	Visit to Britain of the Grand Duke of Oldenburg WEDDERKOP, Captain Curt von, *ADC to HRH* SCHENK ZU SCHWEINSBERG, Lieutenant Baron Gunthram, *ADC to the Landgrave of Hesse*
15 June	Unveiling of Statue of Field Marshal the Duke of Cambridge SCHWICKERATH, Major Adolf, *of German Infantry Regt. von Goeben No.28* HUNOLSTEIN, Captain Egon Vogt, Baron von, *of German Infantry Regt. von Goeben No.28* BAUMBACH, Captain Ludwig von, *ADC to Field Marshal von Hahnke*
27 June	HUGUET, Major Victor Jacques Marie, *Military Attaché to French Embassy*
3 August	Visit of the Coast Squadron of the Royal Swedish Navy to Cowes SPARRE, Lieutenant-Commander Ulf Carl Knutssen, *Royal Swedish Navy*
14 August	King Edward VII's visit to Wilhelmshohe NIESEWAND, Captain Maximilian Maria Joseph Hubert Matthäus von, *Hesse-Homburg Hussar Regiment No. 14* WINTERFELD, Captain Hans von, *Infantry Regt. von Wittich, No.83*
15 August	King Edward VII's visit to Ischl ZELLER, Gustav, MVO, *Paymaster of the Household of the Emperor of Austria, King of Hungary* BAYERL, George, *Commissioner of Police* REPOLUSK, Franz, *Secretary to the Principal ADC*
29 August	For services to Members of the Indian Staff College who visited the Manchurian Battlefields KONO, Captain Tsunekichi, *Imperial Japanese Army* KOTO, Captain Tokutaro, *Imperial Japanese Army* SHIBAYAMA, Captain Shigeichi, *Imperial Japanese Army*

6 September	**King Edward VII's visit to Marienbad**
	ZELLNER, Carl, *Member of the late Empress of Austria's Memorial Committee*
	GURSCHNER, Lieutenant Gustave, *Imperial and Royal Tyrolese Kaiser Jaeger Regiment*
	HANCK, Adalbert, *Chairman, Bavarian State Railway*
	VOORHOEVE, Johannes Marinus, *Chairman, North Brabant German Railway*
	WALRAVEN, Cornelis, *General Manager, Netherlands State Railway*
	WESSEL, Gerhard, *General Manager, State Railway, Cologne*

28 September	**Visit of Field Marshal the Duke of Connaught to Vienna**
	LIECHTENSTEIN, Captain HSH Prince Frederick von und zu

7 October	**Visit of Field Marshal the Duke of Connaught to Karlsruhe to represent HM at the Funeral of The Grand Duke of Baden**
	FREYEND, Major Leopold John von, *1st Baden Grenadier Regiment, No.109*

12 November	**Visit to Windsor of the German Emperor and Empress, King and Queen of Prussia**
	PALESKA, Cdr. William Adalbert Clemens Bernhard, Baron von, *Commanding HIMS Sleipner*
	WIDENMANN, Cdr. William Charles, *Naval Attaché to Imperial German Embassy*
	SEELE, Geheimer Hofrath Frederick Theodore, *of Imperial German Foreign Office*
	ABB, Geheimer Hofrath William, *attached to HIM's Civil Cabinet*
	MASSMANN, Hofrath Emil William Frederick, *attached to HIM's Naval Cabinet*

19 December	**Visit of Prince Arthur of Connaught to Stockholm to represent HM at the Funeral of the King of Sweden**
	ESSEN, Captain Charles Reinhold, Count von, *ADC to the Crown Prince of Sweden*

DEPUTATION TO LONDON on 31 January 1908 of the 5th Prussian Blücher Hussars to congratulate Edward VII on the 25th anniversary of his appointment as their Colonel-in-Chief. (*left to right, seated*) Major the Hon. A.V.F. Russell MVO, Grenadier Guards, Military Attaché, Berlin; Lieutenant-General Alfred von Loewenfeld GCVO, ADC General. (*standing*) Rittmeister Curt Adam Philipp Wilhelm von Zitzewitz MVO (IV), Colonel Max von Bitter KCVO, Commanding Officer; Lieutenant Hugo Claus Ernst von Brockhusen MVO (V), Adjutant.

1908

27 January	**25th Anniversary of King Edward VII's appointment as Colonel-in-Chief** ZITZEWITZ, Captain Curt Adam Philipp Wilhelm von, *Squadron Cdr., 5th (Prince Blücher von Wahlstatt) Hussar Regiment*
8 February	DA SILVA, Captain Manoel Pereira, *Infantry Regiment No.1* DA COSTA E OLIVEIRA, Captain Domingas Augusto Alves, *2nd Portuguese Lancers*
19 March	GOMEZ-COLON, Captain Nivardo Sostrada y, *Spanish Zamora Regiment, No.8*
4 April	**King Edward VII's visit to Biarritz** PONCET, Marius, MVO, *Special Commissary of French Eastern Railway*
25 April	**King Edward VII's visit to Denmark** GRÜT, Captain Torben, *attached to King Edward VII* BLÜCHER-ALTONA, First-Lieutenant Gustavus Bridges Fergus Gotthard Lebrecht, Count, *attached to King Edward VII* MADSEN, Henrik, MVO, *Chief of Detective Police, Copenhagen* PETERSEN, Theodor Christian Magens, *Chief of Municipal Police, Copenhagen* HYRUP, Carl Christian Frederick Peter, *Traffic Manager, Danish State Railways*
27 April	**King Edward VII's visit to Sweden** NAUCKHOFF, Captain John Gustav ADLERSTRÄHLE, Captain Adolf Einar Theodore OTRANTE, Lieutenant Charles Louis, Count d', *attached to Queen Alexandra* ESSEN, Captain Baron Hans Henrik von TAMM, William Adolf, *Assistant Commissioner of Police* FRICK, Harold Otto, *Assistant Commissioner of Police*
2 May	**King Edward VII's visit to Norway** STENERSEN, Captain Erland, *ADC to King Haakon VII* KROGH, Commander John Clasen von, *ADC to King Haakon VII, attached to King Edward VII* METHLIE, Captain Nikolai William Bertonius, *Commanding the Brigade School, Christiania* RAMM, Captain John Etters Beck, *Commanding the Royal Norwegian Guard* SMITH-KIELLAND, Captain Ingvald Mareno, *Norwegian Cavalry* HJORT, Captain Jens Christian Grundt, *Commanding the Cadet Corps* KRAG, William Andreas Wexels, *Director of the National Theatre* AAS, Nils Christian, *Traffic Manager, Norwegian State Railways* SÖRENSEN, John, *Assistant Commissioner of Police* MOSSIN, Ove, *Assistant Commissioner of Police* WELHAVEN, Hjalmar, *Inspector of the Royal Palace*
10 June	**King Edward VII's visit to Russia** KOLOMEITZOFF, Commander Nicolas, *Commanding Russian frigate* Almaz ZILOTI, Commader Serge, *ADC to the Marine HQ Staff* ZIGERSKINE, Captain Leo Gregorevitch, *Chief of the Russian Police, Reval* IVANOFF, Lieutenant Serge Miossoedoff, *Imperial Russian Navy* SABLINE, Lieutenant Nicolas, *Imperial Russian Navy* NENNINGER, Boris, *Assistant Secretary, Ministry of the Court* TCHERNYCHEFF, Constantine, MVO, *Secretariat of the Emperor* MESENTROFF, Colonel Alexandre, *Russian Gendarmerie* MEYER, Lieutenant-Colonel Jean, *Imperial Russian Navy* CHEVELEFF, Lieutenant Claude, *Imperial Russian Navy*
11 August	**King Edward VII's visit to Cronberg** PITSCH, Karl Eugen, *Burgomaster of Cronberg* GERTH, Fritz
18 August	LÜBKE, Walther, *Burgomaster of Homburg*
21 August	**King Edward VII's visit to Ischl** FISCHER, Captain Victor, *59th Infantry Regt. (Archduke Rainer) Austro-Hungarian Army* ZIWSA, Captain Ferdinand, *Court Secretary* STROHMAYER, Anton, *Chief Inspector of the Imperial Palaces* KRÜKL, Doctor Henry, *President, Viennese Choral Society* LEITHNER, Francis, *Burgomaster of Ischl*
4 September	**King Edward VII's visit to Marienbad** TRAUTTMANSDORF-WEINSBERG, Count Charles zu REINIGER, Henry, *Burgomaster of Marienbad* NOHRE, Ernest, *Director of the Prussian State Railways* ERTZBISCHOFF, Albert, *Traffic Manager, Eastern Railway of France* GEBER, William, *Director, Prussian State Railways*
6 November	**On relinquishing the appointment of Naval Attaché at the Italian Embassy** VILLAREY, Lieutenant Count Charles Rey di, *Royal Italian Navy*

17 November	**Visit to Windsor of King Gustav V and Queen Victoria of Sweden** BOSTRÖM, Wollmar Philip, *First Secretary, Swedish Ministry of Foreign Affairs*

1909

12 February	**King Edward VII's visit to Berlin** TSCHIRSCHKY UND BÖGENDORFF von, *Gardes du Corps* ESEBECK, Captain Hermann Augustus Frederick Charles, Baron von, *attached to Master of the Horse's Department, 1st Brandenburg Dragoon Regt. No.2* GOERNE, Captain William von, *1st Regiment of Foot Guards* HARDER, Captain Oskar von, *2nd Regiment of Foot Guards* BACHTENBROCK, Captain William Marschalck von, *1st Regt. of Dragoons of the Guard (Queen Victoria of Great Britain and Ireland)* STUMM, Captain Frederick von JANKE, Captain Hugo, *Commanding 10th Coy Fusilier Guards 'Prince Henry of Prussia' Regiment* POGRELL, Lieutenant Hans Wolf von, *1st Regt. of Dragoons of the Guard (Queen Victoria of Great Britain and Ireland)* EULENBURG, Lieutenant Count Wendt zu, *1st Regiment of Guards* INNHAUSEN UND KNYPHAUSEN, Lieutenant Gisbert Charles Frederick Dodo, Baron zu, *Gardes du Corps* MINTE, Charles John Henry, *Director of the Postal Service to HIM* MÜLLER, Otto Hermann, *Director of the Telegraphic Service to HIM* HENNIGER, Eugene Charles Frederick, *Chief of the Special Police* BURO, Geheimer Hofrath Richard, *Secretary to the Lord Steward* WASMUND, Hofrath Augustus Charles Henry, *Superintendent, Master of the Horse's Department*
15 April	**King Edward VII's visit to Biarritz** GILLIOT, Marie Rudolphe Auguste Paul Martin, *General Manager, Midi Railway*
24 April	**King Edward VII's visit to Malta** ROUDANOVSKY, Basile Constantinovitch, *Russian Consul at Malta* **HM's visit to the King and Queen of Italy at Baia** TORRECUSO, Ferdinand Cito, *Duke of Master of Ceremonies to King Vittorio Emanuele III of Italy*
29 April	PIELLA, Captain Paolo Francesco, *Orderly Officer to the Duke of Aosta*
9 July	LÁSZLÓ, Philip Alexius, *Portrait Painter*
5 August	**Visit of Emperor Nicholas and Empress Alexandra Feodorovna of Russia** ZABOTKINE, Commander Dimitri, MVO, *Imperial Russian Navy* TIMIREFF, Commander Serge, MVO, *Imperial Russian Navy* SCHETININE, Commander Alexis, *Imperial Russian Navy* LEPKO, Commander Vladimir, *Imperial Russian Navy* BESTOUJEFF-RUMIN, Commander Anatole, *Imperial Russian Navy* D'OSTEN-SACKEN, Lieutenant Baron Léon, *Flag Lieutenant to Chief of Staff of the Naval Staff of HIM* SAITANOFF, Lieutenant Alexis, *Imperial Russian Navy* LIALINE, Lieutenant Michel, *Imperial Russian Navy* MIKKOFF, Major-General Alexander, *Chief Engineer, Russian Squadron* PETROFF, Colonel André, *Chief Engineer, Imperial Yacht* Standart KONIOUCHKOF, Lieutenant-Colonel John, *Navigating Officer, Russian Squadron* MAXIMOFF, Lieutenant-Colonel Michael, *Chief Engineer, Imperial Yacht* Polar Star SMIRNOFF, Staff Surgeon John, *Honorary Surgeon to HIM* LENTOVSKY, Staff Surgeon Serge, *Honorary Surgeon to HIM* ANDREEFF, Captain Valdemar, *Russian Gendarmerie* SUSSLOW, Alexandre, *Secretary to the Minister of the Court*
3 September	**King Edward VII's visit to Marienbad** WÜRFL, Father Severin, *Inspector of the Springs, Marienbad* ZÖRKENDÖRFER, Doctor Charles, *Head of the Hygienic Institute* SCHREYER, Adalbert, MVO, *Conductor of the Kurhaus Orchestra*
16 November	**Visit to Windsor of King Manoel II of Portugal** CARVALHO, Amadeu Ferreira d'Almeida, *Second Secretary, Portuguese Legation, London*
22 December	**Visit of the Duke of Connaught to Brussels to represent HM at the Funeral of the late King Leopold II of the Belgians** PERWIN, Captain Ferdinand Charles Jean Albert Stanislas Ghuislain Joseph, Baron de Rennette de Villers, *attached to HRH*

1910

25 January	**Attached to the Special Envoy to King Edward VII to announce the Accession of King Albert of the Belgians** COLONNA DES PRINCES STIGLIANO, Ferdinand (*when conferred was Captain Ferdinand Harfeld*) HARFELD, Ferdinand, *see above*

Attached to Field Marshal Earl Kitchener during his visit to Japan
TAKESHIMA, Colonel Misaku

Attached to the Special Envoy to King Edward VII to announce the Accession of King Albert of the Belgians
URSEL, Jean Hubert Maurice Marie Ghislain, Comte de

25 April **Visit of HM to Biarritz**
LECHELLE, Paul Emile, *General Manager, North of France Railway*

21 May **Funeral of King Edward VII**
ANDRADE, Lieutenant-Colonel José Candido de, *Portuguese Cavalry Regt. No. 3 King Edward VII*
FOMITZKY, Lieutenant-Colonel Ivan, *Russian Hussar Regt.9th (Kieff) King Edward VII*
MARTINEZ-PEÑALVER Y FERRER, Lieutenant-Colonel Don Angel, *Spanish Zamora Regiment No. 8 King Edward VII, of which His late Majesty was Honorary Colonel*
STOSCH, Captain Gustav, Baron von, *5th German Hussar Regiment*
WAITZ VON ESCHER, Captain Carl Sigismund, Baron, *German Cuirassier Regiment No. 8*

1911

2 December **Mission of Prince Alexander of Teck to Bangkok to represent HM at the Coronation of King Vajiravudh of Siam**
INDRAVIJIT, Major-General Phya (formerly Major Luang Yod Awudh), *ADC to the King of Siam*
RAJODAYA, Phya (formerly Nai Cha Yuad), *Gentleman in Waiting to the King of Siam*
CHA YUAD, Ammat Tri Nai, *Gentleman in Waiting to the King of Siam*

1912

23 January **For services rendered as second-in-command of the French cruiser *Friant* in rescue work on the occasion of the wreck of the SS *Delhi*, 13 December 1911**
DRUJON, Rear-Admiral Charles Jérome Alexandre

24 January **Visit to Malta of King George V and Queen Mary**
DUMESNIL, Vice-Admiral Charles Henri, *Chief of Staff to Admiral Commanding French Squadron*
BERTHELOT, Rear-Admiral Charles Alain Marie, *Commanding French Torpedo Destroyer* Lansquenet
MARGUERYE, Cdr. Robert Marie Gabriel Alfred de, *Commanding French Torpedo Flotilla*

30 January **Visit to Gibraltar of King George V and Queen Mary**
SI ALY ZAKY BEY, *of the Mission from the Sultan of Turkey*

31 January ADRIANO PEDRERO BELTRÁN, Captain Don Adriano José Felix, *Commanding Spanish Torpedo Destroyer Asiacho*
SBERT Y CANALS, Captain Don Mariano, *of the Mission from the Sultan of Audaz*

23 March **Inspection by King George V and Queen Mary of the Radium Institute**
WICKHAM, Dr Louis Frederick

15 May **Unveiling of the Queen Victoria Memorial**
KNAUFF, August Eduard Bruno, *Court Secretary to the German Emperor, King of Prussia*
LIVONIUS, Lieutenant Eberhard von, *1st Prussian Regiment of Dragoons of the Guard*
POSTH, Hofrat Paul, *Secretary to the Empress*
SCHLICK, Captain Albert von, *1st Prussian Regiment of Dragoons of the Guard*

23 May **Visit of Prince Arthur of Connaught to Copenhagen to represent HM at the Funeral of King Frederik VIII of Denmark**
MOLTKE, Lieutenant-Colonel Aage, Count

4 September **For services as French Tutor to the Prince of Wales during HRH's residence in France**
ESCOFFIER, Maurice Alexandre

12 September **Visit of Prince Arthur of Connaught to Japan to represent HM at the Funeral of Emperor Mutsuhito of Japan**
KATO, Yasumichi
SHIMOMURA, Lieutenant Chinsuke, *Imperial Japanese Navy*
YAMADA, Colonel Yuichi

1913

2 April **Visit of Prince Alexander of Teck to Athens to represent HM at the Funeral of King George of the Hellenes**
LAMBROS, Rear-Admiral Denis

24 May **Visit to Berlin of King George and Queen Mary to attend the Wedding of the Duke of Brunswick and Luneburg and Princess Viktoria Luise of Prussia**
DOHNA-LAUCK, Captain Count, *Commanding Escort, 1st Prussian Dragoon Guards*
DRUCKLIEB, Gustave
GAUERT, Edward, *Head Superintendent, Prussian Railways*

GAYLING VON ALTHEIM, Captain Charles Henry, Baron, *1st Prussian Dragoon Guards*
HERING, George Albert William, *Inspector of Royal Buildings*
JANCKE, Hans Oscar, *Inspector of Royal Gardens*
KANITZ, Major Charles Richard Andrew, Count von, *1st Prussian Dragoon Guards*
KRIEGER, Dr Bogdan, *Royal Librarian, Berlin*
LIPINSKY, Captain Ernest Adolphus von Rosenberg, *Commanding Guard of Honour*
ROEDER, Captain Otto von, *Commanding Guard of Honour, Berlin*
SETTGAST, John, *Chairman, Prussian State Railways*
THURN UND TAXIS, Captain Max Theodor, Prince, *Assistant Crown Equerry*
TIEDEMANN, Captain Frederick William von, *Guard Cuirassier Regiment*
TOEPPER, Professor Paul, *Head Veterinary Surgeon, Royal Stables*
WERTHERN, Captain Albert, Baron von, *Commanding Salute Battery*
WESTPHALEN, Captain Lubbert Frederick Otto, Count von, *Assistant Crown Equerry*
ZEYSS, Captain Albert Augustus Leopold, *Superintendent of Motor Cars to HIM*

26 May	**Visit to Neu-Strelitz of King George and Queen Mary** BÜLOW, Captain Charles Werny von, *Equerry to the Grand Duke of Mecklenberg-Strelitz*
3 June	**Visit to Britain of the Empress Marie Feodorovna of Russia** ANDRESEN, Captain Andreas, *Secretary to Grand Comptroller of the Household of HIM*
11 June	**Special Mission from the Argentine Republic to HM** PENA, Dr Juan Baptista SALAS, Don Carlos (Junior)
24 June	**Visit to London of the President of the French Republic** VILLET, Félix Victor Eugène, *Secretary to Secretary of State for Foreign Affairs*
21 July	**The Mission to announce the Accession of King Constantine of the Hellenes** PALLIS, Alexis,
25 July	GILLOT, Eugene Louis, *Painted picture of the Coronation Naval Review, presented by French Government to HM*
4 September	**Visit of the Prince of Wales to Sigmaringen to attend the Wedding of King Manoel of Portugal** WEHR, Captain Fritz, Baron von Schönau, *8th Gendarmerie Brigade*
3 November	**King Haakon's visit to Sandringham** OTTO, Captain Edgar, *Equerry to the King of Norway*
17 November	**Visit to Windsor of Archduke Francis Ferdinand of Austro-Hungary** MARES, Zdenko, *Director of Journeys to HI and RH* NIKITSCH, Paul Joseph Nikolaus, *Secretary to HI and RH* STRATEN, Lieutenant Count Rudolph van der, *Equerry to HI and RH*

1914

24 April	**King George V's visit to France** DULINGER, Henri Ernest Joseph, *on Staff of the Protocol, Paris* GRAS, Marcel, *Chief of Private Secretary's Department of the President* JAVARY, Jean Baptiste Paul Emile, *North of France Railways* MOREAU, Auguste, *Contrôleur-Général du Services de Police* MORIEUX, Charles Adolphe, *Mayor of Calais* OUDAILLE, Eugène, *Commissaire Spécial, Gare du St Lazare*
9 May	**King Christian X's visit to Britain** ARNESEN-KALL, Lieutenant-Colonel Harald Valdemar, *ADC to the King of Denmark* KRUSE, John Christian Westergaard, *of the Danish Ministry of Foreign Affairs*

1915

1 November	**King George V's visit to the French Army** HEURTEAU, Captain Charles Emile Edouard, *Officier de Liaison*
10 November	**Coronation of the Emperor of Japan** UNO, Captain Masakata, *Imperial Japanese Navy*

1916

1 April	**Visit to Britain of the Prince Regent of Serbia** JANKOVITCH, Dr Miroslav, *Secretary to President of the Council, Serbia*
26 May	**Visit of the Prince of Wales to the Italian Front** ROSSI, Major Alberto Seribani, Conte di Cerreto, *Captain of the Guards of The King's Squadron*
30 August	**Visit to Britain of Prince Andrew of Greece** METAXA, Colonel Menelas, *ADC to HRH*

1917

5 July   **Visit of the Duke of Connaught to Italy**
SOLARO, Vittorio, dei Marchesi di Borga San Dalmazzo, *ADC to the King of Italy*

26 September   LAUREATI, Captain the Marquese Guilio, *Royal Italian Army Air Force; his flight from Turin to London*

1918

20 June   **Prince Arthur of Connaught's Mission to Japan**
OKAMOTO, Major Masanobu

29 June   NAGAYA, Colonel Shosaku
SHIMADZU, Commander Prince Tadashige

13 August   **HM's visit to his Army in the Field**
DUJARDIN, Colonel Jean Baptiste Marie

Visit to London of King Albert I of the Belgians
PREUD'HOMME, Colonel Léon Nestor

26 September   **Visit to London of the Band of the Italian Royal Caribinieri**
ALBEDI, Lieutenant-Colonel Dario Malchiodi, *Royal Caribinieri*

28 October   **Visit of Prince Yorihito of Japan to Britain**
TAKAHASHI, Akira, *attached to HRH*

30 November   **King George V's State Visit to France**
BAVELIER, Charles, *Archivist, Ministry of Foreign Affairs*
FALCOU, Raphael, *Director of the Paris Museums*
NAZARETH, Alfred, *Officier d'Ordonnance to the President*
RAVIGNAN, Marie André Jean de, *Secretary of the Embassy, Paris*
SAYVE, Lieutenant-Commander Jean de, DSO, *specially attached to Prince Albert*
THIEULEUX, Albéric Florimond, *Secretary at the Presidency*
WEISS, René Isaac, *Chef du Cabinet of President of Municipal Council, Paris*

1919

14 January   **For legal services rendered to the Prince of Wales in France**
MAREAU, Marie Stephane Fernand

28 July   **Reception by HM of a Sudanese Mission**
ABU EL QASIM AHMED HASHIM, El Sheikh
ALI EL TOM, El Sheikh, MBE, *Nazir of the Kabbabish*
AWAD EL KARIM ABDULLAH ABU SIN, El Sheikh, CBE, *Nazir of the Shurria*
IBRAHIM MUSA, El Sheikh, MBE, *Nazir of the Haddendoa*
ISMAEL EL AZHARI, El Sheikh, *Inspector of Mohammedan Courts*

4 November   **Visit to Britain of the Shah of Persia**
HAKIM-ED-DOWLEH, Docteur, *Physician to HIM*
MOCHAR-ES-SOLTAN, *Chamberlain to HIM*

25 November   **Reception by HM of a Uruguayan Mission**
CARRIO, Vicente Mario, *Secretary of Legation*

1 December   **Visit of the Prince of Wales to the USA**
ENRIGHT, Richard Edward, *New York Police*
LEGARÉ, Lieutenant-Commander Alexander Brown
NYE, Joseph Manuel, *Chief Special Agent*
POTTER, Captain John Hamilton, *ADC to Major-General Biddle*
SHARP, Major Edwin Rees
WHALEN, Grover

1920

5 July   **For Services rendered to the late Crown Princess of Sweden**
CEDERSCHIOLD, Lieutenant-Colonel Hugo Montgomery de, *ADC to the Crown Prince of Sweden*
ERNBERG, Dr Johan Harald, *Physician*

1921

9 May   **Visit to Britain of the Crown Prince of Japan**
FUTARA, Count Yoshinori, *Secretary to the Household*
HAMADA, Colonel Toyoki, *ADC to Crown Prince*
INOUE, Captain Baron Kiyosumi, *Commanding HIJMS Kashima*

KITAZIMA, Captain Shusaku, *Second in command HIJMS* Katori
OIKAWA, Rear-Admiral Koshiro, *ADC to the Crown Prince*
TERASHIMA, Rear-Admiral Ken, *Flag Commander, Japanese Third Squadron*

4 July   **Visit to Britain of King Albert and Queen Elizabeth of the Belgians**
GRUNNE, Count Guillaume de Henricourt de, *of the Belgian Foreign Office*

1922

12 March   **Unveiling of Memorial to King Edward VII at Biarritz**
REAL DEL SARTE, Maxime, *Sculptor*

22 April   **Visit of the Prince of Wales to Japan**
HATTORI, Shibataro, *Captain of TSS* Keifuku Maru
IKARIYAMA, Inspector General Susumu, MBE, *of Kanagawa Prefecture Police*
TAKAHASHI, Teitaro, *Architect, Imperial Household*
TAKEI, Morishige, *Master of Ceremonies*

13 May   **HM's visit to Belgium**
CRESPIN, Edmond, *Police Department*
GOFFINET, Captain Robert Théodore Apelin Guislain, *Officier d'Ordonnance*
OOMS, Alphonse Léon Joseph, *of Ministry of Foreign Affairs*

1923

14 May   **King George V's State Visit to Italy**
BALLERINI, Augusto, *Secretary for Royal Journeys*
BIANCARDI, Captain Carmine, *Commanded Guard of Honour at Rome Station*
BOCCI, Giunig, *Secretary of Protocol*
CELLARIO-SERVENTI, Major Giorgio, *Commanded Royal Bodyguard Squadron*
COLONNA, Don Ascanio (Dei Principi), *of the Ceremonial Department*
COSTETTI, Carlo, *Secretary to Minister of the Court*
GEOFFROY, Brig. General Alfredo, *Commanded Royal Caribinieri Legion, Verona*
GOTTI, Nobile Mario Morando Patrizio di Volterra, *Superintendent, Office of Master of the Horse*
LAURENTI, Luigi, *Chef du Cabinet, Royal Commissary of Rome*
MANCINI, Alberto, *Secretary General of Municipality of Rome*
MARINETTI, Colonel Giulio, *ADC to the King of Italy*
PIZZI, Lieutenant Vincenzo, *ADC to Prefect of the Palace, Rome*
RICAGNO, Major Umberto, *Commanded Military Division, Padova*
ROCCO, Guido, *of Italian Ministry of Foreign Affairs*

1924

29 May   **Visit to Britain of King Vittorio Emanuele III of Italy**
BUZZI, Rodolfo, *Commissioner, Italian Police*
CAMPANARI, Major Marchese Francesco, *attached to the Prince of Piedmont*
DOSI, Francesco, *of Italian Public Security Office*

1925

3 June   **Marshal Foch at Trooping the Colour**
L'HOPITAL, Captain René Michel, *ADC to Marshal Foch*

14 September   **Visit to Chile of the Prince of Wales**
EDWARDS, Agustin Robert, *attached to HRH*

23 September   **Visit to Argentina of the Prince of Wales**
MANZANO, Francisco José Ruiz, *Detective Inspector, Argentine Police*

28 November   **Funeral of Queen Alexandra**
HAUG, Major Jacob Hvinden, *ADC to the King of Norway*

1926

1927

19 May   **Visit to Britain of President Doumergue of the French Republic**
DUBOIS, André Germain, *Chief of Military Secretariat*
FRICOT, Edmond Lucien, *Controller, Telegraphic Services of Presidency*
LE ROUX, Jules Paul, *Special Commissary*
PARCHE, Louis, *Chief, Telegraphic Services of Presidency*

6 July	**Visit to Britain of King Fuad I of Egypt** IZZET BEY, Mohamed, *Master of Ceremonies* SAROIT, Ismail, *Private Secretary to Egyptian Prime Minister* TALAÄT BEY, Abd-el Wahhab, *First Secretary Royal Cabinet*

1928

15 March	**Visit to Britain of King Amanullah of Afghanistan** ISLAM BEG, *Dragoman, Afghan Legation, Paris*

1929

27 February	**The Prince of Wales's Journey from Africa at the time of HM's illness** GALLANI, Alfredo, *Chief, Traffic Services, Italian Railways* MUGNIOT, Eugène Nicolas, *Chief Engineer, PLM Railway, France* PATELLA, Domenico, *Railway Engineer, Italian Railways*
10 May	**The Duke of Gloucester's Garter Mission to Japan** SOHMA, Viscount Taketane, *Master of the Ceremonies* TAJIMA, Captain Koremori, *2nd Infantry Regiment*

1930

8 January	**The Duke of York's visit to Rome for the Wedding of the Crown Prince of Italy** PIECHE, Lieutenant-Colonel Giuseppe, *Caribinieri Reale, attached to Duke of York* VERDIANI, Ciro, *Commissioner of Public Security*
28 June	**Visit to London of Prince Takamatsu of Japan** MIZUNO, Commander Kyosuke
30 October	**Visit of the Duke of Gloucester to Ethiopia to represent HM at the Coronation of Emperor Haile Selassie** HERUI, Lij Fakado Sellassé
29 November	**Prince George's visit to Oslo for the Celebration of 25th Aniversary of King Haakon's Accession** CORNELIUSSEN, Captain Elias, *Royal Norwegian Navy, attached to Prince George*

1931–1932

1933

20 June	**Visit of King Feisal I of Iraq to London** SHAKIR AL WADI, Major, *ADC to King of Iraq*

1934

26 September	**Special Mission to announce the Accession of King Leopold II of the Belgians** DE BROQUEVILLE, Baron André Marie Louis Joseph Ghislain D'URSEL, Comte Charles Henri François Joseph Marie

1935–1937

1938

19 July	**State Visit to France of King George VI and Queen Elizabeth** BAILLET, André Charles Ernest, *Commissioner of Police, Paris* BOUQUET, Capitaine d'Infanterie André Florimond Joseph, *of the Ministry of National Defence* BRIDIÉ, Lieutenant-Colonel Alfred François Louis, *Commandant of Republican Guard* BRUNAU, Lieutenant Felix François, *of the Ministry for Foreign Affairs* CANU, Eugène, *Mayor of Boulogne* CHATAIGNEAU, Captain Yves Jean Joseph, *General Secretary of the Presidency Council* DARU, Captain Bruno Marie Joseph Emmanuel, *of the Staff of the Military Governor, Paris* DENAINT, Baron George Henry, *of the Protocol Department* DURIEUX, Colonel Helier Joseph Frederic Jean, MC, *Commanding, Republican Guard Legion* FOURNIER, Lieutenant-Colonel Fernand Marcel, *of the Ministry of National Defence* GENEBRIER, Roger, *Chief of Office of President of the Council* JACQUIN DE MARGERIE, M. Roland

JANNEAU, Charles Guillaume, *of the Ministry of Education*
DE JESSEY, Captain Robert Yves Gatien, *of the Staff of Military Governor of Paris*
LADOUÉ, Pierre Edmond, *Conservator, Versailles National Museum*
MARCHAND, Camille, *Director of Military Police*
PERRIER, Alphonse, *of the Ministry of the Interior*
REBUFFEL, Captain Gabriel Laurent Joseph, *of the Ministry of Marine*
REVILLIOD, Officier d'Artillerie Pierre, *General Secretary of the Prefecture of Police*
ROBELIN, Captain Remi Thomas, *Staff Officer, Paris Region*
SCHILTE, Lieutenant-Colonel André Laurent René, *of the Republican Guard*
DE SEGOGNE, Henry Marie Joseph, *of the Presidency Council*
SIMON, Jacques Edmond, *of the Prefecture of Police*
BAYON-TARGE, Raymond, *Chief of Office of the Presidency of the Council*
TASSIN, Lieutenant-Colonel Charles
VADEZ, Louis Léon Gaston Paul Lucien, *Mayor of Calais*
VERNE, Capitaine d'État-Major Henri Jean François Joseph, *of the Ministry of Education*

15 November   **Visit to Britain of King Carol II of Roumania**
CESIANU, Constantin, *Secretary of Legation*
IIESCU, Capitaine d'État-Major Gheorghe, *Military Attaché, Roumanian Legation*
RADU, Major Ilie, *Orderly Officer to the King*

1939

21 March   **Visit to Britain of President Lebrun of the French Republic**
ALART, Capitaine du Service d'État-Major Antoine Jean Adrien, *Chef du Secretariat Militaire*
SAUTRIAU, François Henry Charles Marie, *Medical Officer*

9 December   **King George VI's visit to France**
DE VOGÜE, Capitaine Robert Jean, *Chief of French Liaison Mission to British Army*

1940

1 June   **800th Anniversary of Portuguese Independence**
GARIN, Vasco Vieira, *First Secretary, Portuguese Legation*

1941–1947

1948

11 June   **Visit to France of Princess Elizabeth, Duchess of Edinburgh and the Duke of Edinburgh**
BONNARDET, Stanislas Marie Louis Joseph Alfred, *Protocol Service*
LESCA, Charles Marie Léon
THURNEYSSEN, Robert

14 September   **Visit of the Duke and Duchess of Gloucester to Denmark to represent HM at the Opening by the King of Denmark of the British Trade Exhibition at Copenhagen**
MENTZ, Ritmester Hugo Ib, *Adjutant to King Frederik of Denmark*

1949

1950

7 March   **Visit to Britain of President Auriol of the French Republic**
ALBAYEZ, Contrôleur Général Georges

21 November   **Visit to Britain of Queen Juliana of the Netherlands and Prince Bernhard**
VAN BOETZELAER, Commander Carel Wessel Theodorus, Baron, *ADC to Queen Juliana*
GEERTSEMA, Major Carel Coenraad, *ADC to the Prince of the Netherlands*

1951

8 May   **Visit to Britain of King Frederik IX and Queen Ingrid of Denmark**
HARHOFF, Major Erik Conrad, *ADC to the King of Denmark*
WERN, Commander Holger Eigil, *ADC to the King of Denmark*

5 June   **Visit to Britain of King Haakon of Norway**
FRODESEN, Commander Fin, *Acting Naval Attaché, Norwegian Embassy*
MALM, Captain Ottar Rolfsson, *ADC to the King of Norway*

1952

1953

2 May Visit of the Duke of Gloucester to Baghdad to attend the Accession Ceremony of King Feisal II of Iraq
MEHDI AHMAD SAMMARRA'I, *Assistant Commandant of Police*

1954

28 June State Visit to Britain of King Gustav VI Adolf and Queen Louise of Sweden
MILLAR, Nils Erik, *Chief Official, Swedish Lord Chamberlain's Office*

14 October State Visit to Britain of Emperor Haile Selassie I of Ethiopia
TSEGAYE, Ato Kifle, *Second Secretary, Ethiopian Embassy*

1955

24 June State Visit to Norway of the Queen and the Duke of Edinburgh
FALSEN, Georg, *Master of Ceremonies, Town Hall, Oslo*
FRØYSTAD, Major Ivar, MC, *ADC to the King of Norway*
GRØNVOLD, Captain Odd, *Private Secretary to the Crown Prince of Norway*
JACOBSEN, Commander Thomas, DSC, RNN Reserve, *General Manager, Port of Oslo*
SIEGWARTH, Commander Fridtjov Karhoff
WAALER, Captain Per, RNAF, *Equerry to Crown Prince of Norway*

25 October State Visit to Britain of President Craveiro Lopez of Portugal
FORTUNATO DE ALMEIDA, Antonio, *Second Secretary, Portuguese Embassy*
CRAVEIRO LOPES, Captain Joào Carlos, *ADC to the President*
PIMENTEL, Captain Octavio Hugo de Almeida e Vasconcelos, *in attendance on President*
POTIER, Antonio, *Third Secretary, Portuguese Embassy*

1956

8 June State Visit to Sweden of the Queen and the Duke of Edinburgh
DANIELSON, Axel Otto, *Commandant, CID, Stockholm*
DYRSSEN, Wilhelm Oscar Gustaf Peder, *Chamberlain*
FOGELMARCK, Stig Fredrik Ugglas Gison, *Deputy Keeper, Royal Collections*
HOLMBERG, Major Henrie Georg, *Adjutant to the Officer Commanding at the Castle*
LINDGREN, Lieutenant-Commander Nils Lennart, *ADC to the Duke of Halland*
LJUNGQUIST, Major Bengt Helge, *Commanding, Royal Swedish Horse Guards*
RUDBECK, Frederic Carl Reinhold, Baron, *Chamberlain*
RUDEBECK, Captain Carl Fredrik Wilhelm Paul Olof, *Horse Guards, Chamberlain*
SKAAR, Commander Nils Eilifson, *Chief of Press Service*

16 July State Visit to Britain of King Feisal II of Iraq
AL-TAK, Colonel Modhaffer Majid, *Assistant Military Attaché*

1957

18 February State Visit to Portugal of the Queen and the Duke of Edinburgh
NATIVIDADE ALVES, Fernando, *of the Ministry of Finance*
CARDOSO, Lieutenant-Commander Leonel Alexandre Gomes, *Liaison Officer*
BARBOSA PEREIRA DA CRUZ, Alberto Manuel, *of the Ministry of Public Works*
GAMITO, José Manuel de Noronha, *of the Protocol Department*
MATOSO, Commander José Francisco Correia, *of the Ministry of Marine*
PINTO DE MESQUITA, Antonio, *Protocol Department*
MALHEIRO REYMÃO NOGUEIRA, Major Antonio Maria, *Commandant, Traffic Police*
BRAGA DE OLIVEIRA, Jorge Adolfo, *in charge of transport and general arrangements*
COSTA VAZ PEREIRA, Antonio Augusto, Marques da, *Private Secretary to Minister for Foreign Affairs*
FREIRE MONIZ PEREIRA, Major Nuno, *Ministry of the Army*
MOURÃO DE MENDONÇA CORTE REAL DA SILVA PINTO, Amandio, *of the Protocol Department*
VENTURA PORFIRIO, Antonio, *Curator of Queluz Palace*
SANTOS PRADO, Lieutenant-Commander Manuel da Rocha, *ADC to the President*
FERREIRA DA SILVA, Captain Alfredo, *Portuguese Navy, of the Office of Under-Secretary for Air*
ABRANCHES DE SOVERAL, Eduardo Silverio, *Protocol Department*
TAVARES, Captain Luiz Manuel, *Public Security Police*
CAYOLLO ZAGALLO, Manuel Carlos de Almeida, *Curator of Ajuda Palace*

8 April State Visit to France of the Queen and the Duke of Edinburgh
ARNOULD, Maurice, *Commandant, Security Police*

AUDOUI, Lieutenant-Colonel Marc Jean, *Military Commandant, Palais d'Elysée*
BERNARD, Gaston Jean, *Commandant, Municipal Police*
BIARD, Henri Louis Marie, *Office Controller of Chief of Police*
BOLLINGER, Armand Charles, *Commandant, Municipal Police*
BOUCHET, Georges, MVO, *Divisional Commissioner, Security Police*
BOUTINEAU, Lieutenant-Colonel Jean Paul Noel, *French Air Force, Commanding, Air Force Base, Bourget*
BRUN, Commandant François Julien, *Bandmaster, Republican Guard*
CAGNARD, Maurice-Edmond René, *Principal Commissioner of Police*
CALON, Capitaine Robert Henri Albert, *Commanding Police Motorcycle Escorts*
CHAMBRILLON, Serge Roland, *Assistant Director, Office of the President*
COT, Pierre Donatien Alphonse, *Director General of the Airport, Paris*
COUHÉ, Louis, KBE, *President Council of Admin., Airport, Paris*
DUFOUR, René Victoir, *of the Protocol Department*
DE FARCY, Commandant Alain Marie Pierre, *Assistant to Chief of Office of Military Governor of Paris*
DE VILLENEUVE-FLAYOSC, Hélion, *of the Ministry of Foreign Affairs*
GENESTIE, Marcel Georges, *Principal Commissioner of Information*
GILLES, Maurice, *Director of Office of Chief of Police*
GLEIZES, Henri
JAPY, André Louis, *Chief Architect, Versailles*
VAN DE KEMP, Gerald Sylvive, *Chief Curator of Museum, Versailles*
LANGLAIS, Henri Jean, OBE, *of the Ministry of Foreign Affairs*
LANTEAUME, Marc Emilien Charles, *Director of Information*
PAPELOUX, Gaston Roger, *Secretary General, National Committee for Preservation of Versailles*
PELOU, Jean-Marie François Alphonse, *Press Officer (Civil)*
PITON, Armand, *Director of Police (Seine et Oise)*
RICHARD, Guy, *of the Ministry of Foreign Affairs*
ROCHES, André, *Director General, Municipal Police*
ROUQUIÉ, Jean Louis, *Director of Police (North)*
SALTET, Marc Louis Lionel, *Keeper of the Palace, Versailles*
SOUTOUS, Lieutenant-Colonel Georges Marcel, *Commanding, Cavalry of Republican Guard*
STABLO, René François, *Counsellor, Ministry of Foreign Affairs*
TERRIER, Commandant Camille Auguste Eugène, *Officer of the Spahis*
VILLENEUVE, André-Jean, *Assistant Director of Office, Prefet de Seine*

21 May — **State Visit to Denmark of the Queen and the Duke of Edinburgh**
ADOLPH, Major Jorgen Asger, *ADC to the King*
BERG, Major Herman, *Royal Life Guards, Commanding Guard at Amalienborg*
BJØRNOW, Ejnar Frants Christensen, *Superintendent, Court Telegraph Service*
CLAUSEN, Captain Arne, *Commander Frigate* Valdemar Sejr
FELDING, Commander Ole, *attached to Flag Officer, Royal Yachts*
GLARBORG, Major Steen, *Royal Danish Air Force, ADC to the King*
IVERSEN, Major Johan Werner Michael, *Staff Officer to Commandant of Copenhagen*
KØNIGSFELDT, Albert Wolff, *Deputy Head, Ministry of Foreign Affairs*
LANGE, Commander Niels Faergemann, *Royal Danish Navy, ADC to the King*
LICHT, Kai Vilhelm de Fine, *Governor of Christiansborg Palace*
LOTZBECK, Major Baron Carl Ferdinand Eugen Ludvig von, *Commanding Guard of Honour*
LOWE, Einar, *Assistant Chief of Section, Ministry of Ecclesiastical Affairs*
MØLLER, Hans Severin, *Private Secretary to Minister of Foreign Affairs*
MUNCK, Commander Johan Christian, *Royal Danish Navy, attached to HM and HRH*
NIELSEN, Major Erik Abildgaard, *ADC to the King*
NYSTROM, Arne Eiler, *Architect and Surveyor, Royal Household Furniture*
RODER, Hans Christian, *Master Mariner*
SCHAUFUSS, Frank, *Director, Royal Danish Ballet*
STAVNSTRUP, Poul Richardt, *Chief Constable, Frederiksberg*
STOLTZE, Major Preben, *ADC to the King*
SUADICANI, Major Bjorn Bertil Emil, *Commanding the Escort*
THØGERSEN, Hans, *Chief Harbour Master, Copenhagen*
THOMSEN, Kaj Straarup, *Assistant Private Secretary to the King*
THORSEN, Sigurd, *Director of Department of Public Affairs*
WOLF, Mogens, *Assistant Commissioner of Police, Copenhagen*

1958

25 March — **State Visit to the Netherlands of the Queen and the Duke of Edinburgh**
AGHINA, Johannes Petrus Maria, *Head of Section, Protocol Department*
DE BEAUFORT, Jonkheer Barthold Willem Floris, *Commander, Mounted Police Escort*
VAN BOKTEL, Colonel Herman, *Commander, Water Police*
EISMA, Major Jan Jacob, *Equerry to the Queen*
VAN ETTINGER, Jan, *Director of Information Centre, Building & Housing*
GREGORY, Commander Niels Joachim Heiberg, *Commander, Rotterdam Naval Base*
HAGDORN, Commander Henric Joan Herman, *Chief of Naval Staff (Operations), The Hague*
LE HEUX, Major Jan, *Equerry to the Queen*
HOOGENBOOM, Pieter Johannes Philippus, *Director of Department of Internal Affairs, Amsterdam*

HOOGENDOORN, Henri Albert, *First Secretary, Netherlands Embassy*
DE JONG, Commander Petrus Josef Sietse, DSC, *ADC to the Queen*
KWINT, Menzo Mattheus, *Burgomaster of Velsen*
DE LOOR, Dirk, *Burgomaster of Delft*
MEURS, Mlle Mieke, *Secretary to Princess Beatrix*
MONTANUS, Captain Willem Adriaan, *Harbour Master of Amsterdam*
POUBLON, Lieutenant-Colonel Charles Alphonse Marie, *Senior Officer in charge of Fly-Past*
RANFT, Lieutenant-Colonel Johann Heinrich, *Commanding Guards Regiment*
VAN ROSSEM, Lieutenant-Commander Willem, *ADC to the Prince of the Netherlands*
VAN SCHENDEL, Arthur François Emile, *Director, Rijks Museum, Amsterdam*
SCHOEMAKER, Paul Wilke, *Commissioner, Rotterdam Municipal Police*
SIX, Willem Cornelis, *Head of Burgomaster's Office, The Hague*
VAN STEENIS, Hendrikus Anthonie, *Commander, Police Escort of State Police*
VEENHUIJS, Major Gerhardus Johannes Bernardus, *Commanding Guard of Honour of the Marines*
WEEKENSTROO, Henricus Jacobus, *Veterinary Surgeon, Royal Mews Department*
WIJSENBEEK, Louis Jacob Florus, *Director of Municipal Museum, The Hague*
VAN YPEREN, Major Rocus, *Director of Music, Royal Military Band*

13 May **State Visit to Britain of President Gronchi of Italy**
SAN GIORGIO, Colonel Corrado, *Deputy Military, Counsellor to the Presidency*
MESCHINELLI, Giuseppe, *First Secretary, Italian Embassy*

20 October **State Visit to Britain of President Heuss of the Federal Republic of Germany**
BRUCKNER, Ernst, *Chief Inspector, CID*
SCHERER, Karl Wilhelm Hans, *First Secretary, German Embassy*

1959

5 May **State Visit to Britain of the Shahanshah of Iran**
ESFANDIARY, Doctor Amir Mohammad, *First Secretary, Iranian Embassy*
FARTASH, Doctor Manoutcher, *First Secretary, Iranian Embassy*
KHOSRODAD, Captain Manoutchehr, *Officer in charge of Codes, Iranian Embassy*
NAJM, Abbas, *First Secretary, Iranian Embassy*

1960

5 April **State Visit to Britain of the President of the French Republic and Madame de Gaulle**
BAEYENS, Baron André Ferdinand, *Second Secretary, French Embassy*
CANTELAUBE, Jacques Marie Joseph, *Controller, Security Dept. of Presidency*
FLOHIC, Capitaine de Corvette François, *ADC to the President*

19 July **State Visit to Britain of King Bhumibol and Queen Sirikit of Thailand**
CHOLASAP, Major Suratana, *Assistant Military Attaché, Royal Thai Embassy*
ISRANGKURA, Commander Lapo, *Assistant Naval Attaché, Royal Thai Embassy*
SIWARAKSA, Sala, *Second Secretary, Royal Thai Embassy*

17 October **State Visit to Britain of King Mahendra and Queen Ratna of Nepal**
HALDAR, Dr Susil Chandra, *Royal Physician*
MANANDHAR, Krishna Prasad, *Private Secretary to the Ambassador*
SHAMSHER JANG BAHADUR RANA, Shushil, *Brother of the Queen*
SHARMA, Poorna Prasad, *Public Relations Officer*
MANANDHAR, Indra Narayan, *Senior Clerk, Royal Nepalese Embassy*
SRESTHA, Subba Kiran Bahadur, *Personal Attendant to the King*

1961

26 February **State Visit to Nepal of the Queen and the Duke of Edinburgh**
KARKI, Vishnu Bahadur, *Engineer*
SHAH, Narain Singh, *Senior Superintendent of Police*
SHAH, Brigadier-General Padma Bahadur, MBE, *Head of CID*
SINGH, Sardar Bhopal, *Deputy, Personal Secretary*
THAPA, Mukund Bahadur, *Electrical Engineer*
THAPA, Rom Bahadur, *Deputy, Inspector General of Police*
UPADHYAYA, Heramba Prasad, *Telecommunications Engineer*

2 March **State Visit to Iran of the Queen and the Duke of Edinburgh**
ASKARI, Major Ali, *of the Imperial Guard*
AMIR BAKHTIARY, Rostam, *Civil ADC to the Shahanshah*
BEIGLARI, Lieutenant-Colonel Mohammad Amin, *Chief of Counter Intelligence, Imperial Guard*
FARTASH, Major Abbas, *of the Imperial Guard*
FATHULLAHI, Major, *of the Iranian Police Force*
GULTAPPEH, Major, *of the Iranian Police Force*
HANJANI, Hasan Ali, *of the Protocol Department*

MALAEKEH, Bahram, *of the Protocol Department*
NAMDAR, Doctor Mostafa, *of the Protocol Department*
NESHAT, Major Ali, *of the Imperial Guard*
QARAGUZLU, Manuchehr, *Civil ADC*
RAKHSHA, Lieutenant-Colonel Ali, *of the Imperial Guard*
RASEKH, Colonel, *of the Iranian Police Force*
SOLEYMANI, Haidarqul Amir, *Civil ADC*
VASIQ, Colonel, *of the Iranian Police Force*

29 April   **State Visit to Italy of the Queen and the Duke of Edinburgh**
CARDUCCI ARTENNISIO, Ludovico, Counsellor, *Ministry of Foreign Affairs*
ADORNI BRACCESI, Renzo Antoniotto Pietro Giovanni, *Attaché for Emigration, Ministry of Foreign Affairs*
CAPOBIANCO, Doctor Antonio Lorenzo, *Supply Office*
CIMA, Doctor Renato, *Secretary to the President*
COGNAZZO, Lieutenant-Colonel Giuseppe, *Attaché to Minister of Foreign Affairs*
COSTANTINI, Ernesto, *Station Master, Rome*
DONNETTI, Doctor Luigi, *Vice-Supt of Police, Quirinale Palace*
FADDA, Doctor Francesco, *Secretary to the President*
FROVA, Colonel Luigi
LATTARI, Francesco, *Assistant Private Secretary to the Presidency*
LAVAGNINO, Professor Emilio, *Director of Lazio Art Gallery, Rome*
MARCHIONI, Felice, *Head of Protocol*
MASARICH, Doctor Alfredo, *Chief of Protocol*
MATTIOLI, Doctor Ivo, *Head of Protocol, Rome*
SANFELICE DI MONTEFORTE, Captain Marcello, *Italian Navy, Military Counsellor*
MUREDDU, Doctor Matteo, *Secretary to the President*
NEVOLA, Doctor Saturno, *Head, Admin. Office of the Presidency*
DEL PRETE, Doctor Renato, *Director, Italian Stationery Office*
MARINUCCI DE REGUARDATI, Costanzo, *Counsellor, Ministry of Foreign Affairs*
ROSSI, Doctor Mario Franco, *Counsellor of Legation*
SANGUINETTI, Doctor Francesco, *Architect, Cultural Department*
SPARISCI, Doctor Emo, *Private Secretary to the President*
TASSONI, Lieutenant-Colonel Bruno, *Commander of the Guards, Quirinale Palace*
VIOLA, Doctor Giovanni, *Secretary to the President*
VITALE, Riccardo, *Director of Rome Opera*
ZACCARINI, Alessandro, *First Secretary, Foreign Relations Branch, Quirinale Palace*

1962

10 July   **State Visit to Britain of the President of Liberia and Mrs Tubman**
BESTMAN, Colonel P. James, *Chief Security Officer*
BIRCH, The Hon. Caesar William, *Private Secretary to the President*
BRUMSKINE, Doctor Walter, *Personal Physician*
DICKERSON, Brigadier-General John Henry, *ADC to the President*
REEVES-GORGLA, Madame Myrtle, *Commercial Attaché*

16 October   **State Visit to Edinburgh of King Olav V of Norway**
ANDERSEN, Major Olav, *RNAF, ADC to the King*
BRUEN, Captain Eigil John, *Naval Attaché*
ELIASSEN, Kjell, *First Secretary, Norwegian Embassy*
GRØNMARK, Lieutenant-Colonel Olai Julius, DFC, *RNAF, Air Attaché*
MOE, Commander Reidar Johan, *Second in Command, HM Yacht* Norge
NORGREN, Commander Knut, *RN Naval Reserve, Physician to the King*
RANDERS, Lieutenant-Colonel Thorvald, *Military Attaché*

1963

14 May   **State Visit to Britain of King Baudouin I and Queen Fabiola of the Belgians**
DE GERLACHE DE GOMERY, Philippe, Baron, *Shipping Counsellor*
DE HEUSCH, Major Raymond Louis Justin, *ADC to the King*
THISSEN, Robert Olivier Pierre, *First Secretary (Press)*

9 July   **State Visit to Britain of King Paul and Queen Frederika of the Hellenes**
KARAGEORGOS, Nicolas Constantine, *First Secretary, Greek Embassy*
SERPIERI, John F., *Master of Ceremonies*
TSELEKIS, Police Lieutenant-Colonel Panaghiotis, *Royal Greek Gendarmerie, Commanding Traffic Police, Athens*

1964

26 May   **State Visit to Britain of President Abboud of the Republic of Sudan**
AGABNA, Sayed Omer Abbas, *Second Secretary Sudanese Embassy*
BEREIR, Sayed Mutasim Ali, *Press Attaché*

BUSHARA, Lieutenant-Colonel El Fatih Mohammed, *Private Secretary*
EL KHIDER, Sayed Bukhari Abdulla, *Commercial Attaché*

1965

1 February   **State Visit to Ethiopia of the Queen and the Duke of Edinburgh**
MICHAEL-BELACHEW, Lieutenant-Colonel Amde, *Chief of Security, Eritrea*
BOGHOSSIAN, Lieutenant-Colonel Kosrof, *Equerry, Imperial Palace*
HAILE, Colonel Angagaw, *in charge of camp arrangements*
INGRIDA, Colonel Loulou, *The Queen's Driver*
KIDANE-MARIAM, Ato Yohannes, *Director General, Ministry of the Pen*
SHENEGALEGN, Colonel Asrat, *in charge of State Coach*
TEKLE, Ato Solomon, *Chief of Protocol, Eritrea*
YIRDATCHU, Colonel Immshaw, *Assistant to Commissioner of Police, Eritrea*

12 February   **State Visit to the Republic of Sudan of the Queen and the Duke of Edinburgh**
ABBAS, Sayed Mubarak, *Town Clerk of Omdurman*
EL AMIN, Sayed Mamoun, *Town Clerk of Khartoum*
EL ARAKI, Sayed Abdel Hamid, *District Commissioner, El Obeid*
BUKHARI, Sayed Idris, *District Commissioner, El Obeid*
BUKHARI, Sayed Mahmoud, *Head of Security Police*
EL FADL, Colonel Murtada, *Military Liaison Officer*
EL HAG, Sayed Ahmed Mohammed, *Executive Officer, Khartoum Rural Council*
HAMMO, Sayed Hussein Mohammed, *Commandant of Police, Khartoum*
IBRAHIM, Sayed Abdullah Mohammed, *Police Commissioner, Kordofan*
KASHAWA, Sayed Osman Ahmed Abu, *Town Clerk, Wad Medani*
KHALIFA, Sayed Abdel Wahab, *Town Clerk, Khartoum North*
MAGID, Colonel Salah el Din Abdel, *of the Honorary Bodyguard*
MOHAMMED, Sayed Abdel Razig Awad El Kareem, *Police Commissioner, Blue Nile*
EL TOM, Sayed Mohammed, *Airport Commandant*
YASSIN, Sayed Ali, *Director of Traffic Police*

18 May   **State Visit to Germany of the Queen and the Duke of Edinburgh**
BARCHEWITZ, Wolf-Dieter, *Head, Private Office of the President*
BÜERGER, Wolfgang, *Senior Security Officer*
BÜSCHER, Rolf Franz Robert, *Security Officer*
FUNCKE, Gustav-Adolf, *Official for Orders*
KOMATOWSKY, Kapitanleutnant Heinz, *Protocol Officer, Ministry of Defence*
KUSTERER, Herr Hermann, MBE
LANGE, Karl Heinrich Martin, *Protocol Officer, Hessen*
MEISWINKEL, Herbert, *Protocol Officer, Rheinland Pfalz*
MICHAEL, Major Friedrich-August von, *Commanding, Guard Battalion*
MONTAG, Werner Georg, *Protocol Dept., Foreign Ministry*
PLEHWE, Frau Helga von, *of the Suite specially attached*
RAUCH, Ruprecht, *Protocol Officer, Berlin*
SCHOLZ, Major Gerhard Theodor Maximilian, *Bandmaster*
STIER, Walter, *Head of Travel Section, Bundesbahn*
WESTERBURG, Werner, *Assistant in Protocol Department*

13 July   **State Visit to Britain of the President of Chile and Señora de Frei**
CASTRO, Señor Guillermo
BUNGE DE CISTERNAS, Señora Elsie

1966

9 May   **State Visit to Belgium of the Queen and the Duke of Edinburgh**
ABRAS, Major Jean Gustave Gabriel Edmond, *Assistant to Chief of Staff, First District*
BAIJOT, Major Marc Emile Auguste Ghislain, *Assistant to Commander of Gendarmerie of the Palaces*
BAUDOT, Lieutenant-Colonel Gustave Philemon, *Prince Philip's helicopter pilot*
BOGAERT, Major Gilbert Roger, *Commanding Royal Mounted Escort*
COCH, Victor Guillaume Louis, *Chief Commissioner of Police, Liège*
CORSUS, Alphonse, *Chief Commissioner of Police, Antwerp*
DEHEM, Albert Roger, OBE, *Burgomaster of Ypres*
DELBECQUE, Ernest Jean, *Chief Commissioner of Police, Bruges*
DELFOSSE, Jean-Marie Michel, *Honorary Consul, Liège*
DUBUCQ, Madame Adrienne, *Assistant, Protocol Department*
VAN ELST, Julius Ludovicus, *Director, Brussels Airport*
HUISMAN, Maurice, *Director, Royal Theatre*
KESTELOOT, Capitaine-Commandant Pierre, *Assistant to Military Household*
LAURENT, Leon G.L., *Assistant, Protocol Department*
LAUWEREINS, John, *Burgomaster of Ostend*
DE MILD, Capitaine-Commandant Jean Ernest, BEM, *ADC to the King*

ROBINS, Lieutenant Hughes, *Belgian Navy*
DE SCHOUTYEETE DE TERVARENT, Philippe, *Head, Press Section, Ministry of Foreign Affairs*
VAN YPERSELE DE STRIHOU, Madame Anne Marie Henriette André Ghislaine, *Assistant to Keeper of the Privy Purse*
TINCHANT, Vincent Jules Joseph, *Chief of Protocol, Brussels Airport*

7 May — **State Visit to Britain of the President of the Federal Republic of Austria and Frau Jonas**
HEIBLE, Dr Gert Guenther, *Secretary of Austrian Embassy*
LOIBL, Dr Wolfgang, *Private Secretary to the President*

19 July — **State Visit to Britain of King Hussein I of Jordan and Princess Muna Al Hussein**
HASSAN, Major Abboud Salim, *Assistant Naval and Air Attaché*
KABARITI, Saleh Alawi, *Third Secretary, Jordanian Embassy*
MOHAMMAD, Lieutenant-Colonel Anwar, *ADC*

1967

9 May — **State Visit to Britain of King Faisal of Saudi Arabia**
JAWAD, Mohammed Said Abdul
SALEH, Ahmed Zaki

1 November — **State Visit to Britain of the President of Turkey and Madame Sunay**
ARIK, Umut, *First Secretary at Embassy*
BALIBEY, Captain Baki, *ADC*
BALKAR, The Hon. Galip, *Director of Presidential Cabinet*
BARAZ, Engin, *Second Secretary at Embassy*
BARUTÇU, Ecmel, *Head of Chancery*
BAYRAK, Staff Lieutenant-Colonel Recep, *Liaison Officer*
ÇAMLIBEL, Ismet Okyay, *Information Attaché*
KICIMAN, Akgün Han, *Second Secretary at Embassy*
ÜZÇERI, Sami Tugay, *Second Secretary at Embassy*
SUNAY, The Hon. Dr Atilla, *Personal Physician*
ÜLGEN, The Hon. Tanju, *Director of the Cabinet, Ministry of Foreign Affairs*
ATLAS, Mustafa, *Attaché at Embassy*
BALCIK, Tacettin, *Security Officer, Presidential Office*
OZNUR, Osman, *Attaché (Cyphers) at Embassy*
SARIOGLU, Necati, *Attaché (Wireless Operator)*
TASCIOGLU, Miss Renan, *Shorthand Typist, Secretary of Chancery*
TEZCAN, Mustafa, *Attaché (Cyphers and Archivist)*

1968

1 November — **State Visit to Brazil of the Queen and the Duke of Edinburgh**
BARBOSA, Rubens Antonio, *Protocol Official*
CASTRIATO DE AZAMBUJA, Marcos, *Official, attached to Ministry of Foreign Affairs*
D'OLIVEIRA, Nuno Alvaro Guilherme, *Official, attached to Ministry of Foreign Affairs*
PACHECO DE ARRUDA, Inspector Firmiano, *Security Officer*
SOARES CARBONAR, Orlando, *Protocol Officer*
VALES HEREDIA, Dr Hugo, *Security Officer*

11 November — **State Visit to Chile of the Queen and the Duke of Edinburgh**
ARELLANO STARK, Colonel Sergio, *Military ADC*
ARIZTIA SWETT, Luis, *Administrator Cousino Palace*
ANDUEZA SILVA, Juan, *Mayor of Vina del Mar*
CONTRERAS ARAYA, Lieutenant-Colonel Dario, *in charge of Motorised Escort of Caribineros*
ESTAY ROJAS, Colonel Hector, *in charge of Caribineros, Carrera Hotel*
GARCIA DE LA HUERTA MATTE, Pedro, *Sub-Manager, Club Hipico*
GONZALES TORRES, Eduardo, *Prefect of Investigaciones*
HENRIQUES GARAT, Commander Victor, *Naval ADC*
MENDOZA DURAN, Colonel Cesar, *Carabineros, in charge of Traffic*
ORREGO VICUÑA, Claudio, *Press Adviser*
RODRIGUEZ LOPEZ, Juan Antonio, *Mayor of Valparaiso*
SOLER MANFREDINI, Wing Commander Juan, *Air ADC*
VARELA, Squadron Leader Alberto Arturo, *Liaison Officer for Royal Flights*

1969

22 April — **State Visit to Britain of President Saragat of Italy**
BELLUSCIO, Constantino, *Private Secretary*
BERLINGUER, Sergio, *First Secretary at Italian Embassy*
BUCALOSSI, Colonel Mario, *Military Attaché*
CROSETTI, Giovanni Battista, *Counsellor at Embassy*

DONINI, Filippo, *Cultural Attaché*
MAROTTA, Colonel Vittorio, *Air Attaché*
MARTUCCI, Captain Giuseppe, *Defence and Naval Attaché*
PRANZETTI, Antonio, *Private Secretary to Minister of Foreign Affairs*
PULCINI, Francesco, *Counsellor at Embassy*

5 May **State Visit to Austria of the Queen, the Duke of Edinburgh and Princess Anne**
BOGNER, Dr Rudolf Johann, *First Secretary, Ministry of Foreign Affairs*
DORREK, Josef, *Head of Dept. of Railways*
HEJKRLIK, Dr Adolf, *Head of Bodyguard*
HENNIG, Dr Georg, *Interpreter for the Queen*
HODICK, Professor Dr Friedrich, *Military Band Master*
KUBISTA, Ernst, *Head of Traffic Department, Ministry of Interior*
PATAY, Lieutenant-Colonel Stephen John von, *Austrian Air Force, of the Central Staff, Ministry of Defence*
PILIPP, Lieutenant-Colonel Heinrich, *Commanding Guard Battalion*
REIDINGER, Dr Karl, *State Police*
REISCH, Frau Monika Maria, *Lady in Waiting to Princess Anne*
SCHÜLLER, Dr Emil, *Security Official*
SCHURZ, Dr Helmut, *Interpreter for Princess Anne*

15 July **State Visit to Britain of the President of Finland and Madame Kekkonen**
CHRISTENSEN, Major Hans Henrik Sweijstrup, *Assistant Military, Naval and Air Attaché*
HEINRICHS, Hilding Axel Erik, *First Secretary, Finnish Embassy*
IMMONEN, Mikko Olavi, *Press Secretary, Finnish Embassy*
LAUKKANEN, Lauri Heikki, *Commercial Secretary, Finnish Embassy*

1970

1971

5 October **State Visit to Britain of Emperor Hirohito and Empress Nagako of Japan**
ARIMA, Tatsuo, *Interpreter for Emperor*
ARISHIMA, Madame Akiko, *Lady in Waiting and Interpreter*
FUJIMAKI, Seitaro, *Chief of Guard Division, Imperial Guard*
HIRAGA, Toshiyuki, *First Secretary, Japanese Embassy*
MATSUURA, Akira, *First Secretary, Japanese Embassy*
OHASHI, Captain Keizo, *Defence Attaché, Japanese Embassy*
SAKA, Koji, *First Secretary, Japanese Embassy*
SAWANO, Hiroshi, *First Secretary, Japanese Embassy*
TOGO, Takehiro, *First Secretary, Japanese Embassy*
YANAGI, Kenichi, *First Secretary, Japanese Embassy*

18 October **State Visit to Turkey of the Queen, the Duke of Edinburgh and Princess Anne**
ALTAN, Kerem, *attached to the Minister in Attendance*
ARAN, Commander Ilhan, *Commanding Naval Escort*
AVUNDUK, Nail, *Ankara Jockey Club*
BAYER, Major Asun, *Bandmaster, Izmir*
ERDAL, Chief Commissioner Umit, *Security, Ministry of the Interior*
GÖKBUDAK, Ilhan, *Deputy Director General, Ministry of Foreign Affairs*
KOÇMAN, Sitki, *Chairman, BMC, Turkey*
ÖZEN, Major Miyazi, *Commander, Guard of Honour*
SILE, Ozcan Saffettin, *of Highways Department, Bosphorus Bridge*
TEMIZER, Dr Raci, *Director, Museum of Anatolian Civilisations*
VERSAN, Miss Belkis, *attached to Princess Anne*
YASA, Major Dursan, *Escorting Officer at Mausoleum*

7 December **State Visit to Britain of King Zahir of Afghanistan**
AFZAL, Mammad Taher, *of Protocol Department*
TARZI, Abdullah, *First Secretary, Afghan Embassy*

1972

10 February **State Visit to Thailand of the Queen and the Duke of Edinburgh**
BUNNAG, Tula, *Director of Royal Household Affairs*
ANIRUTH-DEVA, Colonel Fuangchaloei, *President of Old England Students' Association*
JIRASATIT, Captain Pijit, *Chief of Staff, Sataheep Naval Base*
KASEMSANT, Suprapada, *Chief of Her Majesty's Personal Affairs Division*
KESAKOMOL, Colonel Jitkavi, *Commanding 1st Infantry Regiment, Kings Guard*
KITTIKACHORN, Lieutenant-Colonel Narong, *Assistant Secretary to General P. Charusathiara*
MALAKUL, Mom Luang Piya, *Secretary of Bureau of the Royal Household*
NANDHABIWAT, Mrs Chat-Koo, *Member of the Thai Suite*

NAVARAT, Chet, *Chief of Protocol Division*
PUNKRASIN, Srisward, *Chief of Reception Division*
SNIDVONGS NA AYUTHAYA, Pisith, *Director of Royal Household Division*
SNIDVONGS, Miss Varunyupha, *Member of the Thai Suite*
SUNTHORNNARK, Captain Yongsuk, *Commandant, Sataheep Naval Harbour*
TONGYAI, Mom Rajawongse Tongnoi
VASANTASING, Captain Suthep, *Assistant Commandant, Sataheep Naval Station*
VEJJAJIVA, Nissai, *Chief of Press Division*

22 February	**State Visit to Malaysia of the Queen, the Duke of Edinburgh and Princess Anne**

INCHE ABU BAKAR AZIZ
ZAINAL bin IBRAHIM, *Superintendent, Royal Malaysian Police*
CHELLIAH KAMALANATHAN, *Superintendent, Royal Malaysian Police*
ARIFFIN bin MUDA, *Lieutenant-Colonel*
ABDUL GHANI bin ABDUL RAHMAN, *Superintendent, Royal Malaysian Police*

29 February	**State Visit to Brunei of the Queen, the Duke of Edinburgh and Princess Anne**

PENGIRAN PENGGAWA, *Chief of Protocol*
PENGIRAN DIPA NEGARA PENGIRAN ABDUL NOMIN,*State Secretary*
PEHIN ORANG KAYA LAKSAMANA DATO' SERI UTAMAC AWANG HAJI ABDUL RAHMAN bin P.O.K.
    SHAHBANDAR HAJI MOHAMED TAHA, *Chairman, Public Services Commission*

13 March	**State Visit to the Maldives of the Queen and the Duke of Edinburgh**

MOOSA KALEFANU MANIKU, Ali, *National Security Officer*

11 April	**State Visit to Britain of Queen Juliana and Prince Bernhard of the Netherlands**

LEE, Lieutenant-Commander Henricus Cornelis van der, *ADC to the Prince of the Netherlands*
NIERMAN, Mlle Allegonde Henriëtte Marie, *Second Secretary at the Embassy*
SCHREUDERS, Lieutenant-Colonel Thomas, *ADC to the Prince of the Netherlands*
SPIERENBURG, Lieutenant-Colonel Egbert, *State Police*

15 May	**State Visit to France of the Queen and the Duke of Edinburgh**

AUBRY, Lieutenant-Colonel Pierre, *ADC to the President*
BAYLION, Michel, *Department of State Visits*
BRESSOT, Jean
BRIOTTET, Alain Marcel, *Protocol Department*
DROULERS, M. Daniel Jean Marie
MIMEURE, Lieutenant-Colonel Jacques du Buyer de
MIRMONT, M. Pierre Antoine Henri Mathivet de la Ville de
PARIS, M. Gilbert Leon
PINART, Colonel Jehan André Henri
PLANCHET, M. André
SIRJEAN, M. Roger Charles Leopold
THUILIER, M. Joseph Jules Claude Raymond

13 June	**State Visit to Britain of Grand Duke Jean and Grand Duchess Charlotte of Luxembourg**

MEUNIER, Captain Eugène, *ADC to Grand Duke*
ALEX, M. Julien, *First Secretary, Luxembourg Embassy*

17 October	**State Visit to Yugoslavia of the Queen and the Duke of Edinburgh**

DULOVIC, Velibor, *Counsellor in Protocol*
FILKO, Viktor, *Assistant Director of Centre for Selection of Horses, Croatia*
JOJIC-GAJINOVIC, Mrs Branimira, *Interpreter*
IVIR, Vladimir, *Interpreter*
KOMLJENOVIC, Miss Gordana, *Interpreter*
MILATOVIC, Dragutin, *President's Protocol Officer*
POPOVIC, Mrs Dusanka, *Counsellor in Protocol*
VUCEKOVIC, Mrs Zora, *Counsellor, Ministry of Foreign Affairs*

24 October	**State Visit to Britain of President Heinemann of the Federal Republic of Germany and Frau Heinemann**

BAHN-FLESSBURG, Frau Ruth, *Private Secretary to Frau Heinemann*
HEIDE, Herr Winifried, *First Secretary, Federal Presidency*
MULLERS, Herr Joseph, *Second Secretary, German Embassy*
POPITZ, Herr Peter, *Private Secretary to the President*

1973

3 April	**State Visit to Britain of President Eccheverria Alvarez of Mexico**

CAMPOS, Señora Francisca Celis, *Counsellor Mexican Embassy*
MARTIN, Señor Jorge Eduardo, *Counsellor, Mexican Embassy*
COY, Señor Raul Santos, *First Secretary*

11 December	**State Visit to Britain of President Mobutu of Zaïre**

BOLAMPEMBE, Major-Aviateur Somanza, *Chief of College of Officers*
BONDOY, Citoyen W'Esiba Isawato

PEMBA DI MATANGA, Citoyen
MULUMBA, Citoyen Kaseba wa
NA'KINKELA, Citoyen Yha Tol'ande Gruna la Zingara

1974

3 May **State Visit to Britain of Queen Margrethe II of Denmark and Prince Henrik**
ANDERSEN, Major Henrik Fogh, *Aide-de-Camp*
JESPERSEN, Commander Arne, *Aide-de-Camp*
VOSS, Mr Soren, *First Secretary, Danish Embassy*
SCHMIEGELOW, Mr Ernst Henrik, *First Secretary, Danish Embassy*
HANSEN, Mr Niels Buch, *Commercial Counsellor, Danish Embassy*
BOHR, Mr Erik, *Industrial and Scientific Counsellor*
MUNCH, Mr Mogens, *Agricultural Counsellor*

9 July **State Visit to Britain of the Yang DiPertuan Agung of Malaysia and the Raja Permaisuri Agung**
ENCIK BAHRIN bin HUSSAIN, *Director, Malay Students Department*
ENCIK ABDUL FATAH bin ZAKARIA, *Trade Commissioner*
PEH, Colonel Michael Teck Foo, *Services Adviser*
ENCIK YEOW, Eric Teck Siang, *Deputy Director Malay Students Department*
MOHAMAD ISA bin CHE KAK, Lieutenant-Colonel, *Military ADC*
MAHBOB bin DATUK AHMAD, *Assistant Commissioner, Police ADC*

1975

24 February **State Visit to Mexico of the Queen and the Duke of Edinburgh**
MENDIVIL CABRERA, Tte. Col. Carlos, *Commander, Presidential Flight*
MARTIN DEL CAMPO, Capitan de Corbeta CG Agustin Ortega, *Presidential General Staff*
PAZ DEL CAMPO, Mayor Intendente DEM Rafael, *Presidential General Staff*
CASTILLO, Mayor de Infanteria DEM Agustin Valladares, *Chief of Security*
CABALLERO GARCIA, Señora Doctora Gloria, *Director General, Cultural Affairs*
JIMENEZ LAZCANO, Señor Mauro, *Director of Public Relations*
DE LA BARREDA MORENO, Capitan de Ejercito Luis, *Director of Federal Security*
PENICHE, Mayor de Inf. DEM Antonio Clemente Fernandez, *Presidential General Staff*
OROZCO PERALTA, Commander Jose, *Equerry attached to Duke of Edinburgh*
MEYER PICON, Señor Santiago, *Director General, International Cooperation*
VALDES AGUILAR, Señor Raul, *Director General, Diplomatic Service*

7 May **State Visit to Japan of the Queen and the Duke of Edinburgh**
ITO, Ken, *Assistant to Master of Ceremonies*
SAIGA, Miss Fumiko, *of Protocol Office*
SAITO, Issei, *of Akasaka Palace*
TAKEI, Kazuo, *Assistant to Master of Ceremonies*
TANAKA, Kazuki, *Director General of Affairs, Akasaka Palace*
HONDA, Daisuke, *Official in Kyoto, Imperial Household*

8 July **State Visit to Britain of King Carl XVI Gustaf of Sweden**
BERGÉRUSE, Sture Karl Emanuel, *First Palace Steward*
BERGH, Captain Svante, *ADC to the King*
HASSELGREN, Colonel Curt Wilhelm Brynolf, *Army Attaché, Swedish Embassy*
LUNDQUIST, Arne Erik, *Counsellor*
RYDSTROM, Captain Nils Uno, *Naval Attaché, Swedish Embassy*

1976

4 May **State Visit to Britain of President Geisel of Brazil and Senhora Geisel**
CARVALHO, Captain Mauricio Henrique Bittencourt de, *Naval Attaché, Brazilian Embassy*
CHAVES, Sr Luiz Carlos de Oliveira, *Assistant Press Adviser to Presidency*
MOREIRA DA FONSECA, Colonel Joao Luiz, *Air Attaché, Brazilian Embassy*
PESSOA CAVALCANTI DE ALBUQUERQUE, Lieutenant-Colonel Jose, *Air Force ADC*
DE AZAMBUJA, Lieutenant-Colonel Travano Antonio Morteo, *Assistant to Military Cabinet of President*
DE SMANDECK, Sr Raul, *Counsellor, Brazilian Embassy*
HILGENBERG, Captain Manoel Aldu Teixeira, *Military Member of non-official party*
MELO, Sr Ovidio Andrade, *Minister, Brazilian Embassy*
PEDROZO, Lieutenant-Colonel Germano Arnoldi, *Head, Security Service of Presidency*
SERPA, Major Ibir Fernando, *Military ADC*
VIEGAS, Major Dante Jorge Colangelo, *Assistant, Security Service of Presidency*
VIEIRA, Lieutenant-Colonel Gleuber, *Army ADC*

24 May **State Visit to Finland of the Queen and the Duke of Edinburgh**
OLJEMARK, Mrs Gunvor, *Clerk of the Orders of the White Rose of Finland and of the Lion of Finland*
VESAMAA, Miss Kaija, *Secretary, President's Office*

TAMMI, Mr Tuomo, *Protocol Department*
RAESTE, Mr Arimo, *Superintendent, Presidential Palace*

22 June   **State Visit to Britain of President Giscard d'Estaing of the French Republic and Madame Giscard d'Estaing**
ARNOLD, Lieutenant-General Philippe Claude, *ADC*
DELOCHE DE NOYELLE, Mme. Odette Juliette, *Secretary to Mme Giscard d'Estaing*
JACQUIER, M Michel Fernand Marie Etienne, *Naval Counsellor, French Embassy*
PERROTTE, Général de Brigade Aerienne Francis Edmond Roger, *Air Attaché, French Embassy*
RIGAILLAUD, M. André Marc Philippe, *Commercial Counsellor*
SANTOS, M. Robert de los, *Second Counsellor*
BARDON, Colonel Yves Paul Maurice, *Military Attaché*

8 November   **State Visit to Luxembourg of the Queen and the Duke of Edinburgh**
BLASEN, M. Léon, *of Protocol Department*
MOLITOR, M. Michel, *of Protocol Department*
REUTER, M. Jacques, *of Protocol Department*
THEIN, Captain Egide, *ADC to the Grand Duke*

1977

1978

22 May   **State Visit to Germany of the Queen and the Duke of Edinburgh**
LABOCH, Lieutenant-Colonel Hartmut Alexander Theodor, *Protocol Department*
SCHLINKMEIER, Frau Liselotte, *Second Secretary, President's Office*

14 November   **State Visit to Britain of President Eanes of Portugal**
OLIVEIRA, Captain Rui Faria, *Head of Security Services*
SOUSA PINTO, Captain Alexandre Maria de Castro, *ADC*
SALGUEIRO, Senhor Joao Manuel Guerra, *First Secretary, Portuguese Embassy*
CABRAL CABRAL, Senhor Jose Filipe, *Assistant Counsellor for Information*
GALVAO MEXIA de ALMEIDA FERNANDES, Senhor Alexandre Manuel, *Second Secretary, Portuguese Embassy*
KNOPFLI, Rui Manuel Correia, OBE, *Press Counsellor*
LISBOA, Senhor Eugenio Almeida, OBE, *Cultural Counsellor*

1979

16 May   **State Visit to Denmark of the Queen and the Duke of Edinburgh**
FOGH, Colonel Ole, *Commanding Fly-Past*
GJØDSBØL, Commander Hans, *ADC*
GOTTLIEB, Henning Vincent, *Advisory Officer, Prime Minister's Office*
HERMANSEN, Major Svend Kiilerich, *ADC*
JENSEN, Commander Niels Ebbe, *ADC*
JENSEN, Commander Orla Helmuth, *Captain, HMY* Dannebrog
KAISER, Niels-Jirgen Hermann, *Director, Tivoli*
LJØRRING, Major Henning Baek, *ADC to the Duke of Edinburgh*
RIBER, Major Jørgen, *Governor, Fredensborg Palace*
HARBOE-SCHMIDT, Major Flemming, *ADC*
FREIESLEBEN, Major Carl Erik Gustav von, *ADC to the Queen*

1980

14 October   **State Visit to Italy of the Queen and the Duke of Edinburgh**
ONORY, Cons Leg. Andrea Mochi, *Foreign Affairs Department of Presidency*
GORI, Dott. Sandro, *Protocol Department*
BAZAN, Lieutenant-Colonel Franco, *Deputy Commandant of the Corazzieri*
NICOLETTI, Dott. Maurizio, *Administrator, Quirinale Palace*

    State Visit to Tunisia and Morocco of the Queen and the Duke of Edinburgh
MAGHREBI, M. Mohamed, *of Ministry of Information*
TEBESSI, M. Mohamed Ennaceur, *Assistant Director of Presidential Protocol*
FESSI, M. Hédi El, *Head of Personnel Security at Presidency*

18 November   **State Visit to Britain of King Birendra and Queen Aishwarya of Nepal**
SHAH, Major Vivek, *ADC*
TULADHAR, Mr Ghanashyam Singh, *Attaché*
KHADKA, Mr Khagka Bahadur, *Attaché*

1981

25 May	**State Visit to Norway of the Queen and the Duke of Edinburgh**

PAULSEN, Commander S.R., *ADC*
BORGERSEN, Major Jan-Wilhelm, *ADC*
ASK, Commander Petter Andreas, *Secretary to the Crown Prince*
MOE, Major Knut, *ADC*
GULDBAKKE, Mr Karl H., *Deputy Chief of Protocol*

9 June	**State Visit to Britain of King Khalid of Saudi Arabia**

AL-ANAIZI, Shayeh Mohamed, *HM's Secretariat*
AL-FIHAID, Mohamed, *Leader of Information Delegation*
AL-GHAMEDIE, Ahmed, *HM's Secretariat*
AL-HARIQUI, Abdullah Saad, *HM's Secretariat*
AL-HOMOUDI, Abdul Rahman, *HM's Secretariat*
AL-ISSA, Abdul Wahhab Mohammed, *HM's Secretariat*
AL-KAYYAL, Abdulrahman bin Abdulmohsen, *Attaché*
AL-MOTAIRI, Major-General Saud Mohammed, *Officer of the Royal Guard*
AL-RAJHI, Abdullah Naif, *Counsellor*
AL-ROWAITHEY, Hameed Mohamed Rajah, *Commercial Attaché*
AL-RUWAILI, Mutaib, *HM's Secretariat*
AL-SAYEG, Dr Mohammed O, *Medical Attaché*
ALLADIN, Sami Abdulrahman, *Commercial Attaché*
ALYAHYA, Saud Ahmed M., *Counsellor*
BARRY, Abdullah Omar, *First Secretary*
KURDI, Mamoun, *Counsellor*
ABU LABBAN, Fouad, *HM's Secretariat*
NAZER, Mohammed Osman, *HM's Secretariat*
SEMBAWA, Adel Mohamad, *Counsellor*

1982

16 March	**State Visit to Britain of Qaboos bin Al Said, Sultan of Oman**

AL HAMDAN, Dawood Hamdan, *First Secretary, Oman Embassy*
AL WOHAIBI, Salim Mohamed, *First Secretary, Oman Embassy*

16 November	**State Visit to Britain of Queen Beatrix of the Netherlands and Prince Claus**

OUDWATER, Major A. *ADC*

1983

25 May	**State Visit to Sweden of the Queen and the Duke of Edinburgh**

ADLEN, Commander Ulf, *ADC*
FRIEFELDT, Commander Jan, *ADC to Duke of Halland*
MATTSSON, Fru Wendela, *Lady in Waiting*
TERSMEDEN, Mr Bo, *Gentleman in Waiting*
NORDSTROM, Mr Claes, *Gentleman in Waiting*
LJUNGQVIST, Professor Arne, *Gentleman in Waiting*
PETERSENS, Johan Af, *Gentleman in Waiting*
WAHLBERG, Fru Elisabeth Tarras, *Press Secretary to the Court*
BJORNBERG, Froken Ingrid, *Comptroller of Royal Palace*
LANDERGREN, Fru Ulla, *Curator, Treasury Museum*
WARMING, Lieutenant-Colonel Tomas, *ADC*

1984

26 March	**State Visit to Jordan of the Queen and the Duke of Edinburgh**

AL-JUNDI, Lieutenant-Colonel Abdelqader, *Commander, King's Flight*
AL-SARHANI, Abdulla Warwier, *Assistant Chief of Protocol*
ALKHATIB, Lieutenant-Colonel Issa Dib, *ADC*
ATMEH, Lieutenant-Colonel Mohammed, *ADC*
MAJALI, Ayman H, *Assistant Chief of Protocol*
MAWLA, Nayev Khaled, *of Ministry of Information*
OMET, Moh'd Khair Said, *Assistant Chief of Protocol*
ABOU-SEIR, Darwish Mohammed, *Assistant Chief of Protocol*

10 April	**State Visit to Britain of Shaikh Isa bin Sulman Al-Khalifa, Amir of Bahrain**

AL-KHALIFA, Shaikh Mohammed bin Ali, *First Secretary, Bahrain Embassy*
DARWISH, Mr Fouad Ismail, *Consul*

23 October	**State Visit to Britain of President Mitterand of the French Republic and Madame Mitterand**

LACAU, Général de Brigade Xavier, *Air Attaché*

BISSCHOP, Colonel Claude Bernard Jean Joseph de, *Military Attaché*
TREMEAU, M. Marcel, *First Counsellor*
GALAS, M. Michel A.F., *Consul-General*
JARRIER, M. Dominique Jacques
PAPEGAY, Mlle. Marie-Claire
RICHARD, Mme Evelyne
SCHLUMBERGER, M. Jean Claude
TREMEAU, M. Marcel
VOILLERY, M. Pierre Henri Alexandre

1985

15 March	**State Visit to Portugal of the Queen and the Duke of Edinburgh**

ALBUQUERQUE, Major Anibal Jose, *ADC*
GOMES, Dra. Ana Maria Rosa Martins, CBE, *Assistant Diplomatic Adviser and Interpreter*
BORGES, Senhor Carlos Manuel Baptista, *Deputy Adviser on Diplomatic Affairs*
FIDALGO, Dr Eduardo Dias, *Deputy Adviser on Diplomatic Affairs*
ANTUNES, Dr Manuel Lobo, *Deputy Adviser on Foreign Affairs*

16 April   State Visit to Britain of Life President Dr Banda of Malawi
CHITSAMBA, Lemson Samson, *First Secretary, Malawi High Commission*
KALUMO, Lieutenant-Colonel Charles, *ADC*

11 June   State Visit to Britain of President de la Madrid of Mexico and Señora de la Madrid
HERRERA BRAMBILA, Major-General Vincente, *Military and Air Attaché*
MILLAN DE WASMER, Señora Martha, *Counsellor*
CANSECO GOMEZ, Señor Morelos, *Diplomatic Attaché*
FOURZAN MARQUEZ, Vice Almirante Horacio, *Naval Attaché*
OLGUIN URIBE, Señor Francisco, *First Secretary*

12 November   State Visit to Britain of Shaikh Khalifa bin Hamad Al-Thani, Amir of Qatar
AL-KHARJI, Mr Ali Saad, *First Secretary*
AL-SAHLAWI, Mr Ibrahim Abdul Aziz Mohamed, *First Secretary*
AL-MANNAI, Mr Mohamed Saleh, *First Secretary, Cultural Affairs*

1986

17 February   State Visit to Nepal of the Queen and the Duke of Edinburgh
SINGH, Mr Hem Bahadur, *Deputy Inspector General of Police*
JHA, Mr Keshav Raj, *Under Secretary, Ministry of Foreign Affairs*
KHATRICHHETRI, Lieutenant-Colonel Shashi Pratap, *ADC*
DHAMLA, Major Tika, *ADC*
SINGH, Mrs Prema, *Manager, Household*
SHAH, Lieutenant-Colonel Prakash Bikram, *ADC to Prince Gyanendra*
GURUNG, Lieutenant-Colonel Bharat, *ADC to Prince Dhirendra*
KARKI, Lieutenant-Colonel Yogeshwar, *in charge of Military Secretary for Chief Royal Guest*
RANA, Mrs Renu, *Assistant Secretary*

22 April   State Visit to Britain of King Juan Carlos and Queen Sofia of Spain
MOLLA, Señor Don Jose, *of Military Office*
VALLS, Señor Don Rafael, *Legal Attaché, Spanish Embassy*

1 July   State Visit to Britain of President von Weizsäcker of the Federal Republic of Germany and Freifrau von Weizsäcker
BRAUN, Herr Dr Harald Walter, *Second Secretary, German Embassy*
HAEDELT, Herr Manfred Reinhard, *Second Secretary, German Embassy*
HEIDORN, Herr Dr Joachim, *Second Secretary, German Embassy*
KALTENBACH, Frau Dorothee Ursula, *Interpreter*
REISS, Frau Ursula Sybille, *Private Secretary to Freifrau von Weizsäcker*

1987

14 July   State Visit to Britain of King Hassan II of Morocco
KRIEM, M. Abdellatif, *Moroccan Royal Cabinet*
LAHLOU, M. Abdelkrim, *Moroccan Royal Cabinet*

1988

17 October   State Visit to Spain of the Queen and the Duke of Edinburgh
ARGUELLES, Donna Inés, *Protocol*
ORTIZ, Don Javier, *Deputy Head, Press Section*
GUITART, Captain Miguel, *Chief of Staff, Military Household*

LOPEZ RODRIGUEZ, Commander Manuel, *Motorcade Official*
SACRISTAN, Don Agustin, *Coordinator, State Visits*
BELLACASA, Donna Paz Aznar de Puig de la, *Spanish Lady in Waiting to the Queen*
URBINA, Donna Carmen de Arrospide de, *Spanish Lady in Waiting to the Queen*
RUBIO, Dr Fidel Fernandez, *Spanish Doctor*

8 November **State Visit to Britain of President Abdou Diouf of Senegal and Madame Abdou Diouf**
CISSE, Colonel Lamine, *The President's Doctor*
WANE, Colonel Boubacar, *ADC*
DIOP, Monsieur Seydou, *First Secretary*

1989

9 May **State Visit to Britain of President Babangida of Nigeria**
YUSUFARI, Ambassador Ahmed, *State Chief of Protocol*
SHINKAIYE, Mr J.K., *Minister, Nigerian High Commission*

18 July **State Visit to Britain of Shaikh Zayed bin Sultan Al-Nahyan, President of the United Arab Emirates**
AL-SAAIDI, Salem Rashid, *Protocol Officer*
RASHID, Rashid Mohamed, *Protocol Officer*
AL-HAJ, Dr Saleh Mohamed, *Personal Physician to HH*
AL-HASHEMI, Mr Abdul Bari, *First Secretary*
AL-DALLAL, Mrs Fawziy, *Head, Information Department*

1990

25 June **State Visit to Iceland of the Queen and the Duke of Edinburgh**
BJARNADOTTIR, Mrs Vigdis, *Office of the President*

23 October **State Visit to Britain of President Cossiga of Italy and Signora Cossiga**
MODRONO, Signor Leonardo Visconti di, *First Counsellor, Italian Embassy*
RONCA, Signor Stephano, *First Counsellor, Italian Embassy*
BUONAVITA, Signor Rodolfo, *Consul-General, Edinburgh*

1991

1992

9 June **State Visit to France of the Queen and the Duke of Edinburgh**
AVRIAL, Général de Brigade de Gendarmerie Francis
D'ELLOY DE BONNINGHEN, Antoine, *Head of Naval Supplies*
MARY, Général de Brigade Pierre
MONTAGNE, M. Maurice Jacques Jean-Marie, *Press Officer*
SABATH, M. Gilbert, *of the Quai d'Orsay*
THIERY, M. Christopher Antoine Jacques, *Interpreter*

3 November **State Visit to Britain of the Sultan of Brunei Darussalam and the Raja Isteri**
WAHAB, Pehin Dato Haji, *Official of Royal Household*

1993

27 April **State Visit to Britain of President Soares of Portugal and Senhora Soares**
PIMENTEL QUARTIN-BASTOS, Manuel, *Economic Counsellor*
ALMEIDA-LIMA, Antonio Jose Emauz de, *First Secretary, Portuguese Embassy*
PEREIRA, Antonio Joao Martins Serras, *Tourism and Cultural Attaché*
ALVES-PEREIRA, Joao A. de Brito Castilho, *Commercial Counsellor*
RYDER TORRES PEREIRA, Dr Jorge, *Second Secretary, Portuguese Embassy*

1994

5 July **State Visit to Edinburgh of King Harald and Queen Sonja of Norway**
HEGGE, Miss Tanja, *Secretary, Norwegian Embassy*

1995

1996

17 May **State Visit to Britain of the President of the French Republic and Madame Chirac**
BALOCHE, Monsieur Michel, *Counsellor (Communications)*

DELAHOUSSE, Monsieur Laurent, *of Ministry of Foreign Affairs*
VANKERK-HOVEN, Monsieur Thierry, *Deputy Director, Ministry of Foreign Affairs*
BONNET, Colonel, *Military Attaché, French Embassy*
PASQUIER, Monsieur Jerome, *First Counsellor, French Embassy*
ARVOR, Monsieur Olivier Poivre d', *Cultural Counsellor, French Embassy*
BOTTINE, Colonel, *Air Attaché*

29 October   **State Visit to Thailand of the Queen and the Duke of Edinburgh**
HIRANYASTHITI, Major-General Somchai, *Chief Staff Officer*
THANARAK, Miss Chantanee, *Director of Foreign Affairs Division*
PISONT, Khunying Varnhit, *Secretary, Royal Household Secretariat*

1997

1998

26 May   **State Visit to Britain of Emperor Akihito and Empress Michiko of Japan**
AMAU, Mrs Setsuko, *Lady in Waiting to the Empress*
ONISHI, Dr Hirohide, *Court Physician, Imperial Household*

1 December   **State Visit to Britain of the President of the Federal Republic of Germany and Frau Herzog**
MÜLLER, Frau Petra, *Personal Secretary to the President*
ELLERBECK, Thomas, *Deputy Press Spokesman for the President*
SAUER, Peter, *First Secretary, Office of the President*

1999

22 June   **State Visit to Britain of the President of the Republic of Hungary and Madame Arpad Göncz**
ODZE, György, *Counsellor (Press), Hungarian Embassy*

2000

16 February   **State Visit to Britain of Queen Margrethe II of Denmark and Prince Henrik**
PEDERSEN, Major Frank, *Royal Danish Air Force, ADC to Queen Margrethe*
STAMP, Commander Peter Schinkel, *Royal Danish Navy, ADC to Prince Henrik*
KRISTIANSEN, Verner, *First Secretary, Royal Danish Embassy*

MVO V

1896

8 May   **Queen Victoria's visit to Cimiez**
GRIÈGES, Mons. Henri Louis Maurice Tabard de, *Principal Engineer, French Western Railway*
EDDY, Mons. William, *Dir. of Movements, French Western Railway*
DREYFUS, Mons. Paul, *Dep. Head of Division, Paris, Lyon and Mediterranean Railway*
JULIENNE, Mons. Alfred Armand, *Deputy Inspector, French Western Railway*

30 June   **Visit of Duke of Connaught to Russia representing the Queen at the Coronation of Emperor Nicholas II**
CRICHTON, Serge, *Page of the Chamber*
BROCK, Peter, *Page of the Chamber*
TOURGENEFF, Captain, *attached to the Imperial Stables*
WOLKOFF, Staff Captain, *Imperial Household, Courier Corps*

31 October   HARTING, Arcadi, *Officer for Special Missions, Russian State Police Department*

1897

26 April   HULLY, Mons. Julien Albert, *Station Master at Nice*
VALLET, Mons. Louis Alphonse, *Station Master at Cannes*

2 July   MOELLER-LILIENSTERN, First-Lieutenant Baron von
GERLACH, First-Lieutenant von
STUDNITZ, Second-Lieutenant von

1898

1899

9 May
MASSONI, Mons. Gregoire, *Director of Posts and Telegraphs, Nice*
PONCET, Mons. Marius, *Special Commissary, Gare St Lazare, Paris*
PIATTI, Attilio, *Vice-Consul of USA at Nice*
RUELLE, Mons. Adrien, *Inspector, Paris Lyon Mediterranean Railway*
MITTELHAUSSER, Mons A. V., *Special Commissary, Gare du Nord, Paris*

1900

7 May
The attempt upon the life of the Prince of Wales
CROCIUS, Mons. Charles François, *Stationmaster, Gare du Nord, Brussels*

1901

8 March
GILHAUSSEN, Lieutenant von

King Edward VII's visit to Cronberg
SEELIGMÜLLER, Herr, *Agent at Friedrichshof*

28 May
Funeral of Queen Victoria
SENDEN, Lieutenant Freiherr Max von
ZUYDTWYCK, Lieutenant and Adjutant Freiherr Franz Heereman von, *1st Regt. (Queen Victoria's) of Dragoons of the Guard*
KAMEKE, Lieutenant and Adjutant Ernst Boguslaw von, 5th *(Prince Blücher of Wahlstatt) Hussar Regiment*
MICHAËLIS, Lieutenant Sigismund von, *5th (Prince Blücher of Wahlstatt) Hussar Regiment*

11 October
For medical services rendered to HM on his visit to Homburg
HAMEL, Doctor Gustav

King Edward VII's visit to Homburg
KROHN, Herr Schatoll Rendant, *Private Secretary to Count Seckendorff*
BURVENICK, Herr Anton Mathias, *Assistant Commissioner of Police*
KRUGER, Herr Frederick, *Station Master, Frankfurt-on-Maine*
STIRN, Herr Rudolph, *Station Master, Homburg*

11 October
King Edward VII's visit to Denmark
JUSTRAN, Captain Harold F., *Overseer of the Castle, Fredensborg*
DE NEERGAARD, Lieutenant and Adjutant Peter J. F., *Danish Hussars of the Guard*
ILSOE, Doctor Niels Clausen, *Physician to King Christian IX of Denmark*
MADSEN, Mons. Henrik, *Chief of the Danish Detective Police*
STOCKFLETH, Mons. Frits Emil, *Traffic Inspector, Danish State Railways*
HERMANN, Mons. Emil Johan Wilhelm Victor, *Hof Fourier to King Christian IX*

1902

22 August
King Edward's VII's Coronation
KATERINITCH, Second-Captain Alexander Vasilievitch, *27th (Kieff) King Edward VII Russian Dragoon Regiment*
BROCKHUSEN, Lieutenant Friedrich von, *5th Regt. of Hussars Prince Blücher von Wahlstatt*
PETERSDORFF, Lieutenant Ernst Bodo von, *1st Regt. of Dragoons of the Guard (Queen Victoria of Great Britain and Ireland)*
DE BELLAS, Lieutenant Don Jose Ignacio de Castello Branco, *Portuguese Cavalry Regt. No.3 of King Edward VII*

1903

7 April
King Edward VII's visit to Portugal
MACEDO, Major Ferray de, *Commandant of Police, Lisbon*
SERRA, Second-Lieutenant Antonio Mendes, *Portuguese Cavalry Regt. No. 3 of King Edward VII*
DA SILVA, Senhor Licinio, *Clerk Comptroller of the Household of King Carlos of Portugal*
TEIXEIRA, Senhor Antonio Goncalves, *Yeoman Usher of the Royal Palace, Lisbon*
CALDERA, Second-Lieutenant Dominques Antonio, *Bandmaster, 2nd Regt. of Infantry*
RYDER, Senhor Carlos, *Superintendent of the Royal Stables*
REIS, Senhor Marianno Silva, *Intendant of the Royal Palace*
DE SOUZA, Senhor Joaquim Izidoro, *Intendant of the Palace of Queen Maria Pia of Portugal*
DE CARVALHO, Senhor Augusto Maria, *Intendant of the Palace of Queen Maria Pia of Portugal*
D'ALCANTARA, Senhor Pedro Maria, *Clerk Comptroller of the Household of Queen Maria Pia*

30 April	**King Edward VII's visit to Italy**
	COMANDU, Lieutenant Ricardo, *Royal Body Guard*
	GIANUZZI, Cavalier Enrico, *Courier to King Vittorio Emanuele III of Italy*
	FUROLO, Cavalier Gioacchino, *Commissioner of Police at the Quirinale*
	EGGER, Signor Nicola, *Comptroller of the Household to King Vittorio Emanuele III of Italy*
4 May	**King Edward VII's visit to France**
	PIERRE, Lieutenant Camille, *Commanding Garde Republicaine at the British Embassy*
	MOUQUIN, Mons. Lucien, *Superintendent of the Municipal Police, Paris*
	FISCHESSER, Mons. Paul, *Secretary's Department of the President*
	DE JONGHE, Mons. George, *Secretary's Department of the President*
30 June	VESSELLA, Signor Alessandro, *Conductor of the Municipal Band, Rome*
30 June	**Visit to London of President Loubet of the French Republic**
	THIEULEUX, Adjutant Alberic Florimond, *attached to the Department of the Secretary of the President*
9 October	**King Edward VII's visit to Austria**
	FORCHE, Herr August, *Clerk Comptroller's Department at the Hofburg*
	NEUENSTAMM, Herr Ferdinand Deitenhofen Edler von, *Clerk Comptroller's Department at the Hofburg*
	DITFURTH, Captain Bernhard, Baron von, *1st Arcieran Life Guards on duty in the King's Ante-Chamber*
	SKALISKO, Captain Johann Soukup von, *1st Arcieran Life Guards on duty in the King's Ante-Chamber*
	WORMBRAND-STUPPACH, Captain Ernst, Count, *1st Arcieran Life Guards on duty in the King's Ante-Chamber*
	SZENT-GYÖRGY-VÖLGYE, Captain Bernhard Kiss de, *Royal Hungarian Life Guards on duty in the King's Ante-Chamber*
	TOTH, Captain Geza von, *Royal Hungarian Life Guards on duty in the King's Ante-Chamber*
	KOSZEGHY, Captain Johann von, *Royal Hungarian Life Guards on duty in the King's Ante-Chamber*
	DOCTEUR, Prosper, Baron von, *Traffic Superintendent, Franz Josef Station, Vienna*
	FEHR, Jean Jacques, *Director of HM's Continental Journeys*
	RECKE, First-Lieutenant Baron Karl von der, *Feldjäger Corps, Berlin*
	HM's visit to Marienbad
	NADLER, Doktor Franz, *Burgomaster of Marienbad*
	PETRIDES, Guido, *Post-Master of Marienbad*
	HM's visit to Austria
	JANAUSCHEK, Father Ludwig, *Prefect of the Imperial and Royal Family Vault, Vienna*
	SCHLESINGER, First-Lieutenant Carl, *No. 8 Austrian Infantry Regiment*
	KOCZIAN, First-Lieutenant Rudolf, *No. 8 Austrian Infantry Regiment*
	BERGER, Lieutenant Felix, Ritter von, *No. 8 Austrian Infantry Regiment*
	KOBER, Lieutenant Franz, *No. 8 Austrian Infantry Regiment*
21 November	**Visit to Windsor of King Emanuele III and Queen Elena of Italy**
	VERDESI, Doctor Umberto, *Secretary, Ministry of Italian Royal House*
	LUZZATI, Signor Ricardo, *Delegate of the Sureté Publique*

1904

10 February	**Marriage of Princess Alice of Albany with Prince Alexander of Teck**
	ESCHEN, Lieutenant Baron Charles Sigismund Waitz von, *in attendance on the Duke of Saxe Coburg-Gotha*
23 March	**Funeral of Field Marshal the Duke of Cambridge**
	DRACHENTHAL, Sub. Lieutenant Georg Pausper H. Wladyk von, *ADC to Vice-Admiral Rudolf, Count Montecuccoli*
	RINTELEN, Lieutenant and Adjutant Ernst, *28th Regiment of Prussian Infantry*
18 April	**King Edward VII's visit to Denmark**
	FUNCH, Christian Hulger, *British Vice-Consul, Copenhagen*
	BROCK, Peter Michael Johan, *Inspector of Rosenborg Castle*
	LIISBERG, Henrik Carl Bering, *Inspector of Rosenborg Castle*
	APPELDORN, Lieutenant Carl Mathias, *Danish Life Guards*
	WILLEMÖES, Lieutenant Anton, *Danish Hussars of the Guard*
	LASSON, Lieutenant Kaj Lauge, *Danish Life Guards*
	JOHNKE, Lieutenant Ejnar Viggo, *Danish Hussars of the Guard*
	BILLE-BRAHE-SELBY, Lieutenant Daniel, Baron, *Danish Life Guards*
	OLUFSEN, Aage Thorwald, *Clerk Comptroller of the Household of King Christian IX of Denmark*
	BECK, Alfred Carl, *Hof Fourer to King Christian IX*
	WILSBECH, Captain Jens Christian Erik, *Station Superintendent, Copenhagen*
	BACK, Pieter Samuel de, *Station Superintendent, Flushing*
21 April	**Visit of the Prince of Wales to Austria**
	VAUMANN, First-Lieutenant Louis, *Artillery Regiment 'George, Prince of Wales' No.12*
29 April	FAVRE, Ernest, *Chief Supt. of the Railway Stations, Calais*
11 June	**Visit to Britain of the Archduke Frederick of Austria**
	ZELLER, Gustav, *of the Paymaster's Department at the Hofburg*

1 July	**HM's visit to Kiel** ESMARCH, Lieutenant Charles Frederick John Christian August von, *15th Regiment of Hussars* WEYMANN, Hermann, *Secretary, Lord Steward's Department* WESSELS, Hermann, *Clerk Comptroller, Lord Steward's Department* LEIB, Frederick Charles Otto, *Superintendent of the Rathaus, Hamburg*
6 September	**HM's visit to Marienbad** KRUPICZKA, John, *Traffic Superintendent, Marienbad* SCHOBER, Hans, *Asst. Commissioner, Austrian Police* ZELLER, Mathias, *Commander, Gendarmerie, Marienbad* WAGNER, Albert, *Post Office Controller, Marienbad* METZNER, Fritz, *Chief of the Municipal Police, Marienbad*

1905

23 April	**HM's cruise in the Mediterranean** TILLY, Lieutenant Jean Charles Edmond de, *ADC to the Governor-General of Algeria* BEN-CHERIF, Lieutenant Mohamed, *ADC to the Governor-General of Algeria*
4 May	DALTROFF, Gustave, *Asst. Commissioner of Police, Paris* MURAT, Jean Achille, *Police Superintendent, Paris*
6 June	**Visit of Prince Arthur of Connaught to Berlin to represent HM at the Marriage of the Crown Prince of Germany, Prince Royal of Prussia and the Duchess Cecilie of Mecklenberg-Schwerin** KATT, Lieutenant Hellmuth von, *Queen Elizabeth's Grenadier Guard Regiment No. 3* TIPPELSKIRCH, Second-Lieutenant Willy von, *Queen Elizabeth's Grenadier Guard Regiment No. 3*
4 July	**Visit to Britain of Prince Arisugawa of Japan** MIMURA, Doctor Ishinoské, *Physician to HIH*
19 July	**Coming of age of the Duke of Saxe-Coburg and Gotha** HEUSINGER, Philip, *Secretary in the Grand Marshal's Office, Coburg* IDEN, William, *Station Superintendent at Gotha*
8 Sept	**HM's visit to Marienbad** SCHREYER, Adalbert, *Conductor, Kurhaus Orchestra, Marienbad*
21 October	BUSCH, Hermann Frederick Albert, *President, Veterans Association of 1st Regiment of Dragoons of the Guard 'Queen Victoria of Great Britain and Ireland'*

1906

20 February	**Garter Mission of Prince Arthur of Connaught to the Emperor of Japan** NAKAMURA, Lieutenant Tetsuzo, *1st Infantry Regiment, Imperial Guard* TANI, Lieutenant Hisao, *1st Infantry Regiment, Imperial Guard* SATO, Second-Lieutenant Seiichi, *1st Infantry Regiment, Imperial Guard*
26 February	**Visit of the Lord Chamberlain to Denmark to represent HM at the Funeral of King Christian IX** RICHE, Emile Louis Jules, *Inspector of Belgian State Railways*
2 April	**HM's visit to Biarritz** BACQUÉ, Jean François, *Commissioner of Police, Biarritz* LAFFORCADE, Laurent Antoine Edouard Marie Armand Dupin de, *of the French Ministry of the Interior* BARNIER, Emile Theodore, *Director of the Band, 57th Regiment of Infantry*
24 April	**HM's visit to Greece** KAISSARIE, Lieutenant Joseph, *Conductor of the Royal Band* MACROPOULOS, Dimitri, *Clerk Comptroller to King George of the Hellenes* MONTFERRATOS, Lieutenant Timoleon, *Hellenic Gendarmerie* KAPSALIS, Second-Lieutenant Jean, *Hellenic Gendarmerie* SARATSOGLOU, Second-Lieutenant Basile, *Hellenic Gendarmerie* DIMITRIOU, Second-Lieutenant Evangéle, *Hellenic Gendarmerie*
	HM's cruise in the Mediterranean CASILLI, Giovanni, *Postmaster of Brindisi*
2 May	**HM's visit to France** HADET, Leon Simon, *Chief Inspector, Paris, Lyon and Mediterranean Railway* REURE, Germain Baptiste, *Chief Inspector, Paris, Lyon and Mediterranean Railway*
7 May	BERNARD, Maxime, *Superintendent of Police, Paris* LEBON, Louis, *Superintendent of Police, Paris* SOULLIÈRE, Louis Marius, *Superintendent of Police, Paris*
6 June	**Visit of the Prince of Wales to Madrid to represent HM at the Marriage of King Alfonso XIII of Spain and Princess Victoria Eugenie of Battenberg** REQUEJO Y HERRERO, Lieutenant Don Manuel, *Spanish Cavalry*

RAMIREZ Y RAMIREZ, Lieutenant Pedro, *4th Horse Artillery Regiment, attached to Deputation of Officers of the 16th (The Queen's) Lancers*
MARQUINA-NARRO, Second-Lieutenant Pascual, *Senior Bandmaster at Military Tattoo*

22 June	**Visit of the Prince of Wales to Trondhjem to represent HM at the Coronation of the King of Norway** KJELDSBERG, Francis, *British Vice-Consul*
10 August	PANZLER,Chief Paymaster Peter, *Cuirassier Regiment, (Count Gessler) No. 8*
14 August	**Visit to Britain of King Alfonso of Spain** GUISÔT, Pedro Ruiz, *Conductor of the Band, Spanish Royal Yacht* Giralda
7 September	**HM's visit to Marienbad** MALLY, Lieutenant Franz, *Commanding Gendarmerie , Marienbad* LEIPOLD, Karl, *Post Office Comptroller, Marienbad*
20 September	**Visit of the Duke of Connaught to Karlsruhe to invest the Grand Duke of Baden with the Order of the Garter and to represent HM at the Celebration of the Golden Wedding of the Grand Duke and the Grand Duchess** BRAUN, *Baden Grenadier Guards* LAUER, George Joseph, *Hof Fourer to the Grand Duke* BECK, Salomon, *Hof Fourer to the Grand Duke*
8 November	KECK, Lieutenant Otto Christian August, *of the German Feldjäger Corps*

1907

9 February	**HM's visit to Paris** MALLET, Marc, *Superintendent of Police, Paris (Chemin de fer du Nord)* RAVIN, Louis Victor Jean, *Superintendent of Police, Calais* **HM's visit to Biarritz** AVÉROUS, Siméon Mathieu, *Commissary of Police, Biarritz* DE DÉZERT, Louis Béard, *Chief of Paris Divn., Wagons Lits Company* POURCEL, Auguste, *Engineer, Midi Railway*
9 April	**HM's visit to Spain** ESPINOSA Y LEON, Lieutenant José, *Royal Spanish Navy* DE MENDIVIL Y ELIO, Lieutenant Manuel, *Royal Spanish Navy* SANCHEZ-MACHERO, Julian, *Superintendent of Police* HERRERA, Ignacio Legaza, *Superintendent of Police, Madrid* MARTINEZ, Mariano Bueno, *Superintendent of Municipal Police, Cartagena* CALVO, Santiago, *Superintendent of Municipal Police, Cartagena*
11 April	**HM's cruise in the Mediterranean** ESCUDERO, Bartolomé, *British Vice-Consul, Port Mahon*
26 April	**HM's visit to Palermo** ZUMMO, Claudio, *Chief of Municipal Police, Palermo* GALLO, Giuseppe, *Acting Superintendent of Police, Palermo*
29 April	**HM's visit to Naples** AMATI, Emmanuele, *Superintendent of Police, Naples* CAPOZZI, Massenzio, *Superintendent of Port Police, Naples* CARCATERRA, Armando, *Chief Inspector of Police, Naples*
4 May	**HM's return from cruise in the Mediterranean** GRANDJANY, Albert, *Chief Superintendent of Railway Stations, Calais* **HM's visit to Paris** RIFFART, Marius Hyacinthe Auguste, *Chief of the Postal Service, Rue Boissy District, Paris*
18 May	**Visit of Prince Arthur of Connaught to Madrid to represent HM at the Christening of the Prince of Asturias** IBANEZ-GARCIA, Lieutenant Don José Castor Carmelo TORRES-MARTINEZ, Lieutenant Don José Baldomero PALAZÒN Y YEBRA, Lieutenant Don Gundemaro Godofredo CUERDA FERNANDEZ, Lieutenant Don Fidel Nemesio
15 June	**Unveiling of Statue of Field Marshal the Duke of Cambridge in London** BORNHAUSEN, Lieutenant Eduard, *Adjutant, Infantry Regiment von Goeben No. 28* HEINTZEL, Second-Lieutenant Karl, *Infantry Regiment von Goeben No. 28*
22 July	LANGKILDE, Lieutenant Hans Peter, *5th Regiment, Danish Army attached to HQ Gymnastic Staff, Aldershot*
25 July	HERBST, Lieutenant Leo Arthur, *8th (Count Gessler) Cuirassiers, German Army*
14 August	ZEYSS, Lieutenant Albert August Leopold, *Superintendent of the Motor Cars of the German Emperor*
15 August	**HM's visit to Ischl** ECKMANN, Maximilian, *Clerk Comptroller to the Household of the Emperor of Austria, King of Hungary* LERCHENSTEIN, Gustav Manker von, *Assistant Clerk Comptroller to HIM*

MILIEZEK, Ferdinand, *Inspector of the Railway*
SCAZIGINO, Captain Julius, *4th Tyrolese Kaiser Jäger Regiment*

29 August   **For services to members of the Indian Staff College who visited the Manchurian Battlefields**
MORIMOTO, Mishige, *Interpreter, Japanese Army*

6 September   **HM's visit to Marienbad**
RIEDL, Ludwig, *Member of the late Empress of Austria's Memorial Committee*
DONKER, Joseph William, *Traffic Inspector, N Brabant German Railway*
SIEPEN, Hermann, *Traffic Manager, State Railway, Cologne*
ZEIS, Ernst, *Traffic Manager, Bavarian State Railway*

28 September   **Visit of Field Marshal the Duke of Connaught to Vienna**
HOLZWARTH, Lieutenant Carl, *Austrian Hussar Regiment*
FOGARASSY VON FOGARASS, Lieutenant Alfred, *Austrian Hussar Regiment*

12 November   **Visit to Windsor of the German Emperor and Empress, King and Queen of Prussia for the Unveiling of the Queen Victoria Statue**
KNAUFF, Lieutenant Bruno, *Court Secretary to HIM*
PETERSEN, Matthias, *attached to HIM's Military Cabinet*
POSTH, Paul, *Secretary to Her Imperial Majesty*
CAROW, Ferdinand, *Chancellor, Imperial German Embassy*

25 December   WASMUTH, Second-Lieutenant Sergius, *The Emperor of Russia's Feldjäger Corps*

1908

27 January   **25th Anniversary of HM's appointment as Colonel-in-Chief**
BROCKHUSEN, Lieutenant Hugo Claus Ernst von, *Adjutant, 5th (Prince Blücher von Wahlstatt) Hussar Regiment*

4 March   TCHERNYCHEFF, Constantin, *Secretary to the Comptroller of the Household of the Empress Marie Feodorovna of Russia*

19 March   **Reception by HM at San Sebastian of a Deputation from the Regiment**
CUBEIRO-CEBREIRO, Lieutenant Teodoro, *(Spanish) Zamora Regiment No. 8*
CEVINA CLAT, Lieutenant and Bandmaster, *(Spanish) Zamora Regiment No. 8*

26 March   **Visit of the Prince of Wales to Cologne to inspect the Kurassier Regiment Graf Gessler (Rheinischen) No. 8 of which HRH is Colonel-in-Chief**
KÖNIG, Captain Heinrich Wilhelm Ludwig, *5th Rheinischen Infantry Regiment No. 65*
SÜS, Lieutenant Otto Ludwig August, *Kurassier Regiment Graf Gessler (Rheinischen) No. 8*

14 April   **HM's visit to Biarritz**
CARETTE, Charles Frederick, *Special Commisary, Paris*
CHABANNE, Antoine Firmin Henry, *Station Superintendent, Orleans Railway, Paris*
MUZIO-OLIVI, Lucien, *Special Commissary, Paris*

HM's visit to Paris
PAOLI, Jacques Marie, *of the Sûrété Generale*

HM's visit to Biarritz
PARIES, Bertrand Louis, *Director of Postal and Telegraphic Service, Biarritz*
POMMIES, Vincent, *Station Superintendent, Biarritz*

25 April   **HM's visit to Denmark**
MOLTKE, First-Lieutenant Frederick Josias Valdemar Otto, Count, *Danish Hussars of the Guard*
HEGERMANN-LINDENCRONE, First-Lieutenant John Herman, *Danish Hussars of the Guard*
SEGELCKE, First-Lieutenant Charles, *Danish Hussars of the Guard*
SCHMIDT, Anton Charles Christian, *Secretary, Master of the Horse's Department of King Frederik VIII*
ENGGOIST, Thorvald Frederick, *Clerk Comptroller to the Household of King Frederik VIII*
NOLL, Viggo, *Hof Fourer to King Frederik VIII*
SCHRAM, Charles William, *Superintendent of Police, Copenhagen*
JACOBSIN, Lauritz, *Inspector at the Royal Theatre, Copenhagen*

27 April   **HM's visit to Sweden**
LIDBERG, Charles Gustaf, *Chief of the Detective Department*
KELLERMAN, Anders, *Superintendent of the Stables to the King of Sweden*
WEDHOLM, Eric William, *Hof Fourer to the King of Sweden*
SVÄRD, Gustaf Ferdinand, *Hof Fourer to the King of Sweden*
NILSSON, Nils, *Station Superintendent, Stockholm*
EWALD, Nils Alfred, *Station Superintendent, Malmö*

2 May   **HM's visit to Norway**
NIELSEN, Harold, *Station Superintendent, Christiania*

29 May   **Visit to Britain of President Fallières of the French Republic**
VALLEINS, Georges, *Commissioner, Sureté Générale*

10 June	**HM's visit to Russia**
	BALABIN, Colonel Nicolas Ivanovitch, *Chief of Police at Riga*
	TIMIREFF, Lieutenant Serge, *Imperial Russian Navy*
	ZABOTKINE, Lieutenant Dimitri, *Imperial Russian Navy*
	GENSIOR, Ivan Petroviez, *Assistant Commissioner of Police at Reval*
	KOSTÉRINE, Jean, *Secretary, Chancery of Emperor Nicholas II*
	KOWALENDS, Basile, *Secretary, in the Ministry of the Court*
	RADZIG, Nicolas, *Fourier to Emperor Nicholas II*
	MICHAILOF, Maximilien, *Clerk Comptroller to Emperor Nicholas II*
	TIESENFELD, Alexis, *Clerk Comptroller to Emperor Nicholas II*
	CUBAT, Pierre, *Secretary in the Master of the Household's Department*
	MAXIMOFF, Efim, *Secretary in the Master of the Household's Department*
	DEKSBACH, Captain Constantin, *Russian Gendarmerie*
	YACOVLEFF, Lieutenant Basile, *Imperial Russian Navy*
	SPOLATBOG, Lieutenant Alexandre, *Imperial Russian Navy*
	JABLOUSKY, Michel, *Secretary in the Department of the Russian Ministry of the Interior*
21 August	**HM's visit to Ischl**
	KRANICH, Lieutenant Joseph, *Imperial Gendarmerie*
4 September	**HM's visit to Marienbad**
	DELLA SANTA, Chevalier Luigi, *Director of the Fencing School, Vienna*
	LASKA, Julius, *Director of the Theatre, Marienbad*

1909

12 February	**HM's visit to Berlin**
	LIVONIUS, Lieutenant Eberhard, *1st Regiment of Dragoons of the Guard, 'Queen Victoria of Great Britain and Ireland'*
	KUNTZE, Hubert Augustus Frederick William, *Assistant Commissioner of Police*
	NEUMANN, Ferdinand, *Clerk Comptroller to the Household*
	SEILER, George Ernest Emil, *Secretary, Master of the Horse's Department*
	ROLLFING, Joseph, *Personal Attendant on the Emperor of Germany, King of Prussia*
	RIEGER, Reinhold, *Inspector of the Castle, Berlin*
	BRELL, Hermann, *Electrical Engineer at the Castle*
	SEIBELS, William, *Secretary, Office of Works, Berlin*
	JANCKE, Paul Adolphus, *Inspector of the Royal Gardens, Berlin*
	BUTTMANN, Rudolph, *Inspector of the Royal Gardens, Charlottenburg*
	WEIGAND, Philip, *Superintendent of the Cellars*
	HOFFMAN, Constantine, *Traffic Superintendent, Prussian State Railways, Berlin*
	NEUMANN, Gustavus, *Secretary, Master of the Household's Department*
	SENNEWALD, George Richard, *attached to the Administration of the Prussian State Railways*
	SEIDA, Fritz, *Traffic Superintendent, Prussian State Railways, Rathenow*
	WEBER, Peter, *Traffic Superintendent, Prussian State Railways, Herbesthal*
15 April	**HM's visit to Biarritz**
	TÉTARD, Henry, *Deputy Mayor of Biarritz*
	GALLARD, Doctor Frank, *Deputy Mayor of Biarritz*
	BARTHES, Léon Joseph, *Trafffic Superintendent, Midi Railway of France*
	GUÉRIN, Second-Lieutenant Paul Jean, *Bandmaster, 49th Regiment of Infantry*
5 August	**Visit of Emperor Nicholas II of Russia**
	HLAVÁC, Vojtech, *Conductor of the Band, Imperial Yacht* Standart
	NIKOLAEFF, Alexander, *Secretary to the Minister of the Court*
	SOUSHFOFF, Boris, *Russian Police*
	MONIN, Marcel Bittard, *Russian Police*
3 September	**HM's visit to Marienbad**
	GANGHOFNER, William, *Commissioner of the District, Marienbad*
	BRANDL, Franz, *Assistant Commissioner of Police, Vienna*
16 November	**Visit to Windsor of King Manoel II of Portugal**
	TEIXEIRA, Lieutenant Joao Feijoo, *Superintendent, Lisbon Police Force*

1910

29 April	**HM's visit to Biarritz**
	CHAPTIVE, Paul Marie Joseph Léon, *Special Commissary, Paris*
	GODIER, Jules, *Superintendent of the Line, Paris–Orleans Railway*
	HENNEQUIN, Edouard Ferdinand Octave, *Special Commissary, Paris*
	LEVERVE, Gaston Charles, *Traffic Manager, Paris–Orleans Railway*
21 May	**Funeral of King Edward VII**
	SZAPPANYOS, Lieutenant Paul, *Austro-Hungarian Hussar Regt. No. 12 King Edward VII of which the late King was Honorary Colonel*

NEERGAARD, Lieutenant Frode, *Danish Hussars of the Guard, of which the late King was Honorary Colonel*
VON HELLEFELD, Lieutenant Joachim, *5th German Hussar Regt. (Prince Blücher von Wahlstatt) of which the late King was Colonel-in-Chief*
NATHUSIUS, Lieutenant Martin Joachim, *German Curassier Regt. Graf Gessler No. 8 of which the late King was Colonel-in-Chief*
BRANDEIRO, Captain Antonio Joachim de Mendonca, *Portuguese Cavalry Regt. No. 3 King Edward VII of which the late King was Honorary Colonel*
QUINTANA Y PARDO, Lieutenant Don Guillermo, *Spanish Zamora Regt. No. 8, King Edward VII of which the late King was Honorary Colonel*

20 October **His retirement from the Regiment after fifty years service**
GINSKY, Chief Paymaster Julius Ferdinand Johann, *1st Prussian Regt. of Dragoons of the Guard (Queen Victoria of Great Britain and Ireland)*

1911

30 March **On publication of his history of the 5th (Prince Blücher) Hussar Regiment**
PRETZELL, Lieutenant Gerhard Franz Eugen

15 May **The Unveiling of the Queen Victoria Memorial**
MARTIUS, Lieutenant Walter von, *1st Prussian Regt. of Dragoons of the Guard*

2 December **Mission of Prince Alexander of Teck to Bangkok to represent HM at the Coronation of King Vajiravudh of Siam**
CHAMÜN, Svasti Vinijchaya Amart Tri And Sevok Tri (formerly Chamün Svasdi Vang Raj), *Gentleman in Waiting to the Queen Mother of Siam*
CHAYAKHAN, Rong Amart Ek Nai, *Gentleman in Waiting to the Queen Mother of Siam*
DHIEN, Captain Nai, *Gentleman in Waiting to the Queen Mother of Siam*
INDRATEJ, Phra (formerly Rajamatya, Grand-Lieutenant Chamon And Rong Amart Ek Nai Le Avudh), *Gentleman in Waiting to the Queen Mother of Siam*
RAJASASNA SOBHON, Phaya (formerly Luang Raj Aksara), *Gentleman in Waiting to the Queen Mother of Siam*
RAJMONTRAI, Phya (formerly Phya Desombat), *Gentleman in Waiting to the King of Siam*

1912

23 May **Visit of Prince Arthur of Connaught to Copenhagan to represent HM at the Funeral of King Frederik VIII of Denmark**
BONDE, Commander Niels Knud Harald Falk

1913

24 May **TM's visit to Berlin to attend the Wedding of the Duke of Brunswick and Luneburg and Princess Viktoria Luise of Prussia**
BEERENDSEN, Gerrit John, *Station Superintendent, Flushing*
EYNERN, Lieutenant William Henry von, *1st Prussian Dragoon Guards*
KAESTNER, Charles Emil Paul, *Court Secretary, Hofmarschall's office*
KOSACK, Adolf Hermann Will, *Court Secretary, Hofmarschall's office*
KREUZ, Louis, *Asst. Superintendent, Prussian Railways*
MERTZ, Oscar Richard Kurt, *Secretary, Hofmarschall's office*
REYMANN, Lieutenant Frederick Immanuel, *Special Police attached to the King*
RHEINBABEN, Captain Oswald Moritz George, Baron von, *1st Dragoon Guards*

26 May **TM's visit to Neu-Strelitz**
RÖHR, Lieutenant Wichard von, *Grand Ducal Mecklenberg Grenadier Regiment No. 89*

1914

24 April **King George V's visit to France**
FERRAND, Hippolyte Auguste Léon, *Station Superintendent, Calais*
GAUD, René Gaspard, *Asst. Commissioner of Police, Paris*
LACHAUME, Louis Phillippe, *Inspector on Nord Railway*
LE GRAËT, Yves, *Station Superintendent, Bois de Boulogne, Paris*
PERRIN, Alexandre Claude, *Superintendent, Palace of the Elysée, Paris*
REY, Paul, *Station Superintendent, Les Invalides, Paris*
ROBAGLIA, Marcel, *Chief Engineer, Ceinture Railway, Paris*

1915

10 November **Coronation of Emperor Yoshihito of Japan**
MANYE, Major Katsuichi, *attached to Cavalry Regiment of the Guard*

1916

28 September   The Band's visit to London
BALAY, Captain Guillaume, *Director of Band of Garde Républicaine*

29 September   His visit to Sandringham in connection with installation of Anti-Aircraft guns
SAGET, Lieutenant Lucien Theodore

1917

14 July   HM's visit to Army in the Field
DARU, Ernest, *Special Commissary, British General HQ, France*

1918

11 July   Visit to London of the Band of the 1st Regiment of Zouaves
CHAISE, Lieutenant Interpreter François de la, *attached to 1st Zouaves*
ZIEGLER, Adjutant Jules, *Director of the Band*

26 September   Visit of Band of Royal Carabinieri to Britain
CAJOLI, Lieutenant Luigi, *Bandmaster*

28 October   Visit to Britain of Prince Yorihito of Higashi Fushimi
ADACHI, Daiichi, *Clerk, Imperial Japanese Household*
NAKANE, Nobuo, *attached to Bureau of the Ceremonies*

30 November   King George V's State Visit to France
MONIER, Maurice Just, *of the Ministry of Foreign Affairs*

1919

29 March   Visit to Britain of the Queen of Roumania
COSTESCO, Constantin, *Police Commissioner, attached to Staff of HM*

28 July   Sudanese Mission received by HM
SAMUEL BEY ATIYEH, *Interpreter*

12 November   Visit to Britain of President Poincaré of the French Republic
FERRAND, Léon, *Special Commissary of Police*

1920–1921

1922

22 April   The Prince of Wales's visit to Japan
HARA, Chudo, *Clerk, Imperial Japanese Household*
IMADA, Toshio, *Clerk at British Embassy, Tokyo*
KAMISAGO, Captain Shoshichi, *Captain and Adjutant, Military Police, Tokyo*

13 May   HM's visit to Belgium
DONNAY, Aimé Jean-Baptiste, *Station Superintendent, Gare du Nord, Brussels*
PRÉVOST, Captain Arthur Henry, *Director of Music, Belgian 1st Regt. of Guides*

18 October   The Duke of York's visit to Bucharest to represent HM at the Coronation of King Ferdinand I of Roumania
MANCUS, Captain Remus, *ADC to General Mircescu attached to HRH*

1923

14 May   HM's visit to Italy
BARABASCHI, Gino, Professor, *Director of Band performing at Embassy Dinner*
ANDREANI, Alessandro, *Commissary for Public Security, Rome*
CELLERINI, Ottavio, *Superintendent of Royal Stables*
FERRETTI, Giuseppe, *Station Master, Rome*
FRANCI, Guido, *in charge of Royal Palace of the Quirinal*
GIANDOTTI, Alessandro, *of Department of Secretary General, Royal Stables*
MALESCI, Enrico, *in charge of Royal Gardens of the Quirinal*

1924–1926

1927

19 May   **Visit to Britain of President Doumergue of the French Republic**
ROUSSE, Georges Louis Eugène, *Controller of Telegraphic Services at Presidency*
SUDRE, Robert, *Chief Inspector of Special Police*
VERGER, Pierre, *Inspector of Special Police*

1928

24 September   **For services to the late Viscount Trematon, son of Princess Alice, Countess of Athlone and the Earl of Athlone**
MONTANGE, Dr Jean

1929

27 February   **Prince of Wales's journey from Africa to England at the time of HM's illness**
FOUCAULT, Marie Joseph Edouard Andre, *of Nord Railways*

10 May   **The Duke of Gloucester's Garter Mission to Japan**
AKIYAMA, Tokuzo, *Clerk Comptroller, Imperial Japanese Household*
FUKUHARA, Kaoru, *Superintendent of Police, Kojimachi*
KAMADA, Seiji, *Assistant Technical Expert, Imperial Japanese Household*
TABATA, Sadarobo, *Clerical Assistant, Imperial Japanese Household*
TAMURA, Hideo, *Superintendent of Police, Hibiya*

1930

8 January   **The Duke of York's visit to Rome to represent HM at the Wedding of the Crown Prince of Italy**
ROMEI, Vincenzo, *Commissioner of Police*

30 October   **Visit of the Duke of Gloucester to Ethiopia to represent HM at the Coronation of Emperor Haile Selassie**
MAKURIYA, Balambaras, *Officer of the Guard*
GABRE, Mariam Tessema Balambaras, *Officer of the Guard*
TAFFARA WORQ, Ato Kidane Wold, *Interpreter, British Legation*

1931–1937

1938

19 July   **Visit of King George VI and Queen Elizabeth to France**
ARCHAMBAULT, Marcel Isidore, *Station Master, Boran, Seine et Oise*
BELIN, Jean Jules, *Commanding Division of Mobile Police, Sûreté National*
CHEVREL, Louis Desiré, *Station Master, Bois de Boulogne*
COUÉFFÉ, Francis Victor Eugène, *Station Master, Invalides, Paris*
CUIGNET, Georges Arthur, *Railway Inspector, Northern Region*
DUBOC, Louis Joseph, *Station Master, Gare de Villers Bretonneux*
EHRET, Louis Robert, *Station Master, Boulogne-sur-Mer*
LACROIX, Antoine, *of the Ministry for Foreign Affairs*
MARCHAL, René Louis, *Chef du Service Interieur du Palais de l'Elysée*
MORILIERE, Auguste, *Station Master, Versailles*
POULAIN, Ernest Eugène Edouard, *Principal Station Master, Calais*

1939–1949

1950

7 March   **Visit to Britain of President Auriol of the French Republic**
BEGARD, M., *Divisional Commissioner*
BOUCHET, G., *Principal Commissioner*

21 November   **Visit to Britain of Queen Juliana of the Netherlands and Prince Bernhard**
NIEUWLAND, Captain Gijsbert
SESINK, Commissioner Catherinus, *Head of Security for the Royal Family*

1951

8 May **Visit to Britain of King Frederik IX and Queen Ingrid of Denmark**
HARVEY-SAMUEL, Mme Elsemerete, *Lady Secretary, Royal Danish Embassy*

1952–1953

1954

28 June **State Visit to Britain of King Gustav VI Adolf and Queen Louise of Sweden**
LUTHMAN, Carl Gösta, *Secretary to Swedish Ambassador*

1955

24 June **State Visit to Norway of the Queen and the Duke of Edinburgh**
KARLSEN, Thorleif, *Assistant Commissioner of Police (Traffic), Oslo*
L'ABÉE-LUND, Lars Anton, *Assistant Commissioner (CID), Oslo*
QVALE, John Ottar, *Deputy Commissioner of Police, Oslo*
SKUTLE, Captain Hermann, *Commander, The King's Own Guard*
STÖEN, Karl Ludvig, *Secretary, Royal Norwegian Household*

25 October **State Visit to Britain of President Craveiro Lopes of Portugal**
CASTRO, Mlle Maria Madalena-Ribeiro de, *Head Clerk, Portuguese Embassy*
SALTER DA FONSECA, Mlle Maria Alexandrina, *Secretary to Portuguese Ambassador*
O'DONOVAN, Miss Mairin

1956

8 June **State Visit to Sweden of the Queen and the Duke of Edinburgh**
BERGÉRUS, Sture Karl Emanuel, *Superintendent of the Palace*
DANIELSSON, Otto Daniel, *Criminal Police Commissioner*
EURÉN, Lieutenant-Commander Georg Erik Josua, *Commander, Royal Yacht Vasaorden*
FLEETWOOD, Captain Jan Edvard, Baron, *Commanding Castle Guard*
GUSTAFSSON, Major Ille Alexander Stanislaus, *Inspector of Music, Royal Swedish Life Guards*
JOHANSSON, Johan Ejnar, *Superintendent of the Palace*
JOHANSSON, Johan Oscar, *Commissioner of Police*
STACKELBERG, Count Axel Carl Hjalmar Louis, *ADC to the King*
TORÉN, Lieutenant-Commander Lennart Eriksson, *Commanding Guard of Honour*
WRANG, Captain Carl-Olof, *Commanding Grenadiers at the Castle*

16 July **State Visit to Britain of King Feisal II of Iraq**
IBRAHIM, 1st Lieutenant Mohammed, *ADC Royal Iraqi Air Force*

1957

18 February **State Visit to Portugal of the Queen and the Duke of Edinburgh**
MOREIRA BAPTISTA, Cesar Henrique, *Mayor of Sintra*
LIMA BARROSO, Duarte Nuno de, *Protocol Department*
ALMEIDA SANTOS DE CASTELLO BRANCO, Sebastião Maria de, *Protocol Department*
CARVALHO, Joaquim Augusto de, *Mayor of Alcobaca*
FELGUEIRAS, Maria Eduarda Sarmento de Magalhaes e Menezes, Countess de, *in charge of arrangements, Queluz*
QUADROS FERRO, Antonio Gabriel de, *Secretary to Mayor of Lisbon*
FIGUEIREDO, José B. Duarté de, *Director, Sao Carlos Theatre*
ALMEIDA MONTEIRO, Antonio, *Mayor of Batalha*
MONJARDINO GOMES NEMÉSIO, Jorge, *Protocol Department*
SOARES DE OLIVEIRA, Luis Eduardo de Almeida Campos, *Protocol Department*
VASCONCELLOS E SOUZA PRESTRELLO DE VASCONCELLOS, Bartolomeu dos Martires, *Protocol Department*

8 April **State Visit to France of the Queen and the Duke of Edinburgh**
BAYLION, *Commissioner of Travel*
CHEBROUX, *Principal Officer, Ministry of Interior*
DUVAL, M. Lionel-Raoul, *Press Officer of the President*
JAUBERT, Raymond Louis, *Principal Commissioner, Motorcyclist Service*
JUNG, Jean Charles, *Assistant Commissioner of Police*
LAMONTAGNE, Capitaine François Louis Marie, *Staff Officer, 1st Region*
PIETRI, Ange Marie, *Commissioner, Presidency Security Police*
RICHIEU
SCHMITT, Capitaine, *Chief of Secretariat Service*
SOREAU, Jean Fernand, *Divisional Commissioner for 8th District*

21 May	**State Visit to Denmark of the Queen and the Duke of Edinburgh**

DAMM, Edwin, *Comptroller of Civil List*
DENCKER, Julius Johan Theodor, *Company Commander, Danish Home Guard*
GAMST, Mlle. Birte, *Chief Clerk, Private Secretary's Office, Amalienborg Palace*
GOTFREDSEN, Laurits Peter, *Headmaster, Skovgaard School*
HANSEN, Captain Hans Villy, *Squadron Commander, Royal Danish Air Force*
JAKOBSEN, Andreas Marinus, *Inspector of Child Welfare, Copenhagen*
LARSEN, Mlle. Karen, *Leader of the Nursery School*
LAURITZEN, Martin Østergaard, *Director of Education*
LUND, Major Niels, *Squadron Commander, Royal Danish Air Force*
PEDERSEN, Captain Knud Schnack, *Squadron Commander, Royal Danish Air Force*
THAYSEN, Ejnar Hess, *Deputy Head, Lord Chamberlain's Office*
THIEDE, Lieutenant-Commander Sven Egil, *attached to HM Yacht* Britannia
TRAMPE, Lieutenant-Commander Count Karl-Christian, *Flag Lieutenant to C-in-C Royal Danish Navy*

1958

25 March	**State Visit to the Netherlands of the Queen and the Duke of Edinburgh**

DE BEAUFORT, Jonkheer Romain, *Senior Officer, Protocol Department*
BIJLSMA, Petrus Dirk Nicolaas, *Commissioner, Amsterdam Police*
BLOOT, Jacob, *Chief Inspector, Delft Police*
BREEDVELDT, Pieter, *Comptroller, Office of Master of the Household*
BRON, Hendrik Okko, *Head of Burgomaster's Office, Rotterdam*
BROUWER, Captain Jacobus Gerardus, *Commanding Guard of Honour*
COOVELS, Diederik Johannes Maria van Thiel, *Senior Officer, Protocol Department*
DIEN, Teunis Jacobus van, *Superintendent, Intelligence Department, Hague Police*
GROOT, Dirk, *Secretary to Master of the Household*
LAMMERS, Cornelis Willem, *Administrator, Office of the Crown Equerry*
LOGGERS, Gerrit Gesinus, *Burgomaster of Aalsmeer*
MAN, George Albert, *Harbourmaster North Sea Canal*
MATTHEIJSSEN, Theophilus, *Inspector, Security Service, Royal Household*
VAN NOOTHOORN, Pieter Arend, *Security Officer*
PERFORS, Adriaan, *Supervisor, Royal Palace, The Hague*
VAN DER MOST VAN SPIJK, Captain Albert, *Commanding Amsterdam District*
STERKEN, Captain Hendrik, *Commanding Guard of Honour*
TOUSSAINT, George Johannes Daniel Sijbrand, *Security Officer (Technical Branch) Amsterdam Public Works Department*
VAN DER WETERING, Bastiaan, *Supervisor, Royal Palace, Amsterdam*
ZWIJNEN, Bernardus, *Head Clerk, Military Household*

13 May	**State Visit to Britain of President Gronchi of Italy**

RAPAZZINI, Signorina Ester, *Private Secretary to the Italian Ambassador*

28 October	**State Visit to Britain of President Heuss of the Federal Republic of Germany**

JOERG, Wilhelm, *Assistant Attaché*
MANTWITZ, Alfred, *Employee at Presidency*
RATHJE, Otto, *Official, Protocol Department*

1959

5 May	**State Visit to Britain of the Shahanshah of Iran**

GOODARZI, Mohsen, *Third Secretary, Iranian Embassy*

1960

5 April	**State Visit to Britain of the President of the French Republic and Madame de Gaulle**

ARCHAMBEAUD, Capitaine Philippe Edouard, *French Air Force, Staff Officer attached to President's suite*
DUCRET, André Antoine, *Deputy Security Officer to President*
DE COURS DE SAINT GERVASY, Pierre, Baron, *Secretary to French Ambassador*
GUYOMARD, Paul Alexandre, *Third Secretary French Embassy*
VANETTI, Dr Alexandre Attilio Jean, *Physician to the President*

19 July	**State Visit to Britain of King Bhumibol and Queen Sirikit of Thailand**

ROCHANANOND, Paak, *Third Secretary, Royal Thai Embassy*

17 October	**State Visit to Britain of King Mahendra and Queen Ratna of Nepal**

MANANDHAR, Sri Indra Narayan
SRESTHA, Subba Kiran Bahadur

1961

26 February	**State Visit to Nepal of the Queen and the Duke of Edinburgh**

BASNET, Chintabahadur, *Superintendent of Police, Pokhara*

KARKI, Major Bala Bahadur
KHADKA, Lieutenant-Colonel Man Bahadur, *Military Secretariat*
KHANDKA, Major Premdhoj
LIMBU, Hari, *Superintendent of Police*
RAYA MAJHI, Lieutenant-Colonel Dangambhir Singh, *Military Secretariat*
MALLA, Mlle. Bindashwari, *Section Off., Ministry of Foreign Affairs*
MALLA, Tapta Bahadur, *Superintendent of Police*
SHAMSHER JANG BAHADUR RANA, Lieutenant-Colonel Arvind
RANA, Major Dhruba Nara Simha
SHAMSHER JANG BAHADUR RANA, Nakhul, *Superintendent of Police*
SHAMSHER JANG BAHADUR RANA, Nar Narain, *Superintendent of Police*
BIKRAM RANA, Lieutenant-Colonel Rishi,
SINGH, Lieutenant-Colonel Khadga Bahadur
SUBBA, Jagat Bahadur, *Superintendent of Police*
THAPA, Major Bhairab Bahadur
THAPA, Lieutenant-Colonel Hari Bahadur
THAPA, Lieutenant-Colonel Juddha Bahadur
UPADHYAYA, Harihar Prasad, *Superintendent of Police*

2 March	**State Visit to Iran of the Queen and the Duke of Edinburgh** AKBARI, Captain Jahanshah, *Iranian Police Force* JAHANBINI, Lieutenant Qumars, *Imperial Guard* ZARRIN-KHAMER, Captain Hadi, *Adjutant, Imperial Guard* MAHANPOUR, Captain Abdolah, *Imperial Guard* MUJTABAI, Captain, *Iranian Police Force* NESHATI, Captain Esmael QADERI, Captain, *Iranian Police Force* RAHIMI, Lieutenant, *Iranian Police Force* SHAMS-SHIRAZI, Lieutenant Karim, *Imperial Guard* TURABI, Captain, *Iranian Police*
12 April	**For services in connection with the restoration of statue of Queen Victoria, damaged during the Second World War** PALMERO, Francis, *Mayor of Menton*
29 April	**State Visit to Italy of the Queen and the Duke of Edinburgh** BATISTINI, Doctor Giorgio, *Secretary to the President* CHIANURA, Doctor Giovanni, *Rome Police* ANGUISSOLA DI SAN DAMIENO, Conte Guido, *in charge of baggage, Transport arrangements* MARINI DI SAN LEO, Doctor Artemio Gaetano, *Secretary to the President* MARRONI, Doctor Ermanno, *Secretary to the President* PELLEGRINI, Doctor Domenico, *Secretary to the President* PIACITELLI, Doctor Mario, *Third Secretary of Legation* SABATINI, Giacomo, *Principal Officer, Stationery Office* FARUFFINI DI SEZZADIO, Major Pier Vittorio, *Vice-Commander of the Guards, Quirinale Palace* RIZZO-VENCI, Guido, *Attaché of Legation*

1962

10 July	**State Visit to Britain of the President of the Republic of Liberia and Mrs Tubman** GIBSON, Captain Robert Henri, *President's Personal Guard* KUMEH, Aaron Jlue, *Secretary to the President* RICKS-MARSH, Madame Victoria, *Private Secretary to the Ambassador* BROOKS-UGBOMA, Madame Pandora Evangeline, *Secretary to Mrs Tubman* WESLEY, Madame Julia Benson, *Second Secretary at Embassy*
16 October	**State Visit to Edinburgh of King Olav V of Norway** ERIKSEN, Lieutenant-Commander Leif Ambrosius, *of HM Yacht* Norge JACOBSEN, Lieutenant-Commander Hans-Petter, *of HM Yacht* Norge KARVEL, Lieutenant Lauritz Georg, *of HM Yacht* Norge LUND, Lieutenant-Commander Torleif, *of HM Yacht* Norge REFSHAL, Svenn Ojermund, *Press Attaché, Norwegian Embassy* SAETHER, Halvard Eugen, *Cultural Attaché, Norwegian Embassy* SYVERTSEN, Björn Petter, *Vice-Consul in Glasgow* BØGH-TOBIASSEN, Lieut,-Commander Christian, *of HM Yacht* Norge

1963

14 May	**State Visit to Britain of King Baudouin I and Queen Fabiola of the Belgians** KELLS-RENARD, Madame Liliane Hortense Léonie Ghislaine, *Secretary to Belgian Ambassador* VANDEVELDE, Jean Désiré, *Clerk, Belgian Embassy*
19 July	**State Visit to Britain of King Paul and Queen Frederika of the Hellenes** LAMBROPOULOS, Christos, *Clerk, Greek Embassy*

PIPPAS, Police Captain Andrew John, *Royal Greek Gendarmerie, Security Officer*
STAVRAKAKIS, Second-Lieutenant Stavros John, *Royal Greek Gendarmerie, Security Officer*
VILLIOTIS, John, *Clerk, Greek Embassy*

1964

26 May

State Visit to Britain of President Abboud of the Republic of the Sudan
ABBAS, Sayed Hassan, *Assistant Cultural Attaché*
ALI, Sayed Osman, *Welfare Attaché*
NURI, Sayed Abdulla, *Third Secretary*
TAHIR, Captain Mohamed Hussein, *Assistant. Military, Naval and Air Attaché*

1965

1 February

State Visit to Ethiopia of the Queen and the Duke of Edinburgh
HAILE MARIAM,Ató Fike, *Secretary-General to Governor-General, Eritrea*
MARIAM, Ató Menbere Wolde, *Steward and Valet to the Emperor*
YOHANNES, Ató Fantai Wolde, *Liaison Officer (Transport)*

12 February

State Visit to the Republic of the Sudan of the Queen and the Duke of Edinburgh
ABDULLA, Sayed Mukhtar, *Inspector, Republican Palace*
ABDULLAH, Major Gasmallah, *of the Honorary Bodyguard*
AHMED, Sayed Kamal Hassan, *Security Officer*
ALLAM, Sayed El Tom Hassan, *Senior Book-Keeper*
EL AMIN, Major Muslih Mohammed, *Palace Guard Commander*
FATTAH, Sayed Ibrahim Mustafa Abdel, *Head Staff Clerk*
IBRAHIM, Superintendent Abdel Wahab, *Security Officer*
KHAMIS, Captain Hassan El Nour, *Hon. ADC to the Queen*
EL MAGHRABI, Sayed Kamal Mohammed, *Staff Clerk*
MAHGOUB, Captain Awad, *Palace Guard Commander*
MALIK, Captain Babiker, *Honorary Bodyguard*
EL MUBARAK, Major Nur el Din, *Honorary Bodyguard*
MURJAN, Major Ahmed, BEM, *Bandmaster, Army Band*
RAHIM, 1st Lieutenant Babiker Abdel, *Palace Guard Commander*
SALEEM, Sayed Abdel Azeem Hussein, *Staff Clerk*
EL SIBEITI, Sayed Ahmed Mohammed, *Staff Clerk*

18 May

State Visit to Germany of the Queen and the Duke of Edinburgh
EHLERS, Herbert, *Official in Protocol Department*
GEESE, Heinz Friedrich Wilhelm, *Chief Superintendent, Security Police*
GÖLLNER, Paul, *Official in Protocol Department*
MENZEL, Helmuth, *Official in Protocol Department*
SCHERER, Lieutenant Thomas, *Commanding Guard at the Petersberg*
VON SELCHOW, Wolfgang Hans Rudiger, *Protocol Officer, Berlin*
WALLAU, Theodor, *Assistant in Protocol Department*

13 July

State Visit to Britain of the President of Chile and Señora de Frei
DEBESA, Señor Fernando

1966

9 May

State Visit to Belgium of the Queen and the Duke of Edinburgh
BASTOGNE, Joseph Maurice, *Stationmaster, Liège*
BEAUPREZ, Pierre Edouard, *Chief Commissioner of Police, Ostend*
BEHEYT, Simeon, *Burgomaster of Middelkerke*
BERTRAND, Georges Nicolas Joseph Edmond, *Manager, Royal Estate, Laeken*
CHAILLY, Jean Constance Ferdinand, *Asst. to Commander of Royal Palaces*
CLEMENT, Mlle. Geneviève Marie Paule Hortense Cornélie, *Chief Clerk, Grand Marshal's Department*
CLEMENT, Karolus, *Stationmaster, Ostend*
CORNELLIS, Emile Charles, *Stationmaster, Antwerp*
DEFERIÉRE, Fernand, *Stationmaster, Brussels Central*
DUPORT, Léon Joseph, *Asst. Superintendent of Staff, Palace at Laeken*
RUFFO DE BONNEVAL DE LA FARE, Comte Commandant Guy Sixte Jean Marie Ghislain, *Head, Protocol Section, Armed Forces*
LELOUP-GREGOIRE, Madame Henriette Philomène Mathilde, *Secretary in Grand Marshal's Department*
DE GROEF, Mlle. Jeanne Catherine, *Secretary in Grand Marshal's Department*
HEYVAERT, Willy Philemon, *Secretary to Commander of Royal Palaces*
KINET, Lieutenant Pierre Paul Joseph Antoine, *Royal Mounted Escort*
LEDANT, Major Georges Gustave Deiu Joseph, *Commanded troops, Brussels Palace*
MARTIN, Captain Robert, *Head of Section, Military Movements*
ROTTHIER, Arthur-Léopold, *Inspector at Sûreté*
DE SAHGER, Walter Henri Marthe Leonie Irene, *Burgomaster of Poperinghe*

VERBOIS-SIMON, Madame Marie-José, *Secretary/Librarian, Grand Marshal's Department*
SINNAEVE, Roger Florent, *Stationmaster, Bruges*
STASSEN, Frans Antoine Jean, *Superintendent of Staff, Palace at Laeken*
ZIN-VERWEE, Madame Yvonne Emilienne, *Secretary, Grand Marshal's Department*
VOET, Léon Basile, *Curator, Musée Plantin-Moretus, Antwerp*
VAN DER VORDE, Roger, *Commander, Middlekerke Airport*

| 17 May | **State Visit to Britain of the President of the Federal Republic of Austria and Frau Jonas** |

CALICE, Dr Georg, *Attaché, Austrian Embassy*
HAUER, Viktor, *Chief Clerk, Austrian Embassy*
MUSSI, Dr Ingo, *Press Attaché, Austrian Embassy*

1967

9 May — **State Visit to Britain of King Faisal of Saudi Arabia**
AL-FADL, Abdul Wahab

1 November — **State Visit to Britain of the President of Turkey and Madame Sunay**
ATLAS, Mustafa
BALCIK, Tacettin
OZNUR, Osman
SARIOGLU, Necati
TASCIOGLU, Miss Renan
TEZCAN, Mustafa
MESSERLY, Miss Jacqueline Marie-Louise

1968

1 November — **State Visit to Brazil of the Queen and the Duke of Edinburgh**
AZULAY, Jom Tob de, *Ministry of Foreign Affairs*
BARREIRA CRAVO, Arnaldo Abilio Godoy, *Ministry of Foreign Affairs*
CAMACHO DE VINCENZI, Marcus, *Ministry of Foreign Affairs*
DE CARVALHO, Bernardinho Botelho, *Security Officer*
CEZAR DE ARAUJO, Frederico, *Ministry of Foreign Affairs*
CHOHFI, Osmar Vladimir, *Interpreter*
DIONISIO DE VASCONCELLOS, Paulo, *Ministry of Foreign Affairs*
FRAZÃO, Armando Sergio, *Ministry of Foreign Affairs*
LADEIRA, Jorge, *Ceremonial Department*
MANZOLILO DE MORAES, Victor, *Ministry of Foreign Affairs*
MOREIRA GARCIA, Carlos, *Ceremonial Department*
DE PIMENTEL-BRANDÃO SANCHEZ, João Paulo, *Ministry of Foreign Affairs*
ROITER, Mario da Graça, *Ministry of Foreign Affairs*
SALGADO GAMA FILHO, Jório, *Ministry of Foreign Affairs*
DE SEIXAS CORREA, Luiz Felipe, *Ministry of Foreign Affairs*
DE SOUSA TAPAJOZ, Sergio Luiz, *Ministry of Foreign Affairs*
TAVORA, Ruy Alejandro, *Interpreter*

11 November — **State Visit to Chile of the Queen and the Duke of Edinburgh**
AGUIRRE CHATEAU, Juan Enrique, *Protocol Department*
LEIVA, Captain Humberto, *Officer in charge of Cavalry Escort*

1969

22 April — **State Visit to Britain of President Saragat of Italy**
BARONI, Amedeo, *Administrative Chancellor, Italian Embassy*
FIERMONTE, Vittorio, *Assistant Administrative Attaché at Embassy*
GORGONE, Vincenzo, *Assistant Chancellor, Italian Embassy*

5 May — **State Visit to Austria of the Queen, the Duke of Edinburgh and Princess Anne**
HASCHKE, Maria, *President's Private Office*
HECKL, Dr Richard, *Security Official*
KREUTZER, Adolf, *Ministry of the Interior, in charge of Royal visit arrangements*
KRIEGER, Dr Franz, *Chancellor's Office*
MEISSL, Dr Walter, *Security Official*
PETUTSCHNIG, Lieutenant Dietmar Herman, *Commander of Guard of Honour*
REICHHUBER, Captain Teja Karl Wilhelm, *Flight Commander*
RUCKER, Captain Gustav Adolf Matthias, *Commander of Guard of Honour*
ZAPPE, Dr Wilfried, *Security Official*

15 July — **State Visit to Britain of the President of Finland and Madame Kekkonen**
APPELQVIST, Seppo Villiam, *Attaché, Finnish Embassy*
BÄCKSTROM, Erkki Johannes, *Attaché Finnish Embassy*
LUOSTARINEN, Miss Nelli Maija, *Private Secretary, Finnish Embassy*

SAARIKOSKI, The Reverend Ismo Volevi, *Establishment and Welfare Attaché*
SOLIN, Miss Eeva-Maija, *Head Archivist, Finnish Embassy*
VUORINEN, Miss Taimi Lahja, *Chief Cashier, Finnish Embassy*

1970

1971

5 October **State Visit to Britain of Emperor Hirohito and Empress Nagako of Japan**
IJUIN, Akio, OBE, *Second Secretary, Japanese Embassy*
TAKEUCHI, Yukio, *Private Secretary to Japanese Embassy*

18 October **State Visit to Turkey of the Queen, the Duke of Edinburgh and Princess Anne**
ALTAY, Hadi, *Director, Ayasofya and Kariye Museums*
ANSAY, Engin, *Second Secretary, Ministry of Foreign Affairs*
ÇIG, Kemal, *Director, Topkapi Museum*
EKENLER, Captain Mustapha Kemelettin, *Turkish Navy, Bandmaster, Ankara*
EREN, Ahmet, *Security, Ministry of the Interior*
FALAY, Lieutenant Murat, *Commander, Guard of Honour*
IYIBIL, Nazmi, *Security, Ministry of the Interior*
KOÇAK, Captain Süer, *Bandmaster, Istanbul*
OGUZ, Mehmet, *Traffic Director, Province of Ankara*
ÖZDES, Ahmet Müfit, *Second Secretary, Ministry of Foreign Affairs*
SELEN, Captain Ercümend, *Commander, Guard of Honour at the Queen's Residence*
SENGEZER, Captain Azni, *Commander, Guard of Honour, Istanbul*
TEZOK, Funda, *Second Secretary, Ministry of Foreign Affairs*
TURKOGLU, Sebahattin, *Director, Ephesus and Selçuk Museum*
UNAL, Ismail, *Director, Dolmabahçe Museum*
YIGIT, Yasar, *Security, Ministry of the Interior*

7 December **State Visit to Britain of King Zahir of Afghanistan**
NOWROZ, Mohammed Anwar, *Second Secretary, Afghan Embassy*

1972

10 February **State Visit to Thailand of the Queen and the Duke of Edinburgh**
SURAKARN BANASIDHI, Mrs Ampha, *Matron, Government House Secretariat*
BUNNAG, Tej, *Assistant Chief of Press Division*
CHARUSATHIARA, Captain Prayut
CHINTAKANONDHA, Lieutenant Amornrat, *Special Security Officer*
INTHARASOMBAT, Senior Lieutenant Chamnan, *Special Security Officer*
JAYANAMA, Surapong, *Chief of Press Section*
KATANYU, Somnuk, *Chief of Section, Grand Palace*
KETUPOL, Prapan, *Chief of Household Division*
MAHAKAYI, Verabhand, *Chief of Protocol Division*
PUKKAMAN, Sahas, *Assistant Director of Royal Household Affairs*
SRIYANOND, Mongkol, *Deputy Managing Director, Forest Industry Organisation*
SUNGTONG, Squadron Leader Taweesak, *Special Security Officer*
KESAKOMOL, Colonel Jitkavi

22 February **State Visit to Malaysia of the Queen, the Duke of Edinburgh and Princess Anne**
FOONG YEE KAI, *Security Officer to Princess Anne*
IDRIS bin MOHAMED INCHE, *Government Accommodation Officer*
MOHD. MOKHTAR bin HAJI MOHD. DAUD INCHE, *Assistant Superintendent of Police*
ONG KIM HOE INCHE, *Press Officer*
SALMAH DALIB, *Lady in Waitng to Princess Anne*

29 February **State Visit to Brunei of the Queen, the Duke of Edinburgh and Princess Anne**
MOHAMED ABBAS BIN IBRAHIM, *Chief of Protocol*

13 March **State Visit to Maldives of the Queen and the Duke of Edinburgh**
MANIKU, Adam Naseer, *Minister of State*

11 April **State Visit to Britain of Queen Juliana and Prince Bernhard of the Netherlands**
BEERMAN, Johannes Coenraad, *Senior Steward, Royal Household*
VAN DER HEIDEN, Lieutenant Cornelis, *State Police*
HEIJ, Arend, *Administrator, Office of the Master of the Household*
DE JAGER, Captain Theodorus Gerardus, *Royal Netherlands Air Force*
VAN DER LINDEN, Andreas Casper, *Royal Chef*

13 June **State Visit to Britain of Grand Duke Jean and Grand Duchess Charlotte of Luxembourg**
NIMAX, Lieutenant en premier Pierre, *Bandmaster*

17 October	**State Visit to Yugoslavia of the Queen and the Duke of Edinburgh**
	FEJIC, Goran, *Liaison Officer*
	FLOREANI, Mrs Ankica
	LANG, Nikola, *Secretary in Protocol*
	MIRKOVIC, Mrs Olivera, *Secretary in Protocol*
	MITROVIC, Stojan, *Baggage Master*
	RAICEVIC, Mihajlo, *Secretary, Ministry of Foreign Affairs*
	STEFANOVIC, Miss Slobodanka, *Secretary in Protocol*
	VELASEVIC, Mrs Milica, *Secretary in Protocol*
	VUKICEVIC, Nikola, *Liaison Officer*
24 October	**State Visit to Britain of President Heinemann of the Federal Republic of Germany and Frau Heinemann**
	BERGER, Herr Rolf Dieter, *Assistant Attaché, German Embassy*
	GIEGOLD, Herr Walter, *Assistant Attaché, German Embassy*
	HÄRLE, Fraulein Hildegard, *Assistant Secretary, German Embassy*
	HOCHE, Frau Karin, *Personal Assistant to Head of Presidency*
	HUNDRIESER, Fraulein Annelies Wilfriede Gisele, *Assistant Attaché, Protocol*
	KRUMBIEGEL, Fraulein Ursula Ena, *Chief Assistant to the President*

1973

3 April	**State Visit to Britain of President Eccheverria Alvarez of Mexico**
	RIVAS, Señor Egardo Flores, *Second Secretary, Mexican Embassy*
	BERAIN, Señorita Sandra Fuentes, *Third Secretary*
	GUTIÉRREZ, Señorita Elda Paz, *Third Secretary*
	LITWIN, Señorita Barbara, *Attaché*
	ROMERO, Señor Fernando Rodriguez, *Attaché*
	RAMIREZ CORONA MORAYTA, Señora Italia Rosa, *Interpreter*
11 December	**State Visit to Britain of President Mobutu of Zaïre**
	AZANA, Citoyen Usisazo Unkasinakongo
	LUAFA BALOM'ANKENO, Citoyen
	BIAMUNGU, Citoyenne Rugali, *Private Secretary to Mme Mobutu*
	JAZAB, Docteur Aminollah, *Doctor*
	KAMBALA, Lieutenant Kamudimbi Milambo, *Security Officer*
	KAYEMBE, Capitaine, *Ordinance Officer*
	LONDA, Docteur Mankanda, *Doctor*
	MOZIMO, Citoyen Bosunguma
	NKASAMA, Citoyen Isankunya Iloukele

1974

30 April	**State Visit to Britain of Queen Margrethe II of Denmark and Prince Henrik**
	MOGENSEN, Mr Carsten Sode, *Second Secretary, Danish Embassy*
	POULSEN, Miss Birgitte, *Second Secretary, Danish Embassy*
	ERIKSEN, Commander Ib Edvard, *Assistant to Defence Attaché*
	ALBERTSEN, Mr Niels-Peter, *Press and Cultural Attaché*
	FABRICIUS, The Revd. Poul-Erik, *Embassy Chaplain*
9 July	**State Visit to Britain of the Yang DiPertuan Agung of Malaysia and the Raja Permaisuri Agung**
	SULAIMAN, Encik Zahari, *Second Secretary*
	SANI, Encik Mohamad bin, *Second Secretary*
	HASHIM, Cik Azian, *Second Secretary*
	NAVARATNAM, Encik Sivarajah, *Assistant Trade Commissioner*
	BAHARUDDIN, Encik Wan, *Education Attaché*
	IBRAHIM, Cik Puteh, *Education Attaché*
	ABDULGHANI, Mohd. Arif Fadzillah bin Haji, *Security Officer*
	DADAMEAH, Zulkiflee, *Chief Press Liaison Officer*

1975

24 February	**State Visit to Mexico of the Queen and the Duke of Edinburgh**
	VILLASENOR-ARANO, Señor Ignacio, CMG, *Assistant Deputy Director General, Diplomatic Service*
	BELLO, Señor Jaime Soriano, *Private Secretary to Deputy Minister for Foreign Affairs*
	MARTINEZ CORTÉS, Señor Licenciado Fernando, *Private Secretary to Deputy Minister of Presidency*
	DE ICAZA, Señor Carlos Alberto, *Private Secretary to Deputy Minister for Foreign Affairs*
	RODRIGUEZ GARCIA, Señor Victor Manuel, *Deputy Director General, Diplomatic Service*
	GARCIA, Señora Elizabeth, *Personal Assistant to Minister of Foreign Affairs*
	NAZAR HARO, Señor Miguel, *Deputy Director of Federal Security*
	SALES-HURTADO, Señor Alberto, *Counsellor*
	ROUX-LOPEZ, Señor Francisco, *Deputy Chief of Protocol*

MENDEZ, Señorita Victoria, *of Public Relations Section*
ALONSO MUNOZ, Señor Manuel, *Assistant Director of Public Relations*
ZETINA, Señora Jacqueline, *Assistant Deputy Chief of Protocol*

7 May	**State Visit to Japan of the Queen and the Duke of Edinburgh**

MASAGO, Teruo, *Board of Ceremonies*
NAKAYA, Masayuki, *Board of Ceremonies*
TANAKA, Keiji, *Board of Ceremonies*

8 July	**State Visit to Edinburgh of King Carl XVI Gustaf of Sweden**

ANKARBERG, Hans Goran Gunnar, *Second Secretary, Swedish Embassy*
CLAESSON, Miss Daga Margareta, *Personal Assistant to Swedish Ambassador*
EVANDER, The Reverend Sven, *Chaplain, Swedish Embassy*
REVELIUS, Nils Gunnar, *First Secretary, Swedish Embassy*
WESTIN, Gosta Viktor Axel, *Counsellor, Swedish Embassy*
WIDENFELT, John Staffan, *Trade Commissioner, Swedish Embassy*

1976

4 May	**State Visit to Britain of President Geisel of Brazil and Senhora Geisel**

DUTRA DE MENEZES, Captain Gustavo Adolfo, *Member, non-official party*
FLUSSER, Senhorita Dinah, *First Secretary, Brazilian Embassy*
LOPES, Senhor Jose Ferreira, *First Secretary, Brazilian Embassy*
MERQUIOR, Senhor Jose Guilherme, *First Secretary, Brazilian Embassy*
FRASER NEALE, Senhor Brian Michael, *First Secretary, Brazilian Embassy*
NETO, Lieutenant Oscar de Souza Spinola, *Naval ADC to President*
SOBRINHO, Raphael Valentino, *First Secretary, Brazilian Embassy*

24 May	**State Visit to Finland of the Queen and the Duke of Edinburgh**

HIRVONEN, Lieutenant Teuvo, *of the Presidential Palace*
KIVIMÄKI, *of the Presidential Palace*
FERSEN, Baroness Natalia von, *the Queen's Interpreter*
ERLEWEIN, Mr Rolf, *HRH's Interpreter*

22 June	**State Visit to Britain of President Giscard d'Estaing of France and Madame Giscard d'Estaing**

ANGREMY, M. Jean-Pierre, *Counsellor, French Embassy*
BAUDELOT, M. Réné Marie Georges Maurice, *Head of Security*
COLAS, Mme Paulette, *Secretary to the President*
CONTENAY, M. Daniel Francis, *Press Counsellor, French Embassy*
DE MENTHON, M. Réné, *Protocol Department*
HENNEQUIN, M. Guy, *Intendant of Elysée Palace*
LEJUEZ, M. Roger, *Counsellor*
SODINI, Mme Marie-Françoise, *Press Department, Elysée Palace*
VICARIOT, M. Jean, *Scientific Counsellor, French Embassy*

8 November	**State Visit to Luxembourg of the Queen and the Duke of Edinburgh**

FELTZ, Major Jean Charles, *attached to Palace*
HECK, Captain Jean-Paul, *Commander of Guard of Honour*
THIEL, Major Ernest, *attached to Palace*
WAGNER, Gaston Jean, *Head of Personnel, Grand Duke's Household*

1977

1978

22 May	**State Visit to Germany of the Queen and the Duke of Edinburgh**

ALBRECHT, Herr Sepp, *Protocol Officer, Berlin*
BRUHLER, Lieutenant Hans-Herbert, *Protocol Department Ministry of Defence*
BRUNS, Herr Klaus-Rudiger, *Protocol, Foreign Office*
MONTZKA, Herr Egon, *Protocol, Foreign Office*
SCHONAU, Leutenant zur See Kurt, *Platoon Commander, Guard of Honour, Gymnich*

14 November	**State Visit to Britain of President Eanes of Portugal**

FELNER DA COSTA, Senhor Jorge da Fonseca, *Attaché (Tourism)*
VIANA SIMOES, Senhor Domingos, *Commercial Attaché*
DE MORAES VAZ, Senhor Joao, *Commercial Attaché*
MENDES, Senhor Fernando Manuel Camacho, *Administrative Attaché*

1979

16 May	**State Visit to Denmark of the Queen and the Duke of Edinburgh**

ANDERSEN, Major Flemming Wirzner, *Commanding the Escort*

ANDERSEN, Major Niels Stig Preben, *Commanding Guard of Honour, Tolboden*
BANG, Mogens, *Secretary, Lord Chamberlain's Office*
GRØNBECH, Commander Jens Egede, *Executive Officer HMY* Dannebrog
GREDSTED, Niels Kristian, *Riding Master*
JØRGENSEN, Eigel Korsholm, *Assistant to Governor, Fredensborg Palace*
JØRGENSEN, Major Ole Lysgaard, *Commanding Guard of Honour, Aarhus*
KRISTIANSEN, Sejr Schneekloth, *Head Gardener, Fredensborg Palace*
LARSEN, Poul Anker, RVM, *Comptroller of Supply*
LYKKE, Bent, RVM, *Deputy Comptroller of Supply*
MATHIESEN, Major Bent Otto, *Commanding Guard of Honour, Fredensborg*
NIELSEN, Major Erik Stig, *Keeper of the Cars and Carriages*
PEDERSEN, Peder Richard, *Royal Guard Hussars*
PEDERSEN, Bent Mose, *Consul*
ULRICH, Major Georg Christian, *Commanding Guard of Honour, Amalienborg*

1980

14 October **State Visit to Italy of the Queen and the Duke of Edinburgh**
BRUNO, Dott. Alberto, *Administrator of the Presidency*
NEVOLA, Dott. Fabrizio, *Protocol Department, Presidency*
AGRO, Dott. Bruno, *Press Office, Presidency*
PECORARO, Magg. Giuseppe, *of the Corrazieri*
STEFANO, Dott. Carlo de, *Public Security, Quirinale*
BASTIANELLI, Dott. Alfredo, *Protocol Department, Foreign Ministry*

21 October **State Visit to Tunisia of the Queen and the Duke of Edinburgh**
GARBOUJ, M. Hamda, *Head of Ceremonies*

18 November **State Visit to Britain of King Birendra and Queen Aishwarya of Nepal**
ALE, Captain Dhana Bahadur, *ADC*
RAM, Inspector Bal. KC, *ADC*
PRADHAN, Mr Bir Man, *Accountant*
SHARMA, Mr Madhav, *Secretary*
CASTILLO, Miss Nelia, *Secretary*

1981

5 May **State Visit to Norway of the Queen and the Duke of Edinburgh**
NATAS, Mr Daniel, *Head Gardener, Royal Palace*

9 June **State Visit to Britain of King Khalid of Saudi Arabia**
AL-BASSAM, Mohammed Abdulrahman, *Attaché*
AL-KHAYYAT, Abdullah Mohamed, *Third Secretary*
AL-DAAJANI, Fahad bin Said, *Attaché*
AL-KUHAIMI, Ibrahim Abdulaziz, *Third Secretary*
ALZOGHAIBI, Ahmed Mohammed, *Second Secretary*
BAKHET, Fshad, Abdulrahman, *Third Secretary*
HUSSAIN, Fouad Ahmed Mohammed, *Third Secretary*
MARTINI, Faez Hachem, *of Saudi Arabian Protocol Office*
SARHAN, Salah Ahmed, *Third Secretary*

1982

16 March **State Visit to Britain of Qaboos bin Al Said, Sultan of Oman**
ABDULLA, Sulieman Dawood, *Cultural Attaché, Oman Embassy*
AL-ABRI, Major Abdullah Saif, *Defence Attaché, Oman Embassy*
AL-ABRI, Lieutenant-Colonel Salim Obaid Khamis, *ADC to the Sultan*
AL-HASSANI, Hashil Habib Khalfan, *Attaché, Oman Embassy*
AL-KHANJARI, Anwar Andul Rahman Essa, *Attaché, Oman Embassy*
AL-MA'AMARI, Superintendent Malik Suleiman, *ADC to the Sultan*
BA'OMER, Mohammed Aqeel Alawi, *Second Secretary, Oman Embassy*

16 November **State Visit to Britain of Queen Beatrix of the Netherlands and Prince Claus**
BEAUJEAN, Mr Peter Anne Willem, *Major Domo*
KOTVIS, Mr Paul Donald, *Assistant Clerk*
WESTERA, Mr Arent George, *Inspector, Security Service of Royal House*
UFFORD, Jonkheer A.W.C. Quarles van, *Protocol Officer at Embassy*

1983

25 May **State Visit to Sweden of the Queen and the Duke of Edinburgh**
ENGDAHL, Lars, *Palace Steward*

ANDERSSON, Lennart, *Clerk to the Keeper of the Royal Collections*
WALL, Olof, *Riding Master and Assistant to Master of the Horse*
EKLUND, Fru Cajsen, *Administrative Assistant*
IHRMAN, Fru Carin, *Administrative Assistant*
JERSTAV, Fru Astrid, *Administrative Assistant*
LOMANDER, Fru Anne-Marie, *Accountant*
LAURIN, Lars, *Transport Office, Royal Court*

1984

26 March   **State Visit to Jordan of the Queen and the Duke of Edinburgh**
BAKER, Abdul Muneem, *Manager, Royal Garages*
FALEH, Major Ahmad Mohamad, *Assistant Chief, Royal Guard*
HAMED, Major Fayeis Moussa, *Chief of Staff, Royal Guard*
ODEH, Dawud Mousa Salem Abdullah, *Secretary, Royal Protocol*
RASSAS, Refpat Adeeb Ahmad, *Secretary, Royal Protocol*
SARAIREH, Alkeel Nazzal Jadue, *of Royal Guard, Amman*
SAYER, Captain Abdullah Awad, *of Royal Guard, Aqaba*
SHUKRI, Major Ali Kanj, *Royal Guard Liaison Officer*
ZAZA, Major Hussein Ali, *ADC to King Hussein*

10 April   **State Visit to Britain of Shaikh Isa bin Sulman Al-Khalifa, Amir of Bahrain**
AL-KOOHEJI, Mr Abdul Elah, *Second Secretary, Bahrain Embassy*
AL-SHAALAN, Mr Abdulla Ebrahim Isa, *Third Secretary, Bahrain Embassy*

23 October   **State Visit to Britain of President Mitterand of the French Republic and Madame Mitterand**
D'ARAGON, M. Charles, *Press Counsellor*
CHOURAQUI, M. Gilles, *Cultural Counsellor*
DELBOURGO, M. Ralph, *Scientific Counsellor*
MARC, M. Jean, *Maritime Counsellor*
BURG, M. Jean-Marie, *Defence Procurement Attaché*
GUBLER, M. Dr Claude-Marie

1985

15 March   **State Visit to Portugal of the Queen and the Duke of Edinburgh**
MIGUEIS, D. Ana Luisa Sousa Villas-Boas Potes, *Secretary to Advisor on Foreign Affairs*
NEVES, Dra. Maria do Carmo Leal de Faria Franco de Andrade, *Secretary to Head of President's Civil Household*
AFONSO, Dra. Simonetta Luz, *Curator, Queluz Palace*

16 April   **State Visit to Britain of Life President Dr Banda of Malawi**
CHIGARU, Clement Thaddeus, *Second Secretary, Malawi High Commission*
KADZAMIRA, Miss Beatrice Pamela, *Third Secretary, Malawi High Commission*
KAMBUWA, Marvin Murray, *Second Secretary, Malawi High Commission*

11 June   **State Visit to Britain of President de la Madrid of Mexico and Señora de la Madrid**
ESCOBAR ALENANI, Tte. Coronel Eugenio, *Chief Assistant to Sra. de la Madrid*
HERNANDEZ AVALOS, Coronel de Infanteria Juan, *of the Presidential Staff*
PEREZ SANCHEZ, Tte. Coronel Manuel, *Chief Assistant to the President*

12 November   **State Visit to Britain of Shaikh Khalifa bin Hamad Al-Thani, Amir of Qatar**
AL-SUBAIE, Mr Ibrahim Mohamed, *Medical Attaché*
FANOUS, Miss Leila, *Press Attaché*
SHAMLAN, Mr Tarek, *Amiri Protocol Officer*
AL-KUBAISI, Mr Ghanem, *Amiri Protocol Officer*

1986

17 February   **State Visit to Nepal of the Queen and the Duke of Edinburgh**
BUDHATHOKI, Major Kumar, *ADC*
SHAH, DSP Amer Singh, *ADC*
SWAR, Captain Dilip, *ADC*
RANA, Captain Sunder Pratap, *ADC*
DANGOL, Captain Rajman, *State Coach*
THAPA, Captain Khadga Bahadur, *State Coach Driver*
RANA, Major Binod Jung, *Commander, Guard of Honour*
THAPA, Major Netra Bahadur, *Commander, Guard of Honour*
THAPA, Major Jitendra Jung, *Commander, Guard of Honour at Airport*
SHRESTHA, Inspector Ashok Kumar, *Police ADC*

22 April   **State Visit to Britain of King Juan Carlos and Queen Sofia of Spain**
CALVETE, Señor Andres, *Chancery, Spanish Embassy*
HIDALGO ESCOLANO, Señor Fernando, *HM's Household*
IBANEZ HURTADO, Captain Jose, *HM's Household (Communications)*

1 July	**State Visit to Britain of President von Weizsäcker of the Federal Republic of Germany and Freifrau von Weizsäcker** BERTHOLD, Frau Renate, *Personal Assistant to Head of Presidency* DETTMANN, Kapitanleutnant Ullrich Klaus Eberhard, *Housekeeper, Presidency* LAMLA, Herr Lutz Friedrich, *Assistant, Protocol Department*

1987

14 July	**State Visit to Britain of King Hassan II of Morocco** CHERFAOUI, M. Mohamed, *Moroccan Palace Staff* LOULIDI, M. Mohamed, *Office of Private Secretary to HM* MADANI, Lieutenant Abdelkader, *Office of Private Secretary to HM*

1988

17 October	**State Visit to Spain of the Queen and the Duke of Edinburgh** DOMINGUEZ RAMIREZ, Captain Fernando Javier, *Motorcade Official* DELGADO DIESTRO, Captain Leopoldo, *Motorcade Official* MOTA CAMPOS, Captain Antonio, *Military Household* NUNEZ YANEZ, Lieutenant José Ramon, *Military Household* COLLO, Lieutenant Arturo L. *Military Household* GALLEGO CALVO, Lieutenant Julian, *Military Household* VILLAI NUEVA, Lieutenant Arturo Luis Coeello, *Military Household* MATA, Don Juan Carlos de la, *Administrator, Prado Palace* POBLET, Miss Elena Gonzalez, *Administrator, Escorial* BOTELLA SANCHEZ, Don Rafael, *Administrator, Alcazar Palace* HERNANDEZ GARCIA, Miss Ana Maria, *Protocol* HERRERO GARCIA, Miss Julia, *Protocol* BELZUZ, Don Luis, *ADC to Prime Minister* MORALEJO, Captain Antonio, *ADC to Prime Minister* ANDREV ARDURA, Don Jesus, *Government Spokesman's Office*
8 November	**State Visit to Britain of President Abdou Diouf of Senegal and Madame Abdou Diouf** MBENGUE, Monsieur Aloyse, *Private Secretary to President* SAKHO, Monsieur Abdou, *Private Secretary*

1989

9 May	**State Visit to Britain of President Babangida of Nigeria** BELLO, Lieutenant-Colonel U.K., *ADC* WALI, Dr S.S., *Chief Physician* ONABULE, Chief Duro, *Chief Press Secretary*

1990

25 June	**State Visit to Iceland of the Queen and the Duke of Edinburgh** KRISTJANSDOTTIR, Mrs Vilborg G. *Office of the President* JONSDOTTIR, Mrs Sigridur H. *Special Assistant, Office of the President*
23 October	**State Visit to Britain of President Cossiga of Italy and Signora Cossiga** TOMBOLINI, Signor Felice, *of the Presidency* BISOGNIERO, Signor Claudio, *of the Presidency* BRIZZI, Signora Anna Maria, *Personal Secretary to President* SPOLITI, Signor Dionisio, *of the Presidency* MASSARI, Signor Maurizio, *First Secretary, Italian Embassy* MORRONI, Signor Ciro, *of Italian Embassy* BERTOLOTTI, Signora Anna Maria, *of the Italian Embassy* CRANA, Signora Maria Teresa Romani, *of the Italian Embassy* ATTORRE, Signor Vito, *of the Italian Embassy*

1991

1992

9 June	**State Visit to France of the Queen and the Duke of Edinburgh** BLANC, M. Yannick Stephane, *Deputy Prefect* BREARD, M. Michel BURGOS, M. André, *Director of Mayor of Bordeaux Office* CAMBOURNAC, Lieutenant-Colonel Thierry Jean Tony

CAMPET, Le Commissaire Jean François, *Security Officer*
CAUCHARD, M. Jerome Daniel
CORNO, Lieutenant-Colonel Louis
COTTE, M. Jean-Michel, *Press Officer*
DAVAINE, M. Camille
DU PASQUIER, Mme Isabelle Marie Jenny
ZWANG-GRAILLOT, Mme Michelle
LANDAU, Mme Evelyne
LESCURE, M. Yves
ROLLAND, M. Jean-Luc Michel Gerard, *Director of Office of the Prefect*
ROUSSON, M. Guillaume Jean
CONNES-ROUX, Mme Elizabeth Marguerite, *of the Quai d'Orsay*
TAINGUY, Le Capitaine de Fregate Yann Marie Leopold
VOINDROT, M. Alain

19 October   **State Visit to Germany of the Queen and the Duke of Edinburgh**
ANKERMANN, Herr Rolf, *Assistant Co-ordinator*
ARENDS, Herr Friedrich Wilhelm, *Assistant Secretary, Protocol*
STEINFORT, Miss Elizabeth, *British Interests Section, British Embassy*
RENZ-MORITZ, Mrs Lori Virginia, *Press Officer, British Embassy, Berlin*

3 November   **State Visit to Britain of the Sultan of Brunei Darussalam and the Raja Isteri**
BAGOL, Lieutenant-Colonel Abas, *ADC to the Sultan*

1993

27 April   **State Visit to Britain of President Soares of Portugal and Senhora Soares**
RIBEIRO DE ALMEIDA, Joao, *Protocol Service*
PINHEIRO MARQUES, Antonio, *Protocol Service*

1994

5 July   **State Visit to Britain of King Harald and Queen Sonja of Norway**
SCHREINER, Jon Henrik, *Royal Butler and Head Waiter*
WINNER, Mrs Marianne, *Vice-Consul, Norwegian Embassy*

1995

17 October   **State Visit to Britain of the President of Finland and Mrs Ahtisaari**
KUISMA, Mrs Kaija, *Secretary*

1996

17 May   **State Visit to Britain of the President of the French Republic and Madame Chirac**
CORAIL, Monsieur Louis de, *Protocol Officer*
PETIT, Monsieur Pierre, *Protocol Officer*
MORLOT, *Intendant, Elysée Palace*
CHAPPEDELAINE, Monsieur Bernard, *Second Secretary, French Embassy*
FRIES, Monsieur Charles, *Press Counsellor, French Embassy*
KRAITSWOTS, Madame Janine, *First Secretary, French Embassy*
CHAMBARD, Monsieur Oliver, *First Secretary, French Embassy*
ASVAZADOURIAN, Monsieur Jean-Pierre, *First Secretary*
BARBRY, Monsieur Philippe, *Consul*

28 October   **State Visit to Thailand of the Queen and the Duke of Edinburgh**
KHEAWMEESUAN, Khun Pensri, *Special Grade Official, Royal Chamberlain's Division*
PUSAPARESA, Captain Comsun, *Permanent ADC*
KATANYOO, Mr Prasert, *in charge of Boromabiman Palace*

1997–8

2000

16 February   **State Visit to Britain of Queen Margrethe II of Denmark and Prince Henrik**
SØRENSEN, Henrik, *Attacbé (Administration), Royal Danish Embassy*
LARSEN, Steen Kudsk

AWARDS OF
THE ROYAL VICTORIAN
MEDAL (HONORARY)

═══

These names have been taken from handwritten Registers,
the interpretation of which has not always been clear.
The authors would be pleased to hear of any errors or omissions,
for which they apologise in advance.

QUEEN VICTORIA: RVM, SILVER

1896

30 June	**Czar's Coronation**
	COMSHKINE, Gregory, *Steward*
	DANIKEVSKI, Arlo, *Chief Guard on Train to Moscow*
	OREL, Leonti, *Kammers Kosack der Kaiserin Maria Feodorovna*
	SCHMIDT
30 October	**Czar's visit to Balmoral and at HIM's Coronation**
	JANAW, Jean, *Valet to Empress of Russia*
	KOJINE, Nicolas, *Emperor's Chasseur*
	MIKHAYLOW, Jean, *Emperor's Courier*
	POUSTINNIKOW, Nicolas, *Cossack*
	RADTZIKH, Nicolas, *Emperor's Valet*
	SMIRNOW, Jean, *Chancellor's Clerk*

1897

April	**The Queen's visit to Cimiez**
	ASST, *Telegraphist*
	POULP, *Gendarmerie du Maréchal des Logis*

1898

18 September	VOIGHT, *Staatstrompeter, of The Queen's German Regiment*

1899

November	**German Emperor's visit to Windsor**
	BULKOW, *Sattelmeister*
	HOEPFNER, *Kammerdiener*
	MÜLLER, *Wachtmeister*
	MUSEWALD, *Wachtmeister of the Queen's Prussian Dragoon Guards*
	ROLLFING, *Kammerdiener*
	RUDOLPH, *Wachtmeister*
	SCHULZ, *Kammerdiener*

1900

1901

January	**Duke of Connaught's visit to Berlin – Bicentenary Celebrations of the Foundation of the Prussian Monarchy**
	ASMUS, *Vice-Corporal of Gendarmes*
	DOMBROVSKI, *Kammerdiener*
	WIESE, *Leibjäger*
	WILKEN, *Sergeant Major of the Castle Guard*
February	**Funeral of Queen Victoria**
	BUBLITZ, *Sergeant Major Queen Victoria's Regiment Dragoon Guards*

July	Visit to Britain of Grand Duke Michael of Russia

July   **Visit to Britain of Grand Duke Michael of Russia**
BERNARD, Jules, *Cook to HIH*
ZAHREN, William, *Butler to HIH*

17 December   NIELSEN, Laks, *Cup Bearer to King Christian IX of Denmark*
HANSEN, Niels, *Chasseur to King Christian IX of Denmark*

SOUSA, John Philip, *Bandmaster*

1902

27 January   **The Prince of Wales's visit to Berlin**
DETSON, Wilhelm, *Sergeant-Major, Palace Guards*
HENNECKE, Ernst, *Sergeant-Major, Royal Gendarmarie*
KALBHENN, Artur, *Court Courier*
WINDELBARDT, Carl, *Court Coachman Royal Mews, Berlin*

17 May   **The Duke of Connaught's visit to Madrid**
AFHERA, y Bano Cefurino, *Coachman to the King of Spain*

June   **The Coronation of King Edward VII**
JENSEN, Jens Peter, *Sergeant-Major, Danish Guard Hussar Regt*
MANKE, Hugo, *Sergeant-Major*
WIEST, Hermann, *Sergeant-Major*

14 November   **The German Emperor's visit to Sandringham**
BRUCHMILLER, T., *Jaeger*
CAPPEL, L.
GROSSER, H.
HABY, F., *Hairdresser*
LOTZE, S.
WREDE, A., *Garderobier*

22 November   **The King of Portugal's visit to Britain**
BORGES, D.
RUAST, Amadin

1903-6

1907

11 June   **Visit to Britain of King Frederik & Queen Louise of Denmark**
HANSEN, Niels, *Chasseur to King of Denmark*

1908-12

1913

January   KAKIONSIS, Spiro, *Valet to King of the Hellenes*
VENVRIOS, Soterius, *Laquai de Palais, King of the Hellenes*

QUEEN VICTORIA: RVM, BRONZE

1896

30 June   **Czar's Coronation**
REYROFF, Michael, *Groom at the Imperial Stables*

30 October   **Czar's visit to Balmoral**
LADUNG, Antoine, *Garderobier to the Empress of Russia*
SIPOVITCH, Alexander, *Footman to the Grand Duchess Olga*

1897-8

1899

23 November	German Emperor's visit to Windsor
	DIEGMAN, *Valet*
	WIESE, *Valet*
	DANIEL, *Footman*
	GEHRKE, *Footman*
	LEITSEL, *Footman*
	TABBERT, *Footman*
	VOLZ, *Footman*

1900

1901

February	Funeral of Queen Victoria
	SCHULZE, *Lance-Corporal, Queen Victoria's Regt of Dragoon Guards*
	ZOCHERT, *Lance-Corporal, Queen Victoria's Regt of Dragoon Guards*
	SELIGSOHN, *Queen Victoria's Regt of Dragoon Guards*
July	HOPFNER, Konrad, *Footman to Grand Duke Michael of Russia*
August	EBBRECHT, August, *Frankfurt Police Force*

1902

17 May	Duke of Connaught's visit to Madrid
	PORTER, Orinitive, *Servant, British Embassy*
	CARLOS, Martino
	CORTES, Juan, *Servant to the King of Spain*
	DIAZ, Manuel, *Servant to the King of Spain*
	JIMENER Y JIMENEZ, Petro, *Footman to the King of Spain*
	NAVARO, Salvador, *Servant to the King of Spain*
	PINTO, Ignatis, *Servant to the King of Spain*
June	MICHALS, Hermann, *Private*
	ZOAKE, Otto, *Lance-Corporal*
14 November	German Emperor's visit to Sandringham
	PLAPPERT, *Packer*
	STATTINOPOULOS, Nicholas, *Laquai du Palais*
	SANTAS, Antonio des

EDWARD VII: RVM, SILVER

1903

7 April	King Edward VII's visit to Portugal
	METZENER, Carlos, *Page of Presence*
	QUARESMA, Francisco Rodriguez, *Page of Presence*
	GOMES, Eduardo de Souza, *Page of Presence*
	SANTOS, João Gomes dos, *Page of Presence*
	TERREIRA, Jose do Patrocinio, *Underintendent of the Palace*
	VILLAR, Pedro de Portugal e Andrade de Kuckembuck, *Underintendent of the Palace*
	TERREIRA, Joaquin, *Underintendent of the Palace*
	FORTUNATO, Juce Vicente, *Steward*
	CORRÊA, Antonio Maria, *Steward*
	NEVES, Guilherme, *Steward*
	CORRÊA, Jose Miguel Fernandos, *Steward*
	GOMES, Joaquim, *Steward*
	SIMOES, Pedro, *Coachman*
	CAPARICA, Bento Antonio, *Coachman*
	LIMA, Luiz Nascimento, *Coachman*
	BAPTISTA, Jose Maria, *Coachman*
	SILVA, Manoel Cyra da, *Detective*
	TAVARES, Sergeant-Major João d'Avellar Pinto, *Portuguese Cavalry Regiment, (No3) of King Edward VII*
	JOAQUIM, Sergeant Genesio, *Portuguese Cavalry Regiment, (No3) of King Edward VII*
	COSTA, Sergeant Cipriaco Rodolpho Nunes Martins, *Portuguese Cavalry Regiment, (No3) of King Edward VII*

30 April	**The King's visit to Rome**
	GATTO, Casiniro, *Warrant Officer of Royal Bodyguard*
	MOUDINI, Vittorio, *Warrant Officer of Royal Bodyguard*
	MARZON, Giovanni, *Warrant Officer of Royal Bodyguard*
	SANTAROSA, Giuseppe, *Chief Clerk*
	MANFRINO, Giuseppe, *Head Footman*
	BONATO, Luigi, *Groom of the Chambers*
	BANDIERINI, Primo, *Page*
	SERPE, Arcangelo, *Coachman and Outrider*
	MUSSO, Giovanni Battista, *Coachman and Outrider*
4 May	**The King's visit to Paris**
	TROUDE, Georges, *Coachman to the President*
	CLERC, Jean Marie, *Steward to the President*
	BOUVIER, Charles, *Cook attached to Royal Train*
	FUNCK, Francois, *Guard of Royal Train*
1 July	**The Khedive of Egypt's visit to Britain**
	HALIL, Aga, *Cafetier to the Khedive*
30 August	**The King's visit to Marienbad**
	HOFMAN, Josef, *Wachtmeister, Gendarmerie*
	KRUPIEZKA, Johann, *Station Master*
	LANGHAUS, Johann J., *Photographer*
	PRUSA, Franz, *Wachtmeister, Gendarmerie*
	SCHWARZ, Johann, *Wachtmeister, Local Police*
	SCHOBER, Hans, *Acting Commissaire*
	TAUER, Johann, *Telegraphist*
9 October	**The King's visit to Vienna**
	WUNDERBALDINGER, Heinrich, *Steward in Attendance on the King*
	ESCHNER, Stephan, *Page in Attendance on the King*
	SACHS, Valentin, *Page in Attendance on the King*
	DUSIL, Franz, *Page in Attendance on the King*
	KETTELER, Eugen, *Leibkammerdiener to the Emperor of Austria*
	WEIGL, Stefan, *NCO Trabanten Leibgarde*
	LANGER, Johann, *NCO on guard, The King's Chamber at the Burg Palace*
	WACHTLER, Franz, *NCO on guard, The King's Chamber at the Burg Palace*
	LIEBSCH, Arsenius, *NCO on guard, The King's Chamber at the Burg Palace*
	NAPOKOI, Franz, *NCO on guard, The King's Chamber at the Burg Palace*
	RÄUSCHL, Adolf, *NCO on guard, The King's Chamber at the Burg Palace*
	FRANZEL, Johann, *Leibgarde Infantericompagnie on guard, The King's Chamber at the Burg Palace*
	SCHLIMMEL, Mathias, *Leibgarde Infantericompagnie on guard, The King's Chamber at the Burg Palace*
	HORNY, Hugo, *Leibgarde Infantericompagnie on guard, The King's Chamber at the Burg Palace*
	HANNA, Michael, *Leibgarde Infantericompagnie on guard, The King's Chamber at the Burg Palace*
	HRYMISZAK, Ladislaus, *Leibgarde Infantericompagnie on guard, The King's Chamber at the Burg Palace*
	CVETKO, Andreas, *Leibgarde Infantericompagnie on guard, The King's Chamber at the Burg Palace*
	LUSCHIN, Jakob, *Leibgarde Infantericompagnie on guard, The King's Chamber at the Burg Palace*
	BRODECKY, Josef, *NCO, Leibgarde Infantericompagnie on guard, The King's Chamber at the Burg Palace*
	SCHMIDT, Mathias, *Table Decker, attached to the King's Train*
	BAYERL, Wenzel, *Chancery Servant, British Embassy*
	KOMARCK, Alois, *Senior NCO on guard of Honour at Franz Josef Station*
	HENGGE, Franz, *Outrider*
	WALTER, Josef, *Coachman*
	ZIELBAUER, Johann, *Coachman*
	BAUER, Adolf, *Sichereitswachtinspector*
	HULAK, Anton, *Sichereitswachtinspector*
	SCHEITHAUER, Josef, *Detective Inspector*
	DRESCHER, Robert, *Band Conductor*
	ZIMMERER, Johann, *Keeper at Lobau*
	STUMVOLL, Louis, *Keeper at Lobau*
	VISSER, Karl, *Dutch Pilot*
21 November	**Visit to Britain of King Vittorio Emanuele III of Italy**
	GIARDINA, Achille, *Marshal of Cuirassiers*
	BIACHI, Andrea, *Garderobier*
	BRUSA, Giovanni, *Second Cook*
	BRIZZOLARA, Agostino, *Commis de Voyage*
	NOVELLO, Isidoro, *Brigadier of Secret Police*
	GINFICI, Domenico, *Agent of Secret Police*

1904

10 February	**The Marriage of Princess Alice of Albany and Prince Alexander of Teck**
	HOFMANN, Karl, *Jäger to the Reigning Prince of Waldeck and Pymont*

GUSSMAN, Jakob, *Kammerdiener to the Queen of Württemberg*
SCHUTZ, Edouard, *Kammerdiener to Duke of Saxe-Coburg and Gotha*
BELZ, Gottlob, *Kammerlakai to the Queen of Württemberg*
VERDELMAN, Louis Georges, *Steward to the Queen Mother of the Netherlands*
ROEL, Louis, *Page to the Queen Mother of the Netherlands*
DREUGHAHN, Johannes, *Leibjager to Prince Bentheim und Steinfurt*

23 March **Funeral of the Duke of Cambridge**
FERDINAND, Julius, *Kammerdiener to Prince Albrecht of Prussia (Regent of Brunswick)*
WEISSKIRCHEN, Fusilier Albert, *President, Kriegs Verein, Ehemaliger 28th Regiment*
ATZ, Sergeant Josef, *Cashier, Kriegs Verein, Ehemaliger 28th Regiment*
STEINFELD, Unteroffizer Engelbert, *Secretary, Kriegs Verein, Ehemaliger 28th Regiment*

8 April **The King's visit to Copenhagen**
RASMUSSEN, Christian, *Coachman, King of Denmark's Household*
CHRISTIANSEN, Lars, *Bandmaster, Danish Hussars of the Guard*
HANSEN, Sergeant-Major Peder Otto, *Danish Hussars of the Guard*
BENTSEN, Staff-Sergeant, *Danish Hussars of Guard*
ANDERSEN, Carl August, *Bandmaster, Danish Life Guards*
IBSEN, Staff-Sergeant Jens Henrik, *Danish Life Guards*

18 April JENSEN, Peter, *Yeoman of the Cellars*
VESTERMARK, Erik, *Valet to Prince Waldemar of Denmark*
GLAD, Hans, *Garderobier, King of Denmark's Household*
NIELSEN, Police Sergeant Frederick Martin, *Danish Police Sergeant*
BRUNING, *Danish Police Sergeant*
SCHMIDT, Police Sergeant, *Danish Police Sergeant*
HANSEN, Paul Frederick, *Chief Cook, to King of Denmark*
FREITAG, Julius Ferdinand, *2nd Cook to King of Denmark*
LARSEN, Lauretz, *Lakai, King of Denmark's Household*

21 April **The Prince of Wales's visit to Vienna**
MEIXNER, Hans, *Oberreiter*
BRANNER, Robert, *Page to the Emperor of Austria*
BERGER, Josef, *Page to the Emperor of Austria*
HALLAZEK, Johann, *Loader to the Emperor of Austria*
HARTIG, Richard, *Second Chancery Servant at British Embassy, Vienna*

April **The Prince of Wales's visit to Stuttgart**
REIBER, Martin, *Page to the King of Württemberg*
STAEHLE, Albert, *Jager to the King of Württemberg*
DRÖGMÖLLER, Wilhelm, *Outrider to the King of Württemberg*

11 June **Visit to Britain of the Archduke Frederick of Austria**
GARTNER, Joseph, *Page to HI and RH*
WINGE, Constantin, *Page to HI and RH*

14 June **Visit to Britain of Prince John of Glücksburg**
HENCKEL, Christian, *Jager to HH*
CHRISTENSEN, Christian, *Valet to HH*

Visit to Britain of the Duchess of Saxe-Coburg and Gotha
WIENER, Lorenz, *Kammerdiener to HR and IH*

30 June **The King's visit to Kiel**
GRELLA, Wilhelm, *Steward on board the* Hohenzollern
BARTELT, Max, *Registrar and Military Clerk of 9th Army Corps*
POLLINGER, Franz, *Bandmaster on Board the* Hohenzollern
STROBEL, Edmund, *Bandmaster on Board the* Kaiser Wilhelm II, *1st Coy. of 2nd Marine Division*
POTT, Ernst, *Bandmaster 1st Marine Division*
HAUSLER, Conrad, *Hamburg*
FAJE, Captain H., *in charge of the Revenue Steamer* Hamburg
GOEDE, Johann George, *Registrar of the Baltic Naval Station*
TREUVALD, Gustav, *Chief Pilot of the Canal*
BARTHEL, Ferdinand, *Senior NCO Guard of Honour 2nd Company Hanseatic Infantry 75th Regiment*
SCHRAGE, Robert, *Senior NCO Guard of Honour 1st Guard Regiment zu Fuss*
BERGHOLZ, Paul L.C.B., *Senior NCO 3 Coy 4th Marine Artillery at Brunsbuttel*
KANDZIA, Franz J., *Senior NCO 1st Thuringian Infantry Regiment No31*
WALTHER, Franz, *Senior NCO 3rd Coy Naval Guard of Honour at Kiel*
VANESS, Rudolf O.E., *Senior NCO 2nd Hanseatic Infantry No 76 Guard of Honour Station at Hamburg*
STEFFENS, J.G. Wilhelm, *Bandmaster 2nd Hanseatic Infantry No 76 at Town Hall, Hamburg*
HETTCHE, Johannes G., *Sergeant-Major vom Husaren Regiment Konigin Wilhelmina der Niederlande (Hannoversches) No15*

28 July **Visit of the Duke of Sparta to the King at Goodwood**
BURYANIS, Achilles, *Valet to HRH*

26 August	**Christening of the Cesarevitch**
	TARASSOFF, Wiacheslaw, *Page in attendance on Prince Louis of Battenberg when representing HM in St Petersburg*
	ZANOTTI, Francesco, *Page to Prince Louis of Battenberg*

August	**The King's visit to Marienbad**
	SCHEIBEL, Josef, *Jaeger to the Emperor of Austria*
	INGERTO, Franz, *Coachman to the Emperor of Austria*
	MACH, Franz, *Head Keeper to Prince Trautmansdorff-Weinsberg*
	MANUEL, Berthold, *Detective Inspector, Vienna*
	PFEIFFER, Johann, *Detective Inspector, Vienna*
	KRACH, Ignaz Richard, *Detective Inspector, Vienna*
	BERNDL, Rudolf, *Detective Inspector, Vienna*
	NAPISTEK, Anton, *Detective Inspector, Vienna*
	SPACEK, Franz, *Detective Inspector, Vienna*
	FORT, Anton, *Detective Inspector, Vienna*
	DVORAK, Friedrich, *Detective Inspector, Vienna*

| 19 October | **Prince Christian of Schleswig Holstein representing the King at the Funeral of the King of Saxony** |
| | KEIL, Andreas Trangott, *Sergeant der I Kompagnie in Königlich Sächsichen Schützen I Fusilier Regiment Prince George No 108, attached to HRH* |

| 16 November | **Visit to Britain of King Carlos of Portugal** |
| | MOTTA, Antonio, *1st Valet to the Queen of Portugal* |

4 December	**Prince Arthur of Connaught's visit to Italy to represent the King at the Christening of the Prince of Piedmont**
	AZZALI, Ferdinando, *Page attached to HRH*
	FRAIA, Giovanni, *Coachman attached to HRH*
	BARTOLI, Settimio, *Caretaker of HRH's Apartments*

1905

27 February	**Prince Arthur of Connaught's visit to Berlin for Opening of Protestant Cathedral**
	FRANZ, Carl, *Page*
	EISENBACH, Heinrich, *Footman*
	ENGELBRECHT, Fritz, *Valet*
	THOMEL, Frangott, *Portier*
	GEHRICKE, Wachtmeister, *Hussar Regiment von Zieten (Brandenburg) No 3*
	KAMENSKI, Vice Wachtmeister, *Hussar Regiment von Zeiten (Brandenburg) No 3*

| 8 March | **Prince Ferdinand of Bulgaria's visit to Britain** |
| | MEHMEDOFF, Hassan, *1st Valet de Chambre* |

| 4 April | **The King's Mediterranean Cruise** |
| | COSTE, François, *Maréchal des Logis, in charge of Artillery Horses drawing carriage at Phillipeville* |

4 May	**The King's Mediterranean Cruise**
	LATAPIE, Leon Jules, *Inspector, Direction Generale de Recherches, Préfecture de Police*
	CORTOT, Auguste Paul, *Inspector, Direction Generale de Recherches, Préfecture de Police*

9 May	**Queen Alexandra's visit to Greece**
	CANTOROS, Panayiotio, *Chief Cook*
	KRÖL, Wilhelm, *Outrider*
	ETHIMIOU, Constantine, *1st Postillian*
	MACROPOULOS, Dimitri, *1st Groom of the Chambers*
	SAMOILIS, Constantin, *2nd Groom of the Chambers*
	LALIA, James, *Footman*

6 June	**Visit to Britain of King Alfonso of Spain**
	RODRIGUEZ, Filoteo, *Usher, Lord Chamberlain's Department*
	FERNANDEZ, Sabas, *Usher, Spanish Foreign Office*
	HIJAR, Gorge, *Valet to the King of Spain*
	GARCIA, David, *Military Usher*

15 June	**Marriage of Princess Margaret of Connaught and Prince Gustavus Adolphus of Sweden and Norway**
	BORG, Charles Oscar, *Valet to the Crown Prince of Sweden and Norway*
	NILSSON, Johann Emil, *Valet to Prince Gustavus Adolphus*
	HALLBERG, Gustaf, *Page to the Crown Princess of Sweden and Norway*
	BERGMAN, Gustav Adolf, *Valet to Prince William of Sweden and Norway*
	BREHMER, Nils, *Valet to Prince Eugene of Sweden and Norway*

| 12 July | **The Prince of Wales giving a cup to the Regiment** |
| | FELLENBERG, Reinhold Karl Romanus, *Bandmaster (Staff Trumpeter) 8th Prussian Curassiers Regiment* |

	Prince Arthur of Connaught's visit to Berlin to represent HM at the Marriage of the Crown Prince of Prussia
	SCHASSE, Heinrich, *Jäger*
	FRAEDRICH, Gustav, *Castelan*

REHBINDER, *Page*
SCHACHT, Sergeant Ernst, *Colour Bearer of Guard of Honour, 3rd Garde Grenadier Regiment*
THYSSEN, Wilhelm, *Coachman*
PEINEMANN, *Company Sergeant-Major*

| 19 July | **The Duke of Connaught representing HM at the Coming of Age of the Duke of Saxe-Coburg and Gotha** |

HERKLOTZ, Oscar, *Page to the Duke of Saxe-Coburg and Gotha*
WOLF, Ernst, *Vice Sergeant-Major 3 Coy 6th Thuringen Regiment No95*
GREBHAHN, Paul, *Sergeant-Major 4th Coy 6th Thuringen Regiment No95*
KIRCHHOFER, Hermann, *Castelan of the Ehrenburg Palace, Coburg*
JACOBI, Karl, *Steward of the Cellars, Coburg*

| 16 August | **The King's visit to Marienbad** |

PIETSCH, Ferdinand, *Saalkammerdiener to the Emperor of Austria*
SKODA, Richard, *Head Cook to the Emperor of Austria*
ZEINER, Ludwig, *Chief of Stables to the Emperor of Austria*
HOSCHTALEK, Johann, *Jager to the Emperor of Austria*

| 30 August | **The King's visit to Marienbad** |

IOVANOVITCH, Ilija, *Valet to Prince Nicholas of Montenegro*

| 7 September | **The King's visit to Marienbad** |

BINDL, Georges, *Detective Inspector*
SWOBODA, Henry, *Detective 1st Class*
KUTSCHERA, Francis, *Detective 1st Class*
WÜNSCH, Ferdinand, *Detective 1st Class, Prague Officer*
LEHRER, Wenzel, *Detective 1st Class, Prague Officer*
KOCI, Wenzel, *Detective 1st Class, Prague Officer*
RICHTER, Anton, *Telegraph Clerk*

| 27 November | **Visit to Britain of the King of the Hellenes** |

KAKIOUSIS, Spiro, *Valet to the King of the Hellenes*
VEVRIOS, Sotirios, *Laquai du Palais*
HELIOPOULOS, Basile J., *Valet to Prince Nicholas*

1906

| 26 February | **Queen Alexandra's visit to Denmark** |

HANSEN, Niels, *Restaurateur*

| 6 March | **The King's visit to Paris** |

MAUCEAU, Jules, *Head Facteur in Chancery, HM Embassy, Paris for over 32 years*

| 16 March | **Prince Arthur of Connaught's Garter Mission to Japan** |

EBISAWA, Sergeant-Major Kioji, *1st Infantry Regiment, Imperial Guard Tokyo*
ASAKURA, Yoshitaka, *Exterior Section, Imperial Household*
YAMASHITA, Atsunobu, *Exterior Section, Imperial Household*
OYAGI, Nagamichi, *Cuisine Bureau, Imperial Household*
AGATA, Naoki, *Palace Bureau, Imperial Household*
KAWATSURA, Tokusabura, *Board of Building, Imperial Household*
JAGA, Hajime, *Coachman, Imperial Household*
SAWAGI, Naoyuki, *Hunting Bureau, Imperial Household*
NEBAYASHI, Seiichi, *Hunting Bureau, Imperial Household*
PEACOCK, Mr, *Messenger, British Embassy, Tokyo*

| 19 March | **The Prince of Wales's visit to Cairo returning from the Indian Tour** |

BOEGHIN, François, *The Khedive of Egypt's Head Coachman*
HACHIM, Mohamed, *The Khedive of Egypt's Head Butler*

| 30 March | **The King's visit to Biarritz** |

LAFFONT, Pierre Adrian, *Sous Chef de Musique du 57 d'Infanterie, Bordeaux*

| 2 April | |

TREPIET, Auguste, *Secrétaire au Commissaire Police, Biarritz*
COLLARDEY, Pierre, *Inspecteur Spécial*
CLAUSS, Paul, *Inspecteur Spécial*
CARETTE, Charles Frederic, *Inspecteur Spécial, Paris*
OLIVI, Lucien Muzio, *Inspecteur Spécial, Paris, employed at Biarritz*

| 13 April | **The King's visit to Corfu** |

CACHINZI, Constantine, *Superintendent of Palace, Corfu*

| 22 April | **The visit of their Majesties to Athens** |

THÔMAS, Photios, *2nd Valet to King of the Hellenes*
NERY, Pericles, *Chasseur to King of the Hellenes*
MELANCHRIMOS, André, *Maître d'Hôtel to King of the Hellenes*
MIKES, Christos, *2nd Maître d'Hôtel to King of the Hellenes*
OAPAPOSTOLOU, Jean, *1st Valet de Pieds to King of the Hellenes*
RIZOPOULOS, Panayokis, *Valet de Pieds to the Queen of the Hellenes*

OOLITOPOODY, André, *Valet to Prince George of Greece*
TRIANTAPHYLOPOULO, Jean, *Sergeant of the Gendarmerie*
DALIS, Christos, *Sergeant of the Royal Guard*
BAKALIS, Antonis, *Porter to the King of the Hellenes*
SAMOURIS, Alexis, *Steward to the Duke of Sparta*
MARTIN, Adrien, *Steward to Prince Nicholas of Greece*
ELIAS, Julius, *Coachman for King Edward*
GREK, Josif, *Coachman for Queen Alexandra*
THEODOROPOULOS, George, *Coachman for Princess Victoria*
KASPER, Karl, *Chauffeur*

6 June	**Marriage of the King of Spain**

GOMEZ, Florentino, *Courier, Royal Outrider*
ESCAMILLA, Manuel, *Valet 1st Class*
CACCAMO, Jose, *Maître d'Hôtel*
REISCO, Servando, *Maître d'Hôtel*
TRICAZ, José, *Coachman, 1st Class (drove TM's carriage and was wounded by the bomb explosion)*
MOLINA, Juban, *Usher of Antechamber*

18 August	**The King's visit to Cronberg**

ECK, Ludwig, *Haushofmeister to Prince Frederick Charles of Hesse*
REBMANN, Albert, *Leibkutscher to Prince Frederick Charles of Hesse*
MÖLLER, Wilhelm, *Hofkutscher to Prince Frederick Charles of Hesse*
KRIEGER, Johann, *Schlosser to Prince Frederick Charles of Hesse*
WERNER, Wilhelm, *Chauffeur to the German Emperor*

7 September	**The King's visit to Marienbad**

WOBURKA, Eduard, *Detective Inspector from Vienna*
KÜSS, Josef, *Detective*
KOMOLI, Johann, *Detective*
ZOBL, Karl, *Detective*
LUKESCH, Franz, *Detective*

20 September	**The Duke of Connaught's visit to Karlsruhe**

KRATZMANN, Heinrich, *Lakai (Footman 1st Class)*
GUADIG, Paul, *Sergeant*

1 October	DICKOPF, John Peter, *in celebration of his 50th Anniversary of being in VIIIth Curassiers (Prince of Wales Regiment)*

9 November	**Prince Philip of Saxe-Coburg's visit to Sandringham**

STOCKHAMER, Fridolin, *Leibjäger to Prince Philip*

14 December	**The King and Queen of Norway's visit to Britain**

MOSER, Auguste Emanuel, *Chef to the King of Norway*

1907

28 January	**The visit of Prince Charles of Hohenzollern to Windsor Castle**

SKRIPEK, Johann Friederich, *Corporal in the Landwehr, Valet to HIH*

9 February	**The King's visit to Paris**

LEGRAND, Gabriel Louis, *Police Inspector, Paris*
FAUCON, Abel, *Police Inspector, Paris*
MONTAGUE, Pierre Maxime, *Police Inspector, Paris*
LESTRADE, Jean Alexandre, *Police Inspector, Paris*
LEVET, Eugene, *Controleur des Wagons Lits*

5 March	**Prince Alexander of Teck's Special Mission to invest the Prince of the Netherlands with the Order of the Bath**

VACHER, Pierre Louis Erneste, *Valet to the Prince of the Netherlands*

4 April	**The King's visit to Biarritz**

PERIA, Alfredo, *Commissaire Spécial*

9 April	**The King's visit to Cartagena**

IDOATE, Carlos, *Inspector of Police, Madrid*
ESCRIBANO, Fulgencio, *Police Inspector, Paris*
GARCIA, Fernando Alcon, *Police Inspector, Paris*
GRAS Y PRATS, D. Juan, *Jardinero Mayor*
CHERNOT, Luis, *Cocinero Mayor de Palacio*
CASADO, Mariano Marcos, *Ayuda de Camara del Infante Don Fernando*
BENITO, Sanchez Mariano y, *Porter Mayor de la Inspeccion General*
JIMINEZ, Lorenzo, *Chasseur du Duc de Sotomayor*
FUERTES, Fuertes y, Sancho

26 April	**The King's visit to Palermo**

TOMAJO, Aristide, *Police Agent*

29 April	The King's visit to Naples
	ZIRRILLI, Giovanni, *Inspector of Police, Naples*
	CACCIOPPOLE, Giuseppe, *Telegraph Clerk, Naples*
	NACCIARONE, Enrico, *Telegraph Clerk, Naples*
	GAGLIARDI, Captain Andrea, *Captain of the Police Force, Naples*

7 May — **Visit to Britain of Prince Fushimi of Japan**
ISUDA, Motojiro, *Attaché to the Household of Prince Fushimi*
KIRIOSAWA, Shigetaro, *Attaché to the Bureau of Ceremonies of the Imperial Household*

18 May — **Prince Arthur of Connaught's visit to Madrid for Christening of the Prince of Asturias**
GOMEZ, Sergeant Tomas Garcia, *Batallon de Cazadores, Madrid*
CABOT, Miguel, *Groom of the Chamber to the King of Spain*
COURTENAUT, Antonin, *Chauffeur to the King of Spain*
FERNANDEZ, Rodriguez Pablo, *Coachman to the King of Spain*
PEVELLO Y MORALES, Lucas, *Outrider, Royal Stables, Madrid*

11 June — **Visit to Britain of King Frederik VIII and Queen Louise of Denmark**
JOHANSEN, Niels Peter, *Valet to the Queen of Denmark*
MORTENSEN, Jens August, *Lackey to the King of Denmark*
HANSEN, Hans Jacob Christoffer, *Lackey to the Queen of Denmark*

24 June — **King of Siam's visit to Windsor**
NAI On, *Valet to the King of Siam*
NAI Sri, *Valet to the King of Siam*
HARTMANN, Otto, *Valet to the King of Siam*

2 July — **Visit to Britain of the Grand Duke of Hesse**
DERN, Jakob, *Page to HRH*

14 August — **The King's visit to Wilhelmshöhe**
FALLINSKI, Paul, *Police Detective*
RAU, Alexander, *Hoffourier*
VERGIN, Ferdinand, *Oberkastellan*
FRENZEL, Robert, *Master Saddler*
THIEL, Sergeant Franz, *Orderly 1st Garde Dragoner Regiment*
PEECK, Sergeant Fritz, *Orderly 1st Garde Dragoner Regiment*
BECKER, Sergeant Franz, *Orderly 1st Garde Dragoner Regiment*
PAREY, Sergeant Emil, *Orderly 1st Garde Dragoner Regiment*
UBER, Sergeant Reinhold, *Orderly 1st Garde Dragoner Regiment*
ALBRECHT, Karl, *Wachtmeister, 1st Garde Dragoner Regiment*
BARTZ, Otto R.H., *Vice Wachtmeister, Husaren Regiment Fürst Blücher von Wahlstatt (Pommersches) No 5*
SKRABLIES, August H., *Wachtmeister, Husaren Regiment Fürst Blücher von Wahlstatt (Pommersches) No 5*
PAUKONIN, Gustav Adolf, *Wachtmeister, Husaren Regiment Fürst Blücher von Wahlstatt (Pommersches) No 5*
BIESKE, Karl H.J., *Wachtmeister, Husaren Regiment Fürst Blücher von Wahlstatt (Pommersches) No 5*
EBEL, Karl F.W., *Wachtmeister, Husaren Regiment Fürst Blücher von Wahlstatt (Pommersches) No 5*
PITSIG, Arthur K., *Wachtmeister, Husaren Regiment Fürst Blücher von Wahlstatt (Pommersches) No 5*
HAUKE, Sergeant-Major Richard, *Royal Prussian Castle Guard Company*
RODER, Sergeant Conrad, *Royal Prussian Castle Guard Company*
WANNER, Ernst Friedrich, *Chauffeur to the German Empress*

15 August — **The King's visit to Ischl**
GERSTNER, Rudolf, *Kammerdiener*
MAHR, Bandmaster Gustav, *Military Bandmaster (Tiroler Kaiserjäger Regiment No4)*

6 September — **The King's visit to Marienbad**
DRESCHER, Bandmaster Otto, *Musical Director (Tiroler Kaiserjäger Regiment No3)*
HELLER, Josef, *Gendarmerie Police*
JACKL, Heinrich, *Telephone Clerk*
KOHNHAUSER, Franz, *Maître d'Hôtel, Weimar*
VERERA, Adolf, *Detective*
PONDELICEK, Franz, *Detective*

The Duke of Connaught's visit to Vienna
KATRIEN, Wachtmeister Karl, *4th Austrian Hussars*
BIERSACK, Leopold, *Head Coachman*
RICHTER, Otto Paul, *Steward at British Embassy*

October — **The Duke of Connaught's visit to Karlsruhe**
WIEDEMANN, August, *Page*

9 November — **Visit of the King and Queen of Spain to Sandringham**
COLADO, Jose, *Servant to the King of Spain*

12 November — **Visit to Windsor of the Emperor and Empress, King and Queen of Prussia**
VICKE, Emil, *Servant to the German Emperor*
GAUTZER, Max, *Leibjäger to the German Emperor*
BLESS, Richard, *Leibjäger to the German Emperor*

HABY, Francois, *Leibjäger to the German Emperor*
MULLER, Gustav Adolf, *Servant to the German Emperor*

20 December   **Visit of The King and Queen of Spain to Britain**
RUVIRA, Mauricio, *Servant of the Palace attached to the Prince of Asturias*

1908

8 February   **Prince Arthur of Connaught's visit to Lisbon to attend the Funeral of the Late King of Portugal**
GONCALVES, Antonio, *Page of the Chamber*
ANTUNES, Alberto, *Chauffeur of the King's motor car*

26 March   **The Prince of Wales's Inspection of the Regiment at Cologne**
JUNKER, Friedrich Karl, *Sgt Major 1st Squadron Curassier Regiment Graf Gessler, (Rheinisches) No. 8*
SCHMIDT, Karl Friedrich Wilhelm, *Bandmaster 1st Squadron Curassier Regiment Graf Gessler, (Rheinisches) No. 8*

14 April   **The King's visit to Biarritz**
ETCHEVERRY, Felix, *Commis Principal des Postes Telegraphes, Biarritz*
CULLIERE, Jean Eugene Emile, *Maréchal des Logis, Chef de Gendarmerie*
CAISSO, Emile Frederic, *Sous Chef de Musique au 57 Regiment d'Infanterie*

18 April   **Visit to Britain of Empress Marie Feodorovna of Russia**
PRODEOUS, Sergeant Nicolas, *Agent of Police*
MEYER, Sergeant Charles, *Agent of Police*
KOUDINOFF, André, *Cosaque de Garde*

25 April   **The King's visit to Copenhagen**
PETERSEN, Karl Vilhelm, *Sergeant, Danish Hussars of the Guard*
CHRISTENSEN, Jens Peter Dires Larsen, *Sergeant, Danish Hussars of the Guard*
SIEVERTS, Eduard August Johan Vilhelm, *Sergeant, Danish Hussars of the Guard*
MADSEN, Anders Jacob, *Sergeant, Danish Hussars of the Guard*
HAVONDAL, Hans Pedersen, *Sergeant, Danish Hussars of the Guard*
CHRISTENSEN, Rasmus, *Staff-Sergeant, Danish Hussars of the Guard*
MUNK, S.C., *Page*
CASPERSEN, Niels Martin, *Detective*
MIKKELSEN, Mikkel, *Detective*
NIELSEN, Valdemar, *Bandmaster*
PETERSEN, Rasmus Albert, *Chauffeur to Princess Valdemar of Denmark*
PETERSEN, Niels, *Coachman*
CHRISTENSEN, Therkel, *Coachman (State)*
TIPPERUP, Hans Peter Jürgensen, *Coachman (State)*

27 April   **The King's visit to Stockholm**
OLSSON, Eduard Olof, *Chauffeur*
WRETHOLM, Tor, *Police Detective*
CARLSSON, Carl Arvid, *Sergeant, Royal Göta Footguards*
STRUFUE, Johan Atel Gustaf, *Sergeant, Royal Swedish Horse Guards*
JANASSON, Adolf Hjalmar, *Sergeant, Royal Svea Footguards*
BERGLUND, Wilholm, *Jäger*
STERN, August, *Footman*
GRÜNWALL, Berndt August, *Coachman*
OLSSON, Nils, *Coachman*
BJÖRK, Carl Johann, *Coachman*
JACOBSON, Johan Gustaf, *Butler*
EKBLAD, Carl August, *Table Decker*
OLSSON, Erik Gustaf, *Table Decker*
CARLSSON, Johan, *Page*
HJELM, Johan August, *Page*
LUNDSTRÖM, Lars Gustaf, *Page*
CHRUZANDER, Sergeant Oscar, *Swedish Dragoons of the Guard*

2 May   **The King's visit to Norway**
PAULSEN, Sergeant Hans Peter, *Sergeant of Police*
HUSE, Sergeant Bernt, *Sergeant of Police*
HANSEN, Sergeant Waldemar, *Sergeant of Police*
RÖBERG, Sergeant Nicolai, *Sergeant of Police*
ROED, Sergeant Bernhard, *Sergeant of Police*
LARSSEN, Sergeant Redvald, *Sergeant of Police*
AAGMAES, Sivert Ibs, *Telegraphist*
DOMAAS, Peter, *Telegraphist*
GAARDER, Even, *Vagtmeister*
JOHANSEN, Ludwig, *Vagtmeister*

28 May   **Visit of President Fallières of the French Republic to Britain**
COTIGNAC, Joseph, *Inspector of Police, Paris*

TOUSSAINT, Nicolas, *Inspector of Police, Paris*
DÉCARNELLE, Paul, *Valet de Chambre*
PRIME, Louis Victor, *Valet de Pied*
HUBERT, Pierre Marie Joseph, *Gardien de Bureau*
RIMBAULT, Auguste, *Chef des Huissiers*
JACQUEMOT, Jean, *Huissier*
CHATAIGNON, Pierre, *Argentier*
DIOLEZ, Joseph, *Gardien de Bureau*
PEIGNE, Paul, *Homme de Service*

10 June	**The King's visit to Reval**

ADARDASSOFF, Etienne, *Footman*
AKOULOFF, Nicolas, *Footman*
BERNGARDT, Nicolas, *Footman*
CHWETZ, Potape, *Clerk*
COUPRIANOFF, Dimitri, *Valet to Minister of Marine*
DEREVENKO, André, *Sailor, Private Servant to the Cesarevitch*
DWORETSKY, Nicolas, *Clerk*
GRIGORIEFF, Alexandre, *Clerk*
GROOFF, Abraham, *Clerk*
HERZOG, Jacob, *Valet to the Minister for Foreign Affairs*
IVANOFF, Ivan, *Clerk, Chancellerie Militaire*
IWOUCHKINE, Jean, *Footman*
KORNIKINE, Theodore, *Footman*
KOKITCHEFF, Vladimir, *Cook*
KLIMOFF, Alexander, *Messenger*
KLUEFF, Basile, *Clerk*
KRASTOVSKY, Ignace, *Messenger*
LADOUNGE, Antoine, *Wardrobe man to the Empress of Russia*
LAVRENTIEFF, Ivan, *Messenger to the Minister of Marine*
MAKAROFF, Cosme, *Cellarman*
MALAHOWSKY, Casimir, *Valet to Prime Minister*
NASSOUTA, Alexandre, *Messenger*
NIKITINE, Demetrius, *Clerk*
ONOPRIAINKO, Abdias, *Messenger to Prime Minister*
POLESSKY, Michel, *Cellarman*
SACHALINE, Tercenty, *Valet to the Minister of the Court*
SEMENOFF, Pierre Petrovitch, *Valet to Grand Duke Michael Alexandrovitch*
SKABINSKY, George, *Clerk*
SOKOLOFF, Wladimir, *Valet to Prince Orloff*
TETERIATMIKOFF, Nikita, *Wardrobe man to the Emperor of Russia*
WASSILEVSKY, Jean, *Clerk*
ZAVIALOFF, André, *Messenger*
ATTEMANN, Ernst, *Captain of Reval Ice Breaker (Pilot for Baltic)*

11 August	**The King's visit to Cronberg**

HENNEBERGER, Friedrich Philipp, *Portier to Prince Frederick Charles of Hesse*
FEUERSTEIN, Max, *Kassier to Prince Frederick Charles of Hesse*
HAUSSNEU, Johann, *Castellan to Prince Alexander Frederick of Hesse*
DIENER, Hermann, *Detective from Berlin*
LEUTHOLD, Anton, *Detective from Berlin*
SCHLAF, Wilhelm, *Detective from Berlin*
WEIDNER, Gustav, *Detective from Berlin*
ZIMMERMANN, Karl, *Detective from Frankfurt*

12 August	**The King's visit to Ischl**

BISCHOF, August, *Chief Cellarman*
PFUNDER, Josef, *Table Decker*
HABER, Carl, *Steward*
MUNSCH, Rudolf, *Chief Cook*
REIMITZ, Sergeant-Major Carl, *on Guard of Honour*
ENDL, Alfons, *Chauffeur to Prince Leopold of Bavaria*
PLAYEW, Sergeant Franz, *Gendarmerie*
MEISSNER, Carl, *Inspector of Police*
SCHRÜNK, Rudolf, *Chief Upholsterer*
DÖBER, Rudolf, *Chief Gardener*
TIASCHEK, Charles, *Chief Cook*
BENEDICKTER, Franz, *Pastry Cook*
DAMM, Johann, *Forage Master*
MARKO, Paul, *Valet*
CADA, Josef, *Page*

4 September	**The King's visit to Marienbad**

BORSHICK, Wilhelm Richard, *Bandmaster Ruberzall Hotel*

RESCHAWY, Alois, *Police Agent from Vienna*
BINDER, Wenzel, *Police Agent from Prague*
SCHAAF, Ludwig Balthasar, *Interpreter Cologne Station*

17 November   **Visit to Windsor of King Gustav V and Queen Victoria of Sweden**
RYDEN, Gustaf, *Valet to the Queen of Sweden*

1909

12 February   **The King's visit to Berlin**
DANIEL, Paul, *Footman*
HÜBLER, Paul, *Valet*
FRIEDRICH, Hermann, *Footman*
TURKE, Adolf, *Footman*
TÜLLMAN, Oscar, *Footman*
GOSSMANN, Franz, *Footman*
HEINRICH, Josef, *Porter*
SCHEUNEMANN, August, *Porter*
GÜNSSEL, Emil, *Storekeeper*
NICOLAI, Otto, *Cook*
HUGUENIN, Arthur, *Cook*
MAROTZ, Hermann, *Silver Pantry Man*
WERSING, Ludwig Carl Gustav, *Superintendent of Kitchen Department*
ROGASS, Gustav, *Trotteur*
SCHMIDT, Hugo, *Hoffourier*
BLAPPERT, Karl Heinrich, *Custodian of the Town Hall*
HARTMANN, Heinrich Paul, *In Service of Municipal Authorities, Berlin*
TRAMM, Ferdinand, *Head Coachman*
SCHRODER, Otto August, *Head Chauffeur*
BURMEISTER, Otto Christel Wilhelm Carl, *Head Chauffeur*
BAARZ, Hermann, *Bandmaster, 1st Guard Dragoon Regiment*
BERKER, Wachtmeister Robert Otto, *Sergeant-Major, 1st Guard Dragoon Regiment*
EWALD, Vice Wachtmeister Richard Karl Heinrich, *Acting Sergeant-Major, 1st Guard Dragoon Regiment*
GROTE, Vice Wachtmeister Otto Walter, *Acting Sergeant-Major, 1st Guard Dragoon Regiment*
KRIEN, Vice Wachtmeister Gustaf Albert Karl Hermann, *Acting Sergeant-Major, 1st Guard Dragoon Regiment*
WOLFRAM, Wachtmeister Herman Emil Gustaf, *Sergeant-Major, 1st Guard Dragoon Regiment*
LEHMANN, Sergeant Paul Ernst Rudolf, *Sergeant-Major, 1st Guard Dragoon Regiment*
SALZWEDEL, Sergeant Hans, *1st Guard Dragoon Regiment*
LAMBRECHT, Vice Wachtmeister Alexander Franz, *Hussar Regiment Fürst Blücher von Wahlstatt (Pommersches)*
HASENPUSCH, Vice Wachtmeister Emil Gustav, *Hussar Regiment Fürst Blücher von Wahlstatt (Pommersches)*
PAULINI, Vice Wachtmeister Gustav, *Hussar Regiment Fürst Blücher von Wahlstatt (Pommersches)*
ENDRESATH, Vice Wachtmeister Karl Friedrich, *Hussar Regiment Fürst Blücher von Wahlstatt (Pommersches)*
POMREHN, Vice Wachtmeister Franz Ludwig Wilhelm, *Hussar Regiment Fürst Blücher von Wahlstatt (Pommersches)*
SEGLER, Vice Wachtmeister Otto Friedrich Albert, *Hussar Regiment Fürst Blücher von Wahlstatt (Pommersches)*
KRUCHELDORF, Wachtmeister August, *Hussar Regiment von Zieten*
KARENKE, Feldwebel Gustav, *Fusilier Regiment Prince Henry of Prussia*
LUTKENS, Feldwebel Paul, *2nd Division of the Foot Guards*
FRENTRUP, Feldwebel Heinrich, *1st Division of the Foot Guards*
BARKOW, Vice Feldwebel Wilhelm, *Royal Prussian Castle Guards*
BERENDES, Wachtmeister Martin, *Garde du Corps*
GESCHE, Willi Johannes, *Chief Engineers Mate SMY* Hohenzollern
FELL, Emil, *Chief Engineers Mate SMY* Hohenzollern
MULLER, Karl Christian, *Chief Boatswain's Mate SMY* Hohenzollern
NEUMANN, John, *Chief Boatswain's Mate SMY* Hohenzollern
ZIMMERMANN, Paul, *Chief Coxswain's Mate SMY* Hohenzollern
ASMUS, Paul Edward Christian Willy, *Engineer's Mate SMY* Hohenzollern
STENZIG, Wachtmeister Heinrich, *Police (Potsdam Gendarmerie)*
KORTH, Wachtmeister Karl Gustav Adolf, *Police Sergeant (Berlin)*
BUSSE, Wachtmeister Christoph Ferdinand, *Police Sergeant (Berlin)*

15 April   **The King's visit to Biarritz**
EHERMENAULT, Henri Rene, *Chief Fireman*
RIBES, Jean Bertrand, *Gendarmerie (Sergeant)*

22 May   **The King's visit to Paris**
GAFFAJOLI, Inspector Simon Francois, *Inspector of Police*

5 August   **Visit to Cowes of Emperor Nicholas II of Russia and Empress Alexandra Feodorovna**
ALENCHIKOFF, Chrissandre, *Conductor*
BACHTINE, Nicolas, *Courreur*
BAIBAKOFF, Stepan, *Signalman*
BIAKOFF, Feodor, *Premier Maître*
BOUGONBAIEFF, Ivan, *Conductor*

CHAMOFF, Jacques, *Footman to the Imperial Children*
CHARITONOFF, Jean, *Cook*
CONDRATIEFF, Nicolas
ERMOLAEF, Alexandre, *Baker*
FERBERG, Henry
GALKINE, Alexandre, *Footman to the Empress*
GLAZONNOFF, Victor
IVANOW, Ivan, *Premier Maitre*
KIRILOFF, Gerassime
KORRALEFF, Kassian
LAPSHINE, Egov
MILLED, David
OLEINIK, Peter
OUTCHASTKINE, Wassile
PYRIALOFF, Gregoriy
QUIGORODSKY, Nicolas
SARANA, Jacob, Cosack, *Garde du Corps*
SARANJINE, Constantin, *Footman*
SARAPOFF, Paul
SCHONKALOFF, Feodor
SIASINE, Nicolas, *Cook*
SOLOWIEF, Wladimir, *Footman*
SONDILOFFSKY, Paul
TCHERNOFF, Theodore, *Chief Cook*
TCHERTKOFF, Alexandre
WASSILIEFF, Dimitri
WASSILIEFF, Mathiew

3 September

The King's visit to Marienbad
CHARVAT, Johann, *Detective from Prague*
HOTTINGER, Franz, *Detective from Vienna*

22 December

The Duke of Connaught's visit to Brussels for the Funeral of King Leopold II of the Belgians
MOUSCH, Alfred, *Fournier at the Royal Palace, Brussels*
SALZMANN, Jules, *Valet to the King of the Belgians*
ANTOINE, Georges Jules, *Concierge at the Royal Palace*

1910

25 April

The King's visit to Biarritz
BAIN, Jules Emile, *Controleur, North of France Railway*

21 May

Funeral of King Edward VII; Deputation from Foreign Regiments of which his late Majesty was Colonel in Chief
BOSSING, Sergeant-Major Lars Peter, *Danish Hussars of the Guard*
CHERNICH, Sergeant-Major Trotim, *Russian Hussar Regiment 9th Kieff*

16 November

PETERSEN, Fritz Cato, *Chairman of the Committee which presented the bust of the late King Christian to Queen Alexandra*

1911

6 April

KISTE, Jacob, *Buchsenspanner*

Garter Mission of Prince Arthur of Connaught to the Prince Regent of Bavaria
KOLB, Adolf, *Court Servant*
KRAMER, Max, *Head of Stable Department*
BAWREP, Otto, *First Coachman*
HUBER, Carl, *Upper Court Servant*
SCHRODER, George, *Wachtmeister*

22 April

Prince Arthur of Connaught's visit to Rome for the Jubilee of Italian Unity
RAFFANINI, Raffaele, *Footman-Usher*
GIAQUINTO, Luigi, *Under Footman-Usher*
ROMANI, Oreste, *Coachman*
ROSSINI, Anchise, *Gentleman Porter*
BANDIERINI, Alfredo, *Gentleman Porter*
BOSCO, Giuseppe, *1st Class Footman*
ODDONE, Luigi, *Usher of Ante Room*
BOARON, Benedetto
ADREANI, Giovanni

15 May

Visit of the German Emperor for the unveiling of the Victoria Memorial
FOLLBACH, Jacob, *Wardrobe Man to the Emperor*
RIEGEL, Carl Thomas, *Wardrobe Man to the Emperor*

STRATMANN, Heinrich, *Wardrobe Man to the Emperor*
PURTZ, Otto, *Messenger, Master of Household's Department*
VON DER HEYDE, Ludwig, *Messenger, Admiralty*
MILITZ, Ernst, *Messenger, Foreign Office*
KLOSE, Paul, *Footman, Foreign Office*
SCHLEFFER, Otto, *Footman, Foreign Office*
UNGLAUBE, Georg, *Footman, Foreign Office*
HENSCHKE, Wilhelm, *Footman, Foreign Office*
EHLERS, Friedrich, *Footman, Foreign Office*
JOHANNES, Vice Wachtmeister Friedrich, *Orderly*
BARTELS, Lance Corporal Georg, *1st Prussian Regiment of Dragoons of the Guard*
DETRING, Lance Corporal Wilhelm, *1st Prussian Regiment of Dragoons of the Guard*

EDWARD VII: RVM, BRONZE

1903

7 April **King's Edward VII's visit to Lisbon**
GONCALVES, Antonio (Jnr), *Groom of the Chamber*
FRANCO, Jose da Silva Escobar, *Groom of the Chamber*
LUCAS, Jose (Jnr), *Valet de Pied*
PEREIRA, Antonio, *Valet de Pied*
MIRANDA, Antonio, *Groom*
OLIVEIRA, Joaquim Martius d', *Porter*
LOPES, Joaquim, *Groom in Silver Department*
MOREIRA, Joaquim, *Groom in Silver Department*
ALMEIDA, Jose Maria de, *Valet de Pied*
RODRIGUES, Jose, *Valet de Pied*
FONSECA, Jose M. da, *Mounted Messenger*
ALHO, Henrique Jose de Fiqueiredo, *Mounted Messenger*
PAULO, Antonio, *Mounted Messenger*
MOREAU, Henry, *Chauffeur*
ARANJO, Francisco d', *Valet to the King of Portugal*
NUNES, Manuel, *Footman*
RODRIGUES, Eduardo, *Footman*
ALFARRA, Joaquim Padinha, *Interpreter*

30 April **The King's visit to Rome**
CARPENEDO, Germano, *Vice Brigadier, Royal Bodyguard*
BEGASPARI, Luigi, *Vice Brigadier, Royal Bodyguard*
CALIARI, Enrico, *Apponite, Royal Bodyguard*
PILOTTO, Angelo, *Carabinier*
RIGA, Alessandro, *Carabinier of Royal Bodyguard*
CIONI, Giovanni, *Carabinier of Royal Bodyguard*
CULLINO, Domenico, *Footman*
GARDIN, Andrea, *Footman*
BUTRIO, Carlo, *Footman*
SARTORIO, Everardo, *Footman*
FERRERO, Carlo, *Footman*
DOMENICHELLI, Pietro, *Footman*
CARRARA, Enrico, *Footman*
MOSETTI, Augusto, *Footman*
REGINI, Angelo, *Porter*
SPIRITO, Antonio, *Porter*
AMODIO, Vincenzo, *Coachman to Sir Francis Bertie*
BROSSA, Giorgio, *Chief Postman*

4 May **The King's visit to Paris**
SERIN, Gaston, *Cook to Sir E. Monson*
HONDEBERT, Lucien, *Coachman to Sir E. Monson*
MORAISON, Louis, *Steward to Sir E. Monson*
MANCEAU, J., *Messenger at Embassy*
VAUTHIER, Auguste, *1st Huissier to President Loubet*
DECAN, Andre, *2nd Huissier to President Loubet*
POIGNANT, Ernest, *3rd Huissier to President Loubet*
PICOU, Joseph, *Facteur*
CHAUVIN, Francois, *Facteur*
DUPLAT, Corporal Achille Charles E., *Clerk at the Élysée*
LUCET, Eugene Jules, *Clerk at the Élysée*
JACQUET, Joseph, *Huissier d'Annonce at Élysée*
RAIMBAULT, Auguste, *Huissier d'Annonce at Élysée*

JACQUEMONT, Jean, *Huissier d'Annonce at Élysée*
GIRARD, Prosper, *Huissier d'Annonce at Élysée, Foreign Office*

29 June FLEISCHER, Otto, *Footman to the late Empress Frederick*

1 August **Visit to Britain of President Loubet of the French Republic**
CHATAIGNON, Pierre, *Silver Keeper to President Loubet*
MORO, Alexis, *Valet to President Loubet*
ANGEADR, *Homme de Service to President Loubet*
PEIGNE, Paul, *Homme de Service to President Loubet*
HUBERT, Pierre Marie Joseph, *Valet de Pied to President Loubet*
PRIME, Louis Victor, *Valet de Pied to President Loubet*
ANCEL, *Valet*
LEGER, *Valet*

14 August WURTINGER, Michael, *Forester at Podhornberg*

30 August **The King's visit to Marienbad**
BERNAL, Rudolf, *Detective*
BINDER, Wenzel, *Detective*
DIETSCHE, Jakob, *Detective*
ECKERT, George, *Sergeant, Local Police*
KÜSS, Joseph, *Detective*
PONDELICEK, Franz, *Detective*
PFEIFFER, Johann, *Detective*
SPACEK, Franz, *Detective*
ZOHL, Karl, *Detective*
WURTINGEN, Franz, *Postman*
WURTINGER, Hermann, *Postman*

September **The King's visit to Vienna**
SCHNEIBERG, Gustav, *Leibjager in Attendance on the King*
SCHMALMAUER, Ferdinand, *Lakai in Attendance on the King*
HONISCH, Josef, *Lakai in Attendance on the King*
JAKOB, Julius, *Postman*
IENICIC, Nicolas, *Cellarman attached to the King's Train*
JUAN, Thomas, *Footman*
DOGA, Georg, *Footman*
KOHAJDA, Andreas, *Footman*
LEITNER, Rudolf, *Footman*
SCHELZ, Anton, *Footman*
WAGNER, Wenzel, *Footman*
PLEYER, Wenzel, *1st Sicherheitswachmann*
POSSL, Franz, *2nd Sicherheitswachmann*
NEUBER, Josef, *Detective*
PATEISKY, Otto, *Detective*
ZOHRER, Josef, *Under Keeper at Lobau*

21 November **Visit to Britain of King Vittorio Emanuele III and Queen Elena of Italy**
GRANGE, Delfino, *Loader*
CERNESONI, Edoardo, *Footman*
ROTA, Giovanni, *Footman*
ESPOSITO, Salvatore, *Servant of the Kitchen Staff*
BERRA, Oreste, *Messenger*
PROIA, Alcibiade, *Messenger*
FASULO, Vincenza, *Messenger*
BELSITO, Giuseppe, *Messenger*
MENCHETTI, Francesco, *Messenger at Italian Foreign Office*
PARENTI, Antonio, *Valet to Signor Tommaso Tittoni*
BIARRATTI, Giuseppe, *Valet to Count Gianotti*
FLECCHIA, Leonardo, *Valet to General Ugo Brusati*
BERTAGNA, Alessandro, *Valet to General di Majo*
DEL GALLO, Francesco, *Valet to Lieutenant Colonel Gonsalo Paliere*
FEDERICI, Federico, *Valet to Major Iodini*
TONIETTI, Pietro, *Valet to Count Tozzoni*
CERVELLIERI, Gustavo, *Valet to Dr Quirico*
DOLCI, Ernesto, *Valet to Marchese Calabrini*
GONETTI, Giovanni, *Valet to Count di Trinita*

1904

1 January **The Duke of Saxe-Coburg's visit to Sandringham**
GROSSKWITH, Christoph, *Jaeger to The Duke of Saxe-Coburg and Gotha*

10 February	**Visit to Windsor of the Prince of Waldeck and Pyrmont for the Marriage of Princess Alice of Albany and Prince Alexander of Teck**

FRESE, Wilhelm, *Lakai to HSH*
MENDEL, Ernst, *Lakai to HSH*

The Queen of Württemberg's visit to Windsor Castle for the Marriage of Princess Alice of Albany and Prince Alexander of Teck
BENZ, Wilhelm, *Lakai to HM*
FUNK, Wilhelm, *Lakai to HM*
SCHMID, Christian, *Lakai to HM*
METZ, Christian, *Lakai to HM*

The Prince of Wied's visit to Windsor Castle for the Marriage of Princess Alice of Albany and Prince Alexander of Teck
SCHMIDT, Georg, *Lakai to HSH*

Visit to Windsor of the Queen Mother of the Netherlands for the Marriage of Princess Alice of Albany and Prince Alexander of Teck
ROEL, Johan, *Footman to HM*
VECHT, Hendrik van der, *Footman to HM*

23 March **Funeral of the Duke of Cambridge**
SCHRODER, Otto, *Leibjäger to Prince Albrecht of Prussia (Regent of Brunswick)*
DIEHLE, Wilhelm, *Garderobier to Prince Albrecht of Prussia (Regent of Brunswick)*
BUSCHOW, Fritz, *Garderobier to Prince Albrecht of Prussia (Regent of Brunswick)*
BUCHHOLZ, Wilhelm, *Major Count A. von Schulenberg's Servant*
MULLER, Alfred, *Captain Joachim von Berger Herrendorff's Servant*
STURM, Carl, *Herr Kurt Max von der Osten's Servant*

8 April **The King's visit to Copenhagen**
SORENSEN, Hans Olaf, *Messenger, King of Denmark's Household*
POULSEN, Jorgen, *Surtzer, King of Denmark's Household*
HANSEN, Christen, *Porter, King of Denmark's Household*
BURCHELL, Joseph, *Butler, British Legation*

April **The Prince of Wales's visit to Vienna**
KRASNICKA, Josef, *Jaeger to the Emperor of Austria*
BUCHINGER, Alois, *Footman*
GERINECZ, Josef, *Footman*
SLUKA, Johann, *Footman*
LERCH, Franz, *Footman*
VOGRINESICS, Josef, *Footman*
HENGGE, Franz, *Coachman*
MARCOVITSCH, Martin, *Coachman*
INGERLE, Franz, *Coachman*
DAMM, Johann, *Coachman*
STOLL, Andreas, *Lakai (Kitchen)*
STEINER, Josef, *Cellarman*
SAMADITS, Andreas, *Footman*
SCHLESINGER, Franz, *Kammerdiener*
KOLLER, Johann, *Footman*

April **The Prince of Wales's visit to Stuttgart**
RÜHLE, Friedrich, *Livery Servant to the King of Württemberg*
HAETELE, Friedrich, *Footman to the King of Württemberg*
WARTH, Albert, *Coachman to the King of Württemberg*
MEIER III, Gottleib, *Coachman to the King of Württemberg*
HOFFMANN, Nicolaus, *Hall Porter*
PLESSING, Wilhelm, *Hall Porter*
BERNER, Heinrich, *Footman*
SACKMAN, Adam, *Livery Servant*
SCHERER, Friedrich, *Livery Servant*

11 June **Visit to Britain of the Archduke Frederick of Austria**
SCHON, Maximilian, *Count Saint Quentin's Servant*
MAIER, Joseph, *Captain Pronay's Servant*
BOSCHNER, Martin, *Messenger of the Austro-Hungarian Imperial Caisse*

14 June **Visit to Britain of the Duchess of Saxe-Coburg and Gotha**
KOTTMAN, Karl, *Personal Kammerdiener*

June **The King's visit to Kiel**
KRAUSE, Albert, *Silberdiener on board the* Hohenzollern
LOHSE, Claus, *Postman at Kiel*
MAASS, Ernst, *Postman at Kiel*
ROSENOW, Samuel, *Kellerdiener*
BURANDT, Emil, *Kuchendiener*

OSTERNDORF, Willy, *Elbe Pilot*
OHLSEN, Karl, *Elbe Pilot*
TESSMAN, Heinrich, *Canal Pilot*
BLATT, Heinrich, *Canal Pilot*
SCHULT, Karl, *Silberdiener, Hamburg*

26 August   **Christening of the Cesarevitch**
ALEXIEFF, Ivan, *Coachman in attendance on Prince Louis of Battenberg when representing the King in St Petersburg*
SOKOLOFF, Wladimir, *Footman in attendance on Prince Louis of Battenberg when representing the King in St Petersburg*

August   **The King's visit to Marienbad**
RYBENSKY, Karl, *Interpreter at Marienbad Station*
WILL, Wenzel, *Gamekeeper to Prince Trautmansdorff*
ECKERT, Franz, *Gamekeeper to Prince Trautmansdorff*
ARNOLD. Alfred, *Local Police, Marienbad*
DIEGESSER, Karl, *Local Police, Marienbad*
HAUSE, Karl, *Gendarmerie, Marienbad*
GAMPE, Johann, *Gendarmerie, Marienbad*
HUBER, Andreas, *Postman*
WOLRAB, Alois, *Porter at the Baths*

23 October   **The King's visit to Marienbad**
RICHTER, Otto, *Butler to Sir Francis Plunkett*

16 November   **Visit to Britain of King Carlos of Portugal**
GUERRA, Alfredo, *Valet to the King of Portugal*
PEREIRA, José, *Valet to the Queen of Portugal*
VILLALVA, Carlos José Vieira, *Valet to Senor Villaca*
THOMÉ, Jose, *Valet to Viscount Asseca*
PEREIRA, Manoel, *Valet to Count Jarouca*
GARCIA, Baldomero, *Valet to Count de Ribeira Grande*
MARQUES, Alfredo Silva, *Valet to Rear-Admiral Capello*
ANTUNES, Eduardo, *Valet to Don A. Lancastre*

4 December   **Prince Arthur of Connaught's visit to Italy to represent the King at the Christening of the Prince of Piedmont**
MONETTI, Alessandro, *Footman attached to Prince Arthur of Connaught*
VITALETTI, Luigi, *Footman attached to Prince Arthur of Connaught*

1905

27 February   **Prince Arthur of Connaught's visit to Berlin for opening of Protestant Cathedral**
MÜLLER, Hermann, *Footman*
KÖHLER, Walther, *Outrider*
MEINKE, Georg, *Coachman*
KURTMANN, Max, *Groom*

8 March   **Prince Ferdinand of Bulgaria's visit to Britain**
PETROFF, Misho, *2nd Valet de Chambre*
MILEFF, Kiro, *Laquai*
PETKOFF, Alexandre, *Laquai*

16 April   **The King's visit to Blida, Algeria**
AOUGUEHI, *Chef de Musique Indigène 1er Tirailleurs, Blida*

19 April   **The King's visit to Algiers**
DOIRLET, Francois Auguste, *Huissier du Gouverneur General de l'Algérie*

24 April   **The King's visit to Philippeville, Algeria**
FAIVRE, Sergeant Louis Jean, *Chef de Fanfare 3ème Regiment de Tirailleurs Algériens*

4 May   **The King's visit to Paris**
JACOB, Jean Baptiste, *Night Porter, Hotel Bristol, Paris*

9 May   **Queen Alexandra's visit to Athens**
ELIAS, Julius, *1st Coachman*
MIRTIRIS, Anastasis, *In charge of Steam Pinnace*

6 June   **Visit to Britain of King Alfonso of Spain**
GARZA, Antonio, *Foreign Office Messenger*
PALOMAN, Iacinto, *1st Bodyservant to the King of Spain*
DEL VALLE, Tomas, *Orderly to Dr Jose Alaberu of Raspall*
VILLAMOR, Ballariano, *Servant to the King of Spain*
DORAO, Isaac, *Servant to the King of Spain*
LOPEZ, Angel, *Servant to the King of Spain*
ALVAREZ, Jose, *Valet to the Duke of Sotomayor*

RARRIA, Mauricio, *Valet to the Duke of Santo Mauro*
AAYLOR, Iese, *Valet to the Duke of Alba de Tormes*

| 15 June | **Marriage of Princess Margaret of Connaught and Prince Gustav Adolph of Sweden & Norway** |

DAHL, Axel, *Footman to the Crown Prince of Sweden and Norway*
STROM, Sven, *Footman to the Crown Prince of Sweden and Norway*
NYRKÖM, Johann Auguste, *Footman to the Crown Prince of Sweden and Norway*
RYDEN, Gustaf, *Footman to the Crown Princess of Sweden and Norway*
KALLENBERG, Otto Wilhelm, *Footman to Prince Gustav Adolph*
STERN, August, *Footman to Prince William*
REINHARD, Johann, *Footman to Hereditary Grand Duke of Baden*
SCHAFER, Sebastian, *Footman to Hereditary Grand Duke of Baden*
CHIPÓLA, Pancras, *Footman to Boutros Pacha Ghali*

| 6 June | **Prince Arthur of Connaught's visit to Berlin to represent HM at the Marriage of the Crown Prince of Prussia** |

SCHWEEN, Sergeant, *Orderly, Guard Grenadier Regt. No. 3 Queen Elizabeth*
SPÄHN, Corporal, *Orderly, Guard Grenadier Regt. No. 3 Queen Elizabeth*

| 19 July | **Coming of Age of the Duke of Saxe-Coburg and Gotha** |

GRÜBEL, Hugo, *Lance Corporal 11 Coy, 6 Thüringen Infantry Regiment No95*

| 10 August | LE ROY, Yves Marie, *Cuisinier to Vice-Admiral Commandant of French Northern Squadron* |

| 16 August | **The King's visit to Marienbad** |

STOLLHOF, Jakob, *Coachman to the Emperor of Austria*

| 28 August | **The King's visit to Dachau** |

LEOPOLD, Johann, *Kammerdiener to Prince Windisch-Graetz*

| 4 September | **The King's visit to Marienbad** |

EXNER, Wilhelm, *Kammerdiener in Stift Tepl, Marienbad*

| 7 September | **The King's visit to Marienbad** |

TREML, Otto, *Policeman in Stift Tepl, Marienbad*
GLEISINGER, Johann, *Policeman in Stift Tepl, Marienbad*
WOHBRATH, Leopold, *Gendarmerie in Stift Tepl, Marienbad*
VORACEK, Franz, *Gendarmerie, Marienbad*
JAKOB, George, *Postman, Marienbad*

| 11 September | BORNKAIEFF, Danbek, *Cossack Orderly to General Sir Montague Gerard* |

| 27 November | **Visit to Britain of King George I of the Hellenes** |

STATTINOPOULOS, Nicolai, *Laquai du Palais*
DIAMANTIDES, Pierre, *Valet to Prince Nicholas*

1906

| 16 March | **Prince Arthur of Connaught's Garter Mission to Japan,** |

TSUKADA, Suyemasa, *Exterior Section, Imperial Household*
TOKIOKA, Shigihiro, *Exterior Section, Imperial Household*
ADACHI, Dauchi, *Exterior Section, Imperial Household*
SAKATA, Koya, *Exterior Section, Imperial Household*
SHINAGAWA, Toichiro, *Ceremonial Bureau, Imperial Household*
ONISHI, Tokusahuro, *Cuisine Bureau, Imperial Household*
TUCHIKAWA, Chintaro, *Footman*
MASUMOTO, Moryuki, *Police Inspector*
MATSUMURA, Tomoyuki, *Attaché to the Bureau*
JAKAOKA, Iengiro, *Board of Supply*
FUKUBA, Onzo, *Board of Imperial Gardens*
HATANO, Tominoske, *Superintendent of the Imperial Hunting Enclosure*

| 31 March | **The King's visit to Biarritz** |

LEMAITRE, Louis, *Chef to the Duchess of Manchester*

| 2 April | **The King's visit to Biarritz** |

DUHART, Pierre, *Brigadier de Sûreté, Biarritz*
HARTCANDY, Pierre, *Agent of Police, Biarritz*
PETIT, Pierre, *Agent of Police, Biarritz*
CASTAGNET, Ferdinand, *Agent of Police, Biarritz*
VIGNES, Jean Paul, *Agent de Sûreté, Biarritz*
MARTIN, Hubert, *Agent de Sûreté, Biarritz*

| 19 April | COSCHIERI, Giuseppe, *Chancery Servant at British Legation, Athens since 1874* |

| 22 April | **Visit to Athens of King Edward VII and Queen Alexandra** |

PAPASOTIRION, Christos, *Valet de Pieds to the King of the Hellenes*
FASSITZAS, Jean, *Valet de Pieds to the King of the Hellenes*
DONILIS, Stylianos, *Valet de Pieds to the King of the Hellenes*

GLAROPOULOS, Théodore, *Valet de Pieds to the King of the Hellenes*
EUTHYMIOU, Panayeti, *Valet de Pieds to the King of the Hellenes*
STRARIOJIANOUDAKIS, Jean, *Chasseur to Prince George of Greece*
PLAEAS, George, *Footman to the Duke of Sparta*
PAPADOPOULOS, George, *Valet de Pieds to Queen of the Hellenes*
PROCOPIOS, Dimitri, *Coachman for the Prince of Wales*
OASSOCOS, Nicholas, *Coachman for Princess Victoria*

7 May	**On return of HM from his Mediterranean Cruise** BAUDOUX, Edouard, *Maître d'Hôtel de la Compagnie des Wagons Lits* COUTIN, Georges, *Maître d'Hôtel de la Compagnie des Wagons Lits* GOVART, Adolphe, *Maître d'Hôtel Terminus, Calais*
6 June	**Marriage of the King of Spain** SANTIAGO, Christobal, *Valet 2nd Class* COLAS, Antonio, *Valet 2nd Class* PEREZ, Jose BOCHAS, Faustino FERRER, Gabriel, *Chancery Servant, British Embassy, Madrid*
15 August	**The King's visit to Cronberg** MELZER, Reinhold, *Lakai to Prince Frederick Charles of Hesse* MUNSCH, Adam, *Installateur to Prince Frederick Charles of Hesse* BAUMANN, Joseph, *Wachtmeister to Prince Frederick Charles of Hesse* HENNEBERGER, Friedrich, *Portier*
3 September	**The King's visit to Marienbad** FIALA, Josef, *Forester, Bischofteinitz*
5 September	MAIER, Christof, *Coachman at Hotel Weimar (Drove the King for four years)* SIPPL, Adolf, *Gendarmerie* SIMCHEN, Johann, *Gendarmerie* BAUMANN, Josef, *Telegraph Postman* KONHAUSER, Lorenz, *Town Police* SCHOTT, Karl, *Town Police*
8 September	**The Duke of Connaught's visit to Breslau to attend the German Army Manoeuvres** GOSSMAN, Gustav, *Footman to the German Emperor* HÜBLER, Paul, *Jäger to the German Emperor* SCHULZ, Paul, *Coachman to the German Emperor* HUHNHOLZ, Andreas, *Groom to the German Emperor*
20 September	**The Duke of Connaught's visit to Karlsruhe** LANG, Karl, *Grenadier* IBACH, Bernhard, *Footman (Schlossdiener)*
9 November	**Prince Trauttmansdorff's visit to Sandringham** PATOCKA, Karl, *Jager to HH*
13 November	**Visit to Britain of King Haakon VII and Queen Maud of Norway** HERNAS, Peter, *Footman to the King of Norway* ROKENCES, Hilberg, *Footman to the King of Norway* WOLD, Alexander, *Footman to the King of Norway* HOLTE, Torslein J., *Footman to the King of Norway*

1907

9 February	**The King's visit to Paris** HERVÉ, Emile, *Messenger at British Embassy, Paris* ANGEARD, Adrien, *Postman, Paris* LAIGRES, Anatole, *Postman, Paris* ANDRE, Joseph, *Postman, Paris* CHABEAUD, Henry, *Postman, Paris*
5 March	**Visit of Prince Alexander of Teck to the Hague to invest the Prince of the Netherlands with the Order of the Bath** SCHWEDHELM, Wilhelm C.L.H.F.G., *Chasseur de la Cour* VAN DEN BROEK, Hendrik A.N., *Laquai* JANSEN, Tennis, *Laquai*
4 April	**The King's visit to Biarritz** FAUTONS, Armand, *Agent of Police, Biarritz* LACOSTE, Ambroise, *Agent of Police, Biarritz* CAMAJOR, Jean, *Agent of Police, Biarritz*
9 April	**The King's visit to Cartagena** SANCHEZ DEMOSTIERRE, Rafael, *Official 3° de Cocina (Encargado de la Cava)* SUAREZ Y MENÉNDEZ, Manuel, *Mozo 2° del Guardarropa de S.M.*

ESTEBAN BELTRAN, Toribio, *Mozo de Oficios de los Reales Cuartos*
NAVARRO Y RIQUER, Salvador, *Ayudante 1⁰ de Botilleria y Cava*
JIMENEZ Y HERNANDEZ, Isidoro, *6⁰ de Botilleria y Cava*
COTARELO BOAN, Celso, *7⁰ de Botilleria y Cava*
SIERRA MORALES, Cesar, *Lacayo de la Reina Dona Maria Christina*
MONTERO PACHECO, Emilio, *Portero de Vidrieras*
VILA ROYO, Augustin, *Encargado del Cuarto Cajo*
SAN CRISTOBAL Y CASADO, Miguel, *Mozo Colgador Tapiceria*
RAMOS DE LA VEGA, Enrique, *Mozo Colgador Tapiceria*
CANTARERO SOLANO, Jose, *Barrendero del Real Palacio*
BANTISTA Y CORRAL, Ensebio, *Barrendero del Real Palacio*
PARO Y MELLADO, Sixto, *Barrendero del Real Palacio*
MORENO JIMENEZ, Francisco, *Mozo 2⁰ de Lumpieza y recados del Cuarto de S.M.*
ROMERO SELAS, Pedro, *Ordenanza al Servicio del Cuarto Militar*
FERNANDEZ MARTIN, Francisco, *Mozo de Guardam uebles*
NUNEZ GARCIA, Joaquim, *Mozo de Guardam uebles*
MIGUEL ARGUEDAS, T. Jeodoro, *Ayudante extraordinario de Cocina*
AVA HERNANDEZ, Esteban, *Ayudante extraordinario de Pasteria*

26 April	**The King's visit to Palermo**
	MARTINET, Giovanni, *Royal Carabiniers*
29 April	**The King's visit to Naples**
	BELLISARIO, Beniamino, *Naples Police Agent*
	ROMANO, Roberto, *Naples Police Agent*
	MARCHESE, Marco, *Naples Police Agent*
	TRICOLI, Giuseppe (Senior), *Naples Police Agent*
	SABIO, Giuseppe, *Naples Police Agent*
	DONNARUMMA, Francesco, *Naples Police Agent*
	JUSINI, Carlo, *Naples Police Agent*
	MARINELLI, Francesco, *Naples Police Agent*
	DE RINALDIS, Girolamo, *Naples Police Agent*
	JODARO, Rosario, *Naples Police Agent*
	CAPPELLIERI, Onofrio, *Chief Guard at the Arsenal (Navy)*
	FARA, Giovanni, *Marshal of Gendarmerie*
	CATALANO, Corporal Raffaele, *Corporal of the Municipal Guard*
4 May	**The King's visit to Paris**
	CLERC, Pierre, *Maître d'Hôtel, Wagon Lits Company*
5 May	**Queen Alexandra's visit to Athens**
	PILO, Antonio, *Late Sergeant of Police at Corfu*
7 May	**Visit to Britain of Prince Fushimi of Japan**
	DÜRIG, Fred, *Courier to Baron G. Yamamoto*
	GOTOH, Jakuji, *Servant in Imperial Household*
	IYMURA, Kichiziro, *Servant in Imperial Household*
16 May	DRILIA, Elie, *Footman at Royal Palace, Athens*
18 May	**Prince Arthur of Connaught's visit to Madrid to represent HM at the Christening of the Prince of Asturias**
	ARRIVAS Y ARRIVAS, Augustin, *Ordenanza del Cuarto Militar*
	SANCHEZ CASSO, Jose, *Postillion*
	BELLVER Y PENA, Jose, *Lacayo de primera*
	GARCIA MULA, Enrique, *Delantero de Camara*
11 June	**Visit to Britain of King Frederik VIII and Queen Louise of Denmark**
	BOSERUP, Christian Albert Otto, *Footman*
	PETERSEN, Peder Larsen Wücherpfennig, *Footman*
	HANSEN, Christian, *Footman*
	PETERSEN, Otto, *Footman to Count Brockenhuishack*
	ANDERSEN, Oscar, *Footman to Count Raben Levetzau*
2 July	**Visit to Britain of the Grand Duke of Hesse**
	PFEIFER, Lorenz, *Footman to HRH*
	SCHULER, Wilhelm, *Footman to HRH*
14 August	**The King's visit to Wilhelmshöhe**
	ALTMANN, Gustav, *Police Detective*
	DIETRICH, Otto, *Police Detective*
	BORTH, Robert, *Police Detective*
	KAMENZ, Karl
	FENGE, Jean
	SCHAUB, Karl
	PRETSCHKER, Arthur, *Hofjäger*
	BLASCHKOWSKY, Karl, *Hoflakai*

ADLER, August
SCHLUCKEBRER, Friedrich, *Schlossdiener*

15 August **The King's visit to Ischl**
TRESCHUAK, Leopold, *Page*
MULLER, Josef, *Footman*
MIKULA, Josef, *Footman*
KARNIK, Johann, *Coachman*
MEISSNER, Karl, *Police*
PLOYER, Franz, *Gendarmerie Police*

6 September **The King's visit to Marienbad**
GILL, Wenzel, *Detective*
RICHTER, Gustav, *Gendarmerie*
SEIDLER, George, *Gendarmerie*
LANZENDORFER, Wendelin, *Town Police*
KONHAUSER, Franz, *Town Police*
JANDA, Franz, *Porter at the Station*
KRYS, Wilhelm, *Loader at Bischofteinitz*
SPONER, Leopold, *Butler at Bischofteinitz*

The Duke of Connaught's visit to Vienna
KLING, Joseph, *Coachman to the Emperor of Austria*
LEHNER, Johann, *Leibjäger at British Embassy, Vienna*

The Duke of Connaught's visit to Karlsruhe
BEIDECK, Johann, *Footman*

9 November **Visit of King Alfonso and Queen Eugenie of Spain to Sandringham**
BINDER, Henry, *Palace Servant in Waiting on the Spanish Ambassador*
OLIVANOE, Ange Eugene, *70th Spanish Regiment*
MARTIN, Manuel Villas, *Spanish Artillery*

12 November **Visit to Windsor of the German Emperor and Empress, King and Queen of Prussia**
HOFKEN, Hermann, *Kammerlakai*
RIEGEL, Thomas, *Garderobediener*
STRATMANN, Heinrich, *Garderobediener*
MATZ, Friedrich, *Lakai*
WOLSKE, Friedrich, *Lakai*
BOHRER, Jean, *Servant to Herr von dem Knesebeck*
HOPF, Richard, *Servant to Count Eulenberg*
SCHMERGLASS, August, *Servant to Herr von Ressen*
HEUTSEHELMANN, Hermann, *Servant to Baron Marschall*
PRAUSE, Fritz, *Servant to Captain Rebeur Tachwitz*
KETTLER, Friedrich, *Servant to Dr Ilberg*
BECKER, Anton, *Servant to Count Hulsen Haeseler*
KETTENBACH, Adolf William, *Servant to Admiral von Muller*
WOLFF, William, *Servant to Herr von Schoen*
STELZER, Gustav, *Servant to Herr von Einem*
JÖDLER, William, *Servant to Herr von Winterfeld*
GRUNER, Paul, *Servant to Count Eulenberg's Office*
GUSSON, Frederick William, *Servant to Emperor's Civil Cabinet*
KRAUS, Fritz, *Servant to Military Cabinet*
VON DER HEYDE, Louis M., *Servant to Emperor's Naval Cabinet*
BERGER, Otto, *Servant*
SCHMIDT, Gustav, *Leibgendarme*
PICHAEZECK, Fritz, *Leibgendarme*
KATFORD, James, *Valet to Count H. Hatzfeldt*
LAWRANCE, Arthur William, *Valet to the German Ambassador*

21 December **Visit to Sweden of Prince Arthur of Connaught to represent HM at the King of Sweden's Funeral**
OLSSON, Werner, *Valet*
SCHON, Per Albert, *Valet*
STRAHLE, Oscar Martin, *Footman*
ERIKSSON, Arvid, *Footman*

22 December ROLFE, Walter, *Butler to the Hon George and Mrs Keppel*

1908

14 April **The King's visit to Biarritz**
ROMATET, Guillaume, *Sous-Brigadier de Police, Agent de Ville*
CHRISOSTOME, Jean Baptiste, *(Trompetto), Agent de Ville*
BONNECAZE, Marcel, *Agent de Police*
ONDARS, Antoine, *Agent de Police*
BRUNE, Silvain, *Gendarme*

MENJUZAN, Jean Baptiste, *Gendarme*
FERRON, Jean Baptiste, *Gendarme*
LASSUS, Bernard, *Gendarme*

18 April   **Visit to Britain of the Empress Marie Feodorovna of Russia**
AKOULOFF, Nicolas, *Valet de Chambre*
IVONCHKINE, Jean, *Valet de Chambre*
YOURAWLEFF, Paul, *Valet de la Cour*
KALANDADZÉ, Lemen, *Valet to Prince George Chervachidzé*

25 April   **The King's visit to Copenhagen**
HANSEN, Otto, *Footman*
JORGENSEN, Hans Christian, *Footman*
LINDVANG, Andreas Johan Nikolaj, *Footman*
GREGERSEN, Jens, *Footman*
HEINRICHSEN, Sophus, *Footman*
NIELSEN, Niels Poul, *Porter*
JACKEL, Hans Peter William, *Manservant*
SÖRENSEN, Peter Olüf, *Manservant*
JÜEL, Niels, *Manservant*
ANDERSEN, Anders Peter, *Manservant*
ANDERSEN, Bernhart Olaf, *Manservant*
PETERSEN, Otto Lauritz, *Manservant*
PETERSEN, Hans Peter Valdemar, *Manservant*
STRÜRE, Ferdinand Peter Carl, *Manservant*
JAKOBSEN, Jakob, *Coachman (2nd Class)*
CHRISTIANSEN, Ludwig Lauritz, *Coachman (2nd Class)*

27 April   **The King's visit to Stockholm**
LINDGREN, Hans, *Footman*
LANTZ, Nils Fredrik Laurentius, *Footman*
SVEMFELDT, Gustaf, *Footman*
PETTERSSON, Ernst, *Footman*
ANDERSEN, Sven, *Footman*

2 May   **The King's visit to Christiania**
ANDERSEN, Anders, *Footman*
BERG, Theodor, *Footman*
DÖRUM, Anders, *Footman*
HALSE, Ole, *Footman*
LAKFOSS, Thorvald, *Footman*
LILLEAAS, Carl, *Postman*
LAND, Gerald, *Groom to Queen Maud*
GYLDER, Johan, *Postillion*
PETTERSEN, Johan, *Postillion*
SVENDSEN, Sigvart, *Postillion*
RISER, Harald, *Postillion*
NILSSON, Johan, *Outrider*

28 May   **Visit to Britain of President Fallières of the French Republic**
BRANGIER, Albert Louis, *Valet de Pied*
PEIGNE, Augustin, *Valet to M. Pichon*

10 June   **The King's visit to Reval**
MEYER, R., *Elbe Pilot*
HAASE, Albert, *Pilot, Kiel Canal*
KÖHN, Wilhelm, *Pilot, Kiel Canal*
FAST, Ernest, *Elbe Pilot*
ANDERSON, Theodore, *Valet to Admiral Count Heiden*
BELOOUSSOFF, Basile, *Cook*
BERNADSKY, Nicolas, *Cook*
BOCHINE, Nicolas, *Footman*
CHARITONOFF, Jean, *Cook*
DIMITRIEFF, Alexis, *Hairdresser*
ETTINGSHAUSEN, Joseph, *Valet to Count Benckendorff*
EVDOKIMOFF, Alexandre, *Valet to Prince Galitzin*
GUINZ, Charles, *Wardrobe man to the Grand Duchess Olga*
KANEP, Charles, *Valet to General Daschkoff*
KOBELSKY, Théodore, *Cook*
KRONGLIKOFF, Basile, *Cook*
LOUXGATE, *Valet to Colonel Mordrinoff*
MOSKALENKO, Ivan, *Valet to Prince Gortenekoff*
POURNOFF, Charles, *Footman*
PRINTZEF, Michel Grigorevitch, *Valet to Grand Duke Michael Alexandrovitch*
SACHNO, Alexandre, *Footman*

SAFRONOFF, Jean, *Cook*
SCHMIDT, Auguste, *Footman*
SEMENOFF, Theodore, *Soldier Servant to the Emperor*
SHAMOFF, Yakof, *Footman to the Imperial Children*
SHISHERINE, Aphanasry, *Valet to Admiral Niloff*
SITNIKOFF, Jacques, *Valet to Prince Oldenburg*
SMIRNOFF, Jean, *Cook*
SOLOTOFF, Nicolas, *Clerk*
SOROKINE, Alexandre, *Messenger*
STEPANOFF, Nicolas, *Cook*
TCHOURAK, Jean, *Valet to Baron Osten Sacken*
TÉNISSONN, Andre, *Messenger*
TRAVINE, Arsène, *Valet to Captain Drenteln*
TROFIMOFF, Serge, *Footman*
TROUXHINE, Etienne, *Valet to M. Sawinsky*
WESSOLOVSKY, John, *Valet to General Mossoloff*

| 11 August | **The King's visit to Cronberg** |

BIENERT, Joseph, *Wachtmeister Fuss-Gendarmerie*
UMBREIT, Fritz, *Wachtmeister Fuss-Gendarmerie*
LEZINS, Karl, *Lakai to Prince Frederick Charles of Hesse*
WÜSTENHAGEN, Gustav, *Lakai to Prince Frederick Charles of Hesse*
HUTTENLEHRER, Balthasar, *Chief Postman*

| 12 August | **The King's visit to Ischl** |

POZNANSKI, Leon, *Carriage Caller*
PLATTNER, *Messenger*
POVSIC, Franz, *Footman*
NYERS, Michael, *Footman*
GEIGER, Valentin, *Game Keeper*
PAYERL, Ernest, *Game Keeper*
HITTINGER, Franz, *Police*
PIERINGER, Franz, *Police*
BAUMANN, Wilhelm, *Police*
SIEGEL, Ferdinand, *Police*
WIMMER, Nikolaus, *Senior Veteran, Ischl*
BANDZAUNER, Peter, *Senior Official in the Fire Brigade*
BUCHINGER, Martin, *First Coachman*
WITAK, Rudolf, *Groom*

| 4 September | **The King's visit to Marienbad** |

LERCH, Emil, *Fireman at the Theatre*
TURBER, Anton, *Police*
HOFMANN, Johan, *Police*
FEIL, Michael, *Gendarmerie*
OUTRATA, Anton, *Gendarmerie*
WOKURKA, Josef, *Forester*

| 17 November | **Visit to Windsor of King Gustav V and Queen Victoria of Sweden** |

WILLARS, Julius, *Footman to the King of Sweden*
NOREN, Carl Albert, *Footman to the King of Sweden*
HELGESSON, Johann F., *Footman to the King of Sweden*
GUSTAFSSON, Axel, *Footman to the King of Sweden*
GUSTAFSON, Johan, *Footman to the King of Sweden*
CARLSSON, Carl Oskar, *Footman to the King of Sweden*
ORNSTEDT, Alfred
HAGGLUND, E., *Chasseur*

1909

| 12 February | **The King's visit to Berlin** |

MEINKE, Carl Friedrich, *Postman*
NOACK, Theodor August Oskar, *Postman*
SCHULZ, Georg, *Telegraph Messenger*
FREIER, Hermann, *Telegraph Messenger*
DOBRICZIKOWSKI, Walter Richard Emil, *Messenger*
HERRMANN, Hugo, *Valet*
LAMPE, Albert, *Silver Pantryman*
LEITHAUS, Leopold, *Silver Pantryman*
HERRMANN, Oskar, *Castle Messenger*
LANGE, Walter, *Chauffeur*
KLEINE, Karl, *Chauffeur*
MEYER, Hermann, *Outrider*

WENNER, Franz, *Outrider*
GORLITZ, Friedrich, *Outrider*
MAI, Carl, *Outrider*
SCHÖNEMANN, Oskar Albert, *Chancery Servant at the British Embassy*
RÜHLE, August Heinrich, *Chancery Servant at the British Embassy*

15 April   **The King's visit to Biarritz**
BOURTAYNE, Bernardin, *Gardien de la Paix, Biarritz*
CASTAGNET, Jules, *Agent de Police*
FERRUS, Albert Jerome, *Agent de Police*
HENTY, Adrien, *Agent de Police*
LABADIE, Jean, *Agent de Police*
SUBELET, Jean, *Agent de Police*

22 May   SORET, Pierre, *of the Fire Brigade*
VALLE, Antoine Toussaint, *Postman*
DUSSANT, Arthur, *Ambulance Storekeeper*

20 May   **The King's visit to Naples**
CERZA, Silvio, *Agent de Police, Naples*
PISELLA, Guiseppe, *Agent de Police, Naples*

5 August   **Visit to Cowes of Emperor Nicholas II and Empress Alexandra Feodorovna of Russia**
ALTOUNINE, Frohl, *Footman*
ANDRIEW, Paul
ANTONOFF, Alexis
ARNAOUTOFF, Semen
BODRINE, Ivan
DAVIDKO, Andronik
EGOROFF, Nicolas
EREGIN, Paul
GOUSEFF, Ivan
GRIGORIEFF, Archip
HAILÉ, Gaeques, *Valet to Count Hendrikoff*
KIREIEFF, Peter
KISKA, Feodor
KISSELEFF, Wassili
KLOKOF, Jean, *Cook*
KOBZAR, Ivan
KONOVALOFF, Timoteus
KOVALEFF, Constantin
LOMAKINE, Constantin, *Valet to Prince Belosselsky-Belozersky*
MARAEF, Nicolas, *Cook's Apprentice*
MICHAILOFF, Oulian, *Assistant Butler*
MICHNO, Ivan
MIGAL, Jean, *Assistant Wardrobeman to the Empress*
NIKIFOROF, Gregoire, *Assistant Baker*
OULIANOFF, Olympe, *Assistant in the Kitchen*
PACASSY, Christophe, *Valet to Monsieur Demidoff*
PONOMAREFF, Feodor
PTACHNIKOF Cyprien, *Cook*
ROGATCHOF, Michel, *Footman*
ROMAN, Michailoff
RONDAKOFF, Nikifov
ROUDENKO, Wassili
SMOLIANSKY, Daniel
SARRI, Edward
SPIRIDONOFF, Methodiy
TARASSEVITCH, Feodor
TCHEREMISSINOF, Michel
TCHIJIKOF, Matthieu, *Assistant Wardrobeman*
TREZOUB, Peter
WERECHTCHAGUINE, Dimitry, *Cook*
WOLKOF, Slya, *Tailor*
ZAHAROFF, Serge, *Valet to the Commander of SY Standart*
ZAUTER, Pierre, *Valet to the Minister of Foreign Affairs*
ASPOLM, Eugene Friedrich, *Police Officer*
ESENOFF, Andre Astemir, *Police Officer*
STIER, Daniel Pierre, *Police Officer*
TURTSCH, Basil Jacob, *Police Officer*
POUTILTZER, Gabriel Jean, *Police Officer*

3 September   **The King's visit to Marienbad**
KIRSCH, Rudolf, *Gendarmerie*
ULBRICH, Eduard, *Gendarmerie*

TESCHAUER, Johann, *Town Police*
PSCHIBUL, Ludwig, *Town Police*
MULLER, Georg, *Head Gardener, Stift Tepl*

16 November   **Visit to Windsor of King Manoel II of Portugal**
CASALEIVO, Jose, *Agent de Police*
SOUZA, Julio, *Valet to the King of Portugal*
BARBOZA, Jose Antonio, *Agent de Police*
SOLLERIO, Jose Manuel, *Valet to Senhor du Bocage*
PINTO, Joao, *Valet to Count de Sabugosa*
DAMIAO, Manoel Cosme, *Valet to Marquis du Fayat*
PADRAO, Manuel Corbela, *Valet to Marquis de Lavradio*
SANTOS, Pedro dos, *Valet to Viscount d'Asseca*
SANTOS, Adelino Victorino dos, *Valet to Dr Breyner*

22 December   **Duke of Connaught's visit to Brussels to represent HM at the Funeral of King Leopold II of the Belgians**
WUISBECK, Victor, *Footman*

1910

25 April   **The King's visit to Biarritz**
DEHES, Jean, *Coachman, Hotel Palais*
DUPUY, Bernard, *Brigadier de Gendarmerie*
FOURNIER, Pierre Jean, *Gendarmerie*
DANGÉ, Bernard Vincent, *Agent de Police*
LAURIAC, Louis, *Agent de Police*

GEORGE V: RVM, GOLD

1911–12

1913

24 May   **Their Majesties' visit to Berlin to attend the Wedding of the Duke of Brunswick and Luneberg and Princess Viktoria Luise of Prussia**
BURMEISTER, Otto, *Chauffeur*
DOMKE, Johann, *Page*
EBELING, Friedrich, *Outrider*
JAEZOSCH, Gustav, *Page*
KAHNT, Albin, *Outrider*
NÜSKE, Hermann Gustav Adolf, *Page*
LURKE, Otto, *Riding Master in Royal Stables*
SCHULZ, Rudolf, *Page*
SCHNAACK, Ferdinand Wilhelm Otto, *Coachman*
WANNER, Ernst Friedrich, *Head Chauffeur*
WRIECHEN, Johannes, *Door Porter*
WALTHER, Willy, *Valet*

26 May   **Their Majesties' visit to Neu-Strelitz**
DREWS, Fritz, *Clerk Controller, Lord Steward's Department*
HONNEN, Friedrich, *Valet*
HOFFMAN, Hugo, *Bandmaster*
HARMS, Franz, *Head Footman*
KAHLER, Friederich, *Footman*
RADLOFF, Wilhelm, *Head Footman*
SCHIELE, Ernst, *Outrider*
STEINMANN, Carl Johann Heinrich, *Castle Police*
TIEDT, Wilhelm, *Page*
MICHAEL, Gusttav, *Police Inspector at Neu-Strelitz*

24 June   **Visit to Britain of President Poincaré of the French Republic**
COTIQNAC, Joseph, *Secretaire-Palais de l'Élysée*
MARQUANT, Edouard, *Maître d'Hôtel, Palais de l'Élysée*
CHATAIGNON, Pierre, *Argentier, Palais de l'Élysée*
VACHET, Joseph, *Valet de Chambre to the President*
PRUNE, Louis Victor, *Garçon de Bureau, Palais de l'Élysée*
ANGEARD, Louis Celestin, *Huissier, Palais de l'Élysée*
PEIGNÉ, Paul, *Valet de Pied, Palais de l'Élysée*

| 4 September | Prince of Wales's visit to Sigmaringen for the Wedding of King Manoel of Portugal |
| | WASCHFELD, Wilhelm, *Kammerdiener* |

17 November	Visit to Windsor of Archduke Francis Ferdinand of Austria-Hungary
	BAIERL, Anton, *Messenger*
	JUPTNER, Johann, *Valet to the Archduke*

1914

24 April	Their Majesties' visit to Paris
	VIDON, Louis, *Surveillant M. Personnel de Service au Ministère des Affaires Étrangers*
	BONHOMME, Isidore, *Huissier au Ministère des Affaires Étrangers*
	LONGUET, Georges, *Huissier au Ministère des Affaires Étrangers*
	DECASSUR, Jean Eugene, *Huissier au Ministère des Affaires Étrangers*
	DARRONZÉS, Felix, *Argentier*
	GIRAUDON, Frederic Severin, *Facteur au Ministère des Affaires Étrangers*
	DUBOIS, André Germanj, *Secrétaire à la Présidence de la République*
	LENS, Eugene Louis Joseph, *Ajutant, detaché à la Presidence de la République*
	MORARD, Charles, *Secretaire au Service des Renseignements Généraux*
	LE BRETON, Guy, *Chef de Bureau à la Préfecture de Police*
	FERRAND, Leon, *Commissaire Spécial de Police*
	FENOUILLIERE, Jules Albert, *Portier à la Grille d'honneur du Palais de l'Elysée*
	DECAUX, Andre, *Pigneuro de la Présidence de la République*
	GARAPURI, Camille, *Commis-Calligrapho de Protocole*

| 11 May | Visit to Britain of King Christian X of Denmark |
| | LARSEN, Hans Peter, *Valet to the King of Denmark* |

1915–1918

1919

| 4 November | Visit to Britain of the Shah of Persia |
| | SEIF-US-SULTAN, *Chamberlain to Prince Nosrat es-Sultaneh* |

| 12 November | Visit to Britain of President Poincaré of the French Republic |
| | LE ROUX, Jules Paul, *Commissaire Spécial attached to the President* |

1920

1921

4 July	Visit to Britain of King Albert and Queen Elizabeth of the Belgians
	VAN DYCKE, Théophile, *Valet to the King of the Belgians*
	ANNAERT, Alexandre, *Footman to the Queen of the Belgians*

1922

22 April	The Prince of Wales's visit to Japan
	KIDA, Toshinobu, *Clerk, Japanese Imperial Household*
	SATO, Takeo, *Chauffeur, Imperial Household*
	KITSUGI, Rokuo, *Attendant of Japanese Imperial Table*
	AKIYAMA, Toukzo, *Chief Cook, Japanese Imperial Household*
	IMURO, Haruo, *Police Inspector, Kyoto*
	ARA, Nenotar, *Police Inspector, Kanagawa*
	SAITO, Isami, *Assistant Inspector of Police, Tokyo*
	KUBOTA, Chief Officer Noboru, *T.S.S. Keifuku Maru*
	MIYAZAKI, Warrant Officer Kogoro, *Guard at Tokyo*
	ISHIBASHI, Warrant Officer Rinzaburo, *Guard at Tokyo*

13 May	Their Majesties' visit to Brussels
	MONSCH, Alfred Oscar, *Fourrier at Royal Palace, Brussels*
	LEMAITRE, Joseph, *Chef du Garage at Royal Palace, Brussels*
	DESEY, Leon Henri Joseph, *Chef Argentier, Royal Palace, Brussels*
	ANTOINE, Georges Jules, *Concierge at Royal Palace, Brussels*
	MICHEL, Joseph Aimon, *Maréchal-des-Logis*
	HERMAN, Alphonse, *Chief Electrician, Laeken*

| 18 October | Visit of the Duke of York to Bucharest to represent HM at the Coronation of King Ferdinand I of Rumania |
| | LUPIN, Jules, *Valet de Chambre, Royal Palace, Bucharest* |

1923

14 May **The King's visit to Rome**
MUSSO, Pietro Silvestro, *Maestro della Scuderia da tiro*
NOVELLI, Enrico, *Meccanico dei Reali automobili*
GENTILE, Francesco, *Assistente edile*
CARRARA, Alfredo, *Assistente edile*
ALOTTO, Teofilo, *Brigadiere dei Corrazzieri*
RANIERO, Vincenti, *Mariesciallo Maggiore, Carabinieri Reali*
SALARIS, Pietro, *Appuntato, Carabinieri Reali*
TOCCHI, Orlando, *Appuntato, Carabinieri Reali*
FILIPPI, Giovanni, *Appuntato, Carabinieri Reali*
MORICHINI, Felice, *Deputy Station Master, Rome*

4 November **Visit to Britain of King Gustav V of Sweden for the Marriage of the Crown Prince of Sweden and Lady Louise Mountbatten**
BORG, Carl Oscar, *Valet to the King of Sweden*
NILSSON, Emil, *Valet to the Crown Prince of Sweden*

1924

15 May **Visit to Britain of King Ferdinand and Queen Marie of Rumania**
EDNER, Hermann, *Chef de Cuisine to the King of Rumania*
NEUMANN, Ernest, *Premier Chasseur to the King of Rumania*
SONTAG, Charles, *Valet to the King of Rumania*
STEFANESCU, Francois, *Intendent au Ministère des Affaires Étrangères*
IONESCU, Gheorg, *Chauffeur*

29 May **Visit to Britain of King Vittorio Emanuele III of Italy**
MUSSO, Emanuele, *Valet to the King of Italy*
CHIARIOTTI, Angelo, *Valet to the Italian Minister of the Royal Household*
PIZZINI, Tito, *Head Servant*
NEGRONI, Giovanni, *Typist*
MUSUMECI, Rosario, *Carabiniere Reale Specializzato*
SARTORIO, Everardo, *Staffiere*
MUSSAR, Angelo, *Vice Brigadiere*
BRUTLI, Antonio, *Valet to the Prince of Piedmont*

28 June **Visit to Britain of King Christian X of Denmark**
KOCH, Sören Jensen, *Valet to the King of Denmark*

1925–1926

1927

19 May **Visit to Britain of President Doumergue of the French Republic**
DECARNELLE, Alexandre Paul, *Maître d'Hôtel*
BRANGIER, Albert, *Huissier*
BOURDAIS, Francois, *Valet de Pied*
NICOLLET, Bienaimé, *Valet de Pied*
JALLAT, André, *Valet de Chambre*
LUCIEN, Rene Jean, *Secrétaire d'Etat Major*

6 July **Visit to Britain of King Fuad I of Egypt**
OSMAN, Aly Idris, *Valet to the King of Egypt*
ABDALLAH, Mohamed, *Valet to the King of Egypt*
SALEH, Ahmed, *Chief Maître d'Hôtel to the King of Egypt*

1928

1929

22 March **Marriage of Crown Prince Olav of Norway and Princess Marthe of Sweden**
JOHANSEN, Ludwig, *Steward to the King of Norway*

10 May **The Duke of Gloucester's Garter Mission to Japan**
KAWAGOYE, Norio, *Under Chamberlain, Imperial Japanese Household*
SHIMURA, Shojiro, *Assistant Technical Expert in Japanese Imperial Household*
INUKAI, Noburu, *Attendant at Imperial Japanese Table*

GEORGE V: RVM, SILVER

1911

13 June Coronation of King George V
BECK, Leonhard, *Valet to Herr E.W.E. Hans von Vighan, Chamberlain to the Dowager Duchess of Saxe-Coburg and Gotha*

14 June ROSE, Kammerdiener Friedrich Eduard, *in attendance on the Dowager Duchess of Saxe-Coburg and Gotha*

19 June MAUN, Samuel Thomas, *Station Master at Windsor*

2 December Prince Alexander of Teck's Mission to Bangkok to represent HM at the Coronation of the King of Siam
YON NAI, *Corporal in Siamese Army*
BHERM NAI, *Lance Corporal*
BHAO NAI, *Page Corps, Royal Motor Garage*
SANOA NAI, *Page Corps, Royal Motor Garage*
NGIEM NAI, *Page Corps, Royal Motor Garage*
CHUA NAI, *Page Corps, Royal Motor Garage*
BUN NAI, Chit, *Page Corps, Royal Motor Garage*
PHEN NAI, *Page Corps, Royal Motor Garage*
LIEM NAI, *Page Corps, Royal Motor Garage*
PUY NAI, *Page Corps, Royal Motor Garage*
WAS NAI, *Siamese Police, Under Officer*
KHEN NAI, *Page Corps, Royal Page*

1912

17 January MUSTAFA, Captain Effendi Hamdi, *Guard of Honour from 8th Battalion Egyptian Army at Port Sudan*
ABDULLAH Captain Effendi Kafi, *Guard of Honour from XI Indonese Battalion at Sinkat*
BESHVI, Bey Kembal, *Native Inspector of Kordofan Arabs*
MOHAMMED, Lt. Colonel Bey Ahmed, *Commandant of Police, Suakim*

4 April Prince Alexander of Teck's Mission to Athens to represent HM at the Funeral of King George of the Hellenes
SPIRAOPULOS, Manuel, *Corporal 7th Infantry Regiment, Greek Army*
STAMBOULIS, Theodore, *Sergeant 1st Infantry Regiment, Greek Army*
DESILAS, George, *Private 7th Infantry Regiment, Greek Army*
MICHELLEPIS, Cleobula, *Private 2nd Regiment, Royal Engineers, Greek Army*

11 June Prince Arthur of Connaught's visit to Denmark to represent HM at the Funeral of King Frederik VIII of Denmark
JENSEN, Henry Anton

12 September Prince Arthur of Connaught's Mission to Japan to represent HM at the Funeral of Emperor Mutsuhito of Japan
MURAKANU, Masashi, *Clerk attached to Reception Committee for HRH*
YOSHIMURA, Haruo, *Clerk attached to Reception Committee for HRH*
SAIKI, Takeo, *Clerk attached to Reception Committee for HRH*
WAKIZAKA, Senshiro, *Clerk attached to Reception Committee for HRH*
KABEYA, Yoshinaga, *Clerk attached to Reception Committee for HRH*
UKAI, Nobuzo, *Clerk attached to Reception Committee for HRH*
KANAI, Yoshitada, *Clerk attached to Reception Committee for HRH*
OKAMOTO, Noboru, *Clerk attached to Reception Committee for HRH*
ISHII, Kenkichi, *Clerk attached to Reception Committee for HRH*
ADACHI, Dai-ichi, *Clerk attached to Reception Committee for HRH*
OKUYAMA, Bokushi, *Clerk attached to Reception Committee for HRH*
NAKAYAMA, Matsutaro, *Clerk attached to Reception Committee for HRH*
KUBO, Koshiro, *Clerk attached to Reception Committee for HRH*
KUROZAKI, Genkichi, *Butler, Imperial Household*
SHIMADGU, Hisayoshi, *Police Inspector, Imperial Household*

1913

24 May Their Majesties' visit to Berlin to attend the Wedding of the Duke of Brunswick and Lüneberg and Princess Viktoria Luise of Prussia
JROCKELS, Heinrich, *Cook*
KORSCH, Edward Wilhelm, *Groom*
PODBIELSKI, Karl, *Under Coachman*
DOLL, Emil, *Coachman*
GRUBER, Ignar, *Chauffeur*
MAI, Karl Richard, *Cook*

GILZER, Julius Adolf, *Cook*

JULIUS, Frank, *Butler, Silver Pantry*

BERNDT, Bernhard, *Messenger, Lord Chamberlain's Office, Berlin*

KUTZKE, August, *Masseur*

WIWIANKA, Friedrich, *Page*

SCHULTE, Richard Ernst, *Page*

PETERS, Auguste Carl Theodor, *Page*

JUSTING, Sergeant Heinrich, *Senior NCO Guard of Honour 1st Foot Guards Regiment*

WAGNER, Sergeant Bruno, *3rd Foot Guards Regiment, Senior NCO Guard of Honour*

SCHMIDT, Sergeant Karl, *8th Curassier Regiment, Senior NCO Escort*

JANSEN, Sergeant Bernhard Hermann Wilhelm, *Saluting Battery, Senior NCO*

TSCHAPKE Sergeant Wilhelm, *Royal Bodyguard Orderly attached to the King*

RAHMLOW, Sergeant Hermann, *18th Guard Dragoon Regiment, General Lowenfeld's Servant*

LOEWENSTEIN, Count Wilhelm, *Royal Bodyguard, Orderly attached to King*

ORTMANN, Albert, *of Special Police attached to King*

BÜCHEL, Joseph Franz Jakob Wilhelm Hubert, *of Special Police attached to King*

SCHWANZ, Albert Julius, *of Special Police attached to King*

FUTH, Sergeant Emil Richard Karl, *of Special Police attached to King*

SEELOW, Ernst Karl Friedrich, *Sacristan in St George's Church, Berlin*

SCHÖNEMANN, Albert, *Chancery Servant, British Embassy Berlin*

RÜHLE, Heinrich, *Chancery Servant, British Embassy Berlin*

BOHMS, Sergeant Walter Arnhold Albert Fritz, *Senior NCO, 1st Guard Dragoon Regiment*

SCHLOMSKI, Sergeant Friedrich, *1st Guard Dragoon Regiment*

WESTERMANN Sergeant Charles Henry Wilhelm, *1st Guard Dragoon Regiment*

KOLBERG, Sergeant Rudolf, *1st Guard Dragoon Regiment*

GUNTHER, Sergeant Paul Gustav, *1st Guard Dragoon Regiment*

RAPSEH, Sergeant Franz Theodor Reinhold, *1st Guard Dragoon Regiment*

BLUME, Sergeant Max Gustave, *1st Guard Dragoon Regiment*

BRAUN, Sergeant Hermann, *Blücher Husaren-Regiment Prince Blücher von Wahlstatt (Pommersches) No. 5*

GERSKY, Sergeant Wilhelm, *Blücher Husaren-Regiment Prince Blücher von Wahlstatt (Pommersches) No. 5*

RUKIEK, Sergeant Martin, *Blücher Husaren-Regiment Prince Blücher von Wahlstatt (Pommersches) No. 5*

MÜLLER, Sergeant Hermann, *Blücher Husaren-Regiment Prince Blücher von Wahlstatt (Pommersches) No. 5*

JASBROW, Sergeant Reinhold, *Blücher Husaren-Regiment Prince Blücher von Wahlstatt (Pommersches) No. 5*

NEMITZ, Sergeant Arnold, *Blücher Husaren-Regiment Prince Blücher von Wahlstatt (Pommersches) No. 5*

GRIENHAT, Sergeant Franz, *Blücher Husaren-Regiment Prince Blücher von Wahlstatt (Pommersches) No. 5*

KÄSTNER, Sergeant Ernst, *Blücher Husaren-Regiment Prince Blücher von Wahlstatt (Pommersches) No. 5*

EWERT, Sergeant Max, *Blücher Husaren-Regiment Prince Blücher von Wahlstatt (Pommersches) No. 5*

MILOW, Sergeant Max, *Blücher Husaren-Regiment Prince Blücher von Wahlstatt (Pommersches) No. 5*

GENRICH, Sergeant Ernst, *Blücher Husaren-Regiment Prince Blücher von Wahlstatt (Pommersches) No. 5*

TRUSCKY, Sergeant Karl, *Blücher Husaren-Regiment Prince Blücher von Wahlstatt (Pommersches) No. 5*

PITT, Sergeant Paul, *Blucher Blücher Husaren-Regiment Prince Blücher von Wahlstatt (Pommersches) No. 5*

KALSOW, Sergeant Richard, *Blücher Husaren-Regiment Prince Blücher von Wahlstatt (Pommersches) No. 5*

HELLER, Sergeant Albert, *Blücher Husaren-Regiment Prince Blücher von Wahlstatt (Pommersches) No. 5*

GUSTKE, Sergeant Carl, *Blücher Husaren-Regiment Prince Blücher von Wahlstatt (Pommersches) No. 5*

PAHL, Sergeant Paul, *Blücher Husaren-Regiment Prince Blücher von Wahlstatt (Pommersches) No. 5*

LUERS, Sergeant John, *8th Curassier Regiment*

LIEBECK, Sergeant Ernst, *8th Curassier Regiment*

FLUGERHEIT, Sergeant Wilhelm, *8th Curassier Regiment*

NIEBECKEN, Sergeant Eberhard, *8th Curassier Regiment*

POHLMANN, Sergeant Gerhard, *8th Curassier Regiment*

SCHMIDT, Sergeant Georg, *8th Curassier Regiment*

SCHNACK, Hugo Adolf Christian, *Petty Officer 2nd Class, Sentry in Royal Apartments*

HABICHT, Ernst Willy, *Petty Officer 2nd Class, Sentry in Royal Apartments*

HASS, Friedrich Christian, *Petty Officer 2nd Class, Sentry in Royal Apartments*

FICHT, Paul Emil, *Petty Officer 2nd Class, Sentry in Royal Apartments*

ENGELS, Karl Alfred, *Petty Officer 2nd Class, Sentry in Royal Apartments*

JAHNKE, Herman Martin, *Petty Officer 2nd Class, Sentry in Royal Apartments*

HEYER, Sergeant Paul, *Blucher Hussar Regiment, Sentry, Royal Apartments*

WIEDERSTRASSE, Georg, *Jäger*

AVENDT, Gustav, *Signalman*

26 May   **Their Majesties' visit to Neu-Strelitz**

BÖRMAN, Friedrich, *Head Cellarer*

BUNGER, Franz, *Guard of Honour*

BLANK, Carl, *Footman*

FOSH, Wilhelm, *Footman*

GRABOW, Sergeant Alfred Heinrich Friedrich, *Guard of Honour*

HARKER, Carl, *Footman*

HOLLNAGEL, Hermann, *Footman*

HOLZ, Sergeant Johann Franz, *Salute Battery*

HOLST, Sergeant Wilhelm Hans, *Guard of Honour*

ISRAEL, Sergeant Hermann Eduard Ludwig, *Police*

LÜSSOW, Sergeant Karl Friedrich Johann, *Guard of Honour*

MULLER, Sergeant Amadeus Heinrich Frederick, *Salute Battery*
MOLLER, Franz, *Police*
OHLE, Max, *Wine Butler*
SCHLIZIV, Sergeant Karl Friedrich, *Guard of Honour*
SCHWENN, Sergeant Otto Friedrich Franz, *Guard of Honour*
TELZEROW, Friedrich, *Table Decker*
VOSS, Sergeant Wilhelm August Karl, *Salute Battery*
VOGT, Wilhelm, *Footman*
WILLE, Max, *Coachman*
WIEK, Johann, *Coachman*
WREDE, Arthur, *Head Footman*

24 June   **Visit to Britain of President Poincaré of the French Republic**
LAMOUREUX, Eugene, *Footman*
CHOPARD, Joseph, *Footman*
DAVROUZES, Felix, *Argentier au Ministère des Affaires Étrangères, Paris*
PENHUENÉ, Jean Pierre, *Messenger, French Embassy, London*

4 September   **The Prince of Wales's visit to Sigmaringen to attend the Wedding of King Manoel of Portugal**
HILLER, Eugen, *Footman in Hohenzollern Service*
MALLOW, Friedrich, *Footman in Hohenzollern Service*

October   **Visit to Balmoral in August of Empress Marie of Russia;**
POLIAKOFF, Cyrille Jean, *Cossack in attendance on HIH, 6th Battalion of Cossacks*

15 October   **The Marriage of Prince Arthur of Connaught and Princess Alexandra, Duchess of Fife**
FRAYLING, Fredrick William, *Bandmaster, Royal Scots Greys*

17 November   **Visit to Windsor of Archduke Francis Ferdinand of Austria Hungary**
MELLICK, Karl, *Court Hairdresser*
SCHOCKARTH, Karl, *Leibjäger*
MITTENDORFER, Viktor, *Leibjäger*
HUSZ, Johann, *Footman*

1914

8 March   **The Jubilee of the Kürassier Regt. Graf Geszler (Rheinisches) No. 8**
JOACHIM, Albert, *Polizeiwachter, Veteran Association, 8th Cuirassiers*
DAMMERS, Anton, *Schneidermeister, Veteran Association, 8th Cuirassiers*
KALSOW, Friedrich, *Botenmeister, Veteran Association, 8th Cuirassiers*

6 April   **The Prince of Wales's visit to Christiania**
FLADRAD, Henry, *Footman to the King of Norway*

24 April   **Their Majesties' State Visit to Paris**
LEMESLE, Henri Julien, *Suisse d'Appartement au Ministère des Affaires Étrangères*
CAMBET, Martin Henri, *Suisse d'Appartement au Ministère des Affaires Étrangères*
GUILLON, Gustave, *Suisse du Ministère des Affaires Étrangères*
DESOILE, Alfred, *Concierge, Ministere des Affaires Étrangères*
MESNIL, Louis Eugène, *Concierge*
LEMAIRE, Louis Vilat, *Gardièn de Bureau au Service du Protocole*
GALTIER, Charles Marie, *Gardien de Bureau*
AUBERT, Louis Napoleon, *Chef d'Atelier au Ministère des Postes et Télegraphes*
VERGOS, Louis le, *Gardien de Bureau*
GODBILLE, Ferdinand, *Courier Facteur au Ministère des Affaires Étrangères*
LEROUX, Julian Pierre, *Maître d'Hôtel*
CASTILLON, Paul, *Télephoniste*
PENRICHARD, Francois, *Postillion*
TRAMAUX, Jules, *Brigadier de Sellerie*
BOURGIGNON, Leon Eugène, *Cocher*
VOSS, Ernest Charles Pierre, *Head Chancery Servant, British Embassy, Paris*
VANFERMÉ, Honoré Louis, *Maître d'Hôtel, British Embassy, Paris*
GALAN, Eugene, *Brigadier-Chef*
ZUNFLUH, Ferdinand Charles, *Sous-Brigadier aux Renseignements Generaux et Jeux*
BOURSE, Marc, *Sous-Brigadier*
BERNARD, Leon, *Sous-Brigadier au Service des Renseignements Generaux*
CLARAZ, Honoré André, *Inspecteur au Service des Renseignements Generaux*
GERICH, Louis Roger, *Inspecteur de Police*
CHARDIN, Hilaire, *Inspecteur Principal*
LEBLANC, Louis, *Inspecteur de Police Spéciale*
ROUSSAUD, Léon, *Inspecteur de Police Spéciale*
BOURDAIS, Francois, *Valet de Pied*
NICOLLET, Bienaimé Eugene, *Valet de Pied*
BRANGIER, Albert Louis, *Gardien de Bureau*
AUBEL, Edouard, *Homme de Service, Palais de l'Élysée*
COIRIER, Louis Eugene, *Homme de Service, Palais de l'Élysée*

GRAND, Joseph, *Tapissier*
BAUMARD, Joseph, *Cocher-Postillon*
CAPRON, Maximilien, *Mecanicien*
GONDCHAUX, Marcel, *Chauffeur*
COGNEVILLE, Paul, *Gardien de Bureau*
ARTUS, Valentin Georges, *Gardien de Bureau au Ministère des Affaires Étrangères*
CAPRON, Maximilien Charles Theodore, *Chauffeur Mecanicien*
MARTIN, Auguste Jean, *Commandant du detachement des gardes Planton-Cyclistes du Palais de l'Élysée*
LASSARAT, Philibert, *Adjutant Surveillard Militaire au Palais de l'Élysée*
BOUNI, Louis Achille, *Planton Cycliste de la Présidence*
BATTAILLER, Pierre Hippolyte, *Planton Cycliste de la Présidence*
MORIOT, Henry, *Planton Cycliste de la Présidence*
BOCQUET, Paul Laurent, *Surveillant Militaire, Palais de l'Élysée*
ADONÉ, Joseph, *Surveillant Militaire, Palais de l'Élysée*
MILLOT, Maurice, *Valet de Chambre du Président*

11 May **Visit to Britain of King Christian X of Denmark**
JENSEN, Christian, *Footman to the King of Denmark*
JORGENSEN, Hans Christian, *Footman to the King of Denmark*
PETERSEN, Otto Laurits, *Footman to the King of Denmark*
BOSERUP, Christian Albert Otto, *Footman to the King of Denmark*
JURGENSEN, Peter, *Valet to the Foreign Minister*

1915

18 June **Visit of the Duke of Teck to represent HM at Funeral of the Grand Duke of Mecklenburg Strelitz**
GIPP, Rudolf, *Lakai, Artillery Regiment, No24*

1916

1 April **Visit to Britain of the Crown Prince of Serbia**
MARTINOVITCH, Dushan, *Royal Valet*
ZETCHEVITCH, Vitomir, *2nd Royal Valet*
ROMTCHEVITCH, Miloutin, *Sergeant-Major, Serbian Court Police*
STOITCHITCH, Jacob, *Sergeant-Major, Serbian Court Police*

28 June **Visit of the Prince of Wales to Italy**
FERRERO, Carlo Giovanni, *Servant in Household of King of Italy attached to the Prince of Wales*
SARTORIO, Everardo, *Servant in Household of King of Italy attached to the Prince of Wales*

28 September DELIN, Alfred Henri, *61eme Regiment d'Artillerie de Campagne*

29 September **Visit to London of the Band of the Garde Républicaine**
BOURGEOIS, César, *Sous Chef de la Musique de la Garde Républicaine*

1917

5 July **Duke of Connaught's visit to Italy**
CIMMINO, Mario, *Sergeant-Major Chauffeur*
MOLTENI, Stefano, *Sergeant, Cyclist Battalion Bersaglieri Regiment*
BRAMUCCI, Nazzareno, *Corporal*
GALLOTTI, Pietro, *Private Chauffeur*

14 July **The King's visit to his Army in the Field**
BREUGHON, Frederic, *Adjutant, French Army Interpreter, 2nd Army*
DIGEON, Aurelien, *French Army, Interpreter*
FRANÇOIS, Marcel Jules Odilon, *French Army Interpreter*
LAPIERRE, Jean Marie Louis, *Police Inspector, attached to British GHQ*
SCHUHL, André, *Adjutant, French Army Interpreter, 3rd Army*

1918

29 June **Prince Arthur of Connaught's Mission to Japan**
ADACHI, Shohei, *Chauffeur, Imperial Household*
HASEGAWA, Yoshitaro, *Cooking Department, Imperial Household*
KAMADA, Masaji, *Chauffeur, Imperial Household*
KATO, Ichivoku, *Chauffeur, Imperial Household*
KAWAI, Kennosuke, *Chauffeur, Imperial Household*
KITSUGI, Mutsuo, *Waiter, Imperial Household*
KOIKE, Sagara, *Bureau of Supply, Imperial Household*
KUROKAWA, Tetsuo, *Chauffeur, Imperial Household*
MATSUYAMA, Suretsugu, *Chauffeur, Imperial Household*
MIURA, Jiro, *Architect, Imperial Household*

NAKAMURA, Toshio, *Palace Guard Inspector, Imperial Household*
NAKANE, Nobuo, *Clerk of Bureau of Ceremonies, Imperial Household*
NANJO, Shigeo, *Attaché, Bureau of Imperial Palace*
ONISHI, Seuchiro, *Chauffeur, Imperial Household*
ONISHI, Tokusaburo, *Waiter, Imperial Household*
SATO, Takeo, *Chauffeur, Imperial Household*
SHINAGAWA, Jiuchiro, *Clerk, Bureau of Ceremonies, Imperial Household*
TABATA, Sadanobu, *Attaché, Bureau of Ceremonies, Imperial Household*
YAIRO, Sonosuke, *Attaché, Bureau of Supply, Imperial Household*

6 July   **Visit to Britain of King Albert I of the Belgians**
ANNAERT, Alexandre, *Valet to HM*
VAN DYCK, Théophile, *Valet to HM*

30 November   **The King's State Visit to Paris**
BILLET, Claude Edouard, *Garçon d'Office, Elysée, Paris*
BONNOT, Leon, *Office Keeper, Foreign Ministry, Paris*
BOUILLÉ, Charles, *Office Keeper, Foreign Ministry, Paris*
BOURGNE, Paul, *Police Official*
BRETTES, Prospère, *Messenger, Foreign Ministry, Paris*
CANIVET, Joseph, *Office Keeper, Foreign Ministry, Paris*
CHAVERIAT, Henri, *Orderly*
DARIOT, Sergeant Jean, *Office Keeper, Foreign Ministry, Paris*
DENIS, Louis Henri Eugène, *Chief Cook, Foreign Ministry, Paris*
DUJON, Lucien, *Chief Cook, Presidency of the French Republic, Paris*
DUPONTHIEUX, Louis, *Steward, Foreign Ministry, Paris*
EQUI, Jules André Joseph Marie, *Chauffeur, Elysée, Paris*
FARCACHE, Louis, *Coachman*
FAUQUET, Charles Emile, *Orderly*
FLACON, Alphonse Jules Achille, *Steward, Foreign Ministry, Paris*
GÉLINEAU, Mathurin Louis, *Steward, Foreign Ministry, Paris*
GIRAULT, Aristide, *Gardien de la paix*
HONY, Gustave, *Office Keeper, Foreign Ministry, Paris*
LANGLOIS, Hector Edouard, *Groom*
LORIN, Corporal Jean, *Clerk at the Presidency of the French Republic*
MARCEAU, Pierre, *Garde Républicaine*
MASINGNE, Camille, *Cook, Elysée, Paris*
MAUPIED, Claude, *Steward, Foreign Ministry, Paris*
MÉEUS, Alphonse, *Garçon-de-Bureau, Elysée, Paris*
MORLAT, Louis, *Office Keeper, Foreign Ministry, Paris*
NOIREAU, Corporal Maurice, *Clerk at the Presidency of the French Republic*
PIERRE, Charles Jules, *Valet, Elysée, Paris*
PLASSARD, Pierre Marie, *Groom*
PONCET, Joseph Louis, *Steward, Foreign Ministry, Paris*
ROUAIX, Paul, *Orderly*
TOUSTON, Paul, *Office Keeper, Foreign Ministry, Paris*

10 December   **The King's visit to his Army in the Field**
BRIELET, Leon Charles, *Page to the King of the Belgians*

1919

29 March   **Visit to Britain of Queen Marie of Roumania**
MACHEDON, Ion, *Valet*
CRISTESCU, Petre, *Agent de Sureté*
DELCOURT, Réné, *Interpreter*
MARIN, Nicka, *Valet*
ZOTESCU, Nicolae, *Valet*
LUPIN, Jules, *Valet*
DRĂGOI, Constantin, *Valet*

28 July   **Reception of the Sudanese Mission**
ABDALLAH, Mahil, *Sudanese Follower*
ABDALLAH, Ahmed, *Sudanese Follower*
AHMED, Abdallah, *Sudanese Follower*
EL HAJ EL AMIN, Mohammed, *Sudanese Follower*
BILAL, Ahmed, *Sudanese Follower*
BALAL, Salim, *Sudanese Follower*
HASABALLAH, Abu Amna, *Sudanese Follower*
AHMED SHERFI, Gaafar, *Sudanese Follower*
EL TAYYEB, Ahmed Bashir, *Sudanese Follower*
IBRAHIM, Musa, *Sudanese Follower*
SAYED AHMED, Ismail, *Sudanese Follower*
MOHAMMED, el Nur, *Sudanese Follower*

SHERIF, Abdallah, *Sudanese Follower*
BALIKR, Abdullahi, *Sudanese Follower*

4 November — **Visit to Britain of the Shah of Persia**
JAHAN, Baksh, *Servant to Prince Firuz Mirza Nosrat-ed-Dowlah*
HASSAN KHAN, Homayoun, *Assistant Master of the Robes to the Shah of Persia*
SEYID, Mohammed Khan, Moir-es-Saltaneh, *Valet to the Shah*

12 November — **Visit to Britain of President Poincaré of the French Republic**
PESSAT, Louis, *Valet de Chambre*
DUCHEMIN, Albert Louis Ferdinand, *Valet to M. William Martin*
GABEURE, Jules Cyprien, *Valet to the French Ambassador*

1920

7 December — **Visit to Britain of King Christian X of Denmark**
KOCH, Sören Jensen, *Page in the Service of the King of Denmark*
LARSEN, Johannes Albert, *Valet de Cour in the Service of the King of Denmark*

1921

24 February — **The Duke of York's visit to Brussels**
DE RIDDER, Alphonse Louis, *Footman in the Service of the King of the Belgians*
VAERENBERGH, Alphonse van, *Footman in the Service of the King of the Belgians*
COLMADIN, Camille, *Valet in the Service of the King of the Belgians*
DEMOULIN, Cyrille Joseph, *Steward in the Service of the King of the Belgians*

4 July — **Visit to Britain of King Albert and Queen Elizabeth of the Belgians**
LATTEUR, Arthur Henri, *Footman*
HUNAERTS, Josse Emile, *Footman*
ALLEGOEDT, Paul Guillaume, *Footman*
GUILLAUME, Arthur, *Footman*
COSSI, Joseph Odelin Gilles, *Brusher*

1922

22 April — **The Prince of Wales's visit to Japan**
KUZE, Junkichi, *Clerk, Japanese Imperial Household*
NAITO, Heizaburo, *Chauffeur, Japanese Imperial Household*
ONO, 1st Engineer Makizo, *TSS Keifikumaru*
HAYASHI, Sergeant-Major Susumu, *Guard at Tokyo*
SUZUKI, Sergeant-Major Ushikichi, *Guard at Tokyo*
HIROSE, Sergeant Toyomitsu, *Guard at Tokyo*
HONMA, Sergeant Junji, *Guard at Tokyo*
FUKUSHIMA, Sergeant Fukutaro, *Guard at Kyoto*
DOI, Sergeant Hatsutaro, *Guard at Kyoto*
AOJIMA, Kenichiro, *Clerk, Japanese Imperial Household*
KONO, Junichi, *Clerk, Japanese Imperial Household*
TAKAHASHI, Chiukichi, *Clerk, Japanese Imperial Household*
TAKAKURA, Toshimasa, *Clerk, Japanese Imperial Household*
MUKAI, Noburu, *Attendant, Imperial Japanese Table*
OGASAWARA, Kenkichi, *Sergeant of Police, Tokyo*
ASAGAME, Yoichi, *Police of Tokyo*
YAMASAKI, Makoto, *Attendant, Japanese Imperial Table*
NOMURA, Rikichi, *Attendant, Japanese Imperial Table*
KUNIMATA, Masaji, *Attendant, Japanese Imperial Table*
MOCHIZUHI, Kurasatsu, *Clerk, Imperial Japanese Household*
NINOMIYA, Masaaki, *Clerk, Imperial Japanese Household*
YOSHIZAWA, Akiyeshi, *Clerk, Imperial Japanese Household*

13 May — **Their Majesties' visit to Brussels**
BENKELAERES, Albert, *Postillion*
BORY, Jean, *Messenger*
BRIL, Jean Théodore Henri, *Cook*
BRUNEEL, Guillaume, *Servant*
CAUCHIE, Roger, *Argentier*
CHARLIER, Elisée, *Messenger*
COENEGRACHTS, Jean Herbert, *Maréchal des Logis*
COLLA, Henry, *Valet de Pied*
DE SUTTER, Desiré, *Valet de Chambre*
DHAENENS, Isaie Joseph, *Maréchal des Logis*
DOYE, Leon, *Chauffeur*
GELINNE, Georges, *Messenger*

HAUMONT, Ernest Louis Henri, *Chauffeur*
HOURLAY, Armand Joseph Auguste, *Maréchal des Logis*
MENNE, Dominique, *Maréchal des Logis*
MERTENS, Antoine, *Frotteur*
NULENS, Jean, *Huissier*
POLFLIET, Guillaume, *Postillion*
RAMAEKERS, Antoine Théodore Egide, *Argentier*
SALDEN, François, *Surveillant des Travaux*
SAUVAGE, Henri François Georges, *Cocher*
THOMAS, Joseph Julien, *Argentier*
VAN ANTWERPEN, Jean Pierre, *Postillion*
VANDERSYFEN, Louis, *Frotteur*
WORST, Louis Joseph Emile van der, *Argentier*
GORP, Henri van, *Cocher*
GYSEL, Francois van, *Porter*
VERBEYST, Joseph, *Valet de Pied*
FONTIER, Richard Joseph, *Officier Judiciaire*
STRICHT, Frans van der, *Officier Judiciaire*
LEEMANS, Pierre, *Officier Judiciaire*
CNAEPELINCKX, Jean, *Premier Jardinier au Potage, Laeken*
SMEDT, Jean-Baptiste de, *Jardinier, Laeken*
ERROELEN, Francois, *Jardinier, Laeken*
BELLIRGEN, François van, *Jardinier, Laeken*
CAUWENBERGH, Louis van, *Contremaître au Service des Travaux, Laeken*
VANDERPERREN, Jacques

9 June   **Visit of the Duke of York to Belgrade for the Marriage of King Alexander I of the Serbs, Croats and Slovenes**
STANITCH, Zvetko, *Valet*

1923

27 January   **Visit to Sandringham of Empress Marie Feodorovna of Russia**
POLIAKOFF, Kirill, *Cossack to the Empress*

14 May   **The King's visit to Italy**
SAMPIETRO, Simone, *Assistente di Custodia*
DE VECCHIS, Ettore, *Cocchiere to the Queen of Italy*
JACCHINI, Angelo, *Cocchiere istruttore*
FOGLIANTI, Telemaco
VANNUCCI, Augusto, *Usciere d'Ufficio*
GHELARDONI, Angelo, *Usciere d'Ufficio*
DI DONATO, Salvatore, *Usciere d'Ufficio*
BIANCHI, Carlo, *Usciere d'Ufficio*
BERNARDOTTI, Giovanni, *Usciere d'Ufficio*
BOLTRI, Pietro, *Usciere d'Ufficio*
GALVAN, Gioachino, *Appuntado dei Corazzieri*
ROSA, Nazzareno, *Maresciallo ordinario del Rudlo Reali Carabinieri*
FALCIRELLI, Luigi, *Maresciallo ordinario del Rudlo Reali Carabinieri*
FORTUNA, Vincenzo, *Brigadiere del Rudlo Reali Carabinieri*
BONO, Guiseppe, *Brigadiere del Rudlo Reali Carabinieri*
ABRADO, Valerio, *Magazziniere Reali Magazzini Foraggi*
MACARO, Salvatore, *Capo tapezziere*
CIGNI, Giulio, *Carabiniere Real*
MUSSARI, Angelo, *Carabiniere Real*
MUSSUMECI, Rosario, *Carabiniere Real*
GERUNDA, Angelo, *Carabiniere Real*
AGNELLI, Antonio, *Carabiniere Real*
SFORZA, Antonio, *Carabiniere Real*
TRIOANNI, Giovanni, *Carabiniere Real*
LEONI, Filippo, *Carabiniere Real*
SABATINO, Piergiovanni, *Carabiniere Real*
LUCCHI, Mario, *Carabiniere Real*
PALOMBELLI, Romeo, *Chief Porter at Campidoglio Palace*

14 November   **Visit to Britain of King Gustav V of Sweden for the Marriage of the Crown Prince of Sweden to Lady Louise Mountbatten**
BERG, Carl Johann, *Footman to the King of Sweden*
KARLSSON, Emil, *Footman to the King of Sweden*
MALM, Karl Johann Gunnar, *Footman to the King of Sweden*
AHLIN, Arvid, *Footman to the King of Sweden*
GUSTAFSSON, Knut Erik, *Valet to Prince William of Sweden*
SCHÖN, Albert, *Valet to Prince Gustaf Adolf of Sweden*

1924

15 May **Visit to Britain of King Ferdinand I of Roumania**
STOIAN, Constantin, *Garçon d'Office*
GRACIUNESCU, Nicolae, *Garçon d'Office*
DAMIAN, Aristide, *Footman*
DUMITRESCO, Antofi, *Huissier, Foreign Office*
IANZA, Virgiliu, *Chauffeur*
GLATZETER, Jules, *Chasseur*
BEER, Leon, *Masseur*
SIRBU, Gheorge, *Footman*
SOTIR, Ioan, *Footman*
BUSCUIOC, Nicolae, *Valet*
SAVESCU, Dumitru, *Cook*
EFTIMIU, *Footman*

29 May **Visit to Britain of King Vittorio Emanuele III of Italy**
PARENTI, Vasco, *Footman to the Queen of Italy*
GIACOIA, Carmine, *Valet to General Cittadini*
DI CECCO, Duilio, *Valet to Admiral Bonaldi*
GUNETTI, Giovanni, *Valet to Count Trinita*
CICCARELLI, Ugo, *Valet to Admiral Monaco*
LENZI, Massimo, *Valet*
GAMBINI, Vincenzo, *Valet to Colonel Marzano*
NOVENTA, Carlo, *Valet to Captain Campanari*
CERMESONI, Edoardo, *Staffiere*
SANTONI, Menotti, *Staffiere*
LUCI, Umberto, *Aiutante*
GRECO, Salvatore, *Aiutante*
SALUSTRI, Cesare, *Aiutante*
BERARDI, Marco, *Aiutante*
GRASSINI, Giuseppe, *Real Uffici di bocca*
AGNELLO, Giovanni Battista, *Real Uffici di bocca*
BO, Guiseppe, *R. Uffici di bocca*
MONTEMURRO, Giuseppe, *Vice Brigadiere*
PIACENZA, Bernardo, *Clerk*
GRADI, Augusto, *Usciere*
BASSETTI, Quinto, *Appuntado dei RRCC Specti*
PARIS, Florido, *Ferroviere*

1925

23 September **The Prince of Wales's tour to South America**
LORENZO, Ignacio, *In charge of Presidential Coach, Argentina*

29 November **Funeral of Queen Alexandra**
JOHANSEN, Trode, *Valet to Prince George of Greece*
CARLSEN, Niels, *Valet in the Service of the King of Denmark*
NIELSEN, Jens, *Footman in the Service of the King of Denmark*

1926

19 May **Visit to Britain of President Doumergue of the French Republic**
YUART, André, *Tapissier*
TOULVENT, Michael, *Valet de Pied*
ARLOT, Julien, *Valet de Pied*

10 November **Prince Henry's visit to Brussels for the Marriage of the Crown Prince of Belgium**
DEMOULIN, Pierre, *Footman in the Service of the King of the Belgians*
FLAMME, Auguste, *Chasseur in the Service of the King of the Belgians*

1927

6 July **Visit to Britain of King Fuad I of Egypt**
DIAB, Mohamed Khalil, *Garçon de Table to the King of Egypt*
OSMAN, Ahmed, *Garçon de Table to the King of Egypt*
KHAIRY, Mohamed Khalil, *Garçon de Table to the King of Egypt*
NOUR, Aly Mohamed, *Garçon de Table to the King of Egypt*
HASSAN, Gaafar, *Garçon de Table to the King of Egypt*
ALI, Ahmed, *Garçon de Table to the King of Egypt*
CHERIF, Abou Bakr Taha, *Garçon de Table to the King of Egypt*
SELIM, Abdon Mohamed, *Garçon de Table to the King of Egypt*

AHMED, Fetouhi, *Garçon de Table to the King of Egypt*
SELIM, Soliman Mohamed, *Garçon de Table to the King of Egypt*
TAHA, Mohamed Abdou, *Garçon de Table to the King of Egypt*
CHARKARS, Mohamed Daoud, *Garçon de Table to the King of Egypt*
IDRIS, Mohamed Ahmed, *Garçon de Table to the King of Egypt*
GAAFAR, Hussein, *Garçon de Table to the King of Egypt*
ALI CHAKER, *Garçon de Table to the King of Egypt*
DAHAB, Hussein, *Garçon de Table to the King of Egypt*
SALEH, Khalil, *Garçon de Table to the King of Egypt*
KOURDI, Ahmed, *Garçon de Table to the King of Egypt*
IBRAHIM, Idris, *Garçon de Table to the King of Egypt*
HAROUN, Ahmed, *Garçon de Table to the King of Egypt*
KASSEM, Soliman, *Garçon de Table to the King of Egypt*
IDRIS, Bichir, *Garçon de Table to the King of Egypt*

15 September   **Visit to Balmoral of King Boris III of Bulgaria**
NICOLOFF, Svilen, *Valet to the King of Bulgaria*

1928

15 March   **Visit to Britain of King Amanullah of Afghanistan**
QURBAN, Ali, *Valet to the King of Afghanistan*
SEYYID, Mir, *Valet to the King of Afghanistan*
GHULAM, Sakhi, *Major Domo to the King of Afghanistan*
MAULA, Dad, *Valet to the King of Afghanistan*
SALEH, Mohamed Khan, *Steward to the King of Afghanistan*

1929

21 March   **Visit of the Duke and Duchess of York to Oslo to represent HM at the Marriage of Crown Prince Olav of Norway**
WIDL, Engelbert, *Steward to the British Minister, Oslo*
RÖKERES, Hilberg Olsen, *Footman to the King of Norway*
ANDERSEN, Anders, *Footman to the King of Norway*
NILSEN, Nils, *Footman to the King of Norway*

10 May   **The Duke of Gloucester's Garter Mission to Japan**
KATO, Chonosuke, *Clerk in the Japanese Imperial Household*
KURODA, Minoru, *Clerk in the Japanese Imperial Household*
OHSAWA, Hanazahuo, *Police Inspector, Imperial Japanese Court*
TAKEDA, Suzukichi, *Employed in Imperial Japanese Household Department*
IGURA, Masaji, *Assistant Technical Expert in Imperial Japanese Household Department*
MARUYAMA, Takaichi, *Assistant Technical Expert in Imperial Japanese Household Department*
YANO, Naojiro, *Assistant Technical Expert in Imperial Japanese Household Department*
MAGARA, Umekichi, *Assistant Technical Expert in Imperial Japanese Household Department*
SUZUKI, Rikichi, *Assistant Technical Expert in Imperial Japanese Household Department*
SHIBUYA, Chuji, *Clerk in the Imperial Japanese Household*

1930

8 January   **Visit of the Duke of York to Rome for the Marriage of the Crown Prince of Italy**
BAILO, Antonio, *Police Agent*
PALOMBO, Raffaele, *Police Officer*
BARBERO, Domenico, *Butler at the British Embassy, Rome*

30 October   **The Duke of Gloucester's visit to Addis Ababa to represent HM at the Coronation of Emperor Haile Selassie of Ethiopia**
HAPTA SELLASIE, Andreas, *Driver to the Emperor of Ethiopia*

1931

15 February   **The Prince of Wales's visit to South America**
ERAZO, Celestino, *Messenger, HM Legation, Lima*

31 March   **Prince of Wales's visit to South America**
SANTOS, Tomas, *Head Chancery Servant, British Embassy, Buenos Aires*

1932

27 September   **The Prince of Wales's visit to Denmark and Sweden with Prince George**
LINDRANG, Andreas Johan Nickolaj, *Footman, Royal Palaces, Denmark*

5 October **The Prince of Wales's visit to Denmark and Sweden with Prince George**
ANDERRSON, Knut Johannes, *Footman, Royal Palaces, Stockholm*
SVENBERG, Olof Ragnar Gustaf, *Footman, Royal Palaces, Stockholm*

14 December **Visit of the King of Denmark to Britain**
SIMONSEN, Soren, *Footman to the King of Denmark*

1933

1934

28 November **The Wedding of the Duke of Kent to Princess Marina of Greece**
OECONOMOU, Achille, *Valet to Prince Nicholas of Greece*
NASSALOVITCH, Ouroch, *Valet to Prince Paul of Yugoslavia*
RASMUSSEN, Valdemar, *Valet to Prince George of Greece*

1935

3 June **Visit of Prince Arthur of Connaught to Sweden to represent HM at the Wedding of Princess Ingrid of Sweden to the Crown Prince of Denmark**
JOHANSSON, Carl Gustaf

GEORGE V: RVM, BRONZE

1911

2 December **Prince Alexander of Teck's Mission to Bangkok to represent HM at the Coronation of the King of Siam**
KHEM NAI, *Private, 1st Infantry Regiment, Siamese Army*
RÖL NAI, *Private, 1st Infantry Regiment, Siamese Army*
CHÖE NAI, *Private, 1st Infantry Regiment, Siamese Army*
TO NAI, *Private, 1st Infantry Regiment, Siamese Army*
CHOM NAI, *Private, 1st Infantry Regiment, Siamese Army*
CHERM NAI, *Private, 1st Infantry Regiment, Siamese Army*
SEN NAI, *Private, 1st Infantry Regiment, Siamese Army*
YOD NAI, *Private, 1st Infantry Regiment, Siamese Army*
PHAN NAI, *Private, 1st Infantry Regiment, Siamese Army*
BHERM NAI, *Private, 1st Infantry Regiment, Siamese Army*
WEG NAI, *Private, 11th Infantry Regiment, Siamese Army*
PLENG NAI, *Lance Corporal, 11th Infantry Regiment, Siamese Army*

GEORGE VI: RVM, GOLD

1937

18 November **State Visit to Britain of King Leopold III of the Belgians**
EECKEN, Jos van der, *Chief Valet*

1938

19 July **State Visit to France of King George VI and Queen Elizabeth**
TROWBRIDGE, Louis James Gabriel, *Embassy Servant*
BONNOT, André, *Embassy Servant*
PINAUDIER, Daniel P.H., *Embassy Servant*
DUTHOIT, Louis, *Chief Mechanic, Elysée*
GUILLEMOT, Marcel, *Chef, Quai d'Orsay*
DELBAR, Maurice, *Pilot of Vedette*
CARROU, M. le, *Driver of the Royal Train to Versailles*

15 November **State Visit of King Carol II of Rumania**
ZOPP, Martin, *Personal Servant to the King of Rumania*

1939

21 March **State Visit to Britain of President Lebrun of the French Republic**
DÉCARNELLE, Alexandre Paul, *President's Maître d'Hôtel*

GEORGE VI; RVM, SILVER

1937

18 November   **State Visit to Britain of King Leopold III of the Belgians**
POTIER, M., *Valet de Pied*
VERGAELEN, Maurice, *Valet de Pied*
BROECK, Maurice van den, *Valet de Pied*
LIBERT, Victor, *Valet de Pied*
CLAREN, Jules, *Valet to M. Spaak*

1938

19 July   **State Visit to France of King George VI and Queen Elizabeth**
NOVOTUY, Karl J., *Butler to the British Embassy*
ENFERT, Léon, *Embassy Servant*
LARRALDE, Jean, *Mechanic, Elysée*
MARCHAND, Georges, *Doorkeeper, Elysée*
BROCHIER-CENDRE, Victor, *Doorkeeper, Elysée*
NICOLLET, Eugène, *Office Porter, Elysée*
COUTURIER, Roger Charles, *Office Porter, Elysée*
MASSON, Alfred Camille, *Chef de Cuisine, Elysée*
SANGLAR, Jean, *Valet de Chambre, Elysée*
ROULIER, Emile Eugène, *Footman, Elysée*
HERAULT, Joseph Marie A., *Assistant attached to the Military Secretary, Elysée*
GARÇAIS, Eugène Ernest G., *Chief Assistant to the Military Secretary, Elysée*
CARRÈRE, Louis, *Halberdier, Quai d'Orsay*
AUMEUNIER, Pierre, *Doorkeeper, Quai d'Orsay*
MAZILLIER, Marcel, *Doorkeeper, Quai d'Orsay*
HAMEL, Emile George, *Doorkeeper, Quai d'Orsay*
LE NABAT, Alain René, *Agent of the P.T.T., Quai d'Orsay*
CORNET, Juliette, *Femme de Chambre, Quai d'Orsay*
ALLIBERT, Pierre, *Chef des gardes, Quai d'Orsay*
VIQUIER, Joseph Henri, *Quai d'Orsay*
BOURLON, Pierre, *Chef adjoint du Cabinet, Préfecture of Police*
BLANC, Lucien André François, *Chef adjoint du Cabinet, Préfecture of Police*
LUCE, Charles Louis, *Principal Commissary at the Direction of General Information, Préfecture of Police*
LOUIT, Christian, *Commissary at the Direction of General Information, Préfecture of Police*
DUBRAY, Henri Emile, *Officier de Paix, Préfecture of Police*
COURTOIS, Antonin, *Principal Technical Inspector, Préfecture of Police*
MOTTELET, Jean Georges Gabriel, *Principal Inspector, Préfecture of Police*
DUVOLLET, Emile, *Assistant Principal Inspector, Préfecture of Police*
VANOT, Marceau Alsinder, *Assistant Principal Inspector, Préfecture of Police*
MORICEAU, Louis Roger, *Assistant Principal Inspector, Préfecture of Police*
CHENEVIER, Charles J., *Sûreté*
ARNULF, Raoul Constant Joseph Marcel, *Sûreté*
PERRIN, Maurice Arthur, *Sûreté*
PELLETIER, Marcel François, *Commissary of Police at the Direction of State Police at Versailles*
CORNIER, Henri Placide J., *Inspector of Special Police, Service of Official Journeys, Sûreté*
BALDY, Jean, *Inspector of Special Police, Service of Official Journeys, Sûreté*
LE GAC, Marcel Jean, *Fireman, Royal Train*
DELHAYE, Nestor, *Steward, Royal Train*
JARLAND, Paul, *Chef, Royal Train*
THIL, Lucien Edouard, *Guard, Royal Train*
PICOT, René, *Embassy Chauffeur*

17 November   **State Visit to Britain of King Carol II of Rumania**
OLTEANU, Gheorgue H., *Personal Servant to the Crown Prince of Rumania*
PLATON, Ion, *Personal Servant to Mons. Urdarianu*
WAGNER, Ernest, *Personal Servant to Baron Styrcea*
HOOLOR, Nicolae, *Valet*
SCHAPP, Conrad, *Valet*

1939

21 March   **State Visit to Britain of President Lebrun of the French Republic and Madame Lebrun**
JANOT, Jean, *Footman*
RUCH, Charles, *Footman*
LACABARETE, Jean Pierre, *Footman*
EUDELINE, Louis Ferdinand, *Storekeeper, Elysée*

9 June	Their Majesties' State Visit to the USA
	MADDAMS, Sidney Charles, *Butler,*
9 December	The King's visit to France
	CLERGEOT, Pierre Francis Marcel, *Chauffeur to General Gamelin*

1940

1 June	The Duke of Kent's visit to Lisbon to represent HM at the 800th Anniversary of Portuguese Independence
	CASIMIRO ALVES, Antonio, *Chefe de mesa contratado, da Presidencia da Republica Portuguesa*
	MARTINE, Fructuoso Andion, *Butler, British Embassy, Lisbon*
	ALMEIDA OLIVEIRA, Joao, *Chefe do Pessoal menor da Presidencia da Republica Portuguesa*

1941–1946

1947

21 November	The visit of King Haakon VII of Norway and King Frederik IX of Denmark to Britain to attend the Wedding of Princess Elizabeth
	FURULUND, Sverre Martin, *Valet to the King of Norway*
	NEILSEN, Egon Johanne Vitussen, *Valet to the King of Denmark*

1948

11 October	The visit of Princess Margaret to Holland to represent HM at the Inauguration of Princess Juliana as Queen of the Netherlands
	KOEDAM, Cornelis Gerrit, *Chauffeur to Princess Margaret*
1 November	Visit of the Duke and Duchess of Gloucester to Denmark representing HM at the opening by the King of Denmark of the British Trade Exhibition at Copenhagen
	ANDERSEN, Anders Niels, *Butler*
	BOERJESEN, Gunnar Aage, *Footman*
	JENSEN, Einar Vilhelm, *Chauffeur*

1949

1950

7 March	State Visit to Britain of President Auriol of the French Republic and Madame Auriol
	BALLAIS, Hélène Agnès, *Premier Femme de Chambre de Madame Auriol*
	BARRAUD, Henri
	BARREAU, Albert, *Valet de Chambre du Président*
	BELLANGER, Norbert, *Garçon de Bureau*
	BERQUEZ, Constant
	BLOAS, Inspector, *Security Officer*
	CABANNES, Jean
	DELAFOSSE, Emile
	LE FUR, Clement, *Argentier*
	GONIN, Jean, *The Ambassador's Chef*
	JAVELOT, Georges
	JUNG, Inspector, *Security Officer*
	MOÉSE LACHARTRE, *Valet de Chambre*
	PERRUÇON, Louis, *Garçon de Bureau*
	PIETRI, Inspector Ange Marie, *Security Officer*
	SONTAG, *Footman*
21 November	State Visit to Britain of Queen Juliana of the Netherlands
	ALLEBLAS, Gijsbertus, *Footman*
	VAN DEN AREND, Hendrik Willem, *Footman*
	BEERMAN, Johannes Coenraad, *Housemaster*
	BEKKER, Evert, *Footman*
	BERENDSEN, Karel Johan, *Florist*
	BEYLEVELD, Gerardus Willem, *Yeoman of the Silver*
	BIE, Arie de, *Footman*
	BOSCH, Mademoiselle Hermina, *Head of Linen Room*
	CASTEL, Frans, *Chauffeur*
	DIE, Mademoiselle Lena van, *Linen Maid*
	DULK, Leendert den, *Footman*

ERKELENS, Johannes C., *Footman*
ESSEN, Dirk Jan van, *Yeoman of the Silver*
FIEN, Willem, *State Detective (1st Class)*
FLIER, Elbertus van de, *Housemaster*
GELTINK, Albert Jan, *Footman*
GROOT, Dirk, *Assistant Secretary*
HALSTEIN, Mademoiselle Gerarda Matilda Antoinette, *Personal Maid to the Queen of the Netherlands*
HOFTIJZER, Dirk, *Footman*
HÜSKEN, Johan Martin, *Butler, Royal Netherlands Embassy*
HÜSKEN, Marinus, *First Cook*
JAARSMA, Jacob, *Footman*
JOS, Ferdinand, *Acting Cook*
KOKELAAR, Karel Frederick, *Warrant Officer Bandmaster, Royal Netherlands Marines*
LINDEN , Andreas Aspar van der, *Chief Cook*
LINDEN, Johannes Th.A. van der, *Cook*
LOOIS, Frits, *Footman*
MELIS, Cor Gerardus Maria van, *Footman*
MAGRIJN, J.W., *Acting Cook*
NIJMAN, Gerit Jan, *Footman*
OOSTRUM, Arie van, *Housemaster*
OP'T HOF, Frans, *Acting Footman*
QUAARS, Fransuens Johanus, *Lackey*
RADSTAKEN, Willem I., *Chief Florist*
ROZEMA, Tjaart, *Chief Cook, Royal Netherlands Embassy*
SEITZINGER, Johann Lambertus Antoon, *Footman*
SMIT, Jacques J., *Footman*
SCHAIK, Willem Herman van, *Footman*
STRATEN, Pieter Cornelis N. van, *Acting Footman*
SUKKEL, Jan, *Footman*
TIEL, Klaas, *Footman*
VERBEEK, Wilhelmus C., *Footman*
VISSER, Jelte, *State Detective*
VRIES, Theodorus de, *Footman*
WASSINK, Adriaan, *Footman*
WEES, Willem Hendrik van, *Cook*
WIJK, Anton van, *First Cook*
WIJNHORST, Adrianus, *Footman*
WINTER, Jan, *Footman*
WOEREKOM, Andries van, *Footman*

1951

8 May **State Visit to Britain of King Frederik IX and Queen Ingrid of Denmark**
CHRISTIANSEN, Torben, *Assistant Butler*
LARSEN, Mademoiselle Hederig Nielsene, *Chambermaid*
LARSEN, Helge, *Footman*
MADSEN, Ida Marie, *Chambermaid*
MAURITZEN, Egan Preken, *Footman*
PETERSEN, Lilli, *Cook*

GEORGE VI: RVM, BRONZE

1939

9 June **State Visit to the USA of King George VI and Queen Elizabeth**
BROWNE, Charles Florence Maline, *Chancery Servant, British Embassy, Washington*
BARKSDALE, Chester Howard, *Chancery Servant, British Embassy, Washington*

ELIZABETH II: RVM, GOLD

1957

8 April **State Visit to France of the Queen and the Duke of Edinburgh**
TOULVENT, Michel, *Huissier-en-Chef*
CARTRON, Joseph, *Surveillant Chef à Versailles*
GIRAUD, André, *Adjutant-Chef de la Garde Républicaine*

1958

25 March   **State Visit to the Netherlands of the Queen and the Duke of Edinburgh**
GROOS, K.J., *Usher, Minister of Foreign Affairs*
AGTERBERG, G.M., *Adjutant, River State Police Escort*
SCHEPER, G., *Adjutant, River State Police Escort*
BOKUM, HAH ten, *Adjutant, Hague Municipal Police*
ECK, D.J. van, *Adjutant, Delft Municipal Police*
PLUIM, J., *Adjutant, Rotterdam Municipal Police*
WARENDORP, J. van, *Adjutant, Hague Municipal Police*
MAURIK, H.A. van, *Warrant Officer, Royal Military Band*
PLUGGE, D.M., *Warrant Officer, Fusilier Guards Regiment*
REIJNHOUDT, J.A., *Warrant Officer, Commanding Trumpet Corps of Cavalry*
KOELEWIJN, R., *Warrant Officer,* HMS De Zeven Provincien
MEULMEESTER, K., *Chief Petty Officer, Standard Bearer of the Marines*

1959

1960

5 April   **State Visit to Britain of President de Gaulle of the French Republic and Madame de Gaulle**
LEFEBVRE, Pierre, *Intendant de la Présidence de la République*

1961

2 March   **State Visit to Britain of the Shahanshah of Iran**
SALEHI, Reza, *Butler at Ministry of Foreign Affairs*

5 May   **State Visit to Italy of the Queen and the Duke of Edinburgh**
BONJEAN, Wladimiro, *Head of Antichamber Staff, the Quirinale*
MARROCU, Anacleto, *Head of Custodians, the Quirinale*
FLORA, Michele, *Police Security Officer, Questura*
VITO, Albine di, *Chief Marshal*
PASCUCCI, Espedite, *Ceremoniale*
GIORGI, Duilie, *Ceremoniale*
GHEZZI, Oldine, *Head Gardener*

1962

16 October   **State Visit to Edinburgh of King Olav V of Norway**
HEDENSTAD, Bjarne, *Chief Steward to HM*
HEDENSTAD, Johan, *Valet to HM*
MYHRE, E., *Footman*
GOMSRUD, E., *Footman*
BRATEN, Halvor, *Footman*

1963

9 July   **State Visit to Britain of King Paul and Queen Frederika of the Hellenes**
NANOS, Paul, *Head Butler*

1964

28 May   **State Visit to Britain of President Abboud of the Republic of the Sudan and Madame Abboud**
SALAM, Sergeant Major Ibrahim, *Attendant*

1965

8 February   **State Visit to the Sudan of the Queen and the Duke of Edinburgh**
IBRAHIM, Sayed Mahmoud, *Comptroller, Republican Palace*
RAYAH, Sayed Mahgoub el, *Horticultural Officer*
KHALIL, Sayed Daoud, *Head Suffragi*

18 May   **State Visit to the Federal Republic of Germany of the Queen and the Duke of Edinburgh**
LILL, Ilse, *Specialist in British Affairs in Federal Office*
KUNIS, Eberhard, *Protocol Expert, Bonn*
KLEIN, Karl, *Chief Inspector of Police, Head of Police Escort*
SUDER, Franz Joseph, *State Visit Section, Bavarian State Chancery*

FORSTER, Max, *State Visit Section, Bavarian State Chancery*
GEISLER, Helmut, *Bavarian Security Official*
SCHAFFELDER, Kurt, *Security Police Chief Inspector, Lower Saxony*
BÜGE, Gerhard, *Protocol Official, Berlin Senate Chancery*
BADING, Elisabeth, *Protocol Official, Berlin Senate Chancery*
FUCHS, Eugen, *Senior Official, Schlafwagen Gesellschaft-on train*
GRÖPEL, Heinrich, *2nd Senior official, Schlafwagen Gesellschaft-on train*
BOEMINGHAUS, Walter, *Protocol, City of Cologne*
PADBERG, Theodor, *Post Office, in charge of telephone on train*

1966

9 May **State Visit to Belgium of the Queen and the Duke of Edinburgh**
MATTERNE, Charles, *Regimental Sergeant-Major*
SEVENANT, Georges van, *Battalion Sergeant-Major*
REULLE, Fernand, *Deputy Bandmaster*
SURMONT, Lucianus-Oscar, *Commissioner of Police, Middelkerke*
T'JOENS, Michel-Adelson, *Commissioner of Police, Poperinghe*
DEBEL, Cyriel, *Commissioner of Police, Ypres*
ROL, Henri, *in Department of the Grand Maréchal*
VERELLEN, Frans, *in charge, Royal Garage, Laeken*
SEYS, Valère, *in charge, Royal Garage, Brussels*
LIBERT, Emile, *Usher*
GROOTE, René de, *Usher*
MEYSMAN, Auguste, *Usher*
DERYCKE, Georges, *Caretaker of Brussels Palace*
DERYCKE, Mme Jeanne, *Linen Keeper*
OVART, Edgard, *in charge, Silver Pantry, Brussels*
BRUCKER, Robert de, *Butler*
GOETHALS, Pierre, *Under-Butler*
MULOT, Marcel, *Chef*
ELST, Marcel, *Chief Clerk at Laeken*
LEDIEU, Félix, *Warrant Officer Class 2*

17 May **State Visit to Britain of President Jonas of Austria and Frau Jonas**
ENGEL, Frau Felicitas, *Social Secretary, Austrian Embassy*
FISCHER, Sergeant-Major, *Military Attaché, Austrian Embassy*

1967

1968

1 November **State Visit to Brazil of the Queen and the Duke of Edinburgh**
PINTO, Antonio de Oliveira, *Administration Officer, Ministry of Foreign Affairs*
PADILHA, Delegado Deraldo, *Security Co-ordinator, Rio*
BOMCRISTIANO, Jose Paulo, *Security Co-ordinator, Sâo Paulo*
MARIA, Major Pedro Paulo, *Public Relations Officer, Air Ministry*
NOVONHA, Major Ney, *Commandant, Air Base, Brasilia*
CARDOSO, Hermes, *Liaising with Naval Services, Rio*
MEIRELLES, Captain de Corveta Antonio F., *Naval Administration, Rio*
OLIVEIRA, Major Helio de, *Commanding Military Police Operations, Rio*
RESENDE, Major José Gentil, *Commanding Outriders, Rio*

11 November **State Visit to Chile of the Queen and the Duke of Edinburgh**
PONCE, Jorge Maluenda, *Officer in charge of Security, Valparaiso*
MONDACO, Patricio, *Executive Chef, Carrera Hotel*
PAREDES, Arnoldo Cardenas, *Head Waiter*
COUCHOT, Francisco, *Administrator, Cerro Castillo*

1969

5 May **State Visit to Austria of the Queen and the Duke of Edinburgh**
MIERZINSKI, Maria, *of the Presidential Chancellery*
SCHOPF, Ernst, *Inspector, of the Presidential Chancellery*
WASTL, Josef, *Courier, of the Presidential Chancellery*
KRISCHNIAK, Otto, *Official, of the Presidential Chancellery*
NEUMAYER, Erich, *Lorry Driver, of the Presidential Chancellery*
PODSCHEIDER, Karl, *Official, of the Presidential Chancellery*
HERMANN, Ernst, *Inspector, of the Presidential Chancellery*
KÖNIG, Friedrich, *Secretary, Federal Chancellor's Office*

KEMPINGER, Alfred, *Clerk, Federal Chancellor's Office*
WENINGER, Franz, *Special Inspector, Federal Chancellor's Office*
STOCKREITER, Wilhelm, *Special Inspector, Federal Chancellor's Office*
CERNY, Walter, *Head Clerk, Federal Chancellor's Office*
HIESSBERGER, Emma, *Secretary, Ministry of Foreign Affairs*
SCHMUTZ, Major Rudolf, *Police*
KEPPLINGER, Lieutenant Karl, *Gendarmerie*
IRBINGER, Johann, *Senior Horseman*
ROHATSCH, Robert, *Senior Warrant Officer*
SCHIENER, Karl, *Special Inspector, Ministry for Building*
HÖLZL, Konrad, *Technical Commissioner, Vienna*
FLORIAN, Johann, *Technical Commissioner, Vienna*

15 July   **State Visit to Britain of the President of Finland and Madame Kekkonen**
BAHLSTIN, Albert, *Maître d'hôtel to the President*
SCHAUMAN, Ann-Kristin, *Secretary to Press Department, Finnish Embassy*
SCOTT, Ritva, *Switchboard Operator, Finnish Embassy*

1970–1971

1972

9 February   **State Visit to Thailand of the Queen, the Duke of Edinburgh and the Princess Anne**
WONGSAROT, Damri, *of the Civil Service*
PYRAMARN, Chuan, *of the Civil Service*
VANACHINDA, Powthep, *of the Civil Service*
SONJAROON, Sukasem, *of the Civil Service*
PINSAKUL, Captain Maka, *Royal Thai Army*
KEEREETAWEEP, First-Lieutenant Jane, *Royal Thai Army*
DECHACUPT, Lieutenant Preda, *Royal Thai Navy*
SANGAVICHIAN, Lieutenant Visut, *Royal Thai Navy*
ONCHAN, Flight Lieutenant Viraj, *Royal Thai Air Force*
BANMAI, Flying Officer Sirichai, *Royal Thai Air Force*
SWASDI-KUTO, Major Chumtool, *Police Department*
RAEMVAL, Lieutenant Vira, *Police Department*

22 February   **State Visit to Malaysia of the Queen, the Duke of Edinburgh and the Princess Anne**
SALIHI, Abdullah, *Ceremonial Clerk at Istana Negara*
NGASIMIN, Hashim, *Clerk at Istana Negara*
PHOON, Inche Lee Soon, *of Ceremonial Division of Prime Minister's Department*
WAHAB, Inche Mohd Shaari bin Abdul, *of Ceremonial Division of Prime Minister's Department*
VENKATESH, Inche R., *Protocol Division Ministry of Foreign Affairs*
TEH, Puan Daphne, *Secretary/Stenographer, Protocol Division, Ministry of Foreign Affairs*
SUAN, Puan Chong Poh, *Stenographer, Protocol Division, Ministry of Foreign Affairs*
JIDIN, Wt Officer I. Waheb bin, *Personnel Division, Ministry of Defence*
ISMAIL, Wt Officer I. Malek, *Personnel Division, Ministry of Defence*
AHMAD, Wt Officer I. Kamaruddin bin, *Personnel Division, Ministry of Defence*
MAN, Sub-Inspector Saad bin, *Royal Malaysian Police HQ*
JAMIN, Sergeant-Major Zakaria bin, *Royal Malaysian Police HQ*

11 April   **State Visit to Britain of Queen Juliana of the Netherlands and Prince Bernhard**
SARIS, Miss F.M.J., *Private Secretary to Ambassador*
PAPAVOINE, Warrant Officer Hendrik Theodorus, *Royal Netherlands Air Force*
STARKE, Luurt, *Steward, Royal Household*
CORNELISSE, Klaas, *Steward*
AREND, Hendrik Willem van den, *Head of Silver Room*
DIE, Miss Lena van, *Head Linen Room*
KOL, Pieter, *Head Florist*
DUYN, Buisert van, *Senior Footman*
DE GRAAF, Nicolaas, *Senior Footman*
MELIS, Cor Gerardus Marie van, *Senior Footman*
WEYDE, Pieter van der, *Senior Footman*
REMIJNSE, Warrant Officer Johan, *Senior Footman*
GOUT, Warrant Officer Louis M., *Senior Footman*
LEZER, Samuel George, *Valet to the Prince of the Netherlands*
SCHAIK, Willem Herman van, *Valet*
TERPSTRA-HARTOG, Mrs Cornelia, *Personal Maid to the Queen of the Netherlands*
GROENEVELD, Miss Johanna Margaretha, *Personal Maid to Baroness Sweerts*
DIJKSTRA, Warrant Officer M., *Royal Netherlands Marines*

15 May   **State Visit to France of the Queen and the Duke of Edinburgh**
PAYET, Jean, *Service Intérieur, Ministry of Foreign Affairs*

COULHON, Capitaine Pierre, *Commandant Militaire du Palais, Grand Trianon*
GODARD, André, *Chef du Service Dessin, Palais de l'Elysée*
HENNEQUIN, Guy, *Intendant du Palais de l'Elysée*

13 June — **State Visit to Britain of Grand Duke Jean of Luxembourg**
STEFFEN, Michel, *Palace Steward*
HENGESCH, Aloyse, *Silver Steward*
BIREN, Charles, *Head Chauffeur*
GIERES, Mathias, *Band Sergeant-Major*

17 October — **State Visit to Yugoslavia of the Queen and the Duke of Edinburgh**
PAUNESKU, Panta, *Guard Band, Yugoslav Army*
PETROVIC, Milan, *Guard Band, Yugoslav Army*
AVRAMOVSKI, Dusko, *Sergeant Major, Guard of Honour, Yugoslav Army*
GUBERINIC, Bozo, *Sergeant Major, Guard of Honour, Yugoslav Army*
PESUT, Radoslavi, *Petty Officer 1st Class, Yugoslav Army*
DIMITRIJEVIC, Ljubisa, *Chief Engineer, Yugoslav Army*
SOKCEVIC, Teodor, *Technician, Yugoslav Army*
SKLEMPE, Mirko, *Maître d'Hôtel, Dedinje Palace*
MARKOVIC, Mirko, *Head Waiter, Dedinje Palace*
COZO, Martin, *Chef, Villa Brionka*

24 October — **State Visit to Britain of President Heinemann of the Federal Republic of Germany**
MÜLLER, Margot, *Personal Assistant to Frau Heinemann*

1973

3 April — **State Visit to Britain of President Echeverria of Mexico**
GONZALEZ, Luisa, *Secretary, Mexican Embassy*
DILLON, Rocio Caballero de, *Secretary, Mexican Embassy*

1974

30 April — **State Visit to Britain of Queen Margrethe II of Denmark and Prince Henrik**
SORENSEN, Knud, *Chef, Royal Yacht Dannebrog*
SHEARING, Helga, *Clerk, Danish Embassy*

9 July — **State Visit to Britain of the Yang Di-Pertuan Agong of Malaysia and the Raja Permaisuri Agong**
AWANG, Haji Jaafar bin, *Personal Assistant to the Private Secretary*
MOHAMED, Lieutenant-Commander Tuan Hashim bin Tuan, *Assistant Services Adviser (Navy), Malaysian High Commission*

1975

24 February — **State Visit to Mexico of the Queen and the Duke of Edinburgh**
BUCH, Elisa Diaz Lombardo de, *Assistant, Protocol Dept., Ministry of Foreign Affairs*
ROIG, Susana C. de, *Assistant, Protocol Dept., Ministry of Foreign Affairs*
HAUSSNER, Maria Teresa A. de, *Assistant, Protocol Dept., Ministry of Foreign Affairs*
CABALLEROS, Captain Carlos Henrique M., *responsible for logistics*
CASTRO, Captain Jesús Rangel, *responsible for logistics*
FERNANDEZ, Armando, *President, Pedregal Association of Horsemen*

7 May — **State Visit to Japan of the Queen and the Duke of Edinburgh**
HIRASAWA, Masao, *Assistant Director, Decoration Bureau*
KOIDE, Hideo, *Assistant Director, Decoration Bureau*
TOKITA, Masayuki, *Chief, Inspection Division, Decoration Bureau*
HIRABAYASHI, Yukifusa, *Assistant Director, Decoration Bureau*
ASAKURA, Kiichi, *Assistant Director, Personnel Division*
BEPPU, Shinyu, *Official, Press Division*
HOSHIAI, Inspector Takaki, *Second Public Security Division, National Police Agency*
HAMAMURA, Inspector Yoshiaki, *Second Public Security Division, National Police Agency*
ISHIKAWA, Inspector Kiyoshi, *The Queen's Bodyguard*
SAKURAI, Inspector Tadashi, *Head of Guards, Akasaka Palace*
HAGA, Sgt. Taisuke, *Protection Section, Metropolitan Police Board*
SAKAGUCHI, Sgt. Masahiro, *Protection Section, Metropolitan Police Board*
HOSONO, Kazuo, *Assistant Director, Akasaka Palace*
AONO, Shoichi, *Assistant Director, Akasaka Palace*
SUZUKI, Shinjiro, *Assistant Director, Akasaka Palace*
ENDO, Shintaro, *Assistant Director, Akasaka Palace*
OGAWA, Hiroshi, *Official, Akasaka Palace*
MATSUMURA, Yousuke, *Official, Akasaka Palace*

8 July — **State Visit to Britain of King Carl XVI Gustav of Sweden**
LINDELL, Knut, *Valet de Chambre*

KARLSSON, Karl Erik, *Butler*
BOSTRÖM-MURPHY, Gudrun, *Press and Information Assistant, Swedish Embassy*

1976

4 May   **State Visit to Britain of President Geisel of Brazil and Senhora Geisel**
CISNEROS, Flora Belté, *Protocol Officer, Brazilian Embassy*

24 May   **State Visit to Finland of the Queen and the Duke of Edinburgh**
WAGELLO, Liisa, *Secretary of Bureau, Protocol Department*
VALLILA, Pirkko, *Secretary of Bureau, Protocol Department*
AHORANTA, Vesa, *Chief Constable, Security Police*
BARQVIST, Veikko, *Chief Detective, Security Police*
POUTANEN, Risto, *Chief Constable, Security Police*
PUISTOLA, Antti, *Chief Constable, Security Police*
LEMMETTY, Vilho, *Chauffeur, Presidential Palace*
LINDBLOM, Ragnar, *Chauffeur, Presidential Palace*
VILPAS, Pekka, *Head Steward, Presidential Palace*
BELLMAN, Arnold, *Head Commissionaire, Presidential Palace*

22 June   **State Visit to Britain of President Giscard d'Estaing of France and Madame Giscard d'Estaing**
SELZ, Philippe, *Deuxième Secrétaire*

8 November   **State Visit to Luxembourg of the Queen and the Duke of Edinburgh**
GOERENS, Josette, *Secretary, Protocol Department, Ministry of Foreign Affairs*
COURTE, Leon, *Official, Decorations Service*
ENTZ, M., *of Government Information Service*
DONNERSBACH, Emile, *Official of Public Works Department*
DUMONT, Theo, *Supervisor of Parks and Gardens*
THOMA, Robert, *Assistant to ADCs*
DECKER, Alphonse, *Housekeeper, Grand Duke's Household*
MARTIN, Adjutant-Chef René, *Doorman, Grand Duke's Household*
SCHNITZLER, Roland, *Chef, Grand Duke's Household*
HOFFMAN, Pierre, *Chief Chauffeur, Grand Duke's Household*
HASTERT, R., *Secretary, Committee for Kirchberg Centre*

1977

1978

22 May   **State Visit to the Federal Republic of Germany of the Queen and the Duke of Edinburgh**
VIEWIG, Peter, *Chief Superintendent, Police Inspectorate Schleswig-Holstein*
DELFS, Erika, *Clerk, Protocol Section, Schleswig-Holstein*
JÜRRIES, Friedrich, *Head of Travel Department, Federal Railways*

1979

16 May   **State Visit to Denmark of the Queen and the Duke of Edinburgh**
JENSEN, Leif Richard, *Head Messenger, Ministry of Foreign Affairs*
SØRENSEN, Lieutenant Niels Erik, *Liaison Officer to HMY Britannia*
BARNER, Lieutenant Per Odegaard, *Royal Danish Barge Officer*
BASBALLE, Lieutenant Erik, *Royal Life Guard*
GRAUGAARD, Knud, *Bandmaster at Aarhus*
BANG, Erik Vilhelm Frithjof, *Senior Custodian, The Royal Theatre*
HANSEN, Tage, *Inspector, Municipality of Copenhagen*
DEDING, Ebba, *Head Clerk, Lord Chamberlain's Office*
CLAUSEN, Karen Margrethe, *Clerk, Lord Chamberlain's Office*
PJETURSSON, Sigurdur Bjarnason, *Clerk, Comptroller's Office*
HANSEN, Gunther Moeller, *Senior Messenger, Christiansborg*
THOMSEN, Kurt Rode, *Table Dresser*

1980–1981

1982

16 November   **State Visit to Britain of Queen Beatrix of the Netherlands and Prince Claus**
BERG, Warrant Officer C.L. van den, *Steward, Royal Netherlands Air Force*
FOKS, H., *Chief Chef*
LAAR, P.J.R. van, *Chief Florist*
OOMS, M., *Head of Linen Room*

ZWEEKHORST, G.J.F., *Keeper of the Royal Silverware*
DAAS, W. den, *Chief Florist*
ENDER, S.M. Thesen, *Secretary, Royal Netherlands Embassy*

1983

25 May   **State Visit to Sweden of the Queen and the Duke of Edinburgh**
LINDQUIST, Rolf, *First Groom of the Bedchamber*

1984

10 April   **State Visit to Britain of Sheikh Isa bin Sulman Al-Khalifa, Amir of Bahrain**
KHONJI, Mohamed Sharif, *Medical Attaché, Bahrain Embassy*
MONFARADI, Hasan, *Cultural Attaché, Bahrain Embassy*

23 October   **State Visit to Britain of President Mitterand of France and Madame Mitterand**
KRAITSOWITS, Janine, *Second Secretary, French Embassy*

1985–1991

1992

9 June   **State Visit to France of the Queen and the Duke of Edinburgh**
DOCQUIERT, Madame, *Director of Communications, La Villette*
ARBONNEAU, Capitaine Stanislas Marie d', *Maritime Préfecture, Brest*
LEROLLE, Madame Aggy, *Press Chief, Musée d'Orsay*
LOYRETTE, Henri, *Chief Conservator, Musée d'Orsay*
MARTIN, Jean-Pierre, *Préfecture of Pau*
PERRET, Alain, *Préfecture of Val-de-Marne*
TANDONNET, Maxime, *Préfecture of Tours*
TSCHUMI, Bernard, *Architect*

1993

1994

5 July   **State Visit to Edinburgh of King Harald of Norway and Queen Sonja**
HANSEN, Wenche, *Senior Clerk, Norwegian Embassy*
ANDERSEN, Trond, *Valet*

ELIZABETH II: RVM SILVER

1954

28 June   **State Visit to Britain of King Gustav VI Adolf and Queen Louise of Sweden**
BERGÉRUS, S., *Chief Palace Steward*
LINDELL, K., *Valet de Chambre to the King*
THULIN, Miss J., *Lady's Maid to the Queen*
SKOGH, I., *Footman*
LINDQVIST, R., *Footman*
N, B., *Assistant Footman*
HJELM, Miss E., *Lady's Maid to the Mistress of the Robes*
LINDELL, Miss I., *Assistant Lady's Maid*
HANSSON, Alfons, *Messenger*
LUISARDI, Luigi, *Butler*
LUCIA, Giuseppe de, *Cook*

14 October   **State Visit to Britain of Emperor Haile Selassie of Ethiopia**
ADMASU RETTA, Ato, *Valet*
MANGASHA, Ato, *Valet*
LANTIDEROU, Ato, *Valet*
LEGGESE, Ato, *Valet*

1955

24 June	**State Visit to Norway of the Queen and the Duke of Edinburgh**

BEKKEN, Ole, *Page*
BORCHGREVINK, Henrik Christian, *Head Chauffeur to the King of Norway*
BRATEN, Halvor, *Page*
ERIKSEN, Bjärne, *Head Porter*
FOSSUM, Olaf, *Third Chauffeur to the King of Norway*
GOMSRUD, Einar Villiam, *Page*
HEDENSTAD, Bjärne, *Steward*
HEDENSTAD, Johan, *Page*
INGEBRETSEN, Edvard, *Page*
IVERSEN, Paul Einor, *Porter*
MYHRE, Edvard Johannes, *Footman*
NAESS, Sören, *Porter*
NYBORG, Reidar Sverre, *Chauffeur*
ORMAASEN, Ivar, *Footman*
RAKNERUD, Ingebret, *Chauffeur*
ROED, Torstein Wilhelm, *First Chauffeur to the Crown Prince*
RUUD, Finn, *Footman*
TOFSRUD, Erling Josef, *Steward to the Crown Prince*
VERKET, Haakon, *Page*

25 October	**State Visit to Britain of the President of Portugal and Madame Craveira Lopes**

FREITAS, Jose Felix, *Chief Butler, Portuguese Embassy*
CHABERT, Henrique, *Chef to the Portuguese Ambassador*
CAMARATE PEREIRA, Manuel Agostinho, *Footman*
MARTINHO ROSEIRO, Antonio, *Major-domo*
ALVARO DA CUNHA, Caetano, *Valet de Chambre to the President*
PIEDADE MARTINS, Miss Emilia da, *Lady's Maid to Madame Craveira Lopes*
MENDES, Fernando Manuel Camacho, *Clerk, Portuguese Embassy*

1956

8 June	**State Visit to Sweden of the Queen and the Duke of Edinburgh**

ACKELMAN, N., *Palace Attendant*
LINDAHL, S., *First Palace Attendant*
ARNHOV, H., *Palace Attendant*
ERICSSON, G., *Palace Attendant*
HAGDALEN, A., *Palace Attendant*
KALFJÄLL, G., *Palace Attendant*
WENSTRÖM, M., *Palace Attendant*
KARLSSON, K.E., *Butler*
ANGSTRAND, H., *Butler*
SONDAL, G., *Footman*
MALMBORG, B., *Footman*
HANSSON, B., *Footman*
JANSSON, O., *Chauffeur*
ALVERGARD, E., *Chauffeur*
JOHANSSON, *Footman*
WIGREN, B., *Footman*
ALWERHOLM, A., *Head Housekeeper*
OHLSSON, G., *Upholsterer*
KARLSSON, *Guard*
EDIN, Miss Gerda, *Seamstress*
KARLSSON, K.G., *Coachman*
KARLSSON, E.I., *Chauffeur*
HERVÉN, C.E.L., *Coachman*
ENGSTRÖM, G.A., *Coachman*
ERICSSON, E.A., *Jockey*
ANDERSSON, G.C.F., *Chauffeur*
ANDERSSON, G.L., *Chauffeur*
NITTSJÖ, O.H., *Chauffeur*
FRÄNNE, G.J., *First Machinist*
JANGÖ, A.E.A., *Electrician*
SANDELL, J.A., *Footman of the Castle*
LAGERGREN, S.J.V., *Footman of the Castle*
HARTZELL, E.G., *Carpenter*
ROSÉN, E. *Chauffeur*
STRANDBERG, E., *Messenger, British Embassy*

16 July	**State Visit to Britain of King Feisal II of Iraq**

BASTAWI, Hassan, *Valet to King Feisal*
DAHI, Kadhim, *Valet to King Feisal*

1957

18 February **State Visit to Portugal of the Queen and the Duke of Edinburgh**
SILVA, Anibal Espirito Santo, *Butler, Palace of Queluz*
MELO, Antonio da Silva, *Manservant, Palace of Queluz*
MOCO, Alzira da Purificacao, *Maid, Palace of Queluz*
BOTO, Fernando da Conceicao, *Manservant, Palace of Queluz*
MORAIS, José, *Manservant, Palace of Queluz*
TAVARES, Fernando Miguel de Moura, *Manservant. Palace of Queluz*
JESUS, Manuel de, *Chauffeur of the Queen's car*
SANTOS, Antonio dos, *Doorkeeper, Palace of Queluz*
PEREIRA, Luiz Soares, *Chauffeur, Palace of Queluz*
GOMES, Antonio Agostinho, Jr, *Chauffeur, Palace of Queluz*
ALMEIDA, Manuel de, *Chauffeur's assistant, Palace of Queluz*
SILVA, José Marcal da, *Chauffuer's assistant, Palace of Queluz*

8 April **State Visit to France of the Queen and the Duke of Edinburgh**
CARTIERRE, *Drum Major, Band of the Garde Républicaine*
GOSSET, Adjutant-Chef, *Chef du Fanfare de la Garde Républicaine*
AISSA, Adjutant Merissi, *Senior North African NCO, Spahi Escort*
HOUVENAGHEL, M., *Inspecteur de Police*
DELROUX, Mlle, *Secrétaire du Chef du Protocole*
DUBOIS, M., *Inspecteur-adjoint*
LABAT, M., *Huissier-Chef*
CASIER, M., *Chef-Surveillant*
VIAVANT, M., *Huissier-Chef*
PREVOST, M., *Inspecteur de Police*
RACINAIS, Henri, *Archiviste, Versailles*
CHEP, M. Gabriel, *Surveillant, Louvre*
VITOUX, M. Fernand, *Brigadier, Louvre*
DUPOUY, M., *Lustrier, Service Interieur*
LE CALVE, M., *Surveillant Militaire, Service Interieur*
MOHAMED, M., *Homme de Service, Service Interieur*
BOISSON, M., *Inspecteur, P.T.T.*
COLAS, M., *Contrôleur, P.T.T.*
LEGER, M., *Contrôleur, P.T.T.*
CORMIER, M., *Chef de Cuisines, Personnel Privé*
ROUVRAIS, M., *Huissier, Personnel Privé*
DURET, M., *Huissier, Personnel Privé*
HARRY, M., *Fleuriste, Personnel Privé*
DAVID, Mme Blanche, *Lingère en Chef, Personnel Privé*
TAMINE, M., *Adjutant-Chef, Garde Républicaine*
CAJAC, M., *Adjutant, Garde Républicaine*
VIGNERON, M., *M.D.L. Chef, Garde Républicaine*
ITHURBIDE, M., *Garde, Garde Républicaine*
GIRARD M. A.F., *Adjutant, Garde Républicaine*
GODARD, M., *M.D.L. Chef, Garde Républicaine*
DONDEYNE, M., *M.D.L. Chef, Garde Républicaine*
DUMONT, M., *Garde, Garde Républicaine*
MATHIEU, M., *Garde, Garde Républicaine*
ROCHER, M., *Sergeant-Chef, Garde Républicaine*
ESTEBE, M., *Garde, Garde Républicaine*
CLAIR, M., *Surveillant des Travaux*
YVART, M., *Chef du Service au Mobilier National*
BOUTELET, M., *Officier de Police Principal, Securité*
GRILLOT, M., *Officier de Police Principal, Securité*
PASKA, M., *Officier de Paix, Securité*
GARAGNON, M., *Brigadier, Securité*
GAQUER, M., *Brigadier Chef, Securité*
ROSSIGNOL, M., *Brigadier, Securité*
PEYRE, M., *Officier de Police, Securité*
CHARBUILLET, M., *Officier de Police, Securité*
GUEGAN, M., *Officier de Police, Securité*
TERRIER, M., *Officier de Police, Securité*
BOULANGER, M., *Commandant de l'Aéroport, Lille*
PAGANT, M., *Chef du Service Intérieur de la Préfecture de Lille*
HAUTECOEUR, M., *Chef de Division à la Mairie de Lille*
PLUQUET, Georges, *Directeur à la Mairie de Roubaix*

21 May **State Visit to Denmark of the Queen and the Duke of Edinburgh**
PEDERSEN, Carl Jørgen Nicolaj, *Chief Custodian*
FREDERICK, Jens Fryndling Ditlev, *Senior Custodian*
FLENSTED, Erik Gorm, *Senior Custodian*

ANDERSEN, Hans Jørgen, *Assistant Senior Custodian*
LARSEN, Leif Tage Jens, *Town Hall Custodian*
JOSIASEN, Albert, *Porter*
PAULSEN, Svend Aage, *Inspector of the Danish State Police Forces*
PEDERSEN, Theodor Frederik, *Inspector of the Danish State Police Forces*
ARMFELT, Bode Rupreckt, *Inspector of the Copenhagen Police*
HANSEN, Evald, *Inspector of the Copenhagen Police*
RAMSHOLT, Niels Peter, *Inspector of the Frederiksborg Police*
OLSEN, Oluf Frederik, *Inspector of the Frederiksborg Police*
ERIKSEN, Axel Alexander, *Policeman called in from other districts*
HANSEN, Ernst Ove Ingfred, *Policeman called in from other districts*
BANGSO, Kaj Verner Bang, *Policeman called in from other districts*
GUNDERSEN, Carl Christian Gunder, *Policeman called in from other districts*
RASMUSSEN, Svend Valdemar Lars, *Policeman called in from other districts*
PJETURSSON, S.B., *Chasseur, Palace of Christian VII*
NIELSEN, I.F. Skovdal, *Chasseur, Palace of Christian VII*
ERIKSEN, O., *Courier, Palace of Christian VII*
ESKILDSEN, N.K., *Courier, Palace of Christian VII*
LARSEN, E.H., *Footman, Palace of Christian VII*
PETERSEN, A., *Footman, Palace of Christian VII*
JENSEN, E., *Footman, Palace of Christian VII*
JOHNSTAD, V.H.S., *Footman, Palace of Christian VII*
MEJER, P.R., *Footman, Palace of Christian VII*
BJERRE, B.H., *Office Messenger, Palace of Christian VII*
ENGELHOF, F., *Office Messenger, Palace of Christian VII*
STROMBERG, B., *Office Messenger, Palace of Christian VII*
PEDERSEN, H. Reinholdt, *Keeper of the Plate, Palace of Christian VII*
SØRENSEN, J.P., *Keeper of the Plate, Palace of Christian VII*
LARSEN, P.A., *Livery Servant, Palace of Christian VII*
SØRENSEN, K., *Livery Servant, Palace of Christian VII*
PETERSEN, L.B., *Livery Servant, Palace of Christian VII*
LYKKE, B., *Livery Servant, Palace of Christian VII*
PEDERSEN, J.F., *Door Keeper, Palace of Christian VII*
NIELSEN, A.M., *Door Keeper, Palace of Christian VII*
BOSKOV, P., *Night Door Keeper, Palace of Christian VII*
HANSEN, H.J., *Night Door Keeper, Palace of Christian VII*
LARSEN, A., *Chef, Palace of Christian VII*
HJORTH, Miss E.A.M., *Chief of the Kitchen Staff, Palace of Christian VII*
HANSEN, Miss A.L., *Housekeeper, Palace of Christian VII*
HANSEN, Miss K.K., *Linen Room Maid, Palace of Christian VII*
NORDEN, Miss J.L., *Lady's Maid, Palace of Christian VII*
BERG, Miss A.G.M., *Parlour Maid, Palace of Christian VII*
JOHANSEN, Miss A.S., *Parlour Maid, Palace of Christian VII*
EJSTRUP, N.E., *Office Clerk, Palace of Christian VII*
HANSEN, Hans Ivar, *Doorkeeper at the Christiansborg Palace*
LARSEN, Robert, *Doorkeeper at the Christiansborg Palace*
PEDERSEN, H.P., *Caretaker*
MOGENSEN, K.N., *Chief Coachman*
JENSEN, Th. E., *Coachman*
HENRIKS, P., *Chief Chauffeur*
RECKDORF, R.E., *Chauffeur*
VINSTED, E.B., *Chauffeur*
PETERSEN, A.H., *Chauffeur*
WONGE, G.S., *Chauffeur*
ANDERSEN, P.H. Skovgaard, *Chauffeur*
PEDERSEN, O.P. Jørgensen, *Chauffeur*
PETERSEN, K.A., *Chauffeur*
RASMUSSEN, P.C.K., *Messenger*
HANSEN, N.J. A., *Messenger*
LARSEN, B., *Assistant Courier*
BORG, C., *Assistant Courier*
KRISTENSEN, Mr Egon Gerald Jul, *Police Constable (outrider)*
STENBERG, Mr Bent Leo, *Police Constable (outrider)*
ALBERTSEN, Jens, *Harbour Guard, Port of Copenhagen*
SCHUMACHER, V.C.H., *Harbour Guard, Port of Copenhagen*

1958

25 March   **State Visit to the Netherlands of the Queen and the Duke of Edinburgh**
AALTEN, J., *Florist*
BEEKMAN, W.J., *First Coachman*
BEUSEKOM, G. van, *Usher at the Royal Palace, The Hague*

BLOKDIJK, C., *Electrician at the Royal Palace, The Hague*
BOS, T., *Usher at the Royal Palace, Amsterdam*
BOUWMAN, J., *Footman*
DOL, N.J., *First Coach-house servant*
EEKELEN, F.F.B. van, *First Chauffeur*
FLORESTEIN, D.H.J. van, *First Coachman*
GARDIEN, P.J., *Footman*
GROENEVELD, Miss J.M., *Maid*
HALSTEIN, Miss G., *Waiting-Maid*
HEERDE, J. van, *Chief Mechanic*
JONG, J.W.de, *Mechanic*
KANT, J.M., *First Coachman*
KLOOSTER, M.P. van der, *First Chauffeur*
LUYTEN, J., *Usher and Telephone Operator, Royal Palace, The Hague*
OORD, J.A. van der, *Usher, Royal Palace, Amsterdam*
PAANS, J.A., *Deputy Head, Motor Car Section*
PARLEVLIET, C.M., *Head Gardener, Royal Palace, The Hague*
SIMONS, E.H., *First Chauffeur*
TJADEN, *Electrical Artificer, Royal Palace, Amsterdam*
TOUW, H.P. van der, *First Coachman*
VEERMAN, J., *First Coachman*
VERHEYEN, B.N.G., *First Chauffeur*
VISSER, J., *First Footman*
VISSER, W., *First Coach-house servant*
BOOMKAMP, Mrs P., *Secretary, Royal Palace, Amsterdam*
ZOEST, B.M. van, *First Chauffeur*
BERGAKKER, J., *Police Sergeant, Motor-Escort*
HAGELAAR, Th. G., *Sergeant-Major, Motor-Escort*
HILLEBRAND, *Police Sergeant, Motor-Escort*
VRIES, J.M. de, *Police Sergeant, Motor-Escort*
WAARDT, S. van der, *Police Sergeant, Motor-Escort*
WINTER, A de, *Police Sergeant, Motor-Escort*
WISSE, J.C., *Police Sergeant, Motor-Escort*
EGBERTS, C.W., *Head of Technical Staff, Rotterdam Town Hall*
HOOGEN, Tj. H. van, *Sergeant, Amsterdam Municipal Police*
SLEIJSTER, P.J.A., *Sergeant, The Hague Municipal Police*
VEEN, A van der, *Sergeant, Amsterdam Municipal Police*
VINK, W., *Usher, Burgomaster's Cabinet, The Hague*
WARENDORP, P.F. van, *Sergeant, Rotterdam Municipal Police*
BREETVELD, D., *Chief Instrument Maker, Hydraulics Laboratory, Delft*
EIKELENSTAM, W. *Sergeant, Royal Constabulary*
GESTEL, J.H. van, *Sergeant-Major, Royal Constabulary Standard Bearer*
GROOT, *Sergeant, Royal Constabulary*
REIJNDERS, W.P., *Drum Sergeant, Grenadier Guards Regiment*
KAPEL, H. van, *Drum Sergeant-Major, Marines Band, Royal Netherlands Navy*
TOL, A. van, *Chief Petty Officer, Coxswain of HMS* Utrecht

13 May   **State Visit to Britain of President Gronchi of Italy**
ZAPPIA, Domenico, *Police Officer*
CORAZZA, Antonio, *Police Officer*
LEONARDI, Cav. Uff. Francesco, *of the Presidency*
PACE, Pietro, *of the Ministry of Foreign Affairs*
RANDONE, Luigi, *of the Presidency*
VILLANI, Signora Lilia Zini in, *in attendance on Signora Gronchi*
BARONE, Signorina Anna Maria, *Typist*
SALERANI, Giuseppe, *Butler*
LUCIA, Giuseppe, *Chef*

20 October   **State Visit to Britain of President Heuss of the Federal Republic of Germany**
KRULAK, Karl, *Footman, Ministry of Foreign Affairs*
KUNKEL, Hans, *Butler, German Embassy*
BALOTTARI, Carlo, *Chef, German Embassy*
GLUEK, Willy, *Steward and Doorkeeper, German Embassy*

1959

5 May   **State Visit to Britain of the Shahanshah of Iran**
JESUS, Miss Gracinda de
BEIGLOU, Abolghassem, *Valet*

1960

5 April   **State Visit to Britain of President de Gaulle of the French Republic and Madame de Gaulle**
D'JOUDER, Henri, *of the Security Staff*

COMITI, Paul, *of the Security Staff*
TESSIER, Roger, *of the Security Staff*
AUVRAY, René, *of the Security Staff*
HENNEQUIN, M., *Valet to the President*
BROCK, Mme, *Maid to Madame de Gaulle*
THONE, Robert, *Chef-Huissier*
BUIVAN, Han, *Chef de Cuisine*

19 July **State Visit to Britain of King Bhumibol and Queen Sirikit of Thailand**
SORAVITHI, Miss Phussadi, *Wardrobe and Jewellery Keeper*
DEVAKUL, Miss Dasamai, *Hairdresser*
XUTO, Xubasna, *Valet*
SUWANCHINDA, Uthai, *Valet*
LONDOM, Prakhan, *Butler, Royal Thai Embassy*
PATANALERT, Miss Laor, *Housekeeper, Royal Thai Embassy*

17 October **State Visit to Britain of King Mahendra and Queen Ratna of Nepal**
BAHADUR, K., *Butler, Nepalese Embassy*
ZIMMERLI, Armin, *Chef, Nepalese Embassy*
GAFTA, M., *Footman, Nepalese Embassy*

1961

26 February **State Visit to Nepal of the Queen and the Duke of Edinburgh**
TAPASI, Naib Subba, *Hunter*
PRADHAN, Birishi Man, *Airport Manager*
GIRI, Krishna, *Airport Manager*
LIMBU, Mir Subba Hari Bahadur, *Steward, Lakshmi Nivas Palace*
SHRESTHA, Subba Kedarman, *of the Royal Staff, Royal Palace, Katmandu*
RAJBAHAK, Naib Subba Ram Bahadur, *of the Staff, Royal Palace, Katmandu*
SHAH, Naib Subba Top Bikram
STHAPIT, Naib Subba Moti Ratna, *Personal Attendant, Royal Palace, Katmandu*
SHRESTHA, Naib Ditta Inra Prasad
THAPALIA, Shri Bhanu Prasad
RANA, Captain Kanak Shamsher
TAMRAKAR, Shri Chatur Ratna, *of Staff of Royal Guest House, Katmandu*
RIMAL, Mir Subba Ram Prasad, *of Staff, Royal Guest House, Katmandu*
KARMACHARYA, Shri Kaiser Lal, *Assistant, Hospitality Department*
SINGH, Hira, *Senior Clerk, British Embassy, Katmandu*
SINGH, Subir, *Head Messenger, British Embassy, Katmandu*
RATHAN, Bhaja, *Butler, British Embassy, Katmandu*

2 March **State Visit to Iran of the Queen and the Duke of Edinburgh**
YUSEFI, Warrant Officer Aliakbar, *of the Imperial Guard*
KIANI, Warrant Officer Jalal, *of the Imperial Guard*
MURTAZAVI, Sergeant Hossain, *of the Imperial Guard*
NAUBARI, Sergeant Jalal, *of the Imperial Guard*
SHIROZHAN, Sergeant Abbas, *of the Imperial Guard*
MOSHFEGHI, Sergeant Azizollah, *of the Imperial Guard*
NAJAI-NEZHAD, Sergeant Mehdi, *of the Imperial Guard*
SHEIBANI, Sergeant Khosro, *of the Imperial Guard*
KAZEMI, Warrant Officer Nazar, *of Police and Security Organisation*
SUHRABNEJHAD, Warrant Officer, *of Police and Security Organisation*
MIRPUR, Sergeant, *of Police and Security Organisation*
NEJHAD, Sergeant Muhammad Baqer Muslem, *of Police and Security Organisation*
HUSAINI, Sergeant Muhammad Amir, *of Police and Security Organisation*
SALEHI, Sergeant Asghar, *of Police and Security Organisation*
MABHUTI, Sergeant Mahmud, *of Police and Security Organisation*
TAVAKKULI, Sergeant Muhammad Hasan, *of Police and Security Organisation*
ETEZAD, Kazem, *of the Palace Staff*
SHARIFI, Ali, *of the Palace Staff*
YAZDI, Kamran, *of the Palace Staff*
ESHRATABADI, Khodaverdi, *Coachman*
REZAYI, Abdolhossein, *Coachman*
GHASEMI, Mehdi, *Chauffeur*
VAZIRI, Jamshid, *Chauffeur*
AMIRSADEGHI, Asghar, *Chauffeur*
MEHRAN-HAMADAHI, Ahmad, *Chauffeur*
KABIRI, Ali, *Cook*
GASGARI, Mohsen, *Head Messenger, British Embassy*

2 May **State Visit to Italy of the Queen and the Duke of Edinburgh**
CERRUTTI, Alfredo, *Head of Garage Staff, the Quirinale*

FRASCHINI, Francesco, *The President's Driver*
ZOCCHI, Leopoldo, *Head of Stable Staff, the Quirinale*
PAMPANINI, Aldo, *in charge of China etc, the Quirinale*
FERRI, Mario, *Personal Attendant of the President*
LENARES, Sebastiano, *Police Security Officer*
AUDINO, Vincenzo, *Police Security Officer*
CIVITA, Mario, *Police Security Officer*
COLUCCI, Luigi, *Chief Printer, Italian Stationery Office*
BOLDRINI, Idoro, *Brigadiere, Guardia di Finanza*
ROSA, Antenoro Della, *Brigadiere, Guardia di Finanza*
GIOIA, Stefano, *Brigadiere, Guardia di Finanza*
ROSETTI, Artemio, *Vice Brigadiere, Guardia di Finanza*
BATTISTA, Giuseppe
CIPELLI IN CAMPANA, Signora Giuliana, *of Ministry of Foreign Affairs*
FUGGI, Senora Liliana, *of Ministry of Foreign Affairs*
LAZZARO, Giulio
COLONNESI MARCONI, Signora Luciana, *of Ministry of Foreign Affairs*
MELCHIONDA, Signora Paola, *of Ministry of Foreign Affairs*
NICCHIO, Carlo, *of Ministry of Foreign Affairs*
RICCARDI DI NUNZIO, Senora Maria, *of Ministry of Foreign Affairs*
PETRUCCI, Signora Pia Maria, *of Ministry of Foreign Affairs*
POZNAN, Leon
RADONICH DEI VERUNSICH, Senora Estella, *of Ministry of Foreign Affairs*

1962

10 July   **State Visit to Britain of President Tubman of Liberia and Mrs Tubman**
BARROLLE, Jimmie, *Valet to the President*
SHERMAN, Joseph, *Steward*
MCLEER, Mr J. Janitor, *Liberian Embassy*

16 October   **State Visit to Britain of King Olav V of Norway**
JENSEN, Ragnar, *Chef*
BERSAS, Miss Borghild, *Housemaid*
EBNE, Miss Ingrid Johanne, *Housemaid*
HVAMB, Mr O., *Police Official*
KNUDSEN, Viktor, *Footman*
ARNTZEN, Chief Petty Officer Torstein, *K/S Norge*
SKAR, Chief Petty Officer Kare, *K/S Norge*
SVENDSEN, Chief Petty Officer Odd, *K/S Norge*
RUSTADBAKKEN, Chief Petty Officer Knut, *K/S Norge*
JOHANNESEN, Chief Petty Officer Trygve, *K/S Norge*
HANSEN, Chief Petty Officer Rolf, *K/S Norge*
SORLAND, Petty Officer Magne, *K/S Norge*
FOSSEN, Petty Officer Ole, *K/S Norge*
HAVELAND, Petty Officer Per, *K/S Norge*
HOLSTAD, Petty Officer Age, *K/S Norge*
MARTINSEN, Petty Officer Svein, *K/S Norge*
CHRISTOPHERSEN, Miss Sigrid, *Private Secretary to the Norwegian Ambassador*
SUNDE, Henry, *Chauffeur*
BJONNES, Sverre, *Secretary to Norwegian Consulate, Edinburgh*

1963

14 May   **State Visit to Britain of King Baudouin and Queen Fabiola of the Belgians**
LECEUVE, Victor, *Head Porter, Belgian Embassy*
MULOT, Marcel, *Chef, Belgian Embassy*
CSINTALAN, Andrew, *Chauffeur, Belgian Embassy*
FERNANDEZ, Senorita Josefa, *Personal Maid to the Queen of the Belgians*
BARRENO-VARA, Senorita Rosa, *Personal Maid to the Queen of the Belgians*
VERHELPEN, Jean Elysée, *Valet to the King of the Belgians*
LIBERT, Emile Adolphe, *Valet to Members of the Suite*
GROOTE, René Joseph de, *Valet to Members of the Suite*
RENARD, Jules, *Hairdresser*

9 July   **State Visit to Britain of King Paul and Queen Frederika of the Hellenes**
HATZIANTONIOU, Mme Alex, *Hairdresser to the Queen of the Hellenes*
THEODOROU, Hélène, *Chambermaid to the Queen of the Hellenes*
THOMAS, Vassilios, *Personal Valet to the King of the Hellenes*
BOUZIS, Anastassios, *Personal Valet to the King of the Hellenes*

1964

28 May   **State Visit to Britain of President Abboud of the Republic of the Sudan**
SIBAITI, Sayed Mohammed Hassan el, *Valet*
AZRAG, Sayed Mohamed el Hassan, *Valet*
YOUSIF, Sayed Osman Mohamed, *Senior Messenger, Sudanese Embassy*
KHALIL, Sayed Khalil Mohamed, *Messenger, Sudanese Embassy*
KHEIR, Sayed Dirrar Sabah el, *Valet*
ABDULLA, Sayed Ishag, *Valet*
AHMED, Sergeant-Major Abdel Mejid Sid, *in charge of Police Escort*

1965

1 February   **State Visit to Ethiopia of the Queen and the Duke of Edinburgh**
HAILU, Colonel Tessema, *Imperial Ethiopian Police*
SHIFFERAW, Lieutenant-Colonel Amare, *Imperial Ethiopian Police*
WONDIMU, Lieutenant-Colonel Abebe, *Imperial Ethiopian Police*
SIRAK, Lieutenant-Colonel Tesfa, *Imperial Government Security Department*
TAFESSE, Ato Aklile Berhane Getshun, *Director, Special Branch, HIM's Private Cabinet*
KIDANE, Ato Abay, *Special Driver, Ministry of Imperial Court*
MOHAMMED, Sergeant Abdulshafi, *Sergeant of the Guard, British Embassy, Addis Ababa*
MARIAM, Ato Berhanu Wolde, *Chauffeur, British Embassy, Addis Ababa*

8 February   **State Visit to Sudan of the Queen and the Duke of Edinburgh**
SAYED, Sayed Mohammed Ibrahim el, *Senior Clerk, Republican Palace*
HALFAWI, Sayed Mohammed Hussein, *Senior Clerk, Republican Palace*
HUSSEIN, Sayed Mohammed, *Senior Storekeeper, Republican Palace*
IDRIS, Sayed Ahmed, *Senior Storekeeper, Republican Palace*
RIZGALLAH, Sayed Sharif, *Horticultural Officer, Republican Palace*
MUKHTAR, Sayed Naim, *Head Driver, Republican Palace*
GUBARA, Sayed Ramadan, *Clerk, Republican Palace*
SHAFIE, Sayed Mohammed Zein el, *Clerk, Republican Palace*
FADLALLAH, Sayed Hassan Suleiman, *Clerk, Republican Palace*
CHAYOUM, Sayed Abdullah Abdel, *Book-keeper, Republican Palace*
ABDULLAH, Sayed Mohammed Ahmed, *Assistant Steward, Republican Palace*
IDRIS, Sayed Mirghani Mohammed, *Chef, Republican Palace*
ALI, Sayed Salih Mohammed, *Suffragi, Republican Palace*
BAHAR, Sayed Hassan Ali, *Suffragi, Republican Palace*
BESHIR, Sergeant-Major Hashim el, *Palace Guard*
FADL, Staff-Sergeant Awad Hassan, *Palace Guard*
MEDANI, Sayed Mohammed el, *Head Suffragi, British Embassy*

   State Visit to the Federal Republic of Germany of the Queen and the Duke of Edinburgh
DALADES, Frau Christel, *Protocol, Office of the Federal President*
BAUMEISTER, Fräulein Mathilde, *Secretary to the Federal President*
WITTENBERG, Fräulein Dora, *Expert in Orders Section, Federal President's Office*
POSACK, Albert, *Protocol, Office of Federal Chancellor*
SCHLIEBUSCH, Johannes, *External Section, Office of Federal Chancellor*
HOLLSTEIN, Gerhard, *Inspector, Security Group, travelling with Royal Party*
MEIXNER, Heinrich, *Inspector, Security Group, travelling with Royal Party*
KRAFT, Herbert, *Inspector, Security Group, travelling with Royal Party*
MEYER, Clemens, *Sergeant, Security Group, travelling with Royal Party*
STRING, Martin, *Sergeant, Security Group, travelling with Royal Party*
BAUHAUS, Ulrich, *Sergeant, Security Group, travelling with Royal Party*
EICKENBROCK, Bernhard, *Sergeant, Security Group, travelling with Royal Party*
SAUER, Joseph, *Staff-Sergeant, Leader of Escort*
REICHEL, Max, *Staff-Sergeant, Leader of Escort*
NEUMANN, Hans Dieter, *Sergeant, Leader of Escort*
MÜLLER, Walter-Christoph, *Lance Sergeant, Leader of Escort*
LANGE, Hans, *Sergeant-Major, Trumpeter*
MANTEL, Hans, *Sergeant-Major, Tenor Horn player*
GEISLER, Kurt, *Protocol, City of Cologne*
LINGSCHEID, Heinz, *Security Police Inspector, North Rhine Westphalia*
BOSSE, Hasso, *Superintendent, Schloss Augustusburg*
OCHS, Wilhelm, *Protocol, Hessian State Chancery*
RICHTER, Bernd, *Leader, Police Escort, Hessen*
FRITSCH, Walter, *Leader, Police Escort, Bavaria*
SEYBOLD, Wilhelm, *State visit Section, Baden-Württemberg*
VATTER, Frau Annemarie, *State visit Section, Baden-Württemberg*
SCHUMANN, Erich, *State visit Section, Baden-Württemberg*
LIPPERT, Frau Annaliese, *Press Section, Baden-Württemberg*
MUELLER, Anton, *Leader, Police Escort, Baden-Württemberg*

KOEHN, Werner, *Police Security, Lower Saxony*
JAKOB, Heinz, *Leader, Police Escort, Lower Saxony*
JOHN, Günther, *Protocol, Senate Chancery, Berlin*
SCHOLZ, Wolf-Dieter, *Protocol, Senate Chancery, Berlin*
WULFF, Fräulein Ruth, *Protocol, Senate Chancery, Berlin*
OTT, Hans-Dietrich, *Leader of Police Escort, Berlin*
OVERHEU, Horst, *Wireless Inspector, Federal Post Office – on train*
POETTIG, Wilhelm, *Wireless Inspector, Federal Post Office – on train*
EHRENSPERGER, Theodor, *Wireless Inspector, Federal Post Office – on train*
RAPP, Hans, *Leader, Police Escort, Baden-Württemberg*
ROTH, Herr, *Butler to British Ambassador*
STANSKY, Herr, *Chef to British Ambassador*

13 July   **State Visit to Britain of President de Frei of Chile and Madame de Frei**
PEREZ DE MARTIN-PEÑASCO, Sra Maria del Rosario, *Femme de Chambre de Madame de Frei*
MARTIN-PEÑASCO, Jesús, *Valet de Chambre du President de Frei*

1966

9 May   **State Visit to Belgium of the Queen and the Duke of Edinburgh**
LINT, Christian van, *Foreman at Laeken*
TROOST, Madame Delphine van den, *Chambermaid*
BERGHEN, Jean Vanden, *Chauffeur*
ARCOULIN, Lambert, *Chauffeur*
EECKHOUDT, Gustaaf van, *Chauffeur*
GYSELINCK, Paul, *Chauffeur*
THEELEN, Théophile, *Chauffeur*
SEGERS, François, *Usher*
STUBBE, Cyrille, *Usher*
GRAVE, Constant de, *Porter*
MASSIN, Georges, *Chief Electrician*
ERROELEN, Louis, *Chief Stoker*
KEMPER, Jean de, *Stoker*
DAVIN, Auguste, *Caretaker at Ciergnon*
BUELENS, Eugène, *Footman*
NIEUWENHOVE, Jean van, *Footman*
MEERT, Albert, *Footman*
FRESON, Louis, *Furniture Repairer*
REYSKENS, Mme Maria, *Chief Kitchen Maid*
WIJNS, Henri, *Polisher*
LIERDE, Benigins van, *Police Officer*
DAXHELET, Ferdinand, *Warrant Officer Class 2*
DUFRASNE, Roger, *Police Officer*
PAUWELS, Marcel
DRIES, André
DUYSSENS, George
SALICHI, Carlo, *Butler at Canadian Embassy*
FAENZA, Otello, *Chef at British Embassy*
GARCIA, Antonio, *Butler at British Embassy*

17 May   **State Visit to Britain of the President of Austria and Frau Jonas**
WASSERTHEURER, Gustav, *Head Porter, Austrian Embassy*

19 July   **State Visit to Britain of King Hussein of the Hashemite Kingdom of Jordan and Princess Muna al Hussein**
MARZOUK, Second-Lieutenant Suleiman, *Valet to the King*
HORMIS, Miss Helen, *Chambermaid to Princess Muna*
IANUCCI, Ralph, *Chauffeur*

1967

9 May   **State Visit to Britain of King Faisal of Saudi Arabia**
FAISAL, Saeed al, *The King's Domestic Staff*
ABDURRAHMAN, Salih, *The King's Domestic Staff*
WAHID, Ali Abdul, *The King's Domestic Staff*
MOWEIMEI, Abdullah bin, *The King's Domestic Staff*

1 November   **State Visit to Britain of the President of Turkey and Madame Sunay**
BELET, Orban, *Valet to the President*
MOURA, Enrico de, *Chauffeur to Turkish Ambassador*

1968

1 November	**State Visit to Brazil of the Queen and the Duke of Edinburgh**

PEREIRA, Sylvio José Barroso, *Administration Department, Ministry of Foreign Affairs*
MARTINS, Maria Nanni, *Photocopying Department*
MALVEIRA, Maria Lucinde, *Typing Department*
ELLWANGER, Gessy, *Distinguished Visitors' Section*
BRASIL, Crismélia, *Distinguished Visitors' Section*
JANOT, Regina, *Distinguished Visitors' Section*
GOMES, Maryse Lafayette Tapajos, *Distinguished Visitors' Section*
MENEZES, Mariusha Bezerra de, *Distinguished Visitors' Section*
MELLO, Marise Pavente de, *Distinguished Visitors' Section*
MARQUES, Nelito, *Security Officer*
OLIVEIRA, Rivaldo, *Security Officer*
WILLIAMS, Arinos da Silva, *Security Officer*
FREITAS, Captain Luiz Osiris de Almeida, *in charge of Baggage Services*
WHITE, Captain, *Head of Army Outriders, Brasilia*
FARIA, Epitácio Albuquerque de, *Deputy Customs Chief, Rio*
MELO, José Maria, *Assistant Customs Chief, Rio*
GUIMARÃES, José Salgado, *Senior Customs Chief, Rio*
SANTANELLI, Octavio, *Head of Traffic, Rio*
CASCARDO, Pascoal, *Traffic Control Officer, Rio*
VIANA, Captain Aviador Paul, *Guard Commander, Air base, Rio*
COSTA, F.J. da, *Vice-Consul, Rio*
TIBAU, Miss H., *Assistant, Information Section, British Embassy*
JUNGMAN, R., *Head Translator, Information Section, British Embassy*
LIMA, A., *Radio Producer, Information Section, British Embassy*

11 November	**State Visit to Chile of the Queen and the Duke of Edinburgh**

ARGANDOÑA, Sara Daniel, *Private Secretary to the President*
CAVADA, Rosa Adriana Leiter, *Private Secretary to the President*
OREGO, Amelia Celis de, *Protocol*
ORELLANA, Ramon Villareal, *in charge of Security, Carrera Hotel*
BAÑOS, Luis Caviedes, *in charge of Security, Carrera Hotel*
BENNETTS, David de-Vescovi, *Interpreter*
ARAVENA, Lt José Antonio Pavez, *Officer in charge of Motorcycle Escort*
PINTO, Captain Victor Rolando Torres, *Officer in charge of Traffic*
PANIZZA, Lt. Sergio Roberto Cristoforo, *Press Liaison Officer*
STARKEY, Lt Herbert Stanley William Lake, *Carabinero Press Liaison Officer*
MONTERO, Julia Moreno, *Head Cashier, Carrera Hotel*
JOPIA, Juan Davila, *Receptionist, Carrera Hotel*
RAMDOHR, Gustavo José, *Sub-Manager, Club Hipico*
OYARZÚN, Sergio, *Manager, Club de Polo y Equitacion, 'San Cristobal'*
JIMENEZ, Fernando Hugo Diaz, *Director, Anglo-Chilean Centre INACAP*
BUSTOS, Luis Enrique, *Administrator, National Stadium*
LAMPARD, William John, *Mine Superintendent*
RODENA, Anibal, *in charge of Catering, the Queen's Banquet and Reception*
HERMANSEN, Senor, *in charge of Tent decoration at the Queen's Banquet*

1969

22 April	**State Visit to Britain of President Saragat of Italy**

COLBERTALDO, Giovanni Battista, *Interpreter*
TEMPINI, Giovanna, *Interpreter*
CAPITANI, Bruno, *Clerk in the President's Office*
BOCCINI, Giuliano, *Clerk in the President's Office*
PICICCHE, Olga, *Secretary*
REISINO, Vincenzo, *Head Valet to the President*
BONDI, Carina, *Private Secretary to the Ambassador*
MASCELLANI, Pasquino, *Head Messenger, Italian Embassy*
LOMBARDINI, Marco, *Butler, Italian Embassy*

5 May	**State Visit to Austria of the Queen and the Duke of Edinburgh**

LOPEZ, Angel Maranon, *Butler, British Embassy*
RODLER, Ingeborg, *Assistant, Presidential Chancellery*
ZIDEK, Wilhelm, *Courier, Presidential Chancellery*
MAYERHOFER, Anton, *Receptionist, Presidential Chancellery*
STUHLHOFER, Otto, *Clerk, Federal Chancellor's Office*
STEINER, Franz, *Special Inspector, Federal Chancellor's Office*
RATZESBERGER, Friedrich, *Clerk, Federal Chancellor's Office*
SINGER, Adrienne, *Clerk, Ministry of Foreign Affairs*
HOCHSTATTNER, Helmuth, *Clerk, Ministry of Foreign Affairs*

CECH-MUNTEANU, Margarete, *Clerk, Ministry of Foreign Affairs*
MAYRHUBER, Heinrich, *Clerk, Ministry of Foreign Affairs*
SCHARL, Richard, *Clerk, Ministry of Foreign Affairs*
PROSZNAK, Josef, *Clerk, Ministry of Foreign Affairs*
RUPP, Michael, *Inspector, Ministry for the Interior*
RICHTER, Erwin, *Inspector, Ministry for the Interior*
SCHELLENBACHER, Alois, *Inspector, Ministry for the Interior*
PODRAZIL, Adolf, *Inspector, Ministry for the Interior*
WIMMER, Karl, *Inspector, Ministry for the Interior*
REITER, Ludwig, *Inspector, Ministry for the Interior*
EGGER, Alois, *Railway Inspector*
FASTNER, Franz, *Railway Inspector*
GRASSL, Franz, *Railway Official*
TRAPPL, Josef, *Railway Official*
ENGEL, Andreas, *Warrant Officer*
PILZ, Hubert, *Warrant Officer*
PICHLER, Roman, *Castle Warden, Province of Steiermark*
KANDORA, Maria, *Special Inspector, Province of Salzburg*
SIMURDA, Margarethe, *Special Inspector, Province of Salzburg*
SCHMIED, Kurt, *Factory Inspector, Vienna*
KLICKA, Rudolf, *Inspector, Vienna*
DEKAN, Friedrich, *Head Cook, Vienna*

15 July **State Visit to Britain of President Kekkonen of Finland and Madame Kekkonen**
LAITINEN, Eelis, *Head Porter, Finnish Embassy*
LOPAKKA, Arvo, *Janitor, Finnish Embassy*
LAUHIALA, Ulla-Maija, *Assistant Archivist, Finnish Embassy*
KARPPINEN, Anja, *Shorthand Typist, Finnish Embassy*
PARMI, Ritva, *Shorthand Typist, Finnish Embassy*
KUNNAS, Anja, *Shorthand Typist, Finnish Embassy*
MARKKOLA, Ester, *Chambermaid to Madame Kekkonen*

1970

1971

18 October **State Visit to Turkey of the Queen and the Duke of Edinburgh**
GÜVEN, Erdogan, *Administration Official, Ministry of Foreign Affairs*
TÜRKÖZ, Ali, *Administration Official, Ministry of Foreign Affairs*
TUGRUL, Ergin, *Administration Official, Ministry of Foreign Affairs*
CITLER, Abdullah, *Head of Printing Shop*
PASINLI, Mennan, *Director of Hippodrome, Ankara*
SAYALI, Acar, *Clerk, Commonwealth War Graves Commission*
DEMIREL, Dogan, *Foreman, Commonwealth War Graves Commission*
BALCILAR, Hakki, *Chancery Messenger, British Embassy*
OCAK, Sait, *Butler, British Embassy*
CAKIR, Hassan, *Chef, British Embassy*
GEZEROL, Muhittim, *Chauffeur, British Embassy*
OKSUZ, Cemal, *Head Gardener, British Embassy*
PENADIS, S., *Head Gardener, Consulate General, Istanbul*

7 December **State Visit to Britain of King Mohammad Zahir Shah of Afghanistan**
SADDIQ, Mohammad, *Valet to the King*
RAHIM, Mohammad, *Valet to the King*
MACKAI, Gul, *Lady's Maid*

1972

8 February **State Visit to Thailand of the Queen, the Duke of Edinburgh and the Princess Anne**
CHUTTHONG, Yavas, *of the Civil Service*
NARUEMITYARN, Samarn, *of the Civil Service*
SAKULYINGYAI, Pricha, *of the Civil Service*
KHIAONARONG, Dej, *of the Civil Service*
INTHASANTI, Prasith, *of the Civil Service*
NITYASUTH, Panni, *of the Civil Service*
NILPANICH, Chit, *of the Civil Service*
SRISARAKARM, Boonchuay, *of the Civil Service*
RUNGSUP, Master Sergeant Udom, *Royal Thai Army*
SNONGKLIE, Master Sergeant Aroon, *Royal Thai Army*
ONLAMAI, Master Sergeant Sanguan, *Royal Thai Army*
ON-LAOR, Master Sergeant Suchet, *Royal Thai Army*

SRIPUM, Lieutenant Junior Griangsak, *Royal Thai Navy*
WONGBAIBOOL, Lieutenant Junior Sinthu, *Royal Thai Navy*
NAVAVICHIT, Lieutenant Junior Chart, *Royal Thai Navy*
PIAMFA, Lieutenant Junior Viriya, *Royal Thai Navy*
PETVAW, Flight Sergeant I. Boonmee, *Royal Thai Air Force*
MEMAICHONE, Flight Sergeant I. Chob, *Royal Thai Air Force*
SUWANWAT, Flight Sergeant I. Samudh, *Royal Thai Air Force*
CHOWKONGJAK, Flight Sergeant I. Prasit, *Royal Thai Air Force*
MUSIKATALA, Corporal Chamnian, *Police Department*
SUTHISUP, Corporal Panas, *Police Department*
PATAKINANG, Sergeant Chan, *Police Department*
YAMSAEMGSUNG, Master Sergeant Suksa, *Police Department*

22 February   **State Visit to Malaysia of the Queen, the Duke of Edinburgh and the Princess Anne**
D'CRUZ, Inche J.A., *Chief Clerk, Ceremonial Division, Prime Minister's Department*
HOCK, Inche Cheah Tat, *Senior Clerk, Ceremonial Division, Prime Minister's Department*
RADAKRISHNAN, Inche P., *Stenographer, Ceremonial Divison, Prime Minister's Department*
RAJU, Inche S.A., *Protocol Division, Ministry of Foreign Affairs*
LUKA, Staff Sergaent Aman bin, *Personnel Division, Ministry of Defence*
SAID, Sergeant Mohd.Laza bin Mohd., *Personnel Division, Minsitry of Defence*
RASHID, Sergeant Ahmad Abdul, *Personnel Division, Ministry of Defence*
AWANG, Sergeant Khalid bin, *Royal Malaysian Police HQ*
AHMAD, Sergeant Abdul Hamid bin, *Royal Malaysian Police HQ*
OTHMAN, Corporal Zainudin, *Royal Malaysian Police HQ*
SERINEK, Corporal Hassan bin, *Royal Malaysian Police HQ*
SILVERAJAH, Inche V., *Technician, Public Works Department, Selangor*

29 February   **State Visit to Brunei of the Queen, the Duke of Edinburgh and the Princess Anne**
IBRAHIM, Awang, *The Queen's Driver*
WASULFALAH, Awang, *The Duke of Edinburgh's Driver*
AHMAD, Awang, *The Princess Anne's Driver*

14 March   **State Visit to the Maldives of the Queen, the Duke of Edinburgh and the Princess Anne**
MOHAMED, Kuluduffushi, *The Royal Driver*

24 March   **State Visit to Mauritius of the Queen, the Duke of Edinburgh and the Princess Anne**
GOWRY, Ramchurn, *The Royal Driver*

11 April   **State Visit to Britain of Queen Juliana of the Netherlands and Prince Bernhard**
OOMS-SLAGTER, Mrs Meintje, *Linen Maid*
AALTEN, Jacob, *Florist*
OUWEHAND, Jan, *Florist*
RIJSDAM, Wijnand, *Footman*
DE GRAAF, Cornelis Benjamin, *Footman*
COELE, Sergeant-Major A., *Footman*
VELDE, Sergeant J. van der, *Footman*
SCHAUS, J.C. van der, *Footman*
SCHUERMANS, Martinus Johannes M., *Footman*
SCHREUDER, Adriaan, *Footman*
HENDRIKS, Gradus Karel Evert, *Footman*
DE WIT, Antonius Martinus, *Footman*
ZWEEKHORST, Gregorius Jan P., *Footman*
WIERSMA, Klass, *Footman*
SEIJFFER, Gustaaf Adolf, *Footman*
OORSCHOT, Adriaan Jan van, *Footman*
KLIFMAN, Gerrit, *1st Chef*
HENDRIKS, Pieter Johannes, *1st Chef*
BAEDE, Albertus Alfonsus, *1st Chef*
LEEUW, Robert de, *1st Chef*
FOKS, Hendrik, *1st Chef*
ASSELT, Gijsbertus van, *Patisserie Chef*
HORRIS, Hubertus, *Kitchen Hand*
DIJKHOF, Miss Johanna Sophia F., *Kitchen Maid*
KESTEREN, Sergeant-Major Hendrikus Z. van, *Footman*
WEIDE, Sergeant-Major Cornelis Adriaan van der, *Footman*
KLUTZ, Sergeant-Major Simon Jacobus, *Footman*
TOUSSAINT, Sergeant-Major Johannes W., *Footman*
SMIT, Sergeant-Major Pieter M., *Footman*
RANGE, Sergeant-Major Wilhelmus B., *Footman*
MORAAL, Sergeant-Major Wouter, *Footman*
GREEVEN, Sergeant Willem Christiaan, *Footman*
HAGEN, Sergeant Karel, *Footman*
BUITENHUIS, Sergeant-Major G.D., *Royal Netherlands Marines*
WAARSENBURG, Sergeant H.J.H., *Royal Netherlands Marines*
SEGERS, Sergeant J., *Royal Netherlands Marines*

15 May **State Visit to France of the Queen and the Duke of Edinburgh**
WILMIN, Adrien, *Guardien Chef du Musée de Trianon*
CASIER, Alfred, *Inspecteur du Matérial, Grand Trianon*
GODARD, Robert, *Chef Surveillant, Grand Trianon*
MAUGEY, Edmond, *Huissier Chef, Grand Trianon*
LOISELET, Jean-Marie, *Chef de Cuisine, Grand Trianon*
AUFFRET, Garde Valentin, *Chauffeur, Palais de l'Elysée*
BRETONNET, Garde René, *Chauffeur, Palais de l'Elysée*
SAPPA, Garde Roger, *Chauffeur, Palais de l'Elysée*
LESCOFFY, J., *Ambassador's Chauffeur, British Embassy*

13 June **State Visit to Britain of Grand Duke Jean of Luxembourg and Grand Duchess Charlotte**
ESPEN, Léon, *Police Officer*
WEINACHTER, François, *Chauffeur*
HECK, Nicolas, *Footman*
LOUIS, Joseph, *Footman*
KUGENER, Aloyse, *Footman*
THILL, François, *Footman*
BINDELS, Jean, *Valet*
HOFFMANN, Nelly, *Dresser*
DUSCHINGER, Jean, *Band Sergeant*
MEYER, Gaston, *Band Sergeant*
HIRTZ, Bernard, *Band Corporal*

17 October **State Visit to Yugoslavia of the Queen and the Duke of Edinburgh**
MAGAJNE, Zdenko, *Guard Band*
RISTANOVIC, Luka, *Sergeant Major, Driver of Guard Escort of Honour*
STOJANOVIC, Zivko, *Sergeant Major, Driver of Guard Escort of Honour*
RISTIC, Zlatko, *Head of Escort*
BUJAGIC, Branko, *Technical Inspector*
KOSANOVIC, Pero, *Chief Petty Officer, Driver of Guard of Honour*
PAVKOVIC, Ivo, *Petty Officer, Driver of Guard Escort of Honour*
RALEVIC, Milos, *Petty Officer, Driver of Guard Escort of Honour*
BANJAC, Vojin, *Naval Chief Petty Officer, Member of Yacht Crew*
DRAGISIC, Drago, *Naval Chief Petty Officer, Member of Yacht Crew*
MARIC, Dusan, *Naval Sergeant Major, Member of Yacht Crew*
PUKSIC, Franc, *Naval Sergeant Major, Member of Yacht Crew*
VASIC, Svetozar, *Naval Sergeant Major, Member of Yacht Crew*
FURTULA, Dusanka, *Chambermaid, Dedinje Palace*
JOVANOVIC, Mihajlo, *Head of Kitchens, Dedinje Palace*
NIKODIJEVIC, Danica, *Chambermaid*
PAREZONOVIC, Zivka, *Chambermaid, Dedinje Palace*
TURNOVIC, Ante, *Head of Supply, Dedinje Palace*
ZATKOVIC, Vlando, *Hotel Director, Dedinje Palace*

24 October **State Visit to Britain of President Heinemann of the Federal Republic of Germany and Frau Heinemann**
LIEBERTZ, Gottfried, *Luggage Supervisor, Federal Presidency*
MÜLLER, Willy, *Luggage Supervisor, Ministry of Foreign Affairs*
PERELLA, Signor, *Chef, German Embassy*

1973

3 April **State Visit to Britain of President Echeverria of Mexico and Señora Echeverria**
HERNANDEZ, Maria, *Maid to Señora Echeverria*
ALCAZAR, Rodolfo, *Valet to the President*
GAYOSSO, Rogelio Martinez, *Secretary, Mexican Embassy*

11 December **State Visit to Britain of President Mobutu of Zaïre**
PIRON, Madame, *Nurse*

1974

30 April **State Visit to Britain of Queen Margrethe II of Denmark and Prince Henrik**
ANDERSEN, Anker, *Valet*
THOMSEN, Alice, *Clerk, Danish Embassy*
CHAPMAN, Bente, *Clerk, Danish Embassy*
DAHLSTROM, Benny Bolt, *Chauffeur, Danish Embassy*

9 July **State Visit to Britain of the Yang DiPertuan Agung of Malaysia and the Raja Permaisuri Agung**
WAZIR, Encik Zainal Abidin bin Mohd., *Education Attaché, Malaysian High Commission*
LASSIM, Encik Abdul Hamid bin, *Education Attaché, Malaysian High Commission*
ALI, Encik Talib bin, *Second Secretary, Malaysian High Commission*
ISMAIL, Encik Othman bin, *Valet to His Majesty*

OMAR, Cik Jamilah binti, *Maid to Her Majesty*
JANZ, Cik Lily, *Hairdresser to Her Majesty*

1975

24 February
State Visit to Mexico of the Queen and the Duke of Edinburgh
GUTIERREZ, Ada Esther Guttierez, *Assistant, Protocol Department, Ministry of Foreign Affairs*
MARTINEZ, Guadalupe Ortega, *Assistant, Protocol Department, Ministry of Foreign Affairs*
MIMIAGA, Patricia Montano, *Assistant, Protocol Department, Ministry of Foreign Affairs*
PUENTE, Julieta Garza, *Assistant, Protocol Department, Ministry of Foreign Affairs*
ARRIAGA, Antonio Medina, *Assistant, Protocol Department, Ministry of Foreign Affairs*
TENORIO, Dolores Rebollo, *Assistant, Protocol Department, Ministry of Foreign Affairs*
PEREZ, José S. Ramirez, *Assistant, Protocol Department, Ministry of Foreign Affairs*
MENDEZ, Marta Esther Rico, *Assistant, Diplomatic Service Department*
LÓPEZ, Teniente Carlos Ascenio, *Private Secretary to Head of Section II*
GOMEZ, Captain Inf. DEM Manuel Eliezer Castro, *in charge of Security in Hotels*
OSUNA, Captain Inf. Cipriano Alatorre, *Chief of Escort*
PEREZ, Tte. Inf. Austreberto Luis Ortiz, *Escort*
SOBERANIS, Sub-Tte. de Inf. Carlos GM, *Escort*
URANGA, Sub-Tte de Art Luis Antonio P., *Escort*
CANALES, Roman Zapata, *Manager, Camino Real Hotel, Mexico City*

7 May
State Visit to Japan of the Queen and the Duke of Edinburgh
NAKAJIMA, H. BEM, *Butler, British Embassy*
AMINO, Masatsugo, *Official, Board of Ceremonies*
KOBAYASHI, Assistant-Inspector, Minoru, *The Duke of Edinburgh's Bodyguard*
NAMIKI, Hiroshi, *Chief of Guard Section*
SHIRAI, Tadashi, *Chief, Haneda Branch, Yokohama Protection Station*
UCHIDA, Toshisada, *Director of Haneda Customs*
OGAWA, Katsumi, *Chief of Flight Operations at Airport*
AOYAMA, Atsumu, *Director, Haneda Immigration Office*
AIDE, Toshio, *Chief of Quarantine Station at Airport*

8 July
State Visit to Britain of King Carl XVI Gustaf of Sweden
ADOLFSSON, Christer, *Footman*
ENGDAHL, Lars, *Footman*
FREDERIKSSON, Hans, *Chauffeur*
LINDEWALL, Stina, *Assistant, Defence Department, Swedish Embassy*
HAGELBRANT, Britt-Marie, *Secretary to Baron von Platen*
SANDBERG, Nina, *Secretary to Mr Akerren*

1976

4 May
State Visit to Britain of President Geisel of Brazil and Senhora Geisel
VIEIRA, Maria Cristina de Andrade, *Administrative Officer, Brazilian Embassy*
VASSEUR, Thais, *Administrative Officer, Brazilian Embassy*
ALVES, Nayde Rodrigues, *Private Secretary to the Ambassador*

24 May
State Visit to Finland of the Queen and the Duke of Edinburgh
ANTIKAINEN, Sinikka, *Clerk, President's Office*
HIILESMAA, Tuula, *Clerk, President's Office*
PERKIÖNIEMI, Pirkko, *Clerk, President's Office*
AALTO, Antti, *Senior Constable, Security*
KAUKINEN, Matti, *Detective, Security*
KEKKONEN, Tuomo, *Senior Constable, Security*
LÄHDE, Pentti, *Detective, Security*
MUSTONEN, Ilkka, *Detective, Security*
PILKEVAARA, Onni, *Senior Constable, Security*
VIRTANEN, Matti, *Senior Constable, Security*
WAHLROOS, Matti, *Senior Constable, Security*
SATUKANGAS, Heli, *Chambermaid, Presidential Palace*
HEIKKINEN, Martti, *Caretaker, Presidential Palace*
KOIVISTO, Ruben, *Caretaker, Presidential Palace*
KOIVU, Ossi, *Commissionaire, Presidential Palace*
SALOMAA, Raimo, *Commissionaire, Presidential Palace*
BLÖMQVIST, Carl-Erik, *Head Waiter, Presidential Palace*
HANSEN, Nils, *Head Waiter, Presidential Palace*
SÄRÖ, Heli-Inkeri, *Secretary, Office of City of Helsinki*
TIIHONEN, Kalevi, *Police Officer attached to the Queen*
VESANTO, Matti, *Police Officer attached to Duke of Edinburgh*

22 June	**State Visit to Britain of President Giscard d'Estaing of the French Republic and Madame Giscard d'Estaing**

COLLEU, Pierre, *Assistant Consul*
MACDONALD, Patricia, *Attaché de Presse*

8 November   **State Visit to Luxembourg of the Queen and the Duke of Edinburgh**

DAMIT, Marcel, *of the Government Garage*
WEYDERT, Robert, *Chauffeur, Grand Duke's Household*
NURENBERG, Victor, *Chauffeur, Grand Duke's Household*
REDING, Armand, *Keeper of the Silver, Grand Duke's Household*
KIPS, Joseph, *Gardener, Grand Duke's Household*
SCHAMMEL, Henri, *Deputy Head of Gendarmerie, Diekirch District*
DAHM, Lucien, *Deputy Head of Gendarmerie, Luxembourg District*
GLESENER, J.P., *Deputy Head of Gendarmerie, Esch-sur-Alzette*
STOFFEL, J.P., *Chief Commissaire, Security Service*
HOFFMAN, Joseph, *Chief of Traffic Control*
GRETHEN, A., *Sergeant-Major (Army)*
GOEREND, F., *Sergeant-Major (Army)*
CLEES, J., *Sergeant-Major (Army)*
GODEFROID, M.J., *Departmental Head, Police, Luxembourg*
WILMES, M.C., *Departmental Head, Police, Luxembourg*
ALZIN, M.R., *Departmental Head, Police, Luxembourg*
ANTON, M.C., *Departmental Head, Police, Esch-sur-Alzette*
THEIN, M.J., *Departmental Head, Police, Ettelbruck*
KIEFFER, M.H., *Secretary to Council of Echternach*
KREMER, M.J., *Secretary to Council of Vianden*
CLEMENT, M.J., *Secretary to Council of Esch*
CIGRANG, M.F., *Secretary to Council of Differdange*
FOX, Pierre, *Chief Usher, Grand Duke's Household*

1977

1978

22 May   **State Visit to the Federal Republic of Germany of the Queen and the Duke of Edinburgh**

BEDNARZ, Jürgen, *Clerk, President's Office*
KRÜGER, Charlotte, *Clerk, President's Office*
KÜLPS, Erika, *Clerk, President's Office*
DITTMANN, Ulrich, *Clerk, President's Office*
CHEMORIN, Hannelore, *Clerk, President's Office*
HAAGE, Ingrid, *Clerk, Protocol Department*
PESCH, Katharina, *Clerk, Protocol Department*
VEITH, Anneliese, *Clerk, Protocol Department*
RITTER, Gisela, *Clerk, Protocol Department*
LANGE, Staff-Sergeant Horst, *Member of the Band*
RENTZ, Sergeant Jürgen, *Field Artillery Battalion 110*
BALLA, Petty Officer Horst, *Destroyer Hessen*
PETER, Police Sergeant Andreas, *Federal Border Guard*
BORCHER, Police Sergeant Volker, *Federal Border Guard*
MOTTSCHELLER, Police Sergeant Axel, *Federal Border Guard*
ZEHRER, Police Sergeant Hans, *Federal Border Guard*
PAPE, Constable Hans-Joachim, *Federal Border Guard*
WYSK, Police Sergeant Klaus, *President's Department, Bonn*
LUTZI, Police Sergeant Wilhelm, *President's Department, Bonn*
BRUNE, Police Sergeant Paul, *President's Department, Bonn*
RHEINDORF, Detective Sergeant Toni, *President's Department, Bonn*
STÖLBEN, Detective Sergeant Kurt, *President's Department, Bonn*
HOLTSCHNEIDER, Sergeant Jens-Carsten, *Schleswig-Holstein Police*
BAUMANNS, Hermann, *Head Driver, Protocol Division*

14 November   **State Visit to Britain of President Eanes of Portugal**

MENDONCA, Lopes de, *Private Photographer to the President*
ANDREW, Monteiro, *of Secretariat for Social Communication*
CASTRO, Noronha, *of Secretariat for Social Communication*
SILVA, Macedo, *Official Photographer*
COLAÇO, Gonçalves, *of Secretariat for Social Communication*
CHARTRES, Luis, *Assistant Commercial Attaché, Portuguese Embassy*
SOUSA, Roberto de, *Deputy Director, Tourist Office*
GONÇALVES, Neves, *Vice-Consul*

1979

16 May **State Visit to Denmark of the Queen and the Duke of Edinburgh**
WINTHER, Kirsten, *of the Chancery of the Orders of Knighthood*
HANSEN, Kai, *Messenger, Ministry of Foreign Affairs*
KNUDSEN, Staff-Sergeant Flemming Wrist, *Royal Guard Hussars*
KNUDSEN, Warrant Officer Kurt Weisz, *Royal Life Guard*
DANIELSEN, Staff Tambour Niels, *Combined Band at Aarhus*
TORNEHAVE, Staff Tambour Axel Fritjof, *Combined Band at Aarhus*
ANDERSEN, Jorn Claus Sindal, *Assistant Commissioner, Aarhus Police*
HORN, Carl, *Inspector, Copenhagen Police*
TEILMANN, Kare, *Inspector, Copenhagen Police*
KRISTIANSEN, Ivan Groesen, *Inspector, Aarhus Police*
HORNBAEK, Peter Sten, *Inspector Aarhus Police*
HANSEN, Tage, *Inspector, Municipality of Copenhagen*
HANSEN, Hans Erik, *Senior Custodian, Municipality of Copenhagen*
OLSSON, Svend Christian Lischang, *Senior Custodian, Municipality of Copenhagen*
WULFF, Jens Frederik, *Harbour Assistant, Port of Copenhagen*
JENSEN, Henning Otto, *Custodian, Municipality of Aarhus*
MADSEN, Henning, *Chasseur, Royal Household*
JENSEN, Jonna, *Lady's Maid to Queen Margrethe*
CHRISTIANSEN, Jens, *Coachman*
HANSEN, Gert, *Chef, Royal Household*
VINDING, Jesper Michael, *Chef, Royal Household*
JORGENSEN, Elva Korsholm, *Housekeeper at Fredensborg*
LARSEN, Anni Franck, *Clerk, Private Secretary's Office*
RASMUSSEN, Martin, *Office Messenger, Royal Household*

1980

14 October **State Visit to Italy of the Queen and the Duke of Edinburgh**
FALSO, Coad. Daniele, *Protocol Hospitality*
BONANNI, Coad. Luigi, *Protocol Driver*
PAOLILLI, Canc. Salvatore, *Protocol Administration*
MICUCCI, Coad. Naazareno, *Protocol Baggage*
MAZZARO, Coad. Ornella Coppola, *Protocol Visits*
D'ERAMO LOMBARDOZZI, Coad. Sup. Erminia, *Protocol Visits*
UBALDINI, Canc. Paola Piastra, *Protocol Visits*
SBRACIA, Canc.Giulio, *Protocol*
MOSCATELLI, Cav. Silvio, *Protocol Printing*
CASADEI, Sig. Stefano, *Protocol Honours*
LORENZONI, Sigra. Annamaria, *Protocol Honours*
PETRUCCELLI, Sigra. Rosalba, *Protocol Honours*
FINAZZI, Sig. Fabrizio, *Protocol Villa Madama*
NASTASI, Sigra. Domenica Natalizia, *Protocol*
FERRANDO, Signa. Maria Teresa, *Protocol Visits*

18 November **State Visit to Britain of King Birendra and Queen Aishwarya of Nepal**
GURUNG, Subedar Sarba Dhoj, *Valet to the King*
THAPA, Subedar K.B., *Security*

1981

25 May **State Visit to Norway of the Queen and the Duke of Edinburgh**
BRATHEN, Knut, *Principal Chauffeur*
GOMSRUD, Einar, *Responsible for Silverware*
EINARSBOL, Haakon, *Caretaker, Royal Palace*
SALZER, Günther, *Royal Chef*
BRYN, Anton, *Head Waiter*

1982

16 March **State Visit to Britain of Sultan Qaboos bin Al Said of Oman**
TAWFIQ, Lokhman, *The Sultan's Servant*
SAID, Suleiman, *The Sultan's Servant*
HARTHI, Captain Said Saif Said Al, *The Sultan's Servant*

16 November **State Visit to Britain of Queen Beatrix of the Netherlands and Prince Claus**
BRANDT, C., *Acting Chef*
BUHRMANN, Staff-Sergeant P.C., *RNLAF – Steward*
EEDEN, F.M.P.F. van, *Footman*
GERRING, Sergeant J.G., *RNLN – Steward*

GRAAF, I. de, *Personal Maid to Queen Beatrix*
GRONINGEN, B.H. van, *Acting Chef*
HEUVEL, Staff-Sergeant C. van den, *RNLAF – Steward*
KOOTEN, Sergeant-Major W. van, *RNLAF – Steward*
KRANS, P.H.M., *First Chef*
ROOSE, Sergeant P., *RNLAF – Steward*
SERNE, W.J., *Valet*
SLIK, H.F., *Valet to Prince Claus*
SOEST, Sergeant G. van, *RNLN – Steward*
WIEL, Sergeant, G.J.M. te, *RNLMC – Bandmaster*
MONDFRANS, R., *Detective, Security Service*

1983

25 May **State Visit to Sweden of the Queen and the Duke of Edinburgh**
KRAFTNER, Gunter, *Palace Chef*
VOGELI, Werner, *Court Restaurateur*
FREDERICKSSON, Hans, *Leading Driver*
KELLBERG, Agnes, *Administration Assistant, Office of the Marshal of the Court*
OSTERLUND, Solveig, *Accountant*
OHLSSON, Gosta, *Master Upholsterer*
JOSEPHSSON, Ingrid, *Textile Conservator*
ALMQVIST, Monica, *Textile Conservator*
SAMARK, Ingrid, *Administrative Assistant, Office of Palace Governor*
THILANDER, Kenth, *Chief Engineer*
NEDERMAN, Kapten Leif, *Commanding Guard of Honour*
JOHANSSON, Kapten Beyron, *Second in Command, Mounted Escort*
LUNDQVIST, Kapten Thorbjorn, *Commanding Royal Guard at Palace*
BRISSMAN, Kapten Per, *Commanding Troops lining Processional Route*
CARLSSON, Erik, *Detective Chief Inspector, Senior Personal Protection Officer*
HELLSTROM, Erik, *Detective Chief Inspector, Special Branch Officer*
OLOFSSON, Reidar, *Inspector, Royal Driver*
SAMUELSSON, Ingrid, *Inspector, Royal Driver*
GRANKVIST, Sten, *Chief Inspector, District Police*
JOGERHEIM, Stig, *Chief Inspector, District Police*
KLINTEBERG, Nils, *Police Superintendent, Gothenburg*
ANDERSSEN, Amus Erik, *Leader, Folk Music Orchestra in Palace*
JOHANSSON, Tore, *Head of Transportation Centre*
JERN, Lena, *Clerical Officer, Protocol Department*
AYDIN, Karin, *Clerical Officer, Protocol Department*
GROLL, Elisabeth, *Clerical Officer, Protocol Department*

1984

26 March **State Visit to Jordan of the Queen and the Duke of Edinburgh**
ROLFS, John, *Manager, Royal Palaces*
WILLEMS, Marac, *Food and Beverages Manager, Royal Palaces*
NOVEMBRE, Walter, *Food and Beverages Manager, Royal Palaces*
SCHWARZ, Nick, *Assistant Manager, Royal Palaces*
SEGOVIA, Liesa, *Executive Housekeeper, Royal Palaces*
SCHMITT, Christel, *Assistant Executive Housekeeper, Royal Palaces*
PITCHMANN, Andreas, *Senior Resident Engineer, Royal Palaces*
ILIOPOULOS, Lt. Cdr. Nicholas, *Marine Chief Superintendent Royal Yachts*

10 April **State Visit to Britain of Shaikh Isa bin Sulman Al Khalifa, Amir of Bahrain**
AMEEN, Ali Mohammed, *His Highness' Personal Domestic Staff*
BUBSHAIT, Ahmeed Yousuf, *His Highness' Personal Domestic Staff*
KANOO, Ebrahim, *His Highness' Personal Domestic Staff*

23 October **State Visit to Britain of President Mitterand of the French Republic and Madame Mitterand**
LAMBERT, Georges, *Personal Bodyguard to the President*
QUENARD, Louis, *Personal Bodyguard to the President*
MANOUJIAN, Didier, *Personal Bodyguard to Madame Mitterand*
BERRIER, Philippe, *Personal Bodyguard to Madame Mitterand*
CORDIER, Bruno, *Doctor*
VAUTHIER, Denis, *Major-domo at Elysée Palace*
KERROS, Major Yvan, *Communications*

1985

25 March **State Visit to Portugal of the Queen and the Duke of Edinburgh**
DAVID, Antonio Maria Fernandez, *State Protocol*

GUEDES, Maria Clara Marques, *State Protocol*
AIRES, Commr. Joao Paulo, *Security*
PAULO, Deputy Chief Jose Joaquin, *Security*
CASTRO, Ana Paula Machada, *Queluz Exhibition*
GUARDIOLA, Ana Maria, *Queluz Exhibition*
DIAS, Maria Ines Enes, *Queluz Exhibition*
SERRA, Sergeant-Major Joao de Conceicao, *Driver of the Queen's car in Oporto*
LOURO, Dr Francisco Carvalho, *Ajuda Palace Exhibition*
PINTO, Dra. Graca Mendes, *Ajuda Palace Exhibition*
LAMAS, Dra. Joana, *Ajuda Palace Exhibition*

16 April   **State Visit to Britain of Life President Dr Banda of Malawi**
CHISONGA, H., *Senior Valet*
MWENELUPEMBE, R.C., *Assistant Superintendent of Police*
NANGWALE, F.C., *Presidential Guard*
MALOYA, R., *Inspector of Police*

1986

17 February   **State Visit to Nepal of the Queen and the Duke of Edinburgh**
DANGOL, Subba Bishnu Man, *Driver, Royal Palace*
BISTA, Shanker Raj, *Under Secretary*
BAJRACHARYA, Nahendra Ratna, *Engineer*
SHAH, Bishwo Bikram, *Under Secretary*
BAJRACHARYA, Hira Ratna, *Section Officer*
SHRESTHA, Amrit Bahadur, *Chairman, District Panchayat, Kathmandu*
BAHADUR, Badri, *Chairman, District Panchayat, Lalitpur*
KHATRI, Ganesh Bahadur, *Chairman, District Panchayat, Bhaktapur*
BAJRACHARYA, Buddhiraj, *Chairman, Lalitpur Town Panchayat*
NAICHAI, Gyan Bahadur, *Chairman, Bhaktapur Town Panchayat*
SHRIVASTAV, Sachitanand, *Director-General, Postal Services Department*
NIRAULA, Punya Prasad, *Director-General, Department of Archaeology*
MALLA, Dr Samar Bahadur, *Director-General, Department of Medicinal Plants*
THAPA, Damber Jung, *Director-General, Department of Civil Aviation*
PRADHANANG, Shiva Bahadur, *Chief Engineer, Department of Roads*
RAJBHANDARI, Hajmaniya Lal, *Chief Engineer, Department of Housing and Physical Planning*
RAYMAJHI, Dev Bahadur, *Chief Engineer, Department of Drinking Water and Sewerage*
SHRESTHA, Harshman, *Chief Director, Nepal Electricity Authority*
SHAH, Bhogya Prasad, *Manager, Radio Nepal*
UPADHAYA, Anand Bilash, *Chief Officer, Royal Botanical Garden, Godawari*
AMATYA, Dr Sphalyya, *Deputy Director, National Archives*
GAUTAM, Dhanush Chandra, *Director, Department of Information*
SHRESTHA, Krishna Prasad, *Chief of the National Museum, Bhaktapur*
SHRESTHA, Govinda Man, *Acting Director, Hanuman Dhoka Supervision Office*
BASNET, Bhagirath, *Section Officer, Ministry of Foreign Affairs*
ACHARYA, Gyan Chandra, *Section Officer, Ministry of Foreign Affairs*
PRASAI, Prahlhad Kumar, *Section Officer, Ministry of Foreign Affairs*
PUDASAYANI, Suresh Kumar, *General Manager, Nepal Telecommunications Corporation*
SHEUARMA, Nagendra, *General Manager, Gorkhapatra Corporation*
BISTA, Radhashyam, *General Manager, National News Agency*
SINGH, Mrs Tika, *General Manager, Nepal Film Corporation*
SHAH, Nir, *General Manager, Nepal Television*
NEUPANE, Ramchandra, *Chief Editor, Gorkhapatra*
BAHADUR, Shyam, *Editor, The Rising Nepal*
GAURI, Mrs, *Editor, Radio Nepal*
DHITAL, Arun Prasad, *Protocol Department, Ministry of Foreign Affairs*
BHATTARAI, Dinesh, *Protocol Department, Ministry of Foreign Affairs*
CHUDAL, Inspector Bharat, *Escort Jeep*
ALE, Inspector Shadev, *Escort Jeep*
NEWANG, Inspector Amer, *Escort Jeep*
BAHADUR, Dan, *Senior Steward*
PRADHAN, Gaya Prasad, *Property Services Agency Foreman*

22 April   **State Visit to Britain of King Juan Carlos and Queen Sofia of Spain**
RODENAS, Pablo, *Security, Ministry of Foreign Affairs*
HORCAJUELO, Juan, *Security, Ministry of Foreign Affairs*
HIDALGO, Luis, *Secretary, His Majesty's Household*
GIL, Victor, *Secretary, His Majesty's Household*
JIMENEZ, Rafael, *Secretary, His Majesty's Household*
SALAS, Miguel Angel, *Private Secretary to the Head of His Majesty's Household*
DALDA, Antonio Garcia, *Official Photographer to His Majesty*
GARCIA, Jose Lopez, *His Majesty's Household, Communications*
GALIANA, Juan, *His Majesty's Household, Communications*

MARTIN, Jose M., *His Majesty's Household, Communications*
LEIVA, Blas, *Valet to His Majesty*
BERMEJO, Dona Paulina, *Maid to Her Majesty*
MARTIN, Dona Dolores, *Maid to Her Majesty*
SEGURA, Francisco, *Hairdresser to Her Majesty*
GONZALEZ, Dona Alicia, *Maid to the Marquesa de Mondejar*
CANTOS, Jose, *Assistant to the Marques de Mondejar*
ANTORAZ, Jose, *Assistant to Head of Military Office of HM's Household*
BELLOSO, Jose, *Assistant to the Secretary General of HM's Household*

1 July | **State Visit to Britain of President von Weizsäcker of the Federal Republic of Germany and Freifrau von Weizsäcker**
WEISS, Gerhard, *Luggage Supervisor*
NIESEL, Hans-Jurgen, *Luggage Supervisor*
HILL, Renata, *Clerk, Protocol Department*
STUNKEL, Peter, *Communication Clerk*
KLEINSCHNITTGER, Josef, *Calligrapher*
RAUSCH, Thomas, *Personal Bodyguard of the President*
FORSTER, Herald, *Personal Bodyguard of the Foreign Minister*
BESSEN, Peter, *Attaché, German Embassy*
KOHL, Wilhelm, *Assistant Attaché, German Embassy*
FRANKE, Willy, *Clerk, German Embassy*
CASH, Ilse-Marie, *Shorthand Typist, German Embassy*
BOCKSTALLER, Rolf, *Technician, German Embassy*

1987

14 July | **State Visit to Britain of King Hassan II of Morocco**
EL-ACHRAOUI, Mustapha
RAHMOUNI, Hassan
LINH, Bi-Quang
MOUKALLAF, Abdallah, *Palace Staff*
MARJANE, Abderrahman, *Palace Staff*
GOUJJANE, Mekki, *Palace Staff*
CHERRAJA, Messaoud, *Palace Staff*
BAGGAR, Rahal, *Palace Staff*
SIDKI, Rahal, *Palace Staff*
JAOUHAR, Lachen, *Palace Staff*
TREHART, Jean-Claude, *Palace Staff*
BENZEMROUN, Lieutenant Mokhtar, *Palace Staff*
AMINE, Lieutenant Mohamed, *Palace Staff*

1988

12 July | **State Visit to Britain of King Olav V of Norway**
ANDERSEN, Trond, *Valet*
SKAAR, Edvall, *Footman*
MAGNUS, Inspector Per Munthe, *Security Officer*
REIS, Fernando Jaspar Dos, *Head Waiter*
HANSSEN, Wenche, *Secretary, Norwegian Embassy*

17 October | **State Visit to Spain of the Queen and the Duke of Edinburgh**
CRIADO, Pedro
TOMÉ, Francisco
SANCLEMENTE, Señorita Maria Jesus
HERAS, José de las
MONTES, Alfredo
MONTILLA, Manuel
CASILLAS, Dionisio
GONZALEZ, Julian
FERNANDEZ, Federico
OTERO, José Manuel
CARILLO, Gonzalo
ALMAZAN, Angel, *Palacio de Viana*
ALONSO, José, *Palacio de Viana*
GONZALEZ, Luis
ALARCON, Antonio
RODRIGUEZ, Julian

1989

9 May | **State Visit to Britain of President Babangida of Nigeria**
UDOEYOP, E.F., *Minister, State Visit Unit, Nigerian High Commission*

MUSTAPHA, Hadiza, *Second Secretary, State Visit Unit, Nigerian High Commission*
USMAN, Alhaji D.A.D., *Chief Personal Assistant to President*
OZOCHUKWU, C., *Senior Personal Assistant to President*
TAWASIMI, P., *Personal Assistant to President*

1990

25 June **State Visit to Iceland of the Queen and the Duke of Edinburgh**
DUNGAL, Gunnar, *Dalur Horse Farm*
SIGURDARDOTTIR, Mrs. Thordis, *Dalur Horse Farm*
GUDMUNDSSON, Bjarni V., *Driver*
RAGNARSSON, Thorvaldur, *Driver*
PETURSDOTTIR, Mrs Sigrun, *Housekeeper*
PALSDOTTIR, Mrs. Halldora, *Housekeeper*
ERLENDSSON, Gudmundur, *Driver*
VIGFUSSON, Gunnar Geir, *Photographer*
THORODDSEN, Gisli, *Chef*
JONSSON, Hilmar H., *Chef*
RAGNARSSON, Kristjan, *Car Organiser, Ministry of Foreign Affairs*
STEFANSSON, Kristjan Andri, *Assistant, Prime Minister's Office*
SKAFTASON, Halldor, *Food and Beverage Manager, Hotel Saga*
FRIDJONSSON, Sveinbjorn, *Chef, Hotel Saga*
WESSMAN, Ragnar, *Chef, Hotel Saga*
EGILSSON, Hafsteinn, *Inspector, Hotel Saga*
LUTHERSDOTTIR, Miss Hrefna Dis, *Ministry of Foreign Affairs*
BIRGISDOTTIR, Miss Sigridur, *Ministry of Foreign Affairs*
GUNNARSSON, Saevar, *Chief Inspector*
HALLSSON, Jonas, *Chief Inspector*
VIGFUSSON, Arni, *Chief Inspector*
ALFREDSSON, Thorstein, *Chief Inspector*
JOHANSSON, Karl, *Chief Inspector*
GARDARSSON, Gisli, *Detective Sergeant*
KARLSSON, Asgeir, *Detective Sergeant*
JENSSON, Arnar, *Chief Inspector*
BJORNSSON, Gisli, *Chief Inspector*
JONSSON, Gylfi, *Chief Inspector*
SIGURJONSSON, Hakon, *Detective Sergeant*
NJALSSON, Skarphedinn, *Inspector*
EIDSSON, Eidur, *Sergeant*
JONSSON, Onundur, *Chief Inspector*
ASGEIRSSON, Sigurbjorn, *Inspector*
SVANSSON, Agust, *Inspector*
HJARTARSON, Karl, *Inspector*
HANSSON, Gudbrandur, *Inspector*
GUDMUNDSSON, Aiger, *Inspector*
SIGURDSSON, Gudmundur Ingi, *Inspector*
MAGNUSSON, Karl, *Inspector*
THORSTEINSSON, Thorir, *Inspector*
SIGURDSSON, Sergeant Gudbrandur, *The Duke of Edinburgh's Police Officer*
ELISSON, Holmgrimur Svanur, *Detective Sergeant*
BJORGVINSSON, Rikhard J., *Inspector*

23 October **State Visit to Britain of President Cossiga of Italy and Signora Cossiga**
PICCHI, Marcello, *of the Presidency of the Republic*
PRO, Dino, *of the Presidency of the Republic*
LONIGRO, Carla, *Interpreter*
COSMAI, Antonella, *Interpreter*
ANTONIONI, Dominique, *of the Italian Embassy*
CAVALLARO, Concetta, *of the Italian Embassy*
MAZZEGA, Giulia, *of the Ministry of Foreign Affairs*
LATINI, Aldo, *of the Presidency of the Republic*
STEFANONI, Ivo, *of the Presidency of the Republic*
LAZZARO, Claudia, *of the Presidency of the Republic*
ROHR, Marcello, *of the Italian Embassy*
SOBRERO, Laura, *of the Italian Embassy*
VILLARINI, Saverio, *of the Presidency of the Republic*
AGNELLO, Giovanni, *of the Presidency of the Republic*
PAGLIUCA, Domenico, *of the Presidency of the Republic*
SARGENTI, Umberto, *of the Presidency of the Republic*
DEGNI, Vinicio, *of the Presidency of the Republic*
CICCONI, Antonio, *of the Presidency of the Republic*
COZZOLINO, Pasquale, *of the Ministry of Foreign Affairs*

PABA, Pietro, *of the Ministry of Foreign Affairs*
TELCH, Gianni, *of the Ministry of Foreign Affairs*

1991

1992

9 June   **State Visit to France of the Queen and the Duke of Edinburgh**
FELCOURT, Ghislaine de, *Press, Quai d'Orsay*
MILBERT, Martine, *Press, Quai d'Orsay*
CASAPOPRANA, Seraphin, *Service, Quai d'Orsay*

3 November   **State Visit to Britain of the Sultan of Brunei Darussalam and the Raja Isteri**
MASTURA, Pengiran Hajjah, *Personal Assistant to Princess Amal Umi Kalthum*
AWANG, Haji Ismail, *of the Royal Household Staff*
AHMID, Ismi, *Education Attaché, Brunei High Commission*
MASU'UT, Bujang Haji, *Education Attaché, Brunei High Commission*
ASMAT, Haji Kasim, *Third Secretary, Brunei High Commission*
HUSSEIN, Zulkifli Haji, *Third Secretary, Brunei High Commission*
ALI, Pengiran Haji Omar, *Personal Assistant to High Commissioner*
DAUD, Pengiran Haji Johari, *Education Attaché, Brunei High Commission*
HAMID, Abdullah Haji, *Third Secretary, Brunei High Commission*
SIDUP, Abu Bakar, *Third Secretary, Brunei High Commission*
AJI, Merussin Haji, *Communication Attaché, Brunei High Commission*
DAUD, Pengiran Haji Johari, *Education Attaché, Brunei High Commission*
HAMID, Abdullah Haji, *Third Secretary, Brunei High Commission*

1993

27 April   **State Visit to Britain of President Soares of Portugal and Senhora Soares**
ANDRADE, Margarida
FILIP, Sub-Chefe Carlos Fonseca
SILVA, Francisco Antonio Oliveira e
LEWIS, Anabela
FOX, Roberta

1994

5 July   **State Visit to Edinburgh of King Harald of Norway and Queen Sonja**
AAMODT, Vidar, *Valet*
INAGE, Masaru, *Royal Chef*
STOEN, Aud, *Housekeeper*

1995

17 October   **State Visit to Britain of President Ahtisaari of Finland and Madame Ahtisaari**
MIETTINEN, Miss Leena, *Archivist, Finnish Embassy*
MIEKKONIEMI, Miss Ritva, *Accountant, Finnish Embassy*
BUTLER, Mrs Ritva Marjatta, *Consular Assistant, Finnish Embassy*
MELAS, Mrs Annele, *Press Office Assistant, Finnish Embassy*
VILPAS, Pekka, *Valet, Finnish Embassy*

1996

14 May   **State Visit to Britain of President Chirac of the French Republic and Madame Chirac**
HAULON, Stephan, *Doctor*
MORIN, Commandant de Police Joel Henri André, *Personal Security Officer to the President*
PELOIS, Commandant de Police Jean-Claude, *Personal Security Officer to the President*
PASTOR, M. Valery, *Personal Security Officer to Madame Chirac*
PERROT, Major Alain, *Communications Officer*
CANOVAS, M. Yves, *Superintendent, French Embassy*
MIKHOS, Madame Nicole Maryvonne Annick, *Secretary, French Embassy*
PAIRONE, Madame Eleanor, *Secretary, French Embassy*
PIETROBONI, M. José François, *Valet*
MESTAIS, Madame Anne Elizabeth Edwige Marie Pierre St. Gilles, *Secretary, French Embassy*

1997

31 December   BONICI, Tonio, *Palace Foreman, Buckingham Palace (see also p.119 ante)*

1998–9

2000

16 February	**State Visit to Britain of Queen Margrethe II of Denmark and Prince Henrik**

MADSEN, Kenneth
CHRISTENSEN, Poul Nymark
MEIER, Steen-Flemming
NIELSEN, Torben
HATT, Preben
ERIKSEN, Ms Lisbeth Faber

ELIZABETH II: RVM, CLASPS

1958

25 March   **State Visit to the Netherlands of the Queen and the Duke of Edinburgh**
BOSCH, Miss H., *Head of Linen Room, Royal Palace*
BEERMAN, Mr J.C., *Director, Master of the Household's Office*
LINDEN, Mr A.C. van der, *Chef de Cuisine*
OOSTRUM, Mr A. van, *House Manager*

5 April   **State Visit to Britain of President de Gaulle of the French Republic and Madame de Gaulle**
BLOAS, Jean, *Security Officer*
HARRY, Roger, *Fleuriste en Chef à la Présidence*

ELIZABETH II: RVM, BRONZE

1958

25 March   **State Visit to the Netherlands of the Queen and the Duke of Edinburgh**
BRINK, J., *Janitor, Het Concertgebouw NV*
BOES, F.D., *Chauffeur*
BOLTEN, G.W., *Coachman*
BRUGMAN, Miss P., *Housemaid*
DIJKHOF, Miss S.F., *Kitchenmaid*
GASPAR, A.J., *Coachman*
GRAAF, H., *Chauffeur*
HORST, B.L., van der, *Assistant Coachman*
KEPPEL, W., *Coachman*
LEZER, S.G., *Footman*
OOSTERVEER, B.A.A., *Coachman*
OVERWATER, C.A.G., *General Servant*
REMMERS, H.J., *House Painter, Royal Palace, Amsterdam*
STEENBERGEN, M.W., *Batman*
VEERMAN, P., *Coach House Servant*
WEIJDE, P., van der, *Footman*
WESTERHOUD, J. Th. M., *Coachman*
HEMMINK, H., *Chief Constable, Amsterdam Municipal Police*
KAPEL, P. van, *Chief Constable, The Hague Municipal Police*
NIEUWBUURT, J.S., *Assistant Lock Keeper, Ijmuiden*
SPEYKER, J.C., *Chief Constable, Amsterdam Municipal Police*
STEGMAN, J., *Chief Constable, Rotterdam Municipal Police*
WESTERINK, C.H., *Chief Constable, Rotterdam Municipal Police*

1959

1960

5 April   **State Visit to Britain of President de Gaulle of the French Republic and Madame de Gaulle**
MOUGNEAU, M. Robert, *Maître d'Hôtel*
SOLDA, M. Renato, *Maître d'Hôtel*

1961

26 February **State Visit to Nepal by the Queen and the Duke of Edinburgh**
DANGOL, Kharidar Indra Man, *Bearer*
SHRESTHA, Kharidar Kailas Man, *of Staff of Royal Guest House, Katmandu*
BALAKRISHNA, Shri, *Bearer*
DHANALAL, Shri, *Bearer*
LAKSHMIMAN, Shri, *Bearer*
LAL, Shri Shyam, *Bearer*
KOIRALA, Kharidar Bhola Nath
SHRESTHA, Shri Basant Lal, *Butler*
MAHARJAN, Shri Nir Lal, *Servant*
GOMEZ, Shri J. Ambrosi, *Head Cook*
SHRESTHA, Shri Gopal Krishna, *of Staff of Royal Guest House, Katmandu*
DANGAL, Shri Janak Lal
SHRESTHA, Shri Narayan Prasad, *of Staff of Royal Guest House, Katmandu*
DANGOL, Shri Govind Lal
SINGH, Thakur, *Head Orderly, British Embassy, Katmandu*

2 March **State Visit to Iran of the Queen and the Duke of Edinburgh**
DARVISHIAN, Nosratollah, *of the Palace Staff*
BEGLOO, Abolkassem, *of the Palace Staff*
JAVANSHIR, Esmail, *of the Palace Staff*
POURESHOJAR, Amir, *of the Palace Staff*
SHAHNAZAR, Mehdi, *of the Palace Staff*
HASSASSI, Sayed Hossein, *of the Palace Staff*
ASLANI, Houshang, *of the Palace Staff*
SAFARI, Mehdi, *of the Palace Staff*
SHARAFI, Abbas, *of the Palace Staff*
FATAHI, Hossein, *of the Palace Staff*
NOREHANI, Jafar, *of the Palace Staff*
AMOUI, Abdollah, *of the Palace Staff*
SARDARI, Yahya, *of the Palace Staff*
SARBAZI,

1 May **State Visit to Italy of the Queen and the Duke of Edinburgh**
CIONI, Alfonso, *in charge of Laundry, the Quirinale*
AGOSTINI, Virginio, *in charge of Laundry, the Quirinale*
PACE, Romolo, *Head of Telephone Switchboard, the Quirinale*
ROSA, Eugenio, *Head Cook, the Quirinale*
ANTONUCCI, Aldo, *Chief Doorman, the Quirinale*
BONETTI, Roberto, *Chief of the Workmen, the Quirinale*
CIONCOLONI, Enrico, *Head Gardener, the Quirinale*
CAVALLO, Mario, *in charge of electrical appliances*
JANNUCCELLI, Alfredo, *Chief of the Craftsmen*
DE SANTIS, Vincenzo, *Carabinieri, the Quirinale unit*
TRISOGLIO, Francesco, *Carabinieri, Mounted Group*
FONTANIVE, Silvio, *Carabinieri, Motorcycle Unit*
PROIETTI, Umberto, *Carabinieri, Security Service*
PAOLANTONI, Mario, *Chief Compositor, Italian Stationery Office*

1962

1963

9 July **State Visit to Britain of King Paul and Queen Frederika of the Hellenes**
CHRONOPOULOS, Panayotis, *Personal Valet to the Grand Marshal of the Court*
MACRIS, Thomas, *Footman*
TSIROS, Triphon, *Footman*
VIDINIOTIS, John, *Footman*
CARAYANIS, Constantine, *Footman*
MARTZELIS, Aristides, *Footman*
NIKIFOROS, George, *Footman*
HADJOPOULOS, Nicolas, *Footman*
KITSOS, Panayiotis, *Footman*
GRAMMENOS, Constantine, *Footman*
DILES, M.G., *Butler, Greek Embassy*
DILES, Constantine, *Footman, Greek Embassy*
CONSTANTINIDES, M.K., *Chauffeur, Greek Embassy*

1964

1965

1 February

State Visit to Ethiopia of the Queen and the Duke of Edinburgh

ABEBE, Ato Shiferan, *Butler, British Embassy, Addis Ababa*
HANA, Ato Aderaye Wolde, *Cook, British Embassy, Addis Ababa*
MARIAM, Ato Gebre, *Head Syce, British Embassy, Addis Ababa*
DAMOTE, Ato Kadir, *Clerk/Interpreter, British Embassy, Addis Ababa*
MARIAM, Ato Bayene Gebre, *Driver/Gatekeeper etc, British Consulate*
ARESSIE, Ato Turquabo, *Consular Clerk, Asmara*
KASWII, Ato Munyao, *Consulate Signaller, Asmara*

8 February

State Visit to Sudan of the Queen and the Duke of Edinburgh

AHMED, Sayed Khalil Mohammed, *Telephone Operator, Republican Palace*
HAKEEM, Sayed Mursi Awad el, *Telephone Operator, Republican Palace*
OSMAN, Sayed el Tigani Mohammed, *Telephone Operator, Republican Palace*
HAG, Sayed Sayed el, *Telephone Operator, Republican Palace*
ALI, Sayed el Sir, *Telephone Operator, Republican Palace*
ADAWI, Sayed Nadeem Beshir, *Junior Clerk, Republican Palace*
MOHAMMED Sayed Abdel Gadir, *Junior Clerk, Republican Palace*
NUGUD, Sayed Mohammed, *The Queen's Driver*
MOHAMMED, Sayed Abdel Karim, *The Duke of Edinburgh's Driver*
SALIH, Sayed Abdu, *Suffragi*
ALI, Sayed Mohammed Salih, *Suffragi*
MULA, Sayed Mohammed Abdel, *Suffragi*
ALI, Sayed Magdoub Mohammed, *Suffragi*
AHMED, Mohammed Suléiman Ahmed, *Suffragi*
SUBAHI, Sergeant Abdel Gadir, *Orderly*
DAOUD, Sergeant Osman, *Orderly*
MUBARAK, Sergeant Mohammed el, *of the Palace Police*
ABDULLAH, Sergeant Awad el Karim, *of the Palace Police*
AHMED, Corporal Mahmoud Mohammed, *of the Palace Police*
HAMZA, Corporal Ali Ahmed, *of the Palace Police*
ABDULLAH, Corporal Abdel Rahman, *of the Palace Police*
AHMED, Corporal Ahmed Osman, *of the Palace Police*
TOR, Corporal Said Hamid Arkab el, *of the Palace Police*
IBRAHIM, Corporal Adam Salih, *of the Palace Police*
SHEIKH, Corporal Mohammed el, *of the Palace Police*
ABDULLAH, Corporal Bakheit Keer, *of the Palace Police*
MURJAN, Corporal Idris, *of the Palace Police*
MOHAMMED, Corporal. Abdel Bari, *of the Palace Police*
RAHIM, Corporal Hassan Abdel, *of the Palace Police*
GIDEIL, Corporal Ali Said el, *of the Palace Police*
ALI, Corporal Osman, *of the Palace Police*
SEED, Corporal Abdel Gadir Awad el, *of the Palace Police*
SALIH, Corporal Nur el din Said, *of the Palace Police*
MOHAMMED, Sergeant Abbas Ahmed, *Palace Guard*
MAMOUR, Sergeant Amina, *Palace Guard*
BESHIR, Sergeant Osman, *Palace Guard*
IBRAHIM, Sergeant Abdel Hamid, *Palace Guard*
MOHAMMED, Sergeant el Zubeir, *Palace Guard*
BAKEET, Sayed, *Cook, British Embassy*
IBRAHIM, Sayed Hassan, *Kavass, British Embassy*

18 May

State Visit to the Federal Republic of Germany of the Queen and the Duke of Edinburgh

KREBEL, Herr Otto, *Protocol, Federal Foreign Office*
MATYSIK, Herr Konrad, *Protocol, Federal Foreign Office*
BAUMANNS, Herr Hermann, *Leader of Car Procession*
FEHLING, Herr Albert, *Steward, Schloss Augustusburg*
ULBRICH, Herr Theodor, *Driver to Federal President*
BACHMANN, Herr Gerhard, *Driver to Frau Lübke*
KRAUS, Fräulein Dorothea, *Telephone Operator – on train*
KLATT, Fräulein Edith, *Telephone Operator – on train*
PENIKA, Herr Otto, *Driver of the Royal Car*
KLESS, Herr Michael, *Driver of the Royal Car*
KREUTZAREK, Herr Horst, *Driver of the Royal Car*
TRÄNKLE, Herr Rolf, *Driver of the Royal Car*
KÖHRING, Herr Heinz, *Chef on Special train*
OBST, Herr Erich, *Chef on Special train*
DURSTWITZ, Herr Herbert, *Head Waiter on Special train*
PATSCH, Herr Heinz, *Chef on Special train*

1966

9 May   **State Visit to Belgium of the Queen and the Duke of Edinburgh**
SUWIER, Mme Angèle, *Caretaker at Ostend*
ROCKER, Mme Antoinette de, *Housemaid*
VERBELEN, Georges, *Scullery Assistant*
THOELEN, Eugène, *Silver Pantry Assistant*
VELDER, Jan de, *Silver Pantry Assistant*
CNOP, Mme Anna, *Housemaid*
BONNET, Victor, *Scullery Assistant*
DUTILLEUL, Eugène, *Electrician*
PASTURE, Richard, *Scullery Assistant*
VERSPECHT, Louis, *Stoker*
DRAPS, Georges, *Stoker*
DRAPS, Karel, *Stoker*
TAEYE, Mme Suzanne de, *Housemaid*
ROSSEELS, Mme Clémence, *Housemaid*
ASSELBERGS, Alphonse, *Furniture Repairer*
BUELENS, Frans, *Gardener at Laeken*
GRIETEN, Emile, *Gardener at Laeken*
VEER, Emile van, *Gardener at Laeken*
MILLIANO, Henri de, *Staff-Sergeant*
VERCAMMEN, Jean-Baptiste, *Staff-Sergeant*
CHARLIER, Albert, *Staff-Sergeant*
MOUREAU, Dieudonné, *Staff-Sergeant*
FRONVILLE, Firmin, *Staff-Sergeant*
BEULE, Albinus de, *Staff-Sergeant*
THONET, Paul, *Staff-Sergeant*
VILETTE, Jean, *Staff-Sergeant*
VANACKER, Remy, *Chief Correspondent, Belgian Radio*
CAPPELLAN, Jean van, *Chief Correspondent, Belgian Radio*
LINDEN, Désiré van der, *Chief Correspondent, Belgian Radio*

1967

1968

1 November   **State Visit to Brazil of the Queen and the Duke of Edinburgh**
HUMEO, Doris Barreto Carrilho, *Typist at Ministry of Foreign Affairs*
FERREIRA, Rubisson Fioravante, *Baggage Section at Ministry*
MORAES, José Mario de, *Protocol Section at Ministry*
VIANNA, Sylvia de Silveira, *Protocol Section at Ministry*
MACEDO, Moacyr Albino, *Transport Section at Ministry*
BRAZ, Cloris Martins Ferreira Smith, *Protocol Section at Ministry*
SOUZA, Alcides de, *Protocol Section at Ministry*
MIRANDA, Tenente Murico Israel Correa de, *Bandmaster, Brazilian Marines*
MARQUES, Deoclides Mariano, *of the National Press Agency*
PALHETA, Mario Jesus da Conceicao, *of the National Press Agency*
ARTHUR, Tenente, *Head of Naval Outriders, Brasilia*
OTTONI, Tenente, *Head of Military Outriders, Brasilia*
BESSA, Sargento, *Head of Air Force Outriders, Brasilia*
CHAVES, Esio de Oliveira, *The Queen's Driver, Brasilia*
BARBOZA, Israel Alves, *The Queen's Driver, Recife*
GAERTNER, Tenente Sylvio, *Head of Outriders, Salvador*
SESTARI, Antonio A., *The Queen's Driver, Salvador*
NETTO, Olympio Portugal, *Protocol, São Paulo State*
SILVA, Itaborahy Barbosa da, *Protocol, São Paulo State*
CAMARGO, Tenente Alfredo P., *Head of Outriders, São Paulo*
PATO, Jao de Moraes, *Protocol Section, Guanabara*
NEVES, Aloisio, *Protocol Section, Guanabara*
LEMA, Nelson Pares, *Protocol Section, Guanabara*
PEREIRA, Tenente Heraldo Covas, *Outrider Section, Rio*
SALGADO, Sargento Darcy, *Outrider Section, Rio*
CALZAVARA, Augusto, *Traffic Control Officer, Rio*
OLIVEIRA, Captain Pedro de, *Traffic Control Officer, Rio*
CABRAL, Walfrido, *The Queen's Driver, Rio*
CLEVE, Miss V.M., *Telephonist, British Embassy, Rio*
MANOEL, A., *Doorman/Parker, British Embassy, Rio*
ALMEIDA, M de, *Clerk at Consulate, Rio*
QUEIROZ, Mrs I.H. de, *Telephonist at Consulate, Rio*

ANNICHINI, Constanzo, *Ambassador's Butler*
MORAES, Mrs Benilee Nascimento de, *Ambassador's Head Cook*
BARROS, Mrs Josephina de, *Ambassador's Head Housemaid*
BARROS, Severino Bartolomeu, *Ambassador's Driver*
RESENDE, Pedro, *Ambassador's Electrician*
SOUSA, R.E. de, *Head Messenger, British Embassy*
AZEVEDO, Gil, *Handyman, British Embassy*

11 November **State Visit to Chile of the Queen and the Duke of Edinburgh**
BARRIOS, Inspector Oscar Pizzaro, *Investigaciones Escort to the Queen*
FUENTE, Inspector Eduardo Labra de la, *Investigaciones Escort to the Queen*
REYES, Lidia Merino, *Assistant Housekeeper, Carrera Hotel*
GODOY, Isidro Risi, *Bell Captain, Carrera Hotel*
ALARCON, Manuel Galaz, *Head Painter, Carrera Hotel*
JACQUES, Zoila Latorre, *Telephone Supervisor, Carrera Hotel*
VALDEBENITO, Maria Marchant, *Assistant to Laundry Manager, Carrera Hotel*
MEZA, José Daniel Hernandez, *Associate Chief Engineer, Carrera Hotel*
JEREZ, Ernesto, *Head of Stables, Polo Club*
SAYAGO, José, *Duke of Edinburgh's Groom, Polo Club*
SANDOVAL, Javier Campos, *The Queen's Driver*
REYES, Nibaldo Ramirez, *The Duke of Edinburgh's Driver*

1969

22 April **State Visit to Britain of President Saragat of Italy**
VOLPINI, Umberto, *Valet to the President*
LEGNANI, Ernesto, *Valet to the President*
NATALE, Francesco, *Baggage Officer*
MARANI, Eugenio, *Baggage Officer*
MINELLI, Giuseppina, *Maid to Signora Santacatterina*
CAFARO, Signor, *Clerk, Ministry of Foreign Affairs*

5 May **State Visit to Austria of the Queen and the Duke of Edinburgh**
KRAIF, Johann, *Chauffeur, British Embassy*
THALHAMMER, Friedrich, *Chef, British Embassy*
MACHATSCH, Franz, *Porter, British Embassy*
CERNY, Franz, *Clerk, Federal Chancellor's Office*
HOLLAUS, Johann, *Clerk, Federal Chancellor's Office*
PAUER, Johann, *Official, Federal Chancellor's Office*
STUDENY, Franz, *Official, Federal Chancellor's Office*
RITSCHEL, Viktor, *Clerk, Federal Chancellor's Office*
ZAHRL, Franz, *Official, Federal Chancellor's Office*
KRISPIN, Josef, *Official, Federal Chancellor's Office*
BALUCH, Johann, *CID Officer*
TEMS, Johann, *CID Officer*
PLANETTA, Adolf, *Police Officer*
MUTHSAM, Ernst, *Police Officer*
HOLY, Johann, *Police Officer*
HYDEN, Heinrich, *Gendarmerie Officer*
ORTHABER, Anton, *Police Officer*
WITSCHNIG, Johann, *Superintendent, Ministry for Education*
ZEINER, Karl, *Superintendent, Ministry for Education*
JAGSCHITZ, Gottfried, *Superintendent, Ministry for Education*
BACHINGER, Anton, *Horseman*
PUFFING, Peter, *Stud Groom*
KUTEL, Andreas, *Gardener*
WILD, Emilie, *Gardener*
FENZ, Horst, *Staff-Sergeant*
WERKNER, Franz, *Staff-Sergeant Bandsman*
DRÄGER, Albert, *Staff-Sergeant*
KRUPICKA, Robert, *Inspector, Building Ministry*
ZOLLNER, Gertrude, *Inspector, Building Ministry*
SCHWARZ, Josef, *Provincial Superintendent, Tirol*
VOLLGRUBER, Herbert, *Provincial Superintendent, Tirol*
SCHELLAUF, Alois, *Lorry Driver, Steiermark*
DOLOSCHILL, Johann, *Guard, Vienna*

5 July **State Visit to Britain of President Kekkonen of Finland and Madame Kekkonen**
TIITINEN, Timo, *Porter/Chauffeur, Finnish Embassy*
TUOMINEN, Markku, *Porter, Finnish Embassy*
KAATRANEN, Kaarlo, *Porter, Finnish Embassy*
LOPAKKA, Toini, *Housemaid, Finnish Embassy*

1970–1971

1972

9 February	**State Visit to Thailand of the Queen, the Duke of Edinburgh and the Princess Anne**
	SARASUWAN, Lo, *Staff of the Royal Palace*
	INDRASUT, Nuang, *Staff of the Royal Palace*
	HEMATHAT, Pratuang, *Staff of the Royal Palace*
	PISONT, Varnit, *Staff of the Royal Palace*
	YUANGSRI, Samran, *Staff of the Royal Palace*
	VISVAMITRA, Kriant-Krai, *Staff of the Royal Palace*
	KHWANCHAI, Thanomsri, *Staff of the Royal Palace*
	SUTHISAKDI, Paithoon, *Staff of the Royal Palace*
	PROMMAKOJ, Charunarong, *of the Civil Service*
	SATHAPATAYANON, Rakasakdi, *of the Civil Service*
	GOMOLMISTR, Uthai, *of the Civil Service*
	IMSUWAN, Udom, *of the Civil Service*
	MAKAMONGKOL, Cadet Singkom, *Royal Thai Army*
	PANKLAO, Cadet Manit, *Royal Thai Army*
	TIENSWANG, Cadet Manas, *Royal Thai Army*
	WONGKOET, Cadet Phuchong, *Royal Thai Army*
	YOTHRATIYOTIN, Chief Petty Officer Serun, *Royal Thai Navy*
	CHALERMPONG, Chief Petty Officer Somjit, *Royal Thai Navy*
	YODPRADIT, Chief Petty Officer Pitya, *Royal Thai Navy*
	RUNGPATJHIM, Petty Officer 1st Class Vinai, *Royal Thai Navy*
	NA-NONGKAI, Flight Sergeant Paitoon, *Royal Thai Air Force*
	RUANGRIT, Flight Sergeant Pradit, *Royal Thai Air Force*
	VASINTASHA, Flight Sergeant Nakornchai, *Royal Thai Air Force*
	SUEBNUSORN, Corporal Sermsuk, *Royal Thai Air Force*
	KUMNETR, Corporal Prasert, *Police Department*
	PUNYAHOM, Lance Corporal Prija, *Police Department*
	WONGSWASDI, PC Rawuth, *Police Department*
	LUERPUNYA, PC Sudchai, *Police Department*
	SUWANVICHIEN, Inspector Paitoon, *Police Department*
	SURATHIN, Inspector Mongkol, *Police Department*
	RAI, Ratnabahadur, *Senior Guard, British Embassy*
18 February	**State Visit to Singapore of the Queen, the Duke of Edinburgh and the Princess Anne**
	YUEN, Kelly Chan Kwai, Baggage Master, *British High Commission, Singapore*
11 April	**State Visit to Britain of Queen Beatrix of the Netherlands and Prince Claus**
	DIJK, Corporal Alphons H.M.J. van, *Footman*
	BONNEMA, Corporal Sieberen, *Footman*
	KRAUTH, Corporal Martin Adriaan, *Footman*
	SILIMEIJER, Corporal Cornelis Johannes, *Footman*
	SCHUURMANS, Coenraad, *Military Aide*
	HOEKS, Theodoor, *Assistant Florist*
15 May	**State Visit to France of the Queen and the Duke of Edinburgh**
	VIAÈNE, James, *Chef, British Embassy*
	FIORI, Giovanni, *Butler, British Embassy*
13 June	**State Visit to Britain of Grand Duke Jean of Luxembourg and Grand Duchess Charlotte**
	SCHMITZ, Gaston, *Bandsman*
	FELLOUS, Annie, *Secretary, British Embassy*
17 October	**State Visit to Yugoslavia of the Queen and the Duke of Edinburgh**
	KNEZEVIC, Dragan, *Guard Band, Yugoslav Army*
	SITAR, Janez, *Guard Band, Yugoslav Army*
	JANOSEVIC, Slavoljub, Chief Petty Officer, *Guard Escort of Honour*
	DELETIC, Mileta, Petty Officer, *Driver of Escort of Honour*
	PETROVIC, Dragan, Petty Officer, *Driver*
	PUVACA, Dako, Chief Petty Officer
	SABIC, Radovan, Petty Officer
	SAGONOVIC, Nikola, Petty Officer
	CRNOGORAC, Milan, *Electrician*
	BLAJ, Vinko, Chief Petty Officer, *Member of Yacht Crew*
	CABARKAPA, Drago, Chief Petty Officer, *Member of Yacht Crew*
	GULIN, Josip, Chief Petty Officer, *Member of Yacht Crew*
	SLAMNIK, Matevz, Chief Petty Officer, *Member of Yacht Crew*
	BAKIC, Milka, *Assistant Cook, Dedinje Palace*
	JANKOVIC, Smilja, *of Household Personnel, Dedinje Palace*
	MIHIC, Stojan, *Doorkeeper, Dedinje Palace*

MUHAMEDOVIC, Fadil, *Cook, Dedinje Palace*
PEJOVSKI, Aleksandre, *Doorkeeper, Dedinje Palace*
PINTARIC, Johana, *Chambermaid, Dedinje Palace*
ZGOMBA, Milena, *Chambermaid, Dedinje Palace*

1973

11 December **State Visit to Britain of President Mobuto of Zaïre**
MBAMBA, Citoyenne Makutu, *Femme de Chambre*
NDOMBASI, Citoyen Mpeta, *Valet*
SALABALINGA, Citoyen Kaliba, *Valet*

1974

30 April **State Visit to Britain of Queen Margrethe II of Denmark and Prince Henrik**
MADSEN, Henning, *Footman*
MADSEN, Margit Skovgaard, *Lady's Maid*
CHRISTENSEN, Poul Nymark, *Footman*
MIKKELSEN, Tommy, *Footman*
POULSEN, Benny, *Clerk*
OLESEN, K.M., *Clerical Officer, Danish Embassy*
LARSEN, M. Hoyer, *Stenographer, Danish Embassy*
CHRISTENSEN, A. Hojberg, *Stenographer, Danish Embassy*
SANDBERG, Bernt, *Chef de Cuisine on Royal Yacht*
KJAERGAARD, Mr K. Lykke, *Hairdresser*
KJAERGAARD, Mrs K. Lykke, *Assistant Hairdresser*

9 July **State Visit to Britain of the Yang DiPertuan Agung of Malaysia and the Raja Permaisuri Agung**
ISHAK, Encik Ahmad Arshad bin, *Personal Attendant to His Majesty*
RAHMAN, Encik Baharin bin Abdul, *Personal Attendant to Her Majesty*
DIN, Encik Abdul Majid bin, *HM's Personal Photographer*
CHONG, Encik Lim Teow, *Second Secretary, Malaysian High Commission*
SAMAH, Encik Khamis bin Abu, *Third Secretary, Malaysian High Commission*
DOM, Cik Raziah binti Mohd., *Confidential Secretary, Malaysian High Commission*

1975

7 May **State Visit to Japan of the Queen and the Duke of Edinburgh**
HASHIMOTO, S., *Cook, British Embassy*
TAKAHASHI, Hiroko, *Official, Protocol Office*
SATO, Shoichi, *The Queen's Driver, Kyoto*
KOJIMA, Yasuyuki, *The Queen's Driver, Tokyo*
KOJIMA, Hisao, *The Queen's Driver, Ise and Toba*

8 July **State Visit to Britain of King Carl XVI Gustaf of Sweden**
INGBLAD, Britt-Marie, *Secretary to the Press Counsellor, Swedish Embassy*
RYLIN, Lennart, *Chancery Clerk, Swedish Embassy*
RYDBERG, Bengt, *Chancery Clerk, Swedish Embassy*

1976

4 May **State Visit to Britain of President Geisel of Brazil and Senhora Geisel**
ZANDONADE, Tarcisio, *Communications Officer, Brazilian Embassy*
BROCE, Floriana Sampaio de, *Communications Officer, Brazilian Embassy*

22 May **State Visit to the Federal Republic of Germany of the Queen and the Duke of Edinburgh**
WIENER, Manfred, *Chauffeur, President's Office*
GUND, Walter, *Chauffeur, President's Office*
SCHILLING, Margarete, *of the President's Office*
HALFEN, Rudolf, *Supervisor, Chancellor's Office*
HEINEN, Josef, *Supervisor, Chancellor's Office*
KERP, Anton, *Clerk, Foreign Office*
HALTENBORN, Wilhelm, *Clerk, Foreign Office*
KUNZE, Private Eberhardt, *Guard Battalion*
HELD, Private Kurt Josef, *Guard Battalion*

24 May **State Visit to Finland of the Queen and the Duke of Edinburgh**
SAHANEN, Liisa, *Clerk, President's Office*
PETRAMMA, Annamaija, *Clerk, Protocol Department*
PÄRNÄNEN, *Clerk, Protocol Department*
VÄINÖLÄ, *Clerk, Protocol Department*
PYLSY, Marjatta, *Housekeeper, Presidential Palace*

VUOLIO, Timo, *Head Waiter, Presidential Palace*
HAIKALA, Risto, *Messenger, Presidential Palace*
ILLAK, Ake, *Head Waiter, Presidential Palace*
JEHKONEN, Eero, *Commissionaire, Presidential Palace*
KERÄNEN, Mirja, *Cook, Presidential Palace*
LAAKKONEN, Bertta, *Washer/Ironer, Presidential Palace*
LAHTI, Vieno, *Chambermaid, Presidential Palace*
ROSTI, Pauli, *Caretaker, Presidential Palace*
TANSKANEN, Erkki, *Switchboard Operator, Presidential Palace*

22 June   **State Visit to Britain of President Giscard d'Estaing of the French Republic and Madame Giscard d'Estaing**
COGNÉ, Jacqueline, *Secrétaire de l'Ambassadeur*
TITFORD, Daphne, *Secrétaire*
FRESNEL, Catherine, *Secrétaire*

8 November   **State Visit to Luxembourg of the Queen and the Duke of Edinburgh**
RIES, Emile, *of the Government Garage*
MULLER, Louis, *Usher, Ministry of Foreign Affairs*
ADEMES, Leon, *Usher, Ministry of Education*
BERTEMES, Nicholas, *Usher, Prime Minister's Office*
DOMINICY, Norbert, *Usher, Ministry of Interior*
HOFFMAN, Emile, *Valet, Grand Duke's Household*
GOERGEN, Germain, *Valet, Grand Duke's Household*
DEISCHTER, Fernand, *Valet, Grand Duke's Household*
HEINTZ, Ernest, *Valet, Grand Duke's Household*
STAMMET, Nicolas, *Valet, Grand Duke's Household*
HOFFMAN, Mme N., *Chambermaid, Grand Duke's Household*
BINDELS, Mme J., *Chambermaid, Grand Duke's Household*
THEISEN, R., *Adjudant-Major, Army, Luxembourg*
REUTER, R., *Adjudant-Chef, Army Chauffeur*
UHRES, E., *Adjudant-Chef, Army Chauffeur*
HUBERTY, F., *Adjudant-Chef, Army Chauffeur*
JAEGER, V., *Adjudant-Chef, Army Chauffeur*
REUTER, P., *Adjudant-Chef, Army Chauffeur*
BUTGENBACH, P., *Adjudant, Army Chauffeur*
THILL, J. P., *Adjudant, Army Chauffeur*
BARTHOLMÉ, J., *Adjudant, Army Chauffeur*
TREFFKORN, J., *Sgt-Chef, Army Chauffeur*
KRANTZ, G., *Adjudant-Chef, Brigade Chief, Luxembourg Gendarmerie*
REINARD, J., *Adjudant-Chef, Member of Security Service*
KOHN, R., *Adjudant-Chef, Secretary in Gendarmerie HQ*
JONG, M. P. de, *Member of Echternach School Admin. Staff*
SCHEUER, M. J., *Head Machinist, ARBED-Differdange*
GASPER, M. N., *Foreman, ARBED-Differdange*
MERTZ, M.C., *Foreman, ARBED-Differdange*

14 November   **State Visit to Britain of President Eanes of Portugal**
CUNHA, Alvaro, *President's Butler*
SERRA, Staff-Sergeant Conceição, *Baggage Master of Official Suite*
BASTO, Corporal Pinto, *Baggage Master for Press*
SILVA, Manuel, *Baggage Master of Non-Official Party*
SILVA, Staff-Sergeant Correia da, *Security*
FERREIRA, Staff-Sergeant Herculano, *Security*
MONTEZ, *Baggage Master, Foreign Minister's Office*

1977–8

1979

16 May   **State Visit to Denmark of the Queen and the Duke of Edinburgh**
PROBST, Preben, *Messenger, Ministry of Foreign Affairs*
JØRGENSEN, Svend Skov, *Harbour Guard, Port of Copenhagen*
MEIER, Steen-Flemming, *Livery Servant, Royal Household*
NIELSEN, Torben, *Livery Servant, Royal Household*
JOHANSEN, Flemming, *Livery Servant, Royal Household*
HANSEN, Niels Stentoft, *Livery Servant, Royal Household*
RASMUSSEN, Søren Trier, *Livery Servant, Royal Household*
HANSEN, Kurt Allan Bagge, *Keeper of the Plate, Royal Household*
PEDERSEN, Lennart Herold, *Keeper of the Plate, Royal Household*
FREDERIKSEN, Hans, *Chauffeur, Royal Household*

HANSEN, Torben, *Chauffeur to the Queen*
BUHL, Flemming, *Chauffeur, Royal Household*
HANSEN, Ole Baltzer, *Chauffeur, Royal Household*
NIKOLAJSEN, Bent, *Chauffeur to Prince Philip*
HANSEN, John Erik Otzen, *Chauffeur to Prince Philip*
HATT, Preben Bardenfleth, *Chauffeur, Royal Household*
JØRGENSEN, Kaj Brandt, *Doorkeeper, Royal Household*
LARSEN, Henry Dahl, *Doorkeeper, Royal Household*
ENGEN, Hendrik Lembcke, *Coachman, Royal Household*
KOFOED, Erik Funch, *Coachman, Royal Household*
ANDEREN, Mogens Frederick Christian Lykke, *Coachman, Royal Household*
BENDTSEN, John Frederik, *Coachman, Royal Household*
KONGE, Jørgen Nieslen, *Coachman, Royal Household*
HATTING, Jørn, *Chauffeur, British Embassy*

1980

14 October — **State Visit to Italy of the Queen and the Duke of Edinburgh**
SCAGLIONE, Cav. Uff. Raffaele, *Protocol*
MARTINO, Cav. Uff. Biagio, *Protocol*
PETTI, Cav. Uff. Anna Maria, *Protocol*
GERVASI, Maresciallo Aronne, *Corazzieri*
D'ANDREA, Maresciallo Fausto, *Corazzieri*
MENNITI, Domenico, *Household*
ZUCCACCIA Paolo, *Household*
ANGELI, Brigadiere Vittorio, *Inspectorate*
PIETROPAOLI, Appuntato Luigi, *Inspectorate*
PICCHI, Marcello, *Press*
AGLIECO, Maresciallo Simone, *Press*
ALFANO, Sebastiano, *Press*
RIZZELLO, Rocco, *Press*
SAVIGNANO, Capo I.a classe M.M. Fulvio, *Military Affairs*
DE NOTO, Maresciallo 3. a classe Giorgetto, *Military Affairs*
RONCELLA, Cancelliere Capo Fernando, *Office of the Diplomatic Counsellor*
VERDEROSA, Maresciallo Maggiore Salvatore, *Office of the Diplomatic Counsellor*
SORGONI N. GUGLIELMO, Cancelliere Principale Donatella, *Office of the Diplomatic Counsellor*
AMADIO, Usciere Marcello, *Office of the Diplomatic Counsellor*
MAZZAPICCHIO, Usciere Vittorio, *Office of the Diplomatic Counsellor*
MARANI, Eugenio, *Official*
LATINI, Aldo, *Official*

18 November — **State Visit to Britain of King Birendra and Queen Aishwarya of Nepal**
UPADHYAYA, Hudda B.P., *Security*
KHATRI, Amaldar C.B., *Security*
SHAHI, Amaldar B.B., *Security*
GURUNG, Pyuth C.B., *Security*
ARMAS, Leonardo, *Chauffeur, Nepalese Embassy*
ARMAS, Carmen, *Maid, Nepalese Embassy*
GYAWALI, Suraj Kumar, *Valet, Nepalese Embassy*
SHRESTHA, Prem Lal, *Cook, Nepalese Embassy*
TAMANG, Ram Piya, *Maid, Nepalese Embassy*

1981

5 May — **State Visit to Norway of the Queen and the Duke of Edinburgh**
KNUTSEN, Viktor, *Valet*
ROGSTADMOEN, Arild, *Servant*
SKAAR, Edvall, *Servant*
HANSSEN, Dagfinn, *Servant*
ROM, Bjørn, *Servant*
ANDERSEN, Trond, *Servant*
AARSHEIM, Terje, *Servant*
OLSEN, Torstein, *Servant*
JOHANSEN, Dag Arild, *Servant*
HASLE, Jan Erik, *Servant*
HAAGENSEN, Knut, *Servant*
BORGJORDET, Magne, *Servant*
KOLSETH, Ole Henrik, *Servant*
SØSVEEN, Steinar, *Servant*
TANGEN, Per, *Chauffeur*
GJETSJØ, Leif, *Chauffeur*
SKJOLD, Walter, *Chauffeur*

RAKNERUD, Ingebret, *Chauffeur*
DAHL, Bjørn, *Chauffeur*
MYHRE, Edvard, *Guard*
NYGAARD, Ingvald, *Guard*
MOUM, Albert, *Guard*
TJUGUM, Leif, *Guard*
KJAERSTAD, Herman, *Guard*
EINARSBØL, Egil, *Guard*
BERTHELSEN, Hans Gustav, *Palace Warden*
LARSEN, Oddvar, *Palace Warden*
PEDERSEN, Alf Konrad, *Palace Warden*
LARSEN, Knut Andreas, *Palace Warden*
FRANTZEN, Kjell, *Palace Warden*
BERNTSEN, Bjørn, *Palace Warden*
STORSVEEN, Miss Olaug, *Chauffeur*
WEUM, Miss Jenny, *Parlourmaid*
EBNE, Miss Ingrid, *Parlourmaid*
MOUM, Mrs. Ragnhild, *Parlourmaid*
SØRENSEN, Miss Magda, *Cook*
AMDAM, Miss Oddny, *Assistant Cook*
NØSTRIK, J., *Servant*
HAMMERSETH, Miss Oddny, *Parlourmaid*
SYRINGEN, Miss Oddlaug, *Parlourmaid*
LOTHIGIUS, Mrs. Karen, *Secretary*
HENRIKSEN, Mrs. Eva, *Telephone Operator*
HOLM, Mrs. Wenche, *Telephone Operator*
HOLSTAD, Mrs. Brit, *Secretary*
WILMANN, Mrs Bjørg, *Secretary*
LUND, Mrs. Linge, *Housekeeper, Royal Palace*
GUNDERSEN, Mrs. Gerd, *Secretary*
KONGSTAD, Mrs. Lise, *Librarian Royal Palace*
ANGELL, Miss Katherine, *Secretary*

9 June   **State Visit to Britain of King Khalid of Saudi Arabia**
IDRIS, Mohammed, *Private Companion*

1982

16 November   **State Visit to Britain of Queen Beatrix of the Netherlands and Prince Claus**
BLOM, E.M., *Footman*
DATEMA, A.G., *Linen Maid*
DRIESSEN, C.H., *Footman*
ESSEN, M.A.P. van, *Florist*
HEUVEL, J.C. van den, *Footman*
HOEFF, H.C. van der, *Footman*
HUT, J.T., *Footman*
WASSINK, H.R. Klein, *Footman*
TROUWEE, Cornelis, *Footman*
KOELEWIJN, Z.G., *Footman*
KORTEKAAS, W.J., *Florist*
SCHAGEN, D., *Footman*
JUHREND, Corporal M., *Chauffeur, RNLA*
DIEREN, R., *Florist*
LEYESDORFF, M., *Florist*

1983

25 May   **State Visit to Sweden of the Queen and the Duke of Edinburgh**
ROHRENS, Toni, *Steward of the King's Table*
JONSSON, Erling, *Groom of the Bedchamber*
PREMFORS, Haken, *Valet*
ERIKSSON, Ove, *Driver*
JURLANDER, Stig, *Driver*
SUNDIN, Ingvar, *Royal Coachman*
LINDVALL, Sven Erik, *Outrider*
ORTH, Gunnar, *Palace Guard*
KULL, Sven, *Palace Guard*
ERIKSSON, Sven, *Palace Guard*
DYBECK, Birger, *Palace Guard*
NILSSON, Kurt, *Palace Commissionaire*
OLSSON, Ake, *Maintenance Engineer*
SCHUTZ, Johanne, *Cleaner*

BJUREKLINT, Alf, Sergeant-Major, *Senior NCO, Palace Guard*
ASKLOF, Wille, Sergeant-Major, *Senior NCO, Troops lining route*
MALMEN, Stig, Sergeant-Major, *Senior NCO, Mounted Escort*
HAMMARSTROM, Asta, *Chief of Stockholm's Kvinnliga Bilkar*
NYBERG, Peter, *Driver*
HELLSTROM K., *British Embassy Driver*

1984

23 October **State Visit to Britain of President Mitterand of the French Republic and Madame Mitterand**
CAMERON, Martine, *Secretary, Press Office*
BOUTON, Claudette Rainelli, *Secretary, Press Office*

1985

25 March **State Visit to Portugal of the Queen and the Duke of Edinburgh**
TAVARES, Fernando Miguel de Moura, *Staff, President's Office*
FERREIRA, Jose Pires Vaz, *Staff, President's Office*
PINTO, Jose Madureira, *Staff, President's Office*
COSTA, Joaquim Morais da, *Staff, President's Office*
CARVALHO, Tereza Mayer de, *State Protocol*
RAMALHO, Maria Tereza de Morais S., *State Protocol in charge of Queluz Palace*
CUNHA, Maria Isabel Brito e, *State Protocol*
GALVAO, Guard Ana Maria C.C., *Security*
DEUS, Guard Jose Da Purificacao Avo de, *Security*
OLIVEIRA, Guard Antonio Amalio de, *Security*
SOUSA, Guard Eduardo Augusto Massa de, *Security*
FERREIRA, Guard Jose Manuel Pedro, *Security*
COELHO, Guard Joaquim Silva, *Security*
CARRAPATO, Vicente Massano, *Queluz Exhibition*
REIS, Dra. Ana Batalha, *Ajuda Palace Exhibition*
ALVES, Vanda, *Ajuda Palace Exhibition*
CORREIA, Ana Brito, *Ajuda Palace Exhibition*
SEQUEIRA, Joao Pedro de Desus, *Driver of the Queen's car in Oporto*

16 April **State Visit to Britain of Life President Dr Banda of Malawi**
KABANGO, *Valet*
ZONDWA, *Accountant to the Delegation*

1986

17 February **State Visit to Nepal of the Queen and the Duke of Edinburgh**
GURUNG, Nayab Subba Suk Bahadur, *Nagarjun Bungalow*
DHAVAN, Inder, *Head Cook*
DANGOL, Nayab Subba Ishwar Man, *Driver*
KHATRI, Nayab Subba Kailash Bahadur, *Table and Room Boy*
GHALE, Nayab Subba Pabitra, *Table and Room Maid*
SHRESTHA, Diththa Radhashya, *Table and Room Boy*
SILWAL, Diththa Ran Bahadur, *Table and Room Boy*
THAPA, Diththa Mrs. Bhawani, *Table and Room Maid*
BAN, Diththa Madan Prasad, *Table and Room Boy*
BAISHNAB, Diththa Keshav Das Baishnab, *Table and Room Boy*
JAYARAM, Bahidar, *Table and Room Boy*
GURUNG, Subadar Prem Bahadur, *Military Police*
PAUDEL, Jamadar Khem Bahadur, *Military Police*
RAI, Deputy-Inspector of Police Narendra Kumar, *Driver Escort*
BAHADUR, Deputy-Inspector of Police Shyam, *Outrider*
MAGAR, Deputy-Inspector of Police Mahila, *Outrider*
PANT, Deputy-Inspector of Police Lila Nath, *Outrider*
THAPA, Deputy-Inspector of Police Man Bir, *Pilot Motor Cycle*
BUDHATOKI, Assistant-Inspector of Police Dilbahadur, *Rear Motor Cycle*
THAPA, Hudda Balbahadur, *Military Police*
KARKI, Hudda Hari Bahadur, *Military Police*
SHAHI, Hudda Bishnu Bahadur, *Military Police*
THAPA, Amaldar Navraj, *Military Police*
GHAREL, Puyouth Sitaram, *Military Police*
BASNET, Amaldar Khamba Dhoj, *Military Police*

1 July **State Visit to Britain of President von Weizsäcker of the Federal Republic of Germany and Freifrau von Weizsäcker**
SCHNEIDER, Jutta, *Shorthand Typist, German Embassy*
MULLENBORN, Heinrich, *Clerical Assistant, German Embassy*

1987

1988

12 July	**State Visit to Britain of King Olav V of Norway** AAMODT, Vidar, *Footman*
17 October	**State Visit to Spain of the Queen and the Duke of Edinburgh** CARRION, Esteban RODRIGUEZ, Luciano ORTEGA, José Maria INFANTES, Alberto GISMERA, Luis JIMINEZ, José Luis MONTERO, Miguel Angel GARLITO, Senorita Maria Teresa BLASCO, Arturo ADRADAS, Luis Francisco DIAZ, Onofre BLASCO, Agustin ORTEGA, Felix GUERRA, José Luis HERNANDO, José FERNANDEZ, Gaudencio LOBO, Antonio NAVARRO, Quiterio MERINO, Juan CANETE, Jesus POSADA, José Maria ARTO, Lauro SAIZ, Albino ALONSO, Tomas POVENDANO, Miguel JIMINEZ, Luis CRESPO, Alfredo ROMERO, David JIMINEZ, Pablo Jorge LOPEZ, Manuel GOMEZ, José Luis BERNABE, Gregorio PEREZ, Javier VEGA, José Maria SANCHEZ, Felix RUIZ, Julio

1989

9 May	**State Visit to Britain of President Babangida of Nigeria** JAJA, Mrs. G.A. Andrew, *Personal Assistant to Mrs. Babangida* OMOWA, K., *Personal Assistant to President* KANU, E., *Personal Assistant to President* ATIM, J., *Personal Assistant to President* EKENG, E.B., *Senior Personal Secretary, State Visit Unit, High Commission*

1990

25 June	**State Visit to Iceland of the Queen and the Duke of Edinburgh** SIGMUNDSSON, Gudmundur, *Constable* SKULASON, Gisli, *Constable* EGILSSON, Olafur, *Constable* THRAINSSON, Gudmundur Omar, *Constable* BERNHARDSSON, Adalsteinn, *Constable* BOGASON, Janbjorn, *Constable* MAGNUSSON, Snorri, *Constable* OLASON, Jon S., *Constable* GISLASON, Bjorn, *Constable* BOGASON, Gudmundur, *Constable* ERLENDSSON, Sveinn, *Constable* MAGNUSSON, Bjarni Olasfur, *Constable*

SIGURDSSON, Atli Mar, *Constable*
THORARINSSON, Jakob Sugurjon, *Constable*
MAGNUSSON, Bjarnie Olafur, *Constable*
THORARINSSON, Rikhard, *Embassy Driver, British Embassy*

1991

1992

9 June   **State Visit to France of the Queen and the Duke of Edinburgh**
POUDADE, Danielle, *Secretary to M. Sabathe, Quai d'Orsay*
DAMON, Nathalie, *Secretary*
BOURDIAL, Marc, *Footman, Hotel Marigny*
NORMAND, Joel, *Chef, Elysée Palace*

3 November   **State Visit to Britain of the Sultan of Brunei Darussalam and the Raja Isteri**
ABDULLAH, Hajjah Masnah, *Household Assistant*
IBRAHIM, Hajjah Ainah, *Household Assistant*
YONG, Lydia, *Household Assistant*

1993

1994

5 July   **State Visit to Britain of King Harald of Norway and Queen Sonja**
LINDSTRØM, Einar, *Servant*
ZIMMERMANN, Geir, *Servant*
TOFTE, Hans, *Servant*
HAGBARTSEN, Berit, *Maid*
KEEFE, Janne, *Maid*
ERIKSEN, Tom, *Hairdresser*
SLYNGSTAD, Bodil, *Chamber Maid*
ALBRIGTSEN, Bernt, *Police Inspector*
THOMSEN, Kristin Hatland, *Clerical Assistant, Norwegian Embassy*

1995

17 October   **State Visit to Britain of President Ahtisaari of Finland and Madame Ahtisaari**
RATSULA, Sergeant Olli, *Police Officer*
POHJOLA, Sergeant Juha, *Police Officer*
LEHTONEN, Ms Johanna, *Parlourmaid*
KALTKARI, Mr Matti, *Official Photographer*

Sources

CHAPTER ONE
1. Aspinall, Arthur (ed.), *The Later Correspondence of George III*. Vol. II, London 1962–1970, p.232, Lord Grenville to the King, 19 August 1794.
2. ibid.
3. Aspinall, A. op. cit p.233, The King to Lord Grenville, 23 August 1794.
4. Nicholas, Sir Nicholas Harris, *History of The Orders of British Knighthood*. Vol. II, London, 1842. p.307.
5. Millar, Oliver, *Pictures in the Royal Collection – Later Georgian Pictures*. London, 1969. Number 886, p.65 and Plate 192.
6. Ibid. Number 910. p.74 and Plate 191.
7. Benson, A.C. and Esher, Viscount, Editors, *The Letters of Queen Victoria*. Vol. I, London, 1907. p.16.
8. Fulford, Roger, Editor, *Dearest Child – Letters Between Queen Victoria and the Princess Royal 1858–1861*. London, 1964 p.184 and Note 1. Mr. Fulford says in his footnote that in her diary the Queen added, 'From us the family Order (our cameo with diamonds).' His observation that 'This is probably the earliest example of the gift of the Queen's private family order' was not correct.
9. RA VIC PP 9794.
10. *Rules and Regulations for the Government of the Royal Order of Victoria and Albert*, 1872. p.13.
11. RA R 52 14 and 14a. Sir Albert Woods to Sir Henry Ponsonby, 5 May 1877, with Ponsonby's comment for the Queen.
12. RA L 6 55. Queen Victoria to Sir Henry Ponsonby, 20 January 1880.
13. RA L 6 57. Sir Albert Woods to Sir Henry Ponsonby, 2 March 1880.
14. RA L6 56. Sir Albert Woods to Sir Henry Ponsonby, 15 January 1880.
15. RA L6 54. Doyne C. Bell to Albert Woods, 13 January 1880. RA L6 56. Sir Albert Woods to Sir Henry Ponsonby with Ponsonby's comment for the Queen.
16. RA Addl. Mss. A/12 1543. Sir Henry Ponsonby to Queen Victoria, 10 February 1888.
17. Jehanne Wake, *Princess Louise, Queen Victoria's Unconventional Daughter*. London, 1988, p.345.
18. Rules, p.4.

CHAPTER THREE
1. A fuller account of the Indian tours and a list of recipients of the gold and silver badges or medals is to be found in 'Gifts, Shikar and Medals' by R.B. Magor in *The Miscellany of Honours*, No. 2 (1980) pp. 37-59.
2. Sub-Lieutenant HSH Prince Louis of Battenberg, an officer in *Serapis*, replaced the official *Illustrated London News* artist for the return journey at the artist's request on being sent on to China. Many of Prince Louis' sketches on board were published in the *ILN*. He received the silver medal.

CHAPTER FOUR
1 Detailed information on all Coronation and Jubilee medals may be found in Coronation and Royal Commemorative Medals 1887–1977 by Lieut. Colonel Howard N. Cole OBE, TD, DL, published in 1977 by J.B. Hayward & Son.
2 Based on documents in the Privy Purse, RA PP Vic 6569 (1886) 30 July 1886–18 December 1891.
3 For the figures, see *Monatsblatt der Numismatischen Gesellschaft in Wien*, 1889, Vol. 66, p.210.

CHAPTER FIVE
1. Mabell, Countess of Airlie, *Thatched with Gold*, edited by Jennifer Ellis, London 1962, p.2.
2 Anne Somerset, *Ladies in Waiting*, London 1984, p.96.
3. ibid, p.130.
4. *Clerks of the Closet in the Royal Household* by John Bickersteth and Robert W. Dunning. Alan Sutton, 1991.
5. ibid.

CHAPTER SIX
1. Letter from Sir Ulick Alexander to Sir Robert Knox dated 20 September 1951 in Cabinet Office papers, File V3.
2. A full account of the disaster is to be found in an article by John Wilson in Journal No. 25 of The Lifesaving Awards Research Society of September 1995 and also in Journal No. 27.

Index

The spelling of names has been taken from the original registers and sometimes varies. Where this occurs the original spelling has been maintained; this can result in two entries for the same person.

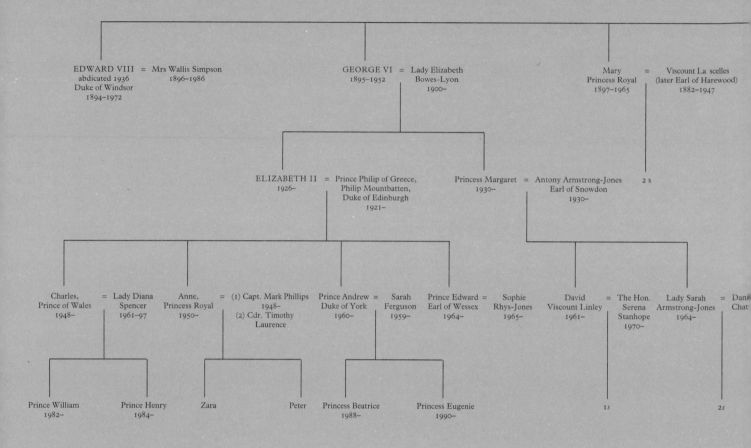

GEORGE
1865–1936

EDWARD VIII = Mrs Wallis Simpson
abdicated 1936   1896–1986
Duke of Windsor
1894–1972

GEORGE VI = Lady Elizabeth
1895–1952   Bowes-Lyon
                 1900–

Mary   =   Viscount La scelles
Princess Royal   (later Earl of Harewood)
1897–1965   1882–1947

ELIZABETH II = Prince Philip of Greece,
1926–   Philip Mountbatten,
               Duke of Edinburgh
               1921–

Princess Margaret = Antony Armstrong-Jones   2 s
1930–   Earl of Snowdon
                    1930–

Charles,   = Lady Diana
Prince of Wales   Spencer
1948–   1961–97

Anne,   = (1) Capt. Mark Phillips
Princess Royal   1948–
1950–   (2) Cdr. Timothy
              Laurence

Prince Andrew = Sarah
Duke of York   Ferguson
1960–   1959–

Prince Edward = Sophie
Earl of Wessex Rhys-Jones
1964–   1965–

David   = The Hon.
Viscount Linley   Serena
1961–   Stanhope
                1970–

Lady Sarah   = Dani
Armstrong-Jones   Chat
1964–

Prince William
1982–

Prince Henry
1984–

Zara

Peter

Princess Beatrice
1988–

Princess Eugenie
1990–

1 s

2 s